A  OF

CHRISTIAN DOCTRINES.

BY THE LATE

DR. K. R. HAGENBACH,

PROFESSOR OF THEOLOGY AT BASEL.

TRANSLATED FROM THE FIFTH AND LAST GERMAN EDITION,

WITH ADDITIONS FROM OTHER SOURCES.

With an Introduction by

E. H. PLUMPTRE, D.D.,

PROFESSOR OF DIVINITY IN KING'S COLLEGE, LONDON; EXAMINING CHAPLAIN
TO THE ARCHBISHOP OF CANTERBURY.

VOL. I

EDINBURGH:
T. & T. CLARK, 38 GEORGE STREET.
1880.

PRINTED BY MORRISON AND GIBB,

FOR

T. & T. CLARK, EDINBURGH.

LONDON, ... HAMILTON, ADAMS, AND CO.
DUBLIN, ... ROBERTSON AND CO.
NEW YORK, . . . SCRIBNER AND WELFORD.

INTRODUCTION.

I AM not the translator or editor of the present volume, but I have compared it here and there with previous translations, and can say with confidence, so far as I have been able to form a judgment, that the Preface of the Editor, who has asked me to take the responsibility of commending it to the English reader, does not overstate its claims. The half-metaphysical, half-theological terms in which Dr. Hagenbach's work abounds are rendered with greater precision; the style is clearer and more flowing. It seems to me altogether a more readable book than any previous translation.

The importance of such a book in its bearing on the work of those who have to enter on the work, not only, or chiefly, of preaching the Gospel to the poor, but of dealing with the intellectual difficulties which in many cases hinder cultivated minds from receiving that Gospel in its fulness, and tracing the underlying unity of the faith of Christendom below the manifold variations which its history presents, can hardly, I imagine, be overrated.

The first impression made on us by the study of the history of dogma in the Christian Church is, it may be freely admitted, disheartening and bewildering. We are almost tempted, as was the Master of Scoffing, of whom Bacon speaks[1] (Rabelais), to label it, as with a cynical despair, as "The Morris Dance of Heretics," each sect and party having "a diverse posture or cringe;" and to feel that it is true not only of "atheists and profane persons," but of many earnest seekers after truth, that "when they hear of so many discordant and contrary opinions in religion, it doth avert them from the Church,"—yes, and not from the Church only,—"and maketh them to sit down in the chair of the scorners." We ask, as

[1] Essay III. *Of Unity in Religion.*

we read the wild speculations of a Basilides or a Swedenborg, perhaps even as we enter into the more systematic teaching of an Augustine or an Aquinas,—Who is this that darkeneth counsel by words without knowledge? It is well if we do not pass on to that other question which came from a jesting or a despairing Pilate, What is truth?

With that scepticism, which we cannot deny to be, in part at least, the result of the study of the history of dogma, there comes, however, a gain which almost counterbalances it. We learn a larger charity and a wider tolerance. If we do not wrap ourselves up in the Lucretian serenity of one who looks out on the wanderings of men in the labyrinth of error, on their strifes and battles in a land of shadows, on their perilous voyages across the stormy sea, driven to and fro by every blast of doctrine, with a supercilious satisfaction, we at least learn to look with pity rather than with horror. We understand each of the contending parties in this or that controversy better than they understand each other. We see the shield both on its gold and its silver side, and discern, not seldom, that men have been disputing about words and names, which they left vague and undefined, or which they defined with an over-sharp preciseness, while they were in reality of one mind and heart in all that is essential. We ask ourselves whether, in these larger and wider thoughts, we are not, at least, drawing a little nearer to the wisdom of the Divine judgment, and the anathemas of passion and of prejudice are hushed as in the calm of the eternal Charity.

And the teaching of the history of the controversies of the past is surely not without its bearing upon those of the present. We learn the limits of our knowledge, and turn back from pushing our inquiries beyond the region of the knowable. What Bacon well calls the "vermiculate questions" that swarm, the "maggots of corrupted texts," in the hot thoughts and distempered imagination of the solitary dreamer, are seen in their right proportions, some of them as belonging to the "infinitely little," which lies below the care of the wise of heart, some to the "infinitely great," which he cannot hope to fathom so long as he knows only "in part," and sees "through a glass darkly." We are content to trace the course of men's thoughts in such matters as part of the intellectual history of mankind, to connect them in their genesis and development with the movements of religious and philosophical thought of which they form a part, with the temperament and personal experience of those who have been their chief exponents, with the influence of their education, and the subtle differences that distinguish one race or nation from another. We learn that, in the evolution of the forms of faith and speculative thought, there has been something like a law of the " survival of the fittest," analogous to that which students of nature recognize in the evolutions of the forms of organized and animated structures, and we see how step by step the thoughts of men have widened with the years, and have become indefinitely nearer approximations to what it is given to man to know of the Being, the attributes, the mind and will of the Eternal. One by one the voices that were loud and clamorous in the strife of tongues, and made sad the hearts of the righteous, whom God had not made sad, have ceased to echo in our ears. The Papal theories of Infallibility and Transubstantiation, of Purgatory and Indulgences, are seen to form no parts of the " faith once delivered to the saints," to have no claims to the character even of developments of that faith, but to have sprung from the early admixture of germs of error, and the half-truths which are the most perilous forms of error, with the truth of God, and which it is our work to distinguish and reject. The dogmatic systems of the Fathers and the Schoolmen, and even of the Reformers, are seen to include the traditions of men as well as the truths of the divine Word, and we are learning slowly but surely to separate the chaff from the wheat. And in that separating and sifting process the history of the dogmas, their rise, development, and in many cases their decay, is a help with which we cannot afford to dispense. In the words which have been chosen as a motto for this volume, words not the less true because they come from the lips of one whose criticisms ended in negation, *Die wahre Kritik des Dogma ist seine Geschichte.*

Nor need the student who is earnestly seeking to know the truth which shall make him free, fear lest the result of the study of that history should only throw him back upon an attitude of sceptical indifference. Rather will he recognize, in the very multiplicity and variety of opinions which have from time to time crystallised round the nucleus of the words and facts in which Christendom recognizes that it has received a revelation from God, a proof of the power of those words and facts over the thoughts and feelings of mankind. A new element was thus introduced into the world's history mightier than any that had gone before or have followed it. There will surely follow upon this thought the conviction that the words and facts themselves must be a worthier object of study than any comments or after-thoughts or inferences from them. The study of any one exhaustive system of theology—such, for instance, as the *Summa Theologica* of Aquinas, or the *Institutes* of Calvin—may narrow a man's thoughts, and lead him to substitute the traditions or speculations of men for the living oracles of God. The study of many such systems in their successive developments will throw him back upon that of the divine Word. A revived and purified Exegesis is the natural outcome of the history of dogmas.

The value of Dr. Hagenbach's *History of Doctrines* has been amply attested by the demand, which from 1841 to the present time has been met by five successive editions. In English theological literature we have, indeed, scarcely any work that can even be compared with it. Dictionaries of religions, sects, and doctrines have, indeed, appeared from time to time in varying degrees of completeness, in which the student might find an account of this or that school of opinions. In works like Newman's *Arians*, or Oxenham's *Catholic Doctrine of the Atonement*, we have had elaborate monographs on single districts of the vast region that lies before us; but a survey of the whole country, tracing, as it were, its physical geography, and the successive changes by which its features have been moulded and fashioned into their present form, we may well note as still among the *desiderata* of our theology.

The excellence of Dr. Hagenbach's work may, indeed, in some degree be measured by its defects. A single glance will show the English student that it is not a volume in which he may look to find light or pleasant reading. It is essentially German in its method and its form, in its exhaustive fulness, its philosophical terminology, its disregard of the graces of composition. The references under every paragraph are almost like the catalogue of a library. The reader has to overcome some difficulties before he finds himself at home. And yet it is believed that few persons who make the effort will find themselves disappointed. Let the student take, for example, such a subject as the Doctrine of the Atonement, or the Eschatology of the early Church, and compare what he finds in Hagenbach with any of the controversial treatises on either point with which he has been hitherto familiar, and I cannot doubt that the result will be, that he will find in this volume far more than all the facts and theories which he finds in them, that he will rise from its perusal with a mind more fully stored and a clearer judgment, and, it may be hoped, also with a larger charity.

E. H. PLUMPTRE, D.D.

February 21, 1880.

ENGLISH EDITOR'S PREFACE.

THE object and method of this work are sufficiently described in the author's prefaces; and the reception already accorded to it in Germany, in England, and in America, has proved its claim to be the most useful of all the manuals hitherto published on the History of Christian Doctrine.

The first edition, which appeared in 1841, was translated by Mr. C. W. Buch, and was published in the Foreign Theological Library in 1846. A second edition and a third of this translation were subsequently put forth, with additions from the second German edition. An eminent American theologian, Dr. H. B. Smith, made additions to Mr. Buch's translation, embodying the whole of the fourth German edition, and giving the titles of many works bearing upon the subject of Christian Doctrine. Dr. Smith has, in the judgment of Dr. Hagenbach, made unnecessary additions to the literature. It is perhaps natural that an English editor should think more favourably of Dr. Smith's work, particularly as his contributions refer, for the most part, to books published in England and America; and he has made free use of his references.

Since the publication of Dr. Smith's translation, the author put forth, shortly before his death, a fifth edition, containing a considerable number of additions, some of less, some of greater importance.

The book now presented to the public is, therefore, the work of many years and of many hands. It may be confidently asserted that it is much more complete, and very much more accurate, than any edition which has hitherto appeared. The translation has been carefully revised; and the whole of the last edition is here, for the first time, presented in English. The mode of quoting the authorities adduced has been made more uniform, and the quotations are given with much greater accuracy. Besides the additions of previous editors, some further contributions have been made to the literature, chiefly by indicating newer editions of the works referred to, and adding any works of importance that have recently appeared. These additions are kept within as narrow limits as possible, for the reason given in the author's preface. It will be understood that the parts in brackets have been added by the various editors.

If it shall appear that the work is still incomplete and imperfect, the critical reader will yet find that much has been done. If the present edition be compared with any previous one, it will be seen that there is hardly a page in which many corrections, emendations, and additions are not found. The editor is confident that those who are the most competent to criticize, will be the most ready to acknowledge what has actually been accomplished.

The reader should be informed that a new and improved edition of Dr. Herzog's "Real-Encyklopädie" (so often quoted in these pages) is now in course of publication. The dictionaries of Christian Biography and Christian Antiquity, now being published under the editorship of Dr. W. Smith, will be found to be of great value.

AUTHOR'S INTRODUCTION TO THE FIRST EDITION.

IN consequence of the careful, and, to a certain extent, profound treatment which the history of dogma has in later times received, there has arisen a more urgent necessity for uniting the abundant results of these searching inquiries, as far as possible, into a harmonious whole,—a task which, in view of the richness of the available materials, and in comparison with the incompleteness of earlier performances, may appear easy, but which, in comparison with the higher requirements of our time, will appear so difficult that he who undertakes it may well despair of the possibility of attaining even approximately the aim which he has set before himself.

As far at least as this attempt is concerned, I beg that it may be considered and judged only as such. It is the simple result of many years' teaching in the department of the History of Doctrine, and a further realization of the idea which I indicated twelve years ago in the hastily sketched tables then published. The leading paragraphs were dictated to my hearers; the commentaries have been drawn partly from excerpts, partly from reflections and observations carried further, and they both need a more exact completion in oral lectures. The same motive which led me to pursue this method in delivering lectures, now, after many years of hesitancy and delay, has decided the publication of this textbook. Of the existing manuals, with all their merits, none satisfied me in respect of *method ;* and intercourse with competent judges has taught me that it has fared with others as with myself.

To begin with *Münscher*: the handbook (and of this only can we speak here) has certainly gained in material utility by the industrious elaboration of *von Cölln* and his successors, especially by the rich collection of quotations. But the conscientiousness with which *von Cölln* retained the plan of *Münscher*, which is in many ways defective, and from which *Neudecker* for the first time deviated in the treatment of the last period, was by no means advantageous to the book. The division into three periods is certainly too general, and the isolated position which the portion on " the kingdom of Jesus and the angels" occupies from the other principal divisions of doctrinal theology, has astonished others as well as myself. We cannot complain that the customary enumeration of *loci* was departed from (which I have attempted myself, for good reasons, in the second period); but that this, which was apparently the original plan, is immediately abandoned, and is by no means thoroughly carried out. At the beginning we seem to enter the grounds of an English park; but scarcely have we made a few steps forward when we find ourselves again in the wide path of a trim French garden. Moreover, the dogmatic point of view which *Münscher* assumed in his time can no longer be ours, and this not only because of our disinclination to do homage either to a fashion of philosophy or of theology, but because we recognize the duty, in representing historical facts, of considering the needs of the present and the signs of the times.

In this respect the handbook of *Baumgarten-Crusius* has unmistakeable advantages over that of *Münscher*. But that which makes his work inferior to *Münscher's* in practical utility, especially for students, is its want of elasticity, which the author himself acknowledges (page vi. of the Introduction). Besides, the division into the general and particular history of dogma is an inconvenient one, as it renders the reference of the whole to the particular difficult, a defect from which *Augusti's* handbook suffers, which besides, with all its earlier merits, may be considered almost too slight for the present requirements of science. The same may be asserted still more unhesitatingly of *Bertholdt* and *Ruperti*. *Lenz* has pursued a more practical aim. Among the most recent Protestant works, I became acquainted with that of *Engelhardt* shortly before the conclusion of my sketch in manuscript; and, on the other hand, with that of *Meier* during the printing. While, however, we acknowledge the learning displayed in *Engelhardt's* history of dogma, and nothing else was to be expected from so thorough a student, the work could little satisfy the demands of those who wish to have a leading thread through the labyrinth of opinions, by means of which they may guide themselves in the confusion. I at least must confess that I have not gained a clear view of the author's plan. What special path does he find for himself through the widely extended history of heresies to the history of dogma?

On the other hand, I have been much interested in *Meier's* idea of combining together the general and particular history of dogma in such a manner that the special history of a dogma appears, when it brings a new movement into the whole, so that the earlier history of the development of any particular doctrine, hitherto concealed from the reader, is recovered in the later periods of its particular growth. This is indisputably advantageous to its artistic treatment. Stiffness and dulness are avoided, the survey of the whole is rendered easy, and only the consideration that the strict synchronistical treatment would be more suitable for the systematic, progressive, and methodic instruction that enters thoroughly into details, and which beginners in knowledge require before everything, has made me overcome my regret at not having attempted a similar method from my own point of view.

How far I have succeeded in bringing that which I failed to find in the earlier productions known to me, in any way nearer to the ideal which arose before me, and in what relation this handbook of mine will stand to the one which has just appeared, it does not become me to judge. But I may certainly acknowledge, that I shall rejoice if my endeavours find some recognition along with those of the others. Every man has received *his own* gift; and even in the department of science and the Church all are not intended for one and the same service. If it is permitted to others, through greater richness of knowledge, through keener criticism, and through deeper views into the essence and connection of divine things, to instruct the wise and learned, and out of their own special resources to erect a royal building which overtops whole races, yet I am willing to render some assistance in the degree appointed to me, without sinking thereby to a thoughtless carrier. Some one said to me once of my Encyclopedia (whether rightly, I leave to be decided), that it was a genuine student's book. If this can be said with any propriety of this history of dogmas, I shall be perfectly contented. *Convivis, non coquis,* should be the motto of every academic teacher. It is at least mine.

Most of the substance of this manual belongs to the investigations of others, whose footsteps I have conscientiously followed as far as possible to the original sources; yet I hope that here and there, where they might be least expected, the traces of my own inquiry and independent combination will be met with. In the quotation of authorities I have endeavoured to keep the mean between a superfluity confusing to the eye, and an excessive scantiness. I have purposely also, in order to avoid printing what has been already printed, often referred to *Münscher, von Cölln*; and, on the other hand, have introduced a considerable number of passages which are not to be found there. Naturally I could not quite avoid coinciding with him and others (*e.g. Gieseler*) in some, especially the principal passages. At times it has also seemed to me more serviceable to give a summary of the meaning instead of the words of the author, and now and then instead of the original passage to give sometimes a more free, sometimes a more literal translation, as the connection required.

I have also, as far as possible, referred to the best monographs or to books of extracts. In the literature of the subject there are certainly some gaps left; but I confess that I set no particular value on the mere quotation of the titles of books which it is often necessary to copy from others. In this respect there is abundance of cheap and useless work in our German literature. The signs * (for particularly good books and editions) † (for Catholic authors) are well known.

As to the theological point of view which I have taken, I consider it the less necessary to explain myself at large, as it will be shown by the work itself; and this ought to be the case in a historical work, where the subjectivity of the historian should not make itself prominent at the expense of truth and justice, nor entirely deny itself at the expense of freedom and vivacity. The time is past when (to speak with *Mosheim*) in the Church teachers one saw "only dark and walled-up heads," and in the history of dogma "only a lumber-room of human follies and foolish opinions," as *Rosenkranz* expresses it. But we are almost in danger of falling into the opposite extreme (as *de Wette* laments in the preface to the third edition of his Dogmatic); while some would like to adorn afresh, and set up as venerable, that which properly belongs to the lumber-room; and others, by arbitrary interpretations and inventions, seek to make clear for our time that which certainly belongs as well to the darker ages as to the darker provinces of thought and feeling.

It is exceedingly difficult for any one, especially in our time, to preserve the exact mean here. The individual stands more or less under the influence of his time. It is indeed truly said that the history of the world is the judgment of the world. But what mortal ventures to accomplish it? To the judgment of the world belongs also, on the ground of history, the resurrection of the dead; and with this also it has its own difficulties. While some (to continue the idea of the history of dogma) would, like the Gnostics, conjure up the spirits and let them swim in the ideal pleroma, in which everything finds a place which can assume a decorous spiritual form; others would, with St. Jerome, awake, if possible, the nails and hair, the skin and bone of the old Church theology from the dead, and carry it all into the heaven which they grant and promise as sufficient only for themselves and their followers.

But we hope with St. Paul that God in His wisdom will transfigure the mortal into the immortal, and will give to the thinking spirit the body which belongs to it. May He give a joyful resurrection to our theology, and send to it the Spirit which guides into all truth.

Written between Easter and Whitsuntide, 1840.

THE AUTHOR.

AUTHOR'S PREFACE TO THE FIFTH AND LAST GERMAN EDITION.

AFTER nearly ten years this handbook, which I sent out for the first time in the year 1840 into the learned, or rather into the studious world, now appears, in a fifth edition, before the tribunal of the public. I hope that the correcting hand will not be missed, even if criticism still finds room enough for corrections, completions, and improvements, both in form and in contents. For these I shall always be grateful.

Besides the numerous monographs, of which unfortunately some were known to me too late, and others not at all, I have made use, as far as they extend, of the "Lectures on the History of Christian Doctrine," by F. Ch. Baur, which have appeared since. I must be pleased with the judgment which is there passed on my handbook (p. 130), inasmuch as in the introduction to the first edition I described my position as being principally one of reference, as collecting together the results of science, and disavowed the glory of an original inquirer who goes forth to new discoveries. Whether, however, I have, by allowing others to speak instead of myself, in the explanatory comments on the paragraphs, when *their* words appeared accurative and expressive, sunk my work to a "mere collection of materials," on this point others may decide. But as regards the utility of the book, at least for the purpose which it was intended to subserve, the result has already decided. At least I can console myself for the reproach that in my work the "independent productive spirit is wanting;" for I am still of the opinion, that the historian has *not* independently to produce,—that is to say, to make histories,—but simply and objectively to furnish as clear and faithful a report as possible of the products of each period, and also to point out its inner connection, but not *a priori* to construct it.

I observe also that the latest English translation of my handbook (Text-book of the History of Doctrines, by Henry Smith, Professor in New York, 1861) has received many valuable additions from the hand of the translator, but especially in relation to the literature. Yet I have made use of these but sparingly, because, on the principle of *suum cuique* I did not wish to enrich myself from other men's property. At the proper places, I have indicated the rich English literature, which will, however, be little accessible to my German readers. I would much rather have lightened the ballast of title-pages than increased it unnecessarily.

In conclusion, may this handbook remain a guide to studious youth through the province of scientific doctrinal history, which is now ever more industriously and carefully cultivated. The more thoroughly and universally this is prosecuted, the less will the cry of "No more dogma," which is now heard from certain sides, find its justification; but rather a new incitement and stimulus will be given to a study of Christian doctrine, corresponding to the requirements of science.

THE AUTHOR.

BASEL, *November* 1866.

CONTENTS.

INTRODUCTION.

§		PAGE
1.	Definition,	1
2.	The Relation of the History of Doctrines to Church History and Dogmatic Theology,	5
3.	Relation to Biblical Theology,	6
4.	Relation to Symbolism,	7
5.	Relation to Patristics,	9
6.	Relation to the History of Heresies and the General History of Religion,	10
7.	Relation to the History of Philosophy, the History of Christian Ethics, and the History of Dogmatic Theology,	13
8.	Auxiliary Sciences,	15
9.	Scientific and Ethical Importance of the History of Doctrines,	16
10.	Treatment of the History of Doctrines,	17
11.	Arrangement,	20
12.	Division into Periods,	22
13.	Sources of the History of Doctrines—(*a*) Public Sources,	27
14.	(*b*) Private Sources,	32
15.	(*c*) Indirect Sources,	36
16.	Works on the History of Doctrines,	37

FIRST PERIOD.

FROM THE APOSTOLIC AGE TO THE DEATH OF ORIGEN, OR FROM THE YEAR 70 TO THE YEAR 254.

THE AGE OF APOLOGETICS.

A. GENERAL HISTORY OF DOCTRINES DURING THE FIRST PERIOD.

17.	Christ and Christianity,	49
18.	The Apostles,	53
19.	Culture of the Age, and Philosophy,	58
20.	Rule of Faith—The Apostles' Creed,	61
21.	Heresies,	63
22.	Judaism and Ethnicism,	66
23.	Ebionites and Cerinthus.—Docetæ and Gnostics,	66

CONTENTS.

§	PAGE
24. Montanism and Monarchianism,	74
25. The Catholic Doctrine,	77
26. The Theology of the Fathers,	78
27. The General Doctrinal Character of this Period,	95

B. SPECIAL HISTORY OF DOCTRINES DURING THE FIRST PERIOD.

FIRST DIVISION.

APOLOGETICO-DOGMATIC PROLEGOMENA.

TRUTH OF CHRISTIANITY—REVELATION AND SOURCES OF REVELATION—SCRIPTURE AND TRADITION.

28. Truth and Divinity of the Christian Religion in general,	97
29. Mode of Proof,	100
30. Sources of Knowledge,	108
31. Canon of the Sacred Scriptures,	109
32. Inspiration and Efficacy of the Scriptures,	114
33. Biblical Interpretation,	123
34. Tradition,	127

SECOND DIVISION.

THEOLOGY.

THE DOCTRINE CONCERNING GOD (INCLUDING THE DOCTRINE OF THE CREATION AND GOVERNMENT OF THE WORLD; ANGELOLOGY AND DEMONOLOGY).

35. The Being of God,	133
36. The Unity of God,	138
37. Whether God can be named and known,	140
38. Idealism and Anthropomorphism—Corporeity of God,	144
39. The Attributes of God,	149
40. The Doctrine of the Logos—(a) Before the Christian Era, and in other Systems,	153
41. (b) The Christian Doctrine of the Logos in the Writings of John,	158
42. (c) The Theologumenon of the Church concerning the Logos, to the Times of Origen,	160
43. (d) Origen's Doctrine of the Logos,	168
44. The Holy Ghost,	171
45. The Triad,	176
46. Monarchianism and Subordination,	178
47. Doctrine of the Creation,	183
48. Providence and Government of the World,	189
49. Angelology and Demonology,	192
50. The Angels,	193
51. The Devil and Demons,	198
52. The same subject continued,	202

THIRD DIVISION.

ANTHROPOLOGY.

§		PAGE
53.	Introduction,	207
54.	Division of Human Nature and Practical Psychology,	208
55.	Origin of the Soul,	211
56.	The Image of God,	214
57.	Freedom and Immortality—(a) Liberty,	217
58.	(b) Immortality,	221
59.	Sin, the Fall, and its Consequences,	223
60.	The Doctrine of Sin in general,	225
61.	Interpretation of the Narrative of the Fall,	226
62.	State of Innocence and Fall,	229
63.	The Effects of the Fall,	231

FOURTH DIVISION.

CHRISTOLOGY AND SOTERIOLOGY.

64.	Christology in general,	237
65.	The God-man,	239
66.	Further Development of this Doctrine,	243
67.	The Sinlessness of Jesus,	250
68.	Redemption and Atonement—(The Death of Jesus),	252
69.	Descensus ad Inferos,	262
70.	The Economy of Redemption,	264

FIFTH DIVISION.

THE CHURCH AND ITS MEANS OF GRACE.

71.	The Church,	271
72.	Baptism,	277
73.	The Lord's Supper,	286
74.	Idea of the Sacrament,	297

SIXTH DIVISION.

THE LAST THINGS.—(ESCHATOLOGY.)

75.	The Second Advent of Christ—Millenarianism—(Chiliasm),	300
76.	The Resurrection,	306
77.	The Last Judgment — Hades — Purgatory — Conflagration of the World,	312
78.	State of the Blessed and the Condemned.—Restitution of all Things,	316

SECOND PERIOD.

FROM THE DEATH OF ORIGEN TO JOHN DAMASCENE, FROM THE YEAR 254–730.

THE AGE OF POLEMICS.

A. GENERAL HISTORY OF DOCTRINES IN THE SECOND PERIOD.

§   PAGE
79. Introduction, ... 323
80. Doctrinal Definitions and Controversies, ... 324
81. The Dogmatic Character of this Period—The Fate of Origenism, . 325
82. Church Teachers of this Period, ... 326
83. The Eastern Church from the Fourth to the Sixth Century—The Schools of Alexandria and Antioch, ... 339
84. The Western Church—Augustinianism, ... 340
85. The Heresies, ... 340
86. Division of the Material, ... 343

B. SPECIAL HISTORY OF DOCTRINES DURING THE SECOND PERIOD.

FIRST CLASS.

DOCTRINAL DEFINITIONS OF THE CHURCH IN CONFLICT WITH HERESIES.

(POLEMICAL PART.)

FIRST DIVISION.

DOCTRINES RESPECTING THEOLOGY AND CHRISTOLOGY.

A. THEOLOGY PROPER.

87. The Hypostatical Relation and Subordination of the Son, . . 344
88. The Consubstantiality of the Son with the Father—Sabellius and Paul of Samosata, ... 348
89. Subordination of the Son to the Father, and the Distinction of Persons in Arianism, ... 352
90. The Hypostatical Relation and Homoousia of the Son—The Nicene Doctrine, ... 355
91. Further Fluctuations until the Synod of Constantinople, . . 357
92. The Causes of these Fluctuations—Arianism and Semi-Arianism on the one hand, and return to Sabellianism on the other—(Marcellus and Photinus), ... 360
93. Godhead of the Holy Spirit, ... 365

§		PAGE
94.	Procession of the Holy Spirit,	371
95.	Final Statement of the Doctrine of the Trinity,	374
96.	Tritheism, Tetratheism,	379
97.	Symbolum Quicumque,	381

B. CHRISTOLOGY.

98.	The True Humanity of Christ—Traces of Docetism—Arianism,	383
99.	The Doctrine of Apollinaris,	386
100.	Nestorianism,	389
101.	Eutychian-Monophysite Controversy,	393
102.	Progress of the Controversy—Theopaschites,	396
103.	Various Modifications of the Monophysite Doctrine—Aphthartodocetæ, Phthartolatri, Agnoëtæ,	398
104.	The Doctrine of Two Wills in Christ—Monothelites,	400
105.	Practical and Religious Significance of Christology during this Period,	402

SECOND DIVISION.

ANTHROPOLOGICAL DEFINITIONS.

106.	On Man in general,	404
107.	On the Doctrine of Sin in general,	411
108.	Consequences of the First Sin, and Freedom of the Will (according to the Teachers of the Greek Church),	413
109.	The Opinions of the Latin Teachers before Augustine, and of Augustine before the Pelagian Controversy,	416
110.	The Pelagian Controversy,	418
111.	First Point of Controversy—Sin—Original Sin and its Consequences,	422
112.	Second Point of Controversy—Liberty and Grace,	426
113.	Third Point of Controversy—Predestination,	429
114.	Semi-Pelagianism and the later Teachers of the Church,	432

INTRODUCTION.

[Comp. *Hagenbach*, Encyklopädie, 7te Aufl. s. 253 ff. *Th. Kliefoth*, Einleitung in die Dogmengeschichte, Parchim 1839. *F. Dörtenbach*, Die Methode der Dogmengesch. in the Studien und Kritiken, 1842. *Kling*, in Herzog's Encyklopädie, under *Dogmengeschichte*. *Baur*, Vorlesungen über die Dogmeng. 1865. [*Baur*, Lehrbuch der christ. Dogmeng. 1867. *Nitzsch*, Grundriss der chr. Dogmeng. Einleit. 1870. *Shedd*, Hist. of Christ. Doctrine, Introd. 1872. *Baur's* works distinguished thus in reff. *Vorles.* has vol. in Rom. numerals. *Lehrb.* has only the page.]

§ 1.

Definition.

THE History of Doctrines is that branch of theological science which exhibits the gradual development and definite shaping of the substance of the Christian faith into doctrinal statements[1] (definitions, dogmas) (1). It also sets forth the different forms which this system of doctrines has assumed in the course of history; the changes it has undergone as influenced by the culture of different periods; and it likewise illustrates the religious significance which it has always maintained, as the imperishable kernel in the midst of all these transformations (2).

(1) On the meaning of the word δόγμα (statutum, decretum, præceptum, placitum), see *Suicer*, Thesaurus, sub voce. *Münscher*, Lehrbuch der christlichen Dogmengeschichte, edit. by von Cölln, s. 1. *Baumgarten-Crusius*, Lehrbuch der christlichen Dogmengesch. s. 1. *Augusti*, Dogmengeschichte, § 1. *Klee*,

[1] [*Lehrgehalt* = didactic contents, into *Lehrbegriff* = doctrinal notions or system.]

Dogmengeschichte, Prolegomena. *Nitzsch,* System der christlichen Lehre, 6th ed. s. 52, 7th ed. s. 254 ff. *Hagenbach,* Encykl., 4th ed. s. 240 ff. *J. P. Lange,* Dogmatik, s. 2. *Gieseler* and *Neander,* Dogmengesch. s. 1 ff. The word δόγμα signifies, in the first place: *decree,* edict, statute. Comp. (Sept. vers.) Dan. ii. 13, vi. 8; Esth. iii. 9; 2 Macc. x. 2; and in the New Testament, Luke ii. 1; Acts xvii. 7 (where it has a political sense only); Acts xvi. 4 (used in a theological sense, denoting the apostolical rule for the Gentile Christians); Eph. ii. 15; Col. ii. 14 (in these passages it has a theological sense, not referring to *Christian* belief and *Christian* doctrine, but to the Old Testament Jewish ordinances; comp. *Winer,* Grammatik des Neutestamentlichen Sprachidioms, 5th ed. s. 250, 6th ed. s. 196 [7th ed. translated by Moulton, 1877, p. 275], and *Neander,* l.c.). Its use in the sense of substance of the Christian faith cannot be established with certainty from any passage in the N. T.; the words employed to express this idea are: εὐαγγέλιον, κήρυγμα, λόγος τοῦ θεοῦ, etc. In the writings of the *Stoics,* δόγμα (decretum, placitum) signifies: *theoretical principle. Marcus Aurelius* εἰς ἑαυτ. 2, 3: Ταῦτά σοι ἀρκέτω, ἀεὶ δόγματα ἔστω. *Cic.* Quaest. Acad. iv. 9: Sapientia neque de se ipsa dubitare debet, neque de suis decretis quae philosophi vocant δόγματα. *Seneca,* Ep. 95, distinguishes decrees (δόγματα) from precepts. The former alone are regarded by him as the root and first cause (decretum) of philosophy. Decreta sunt quae muniant, quae securitatem nostram tranquillitatemque tueantur, quae totam vitam totamque rerum naturam contineant. With this signification is connected the usage of the teachers of the Church, who first in the sphere of Christianity employed the word δόγμα (also with the predicate τὸ θεῖον) to designate the whole substance of doctrine. Compare the passages from *Ignatius* (Ep. ad Magn. c. 13), *Clement* of Alex. (Paed. I. 1, Strom. viii. p. 924, ed. of Potter), *Origen, Chrysostom, Theodoret,* etc., in *Suicer,* Thesaurus, sub voce. These teachers also sometimes called the opinions of heretics δόγματα, with the epithet μυσαρά, or others of similar import, but more frequently δόξαι, νοήματα; comp. *Klee,* l.c. *Cyril* of Jerusalem (Cat. 4, 2) already makes a distinction between the dogmatic and the moral, and understands by δόγμα that which relates to *faith* (conception); by πρᾶξις, that which refers to moral action: Ὁ τῆς θεοσεβείας τρόπος ἐκ δύο τούτων συνέστηκε· δογμάτων εὐσεβῶν καὶ πράξεων ἀγαθῶν. The former are the source of the latter. In a similar way Seneca describes the *dogmas* as the elements of which the body of wisdom is composed, as the heart of life (see above). Thus *Socrates* (Hist. Eccl. ii. 44) says of Bishop Meletius of Antioch: Περὶ δόγματος διαλέγεσθαι ὑπερετίθετο, μόνην δὲ τὴν ἠθικὴν διδασκαλίαν τοῖς ἀκροαταῖς προσήκειν. (Scribendum videtur προσεῖχεν vel προσῆγεν, *Vales.*) So, too, *Gregory* of Nyssa says of Christ and His mode of teaching, Ep. 6: Διαιρῶν γὰρ εἰς δύο τὴν τῶν χριστιανῶν πολιτείαν, εἴς τε τὸ ἠθικὸν μέρος καὶ εἰς τὴν δογμάτων ἀκρίβειαν. According to *Chrysostom*, too (Hom. 27 in Joh. iii.), Christianity requires along with the ὀρθότης δογμάτων a πολιτείαν ὑγιαίνουσαν. A peculiar definition of δόγμα is given by *Basil*, De Spiritu S. c. 27: Ἄλλο γὰρ δόγμα καὶ ἄλλο κήρυγμα· τὸ μὲν γὰρ σιωπᾶται, τὰ δὲ κηρύγματα δημοσιεύεται (esoteric and exoteric doctrine). According to *Eusebius* (Adv. Marc. i. 4), *Marcellus* had already used the word δόγμα in the sense of a human, subjective opinion: Τὸ τοῦ δόγματος ὄνομα ἀνθρωπίνης ἔχεται βουλῆς τε καὶ γνώμης. Only in modern times (*Nitzsch* says, since *Döderlein*) did the usage become general, in accordance with which δόγμα does not designate *ipsa doctrina*, so much as *sententia alicujus doctoris*, that is, doctrinal opinion instead of doctrinal conception. With this explanation of the word is intimately connected the definition of the idea of the science of the History of Doctrines, as well as its value and mode of treatment. (Comp. § 10, and *Gieseler's* Dogmengeschichte, s. 2.) [Gieseler here says, that dogma designates a doctrine, which, as essential to a true faith, claims acceptance among all Christians. The dogmas of any Church express its views of what is essential in the Christian system, in distinction from subjective opinions.]

(2) In respect to this, there is need to beware of two wrong paths. The one is that of those who descry a *perversion* or change of doctrine, in every other manner of apprehending doctrine, in every change of expression and statement, on the false assumption that none but biblical terminology should be introduced into doctrinal theology (*Dogmatik*), which would

make the whole History of Doctrines only a history of deterioration and corruption. The other extreme is that of those who assume that there has been only a constant sound development of truth within the Church, and who will not concede that, together with sound development, diseased conditions have also been generated. Genuine science has respect to both; it finds progress, checks, and retrogression, legitimate developments and those which are illegitimate. (Thus, *e.g.*, it would be incorrect to reject the doctrines of the Trinity, of Original Sin, of the Sacraments, etc., because these exact expressions do not occur in the Bible; although we may lawfully inquire whether foreign ideas may not have crept in with such definite formulas; for with the *development* of a doctrine also grows the danger of contracting or of exaggerating it.) We must, then, distinguish between the *formation*, the *deformation*, and the *reformation* of dogma; and this last, again, is different from mere *restoration* and *repristination.*

It is here that the point of view of the *Catholic* and of the *Protestant* in relation to the History of Doctrines differs. According to the former, dogma has been developed under the constant guidance of the Divine Spirit, and whatever is unsound has been rejected under the form of heresy; so that we cannot really speak of a proper development of doctrine (compare the remarkable concession of *Hermes* of Bonn, as cited in *Neander's* Dogmengeschichte, s. 28) [viz. that it is contrary to the principles of the Catholic Church to treat the history of doctrines as a special branch, since this presupposes the changes made by a developing process; and, consequently, Hermes had doubts as to reading lectures on the subject]. Protestantism, on the other hand, perpetually applies the standard of the Scriptures to the developed dogma, and allows it to be a doctrine of the Church only so far as it reproduces the contents of Scripture. But it is a misunderstanding of the Protestant principle which would lead one to reject everything which is not *verbally* and *literally* contained in the Scriptures. From this standpoint, which finds the whole of dogmatic theology already complete in the Bible, the possibility of a History of Doctrines must be denied, or it must be made to be only a history of errors.

§ 2.

The Relation of the History of Doctrines to Church History and Dogmatic Theology.

The History of Doctrines is a part of Church History, but separated from it on account of its wide ramifications, and treated as an independent science (1). It forms the transition from Church History to ecclesiastical and dogmatic theology (2).

(1) Comp. § 16, and *Hagenbach*, Encyklop. s. 253 ff. Church History also treats of the History of Doctrine; but, in relation to the whole ecclesiastical life, it appears only as the muscles of the living body stand forth to the eye, while the knife of the anatomist lays them bare in the corpse, and proceeds to separate them for scientific uses. " *The difference between the History of Doctrines as a separate branch of theological science, and as a part of ecclesiastical history, is merely formal. For, apart from the difference of extent, which depends on external considerations, the subject of investigation is the same in both cases,—different poles of the same axis. The History of Doctrines treats of the dogma as it developes itself in the form of definite conceptions; ecclesiastical history views the dogma in its relation to external events.*" *Hase*, Church History, pref. Comp. also *Neander*, Dogmengesch. s. 6 : " *Church History judges phenomena by their extensive, the History of Doctrines by their intensive importance. Events are incorporated into Church History only as they have a diffused influence, while the History of Doctrines goes back to the germs of the antagonisms.*" *Baur* (s. 2) distinguishes the History of Doctrines and Church History in this manner, that, "*whilst the latter concerns itself with the external side of Christian life, the former has reference to the internal.*" But the inner life of the Church, which has many other factors, is not expressed in dogma. Baur, too, certainly regards Church History chiefly from the standpoint of dogma, and shows less interest for its inner life, which is not formulated in dogma. *Ebrard* has declared himself as opposed to a History of Doctrines which is separated from Church History (Pref. to his History of the

Church and its Doctrines, 1865; s. viii.). But there is a distinct difference between the inner development of dogma in the laboratory of thought and the visible conflict of differing doctrinal tendencies which appears in history. The History of Doctrines gives up to Church History the external course of doctrinal controversies, and takes for granted that this is already known.[1]

(2) Many regard the History of Doctrines as an *appendix* to dogmatic theology, rather than an *introduction* to it; but this arises from incorrect assumptions respecting the nature of dogmatic theology, and from a misapprehension of its historical character (one-sided conception of dogmatic theology, either from the biblical or from the speculative point of view). The History of Doctrines is the bridge from the sphere of historical theology to that of didactic (systematic) theology. Ecclesiastical history is presupposed; dogmatic theology, both of the present and the future, is the aim and end of its researches. Comp. *Neander*, l.c. 9 : " *The History of Doctrines mediates between pure apostolical Christianity and the Church of the present, by exhibiting the development of Christian doctrine.*" [*Baur* remarks, l.c. s. 2, 3 : " *The object* (of the History of Doctrines and doctrinal theology) *is the same, but the form in which it appears is different. Doctrinal theology is the stream of the History of Doctrines come to rest. What, in the history, is in a continual state of change, doctrinal theology handles at some particular moment as stationary.*"]

§ 3.

Relation to Biblical Theology.

The History of Doctrines presupposes Biblical Theology (the doctrines of the New Testament in particular) as its basis; just as the general history of the Church presupposes the life of Jesus and the apostolic age.

Those writers who reduce dogmatic theology to *biblical*

---

[1] Not so *Baur* in his lectures on the History of Doctrines, in which he introduces a good deal of Church History.

theology, and ignore ecclesiastical theology, are consistent in regarding the History of Doctrines as a mere appendix to biblical theology. But in our view, biblical theology is to be considered as only the *foundation* of the edifice; the History of Doctrines the history of its further *construction;* and dogmatic theology (as a science) is still engaged in its *completion.* It is no more the object of the History of Doctrines to expound the doctrines of the Bible, than of ecclesiastical history to give a complete account of the life of Christ and the apostles. But as the history of primitive Christianity is the only solid foundation and starting-point of Church history, so the History of Doctrines must rest upon biblical theology, beginning with that of the New Testament, and going back to that of the Old Testament. It is, of course, understood that the relation in which biblical theology stands to biblical exegesis and criticism, also applies as a standard to the History of Doctrines.

§ 4.

Relation to Symbolism.

The History of Doctrines comprises the *Symbols* (1) of the Church, since it must have respect not only to the formation and contents of public confessions of faith (2), but also to the distinguishing doctrines set forth in them (3). Symbolism may, however, be separated from the History of Doctrines, and treated as comparative dogmatic theology. It stands in the same relation to the History of Doctrines as the Church statistics of any particular period stand to the continuous history of the Church.

(1) On the ecclesiastical usage of the terms σύμβολον (συμβάλλειν, συμβάλλεσθαι), comp. *Suicer*, Thesaurus, s.v. p. 1084. *Creuzer*, Symbolik, § 16. *Marheineke*, christliche Symbolik, Bd. i. near the beginning. *Neander*, Kirch. Gesch. i. 2, s. 536. [*Pelt*, Theol. Encyclop. s. 456. *Maximus Taurinensis* (about the year 460) says in Hom. in Symb. p. 329: Symbolum tessera est et signaculum, quo inter

fideles perfidosque secernitur.] By *ecclesiastical symbols* (in the doctrinal sense of the word, but not its liturgical or artistic sense) are meant the public confessions of faith, by which those belonging to the same ecclesiastical communion recognize each other, as soldiers by the watchword (tessera militaris). Otherwise *Rufinus*, expos. symb.: Symbolon græce collatio dici potest hoc est, quod plures in unum conferunt.

(2) The *older symbols* of the Church (*e.g.* the so-called Apostles' Creed, the Nicene and Athanasian Creeds) were the shibboleth (Judg. xii. 6) of the Catholics, as opposed to heretics. It is evident that these symbols are deserving of special cônsideration in the history of doctrines. The ecclesiastical confessions are related to the private opinions of individual ecclesiastical teachers, as the mountain-range to the hills and valleys of a country. They are, as it were, the watch-towers from which the entire field may be surveyed, the principal stations in the study of the History of Doctrines, and cannot therefore be arbitrarily separated from it, and consigned to an isolated department. Just as little should the study of the History of Doctrines be restricted to that of symbolism. See *Dorner*, Entwicklungsgeschichte der Lehre von der Person Christi, I. i. s. 32 ff. [Eng. tr. p. 48]. *J. P. Lange*, Dogmatik, i. s. 32 ff.: "*The ecclesiastical dogma has its place between Church doctrine and the Church symbols; it is their living centre, mediating between them: and hence it can be considered as the Church doctrine in a narrower, or as the Church symbol in a wider sense.*"

(3) Since the Reformation, the *Symbols* are to Protestants, not only, as they were to the Catholic Church in ancient times, a barrier erected against heretics,—although Protestantism has also united with the old Church in keeping up this barrier; but Protestants were also forced to give prominence in special confessions to the characteristic peculiarities of their doctrine in opposition to the old Church. These confessions of faith, moreover, had regard to the differences which arose out of controversies within the pale of the Protestant Church itself (between Lutherans and Reformed), and to other opinions at variance with those held by the orthodox party (Anabaptists, Unitarians, and others). And so, too, the Catholics exhibited the doctrine of their Church in a special confession of faith.

All this led to the formation of a separate branch of theological science, which was first known under the name of *Theologia Elenctica* or *Polemics*, and in later times has taken the more peaceful appellation of *Symbolism*, which last name has not so much reference to the progress of the struggle itself, as to the historical knowledge of the points at issue, and the nature of that struggle.[1] When the History of Doctrines comes to the time of the Reformation, it becomes of itself what has been meant by the word symbolism; *i.e.* the stream of history spreads of itself into a sea, the quiet contemplation of the developing process passes over into a complicated series of events, until these lead into a new course of development; and thus the older History of Doctrines is adjusted in relation to the modern. *Baumgarten-Crusius* has also indicated the necessity of uniting Symbolism and the History of Doctrines, Dogmengesch. i. s. 14 f. Comp. *Neander*, Dogmengesch. s. 7: [Symbolism sprung from a dogmatic, and the History of Doctrines from a historical interest: the latter has to do with the historical process leading to the results, which Symbolism compares, etc.]

§ 5.

Relation to Patristics.

As the History of Doctrines has to do with the history of the doctrinal system, as being the common property of the Church, it can consider the private views of individual Church teachers only so far as these have had, or at least have endeavoured to have, a real influence on the formation of the Church doctrine. More precise investigations as to the opinions of any one person in connection with his individual characteristics, and the influence of the former upon the latter, must be left to Patristics (Patrology).

[1] *Sack*, however, has recently published a work on Polemics (Christliche Polemik, Hamburg, 2d ed. 1841) as a distinct science, falling within the historical sphere of Symbolism. Comp. *Hagenbach*, Encykl. s. 298 ff.; and *Hase*, Handbuch der protestantischen Polemik, Halle, 3d ed. 1871.

On the meaning of the indefinite term Patristics as a science, comp. *Hagenbach*, Encyklopädie, s. 262 ff.[1] Even if we enlarge its sphere, so as to make it embrace not only the Church teachers of the first six centuries, but all who have worked upon the Church, either in a creative or reforming spirit,— since Church Fathers must continue as long as the Church (*Möhler*, Patrologie, s. 20),—it is evident that a large proportion of patristic material must be incorporated into the History of Doctrines; the very study of the original documents leads to this. But we would not maintain, with *Baumgarten-Crusius* (Dogmengeschichte, s. 12), that the History of Doctrines already comprises the *essential* part of Patristics; for the individual characteristics, which are the essential part of the latter, can have only a secondary place in the former. Thus the object of the latter is to know Augustinianism, that of Patristics to know Augustine. How the system is related to the person? is a biographical (patrological) question: what is its relation to the doctrine of the Church? is the question in the History of Doctrines. The opinions, too, of individual theologians are of importance in the History of Doctrines, only so far as they have had an appreciable influence upon the formation of the doctrinal system, or have in some way acted upon it. Comp. *Gieseler*, Dogmengesch. s. 11, and *Fr. Nitzsch*, Geschichtliches und Mythologisches zur Patristik (Jahrb. für deutsche Theologie, 1865). On the literature of this subject, see § 14.

§ 6.

Relation to the History of Heresies and the general History of Religion.

Since ecclesiastical dogma has, for the most part, been developed in the conflict with heretical tendencies, it is

---

[1] The distinction made by some writers, especially Roman Catholics, between Patristics and Patrology (*e.g. Möhler*, Patrologie, s. 14), appears to be rather arbitrary. [Protestants usually end the series of the Fathers of the Church with the sixth century, Roman Catholics extend it to the thirteenth. The latter distinguish between fathers, doctors, and authors. The scholastic divines are *Doctores.*]

evident that the History of Doctrines must also include the History of Heresies, giving prominence to those points which have had an essential influence in completing or adjusting the formation of doctrine; or, to such as have set the doctrine itself in a clearer light by their very antagonism (1). To learn the inner formation and ramifications of heretical systems themselves, appeals to a different interest, which is met either in the so-called History of Heresies (2) or in the general History of Religion. Still less is it the object of the History of Doctrines to discuss the relation between Christianity and other forms of religion. On the contrary, it presupposes the comparative history of religion in the same manner as dogmatic theology presupposes *apologetic theology* (3).

(1) From the ecclesiastical point of view, the History of Heresies may be compared to Pathology, the History of Doctrines to Physiology. It is not meant by this that in heresy only disease is to be found, and that full health can be found only in that which has been established as ecclesiastical orthodoxy. For it has been justly observed, that diseases are frequently natural transitions from a lower to a higher stage of life, and that a state of relative health is not unfrequently a product of antecedent disease. Thus the obstinacy of a one-sided error has often had the effect of giving life, and even a more correct form of statement, to the doctrine of the Church. Comp. *Schenkel*, das Wesen des Protestantismus (Schaffh. 1845), i. s. 13. *Baur*, die christliche Lehre von der Dreieinigkeit, i. s. 112. *Neander*, Dogmengesch. s. 16. On the relation of heresy to orthodoxy in general, see *Dorner*, Lehre von der Person Christi, I. i. s. 71, Note [Eng. tr. p. 344]. [See also *Rothe's* Anfänge d. christl. Kirche, s. 333, for the difference between the Church view and the heretical view of doctrines.]

(2) The phrase History of Heresies has been banished by a more humane usage; but not the thing itself, any more than Polemics. The very able publications of recent writers on the Gnostic systems, Ebionitism, Manichæism, Montanism, Unitarianism, etc., and the monographs on some of the Fathers, are of great use to the historian of Christian

doctrine; but he cannot be expected to incorporate all the materials thus furnished into the History of Doctrines. Thus the first period of the History of Doctrines must constantly recur to the phenomena of Ebionitism and Gnosticism, since it was the problem of the Church doctrine to work itself out between these two perilous rocks. But the widespread branches of the Gnostic systems, so far as they differ from one another (*e.g.* as to the number of the æons and the succession of the syzygies), cannot here be traced in detail, unless, indeed, we are to seek in the slime of heresy, as it is collected *e.g.* in the Clementines, for the first living germs of Christianity! Holding fast, on the other hand, from the beginning, to the original biblical type, so far as this heresy is concerned, it will be sufficient to exhibit those forms in which it deviates from this primitive type, and to delineate its physiognomy in general outlines, as they are given in Church History; and the same will suffice for the heresies of the subsequent periods. Thus Nestorianism and Monophysitism are of importance in the Christological controversy of the second period. But after they were overcome by the Catholic spirit, and fixed in sects, which, in consequence of the continued conflict, were themselves divided into smaller parties, it can be no longer the office of the History of Doctrines to follow them in this process. This must be left to monographs on the heresies. For as soon as a sect has lost its doctrine-shaping power, it falls simply into the department of statistics.

(3) Just as it is no part of the functions of dogmatic theology to defend the truth of the Christian religion, since Apologetics must do this work beforehand (see *Hagenbach*, Encyklop. § 81); so, too, the History of Doctrines has nothing to do with the conflict of Christianity with Polytheism, Islamism, etc. But the history of these religions is indispensable as an auxiliary study. The notions of the Jewish sects, the myths and symbols of polytheistic religions, the systems of Mohammed, of Buddha, etc., are still more foreign to the history of Christian doctrines than the heresies of the Church. *Works of reference: Creuzer*, Symbolik und Mythologie der alten Völker, Darmstadt 1819–23, 6 Bde., 3d ed. 1843. *Stuhr*, allgemeine Geschichte der Religionsformen der heidnischen Völker: 1. die Religionssysteme der

heidnischen Völker des Orients, Berlin 1836. 2. die Religionssysteme der Hellenen in ihrer geschichtlichen Entwicklung bis auf die makedonische Zeit, Berlin 1838. *J. Grimm*, deutsche Mythologie, Göttingen 1835, 2 Aufl. 1844–8. *Görres*, Mythengeschichte der Asiatischen Völker. *Richter*, Phantasien des Orients. *Dr. K. Eckermann*, Lehrbuch der Religionsgeschichte und Mythologie der vorzüglichsten Völker des Alterthums, nach der Anordnung von Gottfr. Müller, Halle 1845, 2 Bde. *A. Wuttke*, Gesch. des Heidenthums, 8vo, Breslau 1852–3, 2 Bde. *Hegel*, Phil. der Religion (Werke). *Sepp*, Das Heidenthum, 3 Bde. 1853. *A. von Cölln*, Lehrbuch der vorchristlichen Religionsgeschichte, Lemgo 1853. *L. Preller*, Griech. Mythologie, 2 Bde. 1854. *Baltzer*, allgemeine Religionsgeschichte, Nordhausen 1854. †*Lutterbeck*, das Zeitalter der Religionswende, Mainz 1832. †*J. J. I. v. Döllinger*, Heidenthum und Judenthum, Vorhalle zur Geschichte des Christenthums, Regensburg 1857. [*C. C. J. Bunsen*, Gott in d. Geschichte, 3 Bde., and in English, 1857–8. *Schelling*, Phil. der Mythologie, 2 Bde. 1857. *C. O. Müller*, Mythology, transl. by Leitch, Lond. 1844. *Ch. Hardwick*, Christ and other Masters, four parts, Cambridge 1855–9.]

§ 7.

Relation to the History of Philosophy, the History of Christian Ethics, and the History of Dogmatic Theology.

Although the History of Doctrines has elements in common with the history of philosophy (1), yet they are no more to be confounded with each other than dogmatic theology and philosophy (2). The History of Doctrines is also to be separated from the history of Christian ethics, so far as systematic theology itself is able to make a relative distinction between dogmatics and morals (3). And even to the history of dogmatic theology, it has the relation, at most, of the whole to the part, since the former may indeed have its place in the History of Doctrines (in the general portion), but can by no means be supplanted by it (4).

(1) This is the case, *e.g.*, with the Alexandrian school, the Gnostics, the Scholastics, and modern philosophical schools. Still the object of the History of Philosophy is distinct from that of the History of Doctrines. Comp. *Baumgarten-Crusius*, i. s. 8. Works of reference: *J. Brucker*, Historia Critica Philosophiae, Lips. 1742-4, 5 vols. 4to; 2d ed. 1766-7, 6 vols. 4to. [The History of Philosophy drawn up from Brucker's Hist. Crit. Philos., by *William Enfield*, Lond. 1819, 2 vols.] *W. G. Tennemann*, Geschichte der Philosophie, Leipzig 1798-1819, 11 Bde. [The "Grundriss" of the same author is published in English under the title: "A Manual of the History of Philosophy," translated from the German by the Rev. *Arthur Johnson*, Oxf. 1832; revised edition by *Morell*, in Bohn's Library.] *E. Reinhold*, Geschichte der Philosophie, Jena 1845, 3d ed. 2 vols. *H. Ritter*, Geschichte der Philosophie, Hamburg 1829-53, 12 Bde. [The Ancient Phil. translated into English by *Alex. J. W. Morrison*, Oxf. 1838-9, 4 vols. 8vo.] *Fries*, Geschichte der Philosophie, i., Halle 1837.—(The two latter only for the old history.) *Schleiermacher*, Geschichte der Philosophie, edit. by *H. Ritter* (complete works, iv. 1), Berlin 1839. *T. A. Rixner*, Handbuch d. Gesch. d. Phil., 3 Bde. 1829; Gumposch, Supplement, 1850. *E. Zeller*, Die Philos. d. Griechen, 3 Bde. 1875-7. *J. E. Erdmann*, Gesch. d. neueren Phil., 3 Bde. (6 Theile) 1834-53. *K. Fischer*, Neuere Phil., 6 Bde. 1865-72. *Albert Schwegler*, Hist. of Phil., transl. by J. H. Seelye, New York 1856. *J. D. Morell*, Phil. of the Nineteenth Century. *H. M. Chalybäus*, Hist. Entwickelung . . . von Kant bis Hegel. Trans. (Edinb.) 1856. *H. Ritter*, Die christl. Philosophie . . . in ihrer Geschichte, 2 Bde., Göttingen 1858-9.] *Ueberweg*, Grundriss der Geschichte der Philosophie; 3 Theil, die Christliche Zeit (Patristik und Scholastik), 5th ed. 1877. *A. Stöckl*, Geschichte der Phil. des Mittelalters, 3 Bde., Mainz 1864-7. Further on the literature of the subject, in *Hagenbach*, Encykl. s. 248 ff.

(2) "*The obliteration of the distinction between the History of Philosophy and the History of Doctrines results from a fundamental confusion of the essential nature of Christianity.*" *Dorner*, Person Christi, i. s. 108; comp. *Neander*, Dog-

mengesch. s. 9.:—["Philosophy developes conscious reason of and by itself; theology is employed upon data historically given—the truths that repose in the divine word, and have passed over into Christian consciousness."] On the other side, *Baur*, l.c. s. 78 ff.

(3) Comp. *Baumgarten-Crusius*, s. 9.

(4) Comp. § 11: *Neander*, Dogmengesch. s. 6; *Gieseler*, Dg. s. 16; *Baur*, s. 25 ff.

§ 8.

Auxiliary Sciences.

Although the branches of theological science above enumerated are strictly distinct from the History of Doctrines, they are, nevertheless, in a measure connected with it as auxiliary sciences (1). *Archæology* (2), and, in the second line, the sciences auxiliary to Church History (3), may be added to their number.

(1) *Ecclesiastical History* itself may be viewed in the light of an auxiliary science, since the history of forms of Church government, of worship, of the private life of Christians, etc., are connected with the History of Doctrine. In like manner *Patristics, the History of Heresies, the General History of Religion, the History of Philosophy,* and *the History of Christian* (and *general*) *Ethics* are to be numbered among the auxiliary sciences.

(2) From the connection between the doctrines and the liturgy of the Church, it is obvious that *Archæology* must be considered as an auxiliary science, if we understand by it the complete history of Christian worship. This may easily be seen from the use of certain doctrinal expressions (*e.g.* θεοτόκος, etc.) in the liturgies of the Church, the institution of doctrinal festivals (the feast of Corpus Christi, that of the conception of the Virgin Mary), the reflex influence of the existence or absence of certain liturgical usages on the doctrinal definitions of the Church (*e.g.* the influence of the withholding of the cup on the doctrine of concomitance, comp. § 195), etc. *Works of reference:*

J. Bingham, Origg. s. Antiqu. Ecclesiasticæ, Halæ 1751–61. [*J. Bingham*, Antiquities of the Christian Church, and other works, Lond. 1834 ff., 8 vols.; a new edition by Richard Bingham.] *J. Ch. W. Augusti*, Denkwürdigkeiten aus der christlichen Archäologie, Leipz. 1817–31, 12 vols. [Christian Antiquities, translated and compiled from the works of Augusti, by the *Rev. Lyman Coleman*, Andover 1844; also by Riddle, London 1839.] *F. H. Rheinwald*, kirchliche Archäologie, Berl. 1830. [*K. Schöne*, Geschichtforschungen über die kirchlichen Gebräuche und Einrichtungen der Kirche, Berl. 1819–22, 3 vols.] *W. Böhmer*, christlich-kirchliche Alterthumswissenschaft, Bresl. 1836–9, 2 vols. [*Siegel*, Handbuch d. christl. kirchl. Alterthümer, 4 Bde., Leipz. 1835–8. *Guericke*, Archäologie, 2d ed. 1860. *William Bates*, Lect. on Christ. Antiquities, 1854–7.] *H. Otto*, Handbuch der christlichen Kunstarchäologie, 4th ed. 1868. *Piper*, Mythologie der christlichen Kunst, Weimar 1847, 1 Bd. s. 10 ff.: "*The daily contemplation of the works of religious art, especially when they are executed in the spirit of the age, has always had a great influence on the faith of the multitude, an influence which has certainly been greater on the side of unbelief than of faith.*" Very instructive on this point are several treatises of Piper, in the evangelisches Kalender edited by him. Comp. also das christliche Kunstblatt of *Grüneisen*.

(3) These are, besides those already mentioned, Universal History, Ecclesiastical Philology, Ecclesiastical Chronology, Diplomatics, etc. [Comp. the introductions to works on Ecclesiastical History. *Gieseler*, Text-Book of Church Hist., published by Clark, Edinburgh, also edited by H. B. Smith, New York, vol. i. pp. 19, 20, 560-2.]

§ 9.

Scientific and Ethical Importance of the History of Doctrines.

Ernesti, Prolusiones de Theologiæ Historicæ et Dogmaticæ conjungendæ Necessitate, Lips. 1759, in his Opusc. Theol., Lips. 1773–92. *Ch. F. Illgen*, über den Werth der christlichen Dogmengeschichte, Leipz. 1817. *Augusti*, Werth der Dogmengeschichte, in his Theologische Blätter, II. 2, s. 11 ff. *Hagenbach*, Encyklop. § 69. *Niedner*, Das Recht der Dogmen, in his

Zeitschrift f. d. hist. Theol. 1851. *Baur*, l.c. [Comp. *Kling* in the Studien und Kritiken, 1840. *Niedner*, Zur neuesten Dogmengesch. in the Allg. Monatsschrift, 1851. *Engelhardt* in the Zeitschrift f. d. historische Theologie, 1853.]

The scientific value of the History of Doctrines follows in part from what has already been said. 1. It helps to complete the study of Church History in one of its most important aspects. 2. It is an introduction to the study of systematic theology (1). Its moral and religious influence, its practical benefits, are the result of this purely scientific significance. In general, it exerts a shaping influence, by bringing into view the efforts and struggles of the human spirit in relation to its most important concerns. But it is of special use to the theologian and to the religious man, by preserving him both from a one-sided and rigid adherence to the letter (false orthodoxy), and from the superficial love of novelty which is characteristic of a dogmatic and superficial spirit (heterodoxy and neology) (2).

(1) Comp. § 2.
(2) Comp. § 10. The importance of the History of Doctrines in both these respects has frequently been overrated. Every theological tendency has appealed to it in support of its peculiar views, or dreaded its results, both equally unworthy of the scientific temper. Comp. *Baumgarten-Crusius*, i. s. 16–20.

§ 10.

Treatment of the History of Doctrines.

Daub, die Form der christlichen Dogmen. und Kirchenhistorie in Betracht gezogen, in Baur's Zeitschrift für speculative Theologie, Berlin 1836. Parts 1 and 2. *Th. Kliefoth*, Einleitung in die Dogmengeschichte, Parchim 1839. *Baur*, l.c. s. 29 ff.

These beneficial results, however, can flow only from that treatment of the History of Doctrines which brings to distinct consciousness not only what is changeable in the doctrinal statements, but what is permanent in the midst of the changes; that which moves through the transient with a revivifying energy: in a word, that which is essential and unchangeable in the Christian system of redemption.[1] Only such a treatment of the subject as, in its historical pragmatism, exhibits the external causes of the variation, in union with the dynamical principle, which works from within outwards.

The following are the different methods in which the History of Doctrines may be treated:—

1. *The merely statutory*, which simply accepts what has been confirmed by the Church as established truth, and excludes all that differs from this as confirmed heresy; the logical standpoint of Roman Catholicism. History, in this view, is simply the register of the protocols of the dictatorship of faith, exercised once for all.

2. *The exclusively biblical*, which starts from the position that the *biblical statement of doctrine* in its simple expression is sufficient for all subsequent times, and which then convinces itself either that it finds in the Bible, according to a traditional exegesis, the orthodox formulas that were later developed (*e.g.* those of the Trinity and Original Sin), or, with logical exegetical severity, excludes what is not verbally contained in the Scriptures (biblical supernaturalism on the one side, or biblical rationalism on the other)—the standpoint of a still incomplete Protestantism. With this method of treatment is usually conjoined

3. *The pragmatic and critical*, which explains all which goes beyond the Bible (or even the popular reason) by all sorts of accidents and externalities, by climatic, or social and political relations, personal sympathy and antipathy, passions, cabals of courts, priestly deception, superstition, and the like: the standpoint of vulgar rationalism, in which, however, for a long time, the merely formal biblical supernaturalism shared.

4. *The one-sided speculative treatment*, which sees in the whole development of doctrine a higher but naturalistic process, completed by an internal necessity. Thus, every

---

[1] [For some good remarks on this subject, comp. *Nitzsch*, Grundriss der Dogmeng. Einl. § 3.]

dogma at some period attains its prime, and then fades away and gives place to another. Here the religious and practical significance of doctrine is underrated, as is its speculative significance by the previous modes of treatment. The error at the basis of this method, which was pushed to its extreme by *Strauss* (in his Dogmatik), and which found an ardent scientific advocate in *Baur*, is in considering Christianity as the mere completion of a process of thought—that is, as a kind of philosophy; when it is really a moral and religious force, resting on a historical fact, and continually working on and by personal agents. *Neander* (Dogmengeschichte, s. 15) correctly says: " *While a superficial pragmatism concedes too much influence to the individual, the speculative method sets it wholly aside, regarding individuals as nothing but the blind (?) organs of the idea, and as necessary momenta in its process of development.*"

5. *The theological method* considers the doctrinal substance of the Bible as a living germ, capable of the most prolific development, which, in the midst of the most evidently unfavourable influences, nevertheless retains the productive power, which brings forth new forms of life adapted to the times. It always (like the second method) goes back to the Bible, and measures the products by the canon; but the plant which springs from a biblical root it will neither drive back into the root, nor cut off from it. It has respect (like the third method) to the external circumstances and the conditions of personal life, under which the doctrine has been developed, and is far from denying these influence, often so palpable and tangible; only it does not rank them so high as to get lost, with such pragmatism, in a mere atomistic tendency. Instead of this, it takes for granted (with the fourth method) that there is a dynamic process of development, which, however, is not purely dialectic, and therefore itself again subject to decomposition—for this were only a more refined atomism (as is seen in Strauss' method). But, as *religious* truth can be only approximately expressed in speculative forms,[1] it also seeks after the beatings of the heart of the religious life,

---

[1] Compare the striking remark of *Hamann*, cited in *Neander*, Dogmeng. s. 3 : "The pearl of Christianity is a life hid in God, consisting neither in dogmas, nor in notions, nor in rites and usages."

in the midst of both the coarser and the finer muscular systems, that it may thus grasp the whole organism. This is the *scientific* standpoint which is worthy of a genuine Protestantism; for that alone is truly scientific, which knows the nature of the object which science has to exhibit. He who misconceives the *essential nature of religion* (as distinguished from purely speculative thought), though he may have all historical knowledge and speculative talent, is unequal to a comprehensive and satisfactory account of the History of Doctrines.

§ 11.

Arrangement.

The object of the History of Doctrines is to exhibit, not only the history of *dogma* as a whole, *i.e.* the whole substance of Christian teaching, and the doctrinal *spirit* expressed in its definite statements, but also the history of *dogmas*, *i.e.* the development of those particular *doctrinal statements, opinions*, and *representations of the faith*, in which the Church teaching of each period is unfolded (1). Both these points of view ought then to be so combined that the general shall be made more clear by the special, and the special also by the general. This is the import of the division of the materials into the *General and the Special History of Doctrines.* This division can be vindicated only when the two are not merely placed externally side by side, but are placed in such a relation to each other that the General History of Doctrine is seen to be the root of the Special, and is so proportioned that it forms an introduction to it (2).

(1) " *The Christian dogma (as a whole) approves itself as a thoroughly simple, and, at the same time, as an infinitely varied system of dogmas; it is just as much a single dogma as it is also a world of dogmas. And this is the test of the perfected dogmatic principle, that all genuine dogmas can be derived from it, and referred back to it.*" J. P. Lange, l.c. i. s. 29. " *The*

History of Doctrines has not only to consider how the particular doctrines, one after another, have received an individual, separate existence, and have asserted a right to such existence, but also to show how they are yet in their co-existence only parts of a whole, elements of one and the same conception, members of an organic system." Baur, l.c. s. 28. Comp. s. 75 ff.

(2) The division into the General and Special History of Doctrines has been assailed in recent times (by *Baur* in his review of Münscher's Lehrbuch, von Cölln's edition, in the Berlin wiss. Jahrbücher, Febr. 1836, s. 230, and by *Klee* in his Dogmengesch. s. 9), and rightly, so far as the two are merely co-ordinated without internal relations, and the one treated only after the other has been considered (as in *Augusti* and *Baumgarten-Crusius*); for in this way the one half seems a detailed History of Doctrine, and consequently a chapter of Church History, the other a system of theology in a historical form; and, moreover, repetitions cannot be avoided. But even *Münscher* has the correct view, bringing forward the general and the special in each period, so that the former stands as an introduction to the latter, and the one becomes the test of the other; and this is undoubtedly the best method. (Comp. also *Neander's* Dogmengeschichte.) The so-called General History of Doctrines is the bond which unites into one whole the history of the particular doctrines, since it exhibits the points of view under which they are to be considered, the conditions under which they originated, etc.[1] Or, would it be better, with *Klee*, to treat merely of the history of individual doctrines without prefixing any general summary, and without any division into periods? This leads to dismemberment. The method chosen by *Meier* appeals most strongly to the artistic sense; he tries to mould the historical material in such a way *"that the course of the history may correspond as exactly as possible with the course of development of the dogma itself, in which the general and the special are always acting as conditions, the one upon the other; and so, too,*

---

[1] So far, the General History of Doctrines is like the History of Dogmatics; but yet it is not to be identified with it. It comprises a wider sphere. It is related to it as is the History of Law to the History of Jurisprudence, as is the History of Art to the History of Æsthetics, as is the History of Christian Preaching to the History of Homiletics (as a science).

that the different aspects of the dogma can always be brought forward just at the juncture where there is manifestly some decisive or new point of development." But still, in this mode of treatment, the materials are apt to be too sparingly used. Such artistic handling demands compression, and must demand it; while the History of Doctrines ought to give the materials as completely as possible for the assistance of the student.

§ 12.

Division into Periods.

Comp. *Hagenbach's* Essay in the Theolog. Studien und Kritiken, 1823, Heft 4, and his Encyklop. s. 257. On the other side, *Baur*, l.c. s. 65 ff. [Comp. *Kling* in the Studien und Kritiken, 1841.]

The periods of the History of Doctrines are to be determined by the most important epochs of development in the history of the theological spirit. They do not quite coincide with those adopted in ecclesiastical history (1), and may be divided as follows (2):—

I. *Period.*—From the close of the Apostolic Age to the death of Origen (A.D. 70–254): the Age of *Apologetics* (3).

II. *Period.*—From the death of Origen to John Damascene (254–730): the age of *Polemics* (4).

III. *Period.*—From John Damascene to the Reformation (730–1517): the Age of *Systems* (scholasticism in its widest sense) (5).

IV. *Period.*—From the Reformation to the Rise of the Philosophy of Leibnitz and Wolf in Germany (1517–1720): the Age of Polemico-ecclesiastical *Symbolism,* or of the Conflict of Confessions (6).

V. *Period.*—From the year 1720 to the present day: the Age of *Criticism,* of *Speculation,* and of the *Antagonism* between Faith and Knowledge, Philosophy and Christianity, Reason and Revelation, including the attempts to reconcile them (7).

(1) Events that make an epoch in Church History may not have the same significance in respect to the History of Doctrines; and so conversely. It is true that the development of doctrines is connected with the history of Church government, of Christian worship, etc., but the influences which they exert upon each other are not always contemporaneous. Thus the Arian controversy occurred in the age of Constantine, but it was not called forth by his conversion, which, on the other hand, is of so much importance that it makes an epoch in ecclesiastical history. On the contrary, the views of Arius arose out of the speculative tendency of Origen and his followers, in opposition to Sabellianism. Accordingly, it is better in this instance to determine the epoch by the death of Origen, and the rise of the Sabellian controversy, which are nearly coeval.[1] And so in other periods.

(2) The number of periods adopted is very different. *Baumgarten-Crusius* has twelve periods, *Lenz* eight, etc. *Münscher* follows a different division in his (larger) Handbook from the one in his Text-book: in the former he has seven, in the latter only three periods (ancient, mediæval, and modern times). *Engelhardt* and *Meier* have adopted the same threefold division, with this difference, that the latter, by subdividing each period into two, has six periods.[2] It is alike

[1] This is conceded by *Neander*, although he prefers, as does *Gieseler*, to retain in the History of Doctrines the periods of general Church History. *Baur* divides the whole into the three principal periods of ancient, mediæval, and modern history, but subdivides each of them into two smaller periods. In the ancient Church the division is made by the Synod of Nicæa; in the Church of the Middle Ages, by scholasticism. In the modern period, it commences with the Reformation, by the beginning of the eighteenth century.

[2] [*Neander's* division (Dg. s. 21 ff.) is : 1. To Gregory the Great, subdivided by the times of Constantine, and forming respectively the Apologetic period and the Polemic and Systematic periods. 2. To the Reformation, subdivided by Gregory VII., comprising a transition period and the scholastic era. 3. From the Reformation to the present time. *Gieseler* separates the ancient from the mediæval periods by the Image Controversy, taking A.D. 726 as the epoch. *Baumgarten-Crusius*, in his Compendium, makes six periods, skilfully characterized : 1. Formation of the System of Doctrines by reflection and opinion (to the Council of Nice). 2. Formation by the Church (to Chalcedon). 3. Confirmation of the System by the Hierarchy (to Gregory VII.). 4. Confirmation by the Philosophy of the Church (to the end of the fifteenth century). 5. Purification by Parties (to beginning of the eighteenth century). 6. Purification by Science (to the present time).]

inconvenient to press very different tendencies into long periods, and to have too great a number of divisions. Thus it is one of the chief defects of *Münscher's* Text-book, that the first period extends from A.D. 1 to 600. The periods in the History of Doctrines may be of greater extent than those in ecclesiastical history (see *Baur* in the review above cited), because the whole form of the system of doctrines does not undergo as rapid changes as that of Christian life in general; but boundaries which are as distinct as the age of Constantine should not be lightly disregarded. *Klee* coincides most nearly with us, though he considers the division into periods as superfluous. *Vorländer* also, in his tables, has adopted our terminology. Comp. also the review of *Lenz's* Dogmengesch., in the Litt. Blätter d. allg. Kirch. Zeitung for Jan. 1836. *Rosenkranz* (Encyklopädie, 2d ed. s. 259 ff.) makes, according to philosophico-dialectic categories, the following division: 1. Period of Analytic Knowledge, of substantial feeling (Greek Church). 2. Period of Synthetic Knowledge, of pure objectivity (Roman Church). 3. Period of Systematic Knowledge, which combines analysis and synthesis in their unity, and manifests itself in the stages of symbolical orthodoxy, of subjective belief and unbelief, and in the idea of speculative theology (Protestant Church). The most ingenious division is that of *Kliefoth*, though it is not free from faults peculiar to itself:—

1. The Age of Formation of Doctrines	Greek..........	Analytic ...	Theology.
2. " Symbolical Unity......	Rom. Catholic	Synthetic..	Anthropology.
3. " Completion..............	Protestant....	Systematic	Soteriology.
4. " Dissolution..............	?	?	Church.

On the grounds on which this division rests, see *Kliefoth*, l.c. *Pelt* (Encykl. s. 323) combines this with our division.

(3) In answer to the question, Why not commence with the first year of our era? comp. § 3. The year (of the destruction of Jerusalem) A.D. 70 here assumed is also only approximative. We call this period the age of *Apologetics*, because its theology was chiefly developed in the defence of Christianity against both Judaism and Paganism. The controversies which took place within the Church itself with heretics (Ebionites, Gnostics, etc.) had respect for the most part to the opposition of Judaizing teachers and pagan

philosophers, so that the polemical interest was conditioned by the apologetic. Systematic theology is still more subordinate; and the work of Origen περὶ ἀρχῶν is the only one in which we find any independent attempt to form such a system.

(4) During the second period the conflict became an internal one. Apologetic activity towards those outside the Church ceases almost entirely after the conversion of Constantine, or, at any rate, recedes into the background as compared with polemics (a converse relation to that of the previous period). The history of ecclesiastical controversies, from the rise of the Sabellian down to the close of the Monothelite controversy, forms one chain which cannot easily be broken if we trace the History of Doctrine continuously. It is concluded by the work of John Damascene (ἔκθεσις πίστεως). This period, with its numerous conflicts, its synods for the definition of doctrines, is undoubtedly the most important for the History of Doctrines, if this importance be measured by the efforts put forth to complete the structure whose foundation had been laid in the preceding period. The following periods, too, either elaborated and adorned what was here constructed, or else, by remarkable variations, sometimes restored and sometimes partly overthrew the work of the past.

(5) This period, which we call the *scholastic*, in the widest sense of the word, may be subdivided into three shorter periods. 1. From John Damascene to Anselm, Archbishop of Canterbury, during which period John Scotus Erigena takes the most prominent position in the West. 2. From Anselm to Gabriel Biel (of Tübingen), the age of scholasticism properly so called, which may again be subdivided into three periods (its rise, its prime, and its decay); and, 3. From Gabriel Biel to Luther (the period of transition). But we prefer an arrangement which facilitates a general view of the subject to such a minute articulation. Mystical and scholastic tendencies alternately rule this period; even the forerunners of the Reformation adhered more or less to one or other of these tendencies, though they belong to the next period in the other half of their nature.

(6) We might have fixed upon the year 1521, in which the first edition of *Melanchthon's* Loci Communes was published,

or upon the year 1530, in which the Confession of Augsburg was drawn up, instead of the year 1517; but, for the sake of the internal connection of the events, we make our date agree with the normal epoch of ecclesiastical history, especially as the Theses of *Luther* were of importance in a doctrinal point of view. Inasmuch as the distinguishing principles of the different sections of the Church are brought out very prominently in the Confessions of the age of the Reformation, the History of Doctrines naturally assumes the character of Symbolism; what may be called the statistics of the History of Doctrines, as has already been stated (comp. § 4). From the second half of the sixteenth century the history again assumes the form of a progressive narrative; up to that time it has rather the character of a comparative sketch of opinions—a broad surface and not a process of growth. The age of polemics, and that of scholasticism, may be said to reappear during this period, though in different forms; we also see various modifications of mysticism in opposition to one-sided rationalism. We might commence a new period with *Calixtus* and *Spener*, if their peculiar opinions had then at all prevailed. What both of them wished to effect, from different points of view, shows itself in the sphere of doctrinal theology in the period which we have adopted as the last.

(7) A definite year can here least of all be given. The tendency to a dissolution of the old forms begins with the English Deists as early as towards the close of the seventeenth century. In Germany, the struggle with the established orthodoxy is prepared by *Thomasius* and the *Pietists;* both elements of the opposition (the rationalistic and the pietistic) at first work together, but are separated after *Wolf* begins to teach in Halle. The negative (critical and rationalistic) tendency does not, however, become vigorous until after the middle of the century; and hence many begin a new period from 1750. But, in general, it is very perceptible that the bonds of strict symbolical orthodoxy began to be relaxed even in the first decennia of the century; this is manifest in the abolition of the *Formula Consensus* in Switzerland, and in the attempts at union in Germany; and also in the fact that it was more frequently asked, What are the conditions of a living Christianity? than, What are the differences in the

Confessions of Faith? In the period that preceded the Reformation, apologetic tendencies came first, and were followed by the polemic; now the order is reversed: we first have the polemic period of the sixteenth and seventeenth centuries, and then the apologetic of the eighteenth, in which the question was as to the existence or non-existence oi Christianity. None of these agencies are indeed isolated; and the nearer we come to the present times, the more varied and involved becomes the conflict. Thus we can subdivide this last period into three parts. The first (from *Wolf* to *Kant*) contains the struggles of a rigid and unwieldy dogmatism (in part, too, a supernaturalism on a deistic basis), with an undefined illuminism (*Aufklärung*). The second (from *Kant* onwards) strives to ensure the predominance, in science and the Church, of a rationalism, negative as to doctrine and chiefly restricted to morals, in opposition to both the old and the new faith. In fine, the third period, most fitly dated from *Schleiermacher*, steadily looking at the real and vital questions respecting Christianity, brings into view the most diverse tendencies, partly reactionary to restore the old, partly idealizing and meditating, and again destructive and reconstructive; and thus it is the introduction to a new period, for which history has as yet no name.

§ 13.

Sources of the History of Doctrines.

(a) *Public Sources.*

Everything may be considered as a source of the History of Doctrines which gives sure expression to the religious belief of any given period. In the first rank stand the public confessions of faith or symbols (creeds) of the Church (1); in connection with them, the acts of councils (2), the decrees, edicts, circular letters, bulls, and breves of ecclesiastical superiors, whether clerical or secular (3); and, lastly, the catechisms (4), liturgies (5), and hymns (6) sanctioned by the Church.

(1) Comp. § 4. The ancient creeds may be found in the Acts of Councils mentioned note 2; the three creeds commonly called œcumenical (the Apostles' Creed, the Nicene, and the Athanasian) are also reprinted in the collections of Protestant symbols; comp. *Ch. W. F. Walch*, Bibliotheca Symbolica Vetus, Lemgoviæ 1770. *J. S. Semler*, Apparatus ad Libros Symbolicos Ecclesiæ Lutheranæ, Hal. 1755. [*Guericke*, Allgemeine christliche Symbolik, Leipzig 1846. *Winer*, Confessions of Christendom, Edinr. 1873. *P. Schaff*, History of the Creeds; Creeds of the Greek and Latin Churches; Creeds of the Evang. Prot. Churches, 3 vols., London 1878.] COLLECTIONS OF SYMBOLICAL BOOKS (they become important only since the fourth period): (*a*) *Of the Lutheran Church:* Libri Symbolici Ecclesiæ Evangelicæ ad fidem opt. exempl. recens. *J. A. H. Tittmann*, Misn. 1817, 27. Libri Symbolici Ecclesiæ Evangelicæ, s. Concordia, rec. *C. A. Hase*, Lips. 1827, 37, 46. Die Symbolischen Bücher der Evang. Luther. Kirche, von *J. J. Müller*, Stuttg. 1846. Libri Symbol. Eccl. Luth., ed. *F. Francke*, ed. stereotyp., Lips. 1847. Libri Symbol. Luth. ad edit. princ. etc., ed. *H. A. G. Meyer*, Gött. 1850. Concordia Libri Symbolici Ecclesiæ Evangelicæ ad edit., Lips. 1584, Berol. 1857. (*b*) *Of the Reformed:* Corpus Libror. Symbolicor. qui in Ecclesia Reformatorum Auctoritatem publicam obtinuerunt, ed. *J. Ch. W. Augusti*, Elberf. 1828. Sammlung Symb. Bücher der ref. Kirche, von *J. J. Mess*, Neuwied 1828, 30, 2 vols. **H. A. Niemeyer*, Collectio Confessionum in Ecclesiis Reformatis Publicatarum, Lips. 1840. Die Bekenntniss-schriften der Evangel. ref. Kirche, mit Einleitung und Anmk., von *E. G. A. Böckel*, Leips. 1847. Die Bekenntniss-schriften der ref. Kirche Deutschlands herausgegeben, von *H. Heppe*, Elberf. 1860. [Harmonia Confessionum Fidei Orthodoxarum et Reform. Ecclesiarum, etc., 4to, Genev. 1581: an English translation, Cambr. 1586, Lond. 1643. Corpus et Syntagma Confess. Fidei, etc., 4to, 1612, and Geneva 1654. Sylloge Confess. sub Tempus Reform. Eccl., Oxon. 1801, 27. The Harmony of Prot. Confess. of Faith, edited by *Rev. Peter Hall*, Lond. 1842. *Butler's* Historical and Literary Account of the Formularies, etc., Lond. 1816.] (*c*) *Of the Roman Catholic:* Danz, Libri Symbolici Ecclesiæ Romano-Catholicæ,

Vimar. 1835. *Streitwolf* and *Klener*, Libri Symb. Eccl. Cathol., Gött. 1835. Sacrosancti et Œcumenici Conc. Trid. Canones et Decreta, ed. *W Smets*, Bielefeld, ed. 4, 1854. Canones et Decreta Conc. Trid. ex Bullario Romano, edd. *A. L. Richter* et *Fr. Schulze*, Lips. 1853. (Comp. the works mentioned § 16, note 9.) (*d*) *Of the Greek:* E. T. Kimmel, Libri Symbolici Ecclesiæ Orientalis, Jen. 1843. Append. adj. *H. T. C. Weissenborn*, 1849. (Comp. *Pitzipios*, l'Eglise Orientale de Rome, 1855.)

(2) ACTS OF COUNCILS: *J. Merlin* (Par. 1523, fol. Cöln. 1530, 2 vols. Par. 1535). *Grabbe* (Cöln. 1508, fol.). *L. Surius*, Col. 1577, 4 vols. fol. The edition of Sixtus V., Venice 1585. That of *Binius* (Severinus), Col. 1606, 4 vols. fol. *Collectio Regia*, Paris 1644 (by Cardinal Richelieu), 37 vols. fol. *Phil. Labbeus* and *Gabr. Cossart*, Par. 1671, 72, 17 vols. fol. *Stephani Baluzii*, Nova Collectio Conciliorum, Par. 1683, fol. (Suppl. ad Collect. Labbei); incomplete. *J. Harduin*, Conciliorum Collectio Regia Maxima, seu Acta Conciliorum et Epistolæ Decretales ac Constitutiones summorum Pontificum, græce et latine, ad Phil. Labbei et Gabr. Cossartii labores haud modica accessione facta et emendationibus pluribus additis, Par. 1715, 12 vols. fol. —*Nic. Coleti*, SS. Concilia ad regiam edit. exacta, etc., Venet. 23 vols., with additions by Mansi, 6 vols. fol.—**J. Dom. Mansi*, Sacrorum Conciliorum Nova et Amplissima Collectio, Flor. et Venet. 1759 sqq., 31 vols. fol. Comp. *Ch. W. F. Walch*, Entwurf einer vollständigen Geschichte der Kirchenversammlungen, Leipz. 1759. *Fuchs*, Bibliothek der Kirchenversammlungen des 4 und 5 Jahrhunderts, Leipz. 1788, 4 vols. Bibliotheca Ecclesiastica quam moderante D. Augusto Neander adornavit, *Herm. Theod. Bruns*, I. Canones Apostolorum et Concil. Sæcul. iv.-vii., 2 vols. 1839. [*D. Wilkins*, Conc. Mag. Brit. et Hibern., Lond. 1727, 4 vols. fol.; new ed. Oxford 1869 ff. †*C. J. Hefele*, Conciliengeschichte, 7 vols., Freiburg 1855 ff.; new ed. 1873 ff.; Eng. trans. vols. 1, 2, Edinr. 1872 ff. *E. H. Landon*, Manual of Councils, 1846. *W. A. Hammond*, Definitions of Faith and Canons of Six Œcumenical Councils, New York ed. 1844. *L. Howell*, Synopsis Conciliorum, fol. 1708.] The so-called Apostolical Constitutions belong here for the earlier times: Constitutiones Apostol. Text. Græc. recognovit, *Gulielm. Ueltzen*, Suerini 1853 [transl. in Ante-

Nicene Library, Edinr. 1870]. [Cf. *Bunsen's* Hi,)polytus, vol. 3. The Didascalia or Apost. Const. of Abyssinian Church, by *Thos. P. Platt*, published by the Orient. Transl. Society, vol. xxxix. *Beveridge*, Pandectæ Canonum ss. et Conciliorum ab Eccles. Græc. recept. etc., 2 vols. fol., Oxon. 1672.]

(3) Partly contained in the Acts of Councils.

(*a*) DECREES OF CIVIL GOVERNMENTS EXERCISING AUTHORITY IN ECCLESIASTICAL AFFAIRS (emperors, kings, magistrates): *Codex Theodosianus*, c. perpetuis commentariis Iac. Gothofredi, etc., edit. nova in vi. tom. digesta, cura *Ritteri*, Lips. 1736.— *Codex Justinianus*, edid. *Spangenberg*, 1797. *Steph. Baluzii*, Collectio Capitularium Regum Francorum, etc., Par. 1780, 2 vols. fol. *Corpus Juris Canonici* (editions of *J. H. Böhmer*, 1747, and *A. L. Richter*, 1833). *Codicis Gregoriani* et *Codicis Hermogeniani* Fragmenta, ed. *G. Hänel*, Bonn 1837, 4to. Under this head come also the regulations concerning the Reformation, the ecclesiastical ordinances, and the religious edicts of Protestant states, which, at least formerly, were in a great measure based upon doctrinal principles. *Æm. Ludw. Richter*, Die Evangelischen Kirchenordnungen des 16 Jahrh., Weimar 1846, 4to.

(*b*) PAPAL DECRETALS: Pontificum Romanorum a Clemente usque ad Leonem M. Epistolæ Genuinæ, cur. *C. F. G. Schönemann*, t. i., Gött. 1796.—*Bullarium Romanum* a Leone M. usque ad Benedictum XIII. opus. absolutiss. *Laërt. Cherubini*, a D. Angelo Maria Cherubini al. illustratum et auctum et ad Ben. XIV. perductum, Luxemb. 1727, ss. 19 vols. fol.—Bullarium, Privilegiorum, et Diplomatum Roman. Pontif. amplissima Collect. opera et stud. *Car. Cocquelines*, Rom. 1739-44, 28 vols. fol. The Bullarium is continued by *A. Spetzia*, 1835 ff., 9 vols. fol. *Eisenschmid*, Römisches Bullarium, oder Auszüge der merkwürdigsten päbstlichen Bullen, übersetzt und mit fortlaufenden Anmerkungen, Neustadt 1831, 2 vols.

(4) Catechisms become important only from the period of the Reformation, especially those of Luther, of Heidelberg, the Racovian, the Roman Catechism, etc. Some of them, *e.g.* those just mentioned, may be found in collections of symbolical books (note 1); others are separately published. Comp. *Langemack*, Historia Catechetica, Stralsund 1729-33, 3 vols.; 1740, vol. 4.

§ 13.]   SOURCES OF THE HISTORY OF DOCTRINES.   31

(5) *J. S. Assemani*, Codex Liturgicus Ecclesiæ Universæ, Rom. 1749-66, 13 vols. 4to. *Eus. Renaudot*, Liturgiarum Orientalium Collectio, Paris 1716, 2 vols. fol. *L. A. Muratori*, Liturgia Romana Vetus, Venet. 1748, 2 vols. fol. *M. J. E. Volbeding*, Thesaurus Commentationum select. et antiq. et recent. etc., 2 vols. Lips. 1848. *F. S. Mone*, Lateinische u. griechische Messen, aus dem 2 bis 6 Jahrh., Frankf. 1849. *H. A. Daniel*, Codex Liturg. Eccl. Univ. in Epitomen redact. 4 vols. Lips. 1847-51. Compare the missals, breviaries, liturgies, etc. *Augusti's* Denkwürdigkeiten der christlichen Archäologie, vol. v. *Gerbert*, Vetus Liturgia Allemanica, Ulm 1776, 2 vols. 4to. [*J. Pinius*, Liturg. Ant. Hisp. Goth. etc., 2 vols. fol., Rom. 1749. *W. Palmer*, Origines Liturg. or Antiq. of the Church of England, 2 vols. 1845. *J. M. Neale*, Tetralogia Liturg., Lond. 1848. Eutaxia, or the Presbyterian Liturgies; Historical Sketches, New York 1855. *Bunsen*, Analecta Ante-Nicaena, 3 vols. 1854; Early Liturgies in Ante-Nicene Library, Edinr. 1862.]

(6) *Rambach*, Anthologie christlicher Gesänge aus allen Jahrhunderten der Kirche, Altona 1816-22, 4 vols., and the numerous psalm and hymn books of earlier and later times. How much sacred songs have contributed to the spread of doctrinal opinions, may be seen from the example of Bardesanes [*Gieseler*, i. § 46, n. 2, s. 138], of the Arians, and in later times of the Flagellants, the Hussites, etc.; from the history of the hymns of the Lutheran, and the psalms of the Reformed Church, the spiritual songs of Angelus Silesius, of the Pietists and Moravian brethren, and (negatively) from the dilutions found in many modern hymn-books. Comp. *Augusti*, De antiquissimis Hymnis et Carminibus Christianorum sacris in historia dogmatum utiliter adhibendis, Jen. 1810, and De audiendis in Theologia poëtis, Vratisl. 1812, 1815. *A. Hahn*, Bardesanes Gnosticus, primus Syrorum Hymnologus, 1820. † *Buchegger*, De Origine sacræ Christianorum Poëseos, Frib. 1827, 4to. *Dr. H. Hoffman*, Geschichte des deutschen Kirchenliedes bis auf Luthers Zeit, Breslau 1832. [*J. M. Neale*, Hymni Ecclesiæ e Breviariis, etc., Lond. 1851. *Mohnike*, hymnologische Forschungen, 4 Bde. 1855 ff. *F. S. Mone*, Lateinische Hymnen, 3 Bde. 1853 sq.] *H. A. Daniel*, Thesaurus Hymnologicus, 4 tom. 1856. [*Koch*, Gesch. des

Kirchenlieds, 4 Bde. 2d ed. 1853.] *J. L. König*, die Hauptliturgien der alten Kirche, Neustrelitz 1865. For further hymnological literature (Phil. Wackernagel, Winterfeld, etc.), see in *Hagenbach's* Encyklopädie, s. 379.

§ 14.

(b) Private Sources.

Next in order after these public sources come the private sources of the History of Doctrines. These are: 1. The writings of the Fathers, Church teachers, and ecclesiastical writers of all the Christian centuries (1); but in these we are to distinguish between scientific and strictly doctrinal works on the one hand, and practical (sermons) and occasional writings (letters, etc.) on the other (2). 2. The works of non-theological writers, *e.g.* the Christian philosophers and poets of any period (3). 3. Lastly, the indefinite form of popular belief, which comes out in legends, proverbial sayings, and songs, and in the representations of Christian art, viewed as memorials of certain forms of faith, may also be numbered among those secondary sources (4).

(1) Comp. § 5. Concerning the distinction (which is quite relative) made between Fathers, doctors, and ecclesiastical writers, see the introductions to the works on Patristics, *e.g. Möhler*, s. 17–19. The Fathers of the first centuries are followed by the compilers, the scholastic and mystic divines of the Middle Ages, and these again by the Reformers and their opponents, the polemical writers of the different confessions, and the later theologians in general. Their particular works will be referred to in their proper place. Works of a more general character are: *J. G. Fabricii*, Bibliotheca Ecclesiastica, Hamb. 1718, fol. *W. Cave*, Scriptorum Ecclesiasticorum Historia litteraria, Lond. 1688, 91, Oxon. 1740, 43, Bas. 1749. *C. Oudin*, Comment. de Scriptoribus Ecclesiæ Antiquis, Lips. 1722, 3 vols. *L. El. Dupin*, Nouvelle Bibliothèque des Auteurs Ecclésiastiques, Par. 1686–1714, 47 vols. [transl. by *Wotton*

and *Cotes*, 3 vols. fol., Dublin 1733]. Bibliothèque des Auteurs séparés de la communion de l'église Romaine du 16 et 17 siècle, Par. 1718, 19, 3 vols. Bibliothèque des Auteurs Ecclésiastiques du 18 siècle, par *Claude Pierre Goujet*, Par. 1736, 37, 3 vols. Comp. *Richard Simon*, Critique de la Bibliothèque, etc., Paris 1730, 4 vols. *Remy Ceillier*, Histoire Générale des Auteurs Sacrés et Ecclésiastiques, Paris 1729–63, 23 vols. 4to. *J. G. Walch*, Bibliotheca Patristica, Jen. 1770. Edit. Nova Auctior et Emendatior adornata a *J. T. L. Danzio*, Jen. 1834. *J. S. Assemani*, Bibliotheca Orientalis, Rom. 1719–28, 3 vols. in 4 vols. fol. *J. G. A. Oelrichs*, Commentarii de Scriptoribus Ecclesiæ Latinæ, Lips. 1791. *C. F. G. Schönemann*, Bibliotheca Historico-litteraria a Tertulliano Principe usque ad Gregorium M. et Isidorum Hispal., Lips. 1792–94, 2 vols. *Ch. F. Rössler*, Bibliothek der Kirchenväter, Leipz. 1776–86, 10 vols. *J. Ch. W. Augusti*, Chrestomathia Patristica ad usum eorum, qui Historiam Christianam accuratius discere cupiunt, Lips. 1812, 2 vols. *D. H. I. Royaards*, Chrestomathia Patristica, Pars. I. Traj. ad Rhen. 1831. *Engelhardt*, Literarischer Leitfaden zu Vorlesungen über die Patristik, Erlangen 1823. †*Winter*, Patrologie, München 1814. †*F. W. Goldwitzer*, Bibliographie der Kirchenväter und Kirchenlehrer, vom 1, bis zum 13 Jahrhundert, Landshut 1828. †*J. A. Möhler*, Patrologie oder Christliche Literargeschichte, aus dessen Nachlasse herausgegeben von *Reithmayr*, 1st vol. Regensb. 1839. *J. T. L. Danz*, Initia Doctrinæ Patristicæ Introductionis instar in Patrum ecclesiæ studium, Jen. 1839. *Böhringer*, die Kirche Christi und ihre Zeugen, oder die Kirchengeschichte in Biographien, Zür. 1842–58, 2 Bde. 8 Theile. [A new edition, begun in 1873 (Stuttgard), is now in course of publication, 12 Theile already issued.] Patrologiæ Cursus Compl. accur. *J. B. Migne*, Paris; in the course of publication, 140 vols. issued.

A. BEST COLLECTIONS OF THE WORKS OF THE FATHERS: *Magna Bibliotheca Veterum*, primo quidem a *Margarino de la Bigne* composita, postea studio Coloniens. Theolog. aucta, etc. (with Auctuarium by F. Ducæus and Fr. Combefisius), 1664–72, 5 vols. fol. *Maxima Bibliotheca Vett. Patr.* etc., Lugd. 1677, 27 vols. fol. *And. Gallandii*, Bibliotheca Græcolatina Vett. Patrum, etc., Venet. 1765–81, 14 vols. fol. *Caillon* et *Guillon*, Collectio ss. Patr., Paris 1841 (148 vols. with 25 vols. indices). Corpus Apologetarum, Sec. ii. ed. *J. C. Th. Otto*, ed. 2, Jen. 1848-50, 3 vols. *Biblioth. Patrum Græcor. Dogmatica, cura. *J. C. Thilo*, 2 tom., Lips. 1853 ff. Bibliotheca Patrum Eccles. Latin., ed. *Gersdorf*, Leipz. 1838 ff., 13 tom. 12mo. Bibliothek der Kirchenväter, Auswahl aus deren Werken (Urschrift mit deutsch. Uebersetzung), von *Fr. Oehler*, Leipz. 1858 ff. Bibliotheca patrum selectissima, curavit *G. B. Lindner*, Lips. 1858 ff. Bibl. Patr. Latin., ed. *Reifferscheid*, Wien 1865. See further under § 25. [Corpus Hæreseologicum, ed. *F. Oehler*, tom. ii., Berol. 1856-58. *Angelo Mai*, Patrum Spicilegium Rom., 10 vols., Rom. 1839-44, and Patrum Nova Bibl., 6 tom. 1852 sq. *Martène et Durand*, Vet. Script. Coll., Paris 1724-33, 9 vols. fol. *J. E. Grabe*, Spicilegium ss. Patrum, 2 vols. fol., Oxon 1698. *D'Achery*, Spicilegium, 13 vols. 4to, Paris 1655. Spicilegium Solesmense, ed. *J. Pitra*, 4 tom. 4to, Paris 1853 sq. Comp. *J. G. Dowling*, Notitia Script. ss. Patrum, etc., 1839.] *Philological Aids*: *J. C. Suiceri*, Thesaurus Ecclesiasticus, Amst. 1682 (1728, Traj. 1746), 2 vols. fol. *Charles Du Fresne* (du Cange), Glossarium ad Scriptores Mediæ et Infimæ Latinitatis, Paris 1733-36, 6 vols. fol. [New edition, ed. *G. A. L. Henschel*, Paris, F. Didot, 1840-50, 7 vols. 4to.]

B. COLLECTIONS OF THE WORKS OF ECCLESIASTICAL WRITERS DURING THE MIDDLE AGES (more important for Ecclesiastical History in general than for the History of Doctrines in particular): *Meibomius, Basnage, Muratori, Mabillon,* **Martène et Durand* (Thesaurus Anecd. 5 vols. fol.), *Pertz (Monumenta, 1826-35), etc. Comp. the Literature as to Church History in *Hase's* History of the Church, 5th ed. s. 175 f. *For the East:* Scriptores Byzantini (Par. 1645 ff.), and latest edition by *Niebuhr, Bonn 1829 ff.

C. COLLECTIONS OF THE WORKS OF THE REFORMERS: *Bretschneider*, Corpus Reformatorum, with the continuations by *Bindseil*, Halis et Brunsvici, 1834-77, 42 vols. 4to; the works of individual Reformers will be named in their proper places. (For later doctrinal literature, see § 7.)

D. ON MODERN DOGMATIC LITERATURE: *J. G. Walch*, Bibliotheca Theologica, tom. i., Jen. 1757. *G. B. Winer*, Handbuch der theologischen Literatur, s. 390 ff. *Bretschneider*,

Systematische Entwickelung aller in der Dogmatik vorkommenden Begriffe, u. s. w., 4th ed. Leipz. 1841.

(2) Since the earlier theologians, *e.g.* Origen, drew a distinction between what they taught the people κατ' οἰκονομίαν, and what they propounded in a scientific manner; and since popular language in general does not make any pretension to dogmatic precision, homiletical works are not of so much importance for the History of Doctrines as strictly dogmatic works. But, like all liturgical and ascetic writings, they may be regarded as concrete and living witnesses to the dogmatic spirit of a period.—Homiliarium Patristicum, edid. *Ludov. Pelt* et *H. Rheinwald*, Berol. 1829, deinde *H. Rheinwald* et *C. Vogt*, Ber. 1831.—*E. G. H. Lentz*, Geschichte der Christlichen Homiletik, 2 vols., Braunschw. 1839. *Paniel*, Pragmatische Geschichte der Christl. Beredsamkeit und der Homiletik, i. 1, 2, Leipz. 1839–41. During the Middle Ages the sermons of Berthold, Tauler, etc., in the time of the Reformation those of the Reformers, etc., come into consideration. *W. Beste*, Die bedeutendsten Kanzelredner d. ältern Luth. Kirche, Leipz. 1856. Modern homiletical literature also gives a more or less faithful representation of doctrinal tendencies.

(3) Comp. § 13, note 6. As sacred hymns were numbered among the public sources, so poetical works in general may be considered as a private source, *e.g.* the works of some of the earlier poets, of the so-called Minnesingers, *Dante's* Divina Commedia, and many others. In like manner, a comparison of the poetical views of *Milton, Shakespeare, Göthe, Byron,* or the romantic school, with the doctrinal tendencies of the Church, might lead to interesting results. A history of *Christian* poetry in its whole extent, and in its constant reference to the theological spirit of each period, does not as yet exist.

(4) The influence which popular belief (with its remnants of heathen superstitions) may have exerted upon certain dogmatic notions, *e.g.* concerning the devil and hell, is deserving of particular attention (comp. *Grimm's* deutsche Mythologie). The doctrinal spirit also manifests itself in the silent monuments of art; ecclesiastical buildings, tombs, vasa sacra, paintings, *e.g.* representing the last judgment, or even the Deity (comp. *C. Grüneisen,* über bildliche Darstellung der

Gottheit, Stuttg. 1828), in coins, gems, etc. (*Münter*, Sinnbilder und Kuntsvorstellungen der alten Christen., Altona 1825, 4to. *Bellermann*, die Gemmen der Alten mit dem. Abraxasbilde, Berlin 1817. *Piper*, Mythologie der Christl. Kunst, Weimar 1847. [*Didron's* Christ. Iconography, transl. in Bohn's Lib. 1852. *L. Twining*, Symbols of Early and Mediæval Art, 1852. *Mrs. Jameson*, Sacred and Legendary Art, 3 vols.]).

§ 15.

(*c*) *Indirect Sources.*

We cannot always have access to direct sources, but must frequently have recourse to such as are indirect, *i.e.* accounts or reports which have been transmitted to us by other writers at second or third hand, as is the case, for the most part, with the opinions of heretics (1), whose writings were destroyed at an early period. In like manner, with the teachings of some of the Fathers, whose works are either entirely lost, or have come down to us only in a corrupt form (2). In the use of both the direct and indirect sources, much critical caution is needful (3).

(1) Hence the accounts given by different writers of Cerinthus, the Ebionites, Gnostics, Manichæans, etc., frequently vary from one another, and even contradict each other.

(2) Thus, in the case of Origen, of whose writings we frequently have nothing but the translations of Rufinus, or the relations of Jerome and Eusebius.

(3) Not only the criticism of the text and words, in respect to the genuineness and integrity of the writings (comp. *Danz*, Initia Doctrinæ Patrist. §§ 7–20), but also the criticism of the contents, in relation to the greater or less credibility of the authors. Comp. *Hagenbach*, Encyklop. § 205.

§ 16.

Works on the History of Doctrines.

C. F. Baur, l.c. s. 100 ff.

As all the sources are not at the command of every one, and as their study, generally speaking, will be fruitful only after we have acquired a general outline of the history which we intend more fully to investigate, we must have recourse, in the first instance, to the works of those who, by their own historical researches, and in the application of the historical art, have placed the treasures of science within the reach of all who desire to be learners. The History of Doctrines itself has been treated as an independent branch of theological science only in modern times (1); yet some of the earlier writers of Church History (2), as well as the theologians (3), have prepared the way for it. Besides those works which treat of the History of Doctrines exclusively (4), we have to compare the modern works on ecclesiastical history (5), as well as the monographs on the Fathers and on particular doctrines (6), and also those works on dogmatic theology (7) and Christian ethics (8), which combine the historical with the systematic. Lastly, the literature of symbolism (9) forms (according to § 4) a part of the literature of the History of Doctrines.

(1) The History of Doctrines was formerly treated in connection with ecclesiastical history, or dogmatic theology (comp. § 2); *Semler* and *Ernesti* first showed the necessity of separating the one from the other. The former attempted this in his historical introduction to *Siegm. Baumgarten's* Glaubenslehre, Halle 1759, 3 vols. 4to. His design was (according to i. s. 101): "*to expand the views of divines or studiosi theologiæ in general, and to show the origin, nature, and true object of dogmatic theology.*" In the same year *J. A. Ernesti* published his programme, De Theologiæ Historicæ et Dogmaticæ con-

jungendæ Necessitate et Modo universo, Lips. 1759 (Opusc. Theol., Lips. 1773, ed. 2, 1792, p. 567); he does not indeed speak of the History of Doctrines as a separate science, but it is not difficult to perceive that he felt the necessity of its being so. Comp. also *C. W. F. Walch*, Gedanken von der Geschichte der Glaubenslehre, 2d ed. Gött. 1764.

(2) Eusebius, Socrates, Sozomen, Theodoret, etc. (Editions of *Valesius*, Par. 1659, 3 vols. *Reading*, Cant. 1720, 3 vols. fol. —Manual edition of Eusebius by *Heinichen*, Lips. 1827–28, 3 vols., and an edition by *Laemmer*, Schaffhausen 1862.) [English translations of Euseb. Socrat. Sozom. Theod. and Evagrius, published by Bagster, Lond., 6 vols., also the first three by Bohn.] Rufinus, Sulpicius Severus, Cassiodorus, Epiphanius Scholasticus. *Writers during the Middle Ages:* Gregor. Turonensis, Beda Venerabilis, Adamus Bremensis, Nicephorus Callisti, etc. (comp. the literature in works on ecclesiastical history). *Since the Reformation:* the *Magdeburg Centuriators* under the title: Ecclesiastica Historia per aliquot studiosos et pios viros in urbe Magdeburgica, Basil. 1559–74, 13 vols. fol. †*Cæs. Baronius*, Annales Ecclesiastici, Rom. 1588–1607, 12 vols. fol. †*Odoricus Raynaldus*, Annales Eccles., Rom. 1664–74, 10 vols. fol. (both edited by *Mansi*, along with the Critica Historico-Theologica of Pagi, Luccæ, 1738, 39, 33 vols. fol.).—*J. G. Arnold*, Unparteiische Kirchen- und Ketzerhistorie, Fkft. 1699, 4 vols. fol. †*Nat. Alexander*, Historia Ecclesiastica, Par. 1676–86, 24 vols., Venet. 1759, 77, 9 vols. fol. †*Fleury*, Histoire Ecclésiastique, Paris 1691–1720, 20 vols. 4to (continued by *Jean Claude Fabre*, Paris 1726–40, 16 vols. 4to, and *Al. de la Croix*, Par. 1776–78, 6 vols.), Par. 36 vols. 12mo, 1740, 41. †*Tillemont*, Mémoires pour servir à l'Histoire Ecclésiastique des 6 premiers siècles, justifiés par les Citations des Auteurs Originaux, Paris 1693 ff., 16 vols. 4to. *L. Moshemii*, Institutionum Historiæ Eccles. Antiquioris et Recentioris libri IV., Helmst. 1755, 64, 4to [transl. by *J. Murdock*, New York and London]. *Ch. W. F. Walch*, Historie der Ketzereien, Spaltungen und Religionsstreitigkeiten, Leipz. 1762–85, 11 vols. *J. S. Baumgarten*, Untersuchung theologischer Streitigkeiten mit einigen Anmerkungen, Vorrede und fortgesetzter Geschichte der Christlichen

Glaubenslehre, herausgegeben von *J. S. Semler*, Halle 1762-64, 3 vols. 4to. *By the same:* Geschichte der Religionsparteien, herausgegeben von *J. S. Semler*, ibid. 1766, 4to.

(3) Thus the works of *Irenaeus, Hippolytus, Origen, Tertullian, Epiphanius,* and *Theodoret* contain much material for the History of Doctrines in their refutation of heretics; much, too, is found scattered about in the polemical and dogmatic works of ancient and mediæval times. Thus, in the work of Bishop *Facundus*, of Hermiane, Pro Defensione trium Capitulorum, libri XII. (in *Gallandii*, Bibl. Patrum, tom. xi. p. 665 ff.), in that of the monophysite, *Stephan Gobarus* (in Photii Bibl. Cod. 232), as well as in the treatise of *Abelard*, Sic et Non (edited by *G. L. Henke* and *G. S. Lindenkohl*, Marb. 1851). More definite preparation for the History of Doctrines is found in works published after the Reformation: †*Dion Petavius*, Opus de Theologicis Dogmatibus, Par. 1644–50, 4 vols.; Antw. 1700, 6 vols. *"This work is no less ingenious than profound, and deserves to be more carefully and frequently studied than is generally done."* Dorner. [The first volume of a new edition of *Petau*, expolitum et auctum, collatis studiis C. Passaglia et C. Schrader, was published at Rome, in 4to, 1857; published also in 8 vols. 8vo, ed. by Thomas, Barri-ducis, 1864.] †*L. Thomassin*, Dogmata Theologica, Par. 1684–89. †*Lud. Dumesnil*, Doctrina et Disciplina Ecclesiæ, ex ipsis Verbis ss. codd. concc. PP. et genuinorum Monumentorum sec. seriem temporis digesta, 4 vols., Col. 1730, fol. *Io. Forbesius a Corse*, Instructiones Historico-theologicæ de Doctrina Christiana et vario Rerum Statu Ortisque Erroribus et Controversiis, etc., Amst. 1645, fol., Gen. 1699, and in his Opera, Amst. 1703, 2 vols. fol. (vol. ii.). The design of this work is to prove the agreement between the doctrines of the Reformers and the opinions of the earlier Fathers (especially in opposition to Bellarmin). The various Loci of *Chemnitz, Hutter, Quenstedt, Baier,* and of *Joh. Gerhard* in particular, contain much historical matter: *J. Gerhard*, Loci Theol. (edit. of *Cotta*), Tüb. 1762–98, 22 vols. 4to. [Ed. by *Preuss*, Berol. 1863 ff.] Works which form the transition[1] to the treatment of the History of

---

[1] [*Baur*, Lehrb. (Einl. § 6. 2), says the three greatest leaders in the historical method of studying doctrine were the younger *Walch, Semler,* and *Mosheim.* See above, under 2.]

Doctrines as a separate science: *Lor. Reinhard*, Introductio in Historiam Præcipuorum Dogmatum, Jen. 1795, 4to, and *J. S. Baumgarten*, Evangelische Glaubenslehre, Halle 1759, 60, 4to (the above-mentioned preface to this work by Semler). [On Petavius, Forbes, Gerhard, and Quenstedt, comp. *Baur*, Lehrb. Einl. § 6. 1.]

(4) COMPENDIUMS AND MANUALS OF THE HISTORY OF DOCTRINES: *S. G. Lange*, ausführliche Geschichte der Dogmen, Lpz. 1796 (incomplete). *J. Ch. Wundemann*, Geschichte der christlichen Glaubenslehren vom Zeitalter des Athanasius bis Gregor den Gr., 1st and 2d vols., Leipz. 1798-99 (fragmentary). *W. *Münscher*, Handbuch der christlichen Dogmengeschichte, Marb. vols. i. and ii. 1797 (third edit. without alteration, 1817, 18); vol. iii. 1802, 1804; vol. iv. 1809 (only to the year 604); the first treatment of the History of Doctrine in the pragmatic method. *By the same:* Lehrbuch der christlichen Dogmengeschichte, Marb. 1812, 19, 3d ed., mit Belegen aus den Quellenschriften, Ergänzungen der Literatur, historischen Notizen und Fortsetzungen versehen von **Dan. von Cölln*, 1st part, Cassel 1832, 2d part, ibid. 1834 (edited by *Hupfeld*); 2d part, 2d section (also under the title: Lehrbuch der christlichen Dogmengeschichte von der Reformationszeit bis auf unsere Tage), by *Ch. Gotth. Neudecker*, Cassel 1838 [*Münscher's* Manual, translated by T. Murdock, New Haven, 12mo, 1830]. *Friedr. Münter*, Handbuch der ältesten christlichen Dogmengeschichte, from the Danish, by *Evers*, 1st vol., Gött. 1802 (incomplete). **J. Ch. W. Augusti*, Lehrbuch der christlichen Dogmengeschichte, Leipz. 1805, 4th ed. 1835. *L. Bertholdt*, Handbuch der Dogmengeschichte, herausg. von *Veit Engelhardt*, Erl. 1822, 23, 2 vols. *F. A. Ruperti*, Geschichte der Dogmen, oder Darstellung der Glaubenslehre des Christenthums von seiner Stiftung bis auf die neueren Zeiten, insbesondere für Studierende der Theologie und zu ihrer Vorbereitung auf ihre Prüfung, Berlin 1831. **L. F. O. Baumgarten-Crusius*, Lehrbuch der christlichen Dogmengeschichte, Jena 1832, 2 vols. *C. G. H. Lentz*, Geschichte der christlichen Dogmen in pragmatischer Entwicklung, Helmst. 1834, 1st vol. †*H. Klee*, Lehrbuch der Dogmengeschichte, 1st vol. Mainz 1837, 2d vol. 1838. [German ed. out of print; French transl., Paris, Le Coffre, 1848.]

§ 16.]   WORKS ON THE HISTORY OF DOCTRINES.   41

J. G. V. Engelhardt, Dogmengeschichte, 2 vols., Neust. 1839. *Karl Meier*, Lehrbuch der Dogmengeschichte für akademische Vorlesungen, Giessen 1839. *Baumgarten-Crusius*, Compendium der christlichen Dogmengeschichte, Leipz. vol. i. 1840, ii. 1846 (edited by *Hase*). *F. Ch. Baur*, Lehrb. d. christl. Dogmengesch., Stuttg. 1849 (2d ed. 1858; 3d ed. 1867). *Karl Beck*, Lehrb. d. christl. Dogmengesch., Weimar 1848, Tübingen 1864. *L. Noack*, Die christl. Dogmengesch. nach ihrem organischen Entwicklungsgange, Erlang. 1853, 2d ed. 1856. *J. C. L. Gieseler*, Dogmengeschichte (posthumous, edited by *Redepenning*), Bonn 1855. *A. Neander*, christl. Dogmengesch., edited by *J. L. Jacobi*, 2 Thle., Berlin 1857, 58 (translated by J. E. Ryland in Bohn's Library). *H. Schmid*, Lehrbuch d. Dogmengesch., Nördlingen 1860. *K. F. A. Kahnis*, der Kirchenglaube, historisch-genetisch dargestellt, Leipz. 1864 (2d vol. of his Dogmatik). *F. C. Baur*, Vorlesungen über die christliche Dogmeng. i. 1, herausg. v. *Ferd. Fried. Baur*, Leipz. 1865. [*W. G. T. Shedd*, A History of Christian Doctrine, 2 vols., New York 1863, Edinburgh 1872. Dr. Shedd's method is more like that of Petavius than of the more recent writers. He adopts, so to speak, the vertical and not the horizontal division of the subject, in the following manner:—Book I. Influence of philosophical systems (from Plato to the German philosophy). Book II. History of Apologies. Book III. History of Theology and Christology. Book IV. History of Anthropology. Book V. History of Soteriology. Book VI. History of Eschatology. Book VII. History of Symbols. Each subject is considered under successive periods, but the periods do not coincide. *Nitzsch*, Grundriss der Dogmengeschichte, Berlin 1870; only Part I. (Patrist. period) yet published.]

Tables: *K. R. Hagenbach*, Tabellarische Uebersicht der Dg. bis auf die Reformation, Basel 1828, 4to. *Karl Vorländer*, Tabell. übersichtl. Darstellung der Dogmengesch. nach Neanders dogmengeschichtl. Vorlesungen, Per. i. Hamb. 1835, Per. ii. 1837, Per. iii. and iv. 1855 (Dutch ed. Amsterdam 1850, 4to). *K. Beck*, Zeittafeln für die Dg. mit rücksicht auf Kirchen- u. Culturgeschichte, Tübingen 1864.

(5) WORKS OF MODERN AUTHORS ON CHURCH HISTORY, WHICH INCLUDE THE HISTORY OF DOCTRINES: *J. M. Schröckh*, christliche Kirchengeschichte, Leipz. 1768-1804, 35 vols.,

since the Reformation (continued by *Tzschirner*), 1804-10, 10 vols. *Henke*, Allgemeine Geschichte der Christlichen Kirche nach der Zeitfolge, Braunschw. 1788 ff., continued by *Vater*, 9 vols. (in several editions). *J. E. Ch. Schmidt*, Handbuch der Christlichen Kirchengeschichte, Giessen und Darmstadt 1801 ff., 6 vols. (2d ed. 1825-27), vol. vii. by *Rettberg*, 1834. **Aug. Neander*, Allgemeine Geschichte der Christlichen Religion und Kirche, Hamb. 1825-52, vols. i.-vi. in fourteen parts. [The sixth vol. edited by K. F. H. Schneider, from MSS. 1852. A new edition, with preface by Ullmann, Gotha 1856; translation by Joseph Torrey, 5 vols., Boston 1849-54, and in Clark's For. Theol. Lib.; also in Bohn's Library, London.] **L. Gieseler*, Lehrbuch der Kirchengeschichte, Bonn 1824-57, 3 vols., in several parts (vol. i. 4th ed. in two parts, 1844; vol. ii. in four parts; vol. iii. 1, 1840; 4th ed. of vol. i. 1844). [Of Gieseler's work, vols. iv.-vi. are edited from his MSS. by *E. R. Redepenning*; the 5th vol. to 1848; the 6th vol. is the History of Doctrines to 1517. A translation of this History, to the Reformation, by *Francis Cunningham*, was published in Phil. 1836. *Davidson* and *Hull's* translation, in Clark's Library, Edinburgh, 5 vols. 1846-59. A new edition, revised and ed. by *Henry B. Smith*, New York, 5 vols.] *K. Hase*, Lehrbuch d. Kirchengesch., Leipz. 1833; 10th ed. 1877 [translated from 7th ed. by *C. E. Blumenthal* and *C. P. Wing*, New York 1855]. *H. E. F. Guericke*, Handbuch d. Allg. Kirchengesch., Halle 1833; 9th ed. 1866, 3 vols. [vol. i. comprising six centuries, translated by *W. G. T. Shedd*, Andover 1857]. *Schleiermacher*, Gesch. d. Christl. Kirche (posthumous ed. by Bonnel), Berlin 1840. *A. F. Gfrörer*, Allg. Kirchengesch., Stuttg. 1841-46, 4 vols. *Ch. W. Niedner*, Gesch. d. Christl. Kirche, Leipz. 1846. *J. H. Kurtz*, Lehrb. d. Kirchengesch., Mitau 1840; 7th ed. 2 vols. 1874. [*Same*: Handbuch d. Kirchengesch., vol. i. in three parts, 2d ed. 1858.] *Ph. G. A. Fricke*, Lehrb. d. Kircheng. i., Leipz. 1850. [*W. B. Lindner*, Lehrb. d. Kircheng., 3 vols., Leipz. 1854. *J. G. V. Engelhardt*, Handbuch, 4 vols. 1834. *J. L. Jacobi*, Lehrb. i. 1850. *M. T. Matter*, Histoire universelle de l'Eglise, 4 vols., 2d ed. Paris 1838. *H. H. Milman*, Hist. of Latin Christ., 6 vols., Lond. 1854-57 (various editions). *H. Stebbing's* Hist. of Church to

[§ 16.] WORKS ON THE HISTORY OF DOCTRINES. 43

Eighteenth Cent., 6 vols. 1842. *Philip Schaff*, Hist. of Christ. Church, vol. i., New York 1859. *Foulkes'* Manual, 1851. *Ch. Hardwick*, Middle Ages and Reform., 2 vols. 1853–56. *J. C. Robertson*, to 1517, 4 vols. 1854–73. *Waddington*, through Ref., 6 vols. 1835 sq., New York ed. of first 3 vols. in one.] *F. R. Hasse*, Kirchengeschichte, herausg. v. A. Köhler, Leipz. 1864, 3 vols. *J. H. A. Ebrard*, Handbuch der christlichen Kirchen- u. Dogmengeschichte für Prediger u. Studierende, Erlangen 1865; also *Baur's* works on Church History are, for the most part, of special value for the History of Doctrines (comp. the further literature, as well as the works of the Catholic *Ritter, Locherer, Alzog, Annegarn,* in the Encykl. s. 229 ff.).

[ROMAN CATHOLIC WORKS: *F. L. von Stolberg,* Gesch. d. Rel. Jesu, 15 Bde. 1806–19; continued by *Kerz* and *Brischar*, 52 vols. in all, the last in 1860. *Casp. Sacharelli,* Hist. Eccl., Rom. 1772–95, 25 vols. 4to. *Th. Katerkamp,* Münster, 5 Bde. 1819–34. *J. J. Ritter,* Handb., 2 Bde., 5th ed. 1854. *J. Alzog,* 5th ed. 1850. *Döllinger,* Church Hist. to Ref., transl. by *Ed. Cox,* 4 vols., Lond. 1848. *Rohrbacher,* Hist. Universelle de l'Eglise, Paris 1842 sq., 29 vols.; *Henrion,* in 25 vols. *Palma,* Prælect. Hist. Eccl. Rom., 3 vols. 1838–42.]

Tables of Church History: J. S. Vater, 1803; 6th ed. Thilo 1833. *J. T. L. Danz,* 1838. *Lob. Lange,* 1841. *C. D. A. Douai,* 2d ed. 1850. [*Henry B. Smith,* Hist. of the Church in Synchronistic Tables, fol., New York, new ed. 1860; also by *Möller, Schone, Fiedler, Lange, Danz.*]

WORKS ON THE CHURCH HISTORY OF PARTICULAR PERIODS: (a) *Ancient Times.* *Moshemii,* Commentarius de Rebus Christianorum ante Constantinum M., Helmstad. 1753, 54. [Vol. i. transl. by *R. S. Vidal;* vol. ii. by *Jas. Murdoch,* 2 vols., New York 1852. *Philip Schaff,* Hist. of Apostolic Church, etc., New York 1853. *H. H. Milman,* Hist. of Christ. to Abolition of Paganism in the Rom. Emp., 3 vols. *Rothe,* Anfänge d. Christl. Kirche, 1837. *A. Ritschl,* d. Altkathol. Kirche, 1850. *W. Burton,* Lect. on Eccl. Hist. of First Three Cent., in his Works, vols. iv. and v., Oxf. 1837. *K. R. Hagenbach,* die Christl. Kirche d. drei ersten Jahrh. 1853. *F. C. Baur,* Das Christenthum . . . in d. drei ersten Jahrh. 1853. *H. W. J. Thiersch,* Gesch. d. Christl. Kirche; transl. by Carlyle, Lond.

1852.] Compare also the works of *M. Baumgarten, J. P. Lange, Baur, Lechler, Schwegler, Dietlein, Volkmar, Bunsen, Hilgenfeld, L. Noack,* etc. (*b*) *Middle Ages* (especially in relation to Scholasticism). *J. B. Bossuet,* Einleitung in die Allg. Gesch.; German, transl. by J. A. Cramer, Leipz. 1757–86 [in French and English, numerous editions. *J. T. Damberger,* Synchron. Gesch. d. Kirche u. Welt im Mittelalter, Regensb. 6 Bde. 1850–54; also a French edition]. *Ueberweg* (§ 7). [*M. B. Hauréau,* De la Philos. Scholastique (crowned), 2 vols., Paris 1859. *E. Chastel,* Le Christianisme et l'Eglise au Moyen Age, Paris 1857.] (*c*) *The Time of the Reformation* (in addition to works on the History of the Reformation): *J. G. Planck,* Geschichte der Entstehung, der Veränderungen und Bildung unseres Protestantischen Lehrbegriffs, von Anfang der Reformation bis zur Einführung der Concordienformel, vol. vi. 2d ed., Leipz. 1791–1800, comp. §§ 212, 219. (*d*) *Modern Times: Planck,* Geschichte der Prot. Theol. von der Concordienformel an bis in die Mitte des 18 Jahrh., Gött. 1631. Comp. *J. G. Walch,* Histor. u. Theolog. Einleitung in die Religions-streitigkeiten in und ausserhalb der Lutherischen Kirche, Jena 1733, 10 vols. Further literature under § 272 ff.

(6) Works which treat on particular subjects (monographs) will be mentioned in their proper place. Essays in which the systems of individual Fathers are more fully discussed, will be found in the works of Rössler, Augusti, Möhler, etc., mentioned § 14, note 1.

(7) WORKS ON DOGMATIC THEOLOGY WHICH ALSO CONSIDER THE HISTORY OF DOCTRINES, or include it: *G. J. Seiler,* Theologia Dogmatico - Polemica, cum Compendio Historiæ Dogmatum, ed. 3, Erl. 1789. *J. F. Gruner,* Institutionum Theologiæ Dogmaticæ, lib. iii., Hal. 1777. *J. Ch. Döderlein,* Institutio Theologi Christiani in Capitibus Religionis theoreticis, ed. 6, Alt. 1797, 2 vols. *C. Fr. Stäudlin,* Lehrbuch der Dogmatik und Dogmengeschichte, Gött. (1801, 9), 1822. *J. A. L. Wegscheider,* Institutiones Theol. Christ. Dogmaticæ, addita Singulorum Dogmatum Historia et Censura, Hal. 1815, ed. 8, 1844. *K. G. Bretschneider,* Handbuch der Dogmatik der Evangelischen Kirche, 3d ed. 2 vols., Leipz. 1828, 34. *By the same:* Versuch einer systematischen Entwicklung aller in der Dogmatik vorkommenden Begriffe, nach den Symb. Büchern der

Luth. Kirche, 4th ed., Leipz. 1841. *Karl Hase*, Lehrbuch der Evangelischen Dogmatik, Stuttg. 1826 (6th ed., Leipz. 1870). *By the same:* Gnosis oder Evang. Glaubenslehre für die Gebildeten in der Gemeinde, wissenschaftlich dargestellt, 2d ed. 2 vols., Leipz. 1869-70. [*G. Ch. Knapp*, Vorlesungen über die Christliche Glaubenslehre, herausgeg. von *Thilo*, 2d ed. 1837; translated into English by *Leon. Woods*, And. 1831, and often republished.] *J. D. F. Strauss*, Die Christl. Glaubensl. in ihrer gesch. Entwicklung, 2 vols., Tüb. 1840. *Ch. E. Weisse*, Philos. Dogmatik, oder Phil. des Christenth., 1 vol., Leipz. 1855 (§§ 180-247). [*Dan. Schenkel*, Die Christl. Dogmatik, vom Standpunkte des Gewissens, 2 vols. (in three parts), Wiesbaden 1858-59. *G. Thomasius*, Christi Person u. Werk, 3 Thle., Erlangen 1853 sq. *J. P. Lange*, Christl. Dogmatik, 3 vols., Heidelb. 1849-52. *A. D. C. Twesten*, Dogmatik d. Evang.-Luth. Kirche, 2d ed. 2 vols. 1834-37. *J. H. A. Ebrard*, Christl. Dogmatik, 2d ed. 2 vols. 1862, 63. *F. A. Philippi*, Kirchl. Glaubensl., 5 vols. 1854-75. *Aug. Hahn*, Lehrb. d. Christl. Glaubens, 4te. Aufl. ii. 1858.] *On the History of the Protestant Doctrine:* *W. M. L. De Wette*, Dogmatik der Evangelisch-lutherischen Kirche nach den Symbolischen Büchern und den ältern Dogmatikern (the second part of his Lehrb. der Christ. Dogmatik), 2d ed., Berlin 1821, 3d ed. 1840. *F. A. Klein*, Darstellung des dogmatischen Systems der Evangel. Prot. Kirche, Jena 1822, 3d ed. revised by *Lobegott Lange*, ibid. 1840. *Hase*, Hutterus redivivus, oder Dogmatik der Evangelisch-lutherischen Kirche, Leipz. 1829-58, 9th ed. *Al. Schweizer*, Die Glaubensl. d. Evang. Ref. Kirche, aus den Quellen, vol. i., Zürich 1844 [Die Protestantischen Centraldogmen., vol. ii. 1856]. *D. Schenkel*, Das Wesen des Protest. aus d. Quellen des Reformationszeitalters dargestellt, 3 vols., Schaffh. 1846-51. *H. Schmid*, die Dogmatik der evang.-luther. Kirche, 6th ed., Fkft. 1876. *H. Heppe*, Dogmatik des deutschen Protestantismus im sechzehnten Jahrh., 3 vols., Gotha 1857. *K. F. A. Kahnis*, Lutherische Dogmatik, historisch-genetisch dargestellt, Leipz. 1863, 64 (see above under 4). WORKS ON THE HISTORY OF DOGMATIC THEOLOGY: *Ch. G. Heinrich*, Versuch einer Geschichte der verschiedenen Lehrarten der Christl. Glaubenswahrheiten und der merkwürdigsten Systeme und Compendien derselben, von Christo bis auf unsere Zeiten, Leipz. 1790. *J. H. Schickedanz*, Versuch einer Geschichte der Christ. Glaubenslehre und der merkwürdigsten Systeme, Compendien, Normalschriften und Katechismen der Christ. Hauptparteien, Braunschw. 1827. *Flügge* und *Stäudlin*, Geschichte der theol. Wissenschaften. *Herrmann*, Gesch. d. Prot. Dogmatik, von Melanc. bis Schleiermacher, Leipz. 1842. *Gass*, Gesch. d. Prot. Dogmatik, 3 vols., Berl. 1854-62.

(8) *K. F. Stäudlin*, Geschichte der Sittenlehre Jesu, 3 Bde., Gött. 1799-1812. *De Wette, Christliche Sittenlehre, 3 vols., Berlin 1819-23. The shorter Compendium of the same author: Lehrbuch der Christlichen Sittenlehre und der Geschichte derselben, Berlin 1833.

(9) Comp. § 13, note 1, and § 4 (on the significance of Symbolism). **Phil. Marheineke*, christl. Symbolik, oder historisch-kritische und dogmatisch-comparative Darstellung des katholischen, lutherischen, reformirten und socinianischen Lehrbegriffs, Heidelb., part I. vols. i. ii. 1810, vol. iii. 1813 (also under the title: das System des Katholicismus); new edition by *Matthies* and *Vatke*, 1848. *By the same:* Institutiones symbolicæ, doctrinam Catholicorum, Protestantium, Socinianorum, ecclesiæ Græcæ, minorumque societatt. christ. summam et discrimina exhibentes, Berol. 1812, ed. 3, 1830. *Herb. Marsh.*, The Churches of Rome and England Compared: translated into German by *J. C. Schreiter*, Sulzb. 1821. **G. B. Winer*, comparative Darstellung des Lehrbegriffs der verschiedenen christlichen Kirchenparteien, nebst vollständigen Belegen aus den symbolischen Schriften derselben in der Ursprache (mit angehängten Tabellen), Leipz. 1824, 4to, new ed. 1837. †*J. A. Möhler*, Symbolik, oder Darstellung der dogmatischen Gegensätze der Katholiken und Protestanten, nach ihren öffentlichen Bekenntniss-schriften, Mainz 1832, 6th ed. 1843. On the other side: *Fred. Chr. Baur*, Gegensatz des Katholicismus und Protestantismus nach den Principien und Hauptdogmen der beiden Lehrbegriffe, Tüb. 1833. *K. Im. Nitzsch*, Prot. Beantwort. der Symbolik Möhlers; in reply: *Möhler*, neue Untersuchung der Lehrgegensätze zwischen den Katholiken und Protestanten, Mainz 1834, 35, 7th ed. 1864; and also: *Baur*, Erwiderung auf Möhlers neueste Polemik u. s. w., Tüb. 1834.—*Ed. Köllner*,

Symbolik aller christlichen Confessionen, vol. i. Symbolik der luth. Kirche, Hamb. 1837; vol. ii. Symbolik der römischen Kirche, 1844. *H. E. F. Guericke,* allgem. christl. Symbolik vom luth. kirchl. Standpunkte, Leipz. 1839, 3d ed. 1861. *H. W. J. Thiersch,* Vorlesungen über Kath. u. Protest., 2d ed. 1848. *A. H. Baier,* Symbolik der christ. Confessionem u. Religionsparteien; Part I. Symbolik d. Romisch-Kath. Kirche, vol. i. Greifsw. 1854. *Matthes,* Comp. Symbolik, Leipz. 1854. *N. Hofmann,* Symbolik, oder system. Darstellung d. Symb. Lehrbegriffe, Leipz. 1857. †*Hilgers,* Symbolische Theologie, Bonn 1841. *K. Hase,* Handbuch der protest. Polemik, Leipz. 1862. *A. Neander,* Katholicismus und Protestantismus, herausg. von *Messner,* Berlin 1863. [*M. Schneckenburger,* Vergleichende Darstellung des lutherischen u. reformirten Lehrbegriffs: herausg. von *Ed. Güder,* Zwei Theile, Stuttg. 1855.] For the editions of the symbolical books, see § 13, 1.

FIRST PERIOD.

FROM THE APOSTOLIC AGE TO THE DEATH OF ORIGEN,
OR FROM THE YEAR 70 TO THE YEAR 254.

THE AGE OF APOLOGETICS.

A. GENERAL HISTORY OF DOCTRINES DURING THE FIRST PERIOD.

§ 17.

Christ and Christianity.

On the Life of Christ in general, see the earlier Harmonies of the Gospels [*William Newcome*, Eng. Harmony, repr. Phil. 1809; *Greswell* (ed. 4) and *Slatter*, in Greek, 1845 and 1878; *E. Robinson*, in Greek, 1831, in English, 1846; *L. Carpenter*, Lond. 1835; *J. G. Palfrey*, Bost. 1831; *Stroud's* New Greek Harmony, 1853; Harmony, in Eng., R. Tract Soc. and S. P. C. K. Comp. *S. Davidson* in Kitto, l.c. sub voce], and the modern works of *Hess*, *Hase* (newest ed. 1865), *Paulus*, *Strauss*, and (in reference to the latter) *Weisse*, *Neander*, *Wilke*, † *Kuhn*, *Theile*, *Lange*, *Ebrard*, etc. Since 1863, *Renan*, Vie de Jésus (1863); the new edition of *Strauss'* Leben Jesu (1864); *Schenkel*, Characterbild Jesu (1873); *Schleiermacher*, Leben Jesu, ed. by Rütenick (1864), and the controversial writings occasioned by the works of *Renan*, *Strauss*, and *Schenkel*, which, however, deal less with the doctrinal than the historical aspect of the subject, and therefore have only an indirect bearing upon the History of Doctrine. [*Seeley*, Ecce Homo, Lond. and Camb. 1866; *Keim*, Geschichte Jesu von Nazara, 3 vols., Zürich 1867-72, and new ed.; *Farrar*, Life of Christ, 2 vols. London 1874; *Geikie*, Life and Words of Christ, London 1876, etc.] Concerning the internal or apologetico-dogmatic aspect of his life, which forms the basis of the History of Doctrines, comp. (*Reinhard*) Versuch über den Plan, den der Stifter der christlichen Religion zum Besten der Menschheit entwarf, Wittenberg 1781, new ed., with additions by *Heubner*, Wittenb. 1830 (primarily a reply to the Wolfenbüttel Fragments). [Plan of the Founder of Christ., from the German, by *O. W. Taylor*, 12mo, Andover 1831.] **J. G. Herder*, Vom Erlöser der Menschen, nach den drei ersten

Evangelien, Riga 1796. *By the same:* vom Sohne Gottes, der Welt Heiland, nach Johannes, Riga 1797. (Comp. Werke zur Religion und Theologie, vol. xi., or Christliche Schriften, part 1.) *Ch. F. Böhme,* die Religion Jesu Christi, aus ihren Urkunden dargestellt, Halle 1825-27. **Ullmann,* über die Sündlosigkeit Jesu, in the Studien und Kritiken, 1828, part 1, reprinted, Hamb. 1833, 5th ed. 1845. [*Dr. Ullmann* on the Sinless Character of Jesus, Edinr.] *By the same:* Was setzt die Stiftung der christlichen Kirche durch einen Gekreuzigten voraus? in the Studien und Kritiken, 1832, s. 579-596, and reprinted in his treatise: Historisch oder mythisch? Beiträge zur Beantwortung der gegenwärtigen Lebensfrage der Theologie, Hamb. 1838. *Ch. F. Fritzsche,* de ἀναμαρτησίᾳ Jesu Christi, Commentationes 4 (repr. in Fritzschiorum Opuscula Academica, Lips. 1838, p. 48 seq.). **Alex. Schweizer,* über die Dignität des Religionsstifters, in the Studien und Kritiken, 1834. *F. Lücke,* two programmes (against Hase): Examinatur, quæ speciosus nuper commendata est sententia de mutato per eventa adeoque sensim emendato Christi consilio, Gött. 1831, 4to. On the other side: *Hase,* Streitschriften, Leipz. 1834.—*Strauss* and his opponents. (The Literature in *Theile* and elsewhere.) [*Neander's* Life of Christ, transl. from 4th ed. by J. McClintock and C. E. Blumenthal, New York 1848; London, Bohn. *Hase's* Life of Jesus, transl. by J. F. Clarke, Boston 1860. *Strauss'* Life, transl. 2 vols. Lond. 1854. *W. H. Furness,* History of Jesus, Boston 1850; ibid., Jesus and His Biographers, 1838.—†*Sepp,* Das Leben Jesu, 4 vols. Regensb. 1843 sq.; in French, 1854. *J. P. Lange,* Das Leben Jesu, 3 vols. Heidelb. 1847, and in English (Clark, Edinr.). *A. Ebrard,* Kritik d. evang. Gesch., 3d ed. Erlangen 1868. *C. F. Von Ammon,* 3 vols. 1847. *B. Bauer,* Evang. Gesch., 3 vols., 2d ed. 1855. †*J. Bucher,* Leben Jesu, 1859. *Paulus,* 2 Bde. 1828. Krabbe, 1838. *Weisse,* Evang. Gesch., 2 vols. 1828, 29. *Ewald,* Gesch. Jesu u. seiner Zeit, 1855. *A. Tholuck,* Glaubwürdigkeit, 1837. *T. Young,* The Christ of History, 1855. *Alexander,* Christ and Christianity, 1854. (*Isaac Taylor*) Restoration of Belief, 1855. *W. H. Mill,* Christian Advocate Sermons, Camb. 1844, 49.] *G. Volkmar,* Die Religion Jesu und ihre erste Entwicklung, Leipz. 1857. [*Gess,* Lehre von der Person Christi, 1856.]

WITH the incarnation of the Redeemer, and the introduction of Christianity into the world, the materials of the History of Doctrines are already fully given in germ. The object of all further doctrinal statements and definitions is, in the positive point of view, to unfold this germ; in the negative, to guard it against all foreign additions and influences. We here assume, on the basis of the evidences, that what Jesus Christ brought to light, in relation to the past (1), was new and original, *i.e.* a revelation, and, in relation to the future, is theoretically perfect, not standing in need of correction or improvement (2). This is the principle which we are justified in placing at the very head of the History of

Doctrines, and by which we are to judge all its phenomena. We cannot, therefore, separate Christ's doctrine from His person. For the peculiar and harmonious relation in which Christ, as the Son of God, stood to His heavenly Father, the decision with which He bore witness to this relationship, and the spiritual and moral renovation which were to flow from Himself, as the Saviour, unto mankind, form the kernel and centre of His doctrine. It has not essentially the character of a system made up of certain definitive notions, but it is a fact in the religious and moral sphere, the joyful news (εὐαγγέλιον, κήρυγμα) of which was to be proclaimed to all men for their salvation, on condition of faith, and a willingness to repent and obey in newness of life. Jesus is not the author of a *dogmatic theology*, but the author and finisher of *faith* (Heb. xii. 2); not the founder of a school, but in the most exalted sense the founder of a religion and of the Church. Hence He did not propound dogmas dressed in a scientific garb, but He taught the divine word in a simply human and popular manner, for the most part in parables and proverbs. We find these laid down in the canonical Gospels, though in a somewhat different form in the Gospel of John from that in the synoptical Gospels (3). One of the objects shared by the evangelical interpretation of Scripture, by the histories of the life of Jesus, by apologetics and biblical theology, is to ascertain the peculiar contents of the teaching of Jesus, to reduce it to certain fundamental ideas and one uniform principle.

(1) "*The office of the Saviour was not to propound doctrine, or to set forth doctrinal formulas, but to manifest Himself, and to reveal His unity with the Father. His person was a fact, and not an idea.*" Schwegler, Montanismus, s. 3. Jesus, indeed, adopted many of the current opinions, especially the Mosaic doctrine of one God, and also the prevailing opinions and expectations of the age concerning the doctrine of angels, the kingdom of God, etc. But to consider Him merely as the reformer of Judaism would be to take a too narrow view of

His work, and to speak of Him as an Ebionite; see *Schwegler*, das nachapostolische Zeitalter, s. 89 ff. (das Urchristenthum). On the relation in which the History of Doctrines stands to the teaching of Jesus and His apostles, see *Dorner*, Entwicklungsgeschichte der Lehre von der Person Christi, I. i. s. 68; *Gieseler's* Dogmengeschichte, s. 4, 29 ff.; *Baur*, s. 140.

(2) A perfectibility of Christianity is, from the Christian point of view, unimaginable, if we mean by this an extension or perfection of the *idea* of religion as taught by the Son of God; for this is complete in itself, and realized in the manifestation of the God-man. There is therefore no room within the History of Doctrines for a new revelation, which might supersede the Christianity of its founder. Compare the recent controversy aroused by Strauss upon the question whether and how far the entire *religious life* (and this only as the first point in the debate) can be said to be perfectly realized in any one individual. [This is the point which Strauss debated in the form, that no one individual of a species can fully realize and exhaust any general idea or conception, *e.g.* an incarnation, a perfect religion. See *Dorner, Göschel*, and others in reply.]

(3) How far the synoptical Gospels differ from each other in their accounts of the teaching of Jesus, and how this difference again is connected with the question as to the priority of Matthew or Mark, must be discussed elsewhere. So the important inquiry as to the origin of the fourth Gospel must, for the present, remain for us an open question. We may, however, set down as certain the following points:— In the synoptical Gospels we find more of *doctrina Christi*, in John more of *doctrina de Christo*: hence the former are more objective, the latter is more subjective. But though we concede such a subjective colouring, on the part of the fourth evangelist, in his conception and narration of the words of Jesus, yet this does not affect the *credibility* of his report, or the religious truth of what he imparts; comp. *Ebrard*, das Evang. Johannis, Zür. 1845. Upon the extent to which the divine dignity of Christ is manifested even in the synoptic Gospels, see *Dorner's* work, cited above, s. 79 ff. [Comp. also *W. T. Gess*, Die Lehre von d. Person Christi, 1856, and *Lechler* in Stud. und Kritiken, 1857. *Delitzsch*, Bibl. Psycho-

logie, s. 204 ff. *Hahn*, Theol. des neuen Test. i. 205. *Weizsäcker*, Lebenszeugniss des johanneischen Christus, in Jahrb. f. deutsche Theol. 1857. Comp. also the Commentaries on St. John by *Luthardt* and *Godet*, in Eng., Clark, Edinr.]

§ 18.

The Apostles.

Neander, Geschichte der Pflanzung und Leitung der christlichen Kirche durch die Apostel, vol. ii. sec. 6. [History of the Planting and Training of the Christian Church by the Apostles, translat. by *J. E. Ryland*, Edinr. 1842 (also in Bohn's Library), vol. ii. book vi. : The Apostolic Doctrine.] *G. Ch. R. Matthaei*, der Religionsglaube der Apostel Jesu, nach seinem Ursprunge und Werthe, vol. i. Gött. 1826. *Ch. F. Böhme*, die Religion der Apostel Jesu Christi, aus ihren Urkunden dargestellt, Halle 1829. *Kleuker*, Johannes, Petrus und Paulus, Riga 1785. *T. Ch. E. Schmid*, Dissertationes II. de theologia Joannis Apostoli, Jen. 1801. *L. Usteri*, Entwickelung des Paulinischen Lehrbegriffs in seinem Verhältniss zur biblischen Dogmatik des N. Test., Zürich 1824, 29, 31, 32. *A. F. Dähne*, Entwickelung des Paulinischen Lehrbegriffs, Halle 1835. *F. Ch. Baur*, der Apostel Paulus, Tüb. 1845. *Frommann*, Der johanneische Lehrbegriff, 1839. *K. R. Köstlin*, der Lehrbegriff des Evangeliums und der Briefe Johannis und die verwandten neutestamentlichen Lehrbegriffe, Berl. 1843. *W. Steiger*, der erste Brief Petri, mit Berüksichtigung des ganzen biblischen Lehrbegriffs, Berlin 1832. *Weiss*, Petrin. Lehrb. 1855. *M. Ulrich*, Versuch einer Eintheilung der biblischen Dogmatik des Neuen Testaments, in Röhrs Krit. Predigerbibliothek, xix. 1. [*Tholuck*, Remarks on the Life, Character, and Style of the Apostle Paul, in Clark's Students' Cabinet Library of Useful Tracts.] *In general: Zeller*, Aphorismen über Christenthum, Urchristenthum und Unchristenthum, in *Schwegler's* Jahrbücher der Gegenwart, 1844 (June). *A. Schwegler*, das nachapostolische Zeitalter, 2 vols. Tüb. 1846. *W. O. Dietlein*, das Urchristenthum, eine Beleuchtung der von der Schule des Dr. Baur in Tübingen über das apostolische Zeitalter aufgestellten Vermuthungen, Halle 1845. *Dorner*, l.c. *Schwegler*, Apologetisches und Polemisches (against Dorner), in *Zeller's* Jahrbücher, 1846. *Planck*, Judenthum und Urchristenthum, ibid. 1847, s. 258 ff. *H. W. J. Thiersch*, Die Kirche im apostol. Zeitalter, Frankf., 2d ed. 1858. *Baumgarten*, Die Apostelgesch., Halle, 2d ed. 1859 [in Clark's Library, 1856]. *E. Reuss*, Histoire de la Théologie chrétienne au siècle apostolique, Paris 1852, 3d ed. 1864. *F. Ch. Baur*, Das Christenthum und die christl. kirche d. 3 ersten Jahrh., Tüb. 1853. *Lechler*, Das apostol. und nachapostol. Zeitalter (a prize essay), Haarlem 1854, 2d ed. Stuttgard 1857. *Herm. Messner*, Lehre d. Apostel., Leipz. 1856. *Baur*, Dg. s. 140 ff. *Tripp*, Paulus nach der Apostelgeschichte, Leiden 1866. [*K. Schrader*, Der Apostel Paulus, Leipz. 1830-33, 3 Bde. *Pearson*, Annales Paulini, 1688. *W. T. Conybeare* and *J. Howson*, The Life and Epistles of St. Paul, Lond. 1852, 2 vols. 4to, also ed. in 8vo and 12mo. *Paret*, Paulus und Jesus, Jahrb. f. deutsche Theologie, 1858. On Paul and Seneca: *Chs. Aubertin,* Etude critique, Paris 1858; *Baur* in Zeitschrift f. wiss. Theol. 1858. *H. H. Milman,* Character and Conduct of the Apostles as an Evidence of Christianity, Lond. *Luthardt,* Das Evangelium Johannes, 1853, and in Eng. *K. F. T. Schneider,* Aechtheit d. Evang. Johan. 1854; *G. K. Mayer,* Aechtheit d. Ev. Joh. 1854; comp. *Lechler* in Stud. u. Krit. 1856; *F. C. Baur* in Theol. Jahrb. 54, 1857; *Hilgenfeld* in Zeitschrift f. wiss. Theol. 1858 and 1859, and in Theol. Jahrb. 1855; *Weizsäcker* in Jahrb. f. deutsche Theol. 1859. *Düsterdieck,* Die 3 Joh. Briefe, 2 Bde. 1852-54. *A. Hilgenfeld,* Paulus und die Urapostel, in Zeitschrift f. wiss. Theol. 1860. Comp. also the controversy between Baur and Hase and Hilgenfeld on the principles of the Tübingen School, various pamphlets, 1855-57. *J. P. Lange,* Das apostol. Zeitalter, 1853. *L. Noack,* Der Ursprung des Christenthums, 2 Bde. Leipz. 1852. †*R. C. Lutterbeck,* Die Neutestamentl. Lehrbegriffe, 2 Bde. Mainz 1852. *Schaff's* Apostolic Church. *Köstlin,* Einheit u. Mannigfaltigkeit der neutest. Lehre, in Jahrb. f. deutsche Theol. 1857-58. *Renan,* Les Apôtres, Paris 1866; Saint Paul, 1869; L'Antechrist, 1873. *Lewin,* St. Paul, 3d ed. 1876. *Farrar,* St. Paul, 1879.]

As little as their Master did the first disciples of the Lord propound a dogmatic system. But as they made the original doctrine of Jesus the subject of theoretical contemplation, and as their hearts and lives were practically and experimentally penetrated by it, and as Christ's spiritual personality had been, as it were, formed in each one of them anew, we find, in their discourses and writings (1), the beginnings of a systematic view of Christian doctrines. And this in such a way that while *Peter* and *James* (in this respect to be compared with the synoptical writers) simply relate in an objective manner what was delivered to them (2), an internal and contemplative view of Christianity prevails in the writings of *John,* and a practical and dialectic tendency in those of *Paul,* who was later called to be an apostle (3). And these may be said to be types of the subsequent modes of theological thought and teaching (4).

(1) The apostles are presented to us, partly as simple witnesses and reporters of the teaching of Christ, partly as preachers guided by the Spirit to announce the truths of salvation which they have themselves experienced. But even in this respect we must not forget that we do not refer to the

twelve Apostles, of whose doctrinal views we possess but very imperfect knowledge. For it is yet contested whether the James and Jude, whose Epistles are in the canon, belonged to the twelve apostles, or whether they are the brothers of the Lord. On the doctrinal system of James, see *Dorner*, l.c. s. 91 ff. (Comp. *Herder*, Briefe zweier Brüder Jesu in unserm Kanon; *Wieseler* in the Studien und Kritiken, 1842, I. s. 71 ff.; **Schaff*, das Verhältniss des Jacobus, Bruders des Herrn, zu Jacobus Alphäi, Berl. 1842; and the commentaries.) [*Lardner*, vi. 162-202; *Alford*, Comm. on Ep. of St. James. See also *Herzog*, Real-Encyklopädie, and *Smith*, Dicty. of Bible, s.v.] Accordingly, *Peter* and *John* alone remain; but the second Epistle of the one, and the second and third Epistles of the other, were very early reckoned amongst the Antilegomena; the genuineness of the second Epistle of Peter in particular has again been impugned in modern times; and even his first Epistle, though without sufficient basis, has been the subject of doubts. Comp. *De Wette's* Einleitung ins N. Test. § 172, 173.

(2) If the first Epistle of Peter is genuine, it is undoubtedly of greater doctrinal importance than that of James, who gives a greater prominence to practical Christianity, and seems to ignore its Christological aspects, though he occasionally evinces a profound acquaintance with the nature of faith and the divine economy (ch. i. 13 ff., 25, ii. 10, etc.). [*Dorner*, l.c., contests this position; but *Hagenbach* says that he attributes views to James which are not distinctly his.] On his relation to Paul, see *Neander*, Gelegenheitsschriften, 3d ed. s. 1 ff. But dogmatic ideas appear even in the writings of Peter more as a vast mass of materials as yet in their rough state. "*In vain do we look in his writings for those definite peculiarities, so manifestly impressed upon the works of John and Paul.*" *De Wette*, l.c. Comp., however, *Rauch*, Rettung der Originalität des ersten Briefes Petri, in Winer's and Engelhardt's Krit. Journal, viii. s. 396. *Steiger*, l.c., and *Dorner*, s. 97 ff., and especially *Weiss*, Der Petrinische Lehrbegriff, Beitrag zur biblischen Theologie, Berlin 1855. "*It bears upon it the impress of the apostolic spirit*," *Neander*.

(3) *John* and *Paul* are then the prominent representatives of the doctrinal peculiarities of primitive Christianity. In

estimating the views of the former, besides his Epistles, we have to consider the introduction to his Gospel, and the peculiarities before alluded to in his relation of the discourses of Christ. (On the book of Revelation, and its relation to the Gospel and the Epistles, the opinions of critics have ever been, and still are different.¹) The manifestation of God in the flesh —union with God through Christ—life from and in God, and victory over the world and sin by means of this life, which is a life of love,—these are the fundamental doctrines propounded by John. (Comp. *Lücke's* Commentaries on John's writings; *Rickli's* Predigten über den ersten Brief; *Tholuck's* and *De Wette's* Commentaries on his Gospel [also the Comm. of *Luthardt* and *Godet*, in Clark's For. Theol. Lib.]; *Paulus*, über die 3 Lehrbriefe.) [*Neander*, l.c. s. 240 ff.: "*Hence everything in his view turned on one simple contrast:—Divine life in communion with the Redeemer—death in estrangement from Him.*"] Paul differs from John materially and formally. (*a*) *Materially:* John rather presents the outlines of *theology* and *Christology;* Paul, those of *anthropology* and *soteriology;* nevertheless, the writings of John are also of the highest importance for anthropology, and those of Paul for theology and Christology. But the central point of John's theology is the incarnation of the Logos in Christ; the preponderating element of the Pauline doctrine is justification by faith. (*b*) *Formally:* Paul lets his thoughts rise up before the soul of the reader, reproduces them in him in a genetic order, and unfolds all the resources of dialectic art, in which the traces of his former Rabbinical education are not obliterated. John procceds positively and demonstratively, drawing the reader into the depths of mystic vision, and announces heavenly things in the tone of a seer,

---

¹ While for a long time the Gospel of John was held to be genuine, but not the Apocalypse (*Lücke*), the latest negative criticism has reversed the relation (*Schwegler*); and in opposition to this, the genuineness of both works, including the Epistles of John, has been recently defended by *Ebrard*. Comp., however, *Bleek*, Beiträge zur Evangelienkritik, Berl. 1846, i. s. 182 sq. ; and *Lücke* in the later editions of his work on John. We cannot regard this matter as by any means closed, for, from a wholly impartial standpoint, much may be said in favour of the identity of the evangelist and the author of the Apocalypse. [Comp. *J. T. Zobler*, Ursprung des vierten Evang. in Zeitschrift f. wiss. Theol. 1860. *Hilgenfeld* (Einleitung in das neue Testament, Leipzig 1875) shows that the Apocalypse was at first acknowledged as St. John's, and was only at a later period called in question.]

addressing himself more to the believing mind than to the understanding. John styles his readers *children*, Paul calls them his *brethren*. (Comp. on the difference between Paul and John, *Staudenmaier* on Joh. Scot. Erigena, s. 220 ff.) A peculiar theological tendency is represented, in fine, in the Epistle to the Hebrews. It is related to the Pauline doctrine with a prevailing leaning toward the typical; as to its form, it holds the medium between the modes of Paul and John. (On the conjectures respecting its author, comp. the Commentaries of *Bleek*, [*Stuart*], *Tholuck* [translat. into English by J. Hamilton and J. E. Ryland, Edin. 1842, 2 vols.; also *Delitzsch*, trans. in Clark's For. Theol. Lib.; *Kitto, Herzog,* and *Smith,* s.v.].) On the three primary biblical forms (the Jacobo-Petrine, the Johannean, and the Pauline), see *Dorner*, l.c. s. 77.

(4) The further development of the History of Doctrines will show that the tendency represented by *John* prevailed during the first period, as seen in the unfolding of the doctrine of the Logos, and in its Christology; it was not until the second period that Augustine put the *Pauline* doctrine in the foreground. This statement would need to be entirely changed, and such a view would be a mere optical deception, if the results of modern criticism, like that of the Tübingen school, were as well made out as they might seem to be on a superficial inspection. According to this view, Christianity could not have had any such primitive purity and dignity; that is, it could not have had to maintain from the beginning its character as a specific divine revelation against any possible corruptions and perversions; but it would have had, first of all, to extricate itself from the swaddling-bands of a poverty-stricken Ebionitism before it became purified and elevated, passing through Paulinism to the Johannean *gnosis;* a process for which, according to that theory, more than a full century was needed. We should not in that case find a connected organism existing already in germ, spreading itself out on various sides in the fulness of a rich life, but only a long thin series of differing phenomena, mutually dissolving each other. But, on the contrary, history shows that great epochs (*e.g.* the Reformation) wake up the mind in all directions, and call out different tendencies at one stroke; though they

may occur in a relative succession, yet they follow one another so rapidly that we can comprise them in a synchronistic picture. Thus, *De Wette* says [Wesen des Christl. Glaubens, Basel 1846, s. 256] : "*A more exact acquaintance with the New Testament documents shows us that the primitive Christianity here described had already run through three stadia of its development; that at first (according to the representation of the first three Gospels, particularly that of Matthew) it is a Jewish Christianity; then with the Apostle Paul, it comes into conflict with Jewish particularism; until at last, in John, it wholly overcomes its antagonism with the law.*" It must also be conceded, that in the course of this historical process, now one, and now another of the tendencies pre-formed in primitive Christianity obtains the leading influence; and that a series of centuries not yet closed is necessary, in order that what has actually been revealed in principle may be, in all its relations, wrought into the consciousness of the individual and of the community. Thus the Pauline type of Christianity remained for a long time a hidden treasure in the field of the Church, until in the period of the Reformation it was seen in its full significance. So, too, the more recent philosophy of religion has gone back to the profound spiritual intuition of John. Lastly, in respect to the striking contrast between the apostolic times and the post-apostolic (so much less productive in the sphere of doctrines), it is not unnatural that a period of relaxation should succeed one in which men's souls were thoroughly aroused in all directions; and to this there are also analogies in history, *e.g.* that of the Reformation. Besides this, it has been remarked that the office of the post-apostolic times was not so much to form *doctrines* as to build up the *Church;* whilst, with the period of apologetics, the peculiarly doctrinal work begins. Comp. *Dorner*, ubi supra, s. 130 ff.

§ 19.

Culture of the Age and Philosophy.

Souverain, Le Platonisme dévoilé, Amst. 1700 ; in German, über den Platonismus der Kirchenväter, mit Anmerkungen von Löffler, 2d ed. 1792. In reply : *Keil*, De Doctoribus veteris Ecclesiæ, Culpa corruptæ per Platonicas

§ 19.] CULTURE OF THE AGE AND PHILOSOPHY. 59

Sententias Theologiæ liberandis, Comment. (Opusc. Acad. Pars II.). *Im. Fichte*, De Philosophiæ Novæ Platonicæ Origine, Berol. 1818. *Ackermann*, Das Christliche im Plato und in der platonischen Philosophie, Hamb. 1835. *A. F. Dähne*, Geschichtliche Darstellung der jüdisch-alexandrinischen Religionsphilosophie, in 2 parts, Halle 1834. *F. C. Baur*, Das Christliche des Platonismus, oder Socrates und Christus, in Tüb. Zeitschrift für Theol., Tüb. 1837. *Gfrörer*, Kritische Geschichte des Urchristenthums, vol. i. ; also under the title: Philo und die alexandrinische Theosophie, 2 parts, Stuttgart 1831. *By the same:* Das Jahrhundert des Heils, 2 parts, Stuttg. 1836 (zur Geschichte des Urchristenthums). *Georgii*, über die neuesten Gegensätze in Auffassung der alexandrinischen Religionsphilosophie, insbesondere des jüdischen Alexandrinismus, in Illgen's Zeitschrift für historische Theologie, 1839, 3, s. 1 ff., 4, s. 1 ff. *Tennemann*, Geschichte der Philosophie, Bd. vii. *Ritter*, Gesch. der Philosophie, Bd. iv. s. 418 ff. *Schleiermacher*, Geschichte der Philosophie, s. 154 ff. [*Ritter*, Die Christliche Philos. (1858) i. Kapitel 2 and 3. *Susemihl*, Genetische Entwicklung d. platon. Phil. 1855. Plato contra Atheos; x. Book on Laws, by *Tayler Lewis*, New York 1845 ; cf. President *Woolsey* in Bib. Sacra, 1845. *Cæsar Morgan*, The Trinity of Plato and Philo. *F. Robiou*, de la Philos. chez les Romains, 6 articles in the Annales de la Philos. Chrét., Paris 1857, 58. *R. Ehlers*, Vis atque potestas quam Philosophia Antiqua imprimis Platonica et Stoica in Doctrina Apologetarum Seculi. II. habuerit, Göttin. 1859.] *Baur*, Dg. s. 82 ff., 242 ff. †*Huber*, die Phil. der Kirchenväter, München 1859. *Ueberweg* (§ 7. 1). *M. Schneckenburger*, Vorlesungen über neutestamentl. Zeitgeschichte, Frankf. 1862. †*Becker*, das philosoph. System Plato's in seiner Beziehung zum christlichen Dogma, Freiburg 1862.

Though the peculiar character of Christianity cannot be understood, if it is considered, not as an actual revelation of salvation, but merely as a new system of philosophy, yet, on the other hand, it must be admitted that, in its forms of thought, it attached itself to what was already in existence, though it filled it with its new and quickening spirit, and thus appropriated it to itself (1). This was especially the case with the Alexandrian culture, which was principally represented by *Philo* (2). This already appears in some of the New Testament writings, especially in the doctrine concerning the Logos (3), although in the most general outlines; but afterwards it exercised a decisive influence upon Christian speculation (4).

(1) "*It is a thoroughly unhistorical and untenable assumption, that primitive Christianity was unphilosophical, and as such, undogmatic, and that it had to be indebted to the world for*

the faculty of philosophizing and of forming dogmas." Lange, Dogmatik, s. 41. But it is also historically true that, before Christianity created a new philosophy by its own living energies, it attached itself to the prevalent forms of thought, and that so far the world did "hasten before" the Church in the process of forming doctrines. Comp. *Lange,* l.c. s. 42, and *Gieseler,* Dogmengesch. s. 44. [Gieseler here defends the early Christian teachers in making use of philosophy: 1. Because the times demanded a philosophical treatment of Christianity. 2. That this became injurious only when these philosophical opinions were held to be matters of faith, and not speculations. 3. The Christian philosophers did not intentionally, but unconsciously, introduce philosophical postulates into the Christian system.]

(2) Comp. *Grossmann,* Quæstiones Philoneæ, Lips. 1829. *Theile,* Christus und Philo, in Winer's und Engelhardt's kritisches Journal, Bd. ix. 4, s. 385. *Scheffer,* Quæst. Philon, sec. 2, p. 41 ss. *Lücke,* Commentar zum Joh. i. s. 249. (Comp. § 41 on the Logos.) *Editions of Philo:* Turnebus (1552), Höschel (1613), the Parisian (1640), *Mangey (1742), Pfeiffer (5 vols. Erl. 1820), Richter (1828–30), Tauchnitz's edition, 1851 ff. Comp. the Commentary on Philo's book, De Opificio Mundi, by *J. G. Müller,* Berlin 1841. [*Philo Judæus,* transl. in Bohn's Eccles. Library, by Yonge, 4 vols.] *Edw. von Muralt,* Untersuchungen über Philo in Beziehung auf die der (Petersburger) Akademie gehörigen Handschriften, 1840. [*Creuzer* in the Studien u. Kritiken, 1831. *M. Wolff,* Die Philon 'sche Philos, Leipz. 1849; 2d ed. 1858. *Philonis Judæi* Paralipomena Armena, Venet. 1826; *ibid.* Sermones Tres, ed. Venet. 1832. Articles on Philo, in Christ. R. 1853; North British, 1855; Eclectic (Lond.), Nov. 1855; Journal of Class. and Sacred Philol. 1854. Comp. also *Michel Nicholas,* Des Doctrines Réligieuses des Juifs pendant les deux Siècles antérieurs à l'ère chrétienne, Paris 1860. *S. Klein,* Le Judaisme, ou la Verité sur le Talmud, Paris 1859. *Lutterbeck,* Neutestamentliche Lehrbegriffe, i. s. 393–437.]

(3) That which was a mere abstract and ideal notion in the system of Philo became a concrete fact in Christianity, a spiritual and historical fact in the sphere of the religious life; on this account "*it is alike contrary to historical truth to deny*

the influence of the age upon the external phenomena and the didactic development of the gospel, and to derive its internal origin and true nature from the age."—*Lücke,* l.c.   Comp. *Dorner,* l.c. Einleit. s. 21 ff.

(4) Much of that which was formerly (from the time of *Souverain*) called "the Platonism of the Fathers," is by modern research reduced to this, "*that the general influence exerted by Platonism was the stronger and more definite influence of the general heathen culture.*" *Baumgarten-Crusius,* Compendium, i. s. 67. Comp. *Gieseler,* Dg. s. 44. Thus the charge of Platonism often brought forward against Justin M. is found on closer examination to be untenable; comp. *Semisch,* Justin der M. ii. s. 227 ff. It appears more just in the case of the Alexandrian theologians, especially Origen. But here, too, as well as in reference to the partial influence exerted by Aristotelianism and Stoicism upon certain tendencies of the age, it ought not to be overlooked that during this period "*philosophy appears only in a fragmentary way, and in connection with theology.*" *Schleiermacher,* l.c. s. 154; comp. also *Redepenning,* Origenes (Bonn, 1841), Bd. i. s. 91 ff. [Comp. *Fr. Michälis,* Die Philos. Platons in ihrer inneren Beziehung zur geoffenbarten Wahrheit, 1 Abth., Münster 1859.] *Baur,* l.c.

§ 20.

Rule of Faith.—The Apostles' Creed.

Marheineke, Ursprung und Entwicklung der Orthodoxie und Heterodoxie in den ersten 3 Jahrhunderten (in daub und Creuzers Studien, Heidelb. 1807, Bd. iii. s. 96 ff.). †*Möhler,* Einheit der Kirche oder Princip des Katholicismus im Geiste der Kirchenväter der ersten 3 Jahrhunderte, Tüb. 1825. *J. G. Vossius,* De Tribus Symbolis Dissertt., Amstel. 1701, fol. *Lord King,* History of the Apostles' Creed, with critical observations, 5th ed. Lond. 1738. (Latin translation by *Olearius,* Lips. 1706, Bas. 1768.) *Rudelbach,* die Bedeutung des Apostol. Symbolums, Leipz. 1844. *J. Stockmeyer,* über Entstehung des Apostolischen Symbolums, Zür. 1846. [Bishop *Pearson* on the Apostles' Creed. *H. Witsius,* Dissertation on what is commonly called the Apostles' Creed; transl. from the Latin by *D. Fraser,* Edinr. 1823, Dissert. i.—*P. Heylyn,* The Summe of Christian Theology, contained in the Apostles' Creed, London 1673, fol.—*J. Barrow,* Exposition of the Creed (Theolog. works, vol. v.), Oxf. 1838, sect. 1. *Meyers,* De Symbol. Apostol., Treviris 1849. *Hahn,* Bibliothek. d. Symbole, 1842. *W. W.*

Harvey, History and Theology of the Three Creeds, 2 vols. 1855. *C. A. Swainson, D.D.*, The Nicene and Apostles' Creeds: Their Literary History, London 1875.]

Before a scientific theology, under the form of γνῶσις, developed itself with the aid of philosophical speculation, the faith of the apostles was firmly and historically established as πίστις, by bringing together those elements (στοιχεῖα) of the Christian faith which were accounted essential. The κήρυγμα ἀποστολικόν, the παράδοσις ἀποστολική, was first transmitted by oral tradition, and afterward appeared in a written form (1). What is commonly called the Apostles' Creed (apostolic symbol) is most probably composed of various confessions of faith, used by the primitive Church in the baptismal service. Though it did not proceed from the apostles themselves, yet it preserved the principles of apostolic tradition in broad general outlines (2).

(1) Comp. the rules of faith of *Irenæus*, Adv. Hær. i. c. 10 (*Grabe*, c. 2); *Tertull.* De Virgin. vel. c. 1; De Præscript. Hær. c. 13; Advers. Prax. c. 2. *Orig.* De Princip. prooem. § 4. *Münscher, von Cölln*, i. 16–19. On the importance of tradition and its relation to Holy Scripture, comp. below, §§ 33 and 37. "*The rule of faith was not gained by the interpretation of the Scriptures, but taken from the apostolic tradition handed down in the Churches,*" *Gieseler*, Dogmengesch. s. 50.

(2) The fable of its apostolic origin, mentioned by *Rufinus*, Exposit. Symb. Apost. (in Baron. Annal. anno 44, No. 14 [*Witsius*, l.c. p. 3]), was doubted by Laur. Valla, and afterwards by Erasmus. Some of the earlier Protestants, however, *e.g.* the Magdeb. Centur. (Cent. I. 1, 2, p. 66), still attached credit to it. Comp. *Basnage*, Exercitationes Histor. crit. ad annum 44, No. 17. *Buddei*, Isagoge, s. 441, where the literature is given. *Neander*, Kg. i. 2, s. 535. *Marheineke*, l.c. s. 160 [*Heylyn*, l.c. p. 8 ff.; *Barrow*, l.c. 218, 219; *Gieseler's* Textbook, i. 80, 152. The title *apostolic* was not for several centuries restricted to the shortest of the three creeds, but was given to several other creeds and documents. Comp. *Swainson*, c. 13, p. 154].

§ 21.

Heresies.

Th. *Ittig*, de Hæresiarchis Ævi Apostolici, Lips. 1690, 1703, 4to. [*Edw. Burton*, Theolog. Works, vol. iii. : The Bampton Lecture on the Heresies of the Apostolic Age, Oxf. 1837. Comp. the introduction where the literature is given. *Lardner's* Hist. of Heretics. *Sartori*, Die . . . Secten. 1855. J. B. *Marsden*, Christ. Churches and Sects, 2 vols. 1854, 59. *G. Volkmar*, Die Quellen der Ketzergesch. 1855.]

Every departure from the apostolic canon of doctrine was considered, in relation to the Church, as αἵρεσις, heresy (1). Even in the apostolic age we find false teachers, some of whom are mentioned in the New Testament itself (2), others in the works of early ecclesiastical writers (3). Concerning their personal history and doctrine many points are still involved in obscurity, which, in the absence of trustworthy historical evidence, cannot be easily and satisfactorily cleared up.

(1) Αἵρεσις (from αἱρεῖσθαι) and σχίσμα were at first synonymous (1 Cor. xi. 18, 19), but in later times the one was used to denote a separation in doctrine, the other to designate a disruption in consequence of differences of opinion concerning liturgy, discipline, or ecclesiastical polity. The word αἵρεσις did not originally imply blame; it is used in the New Test. as a *vox media;* comp. Acts v. 17, xv. 5, xxv. 5. [*Burton*, l.c. p. 8.] Ecclesiastical writers themselves call Christianity a *secta* (*Tertull.* Apol. i. 1, and in many other places); and even Constantine gives the Catholic Church the name αἵρεσις (Euseb. x. c. 5). On the contrary, in Gal. v. 20, the same term is used in connection with ἐριθεῖαι, διχοστασίαι, etc., comp. 2 Pet. ii. 1 (ψευδοδιδάσκαλοι). Synonymous terms are: ἑτεροδιδασκαλία, 1 Tim. i. 3, vi. 3 ; ψευδώνυμος γνῶσις, ch. vi. 20 ; ματαιολογία, ch. i. 6 ; the adject. αἱρετικός, Tit. iii. 10. Comp. *Wetstein*, N. T. ii. 147. *Suicer*, Thesaurus, sub voce. On the various etymologies of the German word *Ketzer* (Ital. *Gazzari*, whether from καθαρός, or from the Chazares—like *bougre* from the Bulgares ? or even from Katz ?),

comp. *Mosheim*, Unparteiische und gründliche Ketzergeschichte, Helmst. 1746, s. 357 ff., and *Wackernagel*, Altdeutsches Lesebuch, 1675; *Jac. Grimm's* review of Kling's edition of Berthold's sermons, in the Wiener Jahrb. Bd. xxxviii. s. 216. On the service which heresies may render to science, *Orig.* Hom. 9, in Num. Opp. t. ii. p. 296, says: "Nam si doctrina ecclesiastica simplex esset et nullis intrinsecus hæreticorum dogmatum assertionibus cingeretur, non poterat tam clara et tam examinata videri fides nostra. Sed idcirco doctrinam catholicam contradicentium obsidet oppugnatio; *ut fides nostra non otio torpescat, sed exercitiis elimetur.*" Comp. *August.* De Civit. Dei, xviii. c. 51.

(2) On the different parties in the Church of Corinth (which, however, caused only schisms *in*, but not separations *from* the Church), comp. *Dan. Schenkel*, de Ecclesia Corinthia primæva factionibus turbata, Bas. 1838. *F. Ch. Baur*, die Christuspartei. [*Billroth*, Comment. on the Corinth., transl. by *Alexander*, i. p. 11. *Hilgenfeld*, Hist. Crit. Einleitung ins N. T. 1875, s. 260 ff. *W. L. Alexander*, in Kitto, Cyclop. of Bibl. Lit. *Smith's* Dictionary of the Bible, sub voce.] With respect to the heretics mentioned in the New Testament, the attention of critics has chiefly been directed to those alluded to in the Epistle to the Colossians and in the pastoral Epistles. Concerning the former (were they theosophic Jewish Essenes, or Jewish Christians?), comp. *Schneckenburger* in the appendix to his treatise on the Proselytentaufe, p. 213. *Böhmer*, Isagoge in Epist. a Paulo ad Coloss. datam (1829), s. 131. *Neander*, Apostolische Gesch. ii. [*Alexander*, in Kitto, l.c. sub voce. Especially see Dissertation in *Lightfoot*, Comm. on Ep. to Coloss. 1875, pp. 73-113.] Among the latter, *Hymenæus* and *Philetus* only are mentioned by name as denying the doctrine of resurrection, 2 Tim. ii. 17, 18. [*Burton*, l.c. s. 135 ff. *Ryland*, in Kitto, l.c. sub voce.] But the inquiry relative to the character of these heretics is intimately connected with the critical examination of the Epistles themselves. Comp. *F. Ch. Baur*, die sogenannten Pastoralbriefe des Apostels Paulus, aufs neue kritisch untersucht, Stuttg. 1835. On the other side: *Mich. Baumgarten*, die Aechtheit der Pastoralbriefe, Berlin 1837; comp. also the reply of *Baur* in his treatise, Ueber den Ursprung

§ 21.] HERESIES. 65

des Episcopats, Tüb. 1838, p. 14 ff. Comp. also *Schwegler*, l.c., and *Dietlein*, Urchristenthum. [*Alexander*, in Kitto, l.c., art. Timothy, Titus. *C. E. Scharling*, die neuesten Untersuchungen über die sogenannten Pastoralbriefe. Aus dem Dänischen übersetzt, Jena 1845.] Concerning the *Nicolaitans*, Rev. ii. 6, 15, and those who held the doctrine of Balaam, Rev. ii. 14 (comp. *Iren*. i. 26, and the erroneous derivation from Nicholas, Acts vi. 5), see the commentaries on the Book of Revelation [comp. *Davidson*, in Kitto, l.c.] (Ewald, p. 110). *Neander*, Kg. i. 2, s. 774 ff. [*Gieseler*, i. 88. *Burton*, l.c. Lect. v. p. 145 ff. *Lee*, in Kitto, l.c. *Schaff*, p. 671. *Stuart*, Comm. on the Apoc. ii. p. 62 ff. *Trench* on the Epp. to the Seven Churches, *in loc.*]

(3) The heresiarch *Simon Magus*, who is described in the New Testament (Acts viii.) as a man of an immoral character, but not as a heretic, is nevertheless represented by *Clem. Al.* (Strom. ii. 11, vii. 17) and *Orig.* (Contra Cels. i. p. 57) as the founder of a sect; by *Irenæus* (Adv. Hær. i. 23, 24) and *Epiphanius* (Hær. 21), even as the author of all heresies. Concerning his adventures and disputation with Peter, many fictitious stories were current among the earlier writers (see the Clementine Homilies, and *Justin M.* Apol. i. c. 56).—On Simon Magus and the two Samaritans *Dositheus* and *Menander* (*Euseb*. iii. 26), comp. *Neander*, i. 2. 779. [*Burton*, l.c. Lect. iv. s. 87–118, and note 40. *By the same:* Lectures on the Ecclesiast. Hist. of the First Cent. s. 77 ff. *Schaff*, 215, 376, 655. *Gieseler*, i. 56, § 18, note 8, where the literature is given. *Alexander*, in Kitto, l.c.] *Marheineke* in Daub's Studien, l.c. s. 116. *Dorner* says, l.c. s. 144: "*The accounts given of Simon Magus, Menander, and Dositheus, who have become almost mythical, at least prove that in Syria Gnostic tendencies made their appearance at an early period.*" [*Volkmar*, Simon Magus, in Theol. Jahrbücher, 1856, Heft 2.] The assertion of *Hegesippus* (*Euseb*. iii. 32, iv. 22), that the Church had not been stained with any heresy previous to the time of Trajan (παρθένος καθαρὰ καὶ ἀδιάφθορος ἔμεινεν ἡ ἐκκλησία), is not to be understood as if no heresies at all existed, but that, till the death of Simon (A.D. 108), the poison of heresies had not penetrated into the Church. The judgment of Hegesippus, too, refers to the locality of

Palestine. Comp. *Vatke* in Jahrb. f. wiss. Kritik, 1839, s. 9 ff. *Dorner*, l.c. 223. *Mangold*, Die Irrlehren d. Pastoralbriefe, Marburg 1856, s. 108 ff.

§ 22.

Judaism and Ethnicism.

There were two errors which the new-born Christianity had to guard against, if it was not to lose its own peculiar religious character and disappear in one of the already existing religions: against a relapse into Judaism on the one side, and against a mixture with paganism and speculations borrowed from it, and a mythologizing tendency on the other. Accordingly the earliest heresies, of which we have any trustworthy accounts, appear either as *Judaizing* or as *ethnicizing* (Hellenizing) tendencies. But as Jewish and pagan elements were blended with each other at the time of the rise of Christianity, manifold modifications, and transitions from the one to the other, would be likely to occur.

Concerning the different forms of heathenism (occidental and oriental), as well as the earlier and later periods of the Jewish dispensation, comp. *Dorner*, Entwicklungsgeschichte der Lehre von der Person Christi, s. 4 ff. [*Trench*, Hulsean Lectures on the Unconscious Prophecies of Heathenism, various editions. *Maurice*, The Religions of the World, 1853.]

§ 23.

Ebionites and Cerinthus. Docetæ and Gnostics.

Lequien, Dissertatio de Nazarenis necnon de Ebionitis (in Vogt's Bibliotheca, ii. 1, 1729). *Doederlein*, De Ebionitis, Butsov. et Wismar. 1770.] *Gieseler, von den Nazaräern und Ebioniten, in *Stäudlin's* und *Tzschirner's* Archiv. Bd. iv. st. 2. *Credner*, über Essäer und Ebioniten und einen theilweisen Zusammenhang derselben (in *Winer's* Zeitschrift für wissenschaftl. Theol. 1827, Heft 2 and 3). *Lobeg. Lange*, Beiträge zur ältern Kirchengeschichte, Leipzig 1826, 1 Bd. *Baur*, De Ebionitarum Origine et Doctrina ab Essenis repetenda, Tüb. 1831. *Schneckenburger*, Beiträge zur Einleitung ins Neue Testament, Stuttg. 1832. *A. Schliemann*, Die Clementinen nebst den verwandten Schriften und der Ebionitismus, ein Beitrag zur Kirchen- und Dogmengeschichte der ersten Jahrhunderte, Hamb. 1844. *Schwegler*, ubi supra. *A. Hilgenfeld*, die Clement. Recognitionen und Homilien, Jena 1848. [*Bunsen's* Hippolytus, vol. iii. *A. Ritschl* in Allg. Monatsschrift, Jen. 1852. *Hilgenfeld* in the (Tübingen) Theol. Jahrb. 1854. Clementinorum Epitomæ Duæ, ex Tischendorf (ed. A. R. H. Dressel), Leipz. 1859. *Rossel's* Theologische Schriften, Bd. i. Clement. Homiliæ, ed. Dressel, 1853.] *Schmidt*, Cerinth, ein Judaisirender Christ, in his Bibliothek für Kritik und Exegetik, Bd. i. s. 181 ff. *Paulus*, Historia Cerinthi, in Introduct. in N. Test. Capit. selectiora, Jen. 1799. *A. H. Niemeyer*, De Docetis, Hal. 1823, 4to. *Lewald*, De Doctrina Gnostica, Heidelberg 1819. *F. Lücke* in the Theologische Zeitschrift, Berlin 1820, Heft 2, s. 132. *Neander, Genet. Entwicklung der vornehmsten gnostischen Systeme, Berlin 1818. *Matter*, Histoire Critique du Gnosticisme, Paris 1828, 2 vols. [2d ed. 1840. *Gieseler*, review of *Neander*, in the Hall. Lit. Zeitung, 1823, and of *Matter* in the Stud. u. Krit. 1830]. †*Möhler*, Ursprung d. Gnosticismus, Tüb. 1831. [*Lutterbeck*, Neutest. Lehrbegriffe, Bd. ii. s. 3–79.] *Baur, Christliche Gnosis, oder die christliche Religionsphilosophie in ihrer geschichtlichen Entwicklung, Tüb. 1835. Same : Christenthum u. die Kirchengesch. der 3 ersten Jahrhunderte. *Jacobi* in Herzog, v. 204. *R. A. Lipsius, der Gnosticismus, sein Wesen, Ursprung u. Entwicklungsgang, Leipz. 1860. *A. Hilgenfeld*, Bardesanes der letzte Gnostiker, Leipz. 1864. *Möller*, Geschichte der Kosmologie. Comp. *Gieseler*, i. § 43 ff. *Neander*, i. 344–50, 396–99, 630. *Hase*, §§ 35, 75. *Schleiermacher*, Geschichte der Philosophie, s. 160–65. *Schaff*, 635. The articles in *Herzog's* Real-Encyklopädie. [See especially, Dean *Mansel*, The Gnostic Heresies, London 1875.]

The Judaizing tendency was chiefly represented by the *Ebionites* (1), of whom the *Nazarenes* (2) were a variety more nearly approaching the orthodox faith, and with whom were connected other Judaizing sects of a more indefinite character (3). *Cerinthus* (4) also belonged to this tendency, and makes the transition to that form of Judaism, blended with heathen Gnosis, which we find represented in the so-called *Clementine Homilies* (5). A strict opposition to the Jewish-Ebionitic tendency manifested itself first in the *Docetæ* (6), and afterwards in various ramifications of the *Gnostics* (7). Of the latter, some were more sharply opposed to Judaism (8), others even returned to Ebionitish errors (9), while *Marcion*, who occupied a peculiar position, endeavoured to go beyond the antagonism between Judaism and heathenism; but, despising all historical mediation, he built up a purely imaginary system of Christianity (10).

(1) On the derivation of Ebionites from אֶבְיוֹן, and their history, comp. *Orig.* Contra Celsum II. towards the commencement; *Irenæus,* Adv. Hær. I. 26. *Tert.* Præscr. Hær. 33; De Carne Christi, c. 14. *Euseb.* iv. 27. *Epiph.* Hær. 29, 30. *Hieron.* in Matt. viii. 9, xix. 20, (c. 66), xviii. in Jesaiam; Cat. Script. Eccles. c. 3; and the works on Ecclesiast. History. [*Niedner,* s. 215. *Burton,* l.c. Lect. vi. s. 183 ff.] Different opinions as to the origin of the Ebionites; *Schliemann,* s. 459 ff. (according to Hegesippus in *Euseb.* iii. 32 and IV. 22), dates it after the death of Simeon of Jerusalem. According to the school of Tübingen (*Schwegler*), Ebionitism is as old as Christianity [cf. *Nitzsch,* Dg. § 10], Christ Himself was an Ebionite, and Paul took the first step beyond Ebionitism. The Judaizing tendency, which was firmly rooted in Ebionitism, may indeed be traced back to primitive Christianity: not all Christians were, like Paul, able to comprehend the universal character of their religion. But this Jewish-Christian tendency existed for some time, along with the Pauline, as a more imperfect form of Christianity, without being regarded as heresy. But having once been left behind by the freer spirit of the Pauline doctrine,[1] it had either gradually to wear out (its adherents withering into a Jewish sect), or to grow rank, blended with other (Gnostic) elements (as was the case with the Ebionitism of the Clementine Homilies, comp. note 5). The former kind of Ebionitism has been called "vulgar Ebionitism." Its adherents were characterized by their narrow attachment to Jewish tradition, seeking to impose the yoke of the law upon Christians, and this prevented them from forming a higher idea of Christ than that involved in the Jewish conception of the Messiah. Accordingly, when they declared Jesus to be the Son of Joseph and Mary, this opinion did not proceed (as in the case of the Artemonites, § 24) from a rationalistic source, but had

---

[1] "Orthodoxy, when left behind by the culture of the age, and deserted by public opinion, becomes heresy."—*Hase.* And since there is no standing still, it is natural to infer that Ebionitism became retrograde in the direction of Judaism. *Dorner,* ubi supra, s. 304 ff.

its root in their spiritual poverty and narrow-mindedness. With their Jewish notions concerning the law and the Messiah, would accord the sensual, millennial expectations of which Jerome (l.c., but no other writer) accuses them. ["The common characteristics of the vulgar Ebionites were, as we learn from Irenæus: (1) Observance of the Mosaic law; (2) rejection of the Apostle Paul and his Epistles; (3) a Christology which excluded the doctrine of the pre-existence of Christ taught by Paul and John; (4) the exclusive use of the Gospel of the Hebrews as the source of the evangelical history; and (5) finally, millenarianism," *Nitzsch*, l.c.]

(2) *Origen* (Contra Cels. v. Opp. i. s. 625) mentions two different kinds of Ebionites, of whom the one class approached the orthodox doctrine of the Church more nearly than the other. These more moderate Ebionites were for a long time held to be the same as those to whom Jerome and Epiphanius give the name *Nazarenes*, which was earlier applied to all Christians. They taught that the law (circumcision in particular) was obligatory on Jewish Christians only, and believed Jesus to be the Son of the Virgin, though a mere man, to the extent at least of rejecting His pre-existence. Comp. the treatise of *Gieseler*, l.c. [*Burton*, l.c. p. 184]. According to the most recent researches (of *Schliemann*), however, the Nazarenes were never brought into the same class with the Ebionites, and Origen's distinction refers only to the difference between the common and the Gnostic Ebionites (comp. note 5). According to *Schwegler* (Nachapost. Zeitalter, i. s. 179 ff.), the position of the Nazarenes was only "the earliest primitive stage of the development of Ebionitism." He, as well as *Hilgenfeld* (l.c.), rejects the distinction made by Schliemann. It is simplest, with *Dorner* (ubi supra, s. 301 ff.), to assume that the Ebionites degenerated into Judaism, and thus became heretical Nazarenes (Jewish Christians). [Comp. *Mansel*, p. 123 ff.]

(3) *Elkesaites, Sampsœi*, etc. *Epiph.* Hær. 19. 1–30, 3. 17 (*Euseb.* iv.). "*It seems impossible accurately to distinguish these different Jewish sects, which were perhaps only different grades of the order of the Essenes, assisted, as we are, merely by the confused reminiscences of the fourth century.*" Hase (l.c.

s. 7, 90). [*Ritschl* on Elkesaiten, in Zeitschrift f. hist. Theol. 1853; and *Uhlhorn* in *Herzog's* Real-Encykl., article Elkesaiten; *Mansel*, l.c. p. 234 ff.]

(4) *Iren.* i. 26; *Euseb.* H. E. iii. 28 (according to Caius of Rome and Dionysius of Alexandria); *Epiph.* Hær. 28. Comp. *Olshausen*, Hist. Eccles. Veteris Monumenta Præcipua, vol. i. pp. 223-225. [*Burton*, l.c. Lect. vi. p. 174 ff. *Mansel*, 74 ff., 112 ff.] According to Irenæus, *Cerinthus* is allied to Gnosticism, and remote from Ebionitism, maintaining that the world was not created by the supreme God. He denies, however, in common with the Ebionites, that Christ was born of the Virgin, but on different, viz. rationalistic grounds (*impossible enim hoc ei visum est*). According to the accounts given by Eusebius, his principal error consisted in gross millenarianism, *i.e.* in a Judaistic tendency. Comp. the treatises of *Paulus* and *Schmid*; and on his remarkable, but not inexplicable, mixture of Judaism and Gnosticism, *Baur*, Gnosis, s. 404 f. *Dorner*, l.c. s. 310, claims that there was a peculiar class of Cerinthian Ebionites, who, in his opinion, form the transition to the pseudo-Clementines.

(5) As Cerinthus blended Gnostic elements with Jewish notions, so did that section of the Ebionites represented in the Clementines (*i.e.* homilies of the Apostle Peter, which are said to have been written by Clement of Rome). Comp. *Neander's* Appendix to his work on the Gnostic systems, and Kirchengeschichte, i. 2, 619 f. [*N. Lardner*, Works, ii. 376, 377. *Norton*, l.c. ii. note B, s. xxiii.-xxxvii.] *Baur*, Gnosis, s. 403, and App. s. 760, and his programme referred to above. *Schenkel*, however, has broached a different opinion in his Dissert. (cited § 21, note 2), according to which the Clementine tendency would belong, not to the Judaizing, but to a rationalizing Monarchian tendency (comp. § 24) in Rome (comp. *Lücke's* review in the Göttinger gelehrte Anzeigen, 1838, 50 and 51, and *Schliemann*, u. s., s. 357 ff.). *Dorner*, l.c. s. 324 ff., gives a striking description of this tendency, which passes over from Judaism into paganism. The investigations respecting the Clementines are by no means concluded; comp. *Hilgenfeld*, Clementinorum Epitomæ duæ, altera edita correctior, inedita altera nunc primum integra ex

codd. romanis et excerptis Tischendorfianis, cura *Alb. Rud. Max. Dressel*, Lips. 1859.

(6) The Docetæ whom *Ignatius*, Ad. Eph. c. 7–18, Ad. Smyrn. c. 1–8, already opposed, and probably even the Apostle John (1 John i. 1–3, ii. 22, iv. 2 ff., 2 John 7 [perhaps also St. Paul; see *Mansel*, pp. 55, 76]; on the question whether he also alludes to them in the prologue to his Gospel, comp. *Lücke*, l.c.), may be considered as the rude forerunners of the Gnostics; for, "*although Docetism belongs to the distinctively Gnostic character, yet the Docetæ are sometimes spoken of as a special Gnostic sect.*" *Baur* in his Christ. d. drei ersten Jahrh. s. 207. [*Burton*, l.c. Lect. vi. p. 158 ff.] The Docetæ form the most decided contrast with the Ebionites, so far as this, that they not only maintain (in opposition to them) the divinity of Christ, but also volatilize His human nature, in which the Ebionites exclusively believed, into a mere phantasm (denying that He possessed a *real* body). Ebionitism (Nazareism) and Docetism form, according to *Schleiermacher* (Glaubenslehre, Bd. i. s. 124), *natural* heresies, and mutually complete each other, as far as this can be the case with one-sided opinions; but they quite as easily pass over the one to the other. Comp. *Dorner*, Geschichte der Christologie, s. 349 ff.

(7) What Docetism did in the doctrine concerning Christ alone, the more completely developed system of Gnosticism carried out, in its whole spiritualizing tendency, into the extreme most opposed to Judaizing Ebionitism. It not only contains docetic elements (comp. the Christology in the special History of Doctrines), but in its relation to the Old Test. it possesses a character more or less antinomian, and in its eschatology it is adverse to millenarianism. It opposes the spiritualistic to the literal, the idealistic to the realistic. To resolve history into myths, to dissipate positive doctrines by speculation, and thus to make an aristocratic distinction between those who only believe and those who know, to overrate *knowledge*, especially that which is ideal and speculative ($\gamma\nu\hat{\omega}\sigma\iota\varsigma$) in religion, — these are the principal features of Gnosticism. On the different usages of $\gamma\nu\hat{\omega}\sigma\iota\varsigma$ in a good and a bad sense ($\gamma\nu\hat{\omega}\sigma\iota\varsigma$ $\psi\epsilon\upsilon\delta\acute{\omega}\nu\upsilon\mu\varsigma$), $\gamma\nu\omega\sigma\tau\acute{\eta}\varsigma$, $\gamma\nu\omega\sigma\tau\iota\kappa\acute{o}\varsigma$, comp. *Suicer*, Thesaurus. *Sources: Irenæus*, Adv. Hær. (i. 29, ii.).

Tertullian, Adv. Marcion. lib. v.; Adv. Valentinianos; Scorpiace contra Gnosticos. *Clem. Al.* Strom. in different places, especially lib. ii. iii. vi. *Euseb.* iv.

(8) The different classifications of the Gnostics according to the degree of their opposition to Judaism (*Neander*); according to countries, and the preponderance of dualism, or emanation, Syrian and Egyptian Gnostics (*Gieseler*); or Gnostics of Asia Minor, Syrian, Roman (sporadic), and Egyptian Gnostics (*Matter*); or, lastly, Hellenistic, Syrian, and Christian Gnostics (*Hase*),—present, all of them, greater or less difficulties, and require additional classes (as the Eclectic sects of Neander, and the Marcionites of Gieseler). But *Baur* justly remarks that the mere classification according to countries is too external (Gnosis, s. 106; comp., too, *Dorner*, s. 355), and hence designates the position on which Neander's classification is based as the only correct one, "*because it has regard not only to one subordinate element, but to a fundamental relation which pervades the whole*," s. 109. ["The Gnostic schools have sometimes been divided into two classes of Judaizing and anti-Jewish Gnostics; the one regarding it as the mission of Christ to complete an imperfect revelation, the other supposing Him to be sent to deliver the world from the bondage of an evil creator and governor," *Mansel*, l.c. p. 20.] The three essential forms into which Gnosticism falls, according to *Baur*, are: 1. The *Valentinian*, which admits the claims of paganism, together with Judaism and Christianity; 2. The *Marcionite*, which makes Christianity preponderant; and, 3. The *pseudo-Clementine*, which espouses the cause of Judaism in particular (see s. 120). But respecting the latter, it is yet doubtful whether it should be reckoned among the Gnostic tendencies. It stands upon the borders of Ebionitism and Gnosticism (see note 5); on *Niedner's* classification, see *Lipsius*, l.c. s. 137 ff. *Schwegler* (Montanismus, iv. s. 216), in making Judaism the common root of Ebionitism and Gnosticism, is correct, so far as this, that Gnosticism was shaped in divers ways by the Jewish philosophy. But this philosophy was struggling to get beyond what was merely Jewish and legal. The peculiar and fundamental characteristic of Gnosticism remains in its paganism, though this, too, might react into Judaism, as well as the latter wander off into

§ 23.]   EBIONITES AND CERINTHUS, ETC.   73

paganism. "*Common to all Gnostic sects is their opposition to that merely empirical faith with which they charge the Church, as being founded on authority alone.*" *Dorner*, s. 353. [Further particulars will be found in the special history of heresies (comp. § 6), and in the history of the particular systems of *Basilides* (A.D. 125-140), *Valentinus* (140-160), the *Ophites*, *Carpocrates and Epiphanes, Saturninus, Cerdo, Marcion* (150), *Bardesanes* (170), etc.] The element of knowledge (the speculative) in religion is with it the chief matter; and so far it has its correlate in the Jewish law-works (*Dorner*, s. 354). On the great importance of Gnosticism in the development of theological science and of ecclesiastical art, see *Dorner*, s. 355 ff. On particular points, see further, *Gundert*, Das System des Gnostikers Basilides, in Zeitschrift f. d. luth. Theol., Bd. vi. and vii.; *Uhlhorn*, Das Basilidianische System mit Rücksicht auf die Angaben des Hippolytus dargestellt, Götting. 1855. *A. Hilgenfeld*, Bardesanes, der letzte Gnostiker, Leipz. 1864.

[*Hilgenfeld* on Basilides, in the Theol. Jahrb. 1856, and *Baur*, ibid. 1856. *J. L. Jacobi*, Basilidis . . . Sententiæ ex Hippolyti libro, Berol. 1852. Pistis Sophia, Opus Gnosticum Valentino adjudicatum e codice MS. Coptico . . . ed. *J. H. Petermann*, Berol. 1852; comp. *Köstlin* in Theol. Jahrb. 1854. Colorbasus-Gnosis (the Valentinian Kol-arbas), *Volkmar* in Zeitschrift f. d. hist. Theol. 1855. On Bardesanes in *Cureton's* Spicilegium Syriac., see Journal of Sacred Lit. 1856. Die Philosophumena und die Pertaten (Ophites), *R. Baxmann* in Zeitschrift f. d. hist. Theol. 1860. On the general subject, comp. *Bunsen's* Hippolytus, and especially *Niedner* in his Gesch. d. Kirche, s. 217–253. Niedner's division is the best:—1. Most numerous (in Valentinus and others); Christianity has the primacy, but other religions, Jewish and heathen, are different degrees of the development of the true religion. 2. (Marcion) Christianity sundered from its historical connections; the only revelation. 3. A syncretism, identifying heathenism and Christianity (Carpocrates), or Judaism and heathenism (the Clementines). Gnosticism is an attempt at a philosophy of religion, identifying the history of the world and the history of religion. Comp. *Neander's* Dogmengesch. i. 43–59.]

(9) Comp. *Dorner*, I. i. s. 391 ff.
(10) *Ibid.* s. 381 ff. [*Ritschl*, d. Evang. Marcions, 1847: *Volkmar*, cf. Gersdorf Rep. 1852. *Franck*, d. Evang. M. in Stud. u. Kritiken, 1855. *Hilgenfeld*, Das Apostolikon Marcions, in Zeitschrift f. d. hist. Theol. 1855.]

§ 24.

Montanism and Monarchianism.

Wernsdorf, de Montanistis, Gedani 1751, 4to. *Kirchner*, de Montanistis, Jen. 1852. * *Heinichen*, de Alogis, Theodotianis, Artemonitis, Lips. 1829. * *A. Ritschl*, Entstehung der altkath. Kirche, 2d ed. Bonn 1857. *F. C. Baur*, Das Wesen des Mont., in Zeller's Jahrb. 1851, s. 538 ff. *Gieseler*, Hippolytus, die Monarchianer, und d. romische Kirche, in Stud. u. Krit. 1853. * *F. C. Schwegler*, der Montanismus und die christliche Kirche des zweiten Jahrhunderts, Tüb. 1841 - 48. [*Hase*, § 67. *Niedner*, 253 ff. *Möller* in Herzog's Realencyk. ix. s. 758.]

Besides the antagonism between Judaism and Ethnicism, another might be formed on the basis of the general Christian system; and its opposite extremes likewise run out into heretical tendencies. In the establishment of the peculiar doctrines of the religion of Christ, questions necessarily arose, not only concerning the relation of Christianity to former historical forms of religion, but also respecting its relation to the nature of man and his general capacities of knowledge. Two opposite tendencies might ensue. On the one hand, an exaggerated supernaturalism might manifest itself, passing the boundaries of the historical revelation, making the essence of the inspiration of the Spirit to consist in extraordinary excitement, interrupting the course of the historical development, and endeavouring to keep up a permanent disagreement between the natural and the supernatural. This is seen in what is called *Montanism* (1), which took its rise in Phrygia. On the other hand, an attempt might be made to fill the chasm between the natural and the supernatural, by trying to explain the miracles and mysteries of the faith, adapting them to the understanding, and thus leading to a critico-sceptical rationalism. This appears in one class of the *Monarchians* (Alogi?) (2), whose representatives in the first period are *Theodotus* and *Artemon* (3). The Monarchians, *Praxeas, Noëtus,* and *Beryllus* (4), differ from the preceding in having more profound views of religion, and form the transition to Sabellianism, which we shall have to consider in the following period, as introducing a new (more speculative) mode of thought.

(1) *Montanus* of Phrygia (in which country the fanatical worship of Cybele prevailed from an early period) made his appearance as a prophet (the Paraclete) about the year 170, in Ardaban, on the frontiers of Phrygia and Mysia, and afterwards in Pepuza. He was distinguished rather as an enthusiastic and eccentric character, than for any particular doctrinal heresy; and thus he is the forerunner of all the fanaticism which pervades the history of the Church. "*If any doctrine was dangerous to Christianity, it was that of Montanus. Though noted in other respects only for a strict external morality, and agreeing with the Catholic Church in all its doctrines, he yet attacked the fundamental principle of orthodoxy. For he regarded Christianity, not as complete, but as allowing and even demanding and promising further revelations, as in the words of Jesus concerning the Paraclete.*" Marheineke (in Daub and Creuzer's Studien), s. 150, where he also points out the contradiction in which the earnest and positive Tertullian involved himself by joining this sect. Millenarianism, which the Montanists professed, was in accordance with their carnally-minded tendency. In this respect they were allied to the Ebionites (*Schwegler*). Notwithstanding their anti-Gnostic tendencies, they agree with the Gnostics in going beyond the simple faith of the Church; but still, their eccentricities were seen not so much in speculation as in practical Christianity. Yet Montanism could not keep clear of Gnosticism; but here its peculiarity consists in the position, that this *gnosis* is attained, not by man's faculty of thought, but in an ecstatic state. "*Catholic truth is an evenly flowing stream, gradually swelling from many tributaries; the Montanistic illumination is a spring, suddenly gushing up from the ground; the former is conditioned by the idea of a complex continuity, the latter*

clings to a disconnected and atomistic view of spiritual influences." *Schwegler*, s. 105. This sect (called also Cataphrygians, Pepuzians) existed down to the sixth century, though condemned by ecclesiastical synods. On its connection with the general tendencies of the time, see *Baur* (ubi supra). This does not interfere with a recognition of the individuality of Montanus as an essential element (Neander describes him from this point of view). *Sources: Eusebius* (following Apollonius), v. 18. *Epiphanius*, Hæres. 48. *Neander*, ii. 8. 871 ff. *Neander's* Dogmengesch. s. 49 (against Baur).

(2) This term occurs in *Epiph.* Hær. 51 as a somewhat ambiguous paronomasia on the word Logos (men void of understanding notwithstanding their understanding!), because the Alogi rejected the doctrine concerning the Logos, and the Gospel of John in which it is principally set forth, as well as the book of Revelation, and the millenarian notions which it was used to vindicate. It may be generalized in dogmatic usage so as to be applied to all *those* who rejected the idea of the Logos, or so misunderstood it, as either to regard Christ as a mere man, or, if they ascribed a divine nature to Christ, identified it with that of the Father. It is difficult to decide to which of these two classes the proper Alogi mentioned by Epiphanius belong, comp. *Heinichen*, l.c.; on the other hand, *Dorner*, s. 500, defends them from the charge of denying Christ's divinity, and considers them as being the point of departure for the twofold shape in which Monarchianism showed itself. At all events, we must not lose sight of these two classes of Monarchians (comp. *Neander*, Kg. i. 3, s. 990 ff.; Antignostikus, s. 474. *Schwegler*, Montanismus, s. 268; *Dorner*, l.c.), though it is difficult to make a precise distinction between the one and the other.

(3) *Theodotus*, a worker in leather (ὁ σκυτεύς) from Byzantium, who resided at Rome about the year 200, maintained that Christ (though born of a virgin) was merely a man; and was excommunicated by the Roman bishop Victor, *Euseb.* v. 28. *Theodoret*, Fab. Hær. ii. 5. *Epiph.* Hær. 54 (ἀπόσπασμα τῆς ἀλόγου αἱρέσεως). He must not be confounded with another Theodotus (τραπεζίτης), who was connected with a party of the Gnostics, the Melchisedekites. *Theodor.* Fab. Hær. II. 6. *Dorner*, s. 505 ff. *Artemon* (Artemas) charged

the successor of Victor, the Roman bishop Zephyrinus, with having corrupted the doctrine of the Church, and smuggled in the doctrine of the divinity of Christ. Comp. *Neander*, i. 998. See § 46, below. *Heinichen*, l.c. s. 26, 27. [*Burton*, Lectures on the Ecclesiast. Hist. of the Second and Third Cent. p. 211 ff., 236 ff., 265 ff., 387, and Bampton Lect., notes 100 and 101.] The prevailing rationalistic tendency of this sect (pseudo-Rationalism) may be seen from *Euseb.* l.c. ii. p. 139 (*Heinichen*). Οὐ τί αἱ θεῖαι λέγουσι γραφαὶ ζητοῦντες ἀλλ' ὁποῖον σχῆμα συλλογισμοῦ εἰς τὴν τῆς ἀθεότητος εὑρεθῇ σύστασιν, φιλοπόνως ἀσκοῦντες . . . καταλιπόντες δὲ τὰς ἁγίας τοῦ θεοῦ γραφὰς, γεωμετρίαν ἐπιτηδεύουσιν, ὡς ἂν ἐκ τῆς γῆς ὄντες καὶ ἐκ τῆς γῆς λαλοῦντες καὶ τὸν ἄνωθεν ἐρχόμενον ἀγνοοῦντες. The homage they rendered to Euclid, Aristotle, Theophrastus, and Galen, ὃς ἴσως ὑπό τινων καὶ προσκυνεῖται.

(4) *Praxeas*, from Asia Minor, had gained under Marcus Aurelius the reputation of a confessor of Christianity, but was charged by Tertullian with Patripassianism, and combated by him. *Tertull.* Advers. Praxeam, lib. II. *Noëtus*, at Smyrna, about the year 230, was opposed by Hippolytus on account of similar opinions. *Hippol.* contra Hæresin Noëti. *Theodoret*, Fab. Hær. iii. 3; *Epiph.* Hær. 57.—As to *Beryllus*, bishop of Bostra, in Arabia, whom Origen compelled to recant, *Euseb.* vi. 33 ; comp. *Ullmann*, de Beryllo Bostreno, Hamb. 1835, 4to. Studien und Kritiken, 1836, part 4, s. 1073 (comp. §§ 42 and 46). [For Praxeas, see *Burton*, l.c. p. 221 ff., 234 ff. Noëtus, *Burton*, l.c. p. 312, 364.—Beryllus, *Burton*, l.c. p. 312, 313. *Schleiermacher*, Kirchengesch. 131 ff., 154. *Baur*, Dreieinigkeit, i. 132-341, and in the Jahrb. f. Theologie, 1845. *Bunsen's* Hippolytus.]

§ 25.

The Catholic Doctrine.

The Catholic doctrine (1) was developed in opposition to the heresies. While the orthodox teachers endeavoured to avoid heretical errors, and to preserve the foundation laid by Christ and His apostles, by holding fast to the pure tradition, they yet could not wholly free themselves from the influence which the civilization of the age, personal endowments, and preponderating mental tendencies have ever exerted upon the formation of religious ideas and conceptions. On this account we find in the Catholic Church the same contrasts, or at least similar diversities and modifications, as among the heretics, though they manifest themselves in a milder and less offensive form. Here, too, is, on the one hand, a firm, sometimes painful adherence to external rites and historical tradition, akin to legal Judaism (positive tendency), combined in some cases, as in that of Tertullian, with the Montanist tendency. On the other hand, we find a more free and flexible tendency allied to the Hellenistic; sometimes more ideal and speculative, akin to Gnosticism (the *true* gnosis contrasted with the false), and, again, critico-rationalistic, like Monarchianism, even when not identical with it (2).

(1) On the term *Catholic* in opposition to *Heretic*, see *Suicer*, Thesaurus, sub voce καθολικός, comp. ὀρθοδοξία. *Bingham*, Origg. Eccles. i. 1, sec. 7. *Vales.* ad *Euseb.* vii. 10, tom. ii. p. 333 : "Ut vera et genuina Christi ecclesia ab adulterinis Hæreticorum cœtibus distingueretur, *catholicæ* cognomen soli Orthodoxorum ecclesiæ attributum est."—Concerning the negative and practical, rather than theoretical, character of earlier orthodoxy, see *Marheineke* (in Daub und Creuzer), l.c. s. 140 ff.

(2) This was the case, *e.g.*, with *Origen*, who now and then shows sobriety of understanding along with gnostic speculation. On the manner in which the philosophizing Fathers were able to reconcile *gnosis* with *paradosis* (disciplina arcani), comp. *Marheineke*, l.c. s. 170.

§ 26.

The Theology of the Fathers.

Steiger, La Foi de l'Eglise Primitive d'après les Ecrits des premiers Pères, in the Mélanges de Théologie Réformée, edited by himself and Hävernick, Paris 1833, 1ᵉʳ cahier. *Dorner*, l.c. *Schwegler*, Nachapostolisches Zeit-

§ 26.]   THE THEOLOGY OF THE FATHERS.   79

alter. *A. Hilgenfeld*, Die Apostolischen Väter; Untersuchung über Inhalt und Ursprung der unter ihrem Namen erhaltenen Schriften, Halle 1853. [Patrum Apostol. Opera, ed. *Cotelerius* and *Clericus*, Amst. 1724. *Gebhardt*, *Harnack*, and *Zahn*, Leipz. 1876–78; *Hefele* and *Funk*, Tübing. 1878. *J. H. B. Lübkert*, Theol. d. Apost. Väter, in Zeitschrift f. d. Hist. Theol. 1854. *Hilgenfeld*, Das Urchristenthum, in Zeitschrift f. wiss. Theol. 1858. *E. de Pressensé*, Hist. des trois premiers Siècles de l'Eglise Chrétienne, 2 vols. Paris 1858. *J. J. Blunt*, Lectures on Study of Early Fathers, 2d ed. 1856; ibid. Right Use of Fathers, 1858. *Ginoulhiac*, Hist. du Dogme Cathol. dans les trois prem. Siècles, 2 vols. Paris 1850. *E. Reuss*, Hist. de la Théol. Chrét., 2 vols. 1853, 3d ed. 1864. *Ritschl*, Die Altkath. Kirche, 2d ed. 1857. *Joh. Huber*, Phil. d. Kirchen Väter, 1859. *Abbé Frepel*, Les Pères Apostoliques et leur Epoque, Paris 1859. *Donaldson*, Apostolic Fathers, Camb. 1864, 77; *Lightfoot*, Ep. of Clement, Camb. 1869, 77. Apost. Fathers in Clark's Ante-Nicene Lib., Edin. 1867.]

While the so-called apostolical Fathers (with few exceptions) were distinguished for their direct practical and edifying tendency, preserving and continuing the apostolic tradition (1), the philosophizing tendency allied to Hellenism was in some measure represented by the apologists, Justin Martyr (2), Tatian (3), Athenagoras (4), Theophilus of Antioch (5), and Minucius Felix (6), in the West. On the contrary, Irenæus (7), as well as Tertullian (8), and his disciple Cyprian (9), firmly adhered to the positive dogmatic theology and the compact realism of the Church, the former in a milder and more considerate, the latter in a severe, sometimes in a stiff and sombre manner. Clement (10) and Origen (11), both belonging to the Alexandrian school, chiefly developed the speculative aspect of theology. But these contrasts are only relative; for we find, *e.g.*, that Justin Martyr manifests both a leaning toward Hellenism and also a Judaizing tendency; that the idealism and criticism of Origen are now and then accompanied with a surprising adherence to the letter; and that Tertullian, notwithstanding his anti-Gnosticism, strives in a remarkable way after philosophical ideas.

(1) The name *Patres Apostolici* is given to the Fathers of the first century, who were supposed to be disciples of the apostles. Concerning their personal history and writings, much must be left to conjecture and uncertainty.

1. *Barnabas,* known as the fellow-labourer of the Apostle Paul from Acts iv. 36 (Joses), ix. 27, etc. On the Epistle ascribed to him (formerly in part known only through a Latin translation, now since the publication of the Cod. Sinaiticus by Tischendorf, complete in the original), in which is shown a strong tendency to typical and allegorical interpretations,— though in a quite different spirit from, *e.g.*, the canonical Epistle to the Hebrews,—opinions are still greatly divided; and as the very time of its composition is still uncertain, the arguments against its genuineness must be regarded as preponderating.—Comp. *Ern. Henke,* De Epistolæ quæ Barnabæ tribuitur Authentia, Jenæ 1827. *Rördam,* De Authent. Epist. Barnab., Hafn. 1828 (in favour of its genuineness). *Ullmann,* Studien und Kritiken, 1828, Ht. 2. *Hug,* Zeitschrift für das Erzbisth., Freiburg, Ht. 2, s. 132 ff.; Ht. 3, s. 208 ff. * *Hug* (Zeitschrift für das Erzbisth., Freiburg, Ht. 2, s. 132 ff.; Ht. 3, s. 208 ff.). Against it, *Twesten,* Dogmatik, i. s. 101. *Neander,* i. s. 657 : "*A very different spirit breathes throughout it from that of an apostolical writer.*" *Bleek,* Einleitung in den Brief an die Hebräer, s. 416, note (undecided). *Schenkel* in the Studien u. Kritiken, x. s. 651 (adopting a middle course, and considering one part as genuine and another as interpolated); and on the other side *C. T. Hefele,* [Das Sendschreiben des Apostels Barnabas aufs Neue untersucht, übersetzt und erklärt, Tüb. 1840.—*N. Lardner,* Works, II. s. 17–20, iv. 105–108, v. 269–275 (*for* its authenticity). *W. Cave,* Lives of the most eminent Fathers of the Church, Oxford 1840, i. p. 90–105. *Burton,* Lectures on the Ecclesiastical History of the First Century (Works, iv. p. 164, 343) (*against* it). *S. Davidson,* Sacred Hermeneutics, Edinb. 1843, p. 71 (*for* it). *William Lee,* Discourses on the Inspiration of Holy Scripture, Appendix E, and *Milligan* in *Smith's* Dictionary of Christian Biography, for its genuineness.] The subject has received a new treatment since the discovery of the Codex Sinaiticus. Comp. *Hilgenfeld,* l.c.; *Weizsäcker,* zur Kritik des Barnabasbriefs (Tüb. Univ. Programm, 1863); *Volkmar* (in Hilgenfeld's Zeitschrift, viii. 4, s. 449): "*The latter retains (even according to the Sinaitic) the doctrino-historical significance of an outpost of Gnosticism, standing close and almost forming a transition to it, and yet still untouched*

by the peculiar, i.e. *the consciously dualistic Gnosis." Editions* (see under collective edd. of Ap. Fathers): *Tischendorf* (Cod. N. T. Sinaiticus, Petropoli 1862, Lips. 1863); *Volkmar*, Monumentum vetustatis Christianæ ineditum, Turici 1864, 4to (Univ. Prog.); *Hilgenfeld*, Barnabæ Epistola, integram Græce primum,ed. Lips. 1866. *Same:* Nov. Test. extra canonem receptum, fascic. 2.

2. *Hermas* (Rom. xvi. 14), whose ποιμήν (Shepherd) in the form of visions enjoyed a high reputation in the second half of the second century, and was even quoted as Scripture (γραφή). Some critics ascribe the work in question to a later Hermas (Hermes), brother of the Roman bishop, Pius I., who lived about the year 150. Comp. *Gratz,* Disqu. in Past. Herm., Pt. 1, Bonn 1820, 4to. *Jachmann,* Der Hirte des Hermas, Königsb. 1835. " *The immense difference between the apostolical writings and the immediate post-apostolic literature is more apparent in the work of Hermas than in any other;*" *Schliemann,* Clement. s. 421. *Schwegler,* in his Nachapost. Zeitalter, s. 328 ff., judges differently. Comp. *Dorner,* s. 185 ff. There is a variety of opinion as to the relation of this work to Montanism, Ebionitism, and the Elkesaites; comp. *Uhlhorn* in Herzog's Realwörterb. On the manuscript discovered by Simonides, and published by Anger and Dindorf, 1856, see *Uhlhorn,* l.c. Comp. below, note 6. Comp. on the whole question, *Dr. Ernst Gaab,* Der Hirte des Hermas, ein Beitrag zur Patristik, Basel 1866.

3. *Clement* of Rome (according to some, the fellow-labourer of Paul, mentioned Phil. iv. 3), one of the earliest bishops of Rome (*Iren.* iii. 3 ; *Euseb.* iii. 2. 13, 15). The first Epistle to the Corinthians, ascribed to him, is of dogmatic importance in relation to the doctrine of the resurrection. *Editions:* Clementis Romani quæ feruntur Homil. xx. nunc primum integræ, ed. *Alb. R. M. Dressel,* Gött. 1853. Comp. *R. A. Lipsius,* De Clem. Rom. Ep. ad Cor. priore, Lips. 1855. [*E. Ecker,* Disquisitio—de Cl. Rom. prior. ad Rom. Epist., Traj. ad Rhenum 1853.] The so-called second Epistle is evidently a homily by a later writer. [*Lardner,* l.c. ii. 33–35.] Comp. also *Schneckenburger,* Evangel. der Ægypter, s. 3, 13 ff., 28 ff. *Schwegler,* Nachapostolisches Zeitalter, s. 449; on the other side, *Dorner,* s. 143. [A most important addition has recently

been made to the writings of Clement. Until quite lately both Epistles were incomplete, the first lacking about one-tenth of the whole, and the second fully two-fifths of the whole. In 1875 a complete Greek MS. of the two Epistles was found at Constantinople, and about a year later a Syriac translation in Paris. The discovery has been of great service, not only in completing the works, but in helping to secure a more accurate text. It has also become clear, as had formerly been conjectured, that the so-called second Epistle is a homily. The new ed. of the Ap. Fathers by *Gebhardt* (1876) makes use of the Greek MS. *Lightfoot's* Appendix (1877) uses both the Greek and Syriac. A new edition by *Hefele* and *Funk* (1878) also gives the results of these discoveries.] From a dogmatic point of view, those writings would be of greatest importance which are now universally considered as suppositious, viz. the pseudo-Clementine Homilies (ὁμιλίαι Κλήμεντος, cf. § 23), the Recognitiones Clementis (ἀναγνωρισμοί), the Constitutiones Apostolicæ, and the Canones Apostolici; on the latter, comp. *Krabbe*, über den Ursprung und Inhalt der Apostol. Constit. des Clemen. Rom., Hamb. 1829; and † *Drey*, neue Untersuchungen über die Constitutiones und Canones der Apostol., Tüb. 1832. *Uhlhorn*, Die Homilien u. Recognitionen des Clem. Rom., Götting. 1854. [*Hefele*, Conciliengeschichte, Bd. i., and Eng. Tr. *Hilgenfeld*, Kritische Untersuchungen, 1850. *E. Gundert* in Zeitschrift f. d. Luth. Theol. 1853, 54. *W. Cureton*, Syriac version of Clem. Recognitions, Lond. 1849. *G. Volkmar*, Clem. von Rom. und d. nächste Folgezeit, in Theol. Jahrb. 1856. Clem. Rom. Epistolæ Binæ de Virginitate, ed. *J. T. Beele*, Lovan. 1856, comp. Theol. Quartalschrift, 1856. *Lardner*, ii. p. 29–35, 364–378. *Burton*, l.c. p. 342–344. Art. Apostolical Fathers, by *Lightfoot*, and Clemens. Rom., by *Salmon* in *Smith's* Dict. of Chr. Biog.]

4. *Ignatius* (Θεοφόρος), bishop of Antioch, concerning whose life comp. *Euseb.* iii. 36. On his journey to Rome, where he suffered martyrdom under Trajan (116),[1] he is said to have written seven Epistles to different Churches (Ephesus, Magnesia, Tralles, Rome, Philadelphia, Smyrna) and to Polycarp, which

---

[1] [This is disputed by some writers of the critical school, who maintain that he was put to death at Antioch.]

are extant in two recensions, the one longer, the other shorter. On their genuineness, and the relation of the longer to the shorter, comp. *J. Pearson*, Vindiciæ epp. S. Ign. Cant. 1672 [new edition by *Archdeacon Churton*, in Lib. of Anglo-Cath. Theol., 2 vols. 1852, with preface and notes adapted to the present state of the controversy.] *J. E. Ch. Schmidt*, Die doppelte Recension der Briefe des Ign. (Henke's Magazin. iii. s. 91 ff.). *K. Meier*, Die doppelte Recension der Briefe des Ignat. (Stud. und Kritiken, 1836, Ht. 2). *Rothe*, Die Anfänge der Christl. Kirche, Witt. 1837, s. 715 ff. *Arndt* in Stud. u. Kritiken, 1839, s. 136. *Baur*, Tübinger Zeitschrift, 1838, Ht. 3, s. 148. *Huther*, Betrachtung der wichtigsten Bedenken gegen die Aechtheit der Ignatianischen Briefe, in Illgen's Zeitschrift für historische Theolog. 1841–44. Comp. § 23. *Ch. Düsterdieck*, Quæ de Ignatianarum Epp. Authentia, duorumque Textuum Ratione hucusque prolatæ sunt sententiæ enarrantur, Götting. 1843, 4to.—The whole investigation has entered into a new stadium in consequence of the discovery of a Syriac version, by *W. Cureton*, The Ancient Syriac Version of the Ep. of S. Ignatius, etc., Lond. 1845. Comp. *C. C. J. Bunsen*, Die drei ächten und die vier unächten Briefe des Ign., 4to, Hamb. 1847. *The same:* Ignat. von Antioch, u. seine Zeit, sieben Sendschreiben an Neander, 4to, Hamb. 1847. Against Bunsen, *F. C. Baur*, Die Ignat. Briefe, Tüb. 1848. On the Catholic side, *G. Denzinger*, Die Aechtheit des Textus der Ign. Briefe, Würzb. 1849. *Against* the genuineness, *Vaucher*, Recherches critiques, Gött. 1856. *Latest editions:* *J. H. Petermann*, Lips. 1849; Corpus Ignatianum, by *William Cureton*, 4to, Berl. 1849. *Merx*, Meletemata Ignatiana critica de epistolarum Ignatianarum versione Syriaca commentatio, Hal. 1861. Most important for the History of Doctrines are the polemical writings against the Docetæ (cf. § 23, and *Dorner*, s. 145). [*W. Cureton*, Vindiciæ Ignatianæ, the genuine Writings of Ign. vindicated against the charge of Heresy, Lond. 1846. Comp. the discussion in *Hilgenfeld's* Apostol. Väter, and *Uhlhorn* on the Relation of the Greek to the Syriac Recension, in Zeitschrift f. d. Hist. Theol. 1851, epitomized in the Theol. Critic, 1852. *Weiss* in Reuter's Repertorium, Sept. 1852, and in Deutsche Zeitschrift, 1859 (Nov.). *R. A. Lipsius* in the Zeitschrift f. d. Hist. Theologie,

1856, condensed in the Journal for Sacred Literature (Lond.), 1857; Die Zeitschrift f. Luth. Theologie, 1848 and 1852. See also articles in the Quarterly (Lond.), 1851; the Edinburgh Review, 1849; the British Quarterly, 1856; the Christian Remembrancer, 1857. On the Epistles of Ignatius among the Armenians, see *Neumann*, Gesch. d. Arm. Lit. s. 73 ff.]

5. *Polycarp*, bishop of Smyrna, according to tradition a disciple of the Apostle John, suffered martyrdom under Marcus Aurelius (169). Comp. *Euseb*. iv. 15. An Epistle of his to the Philippians is yet extant, but only a part of it in the original Greek. Comp. *Wocher*, die Briefe der apost. Väter Clemens und Polycarp, mit Einleitung und Commentarien, Tübingen 1830. *Dorner*, s. 171 ff. [*Lardner*, ii. p. 94–109.]

6. *Papias* ($\sigma\phi\acute{o}\delta\rho\alpha$ $\sigma\mu\iota\kappa\rho\grave{o}\varsigma$ $\mathring{\omega}\nu$ $\tau\grave{o}\nu$ $\nu o\hat{u}\nu$, *Euseb*. iii. 39), bishop of Hierapolis in the first half of the second century, of whose treatise $\lambda o\gamma\acute{\iota}\omega\nu$ $\kappa\nu\rho\iota\alpha\kappa\hat{\omega}\nu$ $\grave{\epsilon}\xi\acute{\eta}\gamma\eta\sigma\iota\varsigma$ we have only fragments in *Euseb*. l.c. and *Irenæus* (v. 53). As a millenarian he is of some importance for eschatology. [Fragments of Papias in *Lardner's* Credibility, vol. ii.; supposed fragments in Spicileg. Solesmense, i.]

Complete editions of the writings of the Apostolical Fathers:
* Patrum, qui temporibus Apostolorum floruerunt, Opp. ed. *Cotelerius*, Par. 1672, rep. *Clericus*, Amst. 1698, 1724, 2 vols. fol. Patrum App. Opp. genuina, ed. *R. Russel*, Lond. 1746, 2 vols. Clementis Romani, S. Ignatii, S. Polycarpi, patrum apostolicorum quæ supersunt, accedunt S. Ignatii et S. Polycarpi martyria, ed. *Guol. Jacobson*, Oxon. 1838 [3d ed. 1847]. *J. L. Frey*, Epistolæ Sanctorum Patrum Apostolicorum Clementis, Ignatii et Polycarpi, atque duorum posteriorum Martyria, Bas. 1842. Patrum Apostolorum Opera, textum ex editt. præstantt. repetitum recognovit, brevi annotat. instruxit et in usum prælect. academicar. edid. †**C. J. Hefele*, Tüb. 1839, 4th ed. 1856 [new ed. by *Funk*, 1879]. Comp. Codex N. T. deuteronomius s. Patres Apostolici, rec. ed. *De Muralto*, vol. i. (Barnabæ et Clementis Epistolæ), Tur. 1847. Patrum apostol. Opera, ed. *A. R. M. Dressel*, accedit Hermæ Pastor, ex. frag. græcis, auctore *C. Tischendorf*, Lips. 1857 [new ed. by **Gebhardt, Harnack*, and *Zahn*, 3 vols. Leipz. 1875–78]. *Ittig*, Bibl. Patr. apost., Lips. 1690. Novum

Testamentum extra canonem receptum, ed. *A. Hilgenfeld*, Lips. [*Archbishop Wake*, The Genuine Epistles of the Apostolical Fathers, transl. Lond. 1737, 7th ed. 1840; New York 1810. Also in Clark's Ante-Nicene Library. *W. Chevallier*, Epist. of Apost. Fathers, and Apolog. of Just. Mart. and Tertull., translated 1822, 2d ed. 1851.]

As to the extent to which we can speak of a *theology* of the apostolical Fathers, see *Baumgarten-Crusius*, i. s. 81, note. It is certain that some of them, *e.g.* Hermas, entertained notions which were afterward rejected as heterodox. The older divines, and those of the Roman Catholic Church in particular, endeavoured to evade this difficulty by calling those doctrines *archaisms*, in distinction from *heresies*.[1]

(2) *Justin Martyr* (born about the year 89, †161–168), of Sychem (Flavia Neapolis) in Samaria, a philosopher by vocation, who, even after he had become a Christian, retained the τρίβων, made several missionary journeys, and suffered martyrdom, probably at the instigation of the philosopher Crescens. His *two Apologies* are of special importance; the longer addressed to Antoninus Pius, the other to the Roman Senate (the numbering varies, see *Neander*, i. 3, s. 1111, and *Semisch*, ubi supra, s. 911). *Semisch* still holds that the first of these apologies belongs to the year 138 or 139, the second is after 147; while, according to *Volkmar's* critical investigations on the time of Justin (theol. Jahrb. 1855, 2, 3), both apologies were produced in the same year, 150 [cf. also *Aubé*, St. Justin]. He is the first ecclesiastical writer whose works manifest an acquaintance with the Grecian philosophy (in which he had formerly sought in vain for the full truth and peace of mind).[2] Though he is anxious to prove the superiority of the religion of Christ, and even of the Old Testament

---

[1] It is certain that pseudo-Dionysius, whom some writers number among the apostolical Fathers, belongs to a later period. On the other side, *Möhler* and *Hefele* reckon the author of the Epistle to Diognetus among the apostolical Fathers, which was formerly ascribed to Justin. *Hefele*, PP. App. p. 125. *Möhler*, Patrologie, s. 164; Kleine Schriften, i. s. 19. On the other side: *Semisch*, Justin M. s. 186. [Comp. Just. M. Ep. ad Diogn. and Otto's review in Gersdorf's Rep. 1852. Art. in Church Quarterly Review (1878) seeks to prove that this Ep. is a forgery.]

[2] On his philosophical tendency, see *Schleiermacher*, l.c. s. 155. *Baur*, l.c. s. 256.

dispensation, to the systems of philosophers (by showing that the latter derive their views from Moses), he also perceives something divine in the better portion of the Gentile world. It must, however, be admitted that the tone prevailing in the apologies is much more liberal than that which is found in the Cohortatio ad Græcos (παραινετικὸς πρὸς "Ελληνας). *Neander,* i. 3, 1120, is therefore inclined to consider the latter as spurious, on account of the hard terms in which paganism is spoken of, and *Möhler* (Patrologie, s. 225) agrees with him. Yet the state of mind in which the author wrote his apologies would naturally be very different from that in which he composed a controversial treatise, especially if, as Neander suggests, the latter was written at a later period of his life. These writings, as well as the doubtful λόγος πρὸς "Ελληνας (Oratio ad Græcos) and the 'Επιστολὴ πρὸς Διόγνητον falsely ascribed to Justin M. (see note 1), and also the treatise περὶ μοναρχίας, consisting in great part of Greek excerpts, set the relative position of Christianity and paganism in a clear light. The Dialogus cum Tryphone Judæo has reference to Judaism, which it opposes on its own grounds; its genuineness was doubted by *Wetstein* and *Semler,* but without sufficient reason, comp. *Neander,* i. 3, s. 1125 ff. The principal edition is that published by the Benedictines under the care of **Prud. Maran,* Paris 1742, which also includes the writings of the following three authors, along with the (insignificant) satire of Hermias. Otto's edition, 1846 [new ed. 1879]. Comp. Justin Martyr, His Life, Writings, and Doctrines, by *Carl Semisch,* Breslau 1840-42; transl. by *J. E. Ryland,* Edin. 1844; also *Semisch's* article in Herzog's Realenc. vii. s. 179 ff. [*Lardner,* ii. p. 126-128, 140, 141.] *Otto,* de Justini Martyris scriptis et doctrina commentatio, Jen. 1841. *Schwegler,* nachapostolisches Zeitalter, s. 216 ff. [*John Kaye,* Bishop of Lincoln, Some Account of the Opinions and Writings of Just. M., 2d ed. *A. Kayser,* De Doctrina Just. M. 1850. *Volkmar,* Ueber Just. M. 1853, and Die Zeit Just. M. in Theol. Jahrb. 1855. *Hilgenfeld,* ibid. 1852. The Oratio ad Græcos not by Just., *Nolte* in Theol. Quartalschrift, 1860. *Prof. Stowe,* Sketch of Just. M. in Bib. Sacra, 1852. *W. Reeves,* Transl. of the Apologies, with those of Tertullian and Minucius Felix, etc., 2 vols. Lond. 1716; also in Ante-Nicene Library. *H.*

Browne's of the Dial. cum Tryphone, Lond. 1755. Just. M.'s Opinions in *A. Lamson's* Church of first Three Cent. p. 1–68, Boston 1860.] *Schwegler's* nachapost. Zeitalter, s. 216 ff. [Cf. also *Aubé,* St. Justin, Paris 1875.]

(3) *Tatian* the Syrian (*Dorner,* ii. 1, s. 437, calls him "*the Assyrian Tertullian*"), a disciple of Justin M., became afterward the leader of those Gnostics who are called the Encratites. In his work entitled: λόγος πρὸς "Ελληνας (ed. *Worth,* Oxon. 1700, and *Otto,* Jena 1851), he defends the "*philosophy of the barbarians*" against the Greeks. Comp. *H. A. Daniel,* Tatianus der Apologet, ein Beitrag zur Dogmengeschichte, Halle 1837. [*Lardner,* ii. p. 147–150. *Otto's* Corpus Apologet. 1851; transl. by *Dr. Giles,* Lond. 1837.]

(4) Little is known of the personal history of *Athenagoras,* who was born at Athens in the last half of the second century. Comp., however, *Clarisse,* De Athenagoræ Vita, Scriptis, Doctrina, Lugd. 1819, 4to, and *Möhler,* l.c. s. 267. His works are: Legatio pro Christianis (πρεσβεία περὶ Χριστιανῶν), and the treatise: De resurrectione mortuorum. [*Lardner,* ii. p. 193–200. *J. C. Otto* in Zeitschrift f. d. hist. Theol. 1856; his *Supplicatio,* ed. by *L. Paul,* Hal. 1856; works in *Otto,* Corpus Apolog. vol. vii.; translated in full in *Giles'* Writings of Christ. of Second Century, Lond. 1837, and in Ante-Nicene Library.]

(5) *Theophilus,* Bishop of Antioch (170–180). The work which he wrote against Autolycus: περὶ τῆς τῶν Χριστιανῶν πίστεως (ed. of Otto, Leipz. 1861), manifests a less liberal spirit, but also displays both genius and intelligence. *Rössler* (Bibliothek der Kirchenväter, i. s. 218) numbers it among the most worthless works of antiquity, and *Hase* (Kg. s. 45, 5 Aufl.) calls it a narrow-minded controversial writing, while *Möhler* praises its excellence. There is a German translation of it with notes by *Thienemann,* Leipz. 1833. [Edition by *J. J. Humphrey,* Lond. 1852, and in Ante-Nicene Library. On his use of the N. T., see *Otto* in Zeitschrift f. d. hist. Theol. 1859.]

(6) Ecclesiastical writers vary in their opinions respecting the period in which *Minucius Felix* lived. *Van Hoven, Rössler, Russwurm,* and *Heinrich Meier* (Commentatio de Minucio Felice, Tur. 1824) suppose him to have been contemporary

with the Antonines. *Tzschirner* (Geschichte der Apologetik, i. s. 257-282) thinks that he lived at a later time (about 224-230), which seems to be the more correct opinion. Comp. *Hieron.* Cat. Script. c. 53, 58. *Lactant.* Inst. v. 1. A comparison of the treatise of Minucius, entitled Octavius, with the Apology of Tertullian, and with the work of Cyprian, De Idolorum Vanitate, favours the view that he wrote *after* the former, but *before* the latter. This work of Cyprian appears in some parts to be a copy of the writing of Minucius; that of Tertullian bears the marks of an original. The dialogue between Cæcilius and Octavius is of importance in the history of apologetics, as it touches upon all the objections which we find separately treated by the other apologists, and adds some new ones. In his doctrinal spirit, Minucius is distinguished by a liberal, Hellenistic manner of thinking; but his views are less decidedly Christian than might well be wished. We seek almost in vain in his book for direct Christological ideas. *Editions:* Edit. princeps by *Balduin*, 1560 (before this, considered as the eighth book of Arnobius). Since that time, editions by *Elmenhorst* (1612), *Cellarius* (1699), *Davisius* (1707), *Ernesti* (1773), *Russwurm* (with Introduct. and Notes, 1824), *Lübkert* (with Translation and Commentary, Leipz. 1836). [*Hahn*, in Corpus Scriptor. Eccles. Lat., Vindobonæ 1867. The Octavius of Minucius Felix, ed. by Rev. *H. A. Holden*, Oxf. 1853. Earlier English versions, *James*, Oxf. 1636; *Combe*, 1703; *Reeves*, 1719 (in "Apologies of Fathers"); *Dalrymple*, Edinb. 1781; Ante-Nicene Library, Edinb. Edition in *Gersdorf's* Bibliotheca, vols. xii., xiii.] *Otto*, 1857.

(7) *Irenæus*, a disciple of Polycarp, Bishop of Lyons, about the year 177, died in the year 202, " a *clear-headed, thoughtful, philosophical theologian*" (*Hase, Guericke*). Except a few letters and fragments, his principal work alone is extant, viz. five books against the Gnostics: Ἔλεγχος καὶ ἀνατροπὴ τῆς ψευδωνύμου γνώσεως; the first book only has come down in the original language, the greater part of the remaining four books is now known only in an old Latin translation. The best editions are those of *Grabe*, Oxon. 1702. *Massuet, Paris 1710; Venet. 1734, 47. *A. Stieren*, Leipz. 1853. *Harvey*, Cambridge 1857. Comp. *Euseb.* v. 4. 20–26. *Möhler*, Patrologie, s. 330 ff. *Lardner*, ii. p. 165-193. *Burton*, v.

p. 185, and passim. *Duncker*, des heil. Irenæus Christologie, im Zusammenhange mit dessen theologischen und anthropologischen Grundlehren, Gött. 1843. Comp. also what *Dorner* says concerning him, ii. 1, s. 465, and Erbkam de S. Irenæi principiis ethicis, Regiomont. 1856. [Also edition of *Schaff's* Kirchenfreund, 1852, on Irenæus; *Böhringer's* Kirchengesch. in Biographien, i. Supposed fragments in Spicileg. Solesm. i. 1852. Life and Writings of I., Eclectic (Lond.), Sept. 1854. *J. Beaven*, Account of Life and Writings of St. Iræn., Lond. 1841. *Huber's* Phil. der Kirchenväter, 1858, s. 73-100.] "*Irenæus is a thoughtful writer, in whose doctrinal views there sometimes appears considerable depth. He for the most part opposes the speculation of the Gnostics by sound and pertinent observations, and by his thoughtful moderation and practical circumspection keeps far from the extremes between which Catholic theology had to follow the middle path*," Baur, Dg. s. 262. "*With all his prolixity, in which, however, he never ignores small details, and gives indications of many deep places in Gnosticism, there comes from Irenæus the warm and living breath of a pure spirit; we discern in him moral enthusiasm for truth, sober thoughtfulness, and a sound insight into the very kernel of Christian truth*," Möller, Geschichte der Kosmologie, s. 474.

(8) *Tertullian* (Quintus Septimius Florens) was born in Carthage about the year 160, and died 220; in his earlier life he was a lawyer and rhetorician, and became afterwards the most conspicuous representative of the anti-speculative, positive tendency. Comp. *Neander*, Antignostikus, Geist des Tertullianus und Einleitung in dessen Schriften (Berlin 1825, 2 Ausg. 1849), especially the striking characteristic which he there gives of Tertullian, s. 28 of first edition, cf. s. 9 and following of the new ed., and *Neander's* Kg. iii. 3, s. 1152. *Münter*, Primordia Ecclesiæ Africanæ, Havn. 1829, 4to. *Hesselberg*, Tertullian's Lehre, aus seinen Schriften, Gotha 1851. "*A gloomy, fiery character, who gained for Christianity out of the Punic Latin a literature, in which animated rhetoric, a wild imagination, a gross, sensuous perception of the ideal, profound feeling, and a juridical understanding, struggle with each other*," Hase. *Gfrörer* calls him the Tacitus of early Christianity. "*Notwithstanding his hatred against philosophy, Tertullian is*

certainly not the worst of Christian thinkers," Schwegler, Montanismus, s. 218; compare his further characteristics, ibid. His declaration: ratio autem divina in medulla est, non in superficie (De Resurrec. c. 3), may give us the key to many of his strange assertions, and to his remarkably concise style (quot pæne verba, tot sententiæ, *Vinc. Lir.* in comm. 1). On Tert. as an apologist, cf. *Jepp* (Jahrbuch für deutsche Theol. ix. 4). Of his numerous writings (among which we must distinguish those written *before* and those *after* his transition to Montanism) the following[1] are the most important for the History of Doctrines: Apologeticus (*"one of the finest writings of ecclesiastical antiquity, in which the writer's energy and power are displayed in all their glory,"* Baur, Dg. s. 263)—Ad nationes—(Advers. Judæos?)—*Advers. Marcionem—*Advers. Hermogenem—*Advers. Praxeam—*Advers. Valentinianos— *Scorpiace advers. Gnosticos—(De Præscriptionibus advers. Hæreticos)—De Testimonio Animæ—*De Anima—*De Carne Christi—*De Resurrectione Carnis—(De Pœnitentia)—(De Baptismo)—De Oratione, etc.; his moral writings also contain much that is doctrinal, *e.g.* the treatises: *De Corona Militis —*De Virginibus velandis—*De Cultu Feminarum—*De Patientia—*De Pudicitia, etc.—*Editions of his complete works* were published by *Rigaltius, Paris 1635, fol.; by *Semler* and *Schütz*, Halle 1770 ff., 6 vols. (with a useful Index Latinitatis); by *Leopold*, Leipz. 1841; by *Oehler*, Leipz. 1853, 3 vols. [*Lardner*, ii. p. 267–272, and passim.] The later Church did not venture to number Tert., zealous as he was for orthodoxy, among the orthodox writers, on account of his Montanistic views. In the eyes of *Jerome* (adv. Helvid. 17) he is not a *homo ecclesiæ* (comp. also Apol. contra Rufin. iii. 27), and though he praises his *ingenium*, he still condemns his heresy (Apol. contra Rufinum, iii. 27). [A portion of *Neander's* Antignostikus is published in *Bohn's* edition of *Neander's* Planting and Training. Tertullian in *Böhringer's* Kirchengesch. in Biographien, Bd. i., new ed. Bd. iii. Various treatises translated in the (Oxford) Lib. of Fathers, vol. x. (2d ed.); also complete in Ante-Nicene Library. Bishop *Kaye*, Eccl. Hist. of Second and Third Centuries,

---

[1] The works marked with * were written under the influence of Montanism, those included in ( ) at least tinged with Montanism; comp. *Nösselt*, de Vera ætate Tertulliani Scriptorum (Opusc. Fasc. iii. 1-198).

illustrated in the Life of Tertullian, 3d ed. 1848. *Engelhardt*, Tertullian als Schriftsteller, in Zeitschrift f. d. hist. Theol. 1852. T.'s De Corona Militis, ed. *G. Curry*, Cambr. 1853. Apology, transl. by *H. B. Brown*, Lond. 1655; *W. Reeves*, 1716; edited with English notes by *H. A. Woodham*, 2d ed. Camb., and *Chevallier*. Prescriptions, transl. by *T. Betty*, Oxf. 1772. Address to Scap. Tert., transl. by *Dalrymple*, Edinb. 1790. Oeuvres de Tert. en Français, par *M. de Genoude*, 2d ed. 3 vols. 1852. On *Oehler's* edition, see *Klussmann* in Zeitschrift für wiss. Theol. 1860; and Zeitschrift f. luth. Theol. 1856. *Leopold*, Doctrina Tertull. de Baptismo, in Zeitschrift f. wiss. Theol. 1854. *A. Crés*, Les Idées de Tertull. sur la Tradition, Strasb. 1855. *Huber*, Phil. d. Kirchenväter, s. 100–129.]

(9) *Cyprian* (*Thascius Cœcilius*) was at first a teacher of rhetoric in Carthage; was converted to Christianity in 245; became Bishop of Carthage 248, and suffered martyrdom 258. He possessed more of a practical than doctrinal tendency, and is therefore of greater importance in the history of polity than of doctrine, to which he contributed but little. He did not so much theoretically develope the doctrines respecting the *Church* and the *Sacraments*, as practically carry them out in his life, upholding them in the midst of storms. In his doctrinal opinions he rested on the basis laid by Tertullian, but also sympathized with Minucius Felix, as in his work, De Idolorum Vanitate. Accordingly, along with his numerous letters, his work entitled, De Unitate Ecclesiæ, is of the first importance. Besides these there are: Libri III Testimoniorum, De Bono Patientiæ, De Oratione Dominica, and several of a more practical character. Comp. *Rettberg*, Cyprian nach seinem Leben und Wirken, Göttingen 1834. *Ed. Huther*, Cyprians Lehre von der Kirche, Hamburg 1839. Editions: *Rigaltius*, Paris 1648, fol. *Fell, Oxon. 1682, and the Benedictine edition by *Steph. Baluze* and *Prud. Maran*, Paris 1726, fol. *Goldhorn*, Leipz. 1838, 39, 2 vols. [*Hartel*, in Corpus Script. ecclesiast., Vindob. 1868, 3 vols. *Krabinger's* edition of Cyprian, De Unitate, etc., 1853, and of his Libri ad Donatum, De Domin. Orat., etc., 1859. Life and Times of C., by *Geo. Ayliffe Poole*, Oxf. 1840. *Shepherd*, Hist. of Church of Rome, Lond. 1852, contests the authenticity of all Cyprian's Epistles; ibid., Five Letters to Dr. Maitland, 1853-54. *Nevin*

on Cyprian and his Times, Mercersb. Review, 1852–53. Cyprian's Treatises and Epistles, in Oxford Lib. of Fathers, vols. 3 and 17, and in Ante-Nicene Lib. Articles on Cyprian in *Rudelbach*, christl. Biog., and in *Böhringer*, Kirchengesch. in Biograph. *Dodwell*, Dissertationes Cyprianicæ, 1704. *Bp. Sage*, Principles of Cyprianic Age, 2 vols. Edinb. 1846. C.'s Unity of the Church, by *J. Fell*, Oxf. 1681; Disc. to Donatus, by *J. Tunstall*, 1716; whole Works by *N. Marshall*, 1717. Annales Cyprianici a *J. Pearsono*, rep. in *Fell's* edition of Cyprian, fol. 1700.]

Novatian, the contemporary and opponent of Cyprian (ὁ τῆς ἐκκλησιαστικῆς ἐπιστήμης ὑπερασπιστής, Euseb. vi. 43), must also be considered as belonging to the extreme limit of this period, if the treatise, De Trinitate (De Regula Veritatis s. Fidei), which goes under his name, proceeded from him. It is by no means correct (as Jerome would have it, § 70) that this treatise contains nothing but extracts from Tertullian. " *This author was at all events more than a mere imitator of the peculiar tendency of another; on the contrary, he shows originality; he does not possess the power and depth of Tertullian, but more spirituality,*" Neander, i. 3, s. 1165. *Editions: Whiston*, in his Sermons and Essays upon Several Subjects, Lond. 1709, p. 327. *Welchman*, Oxon. 1724. *Jackson*, Lond. 1728. [*Lardner*, iii. p. 3–20.] Often in connection with Tertullian. Libri de Cath. eccles. unitate, de lapsis et de habitu virg., ed. *Krabinger*, Tüb. 1853.

(10) *Clement* (*Tit. Flav.*), surnamed *Alexandrinus*, in distinction from Clement of Rome (note 3), a disciple of Pantænus at Alexandria, and his successor in his office, died between 212 and 220. Comp. *Euseb.* v. 11, vi. 6, 13, 14. *Hieron.* De Vir. Ill. c. 38. Of his works the following three form a whole:—
1. Λόγος προτρεπτικὸς πρὸς Ἕλληνας. 2. Παιδαγωγός in three books; and 3. Στρώματα (τῶν κατὰ τὴν ἀληθῆ φιλοσοφίαν γνωστικῶν ὑπομνημάτων στρωματεῖς)—so called from the variety of its contents, like a piece of tapestry—in eight books: the eighth of which forms a special homily, under the title: τίς ὁ σωζόμενος πλούσιος, Quis dives salvetur. The ὑποτυπώσεις in eight books, an exegetical work, is lost. Concerning his life and writings, comp. *Hofstede de Groot*, de Clemente Alex., Gröning. 1826. *Von Cölln* in Ersch and

Gruber's Encyklop. xviii. s. 4 ff. *Dähne*, de γνώσει Clem. et de Vestigiis Neoplatonicæ Philos. in ea obviis, Lips. 1831. *Eylert*, Clemens als Philosoph und Dichter, Leipz. 1832. *Baur*, Gnosis, s. 502 ff. *Möhler*, Patrologie, s. 430. *Lämmer* (cf. § 42). [*Lardner*, Works, ii. 220-224.] *Editions by Sylburg*, Heidelberg 1592. Best by *Potter*, Oxon. 1715, fol. Ven. 1757; *smaller ed., R. Klotz*, Lips. 1831, 3 vols. [*Bishop Kaye*, Account of Writings and Opinions of Clem. of Alex., Lond. 1839. Journal of Sacred Lit. 1852. *Leutzen*, Erkennen und Glauben, Cl. v. Alex. und Anselm v. Cant., Bonn 1848. *Reinkens*, De Clem. Alex., Vratislav. 1851. *Reuter*, Clem. Alex. Theol. Moralis, Berol. 1853. *H. Lämmer*, Clem. Alex. de Log. doct., Lips. 1855. Clement and the Alexandrian School, in North British Review, Aug. 1855. *Abbé Herbert-Duperron*, Essai sur la Polémique et la Philos. de Clém. d'Alex., Paris 1855. Alleged fragments of Clem., *Nolte* in Theol. Quartalschrift, 1859, s. 597 ff. Opinions of Cl. Alex. in *Huber's* Phil. d. Kirchenväter, 1859, s. 130-184. *Abbé J. Cognat*, Clément d'Alexandrie, sa doctrine et sa polémique, Paris 1859; transl. in Ante-Nicene Lib.]

(11) *Origen*, surnamed ἀδαμάντινος, χαλκέντερος, was born at Alexandria, about the year 185, a disciple of Clement, and died at Tyre in the year 254. He is undoubtedly the most eminent writer of the whole period, and the best representative of the spiritualizing tendency, though not wholly free from great faults into which he was led by his genius. "*According to all appearance he would have avoided most of the weaknesses which disfigure his writings, if understanding, wit, and imagination had been equally strong in him. His reason frequently overcomes his imagination, but his imagination obtains more victories over his reason,*" Mosheim (translat. of the treatise against Celsus, p. 60). Accounts of his life are given in *Euseb.* vi. 1-6, 8, 14-21, 23-28, 30-33, 36-39, vii. 1. *Hieron.* De Viris Illustr. c. 54. *Gregory Thaumaturg.* in Panegyrico. *Huetius* in the Origeniana. *Tillemont*, Mémoires, art. Origène, p. 356-76. *Schröckh*, iv. s. 29. [*Lardner*, ii. p. 469-486 and passim.] On his doctrines and writings, comp. *Schnitzer*, Origenes, über die Grundlehren der Glaubenswissenschaft, Stuttg. 1835. *Gottf. Thomasius*, Origenes, ein Beitrag zur Dogmengeschichte des 3 Jahrhunderts, Nürnberg 1837.

Redepenning, Origenes, eine Darstellung seines Lebens und seiner Lehre, 2 Bde. Bonn 1841-46. The labours of Origen embraced a wide sphere. We can only refer to what he did for biblical criticism (Hexapla) and exegesis (σημειώσεις, τόμοι, ὁμιλίαι, cf. Philocalia), as well as for homiletics, which appears in his writings in the simplest forms. His two principal works of doctrinal importance, περὶ ἀρχῶν (De Principiis, libri iv.), edit. by *Redepenning* (Lips. 1836), and *Schnitzer's* translation before mentioned; and κατὰ Κέλσου (contra Celsum), lib. viii. (translated, with notes by *Mosheim*, Hamb. 1745). Minor treatises: De Oratione, De Exhortatione Martyrii, etc. Complete editions of his works were published by **Car. de la Rue*, Paris 1733 ff., 4 vols. fol., and by *Lommatzsch*, Berl. 1831 ff., 25 vols. [also by the *Abbé Migne*, Paris 1857, 7 vols. large 8vo. His principal works are translated in the Ante-Nicene Library.]

[*Fischer*, Commentatio de Origenis Theologia et Cosmologia, 1846; Greg. Nyss. Doctrina de hominis Natura cum Origen. comparata, *E. G. Möller*, Halle 1854. Origen and the Alex. School, North British, 1855. *Mosheim's* Comment. in Murdock's edition, ii. p. 143-209. Article on Origen, in British Quarterly, by *R. A. Vaughan*, 1845. *Abbé E. Joly*, Etudes sur Origène, 1860. *Huber's* Phil. d. Kirchenväter, 1859, s. 150-184.]

The doctrinal systems of Clement and Origen unite under a more general aspect, and form what is called the theology of the *Alexandrian* school. The distinguishing characteristics of this theology, in a formal point of view, are a leaning to speculation and the allegorical interpretation of the Scriptures; as to their matter, they consist of an attempt to spiritualize the ideas, and idealize particular doctrines, and they thus form a striking contrast with the peculiarities of Tertullian in particular. Comp. *Guericke*, De Schola quæ Alexandriæ floruit Catechetica, Halæ 1824, 2 vols. [*Baur*, Gnosis, s. 488-543.]

The Philosophumena, ascribed to *Origen*, and published by *Em. Miller*, Oxf. 1851, under his name (᾿Ωριγένους φιλοσοφούμενα ἢ κατὰ πασῶν αἱρέσεων ἔλεγχος, e codice Paris. nunc primum ed.), is with greater probability assigned to *Hippolytus*, who had been held to be a bishop of Arabia (misled by *Eusebius*, vi. 20), but who died, as bishop of Portus Romanus [Döllinger thinks he was an Antipope], a martyr's death, it is said, under Maximin (236–238). This work would then be the same with the ἔλεγχος κατὰ πασῶν αἱρέσεων, ascribed to Hippolytus (edited by *Duncker* and *Schneidewin*, Gött. 1856–59), which is by others attributed to the Roman presbyter Caius (*Baur* in the Theolog. Jahrb. 1853), which is also found under the name λαβύρινθος (*Photius*, c. 48). Comp. Opp. et Fragmenta, ed. *J. A. Fabricius*, Hamb. 1716-18, 2 vols. *Haenel*, De Hippolyto, Gött. 1839. **Jos. Bunsen*, Hippolytus u. seine Zeit, Leipz. 1852–53. [English edition, 7 vols.] *Gieseler*, ubi supra. *Jacobi* in Neander's Dogmengesch. s. 54, and in Zeitschrift f. christl. Wissenschaft, 1831, s. 204. *Döllinger, Hippol. und Callistus, Regensb. 1853 [Eng. trans. Edin. 1877]. *Ritschl* in Theol. Jahrb. 1854. *Volkmar*, Hippolytus, 1855. *F. C. Overbeck*, Quæstionum Hippolytearum specimen, Jena 1864. [Comp. articles in Theol. Critic, 1852; Edinburgh Review, 1852–53; Christ. Rembr. 1853; Dublin Review, 1853, 54; North British, 1853; Journal of Class. and Sacred Philol. 1854; British Quarterly, 1853; Westminster Review, 1853. Comp. also *Ch. Wordsworth*, Church of Rome in Third Cent., 2d ed. 1855. *Lenormant*, Controverse sur les Philos., Paris 1853. *Cruice*, Etudes sur les Philos. 1852.]

§ 27.

Review of the General Doctrinal Character of this Period.

It is the characteristic feature of the apologetic period, that the whole system of Christianity, as a religious and moral fact, is considered and defended on all sides, rather than particular doctrines. Still certain doctrines are more discussed, while others receive less attention. Investigations of a theological and Christological nature are unquestionably more prominent than those of an anthropological character. The Pauline type of doctrine does not come to its rights as fully as does that of John (1). Hence, too, the emphatic prominence given to the doctrine of human freedom, to an extent which could not afterwards be approved (2). Next to theology and Christology, eschatology was more fully developed in the struggle with millenarianism on the one side, and the scepticism of Grecian philosophers on the other (3).

(1) Comp. § 18, note 4.

(2) *Origen* expressly mentions the doctrine concerning the freedom of the will as a part of the prædicatio ecclesiastica; De Princip. procem. § 4 ff.; comp. the Special History of Doctrines, below.

(3) This has its natural grounds. The doctrine of the *Messianic kingdom* ruled the first period. This turned upon the point that the Lord was twice to come; once in His manifestation in the flesh, and again in His future coming to judgment. The doctrine of the resurrection of the body was treated with special predilection. And yet much was left open. Thus Origen expressly says that angelology and demonology, as well as various cosmological questions, had not been adequately defined in the doctrine of the Church; De Princip. procem. § 6, 7, 10.

B. SPECIAL HISTORY OF DOCTRINES DURING THE FIRST PERIOD.

FIRST DIVISION.

APOLOGETICO-DOGMATIC PROLEGOMENA.

TRUTH OF CHRISTIANITY — REVELATION AND SOURCES OF REVELATION — SCRIPTURE AND TRADITION.

§ 28.

Truth and Divinity of the Christian Religion in General.

* *Tzschirner*, Geschichte der Apologetik, vol. i. Leipz. 1808. By the *same:* der Fall des Heidenthums, Bd. i. Leipz. 1829. *H. N. Clausen*, Apologetæ ecclesiæ Christianæ ante-Theodosiani, Havn. 1817. *G. H. van Senden*, Geschichte der Apologetik von den frühesten Zeiten bis auf unsere Tage, Stuttg. 2 vols. [*Bolton*, Apologists of Second and Third Centuries, repr. Boston 1853. *Giles*, Heathen Records and the Script. History, 1857. *Ehrenfenchter*, Apologetik, in Jahrb. f. deutsche Theologie, 1857.]

THE principal task of this period was to prove the divine origin of Christianity as the true religion made known by revelation (1), and to set forth its internal and external character in relation to both Gentiles and Jews. This was attempted in different ways, according to the different ideas which obtained regarding the nature of the Christian religion. The Ebionites considered the principal object of Christianity to be the realization of the Jewish idea of the Messiah (2); the Gnostics regarded it as consisting in breaking away from the traditional connection with the Old Testament (3). Between these two extremes the Catholic Church endeavoured, on the

98 FIRST PERIOD.—APOLOGETICO-DOGMATIC PROLEGOMENA. [§ 28.

one hand, to preserve this connection with the old revelation; on the other, to point out the new and more perfect elements which constituted the peculiarity of the Christian system.

(1) Here we must not expect to find a distinction made between religion itself and the Christian religion (natural and revealed), or look for a precise definition of the term "religion." Such definitions of the schools did not make their appearance until later, when, science and life being separated, learned men speculated on the objects of science, and reduced experimental truths to general ideas. With the first Christians, Christianity and religion were identical (*Augusti*, s. 197); as, again, in modern times, the principal object of apologetics must be the proof that Christianity is *the* religion, *i.e.* the only one which can satisfy man (comp. *Lechler*, über den Begriff der Apologetik, in the Studien und Kritiken, 1839, 3). This view corresponds with the saying of *Minucius Felix*, Oct. c. 38, towards the end: Gloriamur nos consequutos, quod illi (Philosophi) summa intentione quæsiverunt nec invenire potuerunt. *Ignatius*, ad Rom. iii.: Οὐ πεισμονῆς ἔργον ἀλλὰ μεγέθους ἐστὶν ὁ χριστιανισμός, ὅταν μισῆται ὑπὸ κόσμου (cf. *Hefele* on the passage). *Justin M.* also shows that revealed truth, as such, does not stand in need of any proof, Dial. c. Tryph. c. 7, p. 109: Οὐ γὰρ μετὰ ἀποδείξεως πεποίηνταί ποτε (οἱ προφῆται) τοὺς λόγους, ἅτε ἀνωτέρω πάσης ἀποδείξεως ὄντες ἀξιόπιστοι μάρτυρες τῆς ἀληθείας. Fragm. de Resurr. ab init.: Ὁ μὲν τῆς ἀληθείας λόγος ἐστὶν ἐλεύθερος καὶ αὐτεξούσιος, ὑπὸ μηδεμίαν βάσανον ἐλέγχου θέλων πίπτειν, μηδὲ τὴν παρὰ τοῖς ἀκούουσι δι' ἀποδείξεως ἐξέτασιν ὑπομένειν. Τὸ γὰρ εὐγενὲς αὐτοῦ καὶ πεποιθὸς αὐτῷ τῷ πέμψαντι πιστεύεσθαι θέλει ... Πᾶσα γὰρ ἀπόδειξις ἰσχυροτέρα καὶ πιστοτέρα τοῦ ἀποδεικνυμένου τυγχάνει· εἴ γε τὸ πρότερον ἀπιστούμενον πρὶν ἢ τὴν ἀπόδειξιν ἐλθεῖν, ταύτης κομισθείσης, ἔτυχε πίστεως, καὶ τοιοῦτον ἐφάνη, ὁποῖον ἐλέγετο. Τῆς δὲ ἀληθείας ἰσχυρότερον οὐδέν, οὐδὲ πιστότερον· ὥστε ὁ περὶ ταύτης ἀπόδειξιν αἰτῶν ὅμοιός ἐστι τῷ τὰ φαινόμενα αἰσθήσεσι, λόγοις θέλοντι ἀποδείκνυσθαι, διότι φαίνεται. Τῶν γὰρ διὰ τοῦ λόγου λαμβανομένων κριτήριόν ἐστιν ἡ αἴσθησις· αὐτῆς δὲ κριτήριον οὐκ ἔστι πλὴν αὐτῆς. Nor do we find any definitions of the nature

and idea of *revelation* (contrasted with the truths which come to us by nature and reason), nor respecting the abstract possibility and necessity of revelation, etc., because the opposite views did not then exist. Christianity (in connection with the Old Testament) was considered as the true revelation; even the best ideas of earlier philosophers, compared with it, were only the glimmer of anticipation. Comp. *Justin M.*, Dial. c. Tryph. ab initio. *Tert.* Apol. c. 18 (De Test. Animæ, c. 2), pronounces very decidedly in favour of the positive character of the Christian religion (*fiunt*, non *nascuntur* Christiani), though he also calls the human soul, naturaliter christiana (Apol. c. 17), and ascribes to it instinct preceding all teaching, by which it can, as a pupil of nature, attain to a knowledge of the divine in nature; De Test. Anim. c. 5. *Clement* of Alexandria also compares the attempt to comprehend the divine without a higher revelation, to the attempt to run without feet (Cohort. p. 64); and further remarks, that without the light of revelation we should resemble hens that are fattened in a dark cage in order to die (ibid. p. 87). We become a divine race only by the doctrine of Christ (p. 88, 89), comp. Pæd. i. 2, p. 100, i. 12, p. 156, and in numerous other places. *Clement* indeed admits that wise men before Christ had approached the truth to a certain extent (compare the next section); but while they sought God by their own wisdom, others (the Christians) find Him (better) through the Logos; comp. Pæd. iii. 8, p. 279; Strom. i. 1, p. 319, ibid. i. 6, p. 336. The pseudo-Clementines, however, depart from this idea of a positive revelation (17. 8 and 18. 6), and represent the *internal* revelation of the heart as the true revelation, the *external* as a manifestation of the divine ὀργή. Compare *Baumgarten-Crusius*, ii. s. 783; on the other side, *Schliemann*, s. 183 ff., 353 ff.

(2) According to the Clementine Homilies, there is no specific difference between the doctrine of Jesus and the doctrine of Moses. Comp. *Credner*, l.c. Ht. 2, s. 254. *Schliemann*, s. 215 ff. *Hilgenfeld*, s. 283 (?).

(3) As most of the Gnostics looked upon the demiurge either as a being that stood in a hostile relation to God, or as a being of limited powers; as they, moreover, considered the entire economy of the Old Testament as a defective and even a

perverted institution, they could, consistently, look upon the blessings of Christianity only as a deliverance from the bonds of the demiurge. (Comp. the sections on God, the Fall, and Redemption.)

§ 29.

Mode of Proof.

[Comp. *Baur*, Dogmengesch. s. 76–9 ; and his Christenthum in d. drei ersten Jahrhund. s. 357–451.]

Accordingly, the Christian apologists, in opposition to the heathen, defended the history, laws, doctrines, and prophecies of the Old Testament against the attacks of those who were not Jews (1). On this basis they proceeded to prove the superiority of Christianity, in contrast with the Jewish as well as the pagan systems, by showing how all the prophecies and types of the Old Testament had been fulfilled in Christ (2); not unfrequently indulging in arbitrary interpretations and typological fancies (3). But as the apologists found in the Old Testament a point of connection with Judaism, so they found in the Grecian philosophy a point of connection with paganism ; only with this difference, that whatever is divine in the latter is, for the most part, derived from the Old Testament (4), corrupted by the craft of demons (5), and appearing, at all events, very imperfect in comparison with Christianity, however great the analogy (6). Even those writers who, like Tertullian, discarded a philosophical proof of Christianity because they saw in philosophy only an ungodly perversity (7), could not but admit a profound psychological connection between human nature and the Christian religion (the testimony of the soul) (8), and acknowledged, with the rest, that a leading argument for the divine origin of Christianity was to be derived from its moral effects (9). Thus the external argument from miracles (10) was adduced only as a kind of auxiliary proof, and it was even now no longer acknowledged in its full authority (11). Another auxiliary proof was derived from the Sibylline oracles (12), while the almost miraculous spread of Christianity in the midst of persecutions (13), and the accomplishment of the prophecy relative to the destruction of Jerusalem (14), were, like the moral argument, taken from what was occurring at the time.

(1) This argument was founded especially upon the high antiquity of the sacred books, and the wonderful care of God in their preservation; *Josephus* had argued in a similar manner against *Apion*, i. 8. Comp. the section on the Scriptures.

(2) Comp. *Justin M.*, Apol. i. c. 32–35, Dial. cum Tryphone, § 7, 8, 11. *Athenag.* Leg. c. 9. *Orig.* Contra Cels. i. 2; Comment. in Joh. t. ii. 28. Opp. iv. p. 87. [*Aubé*, in his work on St. Justin, has reconstructed the argument of Tryphon.]

(3) Ep. *Barn.* c. 9, where the circumcision of the three hundred and eighteen persons by Abraham (Gen. xvii.) is represented as a prophecy of Christ. The number three hundred and eighteen is composed of three hundred, and eight, and ten. The numeral letters of ten and eight are I and H (η), which are the initials of the name $'I\eta\sigma o \hat{v}s$. The numeral letter of three hundred is T, which is the symbol of the cross. And *Clement* of Rome, in his first Epistle to the Corinthians, which is generally sober enough, says that the scarlet line, which Rahab was admonished by the spies to hang out of her house, was a type of the blood of Christ, c. 12. So, too, *Justin M.* Dialog. cum Tryph. § 111. According to the latter, the two wives of Jacob, Leah and Rachel, are types of the Jewish and Christian dispensations; the two goats on the day of atonement, types of the two advents of Christ; the twelve bells upon the robe of the high priest, types of the twelve apostles, etc. Justin carries to an extreme length the symbolism of the cross, which he sees not only in the O. T. (in the tree of the knowledge of good and evil, the rod of Aaron, etc.), but also in nature, in the horn of the unicorn, in the human countenance, in the posture of a

man engaged in prayer, in the vessel with its sails, in the plough, in the hammer. Comp. Apol. i. c. 55, Dial. cum Tryph. § 97, and elsewhere. Comp. *Minuc. Felix*, c. 29, who, however, does not make it the basis of any further argument. *Irenæus* sees in the three spies of Jericho the three persons of the Trinity, Advers. Hæret. iv. 20. It would be easy to multiply these examples ad infinitum (comp. § 33, note 3). As to the way in which the Septuagint translation was used by Christians in the interpretation of Messianic passages, see *Gieseler*, Dogmengesch. s. 61 ff. [Thus *Clement* of Rome, Epist. § 42, cites the passage Isa. lx. 17 as referring to bishops and deacons; while it reads ἄρχοντας and ἐπισκόπους —which may be only because cited incorrectly from memory. The Christians, too, often accused the Jews of falsifying the Hebrew; for example, the noted passages in *Justin*, Dial. cum Tryph., where he says that they left out, in Ps. xcv. (Heb. xcvi.) 10, ἀπὸ τοῦ ξύλου after ὁ κύριος ἐβασίλευσεν; and Tertullian and Irenæus both cite the passage after Justin; and so in similar passages, alleged to be in Ezra and Jeremiah.] That these arguments were not readily accepted by the philosophically trained heathen is clear from the case of Celsus, who was opposed by Origen from his hermeneutic point of view. Cf. *Baur*, Dg. s. 347 f.

(4) *Justin M.* Apol. i. c. 59, Cohort. ad Græc. c. 14. *Theophil.* Ad Autol. iii. 16, 17, 20, 23. *Tatian*, Contra Græc. ab init. and c. 25. *Tertullian*, Apol. c. 19: Omnes itaque substantias, omnesque materias, origines, ordines, venas veterani cujusque stili vestri, gentes etiam plerasque et urbes insignes, canas memoriarum, ipsas denique effigies litterarum indices custodesque rerum, et puto adhuc minus dicimus, ipsos inquam deos vestros, ipsa templa et oracula et sacra, unius interim prophetæ scrinium vincit, in quo videtur thesaurus collocatus totius Judaici sacramenti, et inde etiam nostri. *Clem. Alexand.* Pæd. ii. c. 1, p. 176; c. 10, p. 224; iii. c. 11, p. 286. Stromata, i. p. 355; vi. p. 752, and many other passages. He therefore calls Plato outright ὁ ἐξ Ἑβραίων φιλόσοφος, Strom. i. 1. Comp. *Baur*, Gnosis, s. 256. *Orig.* Contra Cels. iv. ab init. *Tzschirner*, Geschichte der Apologetik, s. 101, 102.

(5) *Justin M.* Apol. i. c. 54. Thus the demons are said to

have heard Jacob when he blessed his sons. But as the heathen could not interpret the passage, Gen. xlix. 11, "Binding his foal unto the vine," in its true Messianic sense, they referred it to Bacchus, the inventor of the vine, and out of the foal they made Pegasus (because they did not know whether the animal in question was a horse or an ass). In a similar manner a misinterpretation of the prophecy relative to the conception of the Virgin (Isa. vii. 14) gave rise to the fable of Perseus, etc. (comp. § 49 on Demonology).

(6) *Justin M.* calls in a certain sense Christians all those who have ordered their lives according to the laws of the Logos (reason?), Apol. i. c. 46. The Platonic philosophy is in his opinion not absolutely different (ἀλλοτρία) from Christianity. But before the coming of Christ there existed in the world only the scattered seeds (λόγος σπερματικός) of what was afterwards manifested in Christ as absolute truth, comp. Apol. ii. c. 13. *Clem. Alex.* Strom. i. c. 20, p. 376: Χωρίζεται δὲ ἡ ἑλληνικὴ ἀλήθεια τῆς καθ' ἡμᾶς, εἰ καὶ τοῦ αὐτοῦ μετείληφεν ὀνόματος, καὶ μεγέθει γνώσεως καὶ ἀποδείξει κυριωτέρᾳ, καὶ θείᾳ δυνάμει καὶ τοῖς ὁμοίοις. (He speaks, however, of philosophy as such, and not of the Stoic, Platonic, Epicurean, Aristotelian, or any other particular system, Strom. i. 7, p. 338.) Comp. *Baur*, Gnosis, s. 520 ff. On the other contradictions found in *Clement* of Alexandria, in judging of paganism more favourably at one time and less so at another, comp. *Baur*, s. 532. *Minucius Felix,* c. 16, in opposition to the scholastic wisdom of the ancient philosophers, recommends the philosophy of good sense, which is accessible to all (ingenium, quod non studio paratur, sed cum ipsa mentis formatione generatur), and speaks with disdain of mere reliance on authorities; nevertheless, he himself appeals to the doctrines of philosophers, and their partial agreement with Christianity (c. 19, 21, 34). Such language forms a remarkable contrast with the attack he makes upon Socrates (scurra Atticus), c. 38, to whom others assigned the highest rank among the ancient philosophers. Even *Origen* urges that the Christian doctrine equalizes all men, while the philosophy of antiquity was only for the educated. He compares the ancient philosophers with the physicians who heal only the rich, Contra Cels. vi. 2, vii. 60.

(7) *Tert.* De Præscr. 7, 8: Hæ sunt doctrinæ hominum et dæmoniorum, prurientibus auribus natæ de ingenio sapientiæ secularis, quam Dominus stultitiam vocans, stulta mundi in confusionem etiam philosophorum ipsius elegit. Ea est enim materia sapientiæ secularis, temeraria interpres divinæ naturæ et dispositionis. Ipsæ denique hæreses a philosophia subornantur. . . . Quid ergo Athenis et Hierosolymis? quid Academiæ et Ecclesiæ? quid hæreticis et Christianis? Nostra institutio de porticu Salomonis est, qui et ipse tradiderat Dominum in simplicitate cordis esse quærendum. Viderint, qui Stoicum et Platonicum et dialecticum Christianismum protulerunt. Nobis curiositate opus non est post Christum Jesum, nec inquisitione post Evangelium. Cum credimus, nihil desideramus ultra credere. The constant seeking after truth is a proof that it is lost. Above all, it is their duty to hold fast the deposit committed to them. Quæramus ergo in nostro et a nostris et de nostro: idque dumtaxat, quod salva regula fidei potest in quæstionem devenire. The mere libido curiositatis, the curiositas fidei, is to be avoided; the desire for knowledge is to be subordinated to the desire for salvation. Adversus regulam (fidei) nihil scire, omnia scire est (De præscript. 10-14. *Tertullian* calls the philosophers—patriarchæ hæreticorum (De Anima, 3; Adv. Hermog. 8); and Plato, omnium hæreticorum condimentarius (De Anima, 23).

(8) *Tert.* De Test. Anim. 1: Novum testimonium advoco, immo omni litteratura notius, omni doctrina agitatius, omni editione vulgatius, toto homine majus, *i.e.* totum quod est hominis. Consiste in medio, anima. . . . Sed non eam te advoco, quæ scholis formata, bibliothecis exercitata, academiis et porticibus Atticis pasta, sapientiam ructas. Te simplicem et rudem et impolitam et idioticam compello, qualem te habent qui te solam habent, illam ipsam de compito, de trivio, de textrino totam. Imperitia tua mihi opus est, quoniam aliquantulæ peritiæ nemo credit. Ea expostulo, quæ tecum homini infers, quæ aut ex temetipsa, aut ex quocunque auctore tuo sentire didicisti. *Ibid.:* Non es, quod sciam, Christiana: fieri enim, non nasci soles Christiana. Tamen nunc a te testimonium flagitant Christiani, ab extranea adversus tuos, ut vel tibi erubescant, quod nos ob ea oderint et irrideant, quæ te nunc consciam detineant. Non placemus Deum prædicantes

hoc nomine unico unicum, a quo omnia et sub quo universa. Dic testimonium, si ita scis. Nam te quoque palam et tota libertate, quia non licet nobis, domi ac foris audimus ita pronuntiare: Quod Deus dederit, et si Deus voluerit, etc. Comp. Apol. c. 17; De Virgin. veland. c. 5 (tacita conscientia naturæ). *Neander*, Antignost. s. 86–89. *Schwegler*, Montanismus, s. 28 ff.

(9) *Justin M.* Apol. i. c. 14: Οἱ πάλαι μὲν πορνείαις χαίροντες, νῦν δὲ σωφροσύνην μόνην ἀσπαζόμενοι· οἱ δὲ καὶ μαγικαῖς τέχναις χρώμενοι, ἀγαθῷ καὶ ἀγεννήτῳ Θεῷ ἑαυτοὺς ἀνατεθεικότες· χρημάτων δὲ καὶ κτημάτων οἱ πόρους παντὸς μᾶλλον στέργοντες, νῦν καὶ ἃ ἔχομεν εἰς κοινὸν φέροντες, καὶ παντὶ δεομένῳ κοινωνοῦντες· οἱ μισάλληλοι δὲ καὶ ἀλληλοφόνοι καὶ πρὸς τοὺς οὐχ ὁμοφύλους διὰ τὰ ἔθη ἑστίας κοινὰς μὴ ποιούμενοι, νῦν μετὰ τὴν ἐπιφάνειαν τοῦ Χριστοῦ ὁμοδίαιτοι γινόμενοι, καὶ ὑπὲρ τῶν ἐχθρῶν εὐχόμενοι καὶ τοὺς ἀδίκως μισοῦντας πείθειν πειρώμενοι, ὅπως οἱ κατὰ τὰς τοῦ Χριστοῦ καλὰς ὑποθημοσύνας βιώσαντες εὐέλπιδες ὦσι, σὺν ἡμῖν τῶν αὐτῶν παρὰ τοῦ πάντων δεσπόζοντος Θεοῦ τυχεῖν. Dial. cum Tryph. § 8, 30. Orat. ad Græcos, 5. Epist. ad Diognetum, 5. *Athenag.* Leg. c. 11. *Tert.* Apol. ab init. *Minucius Felix*, c. 31, 37, 38. *Orig.* Contra Cels. i. c. 26; Opp. i. p. 345. They were in practice compelled to have recourse to this argument by the accusations of the heathen, which they endeavoured to refute. [Comp. *Tholuck*, Wunder in d. Kirche, in his Vermischte Schriften, i. 28 ff.; the works of *Middleton* and *Warburton; Newman's* Essay, prefixed to his translation of Fleury, i., in opposition to *Isaac Taylor's* Ancient Christianity. *Bp. Kaye* on the Cessation of Miracles, in the preface to his Life of Justin Martyr. *Blunt* on the Early Fathers. Comp. Christ. Rembr. 1858. *Eusebius*, Hist. Eccl. iv. 3, preserves the argument of Quadratus: "The deeds of our Saviour were always at hand, for they were true; those who were healed, those who were raised from the dead, were not merely seen cured and raised, but they were always at hand; and that not merely while our Saviour was on earth, but after He had gone away they continued a considerable time, so that some of them reached even to our times." See *Bolton's* Apologists, u. s.]

(10) Not only were those miracles adduced which are

mentioned in Scripture, but also some which still took place. (*Just. M.* Dialog. c. Tryph. c. 38, 82, 88. *Iren.* ii. 31, 32. *Tert.* Ap. c. 23. *Orig.* Contra Cels. iii. 24, Opp. i. p. 461.) At the same time the Christians did not directly deny the existence of miracles in the heathen world, but ascribed them to the influence of demons (ibid. and *Minucius Felix,* Oct. c. 26); the heathen, on the other hand, attributed the Christian miracles to magic. Comp. *Tatian,* Contra Græcos, c. 18. *Orig.* Contra Cels. i. 38, 67, 68, iii. 24–33. We find, however, that *Minucius Felix* denies the reality of miracles and myths in the pagan world, on the ground of the physical impossibility of such supernatural events,—a ground which might, with equal propriety, have been taken by the opponents of Christianity. Octav. c. 20: Quæ si essent facta, fierent; quia fieri non possunt, ideo nec facta sunt; and c. 23: Cur enim si nati sunt, non hodieque nascuntur?

(11) Though *Origen,* in speaking of the evidence derived from miracles, as compared with that from prophecy, calls the former the evidence of power, and the latter the evidence of the Spirit (Contra Cels. i. 2), yet he subordinates the former to the latter. He was well aware that a miracle has its emphatic effect upon the person we wish to convince, only when it is performed in his presence, but that it loses its direct force as evidence with those whose minds are prejudiced against the veracity of the narrative, and who reject miracles as myths; comp. Comment. in Joh. Opp. iv. p. 87. So, too, the Clementine Homilies do not admit miracles as evidences, while they attach greater value to prophecies. (*Credner,* l.c. Ht. 3, s. 278, comp. with s. 245.) *Origen* spoke also of *spiritual* and *moral* miracles, of which the visible miracles (admitting their importance as facts) may be considered as symbols; Contra Cels. ii. s. 423: "*I may say that, according to the promise of Jesus, His disciples have performed greater miracles than Himself; for still the blind in spirit have their eyes opened, and those deaf to the voice of virtue listen eagerly to the doctrine concerning God and eternal life; many who were lame in the inner man skip like the hart,*" etc. Comp. Contra Cels. iii. 24, where he speaks of the healing of the sick and of prophesying as an indifferent thing ($\mu\acute{\epsilon}\sigma o\nu$), which considered in itself does not possess any moral value.

(12) *Theophilus*, Ad Autolycum, ii. 31, 36, 38. *Clem.* Cohort. p. 66; Stromata, vi. 5, 762. (Celsus charged the Christians with having corrupted the Sibylline books. *Origen*, Contra Cels. vii. 32, 44.) *Editions* of the Sibyll. oracles were published by *Servatius Gallœus*, Amstel. 1699, 4to, and by *Angelo Mai*, Mediolani 1817. On their origin and tendency, comp. *Thorlacius*, Libri Sibyllistarum veteris ecclesiæ, etc., Havniæ 1815, and *Bleek* in the Berliner theolog. Zeitschrift, i. 120 ff., 172 ff. *Piper*, Christ. Mythologie (in Appendix), s. 472 ff. *Friedlieb*, de Codd. Sibyllinorum manuscriptis, 1847; Die Sibyllinischen Weissagungen, 1852. *H. Ewald*, Abhandlung über Entstehung, Inhalt, u. Werth der Sibyll. Bücher (Abhandl. der Kön. Gesellschaft der Wiss. zu Gött.), 1858. *Reuss* in Herzog's Realenc. xiv. [*Mai*, published Books, ix.-xiv. in his Script. Veterum nova Collectio, vol. iii. *Lücke*, Einleitung in die Offenbarung Johan. 2d ed. *M. Stuart* on the Apocalypse, vol. i. *Blondel* on Sibyl. Oracles, transl. by *Davies*, Lond. 1661. Oracula Sibyllina, ed. *P. L. Courier*, Paris 1854; ed. with a German version by *Friedlob*, Leipz. 1852; ed. by *Alexander*, 2 tom. Paris 1841-53. *Volckmann*, De Orac. Sibyl. 1853.] The case of the Ὑστάσπης, to which *Justin M.* Apol. i. 20 and *Clem.* l.c. appeal, is similar to that of the Sibylline books. Comp. *Ch. F. W. Walch*, de Hystaspide, in vol. i. of the Comment. Societ. Reg. Gött. *Lücke*, Einleit. in die Offenb. Joh., 2 Aufl. s. 237 f. But the oracles of the heathen (though a partial use was made of them), as well as of their miracles, were attributed to demoniacal agency; *Minuc. Fel.* c. 26, 27; *Clement.* Homil. iii. 9-13.

(13) *Origen*, Contra Cels. i. p. 321, ii. 361, De Princip. iv. *Justin M.* himself (and many others) had been converted by witnessing the firmness which many of the martyrs exhibited. Comp. his Apol. ii. p. 96, and Dial. cum Tryph. § 121: Καὶ οὐδένα οὐδέποτε ἰδεῖν ἔστιν ὑπομείναντα διὰ τὴν πρὸς τὸν ἥλιον πίστιν ἀποθανεῖν, διὰ δὲ τὸ ὄνομα τοῦ Ἰησοῦ ἐκ παντὸς γένους ἀνθρώπων καὶ ὑπομείναντας καὶ ὑπομένοντας πάντα πάσχειν ὑπὲρ τοῦ μὴ ἀρνήσασθαι αὐτὸν ἰδεῖν ἔστι κ.τ.λ.

(14) *Origen*, Contra Celsum, ii. 13, Opp. i. p. 400.

§ 30.

Sources of Knowledge.

J. C. Orelli, Selecta patrum ecclesiæ capita ad ἰσηγητικήν sacram pertinentia, Turici 1820 ss. Comp. his essay: Tradition und Scription, in *Schulthess*, über Rationalism. und Supranaturalism. *W. L. Christmann*, über Tradition und Schrift, Logos und Kabbala, Tübingen 1825. *D. Schenkel*, über das ursprüngliche Verhältniss der Kirche zum Kanon, Basel 1838. *Sack, Nitzsch*, und *Lücke*, Ueber d. Ansehen d. heiligen Schrift und ihr Verhältniss zur Glaubensregel in der Protest. u. in der alten Kirche: drei theolog. Sendschreiben an Prof. Delbrück, Bonn 1827. *J. L. Jacobi*, Die Kirchliche Lehre von der Tradition, etc., 1 Abth. Berlin 1847. [*J. H. Friedlieb*, Schrift, Tradition, und kirchliche Auslegung (for the first five centuries), Bresl. 1854. *Kuhn*, Die Tradition (early testimonies), in Theol. Quartalschrift, 1848. *Daniel*, Theolog. Controversen. *William Goode*, Divine Rule, 3 vols. *Palmer* on the Church, vol. ii. p. 11–93. *E. B. Pusey*, Rule of Faith. *Perrone*, Protest. and Rule of Faith, 3 vols., Rome 1853; in French, 1854. *Wiseman* (Cardinal), in his Essays, ii. p. 108 sq.] *J. L. Holtzmann*, Kanon und Tradition, ein Beitrag zur neuern Dogmengeschichte u. Symbolik, Ludwigsburg 1859.

The original living source of the knowledge of all Christian truth was the Spirit of Christ Himself, who, according to His promise, guided the apostles and the first heralds of Christianity into all truth. The Catholic Church, therefore, considered herself from the first as possessing this spirit; and consequently, that the guardianship of the true tradition, and the development of the doctrine which it contained, were committed to her (1). A work which only the first Church could perform, was to preserve the oral tradition, and to collect the written apostolical documents into the canon of Scripture. It was not until this canon was nearly completed that the tradition of the Church, both oral and written, came to be considered, along with the sacred canon, as a distinct stream from the one original source (2).

(1) The doctrine concerning the Scripture and tradition can, then, be fully understood only when taken in connection with the dogma concerning the Church (§ 71).

(2) On this account it is not correct to represent Scripture

and tradition as two sources flowing alongside of each other. On the contrary, *both* flow from one *common* source, and separate only after some time. The same term κανών (regula scil. fidei) was first applied to both. For its usage, comp. *Suicer* (Thesaurus Ecclesiast. sub voce) and *H. Planck*, Nonnulla de Significatu Canonis in Ecclesia Antiqua ejusque Serie recte constituenda, Gött. 1820. *Nitzsch*, System der Christlichen Lehre, § 40, 41. [*Lardner*, Works, v. p. 257.] Thus the word παράδοσις (traditio) originally comprehended the whole tradition of the doctrine of salvation, without distinguishing between the oral and the written, cf. *Baur*, Dg. s. 363 ff.

According to the Montanist view, there are various historical stages or periods of divine revelation, viz.:—1. *The law and the prophets;* the period of primitive revelation, which extends to the manifestation of Christ, and corresponds to the duritia cordis. 2. *The period of the Christian revelation,* ending with the person of Christ, and in the circle of the apostles, and corresponding to the infirmitas carnis. 3. *The period of the revelation of the Paraclete,* which completes the remainder of history, and corresponding to the sanctitas spiritualis. Comp. *Tertull.* De Monogam. 14; *Schwegler,* Montanismus, s. 37. (This, however, refers primarily to the moral, and not to the doctrinal.)

§ 31.

Canon of the Sacred Scriptures.

Dillmann, über die Bildung der Sammlung der heiligen Schriften A. T. (Jahrb. für deutsche Theol. 1858, 3 vols.).

[*Cosin,* Scholastic History of the Canon, 4to, Lond. 1657, 72. *Du Pin,* History of the Canon and Writers of the Books of the Old and New Test., 2 vols. fol. Lond. 1699–1700. *Schmid,* Historia Antiq. et Vindicatio Canonis V. et N. T., Lips. 1775. *Jones,* New and Full Method of settling the Canonic. Authority of the N. T., 3 vols. *Alexander,* Canon of the O. and N. T. ascertained, Philad. 1828. **N. Lardner,* Credibility of the Gospel History (Works, i. to iv., and v. to p. 251). *J. Kirchhofer,* Quellensammlung zur Geschichte des neutestamentlichen Kanons bis auf Hieronymus, Zür. 1844, 2 vols. *Hilgenfeld,* der Canon und die Kritik des N. T. in ihrer geschichtlichen Ausbildung u. Gestaltung, Halle 1863. (*Weiss,* Stud. u. Kritik. 1864, 1.) *Hilgenfeld,* Histor. Krit. Einleit. in das N. T., Leipz. 1875.]

[*F. C. Baur* on the primitive sense of Canon (not having the force of law, but writings definitely set apart), in Zeitschrift f. wiss. Theol. 1858. *W. J.*

[Thiersch, Die Kirche im apost. Zeitalter, und die Entstehung der N. T. Schriften, 1852. *Oehler*, art. Kanon. in *Herzog's* Realencykl. B. F. *Westcott*, Hist. of Canon of N. T., Lond. 1845 ; new ed. 1870, 74 ; also in *Smith's* Bible Dicty. Testimonia Ante-Nicæna pro Auctoritate S. Script., in *Routh's* Reliquiæ Sacræ, tom. v. 1848, s. 336–354. Most Anciènt Canon of N. T., *R. Creswell* in Theol. Critic, Sept. 1852. *Credner*, Die ältesten Verzeichnisse der heil. Schriften, in Theol. Jahrb. 1857. *Jan. Van Gilse*, Disp. de antiquis. Lib. Sacr. Nov. Test. Catalog., Amstelod. 1852. *P. Bötticher*, Versuch einer Herstellung des Canon Muratorianus, in Zeitschrift f. d. luth. Theol. 1854. *C. Credner*, Gesch. d. N. T. Canon, ed. Volkmar, Berlin 1860.]

Before the formation of the Canon of the New Testament, that of the Old Testament (1), long since closed, was held in high esteem in the Catholic Church. The Gnostics, however, and among them the Marcionites in particular, rejected the Old Testament (2). Gradually the Christian Church felt the need of having the writings of the apostles and evangelists in a collective form. These writings owed their origin to different causes. The apostolical Epistles were primarily intended to meet the exigencies of the times; the narratives of the so-called evangelists·(3) had likewise been composed with a view to supply present wants, but also with reference to posterity. These testimonies of primitive and apostolical Christianity, in a collected form, would serve as an authoritative standard, and form a barrier against the introduction of all that was either of a heterogeneous nature, or of a more recent date, which was trying to press into the Church (apocryphal and heretical). *The Canon of the New Testament*, however, was only gradually formed, and closed. In the course of the second century the four Gospels were received by the Church in the form in which we now have them (4), with a definite exclusion of the Gospels favoured by the heretics (5). In addition, at the close of our present period, besides the Acts of the Apostles by Luke, there were also recognised thirteen Epistles of Paul, the Epistle to the Hebrews, which, however, only a part of the Church considered to be a work of Paul (6), together with the first Epistle of John and the first Epistle of Peter. With regard to the second and third Epistles of John, the Epistles of James, Jude, and the second of Peter, and, lastly, the Book of Revelation,¹ the opinions as to their authority were yet for some time divided (7). On the other hand, some other writings, which are not now considered as forming a part of the Canon, viz. the Epistles of Barnabas and Clement, and the Shepherd of Hermas, were held by some (viz. Clement and Origen) in equal esteem with the Scriptures, and quoted as such (8). The whole collection, too (so far as it was made), was already called by Tertullian, Novum Testamentum (Instrumentum); and by Origen, ἡ καινὴ διαθήκη (9).

(1) A difference of opinion obtained only in reference to the use of Greek writings of later origin (Libri Ecclesiastici, Apocrypha). The Jews themselves had already made a distinction between the Canon [?] of the Egyptian Jews and the Canon of the Jews of Palestine, comp. *Münscher*, Handbuch, Bd. i. s. 240 ff.; *Gieseler*, Dg. s. 86 ff., and the introductions to the O. T. *Melito* of Sardis (in *Euseb.* iv. 26) and *Origen* (ibid. vi. 25) give enumerations of the books of the O. T., which nearly coincide. [*Lardner*, ii. p. 158, 159, 493–513. *Stuart*, Critical Hist. and Defence of the O. T. Canon, p. 431 ff.] The difference between what was original and what had been added in later times, was less striking to those Christians who, being unacquainted with the Hebrew, used only the Greek version. Yet *Justin M.* does not quote the Apocrypha of the O. T., though he follows the Septuagint version; comp. *Semisch*, II. s. 3 ff. On the other hand, other Church writers cite even the fourth Book of Ezra, and *Origen* defends the tale about Susanna, as well as the Books of Tobit and Judith (Ep. ad Julium Africanum); although he also expressly distinguishes the Book of Wisdom from the canonical books, and assigns to it a lower authority (Prolog. in Cant.). [Comp. *Fritzsche*, Kurzgef. Comm. zu den Apocryph. des alt. Test. 1853–56. *J. H. Thornwell*, Arguments of Rome in behalf of the Apocrypha, 1845. *Volkmar*, Composition des Buchs Judith, Theol. Jahrb. 1857; and on Book of Ezra, Zürich 1858, comp. *Hilgenfeld* in Zeitschrift f. wiss. Theol. 1858. *R. A. Lipsius*, Das Buch Judith, Zeitschrift f. wiss. Theol.

¹ [But see in note 7.]

1859. *A. von Gutschmidt*, Apokalypse des Ezra, ibid. 1860. *Bleek*, Die Stellung d. Apocryphen, in Stud. u. Krit. 1853. *Bleek*, Introd. to O. T., by *Venables*, Lond. 1869.]

(2) Comp. *Neander's* Gnostiche Systeme, s. 276 ff. *Baur*, Christliche Gnosis, s. 240 ff. The Clementine Homilies also regarded many statements in the O. T. as contrary to truth, and drew attention to the contradictions which are found there, Hom. iii. 10, p. 642, and other passages. Comp. *Credner*, l.c., and *Baur*, Gnosis, s. 317 ff., 366, 367; Dg. s. 378. [*Lardner*, viii. 485-489. *Norton*, l.c. iii. p. 238.]

(3) It is well known that the words εὐαγγέλιον, εὐαγγελιστής, had a very different meaning in primitive Christianity; comp. the lexicons to the N. T., and *Suicer*, Thes. p. 1220 and 1234. *Justin M.*, however, remarks (Apol. i. c. 66) that the writings which he called ἀπομνημονεύματα of the apostles, were also called εὐαγγέλια. But it has been questioned whether we are to understand by εὐαγγέλια the four canonical Gospels; see *Schwegler*, Nachapostol. Zeitalter, s. 216 ff. (Against him, *Semisch*, Denkw. des Justin, Hamb. 1848.) Concerning these ἀπομνημ., and the earliest collections of the Gospel narratives (ὁ κύριος), the Diatessaron of Tatian, etc., comp. the Introductions to the N. T. [*Gieseler*, Ueber die Entstehung und frühesten Schicksale der Evangel. 1818. *Lardner* on the Credibility of the Gospel History. (Works, i. iv. v. to p. 251.) *Norton* on the Genuineness of the Gospels, vol. i. Supernatural Religion, new ed., London 1879, 3 vols. *Archbp. Thomson*, art. Gospels, in *Smith's* Dicty., and Pref. to Gospels in *Speaker's* Comm. *Westcott*, Introd. to Study of Gospels, Camb. 5th ed.]

(4) *Irenæus*, Adv. Haer. iii. 11. 7, attempts to explain the number four on cosmico-metaphysical grounds : Ἐπειδὴ τέσσαρα κλίματα τοῦ κοσμοῦ, ἐν ᾧ ἐσμὲν, εἰσὶ, καὶ τέσσαρα καθολικὰ πνεύματα, κατέσπαρται δὲ ἡ ἐκκλησία ἐπὶ πάσης τῆς γῆς. Στῦλος δὲ καὶ στήριγμα ἐκκλησίας τὸ εὐαγγέλιον καὶ πνεῦμα ζωῆς κ.τ.λ. *Tertull.* Adv. Marc. iv. 2. 5. *Clement* of Alex. in *Euseb.* vi. 13. *Origen* in Hom. i. in Johan., Opp. iv. p. 5. For further testimonies of antiquity, comp. the Introductions [and the works of *Lardner* in particular].

(5) *Orig.* Hom. i. in Luc. Opp. t. iii. p. 933, multi conati sunt scribere evangelia, sed non omnes recepti, etc. [The

§ 31.]   CANON OF THE SACRED SCRIPTURES.   113

principal spurious Gospels are the following: The Gospel of the Infancy of Jesus; the Gospel of Thomas the Israelite; the Protevangelion of James; the Gospel of the Nativity of Mary; the Gospel of Nicodemus, or the Acts of Pilate; the Gospel of Marcion; the Gospel of the Hebrews (most probably the same with that of the Nazarenes), and the Gospel of the Egyptians.] On these uncanonical Gospels, and on the Apocryphal Gospels of the Infancy and Passion of Christ, compare the introductions to the N. T. and the treatises of *Schneckenburger, Hahn,* etc., *Fabricius,* Codex Apocryph. N. T., 3 vols. Hamb. 1719, and *D. I. C. Thilo,* Cod. Apocr. N. T., Lipsiæ 1832. *Ullmann,* historisch oder mythisch. [*Lardner,* Works, ii. 91–93, 236, 250, 251, iv. 97, 106, 131, 463, viii. 524–535. *Norton,* l.c. iii. p. 214–286.] The Acts of the Apostles became generally known at a later period. Justin Martyr does not refer to it, nor does he cite any Pauline Epistle, though Pauline reminiscences are found in his works; see *Semisch,* s. 7 sq., and also his Apostolische Denkwürdigkeiten. On the Gospel of Marcion, see the treatises of *Franck* (Studien und Kritiken, 1855), and *Volkmar,* Das Evang. Marcions, Leipz. 1852. [*D. Harting,* Quæst. de Marcione, Trajecti ad Rhenum, 1849. *Hilgenfeld,* Untersuchungen, Halle 1850, and in Niedner's Zeitschrift, 1855. *Ritschl,* Das Evang. Marcion und die Kanon. Evang., Tübing. 1817. Marcion and his Relation to St. Luke, in Church Review, Oct. 1856. Cf. Sup. Religion, and *Dr. Lightfoot's* arts. in Contemporary Review, with Concessions in new ed. of S. R. 1879. *Rud. Hofmann,* Das Leben Jesu nach den Apokryphen, Leipz. 1851. Evangelia Apocrypha, ed. *C. Tischendorf,* Lips. 1853; comp. *Ellicott* in Cambridge Essays, 1856. *Giles,* The Uncanonical Gospels, etc., collected, 2 vols. Lond. 1853. *C. Tischendorf,* Nov. Test. Apoc. 1851–63; translated in Ante-Nicene Liby.]

(6) Comp. *Bleek's* Einleitung zum Briefe an die Hebräer, Berlin 1828. *De Wette,* Einleitung ins N. T. ii. s. 247. [*Stuart's* Comment. on the Epistle to the Heb., 2 vols. Lond. 1828. *Delitzsch,* Comment. on Hebrews, Leipz., and (in Eng.) Edinb. Articles in *Smith, Herzog,* and *Kitto.*]

(7) The Canon of *Origen* in *Euseb.* vi. 25. [*Lardner,* ii. 493–513.] The controversy on the Book of Revelation was connected with the controversy on millenarianism. [*Hilgen-*

feld (Einl. ins N. T. s. 407) says the Apoc. was universally acknowledged as St. John's in the first two centuries.] Comp. *Lücke*, Versuch einer vollständigen Einleitung in die Offenbarung Johannis, und die gesammte apokryphische Literatur, Bonn 1832, s. 261 ff., and 2d ed. [Introd. to Apoc. in *Alford's* Comm. *Stuart*, Comment. on the Apocalypse, i. p. 290 ff. *A. Hilgenfeld*, Die jüdische Apokalyptik in ihrer gesch. Entwicklung, Jena 1857.]

(8) *Clem.* Strom. i. 7, p. 339; ii. 6, p. 445; ii. 7, p. 447 (ii. 15, ii. 18); iv. 17, p. 609; v. 12, p. 693; vi. 8, p. 772, 773. *Orig.* Comment. in Epist. ad Rom. Opp. iv. p. 683. (Comment. in Matt. Opp. iii. p. 644.) Hom. 88, in Num. t. ii. p. 249. Contra Celsum, i. 1, § 63, Opp. i. 378. (Comment. in Joh. t. iv. p. 153). De Princ. ii. 3, t. i. 82. *Euseb.* iii. 16. *Münscher*, Handbuch, i. s. 289. *Möhler*, Patrologie, i. s. 87. [*Lardner*, ii. 18, 247, 528; ii. p. 186, 187, 249, 303, 304, 530–532.] The (apocryphal) Book of Enoch was put by *Tertullian* on a line with Scripture; De Cultu Fem. i. 3. [On Enoch, comp. the treatises of *Dillmann* and *Ewald*, 1854; *Köstlin* in Theol. Jahrb. 1856.]

(9) *Tertullian*, Adv. Marc. iv. 1. *Origen*, De Princip. iv. 1. *Gieseler*, Dogmengesch. s. 93.

§ 32.

Inspiration and Efficacy of the Scriptures.

G. F. N. Sonntag, Doctrina Inspirationis ejusque Ratio, Historia et usus popularis, Heidelberg 1810. *Credner*, De Librorum N. T. Inspiratione quid statuerint Christiani ante seculum tertium medium, Jen. 1828, and his Beiträge zur Einleitung in die Bibl. Schriften, Halle 1832. *A. G. Rudelbach*, die Lehre von der Inspiration der heiligen Schrift, mit Berücksichtigung der neuesten Untersuchungen darüber von *Schleiermacher*, *Twesten*, und *Steudel*. (Zeitschrift für die gesammte lutherische Theologie und Kirche, edited by Rudelbach and Guerike, 1840, i. 1.) *W. Grimm*, Inspiration in Ersch and Gruber, Encyklop. sect. ii. Bd. xix. *Tholuck* in Herzog. [*B. F. Westcott*, Catena on Inspiration, in his Elements of Gospel Harmony, 1851, and Introd. to Gospels, 1860. *C. Wordsworth*, Insp. of Holy Script., 2d ed. 1851 (also on the Canon). *William Lee*, The Insp. of Holy Scripture, Lond. 1854; New York 1857. *A. Tholuck*, Die Inspirationslehre, in Zeitschrift f. wiss. Theol. (transl. in Journal of Sac. Lit. 1854), and in *Herzog's* Realencyklopädie. *R. Rothe*, Offenbarung, and Inspiration, in the Studien und Kritiken, 1859, 60.]

That the prophets and apostles taught as they were moved by the Divine Spirit, was the universal belief of the ancient Church, founded on the testimony of Scripture itself (1). But this living idea of inspiration was by no means confined to the written letter. The Jews, indeed, had come to believe in the verbal inspiration of their sacred writings before the Canon of the New Testament was completed, at a time when, with them, the living source of prophecy had ceased to flow. This theory of verbal inspiration may have been, in its external form, mixed up to some extent with the heathen notions concerning the μαντική (art of soothsaying) (2), but it did not spring from them. It showed itself in an adventurous form in the fable respecting the origin of the Septuagint version, which was believed even by many Christian writers (3). The teachers of the Church, however, in their opinions respecting inspiration, waver between a more and less strict view (4). Verbal inspiration is throughout referred by them more distinctly to the scriptural testimonies of the Old rather than of the New Testament (5); and yet we already find very positive testimonies as to the inspiration of the latter (6). They frequently appeal to the connection existing between the old and the new economies (7), and, tacitly, between the two parts of Scripture. *Origen* goes to the opposite extreme, and maintains that there had been no sure criterion of the inspiration of the Old Testament before the coming of Christ; that this inspiration only follows from the Christian point of view (8). All, however, insisted on the practical importance of the Scripture, its richness of divine wisdom clothed in unadorned simplicity, and its fitness to promote spiritual edification (9).

(1) 2 Tim. iii. 16 ; 2 Pet. i. 19–21.

(2) *Philo* was the first writer who transferred the ideas of the ancients concerning the μαντική (comp. *Phocylides*, v. 121; *Plutarch*, De Pythiæ Oraculis, and De Placitis Philosophorum, v. 1) to the prophets of the O. T. (De Spec. Legg. iii. ed. *Mangey*, ii. 343 ; Quis div. rerum Her., *Mangey*, i. 510, 511 ; De Præm. et Pœn. ii. 417; comp. *Gfrörer*, l.c. s. 54 ff. *Dähne*,

l.c. s. 58). *Josephus*, on the other hand, adopts the more limited view of verbal inspiration, Contra Apion, i. 7, 8. [For a full view of the opinions of Philo and Josephus, see *Lee*, Insp. Append. F.] The influence of heathenism is wholly denied by *Schwegler* (Montan. s. 101, 102 ff.); against this, *Semisch*, Justin Mart. ii. s. 19; *Baumgarten-Crusius*, comp. ii. s. 52 and 53 (with the remarks of *Hase*). At any rate, "*the Jewish and heathen notions of prophecy only gave the forms, into which flowed the Church idea of the Holy Spirit in the Scriptures.*" The idea of the μαντική was carried out in all its consequences by one section of the Christian Church, viz. the Montanists, who attached chief importance to the unconscious state of the person filled with the Spirit, comp. *Schwegler*, Montanismus, s. 99. [Brief and good statement in *Gloag*, Messianic Prophecies, Edin. 1879.] Allusions to it are also found in the writings of some Fathers, especially *Athenagoras*, Leg. c. 9. Κατ' ἔκστασιν τῶν ἐν αὑτοῖς λογισμῶν κινήσαντος αὐτοὺς τοῦ θείου πνεύματος. Comp. *Tert.* Advers. Marc. iv. c. 22. *Origen* speaks very decidedly against it; Contra Cels. vii. 4, Opp. i. p. 596.

(3) The fable given by Aristæus was repeated with more or less numerous additions and embellishments by other writers, comp. *Josephus*, Antiq. xii. c. 2. *Philo*, De Vita Mos. (*Mang.* ii. 139 ff.). *Stahl* in *Eichhorn's* Repertorium für biblische und morgenländische Literatur, i. s. 260 ff. *Eichhorn*, Einleitung ins Alte Test. § 159–338. *Rosenmüller*, Handbuch für Literatur der biblischen Kritik und Exegese, ii. s. 334 ff. *Jahn*, Einleitung ins Alte Test. § 33–67. *Bertholdt*, § 154–190. *De Wette*, i. s. 58. *Münscher*, Handbuch, i. s. 307 ff. *Gfrörer*, s. 49. *Dähne*, i. 57, ii. 1 ff. [*Davidson*, Lectures on Biblical Criticism, Edin. 1839, p. 35–44. *Selwyn*, art. Septuagint, in *Smith's* Dict. of Bible.] According to *Philo*, even the grammatical errors of the LXX. are inspired, and offer welcome material to the allegorical interpreter, *Dähne*, i. s. 58. Comp. *Justin M.* Coh. ad Græc. c. 13. *Irenæus*, iii. 11. *Clem. Alex.* Strom. i. 21, p. 410. *Clement* perceives in the Greek version of the original the hand of Providence, because it prevented the Gentiles from pleading ignorance in excuse of their sins, Strom. i. 7, p. 338.

(4) *Philo* had already taught degrees in inspiration, comp.

De Vita Mos. iii. (tom. ii. p. 161, ed. *Mangey*). The apostolical Fathers speak of inspiration in very general terms; in quoting passages from the O. T., they use indeed the phrase: λέγει τὸ πνεῦμα τὸ ἅγιον, or similar expressions, but they do not give any more definite explanation regarding the manner of this inspiration. Comp. *Clem.* of Rome in several places; *Ignat.* ad Magn. c. 8, ad Philadelph. c. 5, etc. *Sonntag*, Doctrina Inspirationis, § 16. *Justin M.* is the first author in whose writings we meet with a more definite doctrinal explanation of the process, in the locus classicus, Cohort. ad Græc. § 8 : Οὔτε γὰρ φύσει οὔτε ἀνθρωπίνη ἐννοίᾳ οὕτω μεγάλα καὶ θεῖα γινώσκειν ἀνθρώποις δυνατὸν, ἀλλὰ τῇ ἄνωθεν ἐπὶ τοὺς ἁγίους ἄνδρας τηνικαῦτα κατελθούσῃ δωρεᾷ, οἷς οὐ λόγων ἐδέησε τέχνης, οὐδὲ τοῦ ἐριστικῶς τι καὶ φιλονείκως εἰπεῖν, ἀλλὰ καθαροὺς ἑαυτοὺς τῇ τοῦ θείου πνεύματος παρασχεῖν ἐνεργείᾳ, ἵν' αὐτὸ τὸ θεῖον ἐξ οὐρανοῦ κατιὸν πλῆκτρον, ὥσπερ ὀργάνῳ κιθάρας τινὸς ἢ λύρας, τοῖς δικαίοις ἀνδράσι χρώμενον, τὴν τῶν θείων ἡμῖν καὶ οὐρανίων ἀποκαλύψῃ γνῶσιν· διὰ τοῦτο τοίνυν ὥσπερ ἐξ ἑνὸς στόματος καὶ μιᾶς γλώττης καὶ περὶ θεοῦ, καὶ περὶ κόσμου κτίσεως, καὶ περὶ πλάσεως ἀνθρώπου, καὶ περὶ ἀνθρωπίνης ψυχῆς ἀθανασίας καὶ τῆς μετὰ τὸν βίον τοῦτον μελλούσης ἔσεσθαι κρίσεως, καὶ περὶ πάντων ὧν ἀναγκαῖον ἡμῖν ἐστιν εἰδέναι, ἀκολούθως καὶ συμφώνως ἀλλήλοις ἐδίδαξαν ἡμᾶς, καὶ ταῦτα διαφόροις τόποις τε καὶ χρόνοις τὴν θείαν ἡμῖν διδασκαλίαν παρεσχηκότες. Whether Justin here maintains a pure passivity on the part of the writer, or whether the peculiar structure of the instrument, determining the tone, is to be taken into consideration, see *Semisch*, s. 18, who identifies the view of Justin and that of the Montanists; *Schwegler*, Montanism. s. 101; and *Neander*, Dogmengesch. s. 99. ["*Justin transfers the Platonic relation of the* Νοῦς *to the* νοερόν *in man, to the relation of the* λόγος *to the* σπέρμα λογικόν, *the human reason allied to the divine.*"] From the conclusion at which Justin arrives, it is also apparent that he limits inspiration to what is religious, to what is necessary to be known in order to be saved.—The theory proposed in the third book of *Theophilus* ad Autolycum, c. 23, has a more external character; he ascribes the correctness of the Mosaic chronology, and subjects of a similar nature, to divine inspiration [lib. iii. c. 23: ἐπὶ τὴν ἀρχὴν τῆς τοῦ κόσμου κτίσεως, ἣν ἀνέγραψε Μωσῆς ὁ θεράπων τοῦ θεοῦ διὰ πνεύματος Ἁγίου]. Comp. also *Athenag.* Leg. c. 7, and c. 9 (where the same figure occurs; ὡσεὶ αὐλητὴς αὐλὸν ἐμπνεύσας).—The views of *Irenæus* on inspiration were equally strict and positive, Advers. Hæret. ii. 28 : Scripturæ quidem perfectæ sunt quippe a verbo Dei et Spiritu ejus dictæ, and other passages contained in the third book. *Tertullian,* De Præscript. Hæret. 8, 9; Advers. Marc. iii. 6; De Anima, c. 3 ; Apol. c. 18 (comp. however, § 34).—*Clem. Alex.* calls the Sacred Scriptures in different places γραφὰς θεοπνεύστας, or quotes τὸ γὰρ στόμα κυρίου, τὸ ἅγιον πνεῦμα ἐλάλησε ταῦτα, etc. Coh. ad Gr. p. 66, 86 ; ibid. p. 67, he quotes Jeremiah, and then corrects himself in these words : μᾶλλον δὲ ἐν Ἱερεμίᾳ τὸ ἅγιον πνεῦμα, etc., and likewise Pæd. i. 7, p. 134 : Ὁ νόμος διὰ Μωσέως ἐδόθη, οὐχὶ ὑπὸ Μωσέως, ἀλλὰ ὑπὸ μὲν τοῦ λόγου, διὰ Μωσέως δὲ τοῦ θεράποντος αὐτοῦ. [*Clement,* Pæd. lib. i. § 6 : Διὰ τοῦτο ἄρα μυστικῶς τὸ ἐν τῷ Ἀποστόλῳ Ἅγιον πνεῦμα, τῇ τοῦ Κυρίου ἀτοχρώμενον φωνῇ, Γάλα ὑμᾶς ἐπότισα (1 Cor. iii. 2), λέγει.] On the infallibility of the inspired writings, see Strom. ii. p. 432, vii. 16, p. 897. *Cyprian* calls all the books of the Bible divinæ plenitudinis fontes (Advers. Jud. præf. p. 18), and uses in his quotations the same phraseology which *Clement* employs, De Unit. Eccles. p. 111, De Opere et Eleem. p. 201. [De Op. et Eleem. : "Loquitur in Script. Divinis Spiritus Sanctus ;" "Item beatus Apostolus Paulus dominicæ inspirationis gratia plenus." De Unit. Eccl. : "Per Apostolum præmonet Spiritus Sanctus et dicit (1 Cor. xi. 19) : Oportet et hæreses esse."]

(5) Thus *Justin Mart.* speaks only of the inspiration of the O. T. with emphatic interest, although he undoubtedly carried over the idea of inspiration to the N. T., see *Semisch,* ii. s. 12. That he held the evangelists to be inspired, see ibid. s. 22 (against *Credner*). Comp. *Jacobi,* ubi supra, s. 57 ff.

(6) The doctrine of inspiration, as set forth in the N. T. writings, stood in close connection with the doctrine of the Holy Spirit and His operations. But they did not think so much of the apostles as *writers,* as of the power which was communicated to them to *teach* and to perform miracles. It was only by degrees, and after the writings of the N. T.

had also been collected into one codex (see § 31, 9), that they transferred to the N. T. the idea of inspiration which had been connected with the O. T. *Tertullian* first makes mention of this Codex as *Novum Instrumentum*, or (quod magis usui dicere) *Novum Testamentum*, adv. Marc. iv. 1; and he lays so much stress upon the reception of the entire codex as a criterion of orthodoxy, that he denies the Holy Spirit to all who do not receive Luke's Acts of the Apostles as canonical (De Præscr. Hær. 22). The general terms in which *Justin Martyr* speaks of the divine inspiration and miraculous power of the apostles, as in Apol. i. c. 39, and of the spiritual gifts of Christians, Dial. cum Tryph. § 88; and the more general, in which he describes the inspiration of the old poets and philosophers (cited in *Sonntag*, s. 6, 9),—belong to this subject only in a wide sense. *Tertullian*, however (from his Montanistic standpoint ?), draws a distinction between the two kinds of inspiration, viz. the apostolical, and that which is common to all believers (De Exhort. Castit. c. 4), and represents the latter as only partial; but he does not refer the former kind of inspiration to the mere act of writing. According to *Baur's* suggestion (Dg. s. 387), it was Tertullian who first introduced the word "Inspiratio" into theological language. But in the writings of *Irenæus* we find a more definite allusion to *the extraordinary assistance of the Holy Spirit in writing the books*, with a special reference *to the New Testament writers;* Adv. Hær. iii. 16, § 2 : Potuerat dicere Matthæus : *Jesu* vero generatio sic erat; sed prævidens Spiritus Sanctus depravatores, et præmuniens contra fraudulentiam eorum per Matthæum ait: *Christi* autem generatio sic erat. [Comp. *Westcott* on Gospels, 1860, p. 383 ff.]

(7) *Iren.* Adv. Hær. iv. 9, p. 237 : Non alterum quidem vetera, alterum vero proferentem nova docuit, sed unum et eundem. Paterfamilias enim Dominus est, qui universæ domui paternæ dominatur, et servis quidem et adhuc indisciplinatis condignam tradens legem; liberis autem et fide justificatis congruentia dans præcepta, et filiis adaperiens suam hæreditatem. . . . Ea autem, quæ de thesauro proferuntur nova et vetera, sine contradictione duo Testamenta dicit: vetus quidem, quod ante fuerat, legislatio; novum autem, quæ secundum Evangelium est conversatio, ostendit, de qua David

ait: *Cantate Domino canticum novum*, etc. Comp. iii. 11, and other passages. In his fragments (p. 346, *Massuet*), he compares the two pillars of the house under the ruins of which Samson buried himself and the Philistines, to the two Testaments which overthrew paganism. Yet still Irenæus had an open eye for the human side of the Bible. He wrote an essay upon the peculiarities of the style of Paul, in which, among other things, he explains the syntactic defects in the sentences of the apostle by the *velocitas sermonum suorum*, which again he connects with the "impetus" of his mind. Comp. *Neander*, Kirchg. (3d ed.) s. 171. *Clem. Alex.* Pæd. p. 307: Ἄμφω δὲ τὼ νόμω διηκόνουν τῷ λόγῳ εἰς παιδαγωγίαν τῆς ἀνθρωπότητος, ὁ μὲν διὰ Μωσέως, ὁ δὲ δι' Ἀποστόλων. Comp. Strom. i. 5, p. 331, iii. 10, p. 543. *Tertullian* also testifies of the Church: Legem et prophetas cum evangelicis et apostolicis litteris miscet et inde potat fidem. De Præscrip. 36.

(8) *Orig.* De Princip. iv. c. 6, Opp. i. p. 161: Δεκτέον δὲ, ὅτι τὸ τῶν προφητικῶν λόγων ἔνθεον καὶ τὸ πνευματικὸν τοῦ Μωσέως νόμου ἔλαμψεν ἐπιδημήσαντος Ἰησοῦ. Ἐναργῆ γὰρ παραδείγματα περὶ τοῦ θεοπνεύστους εἶναι τὰς παλαιὰς γραφὰς πρὸ τῆς ἐπιδημίας τοῦ Χριστοῦ παραστῆσαι οὐ πάνυ δυνατὸν ἦν, ἀλλ' ἡ Ἰησοῦ ἐπιδημία δυναμένους ὑποπτεύεσθαι τὸν νόμον καὶ τοὺς προφήτας ὡς οὐ θεῖα, εἰς τοὐμφανὲς ἤγαγεν, ὡς οὐρανίῳ χάριτι ἀναγεγραμμένα. From this point of view *Origen* acknowledges the inspiration of both the Old and the New Testaments, De Princip. procem. c. 8, Opp. i. p. 18, lib. iv. ab init.; Contra Cels. v. 60, Opp. i. p. 623; Hom. in Jerem. Opp. t. iii. p. 282: Sacra volumina spiritus plenitudinem spirant, nihilque est sive in lege, sive in evangelio, sive in apostolo, quod non a plenitudine divinæ majestatis descendat. In the 27th Hom. in Num. Opp. t. ii. p. 365, he further maintains that (because of this inspiration) nothing superfluous could have found its way into the Sacred Scriptures, and that we must seek for divine illumination when we meet with difficulties. Comp. Hom. in Exod. i. 4, Opp. t. ii. p. 131: Ego credens verbis Domini mei Jesu Christi, in lege et Prophetis iota quidem unum aut apicem non puto esse mysteriis vacuum, nec puto aliquid horum transire posse, donec omnia fiant. Philocalia (Cantabrig. 1658), p. 19: Πρέπει δὲ τὰ ἅγια γράμματα πιστεύειν μηδεμίαν κεραίαν ἔχειν κενὴν σοφίας Θεοῦ·

ὁ γὰρ ἐντειλάμενος ἐμοὶ τῷ ἀνθρώπῳ καὶ λέγων· Οὐκ ὀφθήσῃ ἐνώπιόν μου κενός (Ex. xxxiv. 20), πολλῷ πλέον αὐτὸς οὐδὲν κενὸν ἐρεῖ. Comp. *Schnitzer*, s. 286. But yet the historical and chronological difficulties attending the attempt to harmonize the Gospels did not escape the critical sagacity of *Origen*. He acknowledges that, taken verbally, there are insoluble contradictions in the narratives of the evangelists (comp. Hom. x. in Joh. Opp. tom. iv. p. 162 ss.), but comforts himself with the idea that truth does not consist in the σωματικοῖς χαρακτῆρσιν. Thus, for example, he notices the difference in the accounts of the healing of the blind men (Matt. xx. 30 ff.; Mark x. 46 ff.; Luke xviii. 35 ff.). But in order not to concede inexactitude, he takes refuge in strange allegories (comp. Comm. in Matth. Opp. tom. iii. p. 372). Another way of escape in respect to doctrinal difficulties was open to him, in the assumption of a condescension of God, training His people, as a teacher, in conformity with their state of culture at each period (Contra Celsum, iv. 71, tom. i. p. 556). Like Irenæus, *Origen* also grants that there are inaccuracies and solecisms in the style of the biblical writers (Opp. iv. p. 93), and so, too, different styles of writing in Paul (Ep. ad Rom. x. Opp. iv. p. 678 *b*). "*In general*," says *Gieseler* (Dogmengesch. s. 98), "*Origen appears to understand by inspiration, not the pouring in of foreign thoughts, but an exaltation of the powers of the soul, whereby prophets [and apostles] were elevated to the knowledge of the truth; and this view was held fast in the school of Origen.*" Comp. also the passages there cited, from which it appears that Origen, with all his exaggerated views of inspiration, also admitted that there were uninspired passages in the Scripture, or at least that there were degrees of inspiration, and thus distinguished between its divine and human elements. [The passages are such as 1 Cor. vii. 6, 10, etc. And *Gieseler* adds, that Origen "*did not follow out such hints any farther, but in other passages declared all the Holy Scriptures, including the writings of the apostles, to be unconditionally inspired.*"] Cf. *Baur*, Dg. s. 388.

(9) *Irenæus* compares the Sacred Scriptures to the treasure which was hid in a field, Adv. Hær. iv. 25, 26, and recommends their perusal also to the laity, but under the direction of the presbyters, iv. 32. *Clem. Alex.* describes their simplicity,

and the beneficial effects which they are calculated to produce, Coh. p. 66: Γραφαὶ δὲ αἱ θεῖαι καὶ πολιτεῖαι σώφρονες, σύντομοι σωτηρίας ὁδοὶ, γυμναὶ κομμωτικῆς καὶ τῆς ἐκτὸς καλλιφωνίας καὶ στωμυλίας καὶ κολακείας ὑπάρχουσαι ἀνιστῶσιν ἀγχόμενον ὑπὸ κακίας τὸν ἄνθρωπον, ὑπεριδοῦσαι τὸν ὄλισθον τὸν βιωτικὸν, μιᾷ καὶ τῇ αὐτῇ φωνῇ πολλὰ θεραπεύουσαι, ἀποτρέπουσαι μὲν ἡμᾶς τῆς ἐπιζημίου ἀπάτης, προτρέπουσαι δὲ ἐμφανῶς εἰς προὖπτον σωτηρίαν. Comp. ibid. p. 71: Ἱερὰ γὰρ ὡς ἀληθῶς τὰ ἱεραποιοῦντα καὶ θεοποιοῦντα γράμματα κ.τ.λ. Clement did not confine this sanctifying power to the mere letter of Scripture, but thought that the λογικοὶ νόμοι had been written, not only ἐν πλαξὶ λιθίναις, ἀλλ' ἐν καρδίαις ἀνθρώπων (Pæd. iii. p. 307); so that at least the effects produced by the Bible depend upon the susceptibility of the mind. The language of *Origen* is similar, Contra Cels. vi. 2, p. 630: Φησὶ δ' ὁ θεῖος λόγος, οὐκ αὔταρκες εἶναι τὸ λεγόμενον (κἂν καθ' αὑτὸ ἀληθὲς καὶ πιστικώτατον ᾖ) πρὸς τὸ καθικέσθαι ἀνθρωπίνης ψυχῆς, ἐὰν μὴ καὶ δύναμίς τις θεόθεν δοθῇ τῷ λέγοντι, καὶ χάρις ἐπανθήσῃ τοῖς λεγομένοις, καὶ αὕτη οὐκ ἀθεεὶ ἐγγινομένη τοῖς ἀνυσίμως λέγουσι. De Princip. iv. 6: ὁ δὲ μετ' ἐπιμελείας καὶ προσοχῆς ἐντυγχάνων τοῖς προφητικοῖς λόγοις, παθὼν ἐξ αὐτοῦ τοῦ ἀναγινώσκειν ἴχνος ἐνθουσιασμοῦ δι' ὧν πάσχει, πεισθήσεται, οὐκ ἀνθρώπων εἶναι συγγράμματα τοὺς πεπιστευμένους θεοῦ λόγους; so that we hear already of the testimonium Spiritus Sancti. Accordingly, the use of the Scripture was universally recommended by the old Christian teachers, and the apologists call upon the heathen to convince themselves out of the Scriptures of the truth of what was told to them. Comp. *Gieseler*, Dogmengesch. s. 105 ff. [On the General Use of the Bible: *Justin*, in his Coh. ad Græc., calls upon the heathen to read the prophetic Scriptures. *Athenagoras*, in his Apology, assumes that the emperors Marcus Aurelius and his son have the Old Testament. All the Scriptures were read in the public services of Christians: *Tertull.* Apol. c. 39. *Origen* against Celsus (vii.) defends the Bible from the charge that it was written in a common style, by the statement that it was written for the common man. Comp. *C. W. F. Walch*, Kritische Untersuchung vom Gebrauch der heiligen Schrift unter den Christen in den vier ersten Jahrh., Leipz. 1779.]

§ 33.

Biblical Interpretation.

Olshausen, über tiefern Schriftsinn, Königsberg 1824. *Rosenmüller,* Historia Interpretat. N. T. t. iii. *J. A. Ernesti,* De Origene Interpretationis grammaticæ Auctore, Opusc. Crit. Lugd. 1764, p. 283 ss. *Hagenbach,* Observat. circa Origenis methodum interpretandæ S. S., Bas. 1823, cf. the review by *Hirzel* in *Winer's* Krit. Journal, 1825, Bd. iii. *Thomasius,* Origenes, Appendix I. [*S. Davidson,* Sacred Hermeneutics, developed and applied; including a Hist. of Biblical Interpretation from the earliest of the Fathers to the Reform., Edinb. 1843. Comp. also *Fairbairn's* Hermeneutics, 1858. *Frankel,* Einfluss der palestin. Exegese auf d. Alexandr. Hermeneutik, Leipz. 1851.]

The tendency to allegorical interpretation (1) was connected in a twofold manner with the theory of verbal inspiration. Some writers endeavoured to *bring* as much as possible *into* the letter of the sacred writings, either on mystical and speculative, or on practical religious grounds; others, from a rationalistic and apologetical tendency, were anxious to *explain away* all that might lead to conclusions alike offensive to human reason and unworthy of the Deity, if taken in their literal sense. This may be best seen in the works of *Origen,* who, after the example of Philo (2), and of several of the Fathers, especially of Clement (3), first set forth a definite system of interpretation, which allowed a threefold sense to Scripture; and, accordingly, they distinguished the anagogical and the allegorical interpretation from the grammatical (4). The sober method of *Irenæus,* who defers to God all in the Scripture that is above human understanding (5), is in striking contrast with this allegorizing tendency, which makes everything out of the Scriptures.

(1) " *With their high opinion of the inspiration of the sacred writings, and the dignity of a revelation, we should expect, as a matter of course, to meet with careful interpretation, diligently investigating the exact meaning. But the very opposite was the fact. Inspiration is done away with by the most arbi-*

trary of all modes of interpretation, the allegorical, of which we may consider Philo the master." (*Gfrörer,* Geschichte des Urchristenthums, i. s. 69, in reference to Philo.) However much this may surprise us at first sight, we shall find that the connection between this theory of inspiration and the mode of interpretation which accompanies it, is by no means unnatural; both have one common source, viz. the assumption that there is a very great difference between the Bible and other books. That which has come down from heaven must be interpreted according to its heavenly origin; must be looked upon with other eyes, and touched with other than profane hands. Comp. *Dähne* on Philo, s. 60. Here it is with the Word as it was afterwards with the Sacraments. As baptismal water was thought to avail more than common water, and the bread used in the Lord's Supper to be different from common bread, so the letter of the Bible, filled with the Divine Spirit, became to the uninitiated a hieroglyph, to decipher which a heavenly key was needed.

(2) Comp. *Gfrörer, Dähne,* l.c., and *J. J. Conybeare:* The Bampton Lecture for the year 1824, being an attempt to trace the history and to ascertain the limits of the secondary and spiritual interpret. of Script., Oxf. 1824. (German in *Tholuck's* Anzeiger, 1831–44.)

(3) Examples of allegorical and typical interpretation abound in the writings of the apostolical and earlier Fathers, see § 29, note 3. [Comp. *Davidson*, Sacred Hermen. p. 71 ff. *Barnabas*, l. 7 : The two goats (Lev. xvi.) were to be fair and perfectly alike; both, therefore, typified the one Jesus, who was to suffer for us. The circumstance of one being driven forth into the wilderness, the congregation spitting upon it and pricking it, whilst the other, instead of being accursed, was offered upon the altar to God, symbolized the death and sufferings of Jesus. The washing of the entrails with vinegar denoted the vinegar mixed with gall which was given to Jesus on the cross. The scarlet wool, put about the head of one of the goats, signified the scarlet robe put upon Christ before His crucifixion. The taking off the scarlet wool, and placing it on a thorn-bush, refers to the fate of Christ's Church. *Clem. Alex.* lib. v. p. 557 : "The candlestick situated south of the altar of incense signified the

movements of the seven stars making circuits southward. From each side of the candlestick projected three branches with lights in them, because the sun placed in the midst of the other planets gives light both to those above and under it by a kind of divine music. The golden candlestick has also another enigma, not only in being a figure of the sign of Christ, but also in the circumstance of giving light in many ways and parts to such as believe and hope in Him, by the instrumentality of the things at first created." Comp. also p. 74, 75, 79, 80.] For a correct estimate of this mode of interpretation, comp. *Möhler*, Patrologie, i. s. 94: "*The system of interpretation adopted by the earlier Fathers may not in many respects agree with our views; but we should remember that our mode of looking at things differs from theirs in more than one point. They knew nothing, thought of nothing, felt nothing, but Christ,—is it then surprising that they met Him everywhere, even without seeking Him? In our present state of culture we are scarcely able to form a correct idea of the mind of those times, in which the great object of commentators was to show the connection between the Old and the New Covenant in the most vivid manner.*" The earlier Fathers indulged unconsciously in this mode of interpretation; but *Clem. Alex.* attempts to establish a theory, asserting that the Mosaic laws have a threefold, or even a fourfold sense, τετραχῶς δὲ ἡμῖν ἐκληπτέον τοῦ νόμου τὴν βούλησιν. Strom. i. 28 (some read τριχῶς instead of τετραχῶς). [Comp. *Davidson*, l.c. p. 79.]

(4) *Origen* supposes that Scripture has a threefold sense corresponding to the trichotomistic division of man into body, soul, and spirit (comp. § 54); and this he finds, too (by a petitio principii), in the Scripture itself, in Prov. xxii. 20; and in the Shepherd of Hermas, which he values equally with Scripture. This threefold sense may be divided into: 1. The *grammatical* [σωματικός] = body; 2. The *moral* [ψυχικός] = soul; and 3. The *mystical* [πνευματικός] = spirit. The literal sense, however, he asserts cannot always be taken, but in certain cases it must be spiritualized by allegorical interpretation, especially in those places which contain either something indifferent in a religious aspect (genealogies, etc.), or what is repulsive to morality (*e.g.* in the history of the patriarchs), or what is unworthy of the dignity of God (the

anthropomorphitic narratives in the Book of Genesis, and several of the legal injunctions of the Old Testament). Comp. Philo's method, *Gfrörer*, u. s.; *Davidson*, p. 63. But Origen found stumbling-blocks not only in the Old, but also in the New Testament. Thus he declared that the narrative of the temptation of our Saviour was not simple history, because he could not solve the difficulties which it presents to the historical interpreter. [The Gospels also abound in expressions of this kind; as when the devil is said to have taken Jesus to a high mountain. For who could believe, if he read such things with the least degree of attention, that the kingdoms of the Persians, Scythians, Indians, and Parthians, were seen with the bodily eye, and with as great honour as kings are looked upon? *Davidson*, l.c. p. 99.] He also thought that some precepts, as Luke x. 4, Matt. v. 39, 1 Cor. vii. 18, could be taken in their literal sense only by the simple (ἀκεραίοις). He does not indeed deny the reality of most of the miracles, but he prizes much more highly the allegory which they include (comp. § 29, note 10); see, besides, the De Princip. lib. iv. § 1–27, where he gives the most complete exhibition of his theory, his exegetical works, and the above-mentioned treatises, with the passages there cited. Both tendencies above spoken of, that of *interpreting into*, and that of *explaining away*, are certainly exhibited in the writings of Origen. Therefore the remark of *Lücke* (Hermeneutik, s. 39), "*that a rationalistic tendency, of which Origen himself was not conscious,*" may account in part for his being addicted to allegorical interpretation, can be easily reconciled with the apparently contrary supposition that the cause of it was mysticism, based on the pregnant sense of Scripture. "*The letter kills, but the spirit quickens; this is the principle of Origen. But who does not see that the spirit can become too powerful, kill the letter, and take its place?*" *Edgar Quinet* on Strauss (Revue des deux Mondes, 1838).

(5) *Irenæus* also proceeded on the assumption that the Scriptures throughout were pregnant with meaning, Adv. Hær. iv. 18 : Nihil enim otiosum, nec sine signo, neque sine argumento apud eum, and made use of typical interpretation. Nevertheless, he saw the dangers of allegorizing, and condemned it in the Gnostics, Adv. Hær. i. 3. 6. We are as

little able to understand the abundance of nature as the superabundance of Scripture, ibid. ii. 28 (*Gr.* 47): Nos autem secundum quod minores sumus et novissimi a verbo Dei et Spiritu ejus, secundum hoc et scientia mysteriorum ejus indigemus. Et non est mirum, si in spiritualibus et cœlestibus et in his quæ habent revelari, hoc patimur nos: quandoquidem etiam eorum quæ ante pedes sunt (dico autem quæ sunt in hac creatura, quæ et contrectantur a nobis et videntur et sunt nobiscum) multa fugerunt nostram scientiam, et Deo hæc ipsa committimus. Oportet enim eum præ omnibus præcellere. . . . Εἰ δὲ ἐπὶ τῶν τῆς κτίσεως ἔνια μὲν ἀνάκειται τῷ θεῷ, ἔνια δὲ καὶ εἰς γνῶσιν ἐλήλυθε τὴν ἡμετέραν, τί χαλεπὸν, εἰ καὶ τῶν ἐν ταῖς γραφαῖς ζητουμένων, ὅλων τῶν γραφῶν πνευματικῶν οὐσῶν, ἔνια μὲν ἐπιλύομεν κατὰ χάριν θεοῦ, ἔνια δὲ ἀνακείσεται τῷ θεῷ, καὶ οὐ μόνον ἐν τῷ αἰῶνι ἐν τῷ νυνὶ, ἀλλὰ καὶ ἐν τῷ μέλλοντι; ἵνα ἀεὶ μὲν ὁ θεὸς διδάσκῃ, ἄνθρωπος δὲ διὰ παντὸς μανθάνῃ παρὰ θεοῦ.

§ 34.

Tradition.

Pelt, über Tradition, in the Theolog. Mitarbeiten, Kiel 1813; *K. R. Köstlin,* Zur Gesch. des Urchristenthums, in Zeller's Jahrb. 1850, 1 ff. *Jacobi,* ubi supra, s. 90 ff. Comp. § 30.

Notwithstanding the high esteem in which Scripture was held, the authority of tradition was not put in the background. On the contrary, in the controversies with heretics, Scripture was thought to be insufficient to combat them, because it maintains its true position, and can be correctly interpreted (*i.e.* according to the spirit of the Church) only in close connection with the tradition of the Church (1). Different opinions obtained concerning the nature of tradition. The view taken by Irenæus and Tertullian was of a positive, realistic kind; according to them, the truth was dependent upon an external, historical, and geographical connection with the mother Churches (2). The Alexandrian school entertained a more ideal view; they saw in the more free and spiritual exchange of ideas, the fresh and ever-living source from which we must draw the wholesome water of sound doctrine (3). It must, however, be acknowledged, that the idea of a secret doctrine (4), favoured by the Alexandrian school, which was said to have been transmitted along with the publicly received truth from the times of Christ and His apostles, betrayed a gnostic tendency, which might easily endanger the adaptation of Christianity to all classes of society. On the other hand, the new revelations of the Montanists in like manner broke loose from the basis of the historical (traditional) development (5). In contrast with these tendencies, it was insisted that tradition is to be measured by Scripture, as well in respect to doctrine as to the usage of the Church (6); this particularly appears in Cyprian.

(1) On the necessity of tradition, see *Irenæus,* i. 10 (p. 49 *M*), ii. 35, p. 171, iii. Pref. c. 1–6, c. 21, iv. 20, 26, 32. (*Orelli,* i. Program. s. 20.) Especially remarkable is the declaration, iii. 4, that the nations had been converted to Christianity, not in the first instance by the *Scriptures* (sine charta et atramento), but by means of the Holy Spirit in their hearts, and the faithfully preserved tradition. See *Tert.* Adv. Marc. iii. 6, v. 5, and particularly De Præscriptione Hæreticorum, where he denies to heretics the right of using Scripture in argument with the orthodox.[1] Comp. c. 13 seq., and c. 19 he says: Ergo non ad scripturas provocandum est, nec in his constituendum certamen, in quibus aut nulla, aut incerta victoria est, aut par (*var.* parum) incertæ. Nam etsi non ita evaderet conlatio scripturarum, ut utramque partem parem sisteret, ordo rerum desiderabat, illud prius proponi, quod nunc solum disputandum est: quibus competat fides ipsa: cujus sint scripturæ; a quo et per quos et quando et quibus sit tradita disciplina, qua fiunt Christiani. Ubi enim apparuerit esse veritatem et disciplinæ et fidei Christianæ, illic erit veritas scripturarum et expositionum et omnium traditionum Christianarum. Comp. c. 37: Qui estis? quando et unde venistis?

[1] On the expression "*Præscriptio,*" Semler in the Index Latin. s. 482: Ex usu forensi significant refutationem, qua, qui postulatur, adversarii accusationem disjicit aut in eum retorquet; and *Tertull.* himself, Præscr. c. 35.

§ 34.] TRADITION. 129

quid in meo agitis, non mei ? The renouncing of tradition is, according to *Tertullian*, the source of the mutilation and corruption of Scripture; comp. c. 22 and 38. But even in its integrity Scripture *alone* is not able to ward off heresies; on the contrary, according to God's providential arrangement, it becomes to heretics a source of new errors, comp. c. 40, 42. — *Clem. Alex.* expresses himself thus (Stromata, vii. 15, p. 887): As an honest man must not lie, so must we not depart from the rule of faith which is handed down by the Church; it is necessary to follow those who already have the truth. As the companions of Ulysses, bewitched by Circe, behaved like beasts, so he who renounces tradition ceases to be a man of God, Strom. vii. 16, p. 890, comp. p. 896.— *Origen*, De Princip. procem. i. p. 47: Servetur vero ecclesiastica prædicatio per successionis ordinem ab Apostolis tradita et usque ad præsens in ecclesiis permanens; illa sola credenda est veritas, quæ in nullo ab ecclesiastica et apostolica discordat traditione.

(2) *Iren.* iii. 4 (2, p. 178 *M*): Quid enim? Et si de aliqua modica quæstione disceptatio esset, nonne oporteret in antiquissimas recurrere ecclesias, in quibus Apostoli conversati sunt, et ab iis de præsenti quæstione sumere quod certum et re liquidum est? Quid autem, si neque Apostoli quidem scripturas reliquissent nobis, nonne oportebat ordinem sequi traditionis, quam tradiderunt iis, quibus committebant ecclesias? etc. *Tertull*. Præscr. c. 20: Dehinc (Apostoli) in orbem profecti eandem doctrinam ejusdem fidei nationibus promulgaverunt, et proinde ecclesias apud unamquamque civitatem condiderunt, a quibus, traducem fidei et semina doctrinæ ceteræ exinde ecclesiæ mutuatæ sunt et quotidie mutuantur, ut ecclesiæ fiant, et per hoc et ipsæ apostolicæ deputantur, ut soboles apostolicarum ecclesiarum. Omne genus ad originem suam censeatur necesse est. Itaque tot ac tantæ ecclesiæ: una est illa ab Apostolis prima, ex qua omnes, etc. Comp. c. 21.

(3) *Clem. Alex.* Strom. i. 1, p. 323: Τὰ φρέατα ἐξαντλούμενα διειδέστερον ὕδωρ ἀναδίδωσι· τρέπεται δὲ εἰς φθορὰν, ὧν μεταλαμβάνει οὐδείς· καὶ τὸν σίδηρον ἡ χρῆσις καθαρώτερον φυλάσσει, ἡ δὲ ἀχρηστία ἰοῦ τούτῳ γεννητική. Συνελόντι γὰρ φάναι· ἡ συγγυμνασία ἕξιν ἐμποιεῖ ὑγιεινὴν καὶ πνεύμασι καὶ σώμασιν.

(4) Ibid.: Αὐτίκα οὐ πολλοῖς ἀπεκάλυψεν (ὁ 'Ιησοῦς) ἃ μὴ πολλῶν ἦν, ὀλίγοις δὲ οἷς προσήκειν ἠπίστατο, τοῖς οἵοις τε ἐκδέξασθαι καὶ τυπωθῆναι πρὸς αὐτά· τὰ δὲ ἀπόρρητα, καθάπερ ὁ θεὸς, λόγῳ πιστεύεται, οὐ γράμματι ... ἀλλὰ γὰρ τὰ μυστήρια μυστικῶς παραδίδοται, ἵνα ᾖ ἐν στόματι λαλοῦντος καὶ ὃ λαλεῖται· μᾶλλον δὲ οὐκ ἐν φωνῇ, ἀλλ' ἐν τῷ νοεῖσθαι κ.τ.λ. Comp. *Euseb.* Hist. Eccl. ii. 1 (from the 7th book of the Hypotyposes), and the notes of *Valesius* and *Heinichen.* *Origen,* Contra Cels. vi. § 6, Opp. t. i. p. 633. The so-called Disciplina Arcani of the ancient Church must not be confounded with this view of a secret doctrine, which is peculiar to the Alexandrians, and pre-eminently to Clement; comp. *G. C. L. Th. Frommann,* De Disciplina Arcani, quæ in Vetere Ecclesia Christiana obtinuisse fertur, Jen. 1833 ; and *Rothe* in *Herzog's* Realencykl. i. s. 469, and *Gieseler,* i. 232, note.

(5) Comp. § 24, § 30, note 2. *Jacobi,* l.c. s. 125 ff. On the Gnostic tradition, see *Köstlin,* l.c. s. 6 ff.

(6) Comp. *Clem. Alex.* Strom. vi. p. 786, vii. p. 891. *Origen,* Hom. in Jerem. i. (Opp. iii. p. 129): Μάρτυρας δεῖ λαβεῖν τὰς γραφάς· ἀμάρτυροι γὰρ αἱ ἐπιβολαὶ ἡμῶν καὶ αἱ ἐξηγήσεις ἄπιστοί εἰσιν (this in relation to the doctrine of the Godhead of Christ). *Hippolytus,* Contra Noëtum, c. 9 (in relation to the doctrine respecting God).

The opinion of *Cyprian* (Ep. 74, p. 215, *Fell*) was developed in the controversy with the Roman bishop Stephen, who appealed to the Roman tradition in support of his views concerning the baptism of heretics. Cyprian, on the contrary, justly went back from the dried-up channel to the source, to the oldest tradition, viz. the Sacred Scriptures (divinæ traditionis caput et origo). In the same place, and in the same connection, he says: Consuetudo sine veritate vetustas erroris est. Comp. Ep. 71, p. 194: Non est de consuetudine præscribendum, sed ratione vincendum. It is interesting to observe that, *e.g., Irenæus* does not as yet know any traditio humana within the Church which could in any way contradict the traditio apostolica; such a tradition is known by *Irenæus* only among the heretics; and *Tertullian* (as Montanist) had already combated the authority of custom with almost the same weapons as Cyprian; comp. De Virgin. Veland. 1: Christus veritatem se, non consuetudinem cognominavit. Quodcunque adversus veritatem sapit, hoc erit hæresis, etiam vetus consuetudo, cf. *Jacobi*, l.c. s. 136 ff. *Huther*, Cyprian, s. 139 ff. *Rettberg*, s. 310. *Pelt*, l.c. *Gess*, Die Einheit der Kirche im Sinne Cyprians, in der Studien der Evangelischen Geistlichkeit, Würtemberg 1838, ii. 1, s. 140 ff. On the ambiguity of the word tradition (a doctrinal, Gnostic, and ritual tradition may be distinguished), see *Gieseler*, Dogmengesch. s. 103. [The Alexandrians claimed to have the Gnostic tradition, which was not the common property of all Christians: this was opposed by Irenæus and Tertullian. *Tertullian* advocated the authority of tradition in respect to rites, but demanded (De Jejunio, c. 10), Tanto magis dignam rationem afferre debemus, quanto carent Scripturæ auctoritate. *Cyprian*, Ep. 74, ad Pompejum, against the Roman claim, says that, ea facienda esse, quæ scripta sunt; and continues: Si ergo aut in Evangelio præcipitur, aut in Apostolorum Epistolis aut Actibus continetur, observetur divina hæc et sancta traditio. And he compares divine tradition to a canal, saying that, when it dries up, the priests must go back to the fountain and the Holy Scriptures; and this in respect to Church rites.]

It was held that *faith* ($\pi i \sigma \tau \iota \varsigma$, fides) is the medium by which we apprehend the revelation made known to us, either by Scripture or by tradition. The question, however, arose in what relation the $\pi i \sigma \tau \iota \varsigma$ stands to the more developed $\gamma \nu \hat{\omega} \sigma \iota \varsigma$? While *Irenæus* does not go beyond faith, but without excluding its scientific exposition (comp. *Duncker*, s. 16), the theologians of the Alexandrian school, *e.g. Clement*, endeavoured to assign a higher position to the $\gamma \nu \hat{\omega} \sigma \iota \varsigma$. But we should mistake him if we were to conclude from some of his expressions that he attached a low value to the $\pi i \sigma \tau \iota \varsigma$. In a certain sense he looks upon it rather as the perfection of knowledge ($\tau \epsilon \lambda \epsilon \iota \acute{o} \tau \eta \varsigma \ \mu a \theta \acute{\eta} \sigma \epsilon \omega \varsigma$), Pæd. i. 6, p. 115. Faith does not want anything, it does not limp (as arguments do); it has the promise, etc. Also, according to Strom. i. 1, p. 320, faith is necessary to attain unto knowledge. It anticipates knowledge, ii. 1, p. 432; comp. ii. 4, p. 436: $Κυριώτερον\ οὖν\ τῆς\ ἐπιστήμης\ ἡ\ πίστις\ καὶ\ ἐστὶν\ αὐτῆς\ κριτήριον.$ In the same place he distinguishes faith from mere opinion, $εἰκασία$, which is related to faith as a flatterer to a true friend, or a wolf to a dog.—Revelation ($διδασκαλία$) and faith depend on each other, as the throwing and catching of a ball in a game; Strom. ii. 6, p. 442.—On the other hand, *Clement* maintained the necessity of a *well-instructed* faith (πίστις περὶ τὴν μάθησιν), Strom. i. 6, p. 336, and insisted, in general, on an intimate connection between πίστις and γνῶσις, ii. 4, p. 436: Πιστὴ τοίνυν ἡ γνῶσις· γνωστὴ δὲ ἡ πίστις θείᾳ τινὶ ἀκολουθίᾳ τε καὶ ἀντακολουθίᾳ γίνεται. Faith is described as an abridged knowledge of necessary truth; γνῶσις is characterized as a firm and stable demonstration of the things already apprehended by faith; Strom. vii. 10, p. 865 sq. From this point of view he valued knowledge more highly than faith, Strom. vi. 14, p. 794. Πλέον δέ ἐστι τοῦ πιστεῦσαι τὸ γνῶναι. Nevertheless, he could distinguish this true gnosis from the false gnosis of the Gnostics; Strom. v. 6, p. 689, 12, p. 695, vi. 7, p. 771, vii. 10, p. 864 (here again faith appears as the basis of true knowledge). On the different names and kinds of knowledge, see Strom. vi. 17, p. 820. Comp. *Neander*, De Fidei Gnoseosque Idea secundum Clementem Alex., Heidelberg, 1811. *Baur*, Gnosis, s. 502 ff. *Origen*, De Princip. procem. 3, Opp. i. 47, concedes that the apostles, who preached to the unlettered, left the investigation of the grounds and reasons of their positions to those who should be endowed by the Holy Spirit with special gifts, particularly with eloquence, wisdom, and science: Illud autem scire oportet, quoniam Sancti Apostoli fidem Christi prædicantes de quibusdam quidem, quæcunque necessaria crediderunt, omnibus manifestissime tradiderunt, rationem scilicet assertionis eorum relinquentes ab his inquirendam, qui Spiritus dona excellentia mererentur: de aliis vero dixerunt quidem, quia sint; quomodo autem, aut unde sint, siluerunt, profecto ut studiosiores quique ex posteris suis, qui amatores essent sapientiæ, exercitium habere possent, in quo ingenii sui fructum ostenderent, hi videlicet qui dignos se et capaces ad recipiendam sapientiam præpararent. Comp. the conclusion, p. 49. *Origen* endeavoured to construct from Christian knowledge an internally complete science, a system of Christian doctrine. Comp. *Baur*, Dg. s. 235. We may, however, question Baur's statement, that, in this attempt, historical Christianity and the historical Christ became to him "*a mere vanishing point.*"

SECOND DIVISION.

THEOLOGY.

THE DOCTRINE CONCERNING GOD (INCLUDING THE DOCTRINE OF THE CREATION AND GOVERNMENT OF THE WORLD; ANGELOLOGY AND DEMONOLOGY).

§ 35.

The being of God.

It can never be the object of a positive religion to prove the existence of God, inasmuch as it always presupposes the knowledge that there is a God. Christianity stood on the basis of the Old Testament idea of God,—now purified and carried beyond the limits of national interests,—as a personal God, who, as the Creator of heaven and earth, rules over the human race: who had given the law, sent the prophets, and manifested Himself most perfectly, and in the fulness of His personal presence, in *Jesus Christ* (1). Consequently the believing Christian needed, as little as his Jewish contemporary, a proof of the being of God. But, in the further development of the Christian consciousness, it became necessary, on the one hand, that Christians should defend themselves (apologetically) against the charge of atheism which was frequently brought against them (2); on the other, they had to demonstrate to the heathen (polemically) that their pagan worship was false, and consequently in its very foundation was a denial of the living God (atheism) (3). When, therefore, the writings of the Fathers contain anything like a proof of the existence of God, it is either the immediate expression of religious feeling in a rhetorical and hymnological form (4), or it is intimately connected with other definitions respecting the nature of God, with the doctrine of His unity, or with the doctrine concerning creation, providence, and the government of the world (5). But the Fathers of this period generally recur to the consciousness of God implanted in the human spirit (testimonium animæ, λόγος σπερματικός), which may be traced even in the heathen (6), and on the purity of which the knowledge of God depends (7). With this they connect, but in a popular rather than a strictly scientific form, what is commonly called the physico-theological, or teleological proof, inferring the existence of a Creator from the works of creation (8). More artificial proofs, such as the cosmological and the ontological, were unknown in this period. Even the more profound thinkers of the Alexandrian school frankly acknowledged the impossibility of a strict proof of the existence of God, and the necessity of a revelation on God's part (9).

(1) The distinction, therefore, between *Theology* and *Christology* is only relative, and made for scientific purposes. The Christian idea of God always depends on faith in the Son, in whom the Father manifests Himself. "*The doctrine of the Logos was the stock out of which Christian theology grew: the divine nature in itself was treated only incidentally and in fragments,*" Semisch, Just. Mart. ii. s. 247. We find, however, in the writings of some of the earliest Fathers (especially Minucius Felix) a kind of theology which bears much resemblance to what was subsequently called *natural* theology, being more reflective than intuitive. Others (*e.g. Clement*) looked at everything as mediated by the Logos; Strom. v. 12, p. 696, comp. note 9 below.

(2) Comp. *e.g. Minuc. Fel.* Oct. c. 8 ; and, on the other side, c. 17, 18, also the Edict. Antonini, in *Euseb.* iv. 13 ; the phrase ὡς ἀθέων κατηγοροῦντες, however, may be differently interpreted. Comp. *Heinichen*, i. p. 328.

(3) This was done by all the apologists, each in his turn; comp. as examples of all, *Minuc. Fel.* c. 20 ss.; *Tertullian*, Apol. c. 8, De Idololatria ; *Cyprian*, De Idolorum Vanitate, etc.

(4) Thus the passage in *Clem. Alex.* Cohort. 54: Θεὸς δὲ πῶς ἂν εἴποιμι ὅσα ποιεῖ; ὅλον ἰδὲ τὸν κόσμον. Ἐκείνου ἔργον ἐστὶν καὶ οὐρανὸς καὶ ἥλιος καὶ ἄγγελοι καὶ ἄνθρωποι, ἔργα τῶν δακτύλων αὐτοῦ. Ὅση γε ἡ δύναμις τοῦ θεοῦ; Μόνον αὐτοῦ τὸ βούλημα κοσμοποιία· μόνος γὰρ ὁ θεὸς ἐποίησεν, ἐπεὶ καὶ μόνος ὄντως ἐστὶ θεός. Ψιλῷ τῷ βούλεσθαι δημιουργεῖ, καὶ τῷ μόνον ἐθελῆσαι αὐτὸν ἕπεται τὸ γεγενῆσθαι κ.τ.λ. Comp. *Tertull.* Apol. c. 17, 18.

(5) Comp. the following sections.

(6) *Tertullian,* Advers. Judæos, c. 2: Cur etenim Deus universitatis conditor, mundi totius gubernator, hominis plasmator, universarum gentium sator, legem per Moysen uni populo dedisse credatur, et non omnibus gentibus attribuisse dicatur? et seq. Comp. Apol. c. 17: Vultis ex operibus ipsius tot ac talibus quibus continemur, quibus sustinemur, quibus oblectamur, etiam quibus exterremur? vultis ex animæ ipsius testimonio comprobemus? Quæ licet carcere corporis pressa, licet institutionibus pravis circumscripta, licet libidinibus ac concupiscentiis evigorata, licet falsis deis exancillata, cum tamen resipiscit ut ex crapula, ut ex somno, ut ex aliqua valetudine, et sanitatem suam potitur, Deum nominat, hoc solo nomine, quia proprio Dei veri: Deus magnus, Deus bonus, et: quod Deus dederit, omnium vox est. Judicem quoque contestatur illum: Deus videt, et: Deo commendo, et: Deus mihi reddet. O testimonium animæ naturaliter christianæ! Denique pronuntians hæc, non ad capitolium, sed ad cœlum respicit, novit enim sedem Dei vivi.—De Testim. Animæ, c. 2: Si enim anima aut divina aut a Deo data est, sine dubio datorem suum novit. Et si novit, utique et timet, et tantum postremo adauctorem. An non timet, quem magis propitium velit quam iratum? Unde igitur naturalis timor animæ in Deum, si Deus non vult irasci? Quomodo timetur qui nescit offendi? Quid timetur nisi ira? Unde ira nisi ex animadversione? Unde animadversio nisi de judicio? Unde judicium nisi de potestate? Cujus potestas summa nisi Dei solius? Hinc ergo tibi, anima, de conscientia suppetit domi ac foris, nullo irridente vel prohibente, prædicare: Deus videt omnia, et: Deo commendo, et: Deus reddet, et: Deus inter nos judicabit, et seq. Comp. *Neander,* Antignost. s. 88, 89. *Justin M.* also speaks of an innate idea of God, Apol. ii. 6: Τὸ θεὸς

προσαγόρευμα οὐκ ὄνομά ἐστιν, ἀλλὰ πράγματος δυσεξηγήτου ἔμφυτος τῇ φύσει τῶν ἀνθρώπων δόξα. Comp. Dial. c. Tr. c. 93.—*Clem. Alex.* Coh. vi. 59: Πᾶσιν γὰρ ἁπαξαπλῶς ἀνθρώποις, μάλιστα δὲ τοῖς περὶ λόγους ἐνδιατρίβουσιν (qui in studiis literarum versati sunt) ἐνέστακταί τις ἀπόρροια θεϊκή. Οὗ δὴ χάριν καὶ ἄκοντες μὲν ὁμολογοῦσιν ἕνα τε εἶναι θεὸν, ἀνώλεθρον καὶ ἀγέννητον· τοῦτον ἄνω που περὶ τὰ νῶτα τοῦ οὐρανοῦ ἐν τῇ ἰδίᾳ καὶ οἰκείᾳ περιωπῇ ὄντως ὄντα ἀεί. Comp. Strom. v. 12, p. 698: Θεοῦ μὲν γὰρ ἔμφασις ἑνὸς ἦν τοῦ παντοκράτορος παρὰ πᾶσι τοῖς εὐφρονοῦσι πάντοτε φυσική· καὶ τῆς ἀϊδίου κατὰ τὴν θείαν πρόνοιαν εὐεργεσίας ἀντελαμβάνοντο οἱ πλεῖστοι, οἱ καὶ μὴ τέλεον ἀπηρυθριακότες πρὸς τὴν ἀλήθειαν.

(7) *Theophilus* ad Autolycum, at the beginning: "If thou sayest, Show me thy God; I answer, Show me first thy man, and I will show thee my God. Show me first whether the eyes of thy soul see and the ears of thy heart hear; for as the eyes of the body perceive earthly things, light and darkness, white and black, beauty and deformity, etc., so the ears of the heart and the eyes of the soul can perceive God. God is seen by those who can see Him when they open the eyes of their soul. All men have eyes, but the eyes of some are blinded, that they cannot see the light of the sun. But the sun does not cease to shine because they are blind, they must ascribe it to their blindness that they cannot see. Thus is it with thee, O man! The eyes of thy soul are darkened by sin, even by thy sinful actions. Like a bright mirror, man must have a pure soul. If there be any rust on the mirror, man cannot see the reflection of his countenance in it: likewise, if there be sin in man, he cannot see God. Therefore, first examine thyself whether thou be not an adulterer, fornicator, thief, robber, etc., for thy crimes prevent thee from perceiving God." Comp. *Clem. Alex.* Pæd. iii. 1, p. 250: Ἑαυτὸν γάρ τις ἐὰν γνώῃ, Θεὸν εἴσεται. *Minuc. Fel.* c. 32: Ubique non tantum nobis proximus, sed infusus est (Deus). Non tantum sub illo agimus, sed et cum illo, prope dixerim vivimus.

(8) *Theophil.* ad Autol. 5: "When we see a well-appointed vessel on the sea, we conclude that she has a pilot on board; so, too, from the regular course of the planets, the rich variety of creatures, we infer the Creator." *Clem. Alex.* (comp. note 4).

Minuc. Fel. c. 32 : Immo ex hoc Deum credimus, quod eum sentire possumus, videre non possumus. In operibus enim ejus et in mundi omnibus motibus virtutem ejus sémper præsentem adspicimus, quum tonat, fulgurat, fulminat, quum serenat, etc. Comp. c. 18 : Quod si ingressus aliquam domum omnia exculta, disposita, ornata vidisses, utique præesse ei crederes dominum, et illis bonis rebus multo esse meliorem : ita in hac mundi domo, quum cœlum terramque perspicias, providentiam, ordinem, legem, crede esse universitatis dominum parentemque, ipsis sideribus et totius mundi partibus pulchriorem. *Novat.* ab init. Similarly also the *pseudo-Clementines*, Hom. vi. 24, 25. After the author has shown how the elements cannot have come together of themselves, he proceeds : Οὕτως ἀνάγκη, τινὰ εἶναι νοεῖν ἀγέννητον τεχνίτην, ὃς τὰ στοιχεῖα ἢ διεστῶτα συνήγαγεν, ἢ συνόντα ἀλλήλοις πρὸς ζῴου γένεσιν τεχνικῶς ἐκέρασεν καὶ ἓν ἐκ πάντων ἔργον ἀπετέλεσεν. Ἀδύνατον γὰρ ἄνευ τινὸς τοῦ μείζονος πάνυ σοφὸν ἔργον ἀπετέλεσεν. Ἀδύνατον γὰρ ἄνευ τινὸς τοῦ μείζονος πάνυ σοφὸν ἔργον ἀποτελεῖσθαι. God is the principle of all motion. Water, out of which everything rises, is moved by the wind (breath, spirit, πνεῦμα), but this spirit itself again proceeds from God. Comp. *Baur*, Dg. s. 400.

(9) *Clem. Alex.* Strom. v. 12, p. 695 : Ναὶ μὴν ὁ δυσμεταχειριστότατος περὶ Θεοῦ λόγος οὗτός ἐστιν· ἐπεὶ γὰρ ἀρχὴ παντὸς πράγματος δυσεύρετος, πάντως που ἡ πρώτη καὶ πρεσβυτάτη ἀρχὴ δύσδεικτος, ἥτις καὶ τοῖς ἄλλοις ἅπασιν αἰτία τοῦ γενέσθαι κ.τ.λ. Ib. in calce et 696 : Ἀλλ᾽ οὐδὲ ἐπιστήμη λαμβάνεται τῇ ἀποδεικτικῇ· αὕτη γὰρ ἐκ προτέρων καὶ γνωριμωτέρων συνίσταται· τοῦ δὲ ἀγεννήτου οὐδὲν προϋπάρχει· λείπεται δὴ θείᾳ χάριτι καὶ μόνῳ τῷ παρ᾽ αὐτοῦ λόγῳ τὸ ἄγνωστον νοεῖν. Strom. iv. 25, p. 635 : Ὁ μὲν οὖν Θεὸς ἀναπόδεικτος ὤν, οὐκ ἔστιν ἐπιστημονικός· ὁ δὲ υἱὸς σοφία τε ἐστὶ καὶ ἐπιστήμη κ.τ.λ. (Comp. above, note 6.) Likewise *Origen*, Contra Cels. vii. 42 (Opp. t. i. p. 725), maintains, in reference to the saying of Plato, that it is difficult to find God : Ἡμεῖς δὲ ἀποφαινόμεθα, ὅτι οὐκ αὐτάρκης ἡ ἀνθρωπίνη φύσις ὁπωσποτανοῦν ζητῆσαι τὸν θεὸν, καὶ εὑρεῖν αὐτὸν καθαρῶς, μὴ βοηθηθεῖσα ὑπὸ τοῦ ζητουμένου· εὑρισκομένου τοῖς ὁμολογοῦσι μετὰ τὸ παρ᾽ αὐτοὺς ποιεῖν, ὅτι δέονται αὐτοῦ, ἐμφανίζοντος ἑαυτὸν οἷς ἂν κρίνῃ εὔλογον εἶναι ὀφθῆναι, ὡς πέφυκε θεὸς μὲν ἀνθρώπῳ γινώσ-

κεσθαι, ἀνθρώπου δὲ ψυχὴ ἔτι οὖσα ἐν σώματι γιγνώσκειν τὸν θεόν.

§ 36.

The Unity of God.

Since Christianity adopted the doctrine of one God as taught in the Old Testament, it became necessary to defend it, not only against the polytheism of the heathen, but also against the dualism, resting on heathenism, and the theory of emanation of the Gnostics (1). Some proved the necessity of one God (2), though not in the most skilful manner, from the relations of space (3), or even from analogies in the rational and also in the animal creation (4). The more profound thinkers, however, were well aware that it is not sufficient to demonstrate the mere numerical unity of the Divine Being, and tried to give expression to this feeling by transporting the transcendental unity into a sphere above the mathematical Monas (5).

(1) Both the hypothesis of an ἄρχων, δημιουργός, Jaldabaoth, etc., who is subordinate to the supreme God (θεὸς ἀκατονόμαστος, βυθός), and that of the unfolding of the one God into manifold simple æons, or pairs of æons, is contrary to monotheism. On the more fully developed systems of Basilides and Valentinus, comp. *Irenæus, Clem. Alex.*, and the works quoted § 23 on the Gnostic systems. Against the Gnostic dualism especially, *Irenæus* (ii. 1); *Origen*, De Princip. ii. 1; *Tert.* Adv. Marcion. i. (As to the mode in which the orthodox Church tried to unite the belief in the Trinity with monotheism, see below.)

(2) *Justin M.* simply acknowledges this necessity, by considering the unity of God as an innate idea, which was afterwards lost. In his opinion, monotheism is the first true criterion of religious principles, Coh. ad Græc. c. 36: Δυνατὸν μανθάνειν ὑμᾶς ἕνα καὶ μόνον εἶναι θεὸν, ὃ πρῶτόν ἐστι τῆς ἀληθοῦς θεοσεβείας γνώριομα.

(3) To this class belongs the proof adduced by *Athenagoras*, Legat. pro Christianis, c. 8 : " If there had been two or several gods from the beginning, they would either be in one and the same place, or each would occupy a separate space. They cannot be in one and the same place, for if they be gods they are not identical (consequently they exclude each other). Only the created is equal to its pattern, but not the uncreated, for it does not proceed from anything, neither is it formed after any model. As the hand, the eye, and the foot are different members of *one* body, as they conjointly compose that body, so God is but one God. Socrates is a compound being, since he is created, and subject to change; but God, who is uncreated, and is incapable of suffering and of division, cannot consist of parts. But if each god were supposed to occupy a separate space, what place could we assign to the other god, or the other gods, seeing that God is *above* the world, and *around* all things which He has made ? For as the world is round, and God surrounds all beings, where would then be room for any of the other gods ? For such a god cannot be *in* the world, because it belongs to another; no more can he be *around* the world, for the Creator of the world, even God, surrounds it. But if he can be neither *in* the world, nor *around* it (for the first God occupies the whole space around it), where is he ? Perhaps above the world, and above God ? *in* another world ? or *around* another world ? But if he is *in* another world, and *around* another world, he does not exist for us, and does not govern our world, and his power, therefore, is not very great, for then he is confined within certain boundaries (after all, a concession !). But as he exists neither *in* another world (for the former God fills the universe), nor *around* another world (for the above God holds all the universe), it follows that he does not exist at all, since there is nothing in which he can exist." Similarly the author of the Clementines. Comp. *Baur*, Dg. s. 401.

(4) *Minuc. Fel.* c. 18 : Quando unquam regni societas aut cum fide cœpit, aut sine cruore desiit ? Omitto Persas de equorum hinnitu augurantes principatum, et Thebanorum præmortuam fabulam transeo ; ob pastorum et casæ regnum de geminis memoria notissima est ; generi et soceri bella toto orbe diffusa sunt, et tam magni imperii duos fortuna non

cepit. Vide cetera: rex unus apibus, dux unus in gregibus, in armentis rector unus. Tu in cœlo summam potestatem dividi credas, et scindi veri illius ac divini imperii totam potestatem? quum palam sit, parentem omnium Deum nec principium habere nec terminum, etc. Comp. *Cyprian*, De Idolorum Vanitate, p. 14.

(5) *Clem.* Pæd. i. 8, p. 140: "Ἐν δὲ ὁ θεὸς, καὶ ἐπέκεινα τοῦ ἑνὸς καὶ ὑπὲρ αὐτὴν μονάδη. Along with the idea of the *unity* of God, *Origen* speaks of the more metaphysical idea of His *simplicity*, De Princip. i. 1, 6 (Opp. t. i. p. 51; *Redepenning*, p. 100): Non ergo aut corpus aliquid, aut *in* corpore esse putandus est Deus (against this, compare *Athenagoras*), sed intellectualis natura simplex, nihil omnino adjunctionis admittens: uti ne majus aliquid et inferius in se habere credatur, sed ut sit ex omni parte μονάς et ut ita dicam ἑνάς, et mens et fons, ex quo initium totius intellectualis naturæ vel mentis est. *Strauss* in his Glaubenslehre (i. s. 404 ff.) gives a compressed sketch of the attempts of the Fathers to prove the unity of God. [*Origen*, Contra Cels. i. 23, in the *a posteriori* method; from the analogy of armies and states. *Lactantius*, Div. Inst. i. 3: Quod si in uno exercitu tot fuerint imperatores, quot legiones, quot cohortes, quot cunei, quot alæ, etc. *Cyprian*, De Idol. Van. 5: Nec hoc tantum de homine mireris, quum in hoc omnis natura consentiat. Rex unus est apibus, et dux unus in gregibus, et in armentis rector unus: multo magis mundi unus est rector, etc. They also derived an *a priori* argument from the infinitude and absolute perfection of the divine essence.]

§ 37.

Whether God can be named and known.

Baur, Dg. s. 392 ff.

The idea of a *revealed* religion implies that so much of the nature of God should be made *manifest* to man as is necessary to the knowledge of salvation; the Church, therefore, has always cultivated the λόγος περὶ θεοῦ (theology). On the

§ 37.] WHETHER GOD CAN BE NAMED AND KNOWN. 141

other hand, the inadequacy of human conceptions has always been acknowledged (in opposition to the pride of speculation), and the unfathomable divine essence admitted to be past finding out; some even entertained doubts as to the propriety of giving God any name. Much of what the Church designated by the term *mystery* is founded partly on a sense of this insufficiency of our conceptions and the inaptitude of our language, and partly on the necessity of still employing certain representations and expressions to communicate our religious ideas.

When the martyr *Attalus*, in the persecution of the Gallican Christians under Marcus Aurelius, was asked during his trial what was the name of God, he replied: Ὁ θεὸς ὄνομα οὐκ ἔχει ὡς ἄνθρωπος, *Euseb.* v. 1 (ed. *Heinichen*, t. ii. p. 29, comp. the note). Such was also the opinion of *Justin M.* Apolog. ii. 6; whatever name may be given to God, he who has given a name to a thing must always be anterior to it. He therefore draws a distinction, with *Philo* (De Confus. Ling. p. 357), between *appellatives* (προσρήσεις) and *names* (ὀνόματα). The predicates πατήρ, θεός, κύριος, δεσπότης, are only appellatives. Therefore he also calls God ἄρρητος πατήρ; other passages are given by *Semisch*, ii. s. 252 ff. When *Justin* further says (Dial. c. Tryph. c. 3) that God is not only above all *names*, but above all *essence* (ἐπέκεινα τῆς οὐσίας), it is to be remembered that he is there speaking as a heathen from the Platonic standpoint. But elsewhere he speaks of an οὐσία of God, *e.g.* Dial. c. Tryph. c. 128, and even ascribes to Him (in a certain sense) a μορφή. Apol. i. 9; comp. *Semisch*, ii. s. 252. *Theoph.* ad Autol. i. 3: Ἄκουε, ὦ ἄνθρωπε, τὸ μὲν εἶδος τοῦ θεοῦ, ἄρρητον καὶ ἀνέκφραστον, καὶ μὴ δυνάμενον ὀφθαλμοῖς σαρκίνοις ὁραθῆναι· δόξῃ γάρ ἐστιν ἀχώρητος, μεγέθει ἀκατάληπτος, ὕψει ἀπερινόητος, ἰσχύϊ ἀσύγκριτος, σοφίᾳ ἀσυμβίβαστος, ἀγαθοσύνῃ ἀμίμητος, καλοποιΐᾳ ἀνεκδιήγητος· εἰ γὰρ φῶς αὐτὸν εἴπω, ποίημα αὐτοῦ λέγω· εἰ λόγον εἴπω, ἀρχὴν αὐτοῦ λέγω (comp. the note to this passage by Maran)· νοῦν ἐὰν εἴπω, φρόνησιν αὐτοῦ λέγω· πνεῦμα ἐὰν εἴπω, ἀναπνοὴν αὐτοῦ λέγω· σοφίαν ἐὰν εἴπω, γέννημα αὐτοῦ λέγω· ἰσχὺν ἐὰν εἴπω, κράτος αὐτοῦ λέγω· πρόνοιαν ἐὰν εἴπω, ἀγαθοσύνην αὐτοῦ λέγω· βασιλείαν ἐὰν εἴπω, δόξαν αὐτοῦ λέγω· κύριον ἐὰν εἴπω, κριτὴν αὐτὸν λέγω· κριτὴν ἐὰν εἴπω, δίκαιον αὐτὸν λέγω· πατέρα ἐὰν εἴπω, τὰ πάντα αὐτὸν λέγω· πῦρ ἐὰν εἴπω, τὴν ἀρχὴν αὐτοῦ λέγω κ.τ.λ.[1] Comp. i. 5 : Εἰ γὰρ τῷ ἡλίῳ ἐλαχίστῳ ὄντι στοιχείῳ οὐ δύναται ἄνθρωπος ἀτενίσαι διὰ τὴν ὑπερβάλλουσαν θέρμην καὶ δύναμιν, πῶς οὐχὶ μᾶλλον τῇ τοῦ θεοῦ δόξῃ ἀνεκφράστῳ οὔσῃ ἄνθρωπος θνητὸς οὐ δύναται ἀντωπῆσαι ; [comp. *Scherer*, Le Dithéisme de Just. Rév. de. Theol. 1856]. According to *Iren.* ii. 25, 4, God is indeterminabilis, nor can any one fully comprehend His nature by thinking He is invisibilis propter eminentiam, ignotus autem nequaquam propter providentiam (ibid. ii. 6). God cannot be known *without* God : we know Him only through the revelation which is made to us of Him (iv. 6). The medium through which we know Him is His revealed love to men. Comp. *Duncker*, s. 11. *Möller*, l.c. s. 475. *Minuc. Fel.* c. 18 : Hic (Deus) nec videri potest, visu clarior est, nec comprehendi, tactu purior est, nec æstimari, sensibus, major est, infinitus, immensus et soli sibi tantus quantus est notus ; nobis vero ad intellectum pectus angustum est, et ideo sic eum digne æstimamus, dum inæstimabilem dicimus. Eloquar, quemadmodum sentio : magnitudinem Dei, qui se putat nosse, minuit ; qui non vult minuere, non novit. Nec nomen Deo quæras : DEUS nomen est ! Illic vocabulis opus est, quum per singulos propriis appellationum insignibus multitudo dirimenda est. Deo, qui solus est, Dei vocabulum totum est. Quem si patrem dixero, terrenum opineris ; si regem, carnalem suspiceris ; si dominum, intelliges utique mortalem. Aufer additamenta nominum, et perspicies ejus claritatem. *Clement* of Alexandria shows very distinctly, Strom. v. 11, p. 689, that we can attain to a clear perception of God only by laying aside, δι' ἀναλύσεως, all finite ideas of the divine nature, till at last nothing but the abstract idea of unity remains. But lest we should content ourselves with the mere negation, we must throw ourselves

---

[1] From these expressions we must not infer that the name of God was indifferent to Christians ; on the contrary, the names given to God in the Scriptures were held to be most sacred : hence *Origen* contends against the position of Celsus, that one might call the highest being, Jupiter, or Zeus, or Sabaoth, or any Egyptian or Indian name : Contra Cels. vi., Opp. i. p. 320.

($ἀπορρίψωμεν$ $ἑαυτούς$) into the greatness of Christ, in whom the glory of God was manifested, in order to obtain to some extent ($ἀμηγέπη$) the knowledge of God (*i.e.* in a practical and religious manner, not by speculation); for even then we learn only what God is *not*, not *what* He is (that is to say, if we speak of absolute knowledge). Comp. also the 12th and 13th chapters of the 5th book, from p. 692; in particular, p. 695, and c. i. p. 647 : $Δῆλον$ $γὰρ$ $μηδένα$ $δύνασθαι$ $παρὰ$ $τὸν$ $τῆς$ $ζωῆς$ $χρόνον$ $τὸν$ $θεὸν$ $ἐναργῶς$ $καταλαβέσθαι$; he therefore gives the advice, ibid. p. 651: $Τὸ$ $δὲ$ $ἄρα$ $ζητεῖν$ $περὶ$ $θεοῦ$ $ἂν$ $μὴ$ $εἰς$ $ἔριν$, $ἀγγὰ$ $εἰς$ $εὕρεσιν$ $τείνῃ$, $σωτήριόν$ $ἐστι$. (Compare on this, *Baur*, Trinitätslehre, s. 191 ff., who remarks that what is *abstract* in the idea of God is not declared by any of the older teachers of the Church, Origen himself not excepted, more strongly and definitely than by Clement. But he by no means confined himself to the abstract.) *Origen*, Contra Cels. vi. 65, Opp. i. p. 681 sq., shows that what is individual cannot be described; for who in words could tell the difference between the sweetness of figs and the sweetness of dates ? And De Princip. i. 1, 5, p. 50 (*Redepenning*, p. 90), he says: Dicimus secundum veritatem, Deum incomprehensibilem esse atque inæstimabilem. Si quid enim illud est, quod sentire vel intelligere de Deo potuerimus, multis longe modis eum meliorem esse ab eo quod sensimus necesse est credere. "As the brightness of the sun exceeds the dim light of a lantern, so the glory of God surpasses our idea of it." Likewise *Novatian* says, De Trinit. c. 2 : De hoc ergo ac de eis, quæ sunt ipsius et in eo sunt, nec mens hominis quæ sint, quanta sint et qualia sint, digne concipere potest, nec eloquentia sermonis humani æquabilem majestati ejus virtutem sermonis expromit. Ad cogitandam enim et ad eloquendam illius majestatem et eloquentia omnis merito muta est et mens omnis exigua est: major est enim mente ipsa, nec cogitari possit quantus sit: ne si potuerit cogitari, mente humana minor sit, qua concipi possit. Major est quoque omni sermone, nec edici possit: ne si potuerit edici, humano sermone minor sit, quo quum edicitur, et circumiri et colligi possit. Quidquid enim de illo cogitatum fuerit, minus ipso erit, et quidquid enuntiatum fuerit, minus illo comparatum circum ipsum erit. Sentire enim illum taciti aliquatenus possumus; ut autem ipse est, sermone explicare non possumus. Sive enim illum dixeris lucem, creaturam ipsius magis quam ipsum dixeris, etc. . . . Quidquid omnino de illo retuleris, rem aliquam ipsius magis et virtutem quam ipsum explicaveris. Quid enim de eo condigne aut dicas aut sentias, qui omnibus et sermonibus major est ? etc. Nevertheless, the Fathers also admit an actual knowledge of God, by faith, which is now mediated by Christ, but will one day be an immediate vision from face to face. Comp. infra, on Eschatology.

§ 38.

Idealism and Anthropomorphism.—Corporeity of God.

The educated mind desires to abstract from the nature of God everything that reminds it of the finite or composite; sometimes it has even taken offence at the idea of the substantiality of God, out of a refined fear of reducing Him to the level of created beings; but thus it runs into danger of dissipating the Deity into a mere abstract negation. In opposition to this idealizing tendency, the necessities of religion demand a real God *for* the world, *for* man, and *for* the human heart; and the bold and figurative language of pious emotion, as well as popular symbolical and anthropomorphite expressions, compensated for what the idea of God lost in the way of negation. Both these tendencies, which have always advanced equal claims in the sphere of religious thought (1), have their respective representatives in the first period of the History of Doctrines. On the one hand, the Alexandrian school, and *Origen* in particular, endeavoured to remove from God everything that seemed to draw Him within the atmosphere of the earthly, or in any way to make Him like men (2). On the other hand, *Tertullian* insisted so much on the idea of the substantiality of God, that he confounded it with His corporeity (though he by no means ascribed to Him a gross, material body, like that of man) (3).

§ 58.] IDEALISM AND ANTHROPOMORPHISM. 145

(1) On this subject even the ancient philosophers entertained differing opinions. The popular, polytheistic form of religion was founded (as is every religion) on anthropomorphism. Xenophanes of Colophon, the founder of the Eleatic school, endeavoured to combat anthropomorphism as well as polytheism. Comp. *Clem. Alex.* Strom. v. 14, p. 714 (*Sylb.* 601 C):

Εἶς θεὸς ἔν τε θειοῖσι καὶ ἀνθρωποῖσι μέγιστος,
Οὔ τι δέμας θνητοῖσιν ὁμοίϊος οὐδὲ νόημα κ.τ.λ.,

and Strom. vii. 4, p. 841; other passages in *Preller*, Hist. Phil. Græco-Rom., Hamb. 1838, p. 84 ss. *Ritter*, i. s. 450. [English translat. by *Morrison*, i. p. 430.] *Schleiermacher*, s. 60.—The Epicureans (though it is doubtful whether Epicurus himself seriously meant to teach this doctrine) imagined that the gods possessed a quasi-human form, but without the wants of men, and unconcerned about human sufferings and pleasures. Thus they retained only what is negative in (the ghost of) anthropomorphism, and lost sight of its more profound significance (the human relation of God to man). Comp. *Cic.* de Natura Deorum, i. 8–12. *Reinhold*, i. s. 404, note. *Ritter*, iii. 490. [Engl. transl. iii. 442.]—Different views were adopted by the Stoics, who represented God as the vital force and reason which govern the universe; but though they avoided anthropomorphic notions, they regarded Him as clothed in an ethereal robe. *Cic.* de Natura Deorum, ii. 24. *Ritter*, iii. s. 576. [English translation, iii. p. 520 ff.]

(2) *Clement* opposes anthropomorphism in different places: "Most men talk and judge of God from their own limited point of view, and measure Him by themselves, as if cockles and oysters were to reason out of their narrow shells, and the hedgehog out of his rolled up self." Strom. v. 11, p. 687; comp. vii. 5, p. 845; c. 7, p. 852, 53: "Ὅλος ἀκοὴ καὶ ὅλος ὀφθαλμὸς, ἵνα τις τούτοις χρήσηται τοῖς ὀνόμασιν, ὁ θεός. Καθ' ὅλου τοίνυν οὐδεμίαν σώζει θεοσέβειαν, οὔτε ἐν ὕμνοις οὔτε ἐν λόγοις, ἀλλ' οὐδὲ ἐν γραφαῖς ἢ δόγμασιν ἡ μὴ πρέπουσα περὶ τοῦ θεοῦ ὑπόληψις, ἀλλ' εἰς ταπεινὰς καὶ ἀσχήμονας ἐκτρεπομένη ἐννοίας τε καὶ ὑπονοίας· ὅθεν ἡ τῶν πολλῶν εὐφημία δυσφημίας οὐδὲν διαφέρει διὰ τὴν τῆς ἀληθείας ἄγνοιαν κ.τ.λ. (on prayer). *Origen* begins his work,

περὶ ἀρχῶν, immediately after the Prooem. with objections to anthropomorphite or material ideas of God: "I know that many appeal even to Scripture to prove that God is a corporeal being; because they read in Moses that He is a consuming fire, and in John, that He is a Spirit (πνεῦμα = רוּחַ). They cannot think of fire and spirit but as something corporeal. I should like to ask them what they say of the passage in 1 John i. 5: "God is light"? He is a light to enlighten those who seek the truth (Ps. xxxvi. 9); for "the light of God" is nothing other than divine power, by means of which he who is enlightened perceives truth in all things, and apprehends God Himself as the truth. In this sense it is also said: "In Thy light we shall see light," *i.e.* in the Word, in the Wisdom, which is Thy Son, we see Thee, the Father. Is it necessary to suppose that God resembles the sunlight, because He is called *Light?* Can any sensible meaning be attached to the idea, that knowledge and wisdom have their source in "the corporeal light"? (Schnitzer's translation, s. 13, 14 ff.) But the spiritualizing tendency of Origen led him frequently so to explain even the more profound sayings of Scripture, as to leave only an abstract idea; this appears in what follows the above extract, where, in order to exclude all conceptions of a divisibility of the Spirit (of God), he compares a participation in the Holy Spirit to "a participation in the medicinal art," although further on he grants that the comparison is inadequate. Here manifestly "the understanding prevails altogether too much over the imagination" (comp. the judgment of *Mosheim,* cited § 26, note 11). *Novatian* also expresses himself in very strong and decided terms against anthropomorphism, De Trin. c. 6: Non intra hæc nostri corporis lineamenta modum aut figuram divinæ majestatis includimus.... Ipse totus oculus, quia totus videt, totus auris, quia totus audit, etc.—Even the definition, that God is a Spirit, has, according to him, only a relative validity: Illud quod dicit Dominus (John iv.) spiritum Deum, puto ego sic locutum Christum de patre, ut adhuc aliquid plus intelligi velit quam spiritum Deum. He thinks that this is only figurative language, as it is said elsewhere, God is light, etc., omnis enim spiritus creatura est.

(3) The first Christian writer who is said to have ascribed

a body to the Deity is *Melito* of Sardis, in his treatise περὶ ἐνσωμάτου θεοῦ, which is no longer extant; comp. *Orig.* Comment. in Genes. (Opp. t. ii. p. 25); *Euseb.* iv. 26, and *Heinichen* on the passage; *Gennadius*, De Dogm. Eccles. c. 4; and *Piper*, über Melito, in the Theologische Studien und Kritiken, 1838, i. s. 71 ff., where a similar view is cited from the Clementine Homilies. [*Cureton*, in his Spicilegium Syriacum, Lond. 1855, published an apology under the name of Melito, which is free from anthropomorphism; but it is the work of a later author.] It is more certain that *Tertullian* ascribed to God (as also to the soul) a body, which he did not, however, represent as a human body, but as the necessary form of all existence (comp. *Schleiermacher*, Geschichte der Philosophie, s. 165, and *Schwegler's* Montanism. s. 171, note), De Carne Christi, c. 11 : Ne esse quidem potest, nisi habens per quod sit. Cum autem (anima) sit, habeat necesse est aliquid per quod sit. Si habet aliquid per quod est, hoc erit corpus ejus. Omne quod est, corpus est sui generis. Nihil est incorporale, nisi quod non est. Advers. Praxeam, c. 7 : Quis enim negabit Deum corpus esse, etsi Deus spiritus est? Spiritus enim corpus sui generis in sua effigie. Sed et invisibilia illa quæcunque sunt, habent apud Deum et suum corpus et suam formam, per quæ soli Deo visibilia sunt; quanto magis quod ex ipsius substantia missum est, sine substantia non erit ! Comp. *Neander*, Antignost. s. 451, and Dogmengesch. s. 109. But *Tertullian* himself draws a definite distinction, which excludes all grosser forms of anthropomorphism, between the divine and the human *corpus*, Advers. Marc. ii. 16 : Discerne substantias et suos eis distribue sensus, tam diversos, quam substantiæ exigunt, licet vocabulis communicare videantur. Nam et dexteram et oculos et pedes Dei legimus, nec ideo tamen humanis comparabuntur, quia de appellatione sociantur. Quanta erit diversitas divini corporis et humani, sub eisdem nominibus membrorum, tanta erit et animi divini et humani differentia, sub eisdem licet vocabulis sensuum, quos tam corruptorios efficit in homine corruptibilitas substantiæ humanæ, quam incorruptorios in Deo efficit incorruptibilitas substantiæ divinæ.[1] On the anthropomorphism of

---

[1] *Münscher, von Cölln,* i. s. 134, wrongly adduces this passage to show that Tertullian is justly chargeable with *real* anthropomorphism. It proves rather

Cyprian, see *Rettberg*, s. 300. In a much more anthropomorphite manner than Tertullian, the author of the Clementines seems to hold the corporeity of God, when he connects the love of God to us with His beauty (for one can love only the beautiful). But how can beauty be imagined without a bodily form? Hom. 17, 2 ff. *Baur*, Dg. s. 412. *Irenæus*, with great sobriety, rejects both anthropomorphism properly so called and false anthropopathism. In no respect is God to be compared to human frailty; though His *love* justifies us in using human phraseology when speaking of Him, nevertheless we feel that, as to His *greatness* and His true nature, He is elevated above all that is human. God is simple, and in all things like Himself (simplex, et non compositus et similimembrius, et totus ipse sibimet ipsi similis et æqualis). Comp. Adv. Hær. ii. 13. 4, and iv. 5. 20. *Duncker*, l.c. s. 25 ff. *Baur*, Christ. Gnosis, s. 466; Trin.-Lehre, s. 190.

the contrary. It must also be borne in mind that the corporeity of God and anthropomorphism are by no means synonymous. It is possible to conceive of God as incorporeal, and yet in a very anthropmorphite way as a very limited spirit, like the spirit of man. On the other hand, the substantiality of God may be taken in so abstract a manner as to exclude all that is human and personal (so the Stoics). Tertullian combines both these modes of representation ; but after all that has been said, it is the awkwardness of his style and mode of thinking, rather than any defective religious views, that has brought him into the repute of being a crude anthropomorphist. [This may be clearly seen from the following passage : "Divine affections are ascribed to the Deity by means of figures borrowed from the human form, not as if He were endued with corporeal qualities : when eyes are ascribed to Him, it denotes that He sees all things ; when ears, that He hears all things ; the speech denotes the will ; nostrils, the perception of prayer ; hands, creation ; arms, power ; feet, immensity ; for He has no members, and performs no office for which they are required, but executes all things by the sole act of His will. How can He require eyes, who is light itself? or feet, who is omnipresent? How can He require hands, who is the silent creator of all things ? or a tongue, to whom to think is to command ? Those members are necessary to men, but not to God, inasmuch as the counsels of man would be inefficacious unless his thoughts put his members in motion ; but not to God, whose operations follow His will without effort."] Tertullian undoubtedly was struggling after more profound views than are even suspected by many who speak of his theology in depreciatory terms. For the same reason, too much is conceded to *Cyprian* by *Rettberg*, l.c. Comp. *Baur's* Trinitätslehre, s. 188, note, and Dg. s. 412. On the distinction between anthropomorphism and anthropopathism, see *Neander*, Dogmengesch. s. 111.

§ 39.

The Attributes of God.

[Comp. *Dorner*, Die Unveränderlichkeit Gottes, in Jahrb. f. deutsche Theologie, i. 2, ii. 3, iii. 3.]

Neither the existence of God, as we have already seen, nor His attributes, were at first defined with scientific precision (1). The Catholic Church simply adopted the concrete idea of a personal God, as propounded in the Old Testament, though under certain modifications (2). But by degrees metaphysical ideas, borrowed from the schools of philosophers, were transferred to the God of the Christians; and on this point, too, opinions are found to oscillate between the philosophical tendencies above described (3). Some connected their notions of the *omnipresence* of God with conceptions of His corporeity, as space-filling and displacing other bodies; others, on the contrary, maintained that He was exalted above space, or that He is to be conceived as abolishing it and taking its place (4). The doctrine of *omniscience* was to some extent mixed up with anthropomorphite ideas, and even Origen put limits to this attribute of God (5), as well as to His *omnipotence* (6). In harmony with the spirit of Christianity, along with the *holiness* of God (7), His *love* and *mercy* were made specially prominent (8). But it was to be expected that collisions would arise, which could be harmonized only by the attempt to take more comprehensive and elevated views; as, for example, to reconcile the omniscience (especially the foreknowledge) of God with His omnipotence and goodness (9), or His punitive justice with His love and mercy (10).

(1) Thus "*Justin Martyr generally makes only a passing reference to the divine attributes, and in contrast with the common humanizing of deity found in the poetic and plastic mythology.*" *Semisch*, ii. s. 258. *Justin*, too, emphasizes the immutability

of God as one of His fundamental attributes, calling Him (Apol. i. 13) τὸν ἄτρεπτον καὶ ἀεὶ ὄντα θεόν.

(2) The Catholic Church preserved in this respect a medium between the anti-Judaizing Gnostics, who spoke of the *Demiurge* as a being either subordinate to the supreme God, or standing in a hostile relation to Him; and the Judaizing Ebionites, who, retaining the rigid physiognomy of Judaism, misapprehended the universality of the Christian doctrine of God. But here, as elsewhere, there is a wide difference between the North African and the Alexandrian schools.

(3) Comp. (§ 36, note 2) the passage cited from Athenagoras on the unity of God. With him agrees *Theophilus* (Ad Autol. i. 5), who compares the world to a pomegranate; as this is surrounded by its peel, so is the world by the Spirit of God, and kept together by His hand. *Cyprian*, De Idol. Vanit. p. 15, reproaches the heathen with attempting to confine the infinite God within the narrow walls of a temple, whilst He ubique totus diffusus est,—the image of a space-filling substance apparently floating before his mind.

(4) *Philo* had previously identified God with absolute space,[1] and called Him His own limit (comp. the passages bearing on this subject in the work of *Dähne*, s. 281–284, and s. 193, 267 ff.); *Theophilus*, too, Ad Autol. ii. 3, calls God His own space (αὐτὸς ἑαυτοῦ τόπος ἐστίν). He does not confine the omnipresence of God to His local presence in one or another spot, but considers it as His uninterrupted activity known only from His works; comp. i. 5. *Clem. Alex.*, too, opposes the localizing of God, Strom. ii. 2, p. 431: Οὐ γὰρ ἐν γνόφῳ (a needless conjecture of Rössler's here is ἐν χρόνῳ) ἢ τόπῳ ὁ θεός, ἀλλ' ὑπεράνω καὶ τόπου καὶ χρόνου καὶ τῆς τῶν γεγονότων ἰδιότητος· διὸ οὐδὲ ἐν μέρει καταγίνεταί ποτε, οὔτε περιέχων οὔτε περιεχόμενος, ἢ κατὰ ὁρισμόν τινα ἢ κατὰ ἀποτομήν. According to *Origen*, God sustains and fills the world (which Origen, like Plato, conceives to be an animate being) with His power; but He neither occupies space, nor does He even move in space, comp. De Princip. ii. 1 (Opp. i. p..77). For an explanation of popular and figurative expres-

---

[1] Comp. the opinions of the Peripatetics (*Sextus Empiricus*, adv. Physicos, x. p. 639, ed. *Fabricius*).

sions, which suggest the occupying of space and change of place, vide Contra Cels. iv. 5, Opp. i. p. 505, and comp. also p. 686. Concerning the expression that God is all in all, see De Princip. iii. 6 (Opp. i. p. 152, 153). *Schnitzer*, s. 231 f. *Baur*, Dg. s. 417.

(5) *Just*. Dial. c. Tryph. c. 127 : Ὁ γὰρ ἄρρητος πατὴρ καὶ κύριος τῶν πάντων οὔτε ποι ἀφῖκται, οὔτε περιπατεῖ, οὔτε καθεύδει, οὔτε ἀνίσταται, ἀλλ' ἐν τῇ αὐτοῦ χώρᾳ ὅπου ποτὲ μένει, ὀξὺ ὁρῶν καὶ ὀξὺ ἀκούων, οὐκ ὀφθαλμοῖς οὐδὲ ὠσὶν, ἀλλὰ δυνάμει ἀλέκτῳ· καὶ πάντα ἐφορᾷ καὶ πάντα γινώσκει, καὶ οὐδεὶς ἡμῶν λέληθεν αὐτόν. *Clement*, Strom. vi. 17, p. 821 : Ὁ γάρ τοι θεὸς πάντα οἶδεν, οὐ μόνον τὰ ὄντα, ἀλλὰ καὶ τὰ ἐσόμενα καὶ ὡς ἔσται ἕκαστον· τάς τε ἐπὶ μέρους κινήσεις προορῶν πάντ' ἐφορᾷ καὶ πάντ' ἐπακούει, γυμνὴν ἔσωθεν τὴν ψυχὴν βλέπων, καὶ τὴν ἐπίνοιαν τὴν ἑκάστου τῆς κατὰ μέρος ἔχει δι' αἰῶνος· καὶ ὅπερ ἐπὶ τῶν θεάτρων γίνεται, καὶ ἐπὶ τῶν ἑκάστου μερῶν, κατὰ τὴν ἐνόρασίν τε καὶ περιόρασιν καὶ συνόρασιν, τοῦτο ἐπὶ τοῦ θεοῦ γίνεται. Ἀθρόως τε γὰρ πάντα καὶ ἕκαστον ἐν μέρει μιᾷ προσβολῇ προσβλέπει. *Origen*, De Princip. iii. 2 (Opp. i. p. 49), proves that the world is finite, because God could not comprehend it if it were infinite; for that only may be understood which has a beginning. But it were impious to say that there is anything which God does not comprehend. For Origen's opinion on the relation between the divine foreknowledge and predestination, see § 70, 9.

(6) *Origen*, De Princip. ii. c. 9, p. 97 (*Redep*. p. 10): Ἐν τῇ ἐπινοουμένῃ ἀρχῇ τοσοῦτον ἀριθμὸν τῷ βουλήματι αὐτοῦ ὑποστῆσαι τὸν θεὸν νοερῶν οὐσιῶν, ὅσον ἠδύνατο διαρκέσαι· πεπερασμένην γὰρ εἶναι καὶ τὴν δύναμιν τοῦ θεοῦ λεκτέον κ.τ.λ. But in other places *Origen* expresses himself in a very appropriate way concerning the divine omnipotence; Contra Cels. v. (Opp. i. p. 595), he shows that God can do all things, but wills nothing which is contrary to nature (παρὰ φύσιν), οὔτε τὰ ἀπὸ κακίας, οὔτε τὰ ἀλόγως γενόμενα.

(7) The holiness of the divine will is the highest law in *Tertullian's* view. His highest moral law is, not to do the good for the sake of the good, but because it is commanded by God. (Comp. De Pœnit. c. 4.)

(8) The notion of *Clement* of Alexandria is remarkable, evidently borrowed from the Gnostic doctrine of an ἀρρενό-

θῆλυς, viz. that the compassion of God presents the female aspect of His character, Quis Div. Salv. p. 956; to which there is an analogy in the Old Testament, Isa. xlix. 15; comp. *Neander's* Gnostische Systeme, s. 209. The works of *Clement*, in particular, abound with passages referring to the love and mercy of God. He loves men because they are kindred with God, Coh. p. 89: Πρόκειται δὲ ἀεὶ τῷ θεῷ τὴν ἀνθρώπων ἀγέλην σώζειν. Comp. Strom. vii. p. 832. God's love follows men, seeks them out, as the bird the young that has fallen from its nest, Coh. 74, Pæd. i. p. 102.

(9) *Origen*, Contra Cels. ii. Opp. i. p. 405, Comment in Gen. Opp. ii. p. 10, 11. For more particulars, comp. the doctrine respecting Human Liberty, § 57.

(10) Here, too, was another point of distinction between Gnosticism and the orthodox Christian view of God; the former did not know how to reconcile the agency of God in inflicting punishment, with His character as loving and redeeming; on this account they felt compelled to separate objectively the just God of the Old Testament from the loving Father of Christians (so Marcion). In opposition to this unwarrantable separation, Irenæus, Tertullian, Clement, Origen, etc., insist particularly on the penal justice of God, and show that it can very well be reconciled with His love. According to *Irenæus*, Adv. Hær. v. 27, penalty does not consist in anything positive which comes from God, but in the separation of the sinner from God (χωρισμὸς δὲ τοῦ θεοῦ θάνατος). God does not punish προηγητικῶς, but ἐπακολουθούσης δι' ἐκείνης (τῆς ἁμαρτίας) τῆς κολάσεως. *Tertullian* considers the penal justice of God first from the judicial standpoint of the inviolability of law; distinguishing between true love and kindly weakness, he shows that the goodness and justice of God are inseparable; Contra Marc. i. 25, 26, ii. 12: Nihil bonum, quod injustum, bonum autem omne quod justum est. Ita si societas et conspiratio bonitatis atque justitiæ separationem earum non potest capere, quo ore constitues diversitatem duorum deorum in separatione? seorsum deputans Deum bonum et seorsum Deum justum? Illic consistit bonum, ubi et justum. A primordio denique Creator tam bonus quam justus.... Bonitas ejus operata est mundum, justitia modulatum est, etc. Comp. c. 13–16 (negabimus Deum, in quo non

omnia, quæ Deo digna sint, constent). Then he draws a distinction between malis supplicii s. pœnæ, and malis culpæ s. peccati. God is the Author only of the former; the devil is the author of the latter.—To defend himself against the charge of anthropomorphism he says: Stultissimi, qui de humanis divina præjudicant, ut quoniam in homine corruptoriæ conditionis habentur hujusmodi passiones, idcirco et in Deo ejusdem status existimentur, etc.—*Clement* of Alexandria adopts partly the same juridical view, Strom. iv. 24, p. 634; but, in enumerating the causes which induce God to inflict penalties, he speaks of the legal principle as being the last. He puts first the educational design to make men better, and to warn and restrain others; comp. Pæd. i. 8, p. 40. This is distinctly set forth, Strom. vii. p. 895: ’Αλλ’ ὡς πρὸς τοῦ διδασκάλου ἢ τοῦ πατρὸς οἱ παῖδες, οὕτως ἡμεῖς πρὸς τῆς προνοίας κολαζόμεθα. Θεὸς δὲ οὐ τιμωρεῖται· ἔστι γὰρ ἡ τιμωρία κακοῦ ἀνταπόδοσις· κολάζει μέντοι πρὸς τὸ χρήσιμον καὶ κοινῇ καὶ ἰδίᾳ τοῖς κολαζομένοις. *Origen*, moreover, says that God is more ready to do good than to punish; Hom. i. in Jerem. (Opp. iii. p. 125): Ὁ Θεὸς εἰς ἀγαθοποιΐαν πρόχειρός ἐστιν, εἰς δὲ τὸ κολάσαι τοὺς ἀξίους κολάσεως μελλητής. He gives the sinner always space for repentance (eodem loco). *Origen* refutes at great length the objections of the Gnostics, De Princ. ii. 5 (Opp. t. i. p. 102, *Schnitzer*, s. 109), by proving (in agreement with Tertullian) that their distinction between "benevolent" and "just" is altogether untenable, and showing that the divine penalties are inflicted for paternal objects by a wise physician; at the same time, he applies the allegorical interpretation to those passages of the Old Testament which speak in an anthropomorphite way of the wrath and vengeance of God; comp. also Contra Cels. iv. 71, 72, p. 556 (see § 48, below).

§ 40.

The Doctrine of the Logos.

(a) *The Doctrine before the Christian Era, and in other Systems.*

Lücke, Historical Examination of the Idea of the Logos, in his Commentar über das Evangelium Joh. Bd. i. 3d ed. s. 249 ff. [*Tholuck*, Commentar zum

Evang. Joh. ch. i. Die Logoslehre, transl. Edin.] *Dorner, Entwicklungs-geschichte der Christologie, Stuttg. 1845, at the beginning. *Von Bohlen*, Das alte Indien mit besonderer Rücksicht auf Ægypten (2 vols. Königsb. 1830), i. s. 201 ff. *Stuhr*, Die Religionssysteme der heidnischen Völker des Orients, s. 99 ff. *Kleuker*, Zendavesta im Kleinen, Th. ii. s. 1 ff. *Bäumlein*, Versuch die Bedeutung des Johann. Logos aus den Religionssystemen des Orients zu entwickeln, Tüb. 1828. [*Colebrooke's* Essays. *J. R. Ballantyne*, Christ. contrasted with Hindu Philos. 1859. *J. Mullens*, Relig. Aspects of Hindu Phil. (prize essay), 1860. *C. F. Köppen*, Die Religion Buddhas, ii. 1858, 59. *Barthélemy St. Hilaire*, Bouddha, 1860.] *J. Bucher*, Des Apostels Johannes Lehre von Logos, Schaffh. 1856. [*Burton*, The Bampton Lecture on the Heresies of the Apostolic Age, Lect. vii. Comp. also *Pye Smith*, Scripture Testimony to the Messiah, 3d ed. i. 522-529, ii. 415, 432, et passim.] *F. Ch. Baur*, Die Christliche Lehre von der Dreieinigkeit und Menschwerdung Gottes in ihrer geschichtlichen Entwicklung, Tüb. 1841-43, 3 Bde., Bd. i. s. 1-128. *G. A. Meier*, Die Lehre von der Trinität., Hamb. 1844, i. s. 1 ff. *Hellway*, Die Vorstellung von der Präexistenz Christi in der ältesten Kirche, in Zeller's Jahrb. 1848. *Duncker*, Zur Gesch. der Logoslehre Justins des Märt. (reprint. from the Göttinger Studien, 1847), Gött. 1848. *Laemmer*, Clement. Alex. de λόγῳ doctrina, Lips. 1855. [*König*, Die Menschwerdung, 1846. *R. J. Wilberforce*, Doctrine of the Incarnation in Relation to Mankind and the Church, 1851. *Maurice*, Religions of the World. *Trench*, Unconscious Prophecies of Heathenism. *Cæsar Morgan*, Trinity of Plato and Philo Judæus, new ed. by Holden, 1853. Comp. also *Liebner's* Christologie, i. 1849; *Thomasius*, Christi Person und Werk, 1853 ff.; Nägelsbach, der Gottmensch, i. 1854; *Kuhn*, Kath. Dogmatik, ii. s. 9-41.] *Delitzsch*, Johannes und Philo (Zeitschr. f. Luth. Theol. 1863, 2), s. 219 ff.

We are obliged to conceive of God, on the one hand, as a purely spiritual essence exalted above all that is finite; and, on the other hand, since He reveals and imparts Himself to the world, as having a definite relation to the created universe. This double necessity in the progress of thought led to the idea of an *organ* (medium) through which God creates the world, works upon it, and reveals Himself to it. This organ was supposed, on the one side, to have its ground in the divine nature itself, to stand in the most intimate connection with it; and, on the other, to be somehow or other distinct from it. In order to ascertain the origin of this idea, we need not go either to remote Oriental sources, the wisdom of India and the religion of Zend (1), nor to the occidental systems of philosophy, that of Plato in particular (2). We may find traces of it in the more definite and concrete form which, at the time when the apocryphal writings were composed, was given to

§ 40.] THE PRE-CHRISTIAN DOCTRINE OF THE LOGOS. 155

the personifications of the Divine Word and the Divine Wisdom found in the Old Testament (3), especially, however, in the doctrine of Philo concerning the Logos (4), and in some other ideas then current (5). Here is prefigured the form into which Christianity was destined to bring the living and fructifying spirit, in giving expression to the profoundest truths of the Christian faith.

(1) "*It is easy to see that the Christian idea cannot be explained by an appeal to the Indian religion.*" *Dorner*, s. 7. The *Trimurti* of the Indian Brahmanism:

Brahma	Vishnu	Siva (Kala).
Sun (Light)	Water (Air ?)	Fire.
Creator	Preserver (progressive development)	Destroyer.
Power	Wisdom	Justice.
Past	Present	Future.
Matter	Space	Time.

Comp. *Von Bohlen* and *Stuhr*, l.c. Among the Egyptians we find the following, corresponding with these deities:—

Brahma = Phtha.
Vishu = Kneph.
Siva = Neith.

The word by which Brahma created the world is Om (Oum), see *Von Bohlen*, i. s. 159 ff., 212. In the system of Zoroaster, Honover is represented as the word by which the world was created (*Duncker*, Logosl. Just. Mart., Gött. 1847), the most immediate revelation of the god Ormuzd; see *Kleuker*, l.c., and *Stuhr*, i. s. 370, 371. [*Burton*, l.c. Lect. ii. p. 14–48.] "*Since, in the pagan systems of religion, the natural is most intimately blended with the divine, their triads are altogether different from the Christian doctrine of the Trinity; in the former the triads only denote the elements (moments) of a developing process, and are therefore most fully found in those religions which occupy a very low position, but disappear when the identification of the divine with the natural is got rid of in the further development of the religious system.*" *Meier*, l.c. s. 4. Comp. *Dorner*, l.c.

(2) The relation in which *Plato* (especially in Timæus) imagined God to stand to the creating νοῦς, presents only a remote analogy; likewise the passage bearing on the λόγος from the Epinomis, p. 986, which *Euseb.* Præp. Evang. xi. 16, professes to quote from Epimenides (given by *De Wette*, Biblische Dogmatik, § 157). Comp. *Tennemann*, das platonische Philosophem vom göttlichen Verstande, in *Paulus'* Memorabilien, Stück i., and his System der platonischen Philosophie, Th. iii. s. 149 ff., 174 ff. *Böckh*, über die Bildung der Weltseele im Timæus des Plato (in Daub und Creuzer's Studien, Bd. iii. s. 1 ff.). *Ritter*, Geschichte der Philosophie, ii. s. 291 ff., 318 ff. [*Burton*, l.c. Lect. vii., and note 90 in particular.] *Neander*, Dg. s. 139. On the doctrine of the Logos among the Stoics (σπερματικὸς λόγος), see *Duncker*, Logoslehre, s. 28 ff.

(3) The oldest form of revelation which we find in the Old Testament is the direct *Theophany*, which, however, was adapted only to the age of childhood. In later times God speaks to His people in general, or to individuals, sometimes by angels (especially the מַלְאַךְ יְהוָה), sometimes by human mediators (Moses and the prophets). But the intercourse of God with the prophets is carried on by the medium of the Word of the Lord (דְּבַר יְהוָה), which descends upon them. This λόγος (ῥῆμα τοῦ θεοῦ, τοῦ κυρίου) is poetically personified in several places: Ps. cxlvii. 15; Isa. lv. 11; in an inferior degree, Ps. xxxiii. 4, cxix. 89, 104, 105; Isa. xl. 8; Jer. xxiii. 28; comp. *Lücke*, l.c. s. 257, 258. Like the Word, so the Wisdom of God (חָכְמָה, σοφία) is personified: Job xxviii. 12–28, and in very strong terms (in contrast with folly), Prov. viii. and ix. On קָנָנִי (Prov. viii. 22) and the signification of אָמוֹן (viii. 30), comp. *Umbreit's* Comment. s. 102, 106; on the personification of Wisdom in the apocryphal writings (Sir. i. 4, 24; Bar. iii. 15 ff., iv. 1; Wisd. vi. 22 to ch. ix.), see *Lücke*, l.c. s. 259 ff., and *Bretschneider*, Systematische Darstellung der Dogmatik der Apokryphen, Leipz. 1805, s. 191 ff. The strongest example of personification is in the Book of Wisdom, so that it is difficult to define exactly the distinction between this personification and the hypostasis properly so called, especially ch. vii. 22 ff. On the relation of this hypostatizing of the word to that of *Philo*, see *Lücke*, l.c. *Dorner*, s. 15 ff. *Grimm*,

Comm. über d. Buch d. Weisheit, Leipz. 1837. [*Gfrörer's* Urchristenthum, Bd. i. See the discussion between *Lücke* and *Nitzsch* in the Theol. Stud. und Kritiken, 1840, 1.]

(4) "*Philo's doctrine of the Logos is the immediate prelude to the Christian idea of the Logos;*" *Semisch*, Just. Mart. ii. s. 267. [Comp. *Jordan Bucher*, Philonische Studien, Tübing. 1848, who discusses in particular the question of the personality of the Logos in *Philo*.] On the question whether *Philo* ascribed personality to the Logos, see *Dorner*, i. s. 21 ff.; while most writers reply in the affirmative, *Dorner* throws doubt upon it. Thus much is certain, that *Philo* makes a distinction between the ὄν as such, and the λόγος τοῦ ὄντος, who is superior to the δυνάμεις, λόγοι, and ἄγγελοι. This Logos he also calls δεύτερος θεός, even θεός directly, but *without* the article,—υἱὸς πρεσβύτερος, υἱὸς μονογενής, πρωτόγονος,—εἰκών, σκιά, παράδειγμα, δόξα, σοφία, ἐπιστήμη τοῦ θεοῦ. According to *Philo*, the Logos is the essence and seat of the ideal world (ἰδέα τῶν ἰδεῶν ὁ θεοῦ λόγος). As an artist first makes a model of that which he purposes to make, so God first shaped the world ideally; see his De Mundi Opif. § 5, and the explanations of *J. G. Müller* (Philo's Buch von der Weltschöpfung, Berl. 1841), s. 149 ff. In the same manner the Logos is the mediator of the revelations of God; the theophanies were possible through him; he is called the παράκλητος, ἀρχιερεύς, ἱκέτης, πρεσβευτὴς ὀπαδὸς τοῦ θεοῦ. He takes care of all that is good, as ἀρχὴ καὶ πηγὴ καλῶν πράξεων. *Philo* was acquainted with the distinction between the λόγος ἐνδιάθετος and the λόγος προφορικός, though he employs these terms only in anthropological relations, De Vita Moys. lib. iii. (Paris, p. 672 c): Ἐν ἀνθρώπῳ δ' ὁ μὲν (λόγος) ἐστὶν ἐνδιάθετος, ὁ δὲ προφορικός, καὶ ὁ μὲν οἷά τις πηγή, ὁ δὲ γεγωνὸς ἀπ' ἐκείνου ῥέων. But he represents the Divine Logos as analogous to the human. Inasmuch as the Logos is the divine idea, all spiritual and sensuous existence derives its origin from Him; as a power of nature He pervades the world, is immanent in it as the world-spirit. That *Philo* frequently personifies the Logos, does not necessarily imply that he ascribes to him a real hypostasis, and hence there should be great caution in the interpretation of single passages. But the more recent researches (since *Dorner*) have shown

that *Philo*, in some places certainly, comes up to the idea of a real hypostasis (Alleg. iii. 93; De Somn. i. 584, 586; Quis Rer. Div. Hær. 509, and elsewhere); comp. *F. Keferstein*, Philo's Lehre von den göttlichen Mittelwesen, Leipz. 1846; also *Semisch*, Justin der M. s. 274. *Baur*, Dreieinigkeits-Lehre, i. s. 59 ff. *Meier*, Trinitätslehre, i. s. 20 ff.; and the works of *Grossmann, Scheffer, Gfrörer, Dähne*, and *Ritter*, referred to in § 19. [*Michel Nicholas*, Les Doctrines religieuses des Juifs, Paris 1860, Pt. 2, ch. 2, p. 178–216, contends that the doctrine respecting the Word (Logos) could not have been derived from either Babylonian or Platonic sources; that it had its origin in Palestine, and passed thence to Alexandria. It is a result of the Jewish views respecting God. "The doctrine of an intermediate being between God and the world is a part of the theology of the Talmud; but this intermediate being is there designated, not by the name of the Word, but by that of the Shekinah," p. 215.]

(5) Traces of the doctrine of the Logos are also found in the Samaritan theology, and in the writings of Onkelos and Jonathan, comp. *Lücke*, l.c. s. 244. Concerning the Adam Kadmon of the Cabbalists, and the Memra and Shekinah, vide *Bretschneider*, l.c. s. 233, 236. *Baur*, Gnosis, s. 332, Anm. *De Wette*, biblische Dogmatik, § 157. [*Burton*, l.c. Lect. ii. p. 51–55.] *Dorner*, l.c. i. 1, s. 59. *Gfrörer*, das Jahrhundert des Heils, Stuttg. 1838, s. 272 ff.

§ 41.

(b) The Christian Doctrine of the Logos in the Writings of John.

Bucher, des Apostel Johannes Lehre vom Logos (§ 40). *Weizsäcker*, die Johanneische Logoslehre (Jahrbuch f. deutsche Theol. 1862), 7 vols. 4to.

Christianity first gave to the speculative idea of the Logos practical and religious relations and significance (1). The Gospel of John, in accordance with the doctrine of Paul (2), which differs only in the form of expression, applied the term *Logos* to the complete and personal revelation of God

§ 41.]   THE CHRISTIAN DOCTRINE OF THE LOGOS.   159

in Christ. This Christian Logos of John was no longer a mere abstract idea, but with all its ideality it was at the same time an historical fact and a religious truth; and on this account it was from the first the peculiar and living root of Christian theology.

(1) It is true that *Philo* himself made use of the idea of the Logos for practical and religious purposes, inasmuch as he accommodated it to the Hebrew religion in connecting it with the idea of the Messiah. But this connection was nevertheless very loose, and the idea of the Messiah itself was altogether abstract, and in the sense of the Jews, not historically realized. (" *The idea of the Messiah becomes in Philo but a dead coal; only the phlegm remains*," Dorner, s. 49.) In contrast with this, the Christian idea of the Logos on the one hand (the speculative and divine), and the idea of the Messiah on the other hand (the national and human), both appear historically realized in the person of Jesus of Nazareth (ὁ λόγος σὰρξ ἐγένετο). *Bucher*, ubi supra, s. 214: " *The Logos* (in John) *is not a mere mediating principle, but also an independent Creator of the world.*" In Philo the Logos is υἱὸς πρωτόγονος, in John υἱὸς μονογενής: ibid. s. 211. On the relation of the Christian doctrine of the Logos to the heathen systems of emanation, see *Duncker*, l.c. s. 23.

(2) Though the term λόγος does not occur in the writings of Paul in the sense in which it is understood by John (cf. John i. 1; Rev. xix. 13), yet the idea of a divine pre-existence of Christ is clearly expressed by him, especially Col. i. 15–17, ii. 9.[1] Similar expressions are used by the author of the Epistle to the Hebrews, ch. i. 4 ff. (Comp. 1 Cor. xv. 47; 2 Cor. iv. 4; Rom. viii. 29.) See *Weizsäcker*, l.c. Concerning the doctrine of the Trinity, as propounded in the New Testament, see *Meier*, l.c. s. 24 ff., and *Hellway*, ubi supra.

---

[1] Those who, with *Baur*, consider the shorter Pauline Epistles as spurious, will, of course, regard the Christology which they contain as a transition intermediate between the genuine Pauline and the pseudo-Johannean doctrine; cf. *Baur*, Dg. s. 425.

§ 42.

(c) *The Theologumenon of the Church concerning the Logos, to the Times of Origen.*

Möller, Geschichte der Kosmologie (§ 47). [*Burton*, Testimonies of the Ante-Nicene Fathers to the Divinity of Christ, etc. (Works, ii.).]

But Christian theology in its further history did not stand still with this idea of the Logos, as historically manifested in the Messiah. That which appears in historical manifestation, it endeavoured to grasp as having its ground in the very nature of God. A deeper religious interest was unquestionably here at work, but it frequently yielded to speculation, and was mixed up with foreign modes of philosophizing. Those heretics who adhered more closely to Judaism (the Ebionites), as well as the Alogi, *Theodotus* and *Artemon*, were most remote from speculations of this nature, but also from the more deeply religious spirit, since they set aside the very substance of this Christian gnosis, the idea of the Logos, by denying the divinity of Christ. The distinction between God the Father and the Logos was likewise abolished by the other section of the Monarchians, *Praxeas, Noëtus,* and *Beryllus,* without, however, denying the actual revelation of God in Christ, which they insisted upon with all emphasis (1). The Gnostics, on the contrary, connected the idea of the Logos with their fanciful doctrine of emanation and of æons, and thus played over into the realm of speculative mythology (2). And so it became incumbent upon the Fathers to defend the speculative element in opposition to the former class of heretics, the historical in opposition to the latter, and to preserve both these elements for the practical religious interests of the Church (3). *Justin* (4), *Tatian* (5), *Theophilus* (6), *Athenagoras* (7), *Clement* of Alexandria (8), endeavoured to illustrate the existence of the Logos, and His relation to the Father, by the aid of figures and analogies, borrowed from the external

§ 42.] THE THEOLOGUMENON OF THE CHURCH, ETC. 161

world and the nature of man. *Tertullian* (9) strove to explain the mystery, wrestling hard with language; while *Irenæus* (10), opposed to all *gnosis*, on the one hand set aside hair-splitting queries, and on the other held fast to the trinitarian faith of the Church as the direct expression of the Christian consciousness.

(1) Compare § 23, note 1, § 25, notes 2 and 3, and the dissertation of *Heinichen* there cited. The orthodox doctrine identified the idea of the Logos and that of the Messiah; but the doctrinal tendency of the Ebionites, as well as of the Gnostics, separated them. The former, adopting the idea of the Messiah alone, lost sight of the spiritual import of the doctrine of the Logos; the reverse was the case with the Gnostics, who held merely an idea of the Logos, but without admitting His incarnation in the Messiah. — Concerning *Artemon*, whose opinions rank him among the Monarchians, *Schleiermacher* (in his essay: Ueber die Sabellianische und Athanasische Vorstellung) observes that he appears to have retained the doctrine of the unity of God with more seriousness, and greater desire to promote the interests of religion, than the more frivolous *Theodotus;* vide Zeitschrift von Schleiermacher, de Wette, and Lücke, iii. s. 303, 304. He there shows also the difference between this tendency and that of *Praxeas* and *Noëtus*, already mentioned § 24, note 4. Comp. also § 46, note 3, and *Gieseler* in Stud. u. Krit. 1853, 4.

(2) Even if we look at it numerically alone, there is a great difference between the Catholic doctrine of the Logos and the views of the Gnostic sects. Before the *doctrine of the Trinity* was further developed (see below), the Logos was considered by Catholics to be the *only* hypostasis; while the Gnostics imagined heaven to be inhabited by a multitude of æons (fœtus æonum, *Tert.*).—According to *Basilides*, there are 365 heavens (οὐρανοί, the lowest of which is under the ἄρχων); and he assigned an intermediate position between the supreme God and the Logos to the νοῦς, and taught that the Logos emanated from the latter. Further emanations of the νοῦς, were the φρόνησις, σοφία, δύναμις, δικαιοσύνη, and εἰρήνη; and these five æons, together with the other two, νοῦς and λόγος,

in all seven, formed, along with the θεὸς ἄρρητος (ἀνωνόμαστος), the first ὀγδοάς.—Still more ingenious is the system of Valentinus. [He asserted that from the great first cause (primitive existence, βυθός, προπάτωρ, προαρχή) successively emanated male and female æons (νοῦς, or μονογενής and ἀλήθεια, λόγος and ζωή, ἄνθρωπος and ἐκκλησία, etc.), so that thirty æons (divided into the ὀγδοάς, δεκάς, and δωδεκάς) form the πλήρωμα. The vehement desire of the last of the æons, the σοφία, to unite itself with the βυθός, gave existence to an immature being (ἡ κάτω σοφία, ἐνθύμησις, ἀχαμώθ) which, wandering outside the pleroma, imparted life to matter, and formed the δημιουργός, who afterwards created the world. In order to restore the harmony of the pleroma, the two new æons, Χριστός and τὸ πνεῦμα ἅγιον, were made; and last of all Ἰησοῦς (σωτήρ) emanated from all the æons, and as the future σύζυγος of the achamoth was appointed to lead back into the pleroma alike the æons and all spiritual natures.] (Comp. *Neander, Matter*, and *Baur*, in the works mentioned, § 23; also *Baur*, Dg. s. 431 ff. On the Syzygies of the Clementines and the Sophia, as χεὶρ δημιουργοῦσα τὸ πᾶν (Hom. xi. 22, xvi. 12), cf. *Hilgenfeld*, l.c. s. 285.) [*Gieseler*, i. § 45. *Niedner*, i. s. 201 ff. *Burton*, l.c. Lect. ii. p. 36–41. *Norton*, Genuineness of the Gospels, vol. ii. note B: On Basilides and the Basilideans, p. xxxviii–xlix. Basilides' System, *G. Uhlhorn*, 1855, cf. *Hilgenfeld*, Judische Apokalyptik, 1857, s. 289 ff. *Baur* in Theol. Jahrb. 1856. On Valentinus, see *Volkmar* in Zeitschrift f. d. hist. Theol. 1855 —the relation to it of the Colorbasus-Gnosis, mentioned by Epiphanius. *Petermann's* edition of the Pistis Sophia, Berlin 1852. *Bishop Hooper* on Valentinus, Works, p. 307–345. *Mansel*, Gnostic Heresies, p. 150 ff.]

(3) The apostolical Fathers hold fast to this practical religious interest; though they do not make any use of the peculiar doctrine of the Logos (*Semisch*, ii. s. 275 ff.), yet there are single, scattered declarations, which offer the outlines of an immanent doctrine of the Trinity (*Meier*, Gesch. d. Trinit. i. s. 47 ff.). Thus particularly, *Ignatius* (in the longer rec.), ad Polyc. i.: Τοὺς καιροὺς καταμάνθανε, τὸν ὑπὲρ καιρὸν προσδόκα τὸν ἄχρονον, τὸν ἀόρατον, τὸν δι' ἡμᾶς ὁρατόν, τὸν ἀψηλάφητον, τὸν ἀπαθῆ, τὸν δι' ἡμᾶς παθητόν, τὸν κατὰ

πάντα τρόπον πάντα δι' ἡμᾶς ὑπομείναντα. Also (in the shorter rec.), ad Magnes. c. 6, in entire conformity with the Johannean doctrine: ὃς πρὸ αἰώνων παρὰ πατρὶ ἦν καὶ ἐν τέλει ἐφάνη.

(4) *Justin*[1] follows Philo to a great extent, yet more as to form than substance, with this difference only, that he identifies the Logos, by whom God has created the world, and manifested Himself in the theophanies, with His incarnate Son, even Christ Jesus. Comp. Apol. ii. 6: Ὁ δὲ υἱὸς ἐκείνου (θεοῦ), ὁ μόνος λεγόμενος κυρίως υἱὸς, ὁ λόγος πρὸ τῶν ποιημάτων, καὶ συνὼν καὶ γεννώμενος, ὅτε τὴν ἀρχὴν δι' αὐτοῦ πάντα ἔκτισε καὶ ἐκόσμησε· Χριστὸς μὲν κατὰ τὸ κεχρίσθαι καὶ κοσμῆσαι τὰ πάντα δι' αὐτοῦ τὸν θεὸν λέγεται· ὄνομα καὶ αὐτὸ περιέχον ἄγνωστον σημασίαν· ὃν τρόπον καὶ τὸ θεὸς προσαγόρευμα οὐκ ὄνομά ἐστιν, ἀλλὰ πράγματος δυσεξηγήτου ἔμφυτος τῇ φύσει τῶν ἀνθρώπων δόξα. Ἰησοῦς δὲ καὶ ἀνθρώπου καὶ σωτῆρος ὄνομα καὶ σημασίαν ἔχει. He then proceeds to the Incarnation itself. *Justin* represents the generation of the Logos as προέρχεσθαι ἀπὸ τοῦ πατρός, as γεννᾶσθαι, προβάλλεσθαι (Dial. c. Tryph. c. 61), and adduces several illustrations in support of his views. Thus man utters words without any loss of his nature; fire kindles fire without undergoing any diminution, etc. (The addition ἀλλ' οὐ τοιοῦτον is not genuine, see the note in the edit. of *Maran*: Si quis tamen retineat hæc verba, scribenda sunt cum interrogationis nota, ut in edit. Lond.) On the other hand, he rejects (Dial. c. Tryph. 128) the illustration taken from the sun and its beams; we can neither speak of an ἀποτέμνεσθαι, nor of an ἐκτείνεσθαι; see *Dorner*, ii. 1, s. 428. On the different understanding of the word *Logos*, now as the creative Word, and now as reason, and on the relation of Justin's doctrine of the Logos, on the one hand to the Old Testament conceptions, and on the other to the Platonic and Stoic philosophy, see *Duncker*, Logoslehre Just. s. 14 ff. [Comp. *Bull*, Judicium Eccles. Cath., App.

[1] "The apostolic *Fathers make no use of the doctrine of the Logos, but adhere to simple aphoristic and undeveloped declarations respecting the divine dignity of Christ*," Semisch, ii. s. 275 ff.; compare, however, *Meier*, Gesch. d. Trinit. i. s. 47 ff., who sees (s. 51) in these most ancient representations an advance from the general ideas of revelation, reconciliation, etc., to the beginnings of the immanent Trinity.

ad c. vii. § 6. *Faber's* Apostolicity of Trinitarianism, 1832, i. 48 ff., 89 ff., 143, ii. 144, et passim.]

(5) *Tatian*, Contra Græc. c. 5, uses illustrations similar to those of Justin. The Logos first existed as immanent (ὑπέστησε) in the Father (God), but derived His existence (προπηδᾷ) from His will, and thus was the ἔργον πρωτότοκον of the Father ἀρχὴ τοῦ κόσμου. He is begotten κατὰ μερισμόν, not κατ' ἀποκοπήν. On this distinction, cf. *Möller*, l.c. s. 170 ff.

(6) *Theoph.* ad Autol. ii. 10, treats most fully of the going forth of the Logos from God, and he is the first writer who uses the distinction between the λ. ἐνδιάθετος and λ. προφορικός in this definite form (*Baur*, s. 167): Ἔχων οὖν ὁ θεὸς τὸν ἑαυτοῦ λόγον ἐνδιάθετον ἐν τοῖς ἰδίοις σπλάγχνοις, ἐγέννησεν αὐτὸν μετὰ τῆς ἑαυτοῦ σοφίας ἐξερευξάμενος[1] πρὸ τῶν ὅλων. Likewise c. 22: Οὐχ ὡς οἱ ποιηταὶ καὶ μυθογράφοι λέγουσιν υἱοὺς θεῶν ἐκ συνουσίας γεννωμένους, ἀλλ' ὡς ἀλήθεια διηγεῖται τὸν λόγον, τὸν ὄντα διαπαντὸς ἐνδιάθετον ἐν καρδίᾳ θεοῦ. Πρὸ γάρ τι γίνεσθαι, τοῦτον εἶχε σύμβουλον, ἑαυτοῦ νοῦν καὶ φρόνησιν ὄντα· ὁπότε δὲ ἠθέλησεν ὁ θεὸς ποιῆσαι ὅσα ἐβουλεύσατο, τοῦτον τὸν λόγον ἐγέννησε προφορικὸν, πρωτότοκον πάσης κτίσεως· οὐ κενωθεὶς αὐτὸς τοῦ λόγου, ἀλλὰ λόγον γεννήσας, καὶ τῷ λόγῳ αὐτοῦ διαπαντὸς ὁμιλῶν.

(7) *Athen.* Leg. c. 10, calls the Son of God (in contrast with the sons of the heathen gods) λόγος τοῦ πατρὸς ἐν ἰδέᾳ καὶ ἐνεργείᾳ· πρὸς αὐτοῦ γὰρ καὶ δι' αὐτοῦ πάντα ἐγένετο, ἑνὸς ὄντος τοῦ πατρὸς καὶ τοῦ υἱοῦ. The distinction between ἐν ἰδέᾳ and ἐν ἐνεργείᾳ corresponds to that between λόγος ἐνδιάθετος and λόγος προφορικός. Comp. *Baur*, s. 170 ff. *Dorner*, s. 440.

(8) In the writings of *Clement* the doctrine of the Logos forms the central point of his whole system of theology, and the mainspring of his religious feelings and sentiments. Without the Logos there is neither light nor life (Coh. p. 87). He is the divine instructor of man (παιδαγωγός). Pæd. iii. 12, p. 310: Πάντα ὁ λόγος καὶ ποιεῖ καὶ διδάσκει καὶ παιδαγωγεῖ· ἵππος ἄγεται χαλινῷ καὶ ταῦρος ἄγεται ζυγῷ· θηρία βρόχῳ ἁλίσκεται· ὁ δὲ ἄνθρωπος μεταπλάσσεται λόγῳ·

---

[1] With reference to Ps. xlv. (xliv.) 1; ἐξηρεύξατο ἡ καρδία μου λόγον ἀγαθόν.

§ 42.] THE THEOLOGUMENON OF THE CHURCH, ETC. 165

ᾧ θηρία τιθασσεύεται καὶ νηκτὰ δελεάζεται καὶ πτηνὰ κατασύρεται κ.τ.λ. Comp. the beautiful hymn, εἰς τὸν παιδαγωγόν, at the end of his work. God has created the world by the Logos; yea, the Logos is the Creator Himself (ὁ τοῦ κόσμου καὶ ἀνθρώπου δημιουργός); He gave the law, inspired the prophets; from Him proceeded the theophanies; Pæd. i. 7, p. 132–134, ii. 8, p. 215, ii. 10, p. 224, 229, iii. 3, p. 264, iii. 4, p. 269; comp. 273, 280, 293, 297, 307. Strom. i. 23, p. 421, 422, vii. 1, p. 833. In his view (as in that of Philo) the Logos is the ἀρχιερεύς, even apart from the Incarnation, Strom. ii. 9, p. 433, 500. He is the face (πρόσωπον) of God, by which God is seen; the peaceful bosom of the Father (λαθικηδὴς μαζὸς τοῦ πατρός) in which His children can take refuge, Pæd. i. 6 and 7, p. 124, 132. The Logos is superior to men and angels, but subordinate to the Father. *Principal passage,* Strom. vii. 2, p. 831: On earth the righteous man is the most excellent being; in heaven, the angels, because they are yet purer and more perfect. Τελειωτάτη δὴ καὶ ἁγιωτάτη καὶ κυριωτάτη καὶ ἡγεμονικωτάτη καὶ βασιλικωτάτη καὶ εὐεργετικωτάτη ἡ υἱοῦ φύσις, ἡ τῷ μόνῳ παντοκράτορι προσεχεστάτη. Αὕτη ἡ μεγίστη ὑπεροχή, ᾗ τὰ πάντα διατάσσεται κατὰ τὸ θέλημα τοῦ πατρός, καὶ τὸ πᾶν ἄριστα οἰακίζει, ἀκαμάτῳ καὶ ἀτρύτῳ δυνάμει πάντα ἐργαζομένη, δι' ὧν ἐνεργεῖ τὰς ἀποκρύφους ἐννοίας ἐπιβλέπουσα. Οὐ γὰρ ἐξίσταταί ποτε τῆς αὐτοῦ περιωπῆς ὁ υἱὸς τοῦ θεοῦ· οὐ μεριζόμενος, οὐκ ἀποτεμνόμενος, οὐ μεταβαίνων ἐκ τόπου εἰς τόπον, πάντῃ δὲ ὢν πάντοτε, καὶ μηδαμῇ περιεχόμενος, ὅλος νοῦς, ὅλος φῶς πατρῷον, ὅλος ὀφθαλμός, πάντα ὁρῶν, πάντα ἀκούων, εἰδὼς πάντα, δυνάμει τὰς δυνάμεις ἐρευνῶν. Τούτῳ πᾶσα ὑποτέτακται στρατιὰ ἀγγέλων τε καὶ θεῶν, τῷ λόγῳ τῷ πατρικῷ τὴν ἁγίαν οἰκονομίαν ἀναδεδειγμένῳ διὰ τὸν ὑποτάξαντα, δι' ὧν καὶ πάντες αὐτοῦ οἱ ἄνθρωποι· ἀλλ' οἱ μὲν κατ' ἐπίγνωσιν, οἱ δὲ οὐδέπω· καὶ οἱ μὲν ὡς φίλοι, οἱ δὲ ὡς οἰκέται πιστοί, οἱ δὲ ὡς ἁπλῶς οἰκέται. (The true knowledge of the Logos is the privilege of the true Gnostic.) Divine worship is due to the Logos, vii. 7, p. 851, Quis Div. Salv. p. 956. [*Burton,* Testimony of the Ante-Nicene Fathers to the Divinity of Christ (Works ii. p. 171 ff.).] On the mode of generation Clement speaks less explicitly than the before-mentioned writers. (On his relation to them, see *Münscher*, Handbuch, i. 422.) He attaches more importance to the immanence of the Logos. In his opinion, the Logos is not only the word of God spoken at the creation, but the *speaking* and creative Word; see *Dorner*, s. 446. He also holds, along with the concrete idea of the individuality of the Logos, another notion of a more general import, according to which the Logos is identical with the higher spiritual and rational life, the life of ideas in general; by this idea of the Logos the ante-Christian world was moved, comp. Strom. v. p. 654; hence the charge of *Photius* (Bibl. Cod. 109), that Clement taught the existence of a twofold Logos of the Father, only the inferior of whom appeared on earth; see *Baur*, Trinit. Lehre, s. 195; Dg. s. 446. Accordingly, those who study the writings of Clement merely for the purpose of deducing a strictly doctrinal system will not be satisfied, and, like *Münscher* (Handbuch, i. s. 418), they will see in him "*mere declamation, from which no definite idea can be derived.*" On the contrary, those who take in his religious system as a whole will feel more inclined to adopt the language of *Möhler*, that Clement "*has written and sung of the dogma of the Logos with greater clearness than all the other Fathers of this period, but especially with unusual depth of feeling, and the most ardent enthusiasm*" (Patrologie, s. 460, 61). Comp. also *Lämmer*, l.c. *Möller*, Gesch. der Kosmol. s. 518 ff.

(9) *Tert.* Adv. Prax. c. 2: Nos unicum quidem Deum credimus, sub hac tamen dispensatione, quam œconomiam dicimus, ut unici Dei sit et filius sermo ipsius, qui ex ipso processerit, per quem omnia facta sunt, et sine quo factum est nihil. C. 5: Ante omnia enim Deus erat solus, ipse sibi et mundus et locus et omnia. Solus autem, quia nihil aliud extrinsecus præter illum. Ceterum ne tunc quidem solus: habebat enim secum, quam habebat in semetipso, rationem suam scilicet, etc. C. 8: Protulit enim Deus sermonem, sicut radix fruticem et fons fluvium et sol radium; nam et istæ species probolæ sunt earum substantiarum, ex quibus prodeunt. In c. 9 the Son is even called a *portio* of the Father. Comp. *Neander's* Antignostikus, s. 476 ff. "*We find in Tertullian, on the one hand, the effort to hold fast the entire equality of the Father and the Son; on the other hand,*

§ 42.] THE THEOLOGUMENON OF THE CHURCH, ETC. 167

the inequality is so manifestly conceded or presupposed, it is everywhere expressed in so marked and, as it were, involuntary a way, and it strikes its roots so deeply into his whole system and modes of expression, that it must doubtless be considered as the real and inmost conception of Tertullian's system." Schwegler, Montanismus, s. 41 [but comp. Meier, Gesch. d. Trin. i. 80 ff.; Dorner, i. 477, 564–601]. According to Dorner (s. 588), Tert. uses the word *filiatio* in a threefold sense; that which is new in the system of Tertullian, and of importance in reference to later times, is this, that he employs the term "Son" (instead of "Word") in order to denote the personal existence of the Logos; see s. 600. At the same time there is in *Tertullian* this peculiarity, that he distinguishes the three factors (*momenta*) of the Trinity as so many periods of time; Adv. Praxeas, c. 12, 13; Baur, Trin. Lehre, s. 176; Meier, s. 80 ff.

(10) Iren. Advers. Hær. ii. 28, p. 158: Si quis itaque nobis dixerit: Quomodo ergo filius prolatus a patre est? dicimus ei: Quia prolationem istam sive generationem sive nuncupationem sive adapertionem, aut quolibet quis nomine vocaverit generationem ejus inenarrabilem existentem, nemo novit, non Valentinus, non Marcion, neque Saturninus, neque Basilides, neque Angeli, neque Archangeli, neque Principes, neque Potestates, nisi solus qui generavit, Pater, et qui natus est, Filius. Inenarrabilis itaque generatio ejus quum sit, quicunque nituntur generationes et prolationes enarrare, non sunt compotes sui, ea, quæ inenarrabilia sunt, enarrare promittentes. Quoniam enim ex cogitatione et sensu verbum emittitur, hoc utique omnes sciunt homines. Non ergo magnum quid invenerunt, qui emissiones excogitaverunt, neque absconditum mysterium, si id quod ab omnibus intelligitur, transtulerunt in unigenitum Dei verbum, et quem inenarrabilem et innominabilem vocant, hunc, *quasi ipsi obstetricaverint*, primæ generationis ejus prolationem et generationem enuntiant, assimilantes eum hominum verbo emissionis (scilicet λόγῳ προφορικῷ). In the opinion of *Irenæus*, faith in the *Son* rests simply on the παράδοσις. The Logos is both reason (wisdom) and the Word (Adv. Hær. iv. 20. 1): Adest enim ei (Deo) semper Verbum et Sapientia (Fil. et Spirit.), per quos et in quibus omnia libere et sponte fecit, ad

quos et loquitur dicens: Faciamus hominem ad imaginem et similitudinem nostram. The Son is in every respect equal to the Father: Adv. Hær. ii. 13 : Necesse est itaque, et eum, qui ex eo est Logos, imo magis autem ipsum Nun, cum sit Logos, perfectum et inpassibilem esse.—In accordance with his practical tendency, *Irenæus* has less to say of the Logos *prior* to His incarnation than of Christ the God-man (of which, infra). In his opinion, the Father is the invisible of the Son, and the Son the visible of the Father (iv. 6. 6); or (after an unnamed author) the Son is the measure of the Father (mensura Patris filius, quoniam et capit eum), iv. 2. 2 ; he even calls the Son and the Spirit the hands of God.[1] Comp. *Möhler*, Patrologie, 357 ff. *Münscher*, Handbuch, i. s. 411 ff. *Duncker*, l.c. s. 40 ff. *Dorner*, s. 467 ff. *Baur*, s. 172 ff., and Dg. s. 439 ff.

§ 43.

(*d*) *Origen's Doctrine of the Logos.*

After *Tertullian* had employed the term "Son" in reference to the personality of the Logos more distinctly than had previously been done (1), *Origen* decisively adopted this terminology (2), and was led to the idea of an eternal generation (3). Though he kept clear with all strictness from any notion of physical emanation (4), yet he was on the other hand pressed to a subordination of the Son to the Father (5). Consequently his definitions by no means satisfied the consciousness of the Church, but led to new misunderstandings, and were the source of new wide-reaching controversies (6).

(1) Comp. § 42, note 9.
(2) Hom. i. in Joh. Opp. iv. p. 22 ss. He finds fault with those who, in a one-sided manner, merely adopt the term Logos (ἐπὶ δὲ μόνης τῆς λόγος προσηγορίας ἱστάμενοι), and are not able to infer the identity of the terms Logos and Son

---

[1] The same idea is found in the Clementines, in which the σοφία appears as χεὶρ δημιουργοῦσα. *Baur*, Dg. s. 441.

from the other predicates applied to Christ; who also restrict the term *Logos* to the *Word*, imagining that the προσφορὰ πατρική consists οἰονεὶ ἐν συλλαβαῖς. In his opinion the Logos is not merely the Word, but a transcendent living hypostasis, the sum of all ideas, the independent personal Wisdom of God; comp. in Joh. i. 39, l.c. p. 39: Οὐ γὰρ ἐν ψιλαῖς φαντασίαις τοῦ θεοῦ τὴν ὑπόστασιν ἔχει ἡ σοφία αὐτοῦ, κατὰ τὰ ἀνάλογα τοῖς ἀνθρωπίνοις ἐννοήμασι φαντάσματα. Εἰ δέ τις οἷος τέ ἐστιν ἀσώματον ὑπόστασιν ποικίλων θεωρημάτον, περιεχόντων τοὺς τῶν ὅλων λόγους, ζῶσαν καὶ οἰονεὶ ἔμψυχον ἐπενοεῖν· εἴσεται τὴν ὑπὲρ πᾶσαν κτίσιν σοφίαν τοῦ θεοῦ, καλῶς περὶ αὐτῆς λέγουσαν· Ὁ θεὸς ἔκτισέ με κ.τ.λ. Comp. De Princip. i. 2. 2: Nemo putet, nos *insubstantivum* dicere, cum filiam Dei sapientiam nominamus, etc.; and thus he calls (Contra Cels. vi. 64) the Logos, οὐσίαν οὐσιῶν, ἰδέαν ἰδεῶν; comp. *Thomasias*, s. 113. What is true of the *Logos* in relation to creation holds good also of the *Son*. He is the organ for the creation of the world. As a house or a vessel is built according to the ideas of the architect, so God created the world according to the ideas which are contained in Wisdom; comp. Hom. xxxii. in Joh. (Opp. iv. p. 449), and De Princip. i. 2 (Opp. i. p. 53). God never existed without the Wisdom (the Son); for, to maintain the contrary, would virtually amount to the assertion, that God either *could* not beget or *would* not beget, either of which is absurd and impious. With all his love for abstractions, *Origen* here calls images to his aid. Besides the already used-up comparison with the sun and its beams, he employs a new one of a statue and a copy on a reduced scale; this comparison, however, he refers rather to the incarnate Son (Christ in the flesh) than to Him as existing before the world (the Logos). But with him both run into each other.

(3) It is difficult to determine whether this idea of generation is consistently carried out, since it is not quite evident whether *Origen* refers it to the *nature* or the *will* of the Father; see *Baur*, s. 204; on the other side, comp. *Dorner*, s. 640 ff.

(4) De Princip. i. 4 (Opp. i. p. 55; *Redep.* p. 110): Infandum autem est et illicitum, Deum patrem in generatione unigeniti Filii sui atque in subsistentia ejus exæquare alicui

vel hominum vel aliorum animantium generanti, etc.; and again (*Redep.* p. 112): Observandum namque est, ne quis incurrat in illas absurdas fabulas eorum, qui prolationes quasdam sibi ipsis depingunt, ut divinam naturam in partes vocent, et Deum patrem quantum in se est dividant, cum hoc de incorporea natura vel leviter suspicari non solum extremæ impietatis sit, verum etiam ultimæ insipientiæ, nec omnino ad intelligentiam consequens, ut incorporeæ naturæ substantialis divisio possit intelligi. "As the will of man proceeds from his reason, and the one is not to be separated from the other, so the Son proceeds from the Father." *Origen* did not make use of the comparison with the human *word*, which was previously employed. He also considers the generation of the Son as *eternal*, because God did not at any time begin to be a Father, like fathers among men. Comp. *Gieseler,* Dogmeng. s. 143 [the passage is in a fragment in *Eusebius,* contra Marcellum, l.c. 4]. According to *Baur,* "*it is not clear whether Origen regards the Son as derived from the essence of the Father or not; statements are found which look both ways, and which do not appear to be capable of reconciliation,*" Dg. s. 451. According to *Baur,* therefore, "*Origen unites the two opposite systems of doctrine, the germs of the Athanasian and the Arian are both found in him,*" Dg. s. 453. [In another passage (in *Athanasius*, De Decretis Conc. Nic. § 27) he says: "As light cannot be without its brightness, so God can never have been without the Son, the brightness of His majesty."]

(5) See below, § 46.

(6) Particularly was the expression υἱὸς τοῦ θεοῦ, which in the New Testament is undeniably used in respect to the historical Christ,[1] confounded with the metaphysical and dogmatic usage of the schools; and here were the germs of new controversies, which in the end led to a recognition of the difference on the biblical basis. On the other hand, from the speculative standpoint, we may, with *Dorner,* in this doctrine of the eternal

[1] "*The more I endeavour to realize the manner of thinking and speaking in the New Testament, the more decided is my opinion, that the historical Son of God, as such, cannot be directly and absolutely called God in the New Testament without completely destroying the monotheistic system of the apostles.*" *Lücke,* Stud. und Krit. 1840, i. s. 91. [But see in reply, *Nitzsch* in the same journal, 1841. Comp. also *G. L. Hahn,* Die Theologie des N. T. 1854, § 87.] Cf. also *Redepenning,* Origenes, ii. p. 88.

generation, descry a thankworthy progress. To attain to this *"mystery, which contains the very kernel of Christianity, subordination has the character of an auxiliary doctrine."* It is (*Dorner* says in his earlier edition, s. 42) *"a necessary aid in the substitution of several actual hypostases in God, for the doctrine of the Logos, as previously held, which only vaguely maintained the distinction of hypostases in God."*

§ 44.

The Holy Ghost.

*Keil, ob die ältesten Lehrer einen Unterschied zwischen Sohn und Geist gekannt? in Flatts Magazin für christliche Dogmatik und Moral, Bd. iv. s. 34 ff. [*Burton*, Testimonies of the Ante-Nicene Fathers to the Trinity, the Divinity of the Holy Ghost (Works, ii.). Comp. the Introduct. where the literature is given.] *Georgii*, dogmengeschichtliche Untersuchungen über die Lehre vom h. Geist bei Justin M., in the Studien der Geistlichkeit, Würtembergs, by Stirm, x. 2, s. 69 ff. *Hasselbach* in the theolog. Stud. und Krit. 1839, s. 378 ff. *Semisch*, Justin d. Märt. ii. s. 305 ff. *Kahnis*, Die Lehre vom heiligen Geiste, i., Halle 1847. [*H. B. Swete*, Early History of the Doctrine of the Holy Spirit, Camb. 1873.]

The doctrine concerning the Holy Ghost, like that of the Son, was considered important from the practical point of view (1), in reference to His prophetic agency (in the more comprehensive sense of the word), to the witness which He bears in the hearts of believers, and, in fine, to His living power in the Church (2). As soon, however, as the attempt was made to go beyond the Trinity of revelation (*i.e.* the Trinity as it manifests itself in the work of redemption), and to comprehend and define the nature of the Holy Spirit, and the relation in which He stands to the Father and the Logos, difficulties sprung up, the solution of which became problems of speculative theology. By some, the *Wisdom* of the Old Testament, from which the doctrine of the Logos was developed, was called πνεῦμα ἅγιον, and made co-ordinate with the Word (3). Others either identified the Logos with the Spirit, or expressed themselves in a vague manner as to the distinction between them (4), and the Holy Ghost (impersonally viewed) appears as a mere divine attribute, gift, or agency (5). But the pressure of logical consistency led gradually to the view of the personality of the Holy Ghost, and his definite distinction from the Word (6).

(1) In the O. T. the רוּחַ אֱלֹהִים (Gen. i. 3) appears already as the creative power of life, comp. Ps. civ. 30, and other passages; as the Spirit of heroism, Judg. vi. 34, xi. 29, xiii. 25, etc.; as the Spirit of insight and wisdom, Ex. xxxi. 3, xxxv. 31; Job xxxii. 8; Isa. xi. 2; especially as the Spirit of prophecy, Num. xxiv. 2; 1 Sam. x. 6, 10, xix. 20, 23, etc.; also as the good, holy Spirit, Ps. li. 13, cxliii. 10. In the N. T., too, the $\pi\nu\epsilon\hat{u}\mu a$ $\ddot{a}\gamma\iota o\nu$ is made equivalent to the $\delta\acute{u}\nu a\mu\iota s$ $\dot{u}\psi\acute{\iota}\sigma\tau o\nu$, Luke i. 35, and to the $\sigma o\phi\acute{\iota} a$, Acts vi. 3, 10. Specifically Christian is the making the Holy Spirit equivalent to the *Spirit of Christ*, as when it is said that the Spirit descends upon Christ (Matt. iii. 16 and the parallel places), and is given to Him without measure (John iv. 34), or that He proceeds from Christ and is given to the disciples (John xx. 22), or is promised to them as the Paraclete, John xv. 26, etc. It has been held essential to the Christian faith to believe that the Spirit from the time of the pentecostal outpouring (Acts ii.), and other extraordinary manifestations of His presence (Acts viii. 14, 17, xix. 1–6), abides in the Church (2 Cor. xiii. 13), and thus that all believers have part in the Spirit, who manifests Himself as *one*, externally in the different gifts (*charismata*, 1 Cor. xii. 4, etc.), and internally working as the Spirit of sanctification, of trust, and of love; and who is also a pledge and seal of the grace of God, 2 Cor. i. 22, v. 5; Eph. i. 14, etc. Compare the works on Biblical Theology.

(2) It is not to be forgotten that the *trias of revelation* was held in a complete form long before the Church came to clear statements respecting the *essential trias*. (Comp. note 1 of the next section.) In the former the Holy Ghost has His definite position along (co-ordinate) with the Father and the Son, 2 Cor. xiii. 13; Matt. xviii. 19. In the apostolic Fathers, we find only isolated declarations as to the Holy Ghost. *Justin M.* makes particular mention of the $\pi\nu\epsilon\hat{u}\mu a$ $\pi\rho o\phi\eta\tau\iota\kappa\acute{o}\nu$ (the term in question occurs twenty-two times in his Apology, nine times in Trypho; see *Semisch*, ii. s. 332, note), while he

does not speak of the influence which He continues to exert upon believers (ibid. s. 329). On the other hand, in *Justin* the Logos, as the λόγος σπερματικός, takes the place of the Holy Spirit, since to Him are ascribed good impulses in the minds of believers. (Comp. *Duncker*, Christl. Logoslehre, s. 37.) *Irenæus*, iii. 24. 1, calls the Holy Ghost the "communitas Christi, confirmatio fidei nostræ, scala ascensionis ad Deum;"[1] comp. iii. 17, v. 6, v. 10, and § 71. At the same time he considers Him as the prophetic Spirit, and makes a distinction between Him as the principle which animates and inspires, and that animation and inspiration itself, Adv. Hær. v. 12. 2: Ἕτερόν ἐστι πνοὴ ζωῆς, ἡ καὶ ψυχικὸν ἀπεργαζομένη τὸν ἄνθρωπον, καὶ ἕτερον πνεῦμα ζωοποιοῦν, τὸ καὶ πνευματικὸν αὐτὸν ἀποτελοῦν . . . ἕτερον δέ ἐστι τὸ ποιηθὲν τοῦ ποιήσαντος· ἡ οὖν πνοὴ πρόσκαιρος, τὸ δὲ πνεῦμα ἀένναον. Comp. *Duncker*, s. 60 ff.; *Kahnis*, s. 255 ff.

(3) *Theoph.* ad Autol. i. 7: Ὁ δὲ θεὸς διὰ τοῦ λόγου αὐτοῦ καὶ τῆς σοφίας ἐποίησε τὰ πάντα; here σοφία is either synonymous with λόγος, or forms the second member; in the former case, there would be no mention of the Spirit; in the latter, He would be identified with the σοφία; and this agrees with ii. 15, where θεός, λόγος, and σοφία are said to compose the Trinity; comp. § 45. · *Iren.* iv. 20, p. 253: Adest enim ei (Deo) semper verbum et sapientia, Filius et Spiritus . . . ad quos et loquitur, dicens: Faciamus hominem ad imaginem et similitudinem nostram; and again: Deus omnia *verbo* fecit et *sapientia* adornavit. [*Burton*, l.c. p. 49–51.] Comp. iv. 7, p. 236: Ministrat enim ei ad omnia sua progenies et figuratio sua, *i.e.* Filius et Spiritus Sanctus, verbum et sapientia, quibus serviunt et subjecti sunt omnes angeli. *Tert.* Adv. Prax. c. 6: Nam ut primum Deus voluit ea, quæ cum Sophiæ ratione et sermone disposuerat intra se, in substantias et species suas edere, ipsum primum protulit sermonem, habentem in se individuas suas, Rationem et Sophiam, ut per ipsum fierent universa, per quem erant cogitata atque disposita, immo et facta jam, quantum in Dei sensu. Hoc enim eis deerat, ut coram quoque in suis speciebus atque substantiis cognoscerentur

---

[1] A similar image is made use of by *Ignatius*, Ep. ad Ephes. 9, when he says: Ἀναφερόμενοι εἰς τὰ ὕψη διὰ τῆς μηχανῆς Ἰησοῦ Χριστοῦ, ὅς ἐστιν σταυρός, σχοινίῳ χρώμενοι τῷ πνεύματι τῷ ἁγίῳ.

et tenerentur. Comp. c. 7, and the formula De Orat. i. ab initio: Dei Spiritus et Dei sermo et Dei ratio, sermo rationis et ratio sermonis et spiritus utrumque Jesus Christus, dominus noster.

(4) From the time of *Souverain* (Platonismus der Kirchenväter, s. 329 ff.), most historians of doctrines have supposed that the Fathers[1] in general, and *Justin M.* in particular, made no real distinction between the Logos and the Spirit. Several of the more recent investigators have also come to the same conclusion. Thus *Georgii* (in the work referred to above), s. 120: "*This much is evident, that in Justin the relation between the Logos and the Pneuma is indefinite, in flowing lines; as in him the Spirit has little, if any, different functions from those of the Logos, so a distinction between them could not, in his view, be demanded by any dogmatic necessity, but could only be occasioned by the conflict, in which the doctrine of the Spirit, as handed down by the Fathers, stood in relation to that of the Logos.*" Comp. *Hasselbach*, ubi supra. With them *Baur* (Dg. s. 504, and elsewhere) is in most distinct agreement. He considers this identifying of the Logos and Pneuma as belonging to the stage of Jewish Christianity. According to him, the πνεῦμα and the λόγος unite in the idea of the σοφία. On the other hand, *Semisch* and *Kahnis* (s. 238 ff.) have tried to defend the Martyr against this objection. One of the principal passages is Apol. i. 33: Τὸ πνεῦμα οὖν καὶ τὴν δύναμιν τὴν παρὰ τοῦ θεοῦ οὐδὲν ἄλλο νοῆσαι θέμις, ἢ τὸν λόγον, ὃς καὶ πρωτότοκος τῷ θεῷ ἐστι, comp. c. 36. He indeed there speaks of the πνεῦμα in Luke i. 35; and it cannot be inferred that he thoroughly identifies the Logos with the Spirit. But still there is here this confounding of the two; and it cannot be explained by saying that the Logos is conceived of as a spiritual being in general, nor by assuming that the Logos forms the body for Himself in the womb of Mary. And when *Tertullian*, Adv. Prax. c. 26, uses similar expressions, this goes to prove that other Fathers besides *Justin* are chargeable with the same want of distinctness. The same is true as regards the manner in which *Justin* ascribes the inspiration of the prophets, sometimes to the Logos, sometimes to the Pneuma, Apol. i. 36,

---

[1] With reference to the apostolic Fathers, *Baur* (Dg. s. 507) refers to a remarkable passage in the "Shepherd" of *Hermas* (Simil. 5) which must not be overlooked.

and elsewhere. (Only it should not be forgotten that, even in the biblical usage, the distinction is not held with sharp doctrinal consistency.) The confusion of agencies leads to a (relative) confounding of the Persons. That *Justin* (in opposition to the baptismal formula and the common confession of the Church) formally put a dyas (two persons) in place of the trias, cannot be justly alleged; for he himself in other passages names the Father, Son, and Spirit (Apol. i. 6, 30, 60), and assigns the third place to the Spirit (comp. § 46): "*but still it is none the less true, that his philosophical principles, logically carried out, lead only to a dyas, and that he could not doctrinally establish the difference between the Son and the Spirit,*" Duncker, l.c. s. 38. There is unquestionably a formal confusion in *Theophilus* ad Autol. ii. c. 10: Οὗτος (ὁ λόγος) ὢν πνεῦμα θεοῦ καὶ ἀρχὴ καὶ σοφία καὶ δύναμις ὑψίστου κατήρχετο εἰς τοὺς προφήτας, καὶ δι' αὐτῶν ἐλάλει τὰ περὶ τῆς ποιήσεως τοῦ κόσμου καὶ τῶν λοιπῶν ἁπάντων· οὐ γὰρ ἦσαν οἱ προφῆται, ὅτε ὁ κόσμος ἐγένετο· ἀλλὰ ἡ σοφία ἡ ἐν αὐτῷ οὖσα ἡ τοῦ θεοῦ, καὶ ὁ λόγος ὁ ἅγιος αὐτοῦ, ὁ ἀεὶ συμπαρὼν αὐτῷ. Comp. the passage in note 3, above; and *Möller,* Gesch. der Kosmologie, s. 138, who sees in this wonderful mixture of names, not indeed " a definite doctrinal representation," but an *embarras de richesses!*

(5) *Justin M.* incidentally calls the Holy Ghost simply δωρεά, Coh. ad Græc. c. 32, though he assigns to Him (Apol. i. 6) the third place in the Trinity. On the question: What relation was the Holy Spirit thought to sustain to the angels? comp. *Neander,* Kg. i. s. 1040, and Dg. s. 182; Studien und Kritiken, 1833, s. 773 ff.; the latter essay was written in opposition to *Möhler,* Theolog. Quartalschrift, 1833, i. s. 49 ff. (comp. § 50, below). *Athenagoras* calls the Holy Spirit ἀπόῤῥοια, Leg. c. 10 and 24, comp. *Kahnis,* s. 245. In general, there are many passages in the Fathers "*which bring the Holy Spirit very near to the creature,*" *Kahnis,* s. 249.

(6) *Tert.* Adv. Prax. 4: Spiritum non alicunde puto, quam a Patre per Filium. Ibid. 8: Tertius est Spiritus a Deo et Filio, sicut tertius a radice fructus ex frutice, et tertius a fonte rivus ex flumine, et tertius a sole apex ex radio. Ibid. 30: Spiritus S. tertium nomen divinitatis et tertius gradus majestatis. But a subordinate position is assigned to the Spirit

when He is considered as Dei villicus, Christi vicarius, Præscr. 28 [could this properly be said to represent a *subordinate* position?]; comp. *Schwegler*, Montanismus, s. 14. *Origen*, Comm. in Joh. t. ii. 6 (Opp. t. iv. p. 60, 61), acknowledges the personality of the Holy Spirit, but subordinates Him to both the Father and the Son, by the latter of whom He is *created*, like all other things, though distinguished from all other creatures by His divine dignity: 'Ἡμεῖς μέντοιγε τρεῖς ὑποστάσεις πειθόμενοι τυγχάνειν, τὸν πατέρα καὶ τὸν υἱὸν καὶ τὸ ἅγιον πνεῦμα, καὶ ἀγέννητον μηδὲν ἕτερον τοῦ πατρὸς εἶναι πιστεύοντες, ὡς εὐσεβέστερον καὶ ἀληθὲς προσιέμεθα, τὸ πάντων διὰ τοῦ λόγου γενομένων, τὸ ἅγιον πνεῦμα πάντων εἶναι τιμιώτερον, καὶ τάξει πάντων τῶν ὑπὸ τοῦ πατρὸς διὰ Χριστοῦ γεγεννημένων. [*Burton*, l.c. p. 99 ff.] Comp. t. xiii. 25, p. 234, and 34, p. 244: Οὐκ ἄτοπον δὲ καὶ τὸ ἅγιον πνεῦμα τρέφεσθαι λέγειν.[1] Nevertheless, there is an infinite chasm between the Spirit of God and other spirits created by God; comp. Comm. in Ep. ad. Rom. vii. (Opp. iv. p. 593). But in another passage (which is extant only in the translation of *Rufinus*, De Princip. i. 3. 3, Opp. i. 1, p. 61, *Redep.* p. 123) *Origen* says, that he had not as yet met with any passage in the sacred Scriptures in which the Holy Spirit was called a created being; though afterwards *Epiphanius, Justinian*, etc., blamed him for maintaining this opinion; comp. *Epiphan.* 64, 5, *Hieron.* ad Avit. Ep. 94, quoted by *Münscher* (*von Cölln*), s. 194. *Schnitzer*, s. 43. *Neander*, Kirchg. i. 3, s. 1040. *Thomasius*, s. 144 ff. (*Redepenning*, Origenes, ii. p. 309 ff., and the other passages there adduced). [*Burton*, l.c. p. 89.] Also *Baur*, Dg. s. 516.

§ 45.

The Triad.

[*Waterland's* Works, new ed. Oxford 1842, vols. ii. and iii. *G. S. Faber*, Apostolicity of Trinitarianism, 2 vols. Lond. 1832. *William Jones* (of Nayland), Works, new ed. 1826, vol i., The Catholic Doctrine of the Trinity. *Bishop Bull*, Defensio Fidei Nicænæ, and his Judicium Eccl. Cath.; Works, by *Burton*, 8 vols. 1846.]

---

[1] *Origen's* principal work, De Principiis, i. 3, also treats of the Holy Ghost; but, as it exists only in the translation of Rufinus, it is not available for our purpose.

The doctrine of God *the Father, Son,* and *Holy Ghost,* is the doctrine of primitive Christianity (1), but has in the New Testament a bearing only upon the Christian economy, without any pretension to speculative significance, and therefore cannot be rightly understood but in intimate connection with the history of Jesus, and the work which He accomplished (2). Accordingly, the belief in the *Father, Son,* and *Holy Ghost* belonged to the *Regula fidei,* apart from all speculative development of the doctrine of the Logos, and appears in what is commonly called the Apostles' Creed, in this historico-epic form, without being summed up in a unity. The Greek name τριάς appears first in Theophilus (3); the Latin term *Trinitas,* of a more comprehensive doctrinal import, is found in Tertullian (4).

(1) Matt. xxviii. 19 (if the baptismal formula be genuine); 1 Cor. xii. 4-6; 2 Cor. xiii. 13, and elsewhere. Comp. the commentaries on these passages, *de Wette's* biblische Dogmatik, § 238, 267, and especially *Lücke* in the Studien und Kritiken, 1840, 1. [*Pye Smith,* the Script. Testim. to the Messiah, iii. p. 13 ff., iii. p. 258 ff.; *Knapp,* l.c. s. 119 ff., 132 ff.] *Gieseler,* Dg. s. 118, and *Neander,* Dg. s. 137, also distinguish correctly the practical element of the doctrine and its relation to the economy of the divine dispensations, from its speculative construction. *Neander:* "This doctrine of God, the Creator, Redeemer, and Sanctifier of humanity in Christ, was essential to the Christian consciousness, and therefore has existed from the beginning in the Christian Church."

(2) On this account some of the more recent writers on doctrinal theology, as *Schleiermacher* and *Hase* (2d ed. s. 626), handle the doctrine of the Trinity at the end of their system. A purely economic view of the doctrine is found in *Ignatius,* Epistle to the Ephesians, 9, where he says: " We are raised on high to the Father by the cross of Christ, as by an elevating engine, the Holy Spirit being the rope,"—a massive, but striking comparison. See above, § 44.

(3) *Theoph.* ad Autol. ii. 15: Αἱ τρεῖς ἡμέραι [πρὸ] τῶν φωστήρων γεγονυῖαι τύποι εἰσὶν τῆς τριάδος τοῦ θεοῦ καὶ τοῦ λόγου αὐτοῦ καὶ τῆς σοφίας αὐτοῦ. Τετάρτῳ δὲ τύπῳ [τόπῳ]

ἐστιν ἄνθρωπος ὁ προσδεὴς τοῦ φωτός. "Ἵνα ᾖ θεὸς, λόγος, σοφία, ἄνθρωπος. Here we have indeed the word τριάς, but not in the ecclesiastical sense of the term Trinity; for as ἄνθρωπος is mentioned as the fourth term, it is evident that the τριάς cannot be taken here as a perfect whole, consisting of three joined in one; besides, the term σοφία is used instead of τὸ πνεῦμα ἅγιον. Comp. *Suicer*, Thesaurus, s.v. τριάς, where the passage from the (spurious) treatise of *Justin*, De Expositione Fidei, p. 379, is cited (Μονὰς γὰρ ἐν τριάδι νοεῖται καὶ τριὰς ἐν μονάδι γνωρίζεται κ.τ.λ.); this passage, however, proves as little concerning the use of language during that period, as the treatise φιλόπατρις erroneously ascribed to Lucian, from which passages are cited. *Clem.* Strom. iv. 7, p. 588, knows a ἁγία τριάς, but in an anthropological sense (Faith, Love, Hope). On the terminology of Origen, comp. *Thomasius*, s. 285. [Comp. *Burton*, l.c. p. 34–36, where the subject is treated at great length.]

(4) *Tertullian*, De Pudic. c. 21: Nam et ecclesia proprie et principaliter ipse est spiritus, in quo est *Trinitas* unius divinitatis, Pater et Filius et Spiritus S. Accordingly, the Holy Spirit is the principle which constitutes the unity of the persons, or (according to *Schwegler*, Montan. s. 171) the spiritual substance common to the persons; comp. Adv. Praxeam, 2 and 3. [*Burton*, l.c. p. 68 ff.] *Cyprian* and *Novatian* immediately adopted this usage. *Cypr.* Ep. 73, p. 200 (with reference to baptism). *Novat.* de Trinitate. [*Burton*, l.c. p. 107–109, 116-123.]

§ 46.

Monarchianism and Subordination.

The strict distinction which was drawn between the hypostases (persons) in the Trinity led, in the first instance, to that system of *Subordination* in which the Son was made inferior to the Father, and the Holy Spirit to both the Father and the Son (1), which system also carried with it the appearance of tritheism (2). The orthodox were obliged to clear themselves from all appearance of tritheism, in opposition to the

Monarchians, who abandoned the personal distinctions in order to hold fast the unity of the Godhead, and thus exposed themselves to the charge of confounding the persons (Patripassianism), or even to the imputation of a heretical tendency denying the divinity of Christ (3). *Origen* now carried to such an extreme the system of hypostatizing, including the subordination scheme (4), that orthodoxy itself threatened to run over into heterodoxy, and thus gave rise to the Arian controversy in the following period.

(1) *Justin M.* Apol. i. c. 13: . . . υἱὸν αὐτοῦ τοῦ ὄντως θεοῦ μαθόντες (*scil.* τὸν Ἰησοῦν Χριστὸν) καὶ ἐν δευτέρᾳ χώρᾳ ἔχοντες, πνεῦμά τε προφητικὸν ἐν τρίτῃ τάξει, comp. i. 6 and i. 60. There are also passages in the writings of *Irenæus* which appear favourable to the idea of subordination, *e.g.* Adv. Hær. ii. 28. 6, 8; v. 18. 2: Super omnia quidem pater, et ipse est caput Christi; but elsewhere he represents the Logos as wholly God, and not a subordinate being (comp. § 42, note 9). "*It cannot be denied that Irenæus here contradicts himself, and it would be a useless labour to remove this contradiction by artificial interpretation.*" Duncker, s. 56; comp. s. 70 ff. *Dorner,* s. 409 ff. *Tert.* Advers. Prax. c. 2: Tres autem non statu, sed gradu, nec substantia, sed forma, nec potestate, sed specie: unius autem substantiæ et unius status et unius potestatis, quia unus Deus, ex quo et gradus isti et formæ et species in nomine Patris et Filii et Spiritus Sancti deputantur. Comp. c. 4 ff.

(2) Thus *Justin M.* says, Dial. cum Tryph. c. 56: The Father and the Son are distinct, not γνώμῃ, but ἀριθμῷ; and *Tertullian* (Adv. Prax. c. 10), from the proposition that, if I have a wife, it does not necessarily follow that I am the wife herself, draws the conclusion that, if God has a Son, He is not the Son Himself. He repels the charge of tritheism, Adv. Prax. 3: Simplices enim quique, ne dixerim impudentes et idiotæ, quæ major semper credentium pars est, quoniam et ipsa regula fidei a pluribus Diis seculi ad unicum et Deum verum transfert, non intelligentes *unicum* quidem, sed *cum sua œconomia* esse credendum, expavescunt ad œconomiam. Numerum et dispositionem trinitatis, divisionem præsumunt unitatis;

quando unitas ex semetipsa derivans trinitatem, non destruatur ab illa, sed administretur. Itaque duos et tres jam jactitant a nobis prædicari, se vero unius Dei cultores præsumunt, quasi non et unitas irrationaliter collecta hæresin faciat, et trinitas rationaliter expensa veritatem constituat. Comp. c. 13 and 22, where he expressly appeals to the point, that Christ did not say that He and the Father were one (*unus*, masculine), but one (*unum*, neuter), and he refers this unity to a moral relation—the dilectio patris and the obsequium filii. In the same way *Novat.* De Trin. 22 : Unum enim, non unus esse dicitur, quoniam nec ad numerum refertur, sed ad societatem alterius expromitur . . . Unum autem quod ait, ad concordiam et eandem sententiam et ad ipsam caritatis societatem pertinet, ut merito unum sit pater et filius per concordiam et per amorem, et per dilectionem. [*Burton*, l.c. p. 120, 121.] He also appeals to Apollos and Paul, 1 Cor. iii. 8 : qui autem plantat et qui rigat, unum sunt.

(3) Concerning the different classes of Unitarians, comp. § 24 and § 42.[1] It is self-evident that all who held Christ to be a mere man could know nothing of any Trinity. These may be called deistico-rationalistic *Antitrinitarians;* God in His abstract unity was, in their view, so remote from the world, and confined to His heaven, that there was no abode for Him even in Christ. Widely different were those who, apprehensive of lessening the dignity of Christ, taught that God Himself had assumed humanity *in* Him, but did not think it necessary to suppose the existence of a particular hypostasis. The name *modalistic* Antitrinitarians would be more appropriate in their case (thus *Heinichen*, de Alogis, s. 34) ; or, if the relation of God to Christ be compared to that in which He stands to the world, they might be called *pantheistic* Antitrinitarians, for they imagined God, as it were, expanded or extended into the person of Christ. Among their number are *Praxeas* and *Beryllus*, the forerunners of *Sabellius*, the former of whom was combated by Tertullian, the latter by Origen. The opinion of

[1] *Origen* already distinguishes two classes of Monarchians ; the one spoke of Jesus merely as a praecognitum et prædestinatum hominem, while the other class taught the Godhead of Christ, but identified the Godhead of the Son with that of the Father. See *Origen*, Epist. ad Tit. fragm. ii. ed. *Lommatzsch*, tom. v., in *Neander*, Dg. s. 158. Comp. the remaining passages in *Baur*, Dg. s. 454. *Novatian*, De Trin. 30.

Praxeas, that the Father, the Son, and the Holy Spirit are one and the same (ipsum eundemque esse), which virtually amounted to the later ὁμοούσιος, was interpreted by *Tertullian* as implying, ipsum patrem passum esse (Adv. Prax. c. 20, 29),[1] whence the heretical appellation *Patripassiani*. [*Burton*, Bampton Lecture, note 103, p. 588, and Testim. of the Ante-Nicene Fathers to the Trinity, etc., p. 68-83.] *Philastr.* Hær. 65. The views of *Noëtus* were similar: Theod. Fab. Hær. iii. 3 : "Ἕνα φασὶν εἶναι θεὸν καὶ πατέρα, τῶν ὅλων δημιουργόν, ἀφανῆ μὲν ὅταν ἐθέλῃ, φαινόμενον δὲ ἡνίκα ἂν βούληται· καὶ τὸν αὐτὸν ἀόρατον εἶναι καὶ ὁρώμενον, καὶ γεννητὸν καὶ ἀγέννητον· ἀγέννητον μὲν ἐξ ἀρχῆς, γεννητὸν δὲ ὅτε ἐκ παρθένου γεννηθῆναι ἠθέλησε· ἀπαθῆ καὶ ἀθάνατον, καὶ πάλιν αὖ παθητὸν καὶ θνητόν. Ἀπαθὴς γὰρ ὤν, φησί, τὸ τοῦ σταυροῦ πάθος ἐθελήσας ὑπέμεινε· τοῦτον καὶ υἱὸν ὀνομάζουσι καὶ πατέρα, πρὸς τὰς χρείας τοῦτο κἀκεῖνο καλούμενον. Comp. *Epiph.* Hær. vii. 1. [*Burton*, Bampton Lecture, note 103, p. 589, 590.] *Dorner*, s. 532 : "*It is worthy of recognition and consideration, that Noëtus already completes Patripassianism, and takes away from it the pagan illusion, whereby the divine nature is made directly finite, which we find in the system of Praxeas.*" Beryllus endeavoured to evade the inferences which may be drawn alike from Patripassianism and from Pantheism, by admitting a difference *after* the assumption of humanity, *Euseb.* vi. 33 : Βήρυλλος ὁ μικρῷ πρόσθεν δεδηλωμένος Βοστρῶν τῆς Ἀραβίας ἐπίσκοπος, τὸν ἐκκλησιαστικὸν παρεκτρέπων κανόνα, ξένα τινὰ τῆς πίστεως παρεισφέρειν ἐπειρᾶτο, τὸν σωτῆρα καὶ κύριον ἡμῶν λέγειν τολμῶν μὴ προϋφεστάναι κατ' ἰδίαν οὐσίας περιγραφὴν πρὸ τῆς εἰς ἀνθρώπους ἐπιδημίας μηδὲ μὴν θεότητα ἰδίαν ἔχειν, ἀλλ' ἐμπολιτευομένην αὐτῷ μόνην τὴν πατρικήν. Comp. *Ullmann* in the Dissert., quoted § 24, note 4, and *Fork*, Diss. Christ. Beryll. Bostr. According to *Baur* (Trin.-Lehre, s. 289, and Dg. s. 474), Beryllus ought to be classed with Artemon and Theodotus;

---

[1] As *Praxeas* was also a decided opponent of Montanism, he had to endure the reproach of *Tertullian*, that, during his residence in Rome, he had done the work of the devil in two respects: prophetiam expulit, et hæresin intulit, Paracletum fugavit et Patrem crucifixit, Adv. Prax. i. The argument of *Tertullian* is strikingly drawn out by *Baur*, Dg. s. 457.

Meier (Trin.-Lehre, s. 114), however, supposes a certain distinction between them. Comp. *Dorner*, s. 545, and *Neander*, Dg. s. 161: " The most natural conclusion is, that Beryl did not wholly belong to either of the two classes (of Monarchians), but held a mediating view, which agrees with his historical position." Against this mediating position *Baur* protests (l.c.) most emphatically. A *mediating* position he certainly did not adopt, but an *intermediate* one between the two schools. To those who adopted the tendency of Noëtus belong *Beron* and his followers, who were combated by Hippolytus; comp. *Dorner*, s. 536 ff.

(4) On the one hand, *Origen* asserts that the Son is equal to the Father, Hom. viii. in Jerem. ii. Opp. iii. p. 171: Πάντα γὰρ ὅσα τοῦ θεοῦ, τοιαῦτα ἐν αὐτῷ (υἱῷ) ἐστίν. He also speaks of the three persons in the Trinity as the three sources of salvation, so that he who does not thirst after all three cannot find God, ibid. Hom. xviii. 9 (Opp. iii. p. 251, 252). Nevertheless, the subordination of the Son is prominently brought forward, and forms, together with the strict hypostatic distinction, the characteristic feature of *Origen's* doctrine. The Son is called δεύτερος θεός, Contra Cels. v. 608; comp. vii. 735: Ἄξιος τῆς δευτερευούσης μετὰ τὸν θεὸν τῶν ὅλων τιμῆς. De Orat. i. p. 222: Ἕτερος κατ' οὐσίαν καὶ ὑποκείμενός ἐστι ὁ υἱὸς τοῦ πατρός. The kingdom of the Father extends to the whole universe, that of the Son to rational creatures, that of the Holy Spirit to the holy (Christians), De Princip. i. 3. 5: Ὅτι ὁ μὲν θεὸς καὶ πατὴρ συνέχων τὰ πάντα φθάνει εἰς ἕκαστον τῶν ὄντων, μεταδιδοὺς ἑκάστῳ ἀπὸ τοῦ ἰδίου τὸ εἶναι· ὢν γὰρ ἔστιν. Ἐλάττων δὲ πρὸς τὸν πατέρα ὁ υἱὸς φθάνων ἐπὶ μόνα τὰ λογικά· δεύτερος γάρ ἐστι τοῦ πατρός. Ἔτι δὲ ἧττον τὸ πνεῦμα τὸ ἅγιον ἔτι μόνους τοὺς ἁγίους διϊκνούμενος. Ὥστε κατὰ τοῦτο μείζων ἡ δύναμις τοῦ πατρὸς παρὰ τὸν υἱὸν καὶ τὸ πνεῦμα τὸ ἅγιον, πλείων δὲ ἡ τοῦ υἱοῦ παρὰ τὸ πνεῦμα τὸ ἅγιον, καὶ πάλιν διαφέρουσα μᾶλλον τοῦ ἁγίου πνεύματος ἡ δύναμις παρὰ τὰ ἄλλα ἅγια. Comp. also in Joh. tom. ii. 2 (Opp. t. iv. p. 50), where stress is laid upon the distinction made by Philo between θεός and ὁ θεός. How far this system of subordination was sometimes carried, may be seen from *Origen*, de Orat. c. 15 (Opp. t. i. 222),

where he entirely rejects the practice of addressing prayer to Christ (the Son); for, he argues, since the Son is a particular hypostasis, we must pray either to the Son only, or to the Father only, or to both. To pray to the Son, and not to the Father, would be most improper (ἀτοπώτατον); to pray to both is impossible, because we should have to use the plural number: παρασχέσθε, εὐεργετήσατε, ἐπιχορηγήσατε, σώσατε, which is contrary to Scripture, and to the doctrine of one God. And thus nothing remains but to pray to the Father alone. To pray to the Father through the Son, a prayer in an improper sense (invocatio?), is quite a different thing; Contra Cels. v. 4 (Opp. i. p. 580): Πᾶσαν μὲν γὰρ δέησιν καὶ προσευχὴν καὶ ἔντευξιν καὶ εὐχαριστίαν ἀναπεμπτέον τῷ ἐπὶ πᾶσι θεῷ διὰ τοῦ ἐπὶ πάντων ἀγγέλων ἀρχιερέως, ἐμψύχου λόγου καὶ θεοῦ. Δεησόμεθα δὲ καὶ αὐτοῦ τοῦ λόγου, καὶ ἐντευξόμεθα αὐτῷ, καὶ εὐχαριστήσομεν καὶ προσευξόμεθα δὲ, ἐὰν δυνώμεθα κατακούειν τῆς περὶ προσευχῆς κυριολεξίας καὶ καταχρήσεως (si modo propriam precationis possimus ab impropria secernere notionem). Comp. however, § 43. *Redepenning*, Origenes, ii. s. 303. *Neander*, Dg. 161. On the subordinationist doctrine of the Trinity in *Hippolytus*, see ibid. s. 172, *Jacobi's* Note [and *Bunsen's* Hippolytus].

§ 47.

Doctrine of the Creation.

C. F. *Rössler*, Philosophia veteris ecclesiæ de mundo, Tubingæ 1783, 4to. [*Weisse*, Philosophische Dogmatik, 1855, s. 670-712. H. *Ritter*, Die christliche Philosophie, i. s. 266 sq.] *Möller*, Geschichte der Kosmologie in der griech. Kirche bis auf Origenes, Halle 1860. J. W. *Haune*, die Idee der absoluten Persönlichkeit, oder Gott und sein Verhältniss zur Welt, 1861, 2 vols. (2 Aufl. 1865).

Concerning the doctrine of creation, as well as the doctrine of God in general, the early Christians adopted the monotheistic views of the Jews, and, in simple faith, unhesitatingly received the Mosaic account of the creation (Gen. i.) as a revelation (1). Even the definition ἐξ οὐκ ὄντων, which was introduced late into the Jewish theology (2 Macc. vii. 28), found sympathy in the primitive Christianity (2). The orthodox firmly adhered to the doctrine that God, the Almighty Father, who is also the Father of the Lord Jesus Christ, is at the same time the Creator of heaven and of earth (3), and rejected the notion of the eternity of matter (4), in opposition to the Gnostics, according to whom the Creator of the world is distinct from the Supreme God, as well as to the opinion of some (5) Christian teachers, and of *Hermogenes* (6), that matter is eternal. But the speculative tendency of the Alexandrian school could not be satisfied with the empirical notion of a creation in time. Accordingly, *Origen* resorted to an allegorical interpretation of the work of the six days (Hexaëmeron) (7); and, after the example of *Clement* (8) (who, however, is doubtful, or at least hesitating), he propounded more definitely the doctrine of an *eternal creation*, yet not maintaining the eternity of matter as an independent power (9). On the contrary, *Irenæus*, from his practical position, reckoned all questions about what God had done before the creation among the improper questions of human inquisitiveness (10).

(1) *Theophilus* (ad Autol. ii. 10 sq.) first gives a fuller exposition of the Mosaic narrative of the creation. The Alexandrian school, on the other hand, deviated from his literal interpretation; comp. notes 7-9.

(2) Comp. Heb. xi. 3, and the commentaries upon that passage. Accordingly, the Shepherd of *Hermas* teaches, lib. ii. mand. 1: Πρῶτον πάντων πίστευσον, ὅτι εἷς ἐστιν ὁ θεὸς, ὁ τὰ πάντα κτίσας καὶ καταρτίσας, καὶ ποιήσας ἐκ τοῦ μὴ ὄντος εἰς τὸ εἶναι τὰ πάντα. Conf. *Euseb.* v. 8. But the idea of creation does not come out as distinctly in all the Fathers. Thus " *in Justin the Christian belief in the creation from nothing is never definitely brought forward against the opposing views of emanation and of dualism,*" Duncker, Zur christl. Logoslehre, s. 19. He uses the expression δημιουργῆσαι ἐξ ἀμόρφου ὕλης, Apol. i. 10. Yet God produced the material itself, and from this shaped the world; Coh. ad Græc. c. 22.

(3) The popular view was always, that the *Father* is the

§ 47.]   DOCTRINE OF THE CREATION.   185

Creator, though the creation *through* the Son also formed a part of the orthodox faith. Accordingly, we find that sometimes the Father, sometimes the Logos, is called the Creator of the world (δημιουργός, ποιητής). Thus *Justin M.* says (Dial. c. Tryph. c. 16): Ὁ ποιητὴς τῶν ὅλων θεός, comp. Apol. i. 61: Τοῦ πατρὸς τῶν ὅλων καὶ δεσπότου θεοῦ. On the other hand, Coh. ad Græc. c. 15: Τὸν τοῦ θεοῦ λόγον, δι' οὗ οὐρανὸς καὶ γῆ καὶ πᾶσα ἐγένετο κτίσις, comp. Apol. i. 64. Likewise *Theophilus*, ad Autol. ii. 10: Ὅτε ἐν τῷ λόγῳ αὐτοῦ ὁ θεὸς πεποίηκε τὸν οὐρανὸν καὶ τὴν γῆν καὶ τὰ ἐν αὐτοῖς, ἔφη· Ἐν ἀρχῇ ἐποίησεν. The phrase ἐν ἀρχῇ was understood in the same sense as διὰ τῆς ἀρχῆς, and ἀρχή explained to denote the Logos, see *Semisch*, s. 335. Thus *Irenæus* also taught, iii. 11: Et hæc quidem sunt principia Evangelii, unum Deum fabricatorem hujus universitatis, eum qui et per prophetas sit annunciatus et qui per Moysem legis dispositionem fecerit, *Patrem Domini nostri Jesu Christi* annunciantia et præter hunc alterum Deum nescientia, neque alterum patrem.   On the other hand, he says, v. 18. 3: Mundi enim factor vere verbum Dei est; hic autem est Dominus noster, qui in novissimis temporibus homo factus est, in hoc mundo existens et secundum invisibilitatem continet quæ facta sunt omnia, et in universa conditione infixus, quoniam verbum Dei gubernans et disponens omnia et propter hoc in sua venit.   *Irenæus* often speaks of the Son and Spirit as the hands of God, by which He created all things; on this see *Duncker*, s. 68, against *Baur*. That *Clement* of Alexandria called the Logos, as such, the Creator of the world (with Philo), has already been remarked, § 42, note 8. For the various appellations, ποιητής, κτιστής, δημιουργός, see *Suicer* under the latter word. [*Burton*, Bampton Lecture, note 21, p. 320, note 50, p. 410.]

(4) *Theoph.* ad Autol. ii. 4, says against the followers of Plato: Εἰ δὲ θεὸς ἀγέννητος καὶ ὕλη ἀγέννητος, οὐκ ἔτι ὁ θεὸς ποιητὴς τῶν ὅλων ἐστί. Comp. iii. 19 sq., and *Iren.* fragm. sermonis ad Demetr. p. 348 (p. 467 in *Grabe*). [Comp. *Burton*, l.c. note 18.]   *Tert.* adv. Hermogenem, see the following note.   *Justin M.* and *Athenagoras*, on the contrary, fall in more with the Platonic view; not, indeed, as agreeing with *Philo* (De mundi opif. 2) in putting God and Hyle

expressly opposite to each other as δραστήριον and παθητικὸν αἴτιον, or as regarding matter generally as coeternal with God; but they do not set forth with sufficient clearness the thought that the ὕλη itself is created by God; it seems to them sufficient to say that God created the world from the formless matter which lay before Him. *Justin*, Apol. i. 10 : Πάντα τὴν ἀρχὴν ἀγαθὸν ὄντα δημιουργῆσαι αὐτὸν (θεὸν) ἐξ ἀμόρφου ὕλης . . . δεδιδάγμεθα, cf. c. 59. *Athenag.* (Legat. 15) compares the creative activity of God to the art of the potter, who forms a vessel of clay. Without the forming hand of the artist the matter would not have become κόσμος, it would have lacked organization and form (διάκρισις, σχῆμα). Cf. c. 19, and *Möller*, l.c. s. 146 ff. In the Cohortatio ad Græcos (c. 22) it is different; there we find the most precise distinction between δημιουργός and ποιητής : ὁ μὲν γὰρ ποιητὴς οὐδενὸς ἑτέρου προσδεόμενος ἐκ τῆς ἑαυτοῦ δυνάμεως καὶ ἐξουσίας ποιεῖ τὸ ποιούμενον· ὁ δὲ δημιουργός, τὴν τῆς δημιουργίας δύναμιν ἐκ τῆς ὕλης εἰληφώς, κατασκευάζει τὸ γινόμενον. So *Tatian* most decidedly rejects the notion of pre-existing matter. Orat. 3 (5). *Möller*, s. 156 f.

(5) On the dualistic and emanatistic theories of creation of Cerinthus, Basilides, Valentinus, and the other Gnostics, as well as of the pseudo-Clementines, see *Baur*, Dg. 520 ff., and *Möller*, s. 189 ff.

(6) *Hermogenes*, a painter, lived towards the end of the second century, probably at Carthage. According to *Tertullian* (adv. Hermog.), he maintained that God must have created the world either out of Himself, or out of nothing, or out of something. But He could not create the world out of Himself, for He is indivisible; nor out of nothing, for as He Himself is the Supreme Good, He would then have created a perfectly good world; nothing, therefore, remains but that He created the world out of matter already in existence. This matter (ὕλη) is consequently eternal, like God Himself; both principles stood over against each other from the beginning, God as the creating and working, matter as the receptive principle. Whatever in matter resists the creating principle, constitutes the evil in the world. In proof of the eternity of matter, *Hermogenes* alleges that God was Lord from eternity, and must therefore from eternity have an object for the exercise

of His lordship. To this *Tertullian* replies (adv. Hermog. c. 3), God is certainly *God* from eternity, but not *Lord;* the one is the name of His essence, the other of power (a relation). Only the essence is to be viewed as eternal. But it was only on this point of the eternity of matter that *Hermogenes* agreed with the Gnostics; in other respects, and especially in reference to the doctrine of emanation, he joined the orthodox in opposing them. He compared the relation of God to the world, to that of the magnet to iron; so that God operates upon matter not by the act of His will, but by the proximity of His essence. Comp. *Guil. Böhmer*, de Hermogene Africano, Sundiæ 1832. *Neander*, Kg. i. 3, s. 974 ff.; Antignosticus, s. 236 ff. *Leopold*, Hermogenis de origine mundi sententia, Budissæ 1844. *Baur*, Dg. s. 524.

(7) De Princip. iv. 16 (Opp. i. p. 174, 175): Τίς γὰρ νοῦν ἔχων οἰήσεται πρώτην καὶ δευτέραν καὶ τρίτην ἡμέραν, ἑσπέραν τε καὶ πρωΐαν χωρὶς ἡλίου γεγονέναι καὶ σελήνης καὶ ἄστρων κ.τ.λ. Comp. § 33, note 4.

(8) According to *Photius*, Bibl. Cod. c. 9, p. 89, *Clement* of Alex. is said to have taught that matter had no beginning (ὕλην ἄχρονον); with this statement comp. Strom. vi. 16, p. 812, 813: Οὐ τοίνυν, ὥσπερ τινὲς ὑπολαμβάνουσι τὴν ἀνάπαυσιν τοῦ θεοῦ, πέπαυται ποιῶν ὁ θεός· ἀγαθὸς γὰρ ὤν, εἰ παύσεταί ποτε ἀγαθοεργῶν, καὶ τοῦ θεὸς εἶναι παύσεται; and p. 813: Πῶς δ' ἂν ἐν χρόνῳ γένοιτο κτίσις συγγενομένου τοῖς οὖσι καὶ τοῦ χρόνου. This is certainly against a creation in time. But in other passages *Clement* most distinctly acknowledges that the world is a work of God; *e.g.* Coh. p. 54, 55: Μόνος γὰρ ὁ θεὸς ἐποίησεν, ἐπεὶ καὶ μόνος ὄντως ἐστὶ θεός· ψιλῷ τῷ βούλεσθαι δημιουργεῖ, καὶ τῷ μόνον ἐθελῆσαι αὐτὸν ἕπεται τὸ γεγενῆσθαι.

(9) *Origen*, indeed, opposes the eternity of matter (in the heathen and heretical sense), De Princip. ii. 4 (*Redep.* 164), and in other places, *e.g.* Comment. in Joh. xxxii. 9 (Opp. t. iv. p. 429); but though, from his idealistic position, he denied eternity to *matter*, which he held to be the root of evil, he nevertheless assumed the eternal creation of innumerable ideal worlds, solely because he could, as little as *Clement*, conceive of God as unoccupied (otiosam enim et immobilem dicere naturam Dei, impium enim simul et absurdum), De Princip.

iii. 5 (Opp. t. i. p. 149, *Redep.* 309): Nos vero consequenter respondebimus, observantes regulam pietatis et dicentes: Quoniam non tunc primum, cum visibilem istum mundum fecit Deus, coepit operari, sed sicut post corruptionem hujus erit alius mundus, ita et antequam hic esset, fuisse alios credimus. It might be questioned whether *Origen*, in the use of the pronoun "*nos*" in the subsequent part of the passage, intended to enforce his own belief as that of the Church, or whether he employed the plural number merely in his character as author; comp. *Rössler*, Bibliothek der Kirchenväter, i. s. 177, and *Schnitzer*, l.c. s. 228 f. Comp. also *Thomasius*, s. 153 ff., 169 ff., *Redep.* ii. 292 ff. On the connection of *Origen's* doctrine of creation with his notion of the pre-existence and the fall of souls (§ 55, 63), see *Baur*, Dg. s. 537, and *Möller*, s. 554. This fall *Origen* sees in the biblical expression καταβολὴ κόσμου. But *Origen* does not understand by this the falling away of God from Himself. The world still remains the sphere of the divine power, and the manifestation of the divine love.

(10) *Iren.* ii. 28, p. 157 (ii. 47, p. 175, *Grabe*): Ut puta si quis interroget: Antequam mundum faceret Deus, quid agebat? dicimus: Quoniam ista responsio subjacet Deo. Quoniam autem mundus hic factus est apotelestos a Deo, temporale initium accipiens, Scripturae nos docent; quid autem ante hoc Deus sit operatus, nulla scriptura manifestat. Subjacet ergo haec responsio Deo. Respecting the important position which the doctrine of *Irenæus* concerning the creation of the world occupies in his theological system (in opposition to the Gnostics), see *Duncker*, s. 8.

In close connection with the *creation* of the world stands its *preservation*. As the world is created by the Logos, so its permanence is secured by Him. More especially is its preservation ascribed to the *Spirit* of God, as the Spirit of life. According to *Theophilus* (ad Autol. ii.), all creation is embraced by the πνεῦμα θεοῦ. *Tatian* distinguishes this cosmic πνεῦμα (πν. ὑλικόν) from the Holy Ghost in the more strict sense of the word (Orat. ad Græc. 12). According to *Athenagoras* (Legat. 16), God Himself comes into immediate causative connection with the world. It was also common to regard the preservation of the world as under the care of the angels. Cf. *Möller*, l.c. s. 174 ff.

§ 48.

Providence and Government of the World.

Though the doctrine that the world exists for the sake of the human race may degenerate into a selfish happiness scheme (eudemonistic egoism), yet it has a deeper ground in the consciousness of a specific distinction between man and all other creatures, at least on this earth, and is justified by hints in the sacred Scriptures (1). Accordingly, the primitive Christians considered creation as a voluntary act of divine love, inasmuch as God does not stand in need of His creatures for His own glory (2). But man, as the end of creation (3), is also pre-eminently the subject of Divine Providence, and the whole vast economy of creation, with its laws and also its miracles, is made subservient to the higher purpose of the education of mankind. The Christian doctrine of *providence*, as held by the Fathers of the Church, in opposition to the objections of ancient philosophy (4), is remote, on the one hand, from Stoicism and the rigid dogma of an εἱμαρμένη held by the Gnostics (5), and, on the other, from the system of Epicurus, according to which it is unworthy of the Deity to concern Himself about the affairs of man (6). Yet here, again, the teachers of the Alexandrian school in particular endeavoured to avoid as much as possible the use of anthropomorphism (7) in connection with the idea that God takes care even of individuals, and to uphold in their theodicy the liberty of man (8), as well as the love and justice of God (9).

(1) Matt. vi. 26 ; 1 Cor. ix. 9, 10.
(2) *E.g. Clement* of Alex. Pæd. iii. 1. 250 : Ἀνενδεὴς δὲ μόνος ὁ θεὸς καὶ χαίρει μάλιστα μὲν καθαρεύοντας ἡμᾶς ὁρῶν τῷ τῆς διανοίας κοσμῷ.
(3) *Justin M.* Apol. i. 10 : Καὶ πάντα τὴν ἀρχὴν ἀγαθὸν ὄντα δημιουργῆσαι αὐτὸν ἐξ ἀμόρφου ὕλης δι᾽ ἀνθρώπους δεδιδάγμεθα. Comp. *Athen.* De Resurr. c. 12 : God, he says,

has made man, not διὰ χρείαν ἰδίαν; yet not μάτην, but δι' ἑαυτόν, i.e. "*He has created him, not in order to obtain something from him, but in order to give him something, and to make him participate in His own wisdom and goodness,*" Möller, l.c. s. 144. Similarly *Iren.* v. 29. 1, iv. 5. 1, iv. 7. 4 (comp. *Duncker,* s. 78, 79). *Tert.* Advers. Marc. i. 13: Ergo nec mundus Deo indignus, nihil etenim Deus indignum se fecit, etsi mundum homini, non sibi fecit. *Orig.* Contra Cels. iv. 74, p. 558, 559, and ibid. 99, p. 576: Κέλσος μὲν οὖν λεγέτω, ὅτι οὖν ἀνθρώπῳ, ὡς οὐδὲ λέοντι, οὐδ' οἷς ὀνομάζει. Ἡμεῖς δ' ἐροῦμεν· Οὐ λέοντι ὁ δημιουργὸς, οὐδὲ ἀετῷ, οὐδὲ δελφῖνι ταῦτα πεποίηκεν, ἀλλὰ πάντα διὰ τὸ λογικὸν ζῶον.

(4) See the objections of Caecilius in *Minucius Felix,* c. 5 ff.; and, on the other hand, the oration of *Octavius,* c. 17, 18, 20, 32, and especially the beautiful passage, c. 33: Nec nobis de nostra frequentia blandiamur; multi nobis videmur, sed Deo admodum pauci sumus. Nos gentes nationesque distinguimus: Deo una domus est mundus hic totus. Reges tantum regni sui per officia ministrorum universa novere: Deo indiciis non opus est; non solum in oculis ejus, sed et in sinu vivimus. Comp. *Athen.* Leg. c. 22, in calce. It has, however, been correctly remarked, that "*in all ages of the Church the doctrine of providence has not been so much doctrinally developed as set forth apologetically, and for edification,*" Kahnis, Kirchengl. s. 47.

(5) On the opinion of the Gnostic *Bardesanes* respecting the εἱμαρμένη (fate) and the influence of stars, comp. *Photius,* Bibl. Cod. 223. *Euseb.* Praep. vi. 10. *Neander,* Gnostische Systeme, s. 198. [*Neander:* "He (Bardesanes), therefore, although, like many of those who inclined to Gnosticism, he busied himself with astrology, contended against the doctrine of such an influence of the stars (εἱμαρμένη) as should be supposed to settle the life and affairs of man by *necessity. Eusebius,* in his great literary treasure-house, the Præparatio Evangelica, has preserved a large fragment of this remarkable work; he here introduces, among other things, the Christians dispersed over so many countries, as an example of the absurdity of supposing that the stars irresistibly influenced the character of a people."] *Baur,* Gnosis, s. 234, Dg. s. 539. *C. Kühner,* Astronomiae et Astrologiae in doctrina Gnostic.

Vestigia, P. I. Bardesanis Gnostici numina astralia, Hildburg. 1833. As to how far *Bardesanes* is the author of the "Dialogue on Fate," published as the "book of the laws of the lands" (Syr. in *Cureton's* Spicileg. Syriacum, Lond. 1855, and in Germ. by *Merx*, Halle 1863), see *Hilgenfeld*, Bardesanes der letzte Gnostiker, Leipz. 1864, who opposes it, and (s. 29 ff.) gives a sketch of the doctrine of Bardesanes on his astrological fatalism in particular, cf. s. 56 ff. If the dialogue were genuine, Bardesanes would have to be reckoned among the opponents rather than the defenders of fatalism. On the relation of the dialogue to the Recognitions of the pseudo-Clement, see s. 123 ff. [Comp. also *Gieseler*, l.c. i. § 49, note 2, and *Burton*, Lect. on Ecclesiast. hist., Lect. xx. p. 182, 183.]

(6) Comp. especially the objections of Celsus in the work of *Origen*: God interferes as little with the affairs of man as with those of monkeys and flies, etc., especially in lib. iv. Though Celsus was not a disciple of Epicurus, as Origen and Lucian would have him to be, but rather a follower of Plato (according to *Neander*), yet these expressions savour very much of Epicureanism. [Comp. *Lardner*, Works, vii. 211, 212.]

(7) According to *Clement*, there is no antagonism of the whole and its parts in the sight of God (comp. also *Minuc. Felix*, note 4): Ἀθρόως τε γὰρ πάντα καὶ ἕκαστον ἐν μέρει μιᾷ προσβολῇ προσβλέπει, Strom. vi. p. 821. Comp. the work of *Origen*, Contra Cels.

(8) The doctrine of the *concursus*, as it was afterwards termed, is found in *Clem.* Strom. vi. 17, p. 821 ss. Many things owe their existence to human calculation, though they are kindled by God, as if by lightning (τὴν ἔναυσιν εἰληφότα). Thus health is preserved by medical skill, the carriage of the body by fencing, riches by the industrial art (χρηματιστικὴ τέχνη); but the divine πρόνοια and human συνέργεια always work together.

(9) Comp. § 39, note 8. In opposition to the Gnostics, who derived evil, not from the supreme God, but from the demiurge, *Irenæus* observes, Adv. Hær. iv. 39, p. 285 (iv. 76, p. 380 *Gr.*), that, through the contrast of good and evil in the world, the former shines more brightly. Spirits, he further remarks, may exercise themselves in distinguishing between good and evil; how could they know the former without

having some idea of its opposition? But, in a categorical manner, he precludes all further questions: Non enim tu Deum facis, sed Deus te facit. Si ergo opera Dei es, manum artificis tui expecta, opportune omnia facientem: opportune autem, quantum ad te attinet, qui efficeris. Præsta autem ei cor tuum molle et tractabile, et custodi figuram, qua te figuravit artifex, habens in temetipso humorem, ne induratus amittas vestigia digitorum ejus. . . . And further on: Si igitur tradideris ei, quod est tuum, *i.e.* fidem in eum et subjectionem, recipies ejus artem et eris perfectum opus Dei. Si autem non credideris ei et fugeris manus ejus, erit causa imperfectionis in te qui non obedisti, sed non in illo, qui vocavit, etc. At all events, the best and soundest theodicy! *Athenagoras* (Leg. c. 24) derives the disorders of the world from the devil and demons (comp. § 51); and *Cyprian* (Ad Demetrianum) from the very constitution of the world, which begins to change, and is approaching its dissolution. To a speculative mind like that of *Origen*, the existence of evil would present a strong stimulus to attempt to explain its origin, though he could not but be aware of the difficulties with which this subject is beset. Comp. especially De Princip. ii. 9 (Opp. i. p. 97, *Redep.* 214; *Schnitzer*, 140); Contra Celsum, iv. 62, p. 551 (an extract of which is given by *Rössler*, i. 232). Different reasons are adduced in vindication of the existence of evil in the world; thus it serves to exercise the ingenuity of man (power of invention, etc.); but he draws special attention to the connection between moral and physical imperfections, evil and sin. Comp. the opinion of *Thomasius* on the theodicy of Origen, s. 57, 58.

§ 49.

Angelology and Demonology.

Suicer, Thesaurus, s.v. ἄγγελος. *Cotta*, Disputationes 2, succinctam Doctrinæ Angelis Historiam exhibentes, Tüb. 1865, 4to. *Schmid*, Hist. dogm. de Angelis tutelaribus, in Illgens histor. theol. Abhandlungen, i. s. 24-27. *Keil*, De Angelorum malorum et Dæmoniorum Cultu apud Gentiles, Opusc. Acad. p. 584-601. (*Gaab*), Abhandlungen zur Dogmengeschichte der ältesten griechischen Kirche, Jena 1790, s. 97-126. *Usteri*, Paulin. Lehrbegriff, 4 Ausg. Anhang 3, s. 421 ff.—[*Dr. L. Mayer*, Scriptural Idea of Angels, in Amer. Biblic. Reposit. xii. 356-388. *Moses Stuart*,

Sketches of Angelology in *Robinson's* Bibliotheca Sacra, No. 1, 1843. *L. F. Voss*, Zeitschrift f. Luther. Theologie, 1855. *Lücke* in the Deutsche Zeitschrift, 1851, review of Martensen. *Twesten*, transl. in Bibliotheca Sacra, by *H. B. Smith*, vols. i. and ii. 1844, 1845. *Smith's* Dicty. *Herzog*, etc.]

The doctrine of angels, the devil, and demons, forms an important appendix to the statements respecting creation, providence, and the government of the world; partly because the angels (according to the general opinion) belong as creatures to the creation itself; partly because, as others conceive, they took an active part in the work of creation, or are the agents of special providence. The doctrine of the devil and demons also stands in close connection with the doctrine of physical and moral evil in the world.

§ 50.

The Angels.

Though the primitive Church, as Origen asserts, did not establish any definite doctrine on this subject (1), we nevertheless meet with several declarations respecting the nature of angels (2). Thus many of the earlier Fathers rejected the notion that they took part in the work of creation (3), and maintained, on the contrary, that they are created beings and ministering spirits (4). In opposition to the doctrine of emanation and of æons (5), even bodies were ascribed to them, of finer substance, however, than human bodies (6). The idea of guardian angels was connected in part with the mythical notion of the genii (7). But no sure traces are to be found during this period of a real cultus of angels within the pale of the Catholic Church (8).

(1) De Princip. proœm. 10 (Opp. i. p. 49, *Redep.* p. 95): Est etiam illud in ecclesiastica prædicatione, esse angelos Dei quosdam et virtutes bonas, qui ei ministrant ad salutem hominum consummandam; sed quando isti creati sint, vel quales aut quomodo sint, non satis in manifesto designatur.

(2) "*The doctrine respecting angels, though a very wavering element of the patristic dogmatics, is yet handled with manifest predilection,*" Semisch, Just. Mart. ii. s. 339. Comp. *Athenagoras*, Leg. 24, and note 1 to the next section.

(3) *Iren.* i. 22 and 24 (against the opinions of Saturninus and Carpocrates), comp. ii. 2, p. 117: Si enim (Deus) mundi fabricator est, angelos ipse fecit, aut etiam causa creationis eorum ipse fuit. iii. 8. 3: Quoniam enim sive angeli, sive archangeli, sive throni, sive dominationes ab eo, qui super omnes est Deus, et constituta sunt et facta sunt per verbum ejus. Comp. also iv. 6. 7: Ministrat ei (patri) ad omnia sua progenies et figuratio sua, *i.e.* Filius et Spir. S., verbum et sapientia, *quibus serviunt et subjecti sunt* omnes angeli. Comp. *Duncker*, s. 108 ff., and *Baur*, Trin.-Lehre, s. 175. The latter, from the manner in which the earliest Fathers frequently bring the angels into close connection with the persons of the Trinity, sees evidence that their views respecting this great mystery itself were yet very indefinite. *Origen*, however, teaches with reference to the passage in Job xxxviii. 7, in his Comm. on Matt. xviii. 27 (Opp. iii. p. 692), that angels, although created, yet belong to an earlier creation.

(4) "*Justin M. regards the angels as personal beings who possess a permanent existence,*" Semisch, ii. s. 341. Dial. c. Tryph. c. 128: "Ὅτι μὲν οὖν εἰσὶν ἄγγελοι, καὶ ἀεὶ μένοντες, καὶ μὴ ἀναλυόμενοι εἰς ἐκεῖνο, ἐξ οὗπερ γεγόνασιν, ἀποδέδεικται.... Athenagoras, Leg. c. 10: Πλῆθος ἀγγέλων καὶ λειτουργῶν φαμέν, οὓς ὁ ποιητὴς καὶ δημιουργὸς κόσμου θεὸς διὰ τοῦ παρ' αὐτοῦ λόγου διένειμε καὶ διέταξε περί τε τὰ στοιχεῖα εἶναι καὶ τοὺς οὐρανοὺς καὶ τὸν κόσμον καὶ τὰ ἐν αὐτῷ καὶ τὴν τούτων εὐταξίαν. Comp. c. 24, and *Clem.* Strom. vi. 17, p. 822, 824; according to him, the angels have received charge over provinces, towns, etc. *Clement*, however, distinguishes *the* ἄγγελος (singular), מַלְאַךְ יְהוָה, from the other angels, and connects him in some degree with the Logos, though assigning to him an inferior rank. Comp. Strom. vii. 2, p. 831–833. He also speaks of a mythical Angelus Jesus, Pæd. i. 7, p. 133, comp. *G. Bulli*, Def. Fidei Nic. § 1, c. 1 (de Christo sub angeli forma apparente). Opp. Lond. 1703, fol. p. 9. [*Pye Smith*, Scripture Test. to the Messiah, i. p. 445-464.]—On the employments of angels, *Origen* can already

say what sphere is assigned to each angel. Raphael has to do with diseases, Gabriel with war, Michael with prayer, De Princip. i. 8. 1. The angels are the invisible γεωργοί and οἰκονόμοι who rule in nature, Contra Celsum, viii. 31 (Opp. i. p. 764), ibid. v. 29 (Opp. i. p. 598), and Hom. xii. in Luc. (Opp. iii. p. 945).

(5) *Philo* had already transformed personal angels (*e.g.* the cherubim) into divine powers, see *Dähne*, 227 ff. *Justin M.* also informs us, that in his time some had compared the relation in which the angels stand to God to that which exists between the sun and its beams (analogous to the Logos); but he decidedly rejects this opinion, Dial. c. Tryph. c. 128. Comp. *Tert.* Adv. Prax. c. 3 (in connection with the doctrine of the Trinity): Igitur si et monarchia divina per tot legiones et exercitus angelorum administratur, sicut scriptum est: Millies millia adsistebant ei, et millies centena millia apparebant ei: nec ideo unius esse desiit, ut desinat monarchia esse, quia per tanta millia virtutum procuratur, etc.

(6) *Justin M.* attaches most importance to the body of angels as analogous to that of man. Their food is manna, Ps. lxxviii. 25; the two angels who appeared to Abraham (Gen. xviii. 1 ff.) differed from the Logos who accompanied them, in partaking of the food set before them, in reality and after the manner of men, comp. Dial. c. Tryph. c. 57, and *Semisch*, ii. s. 343. As regards their intellectual powers and moral condition, *Justin* assigns an inferior position to the angels, *Semisch*, s. 344, 345. *Tertullian* points out the difference between the body of Christ and that of the angels, De Carne Christi, c. 6: Nullus unquam angelus ideo descendit, ut crucifigeretur, ut mortem experiretur, ut a morte suscitaretur. Si nunquam ejusmodi fuit causa angelorum corporandorum, habes causam, cur non nascendo acceperint carnem. Non venerant mori, ideo nec nasci. . . . Igitur probent angelos illos, carnem de sideribus concepisse. Si non probant, quia nec scriptum est, nec Christi caro inde erit, cui angelorum accommodant exemplum. Constat, angelos carnem non propriam gestasse, utpote naturas substantiæ spiritalis, et si corporis alicujus, sui tamen generis; in carnem autem humanam transfigurabiles ad tempus videri et congredi cum hominibus posse. Igitur, cum relatum non sit, unde sumpserint carnem, relinquitur intellectui

nostro, non dubitare, hoc esse proprium angelicæ potestatis, ex nulla materia corpus sibi sumere. . . . Sed et, si de materia necesse fuit angelos sumpsisse carnem, credibilius utique est de terrena materia, quam de ullo genere cœlestium substantiarum, cum adeo terrenæ qualitatis extiterit, ut terrenis pabulis pasta sit. *Tatian*, Or. c. 15: Δαίμονες δὲ πάντες σαρκίον μὲν οὐ κέκτηνται, πνευματικὴ δέ ἐστιν αὐτοῖς ἡ σύμπηξις, ὡς πυρὸς, ὡς ἀέρος. But these ethereal bodies of the angels can be perceived only by those in whom the Spirit of God dwells, not by the natural man (the psychical). In comparison with other creatures they might be called incorporeal beings, and *Ignat.* ad Trall. calls them ἀσωμάτους φύσεις. *Clement* also says, Strom. vi. 7, p. 769, that they have neither ears, nor tongues, nor lips, nor entrails and organs of respiration, etc. Comp. *Orig.* Princip. in procem. § 9, who, however, also wavers between corporeal and incorporeal existence. On the question, whether the Fathers taught the spiritual nature of the angels at all, see *Semisch*, ii. s. 342. The moral nature of the angels was also debated, and the question discussed, whether they were good essentially, or only by habit, freely exercised. *Origen* held decidedly the latter view, De Princip. i. 5. 3.

(7) This idea is already found in the Shepherd of *Hermas*, lib. ii. mand. vi. 2: Δύο εἰσὶν ἄγγελοι μετὰ τοῦ ἀνθρώπου, εἷς τῆς δικαιοσύνης καὶ εἷς τῆς πονηρίας· καὶ ὁ μὲν τῆς δικαιοσύνης ἄγγελος τρυφερός ἐστι καὶ αἰσχυντηρὸς καὶ πρᾶος καὶ ἡσύχιος. Ὅταν οὖν οὗτος ἐπὶ τὴν καρδίαν σου ἀναβῇ, εὐθέως λαλεῖ μετὰ σοῦ περὶ δικαιοσύνης, περὶ ἁγνείας, περὶ σεμνότητος καὶ περὶ αὐταρκείας, καὶ περὶ παντὸς ἔργου δικαίου, καὶ περὶ πάσης ἀρετῆς ἐνδόξου. Ταῦτα πάντα ὅταν εἰς τὴν καρδίαν σου ἀναβῇ, γίνωσκε, ὅτι ὁ ἄγγελος τῆς δικαιοσύνης μετὰ σοῦ ἐστιν. Τούτῳ οὖν πίστευε καὶ τοῖς ἔργοις αὐτοῦ, καὶ ἐγκρατὴς αὐτοῦ γενοῦ. Ὅρα οὖν καὶ τοῦ ἀγγέλου τῆς πονηρίας τὰ ἔργα. Πρῶτον πάντων ὀξύχολός ἐστι καὶ πικρὸς καὶ ἄφρων, καὶ τὰ ἔργα αὐτοῦ πονηρὰ καταστρέφοντα τοὺς δούλους τοῦ θεοῦ· ὅταν αὐτὸς ἐπὶ τὴν καρδίαν σου ἀναβῇ, γνῶθι αὐτὸν ἐπὶ τῶν ἔργων αὐτοῦ. (Frag. ex doctr. ad Antioch.) Comp. the Latin text. *Justin Mart.* Apol. ii. 5: Ὁ θεὸς τὸν πάντα κόσμον ποιήσας καὶ τὰ ἐπίγεια ἀνθρώποις ὑποτάξας . . . τὴν μὲν τῶν ἀνθρώπων καὶ τῶν ὑπὸ τὸν οὐρανὸν πρόνοιαν ἀγγέλοις,

οὒς ἐπὶ τούτοις ἔταξε, παρέδωκεν. We have already seen (note 4) that *Clement* and *Origen* assign to angels the office of watching over provinces and towns; this is connected with the notion of individual guardian angels; comp. *Clem.* Strom. v. p. 700, and vii. p. 833, and the passages quoted above from *Origen. Schmid,* l.c. A principal occupation of the angels is also to bring the prayers of men before God. *Origen,* Contra Cels. v. 4, and *Tertull.* De Orat. c. 12, who speaks of a special angel of prayer.

(8) Col. ii. 18, mention is made of a θρησκεία τῶν ἀγγέλων which the apostle disapproves; comp. Rev. xix. 10, xxii. 9. The answer to the question whether *Justin M.* numbered the angels among the objects of Christian worship, depends upon the interpretation of the passage, Apol. i. 6 : Ἄθεοι κεκλήμεθα καὶ ὁμολογοῦμεν τῶν τοιούτων νομιζομένων θεῶν ἄθεοι εἶναι, ἀλλ' οὐχὶ τοῦ ἀληθεστάτου καὶ πατρὸς δικαιοσύνης καὶ σωφροσύνης καὶ τῶν ἄλλων ἀρετῶν, ἀνεπιμίκτου τε κακίας θεοῦ· ἀλλ' ἐκεῖνόν τε καὶ τὸν παρ' αὐτοῦ υἱὸν ἐλθόντα καὶ διδάξαντα ἡμᾶς ταῦτα καὶ τὸν τῶν ἄλλων ἑπομένων καὶ ἐξομοιουμένων ἀγαθῶν ἀγγέλων στρατόν, πνεῦμά τε τὸ προφητικὸν σεβόμεθα καὶ προσκυνοῦμεν, λόγῳ καὶ ἀληθείᾳ τιμῶντες. The principal point in question is, whether the accusative τὸν τῶν ἄλλων ... στρατόν is governed by σεβόμεθα καὶ προσκυνοῦμεν or by διδάξαντα, and consequently where the punctuation is to fall. Most modern writers adopt the former interpretation, which is probably the more correct one. Thus *Semisch,* s. 350 ff. *Möhler* (Patrologie, s. 240)[1] finds in this passage, as well as in *Athen.* Leg. 10, a proof of the Roman Catholic adoration of angels and saints. But *Athenagoras* (c. 16) rejects this doctrine very decidedly in the following words : Οὐ τὰς δυνάμεις τοῦ θεοῦ προσιόντες θεραπεύομεν, ἀλλὰ τὸν ποιητὴν αὐτῶν καὶ δεσπότην. Comp. *Clem.* Strom. vi. 5, p. 760. *Orig.* Contra Cels. v. 4. 5 (Opp. i. p. 580), and viii. 13 (ib. p. 751), quoted by *Münscher, Von Cölln,* i. s. 84, 85. [*Gieseler,* i. § 99, and note 33. *Burton,* Testimonies of the Ante-Nic. Fath. to the Trinity, etc., p. 15-23. On the Gnostic worship of angels, comp. *Burton,* Bampton Lect., note 52.] According to *Origen,* the angels rather pray

---

[1] In an earlier essay in the Tübingen Quartalschrift, 1833, s. 53 ff., Möhler rejected the interpretation, that the worship of angels is here spoken of.

with us and *for* us, comp. Contra Cels. viii. 64, p. 789; Hom. in Num. xxiv. (Opp. iii. p. 362). If, however, not worthy of divine honour, yet, according to *Origen*, the angels are πρεσβύ-τεροι καὶ τιμιώτεροι οὐ μόνον τοῦ ἀνθρώπου, ἀλλὰ καὶ πάσης μετ' αὐτοὺς κοσμοποιΐας (Comm. in Matt. xv. 27). The εὐφη-μεῖν and μακαρίζειν, which he claims for angels, would soon lead to invocation and finally to worship. On the order and rank of angels in *Origen*, see *Redep*. ii. s. 348 ff.

§ 51.

The Devil and Demons.

The Bible does not represent the prince of darkness, or the wicked one (Devil, Satan), as an evil principle which existed from the beginning, in opposition to a good principle (dualism); but, in accordance with the doctrine of one God, it speaks of him as a creature, viz. an angel who was created by God good, but who, in the exercise of his free will, fell away from his Maker. This was also the view taken by the orthodox Fathers (1). Everything which was opposed to the light of the gospel and its development, physical evils (2), as well as the numerous persecutions of Christians (3), was thought to be the work of Satan and his demons. The entire system of paganism, its mythology and worship (4), and, according to some, even philosophy (5), were supposed to be subject to the influence of demons. Heresies (6) were also ascribed to the same agency. Moreover, some particular vices were considered to be the specific effects of individual evil spirits (7).

(1) Concerning the appellatives שָׂטָן, σατᾶν, σατανᾶς, διάβολος, ὁ ἄρχων τοῦ κόσμου τούτου, δαίμονες, δαιμόνια, βεελζεβούλ, etc., the origin of the doctrine and its develop-ment in the Scriptures, comp. *de Wette*, biblische Dogmatik, § 142–150, 212–214, 236–238; *Baumgarten - Crusius*, biblische Theologie, s. 295; *Von Cölln*, biblische Theologie, s. 420; *Hirzel*, Commentar zum Hiob, s. 16. The Fathers

generally adopted the notions already existing. *Justin M.* Apol. min. c. 5. *Athenag.* Leg. 24: Ὡς γὰρ θεόν φαμεν καὶ υἱὸν τὸν λόγον αὐτοῦ καὶ πνεῦμα ἅγιον ... οὕτως καὶ ἑτέρας εἶναι δυνάμεις κατειλήμμεθα περὶ τὴν ὕλην ἐχούσας καὶ δι' αὐτῆς, μίαν μὲν τὴν ἀντίθεον, οὐχ ὅτι ἀντιδοξοῦν τι ἐστὶ τῷ θεῷ, ὡς τῇ φιλίᾳ τὸ νεῖκος κατὰ τὸν Ἐμπεδοκλέα, καὶ τῇ ἡμέρᾳ νὺξ κατὰ τὰ φαινόμενα (ἐπεὶ κἂν εἰ ἀνθειστήκει τι τῷ θεῷ, ἐπαύσατο τοῦ εἶναι, λυθείσης αὐτοῦ τῇ τοῦ θεοῦ δυνάμει καὶ ἰσχύϊ τῆς συστάσεως) ἀλλ' ὅτι τῷ τοῦ θεοῦ ἀγαθῷ, ὃ κατὰ συμβεβηκός ἐστιν αὐτῷ, καὶ συνυπάρχον, ὡς χρόα σώματι, οὗ ἄνευ οὐκ ἔστιν (οὐχ ὡς μέρους ὄντος, ἀλλ' ὡς κατ' ἀνάγκην συνόντος παρακολουθήματος ἡνωμένου καὶ συγκεχρωσμένου· ὡς τῷ πυρὶ, ξανθῷ εἶναι, καὶ τῷ αἰθέρι, κυανῷ) ἐναντίον ἐστὶ τὸ περὶ τὴν ὕλην ἔχον πνεῦμα, γενόμενον μὲν ὑπὸ τοῦ θεοῦ, καθὸ οἱ λοιποὶ ὑπ' αὐτοῦ γεγόνασιν ἄγγελοι καὶ τὴν ἐπὶ τῇ ὕλῃ καὶ τοῖς τῆς ὕλης εἴδεσι πιστευσάμενον διοίκησιν. *Iren.* iv. 41, p. 288: Quum igitur a Deo omnia facta sunt, et diabolus sibimet ipsi et reliquis factus est abscessionis causa, juste scriptura eos, qui in abscessione perseverant, semper filios diaboli et angelos dixit maligni. *Tert.* Apol. c. 22: Atque adeo dicimus, esse substantias quasdam spiritales, nec nomen novum est. Sciunt dæmonas philosophi, Socrate ipso ad dæmonii arbitrium exspectante, quidni ? cum et ipsi dæmonium a pueritia adhaesisse dicatur, dehortatorium plane a bono. Dæmonas [omnes] sciunt poëtæ, et jam [etiam] vulgus indoctum in usum maledicti frequentat; nam et Satanam, principem hujus mali generis, proinde de propria conscientia animæ eadem execramenti voce pronuntiat. Angelos quoque etiam Plato non negavit. Utriusque nominis testes esse vel magi adsunt. Sed quomodo de angelis quibusdam sua sponte corruptis corruptior gens dæmonum evaserit damnata a Deo cum generis auctoribus et cum eo quem diximus principe, apud litteras sanctas ordine cognoscitur. Comp. *Orig.* De Princip. procem. 6 (Opp. t. i. p. 48), who, however, leaves all other points problematical, as he does in the doctrine respecting angels; it is sufficient to believe that Satan and the demons really *exist*—quæ autem sint aut quo modo sint(ecclesla), non clare exposuit. It was not until the following period that the Manichees developed the dualistic view, that the devil is a distinct and essential evil principle, in the form of a regular system, although traces of it may be found in some earlier ·Gnostic notions, *e.g.* the Jaldabaoth of the Ophites, comp. *Neander's* Gnostische Systeme, s. 233 ff. *Baur*, Gnosis, s. 173 ff., Dg. s. 557. In opposition to this dualistic view, *Origen* maintains that the devil and the demons are creatures of God, though not created *as* devils, but as spiritual beings; Contra Cels. iv. 65 (Opp. i. p. 563).—As to the extent in which Platonism and Ebionitism participated in the Christian demonology, see *Semisch*, Just. Mart. s. 387 ff.

(2) *Tertullian* and *Origen* agree in ascribing failures of crops, drought, famine, pestilence, and murrain to the influence of demons. *Tert.* Apol. c. 22 (operatio eorum est hominis eversio). *Orig.* Contra Cels. viii. 31, 32 (Opp. i. p. 764, 765). He calls the evil spirits the executioners of God (δήμιοι). Demoniacal possessions were still considered as phenomena of special importance (as in the times of the N. T.). *Minuc. Fel.* c. 27 : Irrepentes etiam corporibus occulte, ut spiritus tenues, morbos fingunt, terrent mentes, membra distorquent. Concerning these δαιμονιόληπτοι, μαινόμενοι, ἐνεργούμενοι, comp. in particular Const. Apost. lib. viii. c. 7. A rationalistic explanation is already given in the Clementine Hom. ix. § 12 : "Οθεν πολλοὶ οὐκ εἰδότες, πόθεν ἐνεργοῦνται, ταῖς τῶν δαιμόνων κακαῖς ὑποβαλλομέναις ἐπινοίαις, ὡς τῷ τῆς ψυχῆς αὐτῶν λογισμῷ συντίθενται. Comp., moreover, *Orig.* ad Matt. xvii. 5 (Opp. t. iii. p. 574 ff.), De Princip. iii. 2 (Opp. t. i. p. 138 ff., de contrariis potestatibus). *Schnitzer*, s. 198 ff. ; *Thomasius*, s. 184 ff., and the passages cited there.

(3) *Justin M.* Apol. c. 5, 12, 14 (quoted by *Usteri*, l.c. s. 421). *Minuc. Fel.* l.c. : Ideo inserti mentibus imperitorum odium nostri serunt occulte per timorem. Naturale est enim et odisse quem timeas, et quem metueris, infestare, si possis. *Justin M.* Apol. ii. towards the commencement, and c. 6. Comp. *Orig.* Exhort. ad Martyr. § 18, 32, 42 (Opp. t. i. p. 286, 294, 302). But *Justin M.*, Apol. i. c. 5, also ascribes the process against Socrates to the hatred of the demons. The observation of *Justin*, quoted by *Irenæus* (Advers. Hær. v. c. 26, p. 324), and *Euseb.* iv. 18, is very remarkable : "Οτι πρὸ μὲν τῆς τοῦ κυρίου παρουσίας οὐδέποτε ἐτόλμησεν ὁ Σατανᾶς βλασφημῆσαι τὸν θεόν, ἅτε μηδέπω εἰδὼς αὐτοῦ τὴν κατάκρισιν (comp. *Epiph.* in Hær. Sethianor. p. 289); thus the

efforts of the powers of darkness against the victorious progress of the Christian religion could be more satisfactorily explained.

(4) Ep. *Barn.* c. 16, 18; *Justin M.* Apol. i. 12, and elsewhere; *Tatian,* c. 12, 20, and elsewhere (comp. *Daniel,* s. 162 ff.); *Athen.* Leg. c. 26; *Tert.* Apol. c. 22, De Præscr. c. 40; *Minuc. Fel.* Octav. c. 27, 1; *Clem. Al.* Cohort. p. 7; *Origen,* Contra Cels. iii. 28, 37, 69, iv. 36, 92, v. 5, vii. 64, viii. 30. The demons are present in particular at the offering of sacrifices, and relish the smoke of the burnt-offering; they speak out of the oracles, and rejoice in the licentiousness and excess which accompany these festivals. (Comp. *Keil,* De Angelorum malorum s. Dæmoniorum Cultu apud Gentiles; Opusc. Academ. s. 584–601. *Münscher, Von Cölln,* i. s. 92 ff.)

(5) According to *Minuc. Fel.* c. 26, the demon of Socrates was one of those evil demons. *Clement* also says of a sect of Christians, Strom. i. 1, p. 326: Οἱ δὲ καὶ πρὸς κακοῦ ἂν τὴν φιλοσοφίαν εἰσδεδυκέναι τὸν βίον νομίζουσιν, ἐπὶ λύμῃ τῶν ἀνθρώπων, πρός τινος εὑρετοῦ πονηροῦ, which is manifestly nothing but an euphemism for διαβόλου; comp. Strom. vi. 882: Πῶς οὖν οὐκ ἄτοπον τὴν ἀταξίαν καὶ τὴν ἀδικίαν προσνέμοντας τῷ διαβόλῳ, ἐναρέτου πράγματος, τοῦτον τῆς φιλοσοφίας, δωτῆρα ποιεῖν; comp. also Strom. i. 17, p. 366, and the note in the edition of *Potter.* Astrology, etc., was also ascribed to demoniacal influence; comp. the same note.

(6) Comp. *Justin M.* Apol. i. 56, 58. *Cyprian,* De Unitate Ecclesiæ, p. 105: Hæreses invenit (diabolus) et schismata, quibus subverteret fidem, veritatem corrumperet, scinderet unitatem, etc.

(7) *Hermas,* ii. 6, 2, comp. the preceding section. *Justin M.* Apol. ii. c. 5 (*Usteri,* s. 423) . . . καὶ εἰς ἀνθρώπους φόνους, πολέμους, μοιχείας, ἀκολασίας καὶ πᾶσαν κακίαν ἔσπειραν. *Clem. Alex.* designates as the most malicious and most pernicious of all demons the greedy belly-demon (κοιλιοδαίμονα λιχνότατον), who is related to the one that works in ventriloquists (τῷ ἐγγαστριμύθῳ), Pæd. ii. 1, p. 174. *Origen* follows *Hermas* in classifying the demons according to the vices which they represent, and thus unconsciously prepares the way for more intelligible views, gradually resolving these concrete representations of devils into abstract notions.

Comp. Hom. 15, in Jesum Nave (Opp. t. ii. p. 333): Unde mihi videtur esse infinitus quidem numerus contrariarum virtutum, pro eo quod per singulos pene homines sunt spiritus aliqui, diversa in iis peccatorum genera molientes. Verbi causa, est aliquis fornicationis spiritus, est iræ spiritus alius, est avaritiæ spiritus, alius vere superbiæ. Et si eveniat esse aliquem hominem, qui his omnibus malis aut etiam pluribus agitetur, omnes hos vel etiam plures in se habere inimicos putandus est spiritus. Comp. also the subsequent part, where it is said, not only that every vice has its chief demon, but also that every vicious person is possessed with a demon who is in the service of the chief demon. Others refer not only crimes, but also natural desires, as the sexual impulse, to the devil. *Origen*, however, objects to this, De Princip. iii. 2, 2 (Opp. t. i. p. 139, *Redepenning*, p. 278 ss.).

§ 52.

The same Subject continued.

The Fathers held different opinions as to the particular sin which caused the apostasy of the demons (1). Some thought that it was envy and pride (2), others supposed lasciviousness and intemperance (3). But it is of practical importance to notice, that the Church never held that the devil can compel any soul to commit sin without its own consent (4). *Origen* went so far, that, contrary to the general opinion, he allowed even to Satan the glimmer of a hope of future pardon (5).

(1) The Fathers do not agree as to the time at which this took place. On the supposition that the devil seduced our first parents, it is necessary to assign an earlier date to his apostasy than to the fall of man. But, according to *Tatian* (Orat. c. 11), the fall of Satan was the punishment which was inflicted upon him in consequence of the part he had taken in the first sin of man (comp. *Daniel*, s. 187, 196). From the language of *Irenæus* (comp. note 2), one might suspect that he

entertained similar views; but it is more probable that he fixed upon the period which elapsed between the creation of man and his temptation, as the time when the devil apostatized. Thus *Cyprian* says, De Dono Patient. p. 218: Diabolus hominem ad imaginem Dei factum impatienter tulit; inde et periit *primus* et perdidit.

(2) *Iren.* Adv. Hær. iv. 40, 3, p. 207: Ἐζήλωσε τὸ πλάσμα τοῦ θεοῦ, and *Cyprian*, l.c. *Orig.* in Ezech. Hom. 9, 2 (Opp. t. iii. p. 389): Inflatio, superbia, arrogantia peccatum diaboli est et ob hæc delicta ad terras migravit de cœlo. Comp. *Phot.* Bibl. Cod. 324, p. 293 (ed. *Bekker*): Οἱ μὲν λοιποὶ (ἄγγελοι) ἐφ' ὧν αὐτοὺς ἐποίησε καὶ διετάξατο ὁ θεὸς ἔμειναν· αὐτὸς δὲ (sc. ὁ διάβολος) ἐνύβρισε.

(3) The passage in Gen. vi. 2 (according to the reading οἱ ἄγγελοι τοῦ θεοῦ instead of οἱ υἱοὶ τοῦ θεοῦ) had already been applied to the demons, and their intercourse with the daughters of men. (Comp. *Wernsdorf*, Exercitatio de Commercio Angelorum cum Filiabus Hominum ab Judæis et Patribus Platonizantibus credito, Viteb. 1742, 4. *Keil*, Opusc. p. 566 ss. *Münscher, Von Cölln,* s. 89, 90. *Suicer*, s.v. ἄγγελος, i. p. 36, and ἐγρήγορος, p. 1003.) Thus *Philo* wrote a special treatise "De Gigantibus;" and all the Fathers of the first period (with the exception of Julius Africanus, see *Routh*, Reliquiæ Sacræ, ii. p. 127 ss.) referred the passages in question to the sexual intercourse of the angels with the daughters of men. This, however, holds only of the later demons, who became subject to the devil, and not of the apostasy of Satan himself, which falls in an earlier period (note 1). With him lust is unknown; see *Semisch*, ii. s. 380. Concerning the apparent parachronism, comp. *Münscher*, Handb. ii. s. 30, 31. In accordance with this notion, *Clement*, Strom. iii. 7, p. 538, designates ἀκρασία and ἐπιθυμία as the causes of the fall.—The above-mentioned views of pagan worship, and the temptation to sensuality (§ 51, and ibid. note 7), were connected with these notions respecting the intercourse of the demons with the daughters of men. The fallen angels betrayed the mysteries of revelation to them, though in an imperfect and corrupt form, and the heathen have their philosophy from these women. Comp. *Clem.* Strom. vi. 1, p. 650. [Comp. on Gen. vi. 1–4, *S. R. Maitland* on False Worship, 1856, p. 19 sq., and in British Magazine, vol.

xxi. p. 389 ; also in his essays, "Eruvin." *C. F. Keil* in the Zeitschrift f. luth. Theol. 1855 and 1859 ; *Engelhardt* in the same (against *Keil*), 1856, for the angels. *Kurtz's* Essay on the subject, 1856, and in his Hist. of the O. T., and *Delitzsch* in reply to *Kurtz*, in Reuter's Repertorium, 1857; also in his Comm. on Genesis.]

(4) *Hermas*, lib. ii. mand. 7 : Diabolum autem ne timeas, timens enim Dominum dominaberis illius, quia virtus in illo nulla est. In quo autem virtus non est, is ne timendus quidem est; in quo vero virtus gloriosa est, is etiam timendus est. Omnis enim virtutem habens timendus est; nam qui virtutem non habet, ab omnibus contemnitur. Time plane facta Diaboli, quoniam maligna sunt: metuens enim Dominum, timebis, et opera Diaboli non facies, sed abstinebis te ab eis. Comp. 12, 5 : Potest autem Diabolus luctari, sed vincere non potest. Si enim resistitur, fugiet a vobis confusus.—[For as a man, when he fills up vessels with good wine, and among them puts a few vessels half full, and comes to try and taste of the vessels, does not try those that are full, because he knows that they are good, but tastes those that are half full, lest they should grow sour; so the devil comes to the servants of God to try them. They that are full of faith resist him stoutly, and he departs from them because he finds no place by which to enter into them: then he goes to those that are not full of faith, and because he has a place of entrance, he goes into them, and does what he will with them, and they become his servants. Hermas, 12, 5, *Archbishop Wake's* transl.] Comp. *Tatian*, c. 16 : Δαίμονες δὲ οἱ τοῖς ἀνθρώποις ἐπιτάττοντες, οὔκ εἰσιν αἱ τῶν ἀνθρώπων ψυχαί κ.τ.λ. *Iren.* ii. c. 32, 4, p. 166. *Tert.* Apol. c. 23 : Omnis hæc nostra in illos dominatio et potestas de nominatione Christi valet, et de commemoratione eorum quæ sibi a Deo per arbitrum Christum imminentia exspectant. Christum timentes in Deo, et Deum in Christo, subjiciuntur servis Dei et Christi. *Orig.* De Princip. iii. 2, 4 ; Contra Cels. i. 6, and viii. 36 (Opp. i. p. 769): Ἀλλ' οὐ χριστιανὸς, ὁ ἀληθῶς χριστιανὸς καὶ ὑποτάξας ἑαυτὸν μόνῳ τῷ θεῷ καὶ τῷ λόγῳ αὐτοῦ πάθοι τι ἂν ὑπὸ τῶν δαιμονίων, ἄτε κρείττων δαιμόνων τυγχάνων, and in lib. Jesu Nave, xv. 6. In the former passage, De Princip., *Origen* calls those simple (simpliciores) who believe that sin would not exist if there was no

devil. Along with the moral power of faith, and the efficacy of prayer, the magical effects of the sign of the cross, etc., were relied on. But what was at first nothing more than a symbol of the power of faith itself, became afterwards a mechanical opus operatum.

(5) Even *Clement*, Strom. i. 17, p. 367, says: Ὁ δὲ διάβολος αὐτεξούσιος ὢν καὶ μετανοῆσαι οἷός τε ἦν καὶ κλέψαι, καὶ ὁ αἴτιος αὐτὸς τῆς κλοπῆς, οὐχ ὁ μὴ κωλύσας κύριος, but from these words it is not quite evident whether he means to say that the devil is yet capable of being converted. The general opinion, as earlier held, is expressed by *Tatian*, Orat. c. 15 : Ἡ τῶν δαιμόνων ὑπόστασις οὐκ ἔχει μετανοίας τόπον. *Justin M.* Dialog. c. Tryph. c. 141.—*Origen* himself did not very clearly propound his views; De Princip. iii. c. 6, 5 (Opp. i. p. 154): Propterea etiam novissimus inimicus, qui mors appellatur, destrui dicitur (1 Cor. xv. 26), ut neque ultra triste sit aliquid ubi mors non est, neque adversum sit ubi non est inimicus. Destrui sane novissimus inimicus ita intelligendus est, non ut substantia ejus, quæ a Deo facta est, pereat, sed ut propositum et voluntas inimica, quæ non a Deo sed ab ipso processit, intereat. Destruitur ergo non ut non sit, sed ut inimicus non sit et mors. Nihil enim omnipotenti impossibile est, nec insanabile est aliquid factori suo. § 6. *Omnia restituentur ut unum sint, et Deus fuerit omnia in omnibus* (1 Cor. xv. 28). Quod tamen non ad subitum fieri, sed paulatim et per partes intelligendum est, infinitis et immensis labentibus sæculis, cum sensim et per singulos emendatio fuerit et correctio prosecuta, præcurrentibus aliis et velociori cursu ad summa tendentibus, *aliis* vero proximo quoque spatio insequentibus, tum deinde aliis longe posterius : et sic per multos et innumeros ordines proficientium ac Deo se ex inimicis reconciliantium pervenitur usque ad novissimum inimicum qui dicitur mors, et etiam ipse destruitur ne ultra sit inimicus. He here speaks of the last enemy, death, but it is evident from the context that he identifies death with the devil (this is signified, as cited, *e.g. Münscher*, Handbuch, ii. s. 39, by the use of the parenthesis); he speaks of a substance which the Creator would not destroy, but heal. Comp. § 3, and *Schnitzer* in the passage ; *Thomasius*, s. 187. On the possibility of the conversion of the other demons, comp. i.

6, 3 (Opp. i. p. 70; *Redep.* p. 146): Jam vero si aliqui ex his ordinibus, qui sub principatu diaboli agunt, militiæ ejus obtemperant, poterunt aliquando in futuris sæculis converti ad bonitatem, pro eo quod est in ipsis liberi facultas arbitrii (?) . . .

THIRD DIVISION.

ANTHROPOLOGY.

§ 53.

Introduction.

To bring man back to himself and to the knowledge of his own nature, was the essential object of Christianity, and the condition of its further progress (1). Hence the first office of Christian anthropology must be to determine, not what man is in his natural life in relation to the rest of the visible creation, but what he is as a spiritual and moral being in relation to God and divine things. But since the higher and spiritual nature of man is intimately connected with the organism of both body and soul, a system of *theological* anthropology could be constructed only on the basis of physical and psychical anthropology, which, in the first instance, belongs to natural science and philosophy, rather than to theology. The history of doctrines, therefore, must also consider the opinions held as to man in his natural relations (2).

(1) Comp. *Clem.* Pæd. iii. 1, p. 250 : Ἦν ἄρα, ὡς ἔοικε, πάντων μεγίστων μαθημάτων τὸ γνῶναι αὑτόν· ἑαυτὸν γάρ τις ἐὰν γνῷη, θεὸν εἴσεται.

(2) At first sight it might appear indifferent, so far as theology is concerned, whether man consists of two or three parts; and yet these distinctions are intimately connected with the theological definitions of liberty, immortality, etc. This is the case also with the doctrine of pre-existence, in

opposition to traducianism and creationism, in relation to original sin, etc. Thus it can be explained why *Tatian*, on religious grounds, opposes the common definition, according to which man is a ζῶον λογικόν, Contra Græcos, c. 15: Ἔστιν ἄνθρωπος, οὐχ ὥσπερ κορακόφωνοι δογματίζουσιν, ζῶον λογικὸν, νοῦ καὶ ἐπιστήμης δεκτικόν· δειχθήσεται γὰρ κατ' αὐτοὺς καὶ τὰ ἄλογα νοῦ καὶ ἐπιστήμης δεκτικά. Μόνος δὲ ἄνθρωπος εἰκὼν καὶ ὁμοίωσις τοῦ θεοῦ, λέγω δὲ ἄνθρωπον οὐχὶ τὸν ὅμοια τοῖς ζώοις πράττοντα, ἀλλὰ τὸν πόρρω μὲν ἀνθρωπότητος, πρὸς αὐτὸν δὲ τὸν θεὸν κεχωρηκότα.

§ 54.

Division of Human Nature and Practical Psychology.

Keil, Opusc. Academ. p. 618-647. *Duncker*, Apologetarum secundi Sæculi de Essentialibus Naturæ humanæ Partibus Placita. P. I. 11, Gött. 1844-50, 4to. [*Olshausen*, in Opuscula, 1834. *Franz Delitzsch*, System der biblischen Psychologie, Leipz. 1855, 2d ed. 1862. *J. T. Beck*, Umriss d. biblischen Seelenlehre, Stuttg. 1843, 2d ed. 1871, 3d ed. 1877. Both translated into Eng., Edin.]

That man is made up of body and soul, is a fact which we know by experience previous to all speculation, and before we express it in precise scientific terms. But it is more difficult to define the relation between body and soul, and to assign to each its boundaries. Some regarded the ψυχή as the medium by which the purely spiritual in man, the higher and ideal life of reason, is connected with the purely animal, the grosser and sensuous principle of the natural life. They also suppose that this human triad was supported by the language of Scripture (1). Some of the earlier Fathers (2), those of the Alexandrian school in particular (3), adopted this trichotomistic division, while others, like *Tertullian*, adhered to the opinion that man consists only of body and soul (4). Some Gnostic sects, *e.g.* the Valentinians, so perverted the trichotomistic division, as to divide men themselves into three classes, χοϊκοί, ψυχικοί, and πνευματικοί, according as one or the other of the three constituents preponderated, to the

§ 54.] DIVISION OF HUMAN NATURE AND PSYCHOLOGY. 209

apparent exclusion of the others. Thus they again sundered the bond of union with which Christ had encircled men as brethren (5).

(1) בָּשָׂר, נֶפֶשׁ, רוּחַ; σάρξ, ψυχή, πνεῦμα. Comp. the works on Bibl. Theol., and the commentaries on 1 Thess. v. 23; Heb. iv. 12, etc.; also *Ackermann*, Studien und Kritiken, 1839, part 4. *Olshausen, Beck*, and *Delitzsch*, l.c. The Platonists also hold this trichotomy.

(2) *Justin M.* fragm. de Resurr. § 10 : Οἶκος τὸ σῶμα ψυχῆς, πνεύματος δὲ ψυχὴ οἶκος. Τὰ τρία ταῦτα τοῖς ἐλπίδα εἰλικρινῆ καὶ πίστιν ἀδιάκριτον ἐν τῷ θεῷ ἔχουσι σωθήσεται. Comp. Dial. cum Tryph. § 4. *Tatian* (Contra Græc. Or. c. 7, 12, 15) knows two different πνεύματα, the one of which he calls ψυχή, while the other is of divine nature, but in consequence of sin does not belong to all men. *Irenæus*, v. 9, 1: Tria sunt, ex quibus perfectus homo constat, carne, anima et spiritu, et altero quidem salvante et figurante, qui est spiritus, altero, quod unitur et formatur, quod est caro; id vero quod inter hæc est duo, quod est anima, quæ aliquando quidem subsequens spiritum elevatur ab eo, aliquando autem consentiens carni decidit in terrenas concupiscentias. Comp. v. 6, 1. 298: Anima autem et spiritus pars hominum esse possunt, homo autem nequaquam : perfectus autem homo commixtio et adunitio est animæ assumentis spiritum Patris et admixta ei carni, quæ est plasma secundum imaginem Dei. Accordingly, not every man is by nature made up of three parts, but he only who has received the gift of the Holy Spirit, as the third. Concerning the distinction between Pnoë and Pnuema, comp. § 44, and *Duncker*, s. 97, 98.

(3) *Clement* (Strom. vii. 12, p. 880) makes a distinction between the ψυχὴ λογική and the ψυχὴ σωματική; he also mentions a *tenfold* division of man (analogous to the decalogue), ibid. vi. 16, p. 808: Ἔστι δὲ καὶ δεκάς τις περὶ τὸν ἄνθρωπον αὐτόν· τά τε αἰσθητήρια πέντε καὶ τὸ φωνητικὸν καὶ τὸ σπερματικόν, καὶ τοῦτο δὴ ὄγδοον τὸ κατὰ τὴν πλάσιν πνευματικόν, ἔννατον δὲ τὸ ἡγεμονικὸν τῆς ψυχῆς, καὶ δέκατον τὸ διὰ τῆς πίστεως προσγινόμενον ἁγίου πνεύματος χαρακτηριστικὸν ἰδίωμα κ.τ.λ.; the more general division into body, soul, and spirit forms, however, the basis of this. *Clement*,

after the example of Plato (comp. *Justin M. Coh. ad Gr.* 6), divides the soul itself into these three faculties: τὸ λογιστικόν (νοερόν), τὸ θυμικόν, τὸ ἐπιθυμητικόν, Pæd. iii. 1, ab init. p. 250. The knowing faculty he subdivides into four functions: αἴσθησις, νοῦς, ἐπιστήμη, ὑπόληψις, Strom. ii. 4, p. 445. *Clement* regards body and soul as διάφορα, but not as ἐναντία, so that neither is the soul as such good, nor is the body as such evil. Comp. Strom. iv. 26, p. 639. For the psychology of *Origen*, see De Princip. iii. 3 (Opp. i. 145, *Redep.* p. 296–306). On the question whether *Origen* believed in the existence of two souls in man, see *Schnitzer*, s. 219 ff.; *Thomasius*, s. 190, 193–195; *Redep.* ii. s. 369, Anm. 3. In the view of *Origen*, the ψυχή as such, which he derives from ψύχεσθαι, is intermediate between body and spirit; "*a defective, not fully developed power*" (*Redep.* ii. s. 368). He affirms that he has found no passage in the sacred Scriptures in which the soul, as such, is spoken of with honour; while, on the contrary, it is frequently blamed, De Princip. ii. 8, 3–5 (Opp. i. p. 95 ff., *Redep.* p. 211 ss.). But this does not prevent him from comparing the soul to the Son, when he draws a comparison between the human and the divine triad, ibid. § 5. For the trichotomistic division, comp. also Comment. in Matt. t. xiii. 2 (Opp. iii. p. 570), and other passages in *Münscher* (*VonCölln*), i. s. 319, 320. *Origen* sometimes employs the simple term "man" to designate man's nobler spiritual part, so that man appears not so much to consist of body and soul, as to be the soul itself, which governs the body as a mere instrument; Contra Cels. vii. 38: Ἄνθρωπος, τουτέστι ψυχὴ χρωμένη σώματι (comp. *Photius*, Cod. 234; *Epiph.* Hær. 64, 17). Consequently he calls the soul homo, homo = homo interior, in Num. xxiv.; comp. *Thomasius* and *Redepenning*, l.c.

(4) De Anima, c. 10, 11, 20, 21, 22: Definimus animam *Dei flatu* natam, immortalem, *corporalem*, effigiatam, *substantia simplicem*, de suo patientem varie procedentem, [sapientem] liberam arbitrii, accidentiis obnoxiam, per ingenia mutabilem, rationalem, dominatricem, divinatricem, ex una redundantem (c. 22); Adv. Hermog. c. 11, and *Neander*, Antignostikus, s. 457. Concerning the value which, from his strong realistic position, he attached to the senses (the key to his theological opinions), comp. ibid. s. 452 ff. The soul is to *Tertullian*

something corporeal, as its form (effigies), analogous to the body, proves: it has corporeal outlines (corporales lineas). In support of this view he appeals to the parable of Dives and Lazarus, and to visions. Cf. De Anima, c. 7-10.

(5) *Iren.* i. 5, 5 (*Münscher, Von Cölln,* i. s. 316, 317); comp. also *Neander,* Gnostische Systeme, s. 127 ff. *Baur,* Gnosis, s. 158 ff., 168 ff., 489 ff., 679 ff.; and Dg. s. 565 ff.

§ 55.

Origin of the Soul.

J. F. *Bruch,* Die Lehre von der Präexistenz, Strasb. 1859. [*Julius Müller,* Lehre von der Sünde, 1te Ausg. 1844, 6te 1877. J. *Frohschammer,* Ueber den Ursprung d. menschlichen Seele, München 1854. *Joh. Marcus,* Lehrmeinungen über d. Ursprung d. menschl. Seele, in d. ersten Jahrh. d. Kirche, 1854.]

The inquiry into the origin of the human soul, and the mode of its union with the body, seems to be purely metaphysical, and to have no bearing upon religion (1). But, in a religious point of view, it is always of importance that the soul should be considered *as a creature of God.* This doctrine was maintained by the Catholic Church in opposition to the Gnostic and heretical theory of emanations (2). *Origen's* hypothesis of the *pre-existence of the soul* is allied with Platonic views (3). On the other hand, *Tertullian* maintained the propagation of the soul *per traducem* in connection with his realistic and materializing conceptions of its corporeity (*Traducianism*) (4).

(1) Thus, *Origen* says, De Princip. procem. 5 (Opp. i. p. 48): De anima vero utrum ex seminis traduce ducatur, ita ut ratio ipsius vel substantia inserta ipsis seminibus corporalibus habeatur, an vero aliud habeat initium, et hoc ipsum initium si genitum est aut non genitum, vel certe si extrinsecus corpori inditur, necne: non satis manifesta prædicatione distinguitur.

(2) Traces of the theory of emanation are found in the

writings of some of the earlier Fathers. *Justin M.* fragm. de Resurr. 11 : Ἡ μὲν ψυχή ἐστιν ἄφθαρτος, μέρος οὖσα τοῦ θεοῦ καὶ ἐμφύσημα. (Whether this is *Justin's* own opinion, or a thesis of the Gnostics, which he combats, see *Semisch*, Just. Mart. s. 364.) Comp. the Clementine Homilies, Hom. xvi. 12. On the other hand, *Clement* of Alex. adheres to the idea of *creation* in Coh. p. 78 : Μόνος ὁ τῶν ὅλων δημιουργὸς ὁ ἀριστοτέχνας πατὴρ τοιοῦτον ἄγαλμα ἔμψυχον ἡμᾶς, τὸν ἄνθρωπον ἔπλασεν ; and Strom. ii. 16, p. 467, 468, where he rejects the phrase μέρος θεοῦ, which some employed, in accordance with the principle : Θεὸς οὐδεμίαν ἔχει πρὸς ἡμᾶς φυσικὴν σχέσιν. Comp. *Orig.* in Joh. t. xiii. 25 (Opp. t. iv. p. 235) : Σφόδρα ἐστὶν ἀσεβὲς ὁμοούσιον τῇ ἀγεννήτῳ φύσει καὶ παμμακαρίᾳ εἶναι λέγειν τοὺς προσκυνοῦντας ἐν πνεύματι τῷ θεῷ. Comp. De Princip. i. 7, 1.

(3) *Clement,* Coh. p. 6: Πρὸ δὲ τῆς τοῦ κόσμου καταβολῆς ἡμεῖς οἱ τῷ δεῖν ἔσεσθαι ἐν αὐτῷ πρότερον γεγεννημένοι τῷ θεῷ· τοῦ θεοῦ λόγου τὰ λογικὰ πλάσματα ἡμεῖς· δι' ὃν ἀρχαΐζομεν, ὅτι ἐν ἀρχῇ ὁ λόγος ἦν ; this perhaps should rather be understood in an ideal sense. [*Clement* rejects the view that the soul is generated, in Strom. lib. vi. c. 16: ... οὐ κατὰ τὴν τοῦ σπέρματος καταβολὴν γενώμενον, ὡς συνάγεσθαι καὶ ἄνευ τούτου τὸν δεκατὸν ἀριθμὸν, δι' ὧν ἡ πᾶσα ἐνέργεια τοῦ ἀνθρώπου ἐπιτελεῖται. So, too, *Athenagoras,* De mort. Resur. c. 17.] But *Origen,* following the Pythagoræan and Platonic schools, as well as the later Jewish theology, first spoke of the pre-existence of the soul as something real (comp. *Epiph.* Hær. 64, 4 : Τὴν ψυχὴν γὰρ τὴν ἀνθρωπείαν λέγει προϋπάρχειν). He brought his doctrine into connection with that of human liberty and divine justice, by maintaining that the soul comes into the body as a punishment for former sins : comp. De Princip. i. 7, 4 (Opp. i. p. 27, *Redep.* p. 151; *Schnitzer,* s. 72).—"If the soul of man is formed only with the body, how could Jacob supplant his brother in the womb, and John leap in the womb at the salutation of Mary?" Comp. also t. xv. in Matth. c. 34, 35, in Matt. xx. 6, 7 (Opp. t. iii. p. 703), and Comment. in Joh. t. ii. 25 (Opp. iv. p. 85, *Redep.* ii. 20 ff.). [*Origen* says his view is not directly contained in Scripture : De Princip. i. c. 7 : Nam per conjecturam facilis assertio esse videbitur ; scripturarum autem testimoniis

utique difficilius affirmatur. Nam per conjecturas ita possibile est ostendi. He also speaks in some passages as if his opinion was undecided; lib. ii. in Cant. Cantic.: Et si ita sit, utrum nuper creata veniat, et tunc primum facta, cum corpus videtur esse formatum, sed causa facturæ ejus animandi corporis necessitas extitisse credatur; an prius et olim facta, ob aliquam causam ad corpus sumendum venire existimetur: et si ex causa aliqua in hoc deduci creditur, quæ illa sit causa ut agnosci possit, scientiæ opus est.]

(4) De Anima, c. 19 : Et si ad arbores provocamur, amplectemur exemplum. Si quidem et illis, necdum arbusculis, sed stipitibus adhuc et surculis etiam nunc, simul de scrobibus oriuntur, inest propria vis animæ . . . quo magis hominis? cujus anima, velut surculus quidam ex matrice Adam in propaginem deducta et genitalibus feminæ foveis commendata cum omni sua paratura, pullulabit tam intellectu quam sensu? Mentior, si non statim infans ut vitam vagitu salutavit, hoc ipsum se testatur sensisse atque intellexisse, quod natus est, omnes simul ibidem dedicans sensus, et luce visum et sono auditum et humore gustum et aere odoratum et terra tactum. Ita prima illa vox de primis sensuum et de primis intellectuum pulsibus cogitur. . . . Et hic itaque concludimus, omnia naturalia animæ, ut substantiva ejus, ipsi inesse et cum ipsa procedere atque proficere, ex quo ipsa censetur, sicut et Seneca sæpe noster (De Benef. iv. 6): Insita sunt nobis omnium artium et ætatum semina, etc. Comp. c. 27. *Neander*, Antignost. s. 455, and the whole section. [*Tertullian*, De Anima, c. 36 : Anima in utero seminata pariter cum carne, pariter cum ipsa sortitur et sexum, ita pariter ut in causa sexus neutra substantia tenetur. Si enim in seminibus utriusque substantiæ, aliquam intercapedinem eorum conceptus admitteret, ut aut caro, aut anima prior seminaretur, esset etiam sexus proprietatum alteri substantiæ adscribere per temporalem intercapedinem seminum; ut aut caro animæ, aut anima carni insculperet sexum.]

§ 56.

The Image of God.

[*Thomasius*, Christi Person und Werk, i. 185 ff. *Bp. Bull*, Treatise on the State of Man before the Fall. *Delitzsch*, Bibl. Psychol. ut sup.]

Man's bodily pre-eminence, as well as his higher moral and religious nature, frequently referred to by the Fathers in a variety of forms (1), is appropriately described in the simple and striking words of Scripture (Gen. i. 27): "So God created man in His own image: in the image of God created He him." This form of expression has been always employed by the Church (2). But it was a point of no little difficulty to determine precisely in what this image of God consists. As body and soul could not be absolutely separated, it was represented by some that even the body of man is created after the image of God (3), now in a more gross, and again in a more refined figurative sense; while others rejected this view altogether. All, however, admitted, as a matter of course, that the image of God has a special reference to the spiritual endowments of man. But inasmuch as there is a great chasm between the mere natural properties, and their development by the free use of the powers which have been granted to man, *Irenæus*, and especially *Clement* and *Origen*, still more clearly distinguished between the image of God and likeness to God. The latter can only be obtained by a moral conflict (under the ethical point of view), or is bestowed upon man as a gift of grace, through union with Christ (in the religious aspect) (4).

(1) *Iren.* iv. 29, p. 285: Ἔδει δὲ τὸν ἄνθρωπον πρῶτον γενέσθαι, καὶ γενόμενον αὐξῆσαι, καὶ αὐξήσαντα ἀνδρωθῆναι, καὶ ἀνδρωθέντα πληθυνθῆναι, καὶ πληθυνθέντα ἐνισχῦσαι, καὶ ἐνισχύσαντα δοξασθῆναι, καὶ δοξασθέντα ἰδεῖν τὸν ἑαυτοῦ δεσπότην. Yet in other places *Irenæus* distinguishes less exactly; see *Duncker*, s. 99 ff. *Min. Fel.* 17 and 18, ab init. *Tatian*, Or. Contra Gr. c. 12 and 19. *Clem.* Coh. p. 78.

§ 56.] THE IMAGE OF GOD. 215

According to the latter, man is the most beautiful hymn to the praise of the Deity, p. 78; a heavenly plant (φυτὸν οὐράνιον), p. 80, and, generally speaking, the principal object of the love of God, Pæd. i. 3, p. 102, comp. p. 158. Pæd. iii. 7, p. 276: Φύσει γὰρ ὁ ἄνθρωπος ὑψηλόν ἐστι ζῶον καὶ γαῦρον καὶ τοῦ καλοῦ ζητητικόν; ib. iii. 8, p. 292. But all the good he possesses is not innate in such a way, but that it must be developed by instruction (μάθησις). Comp. Strom. i. 6, p. 336, iv. 23, p. 623, vi. 11, p. 788, vii. 4, p. 839, and the passages on human liberty, which will be found below.

(2) Some of the Alexandrian theologians, however, speaking more definitely, taught that man had been created, not so much after the image of *God* Himself, as after the image of the *Logos*, an image after an image! Coh. p. 78: Ἡ μὲν γὰρ τοῦ θεοῦ εἰκὼν ὁ λόγος αὐτοῦ, καὶ υἱὸς τοῦ νοῦ γνήσιος ὁ θεῖος λόγος, φωτὸς ἀρχέτυπον φῶς· εἰκὼν δὲ τοῦ λόγου ὁ ἄνθρωπος· ἀληθινὸς ὁ νοῦς ὁ ἐν ἀνθρώπῳ, ὁ κατ᾽ εἰκόνα τοῦ θεοῦ καὶ καθ᾽ ὁμοίωσιν διὰ τοῦτο γεγενῆσθαι λεγόμενος, τῇ κατὰ καρδίαν φρονήσει τῷ θείῳ παρεικαζόμενος λόγῳ, καὶ ταύτῃ λογικός (remark the play on the word λογικός). Comp. Strom. v. 14, p. 703, and *Orig.* Comment. in Joh. p. 941 (Opp. t. iv. p. 19, 51); in Luc. Hom. viii. (Opp. t. iii.).

(3) This notion was either connected with the fancy that God Himself has a body (see above), or with the idea that the body of Christ was the image after which the body of man had been created. (The author of the Clementine Homilies also thought that *the body in particular* bore the image of God, comp. *Piper* on Melito, l.c. p. 74, 75; *Baur*, Dg. s. 577.) *Tert.* De Carne Christi, c. 6; Adv. Marc. v. 8; Adv. Prax. 12. *Neander*, Antign. s. 407 ff. [*Just. Mart.* makes the image to consist in the whole man, including the body. *Tertullian*, Adv. Marcion, lib. ii.: Homo est a Deo conditus, non imperiali verbo, ut cætera animalia, sed familiari manu, etiam præmisso blandiente illo verbo: Faciamus hominem ad imaginem et similitudinem nostram.] The more spiritual view was, that the life of the soul, partaking of the divine nature, shines through the physical organism, and is reflected especially in the countenance of man, in his looks, etc. *Tatian*, Or. c. 15 (*Worth*, c. 24): Ψυχὴ μὲν οὖν ἡ τῶν ἀνθρώπων πολυμερής ἐστι καὶ οὐ μονομερής. Συνθετὴ (al.

συνετή, according to Fronto Ducæus, comp. *Daniel*, s. 202) γάρ ἐστιν ὡς εἶναι φανερὰν αὐτὴν διὰ σώματος, οὔτε γὰρ ἂν αὐτὴ φανείη ποτὲ χωρὶς σώματος οὔτε ἀνίσταται ἡ σὰρξ χωρὶς ψυχῆς. *Clem.* Coh. p. 52, Strom. v. 14, p. 703 : Ψυχὴν δὲ τὴν λογικὴν ἄνωθεν ἐμπνευσθῆναι ὑπὸ τοῦ θεοῦ εἰς πρόσωπον. On this account the Fathers of the Alexandrian school very decidedly oppose the more material conception of a bodily copy of the divine image. *Clem.* Strom. ii. 19, p. 483 : Τὸ γὰρ κατ' εἰκόνα καὶ ὁμοίωσιν, ὡς καὶ πρόσθεν εἰρήκαμεν, οὐ τὸ κατὰ σῶμα μηνύεται· οὐ γὰρ θέμις θνητὸν ἀθανάτῳ ἐξομοιοῦσθαι· ἀλλ' ἡ κατὰ νοῦν καὶ λογισμόν. On the other hand, it is surprising that the same *Clement*, Pæd. ii. 10, p. 220, should recognize the image of God in the procreative power of man, which others connected with demoniacal agency (§ 51): Εἰκὼν ὁ ἄνθρωπος τοῦ θεοῦ γίνεται, καθὸ εἰς γένεσιν ἀνθρώπου ἄνθρωπος συνεργεῖ. *Origen* refers the divine image exclusively to the spirit of man; Contra Cels. vi. (Opp. i. p. 680), and Hom. i. in Genes. (Opp. t. ii. p. 57).

(4) The tautological phrase, Gen. i. 26 : בְּצַלְמֵנוּ כִּדְמוּתֵנוּ, induced the Fathers in their acumen to make an arbitrary distinction between צֶלֶם (εἰκών) and דְּמוּת (ὁμοίωσις ; comp. *Schott*, Opuscul. t. ii. p. 66 ss.). *Neander* sees in this (Dg. s. 190) "*the first germ of the distinction, afterwards so important, between the dona naturalia and supernaturalia.*" *Irenæus*, Adv. Hær. v. 6, p. 299, v. 16, p. 313 : Ἐν τοῖς πρόσθεν χρόνοις ἐλέγετο μὲν κατ' εἰκόνα θεοῦ γεγονέναι τὸν ἄνθρωπον, οὐκ ἐδείκνυτο δέ· ἔτι γὰρ ἀόρατος ἦν ὁ λόγος, οὗ κατ' εἰκόνα ὁ ἄνθρωπος ἐγεγόνει. Διὰ τοῦτο δὴ καὶ τὴν ὁμοίωσιν ῥᾳδίως ἀπέβαλεν. Ὁπότε δὲ σὰρξ ἐγένετο ὁ λόγος, τοῦ θεοῦ τὰ ἀμφότερα ἐπεκύρωσε· καὶ γὰρ καὶ τὴν εἰκόνα ἔδειξεν ἀγηθῶς, αὐτὸς τοῦτο γενόμενος, ὅπερ ἦν ἡ εἰκὼν αὐτοῦ· καὶ τὴν ὁμοίωσιν βεβαίως κατέστησε συνεξομοιώσας τὸν ἄνθρωπον τῷ ἀοράτῳ πατρί. According to some, the language of *Clem.* Strom. ii. 22, p. 499 (418, *Sylb.*), implies that the image of God is communicated to man εὐθέως κατὰ τὴν γένεσιν, and that he obtains the likeness ὕστερον κατὰ τὴν τελείωσιν. According to *Tert.*, De Bapt. c. 5, man attains unto likeness to God by *baptism*. According to *Origen*, who everywhere insists upon the self-determination of man, the likeness of God which is to be obtained consists in this, ut

(homo) ipse sibi eam sibi eam propriæ industriæ studiis ex Dei imitatione conscisceret, cum possibilitate sibi perfectionis in initiis data per imaginis dignitatem in fine demum per operum expletionem perfectam sibi ipse similitudinem consummaret; De Princip. iii. 6, 1 (Opp. t. 1, p. 152; *Redep.* p. 317; *Schnitzer*, p. 236). Comp. Contra Cels. iv. 20, p. 522, 23. But *Origen* again uses both terms indifferently, Hom. ii. in Jer. (Opp. t. iii. p. 137); Contra Cels. vi. 63.

§ 57.

Freedom and Immortality.

(a) *Liberty.*

Wörter, die christl. Lehre über d. Verhältniss von Gnade und Freiheit von den apostolischen Zeiten bis auf Augustinus. 1. Hälfte, Freiburg im Breisg. 1856. [*Landerer*, Verhältniss von Gnade und Freiheit, in the Jahrbücher f. deutsche Theologie, 1857, s. 500–603. *Kuhn*, Der vorgebliche Pelagianismus der voraugustinischen Kirchenväter, in the (Tübingen) Theol. Quartalschrift, 1853. *J. B. Mozley*, Augustinian Doctrine of Predestination, Lond. 1855, p. 398 ff. *Neander*, Kg. and Dg.]

Freedom and immortality are those prerogatives of the human mind in which the image of God manifests itself; such was the doctrine of the primitive Church, confirmed by the general Christian consciousness. All the Greek Fathers, as well as the apologists *Justin* (1), *Tatian* (2), *Athenagoras* (3), *Theophilus* (4), and the Latin author *Minucius Felix* (5), also the theologians of the Alexandrian school, *Clement* (6), and *Origen* (7), exalt the αὐτεξούσιον (the autonomy, self-determination) of the human soul with the freshness of youth and a tincture of Hellenistic idealism, but also influenced by a practical Christian interest. They know nothing of any imputation of sin, except as a voluntary and moral self-determination is presupposed. Even *Irenæus* (8), although opposed to speculation, and the more austere *Tertullian* (9), strongly insist upon this self-determination in the use of the freedom of the will, from the practical and moral point of view. None but heretics ventured to maintain that man is subject to the influence of a foreign power (the stars, or the εἱμαρμένη) (10); and on this very account they met with the most decided opposition on the part of the whole Church.

(1) *Justin M.* speaks in the most decisive way against determinism, Apol. i. c. 43 : Εἱμαρμένην φαμὲν ἀπαράβατον ταύτην εἶναι, τοῖς τὰ καλὰ ἐκλεγομένοις τὰ ἄξια ἐπιτίμια, καὶ τοῖς ὁμοίως τὰ ἐναντία, τὰ ἄξια ἐπίχειρα. Οὐ γὰρ ὥσπερ τὰ ἄλλα, οἷον δένδρα καὶ τετράποδα, μηδὲν δυνάμενα προαιρέσει πράττειν, ἐποίησεν ὁ θεὸς τὸν ἄνθρωπον· οὐδὲ γὰρ ἦν ἄξιος ἀμοιβῆς ἢ ἐπαίνου, οὐκ ἀφ' ἑαυτοῦ ἑλόμενος τὸ ἀγαθὸν, ἀλλὰ τοῦτο γενόμενος, οὐδ' εἰ κακὸς ὑπῆρχε, δικαίως κολάσεως ἐτύγχανεν, οὐκ ἀφ' ἑαυτοῦ τοιοῦτος ὤν, ἀλλ' οὐδὲν δυνάμενος εἶναι ἕτερον παρ' ὃ ἐγεγόνει.

(2) *Tatian*, Or. c. 7 : Τὸ δὲ ἑκάτερον τῆς ποιήσεως εἶδος αὐτεξούσιον γέγονε, τἀγαθοῦ φύσιν μὴ ἔχον, ὃ πλὴν [πάλιν] μόνον παρὰ τῷ θεῷ, τῇ δὲ ἐλευθερίᾳ τῆς προαιρέσεως ὑπὸ τῶν ἀνθρώπων ἐκτελειούμενον· ὅπως ὁ μὲν φαῦλος δικαίως κολάζηται, δι' αὐτὸν γεγονὼς μοχθηρός· ὁ δὲ δίκαιος χάριν τῶν ἀνδραγαθημάτων ἀξίως ἐπαινῆται κατὰ τὸ αὐτεξούσιον τοῦ θεοῦ μὴ παραβὰς τὸ βούλημα. Concerning the critical and exegetical difficulties connected with this passage, see *Daniel*, Tatian der Apologet. s. 207.

(3) *Athen.* Leg. 31 ; comp. De Resurr. 12, 13, 15, 18 ss.

(4) Ad Autol. ii. 27 : Ἐλεύθερον γὰρ καὶ αὐτεξούσιον ἐποίησεν ὁ θεὸς ἄνθρωπον, in connection with the doctrine of immortality, of which in the next section.

(5) Octav. c. 36, 37 : Nec de fato quisquam aut solatium captet aut excuset eventum. Sit sortis fortuna, mens tamen libera est, et ideo actus hominis, non dignitas judicatur. . . . Ita in nobis non genitura plectitur, sed ingenii natura punitur. The liberty of man gets the victory in the contest with all the adversities of destiny : Vires denique et mentis et corporis sine laboris exercitatione torpescunt ; omnes adeo vestri viri fortes, quos in exemplum prædicatis, ærumnis suis inclyti floruerunt. Itaque et nobis Deus nec non potest subvenire, nec despicit, quum sit et omnium rector et amator suorum ; sed in adversis unumquemque explorat et examinat ; ingenium singulorum periculis pensitat, usque ad extremam mortem

voluntatem hominis sciscitatur, nihil sibi posse perire securus. Itaque ut aurum ignibus, sic nos discriminibus arguimur. Quam pulcrum spectaculum Deo, quum Christianus cum dolore congreditur, quum adversum minas et supplicia et tormenta componitur! quum strepitum mortis et horrorem carnificis irridens insultat! quum libertatem suam adversus reges et principes erigit, soli Deo, cujus est, cedit, etc.! Moreover, in *Minucius*, xi. 6, it is intimated (though the opinion is put in the mouth of his opponent) that the Christians believed that God judges man not so much according to his conduct, as according to predestination; but he refutes this, as a false accusation.

(6) *Clem.* Coh. p. 79 : Ὑμῶν ἐστιν (ἡ βασ. τῶν οὐρανῶν) ἐὰν θελήσητε, τῶν πρὸς τὸν θεὸν τὴν προαίρεσιν ἐσχηκότων. He then shows (p. 80) how man himself, in accordance with his own nature, ought to cultivate the talents which God has given him. As the horse is not for the plough (after the custom of the ancients), nor the ox for riding, as none is required to do more than his nature will allow, so man alone can be expected to strive after the divine, because he has received the power of doing it. According to *Clement*, too, man is accountable for *that sin* alone which proceeds from free choice, Strom. ii. p. 461; it is also frequently in our power to acquire both discernment and strength, ibid. 462. *Clement* knows nothing of a gratia irresistibilis, Strom. vii. p. 855 : Οὔτε μὴν ἄκων σωθήσεται ὁ σωζόμενος, οὐ γάρ ἐστιν ἄψυχος· ἀλλὰ παντὸς μᾶλλον ἑκουσίως καὶ προαιρετικῶς σπεύσει πρὸς σωτηρίαν· διὸ καὶ τὰς ἐντολὰς ἔλαβεν ὁ ἄνθρωπος, ὡς ἂν ἐξ αὐτοῦ ὁρμητικὸς πρὸς ὁπότερον ἂν καὶ βούλοιτο τῶν τε αἱρετῶν καὶ τῶν φευκτῶν κ.τ.λ.

(7) Comp. the third book of the work De Princip. in its whole connection. According to *Origen*, there is no accountability without liberty, De Princip. ii. 5 (*Redep.* p. 188): "If man were corrupt *by nature*, and could not possibly do good, God would appear as the judge, not of *actions*, but of *natural capacities*" (comp. what Minucius says on this point). Comp. De Princip. i. 5, 3, and Contra Cels. iv. 3 (Opp. i. p. 504): Ἀρετῆς μὲν ἐὰν ἀνέλῃς τὸ ἑκούσιον, ἀνεῖλες αὐτῆς καὶ τὴν οὐσίαν. Nevertheless, this liberty is only relative; every moral action is a mixture of free choice and divine aid. Comp

§ 70, and the passages quoted by *Redepenning*, Orig. ii. s. 318.

(8) *Iren.* iv. 4, p. 231, 232 (*Gr.* 281): Sed frumentum quidem et paleæ, inanimalia et irrationabilia existentia, naturaliter talia facta sunt: homo vero, rationabilis et secundum hoc similis Deo, liber in arbitrio factus et suæ potestatis ipse sibi causa est, ut aliquando quidem frumentum, aliquando autem palea fiat; *Irenæus* then founds the accountability of man upon this argument. Comp. iv. 15, p. 245 (*Gr.* 318), iv. 37, p. 281, 282 (*Gr.* 374, 375): Εἰ φύσει οἱ μὲν φαῦλοι, οἱ δὲ ἀγαθοὶ γεγόνασιν, οὔθ᾽ οὗτοι ἐπαινετοὶ, ὄντες ἀγαθοὶ, τοιοῦτοι γὰρ κατεσκευάσθησαν· οὔτ᾽ ἐκεῖνοι μεμπτοὶ, οὕτως γεγονότες. Ἀλλ᾽ ἐπειδὴ οἱ πάντες τῆς αὐτῆς εἰσι φύσεως, δυνάμενοί τε κατασχεῖν καὶ πρᾶξαι τὸ ἀγαθὸν, καὶ δυνάμενοι πάλιν ἀποβαλεῖν αὐτὸ καὶ μὴ ποιῆσαι· δικαίως καὶ παρ᾽ ἀνθρώποις τοῖς εὐνομουμένοις, καὶ πολὺ πρότερον παρὰ θεῷ οἱ μὲν ἐπαινοῦνται, καὶ ἀξίας τυγχάνουσι μαρτυρίας τῆς τοῦ καλοῦ καθόλου ἐκλογῆς καὶ ἐπιμονῆς· οἱ δὲ καταιτιῶνται καὶ ἀξίας τυγχάνουσι ζημίας τῆς τοῦ καλοῦ καὶ ἀγαθοῦ ἀποβολῆς. Comp. also iv. 39, p. 285 (*Gr.* 380), v. 27, p. 325 (*Gr.* 442). But, according to *Irenæus*, the freedom of man is not only seen in his works, but also in his faith, iv. 37, p. 282 (*Gr.* 376); comp. also the fragment of the sermon, De Fide, p. 342 (*Gr.* 467). On *Hippolytus* and his view of freedom, see *Jacobi* in Neander, Dg. s. 193.

(9) *Tertullian* defended the idea of liberty especially in opposition to Marcion: " How could man, who was destined to rule over the whole creation, be a slave in respect to himself, and not have the faculty of reigning over himself?" Advers. Marcion, ii. 8, 6, 9; comp. *Neander*, Antignost. s. 372, 373.[1]

(10) "*According to the Gnostics, there is a fate which stands in intimate connection with the stars, and is brought about by their instrumentality,*" etc. *Baur*, Gnosis, s. 232. But the doctrine of human freedom is of importance in the opinion of

[1] Even the opponents of the doctrine of human liberty, as Calvin, are compelled to acknowledge this remarkable consensus Patrum of the first period; and in order to account for it, they are obliged to suppose a general illusion about this doctrine! "*It is at any rate a remarkable phenomenon, that the very doctrines which afterwards caused disruptions in the Christian Church, are scarcely ever mentioned in the primitive Church,*" *Daniel*, Tatian, s. 200.

the author of the Clementine Homilies, *e.g.* Hom. xv. 7 : "Ἕκαστον δὲ τῶν ἀνθρώπων ἐλεύθερον ἐποίησεν ἔχειν τὴν ἐξουσίαν ἑαυτὸν ἀπονέμειν ᾧ βούλεται, ἢ τῷ παρόντι κακῷ, ἢ τῷ μέλλοντι ἀγαθῷ; comp. also c. 8, Hom. ii. 15, iii. 69, viii. 16, xi. 8. *Credner*, l.c. iii. s. 283, 290, 294. *Schliemann*, s. 182 ff., 235 ff., 241.

§ 58.

(b) *Immortality.*

* *Olshausen*, antiquissimorum ecclesiæ græcæ patrum de immortalitate sententiæ recensentur, Osterprogramm 1827, reviewed by *Ullmann* in Studien und Kritiken, i. 2, s. 425. *H. Schultz*, die Voraussetzungen der Christlichen Lehre von der Unsterblichkeit, Göttingen 1861.

The theologians of the primitive age did not so completely agree concerning the immortality of the soul. They were far from denying the doctrine itself, or doubting its possibility. But some of them, *e.g. Justin*, *Tatian*, and *Theophilus* (1), on various grounds supposed that the soul, though mortal in itself, or at least indifferent in relation to mortality or immortality, either acquires immortality as a promised reward, by its union with the spirit and the right use of its liberty, or, in the opposite case, perishes with the body. They were led to this view, partly because they laid so much stress on freedom, and because they thought that likeness to God was to be obtained only by this freedom; and partly, too, because they supposed (according to the trichotomistic division of human nature) that the soul receives the germ of immortal life only by union with the Spirit, as the higher and free life of reason. And, lastly, other philosophical hypotheses concerning the nature of the soul doubtless had an influence. On the contrary, *Tertullian* and *Origen*, whose views differed on other subjects, agreed in this one point, that they, in accordance with their peculiar notions concerning the nature of the soul, looked upon its immortality as essential to it (2).

(1) On the question whether the view advocated by the

aged man in *Justin*, Dial. c. Tryph. § 4, is the opinion of the author himself or not?—as well as on the meaning of the passage: Ἀλλὰ μὴν οὐδὲ ἀποθνήσκειν φημὶ πάσας τὰς ψυχὰς ἐγώ, comp. his commentators, *Olshausen*, l.c.; *Rössler*, Bibl. i. s. 141; *Möhler*, Patrologie, i. s. 242; *Daniel*, Tatian, s. 224; *Semisch*, ii. 368. *Tatian* speaks more distinctly, Contra. Græc. c. 13: Οὔκ ἐστιν ἀθάνατος ἡ ψυχὴ καθ' ἑαυτήν,[1] θνητὴ δέ. Ἀλλὰ δύναται ἡ αὐτὴ καὶ μὴ ἀποθνήσκειν. Θνήσκει μὲν γὰρ καὶ λύεται μετὰ τοῦ σώματος μὴ γινώσκουσα τὴν ἀλήθειαν. Ἀνίσταται δὲ εἰς ὕστερον ἐπὶ συντελείᾳ τοῦ κόσμου σὺν τῷ σώματι, θάνατον διὰ τιμωρίας ἐν ἀθανασίᾳ λαμβάνουσα. Πάλιν δὲ οὐ θνήσκει, κἂν πρὸς καιρὸν λυθῇ, τὴν ἐπίγνωσιν τοῦ θεοῦ πεποιημένη. Καθ' ἑαυτὴν γὰρ σκότος ἐστὶ καὶ οὐδὲν ἐν αὐτῇ φωτεινόν ... (Joh. i.) ... Ψυχὴ γὰρ οὐκ αὐτὴ τὸ πνεῦμα ἔσωσεν, ἐσώθη δὲ ὑπ' αὐτοῦ κ.τ.λ. ... Συζυγίαν δὲ κεκτημένη τὴν τοῦ θείου πνεύματος, οὔκ ἐστιν ἀβοήθητος, ἀνέρχεται δὲ πρὸς ἅπερ αὐτὴν ὁδηγεῖ χωρία τὸ πνεῦμα. According to *Tatian* also, the soul is not a simple nature (πολυμερής ἐστι καὶ οὐ μονομερής), c. 15. *Theophilus* (ad Aut. ii. 27) starts the question: was Adam created with a mortal or immortal nature? and replies: neither the one nor the other, but he was fitted for both (δεκτικὸν ἀμφοτέρων), in order that he might receive immortality as a reward, and become God (γένηται θεός), if he aspired after it by obeying the divine commandments; but that he might become the author of his own ruin, if he did the works of the devil, and disobeyed God.[2] *Irenæus* also speaks only of an immortality which is given to man, see Adv. Hær. ii. 64: Sine initio et sine fine, vere et semper idem et eodem modo se habens solus est Deus.... Et de animalibus, de animabus, et de spiritibus et omnino de omnibus his quæ facta sunt, cogitans quis minime peccabit, quando omnia, quæ facta sunt, initium quidem facturæ suæ habeant, perseverant autem, *quoadusque ea Deus et esse et perseverare voluerit. Non enim ex nobis, neque ex nostra natura vita est, sed secundem gratiam Dei datur.* Sicut

---

[1] Καθ' ἑαυτήν is wanting in the most recent manuscripts; vide *Daniel*, s. 228, on this passage.

[2] Whether an absolute annihilation is here intended, or only a loss of consciousness, see *Baur*, Dg. s. 575, who adopts the latter view. On the cognate view of the Thnetopsychites (Arabici), compare below, on Eschatology, § 76, note 8.

autem corpus animale ipsum quidem non est anima, participatur autem animam, quoadusque Deus vult, sic et anima ipsa quidem non est vita, participatur autem a Deo sibi præstitam vitam.

(2) The opposition which *Tertullian* raised to the above doctrine was connected with his twofold division of the soul; that of *Origen*, with his views on pre-existence. (For the latter could easily dispose of the objection that the soul must have an end, because it has had a beginning.) Comp., however, *Tert.* De Anima, 11, 14, 15. Among other things, *Tertullian* appeals to the fact that the soul continues active even in dreams. On the connection of sleep and death generally, see De Anima, c. 43 ff. According to *Orig.* Exhort. ad Mart. 47 (Opp. i. p. 307), De Princip. ii. 11; 4, p. 105, and iii. 1, 13, p. 122, it is both the inherent principle of life in the soul, and its natural relation to God, which secures its immortality. To this is to be added his view about self-determination, and the retribution based thereon. Comp. *Thomasius*, s. 159; *Redepenning*, ii. s. 111.

<small>The whole question, however, had more of a philosophical than Christian bearing, as the idea of immortality itself is abstract negative. On the other hand, the believer by faith lays hold of eternal life in Christ as something real and concrete. The Christian doctrine of immortality cannot therefore be considered apart from the person, work, and kingdom of Christ, and rests upon Christian views and promises; see, below, in the Eschatology. Comp. the writing of *Schultz*, noted above.</small>

§ 59.

Sin, the Fall, and its Consequences.

<small>J. G. Walch (*Th. Ch. Lilienthal*), De Pelagianismo ante Pelagium, Jen. 1738, 4to. *Ejusdem*, Historia Doctrinæ de Peccato Originali; both in his Miscellanea Sacra, Amstel. 1744, 4to. J. *Horn*, Commentatio de sententiis eorum patrum, quorum auctoritas ante Augustinum plurimum valuit, de peccato originali, Gött. 1801, 4to. †*Wörter* [*Landerer and Huber*], u. s. § 57. †*Kuhn*, der vorgebliche Pelagianismus der voraugustinischen Väter (Tüb. Quartalschrift, 1853).</small>

However much the primitive Church was inclined, as we have already seen, to look with a free and clear vision at the bright side of man (his ideal nature), yet it did not endeavour to conceal the dark side by a false idealism. Though it cannot be said that the consciousness of human depravity was the exclusive and fundamental principle upon which the entire theology of that time was founded, yet every Christian conscience was convinced of the opposition between the ideal and the real, and the effects of sin in destroying the harmony of life; and this, too, in proportion to the strictness of the claims set up for human freedom.

Thus *Justin M.* complains of the universality of sin, Dial. c. Tryph. c. 95. The whole human race is under the curse; for cursed is every one who does not keep the law. The author of the Clementine Homilies also supposes that the propensity to sin is made stronger by its preponderance in human history, and calls men the slaves of sin (δουλεύοντες ἐπιθυμίᾳ), Hom. iv. 23, x. 4, *Schliemann*, s. 183.—*Clement* of Alexandria directs our attention, in particular, to the internal conflict which sin has introduced into the nature of man; it does not form a part of our nature, nevertheless it is spread through the whole race. We come to sin without ourselves knowing how; comp. Strom. ii. p. 487. *Origen* also conceives of sin as a universal corruption, since the world is apostate, Contra Cels. iii. 66, p. 491: Σαφῶς γὰρ φαίνεται, ὅτι πάντες μὲν ἄνθρωποι πρὸς τὸ ἁμαρτάνειν πεφύκαμεν, ἔνιοι δὲ οὐ μόνον πεφύκασιν, ἀλλὰ καὶ εἰθισμένοι εἰσὶν ἁμαρτάνειν. Comp. iii. 62, p. 488: Ἀδύνατον γάρ φαμεν εἶναι ἄνθρωπον μετ' ἀρετῆς ἀπ' ἀρχῆς πρὸς τὸν θεὸν ἄνω βλέπειν· κακίαν γὰρ ὑφίστασθαι ἀναγκαῖον πρῶτον ἐν ἀνθρώποις (with reference to Rom. vii. 9). Cf. *Redep.* ii. s. 360. Nevertheless the writers of this period do not express as strong a sense of sin as those of the following. On the contrary, jubilant feelings preponderated in view of the finished work of the Saviour. It would be as one-sided to demand in the first centuries the experience of later times, as it is to misconceive the necessity of the later developments.

§ 60.

The Doctrine of Sin in General.

Suicer, Thesaurus, sub ἁμαρτάνω, ἁμάρτημα, ἁμαρτία, ἁμαρτωλός. *Krabbe*, die Lehre von der Sünde und dem Tode, Hamburg 1836 (dogmatico-exegetical). *Julius Müller, die Christliche Lehre von der Sünde, Breslau 1844, 2 vols. 6te Aufl. 1877 [transl. in Clark's Foreign Theol. Library].

Though sin was recognized as a fact, yet definitions of its precise nature were to a great extent indefinite and unsettled during this period (1). The heretical sects of the Gnostics in general (and in this particular they were the forerunners of Manichæism), with their dualistic notions, either ascribed the origin of evil to the demiurge, or maintained that it was inherent in matter (2). On the other hand, the Christian theologians, generally speaking, agreed in seeking the source of sin in the human will, and clearing God from all responsibility (3). Such a view easily led to the opinion of *Origen*, that moral evil is something negative (4).

(1) A definition, allied to that of the Stoics, is given by *Clement* of Alexandria, Pæd. i. 13, p. 158, 159 : Πᾶν τὸ παρὰ τὸν λόγον τὸν ὀρθὸν, τοῦτο ἁμάρτημά ἐστι. Virtue (ἀρετή), on the contrary, is διάθεσις ψυχῆς σύμφωνος ὑπὸ τοῦ λόγου περὶ ὅλον τὸν βίον. Hence sin is also disobedience to God, Αὐτίκα γοῦν ὅτε ἥμαρτεν ὁ πρῶτος ἄνθρωπος, καὶ παρήκουσε τοῦ θεοῦ. He further considers sin, urging its etymology, as error ... ὡς ἐξ ἀνάγκης εἶναι τὸ πλημμελούμενον πᾶν διὰ τὴν τοῦ λόγου διαμαρτίαν γινόμενον καὶ εἰκότως καλεῖσθαι ἁμάρτημα. Comp. Strom. ii. p. 462 : Τὸ δὲ ἁμαρτάνειν ἐκ τοῦ ἀγνοεῖν κρίνειν ὅ τι χρὴ ποιεῖν συνίσταται ἢ τοῦ ἀδυνατεῖν ποιεῖν. The different kinds of sin are ἐπιθυμία, φόβος, and ἡδονή. One consequence of sin is the λήθη τῆς ἀληθείας, Coh. p. 88, and, lastly, eternal death, ib. p. 89. *Tertullian* puts sin in the *impatience* (inconstancy) of man, De Pat. 5 (p. 143): Nam ut compendio dictum sit, omne peccatum impatientiæ adscribendum. Comp. *Cypr.* De Bono Pat. p. 218. *Orig.* De Princip. ii. 9, 2 (Opp. t. i. p. 97,

Redep. p. 216), also believes that laziness and aversion to efforts for preserving the good, as well as turning from the path of virtue (privative), are causes of sin; for going astray is nothing but becoming bad; to be bad only means not to be good, etc.; comp. *Schnitzer*, s. 140.

(2) Now and then even orthodox theologians ascribe the origin of evil to the sensuous nature: thus *Justin M.* Apol. i. 10 (?); De Resurr. c. 3, see *Semisch*, s. 400, 401. On the other hand, comp. *Clem.* Strom. iv. 36, p. 638, 639: Οὔκουν εὐλόγως οἱ κατατρέχοντες τῆς πλάσεως καὶ κακίζοντες τὸ σῶμα. οὐ συνορῶντες τὴν κατασκευὴν τοῦ ἀνθρώπου ὀρθὴν πρὸς τὴν οὐρανοῦ θέαν γενομένην, καὶ τὴν τῶν αἰσθησέων ὀργανοποιἴαν πρὸς γνῶσιν συντείνουσαν, τά τε μέλη καὶ μέρη πρὸς τὸ καλὸν, οὐ πρὸς ἡδονὴν εὔθετα. Ὅθεν ἐπιδεκτικὸν γίνεται τῆς τιμιωτάτης τῷ θεῷ ψυχῆς τὸ οἰκητήριον τοῦτο κ.τ.λ.... Ἀλλ' οὔτε ἀγαθὸν ἡ ψυχὴ φύσει, οὐδὲ αὖ κακὸν φύσει τὸ σῶμα, οὐδὲ μὴν, ὃ μή ἐστιν ἀγαθὸν, τοῦτο εὐθέως κακόν. Εἰσὶ γὰρ οὖν καὶ μεσότητές τινες κ.τ.λ. Comp. *Origen*, Contra Celsum, iv. 66: Τόδε, τὴν ὕλην ... τοῖς θνητοῖς ἐμπολιτευομένην αἰτίαν εἶναι τῶν κακῶν, καθ' ἡμᾶς οὐκ ἀληθές· τὸ γὰρ ἑκάστου ἡγεμονικὸν αἴτιον τῆς ὑποστάσης ἐν αὐτῷ κακίας ἐστίν, ἥτις ἐστὶ τὸ κακόν.

(3) *Clem.* Strom. vii. 2, p. 835: Κακίας δ' αὖ πάντως ἀναίτιος (ὁ θεός). *Orig.* Contra Cels. vi. 55, p. 675: Ἡμεῖς δέ φαμεν, ὅτι κακὰ μὲν ἡ τὴν κακίαν καὶ τὰς ἀπ' αὐτῆς πράξεις ὁ θεὸς οὐκ ἐποίησε. Comp. iii. 69, p. 492. Nevertheless, he holds that evil is under God's providence; comp. De Princip. iii. 2, 7 (Opp. i. p. 142).

(4) *Orig.* De Princip. ii. 9, 2 (Opp. i. p. 97), and in Joh. t. ii. c. 7 (Opp. iv. p. 65, 66): Πᾶσα ἡ κακία οὐδέν ἐστιν (with reference to the word οὐδέν in John i. 3), ἐπεὶ καὶ οὐκ ὂν τυγχάνει. He terms evil ἀνυπόστατον, and the fall μείωσις (diminutio). *J. Müller*, 1st ed. 132; comp. *Redepenning*, ii. s. 328.

§ 61.

Interpretation of the Narrative of the Fall.

The documents contained in the five books of Moses were to the early Church the *historical* foundation, not only of the

§ 61.] INTERPRETATION OF THE NARRATIVE OF THE FALL. 227

doctrine of the creation of the world and of man, but also of the doctrine of the origin of sin, which appears as a fact in the history of Adam. Some writers, however, rejected the literal interpretation of this narrative. Thus *Origen* (after the example of *Philo*) (1) regarded it as a type, historically clothed, of what takes place in free moral agents everywhere, and at all times (2). It is difficult to ascertain how far *Irenæus* adhered to the letter of the narrative (3). *Tertullian* unhesitatingly pronounced in favour of its strict historical interpretation (4). Both the Gnostics and the author of the Clementine Homilies rejected this view on dogmatic grounds (5).

(1) *Philo* sees in the narrative τρόποι τῆς ψυχῆς, see *Dähne*, s. 341, and his essay in the Theologische Studien und Krit. 1833, 4.

(2) *Clement* considers the narrative of the fall partly as fact and partly as allegory, Strom. v. 11, p. 689, 690. (Serpent = image of voluptuousness.[1]) On the other hand, *Origen* regards it as purely allegorical, De Princip. iv. 16 (Opp. t. i. p. 174); Contra Cels. iv. 40, p. 534. Adam is called man, because : Ἐν τοῖς δοκοῦσι περὶ τοῦ Ἀδὰμ εἶναι φυσιολογεῖ Μωϋσῆς τὰ περὶ τῆς τοῦ ἀνθρώπου φύσεως ... οὐχ οὕτως περὶ ἑνός τινος, ὡς περὶ ὅλου τοῦ γένους ταῦτα φάσκοντος τοῦ θείου λόγου. Concerning the further application of allegorical interpretation to the particulars of the narrative (the clothing our first parents in skins as a symbol of the clothing of the soul?), comp. *Meth.* in *Phot.* Bibl. Cod. 234 and 293. On the other side, see *Orig.* Fragm. in Gen. t. ii. p. 29, where both the literal interpretation is excluded, and this allegorical exposition is called in question.

(3) According to the fragment of Anastasius Sinaïta in *Massuet*, p. 344, *Irenæus* must be understood as having explained the temptation by the serpent (in opposition to the Ophites), πνευματικῶς, not ἱστορικῶς, but it is not evident to

[1] That the serpent was the devil, or the devil was *in* the serpent (which is not expressly declared in Genesis), was generally assumed, in accordance with Wisd. ii. 24 and Rev. xii. 9 (ὁ ὄφις ὁ ἀρχαῖος); probably also with reference to John viii. 44.

what extent he did so. Besides, objections have been urged to the genuineness of this passage; see *Duncker*, s. 115, Anm. But *Irenæus* speaks elsewhere plainly enough of the fall of Adam as an historical fact, iii. 18 (*Gr.* 20), p. 211 (*Gr.* 248), iii. 21 (*Gr.* 31), p. 218 (*Gr.* 259) ss. Thus he labours to defend the threatening of God: "For in the day that thou eatest thereof, thou shalt surely die," from the chronological point of view, by taking the word "day" (as in the account of the creation) in the sense of "period," for "one day is with the Lord as a thousand years, and a thousand years as one day." Adam and Eve died during that period on the same day of the week on which they were created and disobeyed the command of God, viz. on a *Friday* within the first one thousand years; Adv. Hær. v. 23, 2. See *Duncker*, s. 129.

(4) *Tert.* Adv. Judæos, ii. p. 184; De Virg. vel. 11; Adv. Marc. ii. 2 ss., and other passages. He insists upon the literal interpretation of the particulars of the narrative, as they succeeded each other in order of time, in his De Resurr. Carn. 61: Adam ante nomina animalibus enunciavit quam de arbore decerpsit; ante etiam prophetavit quam voravit.

(5) On the Gnostic (Basilidian) doctrine of the fall ($\sigma \dot{v}\gamma$-$\chi v\sigma\iota\varsigma$ $\dot{a}\rho\chi\iota\kappa\dot{\eta}$), comp. *Clem.* Strom. ii. 20, p. 488. *Gieseler*, Studien und Kritiken, 1840, s. 396. *Baur*, s. 211. The author of the Clementine Homilies goes so far in idealizing Adam, as to convert the historical person into a purely mythical being (like the Adam-Cadmon of the Cabbalists), while he represents Eve as far inferior to him. Hence Adam could not sin, but sin makes its first appearance in *Cain*. See *Credner*, ii. 258, iii. 284. *Baur*, Gnosis, s. 339. *Schliemann*, s. 177 ff. *Hilgenfeld*, s. 291. *Baur*, Dg. s. 582. The origin of sin is derived from the disorder introduced by the domination exercised by the feminine principle. On the other hand, the Gnostic Cainites rendered homage to Cain, as the representative of freedom from the thraldom of the demiurge; while the Gnostic Sethites considered Cain as the representative of the hylic, Abel as that of the psychical, and Seth as that of the pneumatic principle, the ideal of humanity. *Neander*, Kircheng. i. 2, s. 758 ff.

§ 62.

State of Innocence and Fall.

With all their differences of opinion respecting the original endowments of the first man (1), and the nature of his sin (2), all the Catholic teachers agreed in this, that the temptation of the serpent was a real temptation to sin, and, accordingly, that the transgression of the command given by Jehovah was a *fall* from a state of innocence, followed by disasters to the human race (3). On the other hand, the Clementine Ebionites denied that Adam could have sinned (4); and the Ophites thought that by this event (at least in one respect) man was elevated to his proper dignity,—a transition to freedom; inasmuch as the prohibition had proceeded from the envy of Jaldabaoth, but the act of disobedience had been brought about by the influence of wisdom (Sophia), the symbol of which is the serpent (5).

(1) These were especially exaggerated by the author of the Clementine Homilies (see the preceding section). Adam possessed prophetic gifts, Hom. iii. 21, viii. 10 (*Credner*, ii. s. 248; *Baur*, s. 363; *Schliemann*, s. 175; *Hilgenfeld*, s. 294), which, however, *Tertullian*, De Resurr. Carn. c. 61, also ascribed to him. The Ophites taught that Adam and Eve had light and luminous bodies, see *Baur*, s. 187. The theologians, previous to the time of Augustine, attached less weight to what was afterwards called *justitia originalis.* According to *Theophilus* of Antioch (ad Aut. ii. 24, 27), Adam was νήπιος, and had to be treated as a child; he was neither mortal nor immortal, but capable of either mortality or immortality. *Clement* of Alexandria maintains the same, Strom. vi. 12, p. 788: "They may learn from us (he says in opposition to the Gnostics), that Adam was created perfect, not in relation to his moral excellences, but in respect to his *capacity* of receiving virtue; for there is certainly a difference between a capacity for virtue and the real possession of it. God will have us attain to

bliss by our own exertions, hence it belongs to the nature of the soul to determine itself," etc. (in *Baur*, Gnosis, s. 493). *Clement* accordingly restricts the original endowments (Strom. iv. p. 632) to what is purely human as a basis for action: Οὐδὲν γὰρ τῶν χαρακτηριζόντων τὴν ἀνθρώπου ἰδέαν τε καὶ μορφὴν ἐνεδέησεν αὐτῷ.

(2) *Justin M.* attributes the fall mainly to the cunning malignity of Satan; Dial. c. Tryph. c. 119, p. 205. A beast (θηρίον) seduced man. On his own part he added disobedience and misbelief; comp. *Semisch*, l.c. s. 393, 394. *Clement* of Alexandria conceives that it was sensuality which caused the fall of the first man; Coh. p. 86: Ὄφις ἀλληγορεῖται ἡδονὴ ἐπὶ γαστέρα ἕρπουσα, κακία γηΐνη εἰς ὕλας τρεφομένη. (*Thiersch* conjectures the reading τρεπομένη in Rudelbach's Zeitschrift f. d. luth. Theol. 1841, 2, s. 184.) Comp. Strom. iii. 17, p. 559 (470, *Sylb.*). *Clement* does not (like the Encratites whom he combats) blame the cohabitation of our first parents as in itself sinful, but he objects that it took place too soon; this is also implied in the passage, Strom. ii. 19, p. 481: Τὰ μὲν αἰσχρὰ οὗτος προθύμως εἵλετο, ἑπόμενος τῇ γυναικί. Comp. § 61, 2.

(3) The notion that the tree itself was the cause of death (its fruit being venomous), is rejected by *Theophil.* of Antioch, ad Autol. ii. 25: Οὐ γὰρ, ὡς οἴονταί τινες, θάνατον εἶχε τὸ ξύλον ἀλλ' ἡ παρακοή.

(4) Comp. § 61, note 5. Adam could not sin, because the θεῖον πνεῦμα, or the σοφία itself, having been manifested in him, the latter must have sinned; but such an assertion would be impious; comp. *Schliemann*, u. s. Yet the Clementines seem to adopt the view, that the image of God was defaced in the descendants of the first human pair; comp. *Hilgenfeld*, s. 291.

(5) The Ophites are in confusion about their own doctrines; for at one time they render divine homage to the serpent, at another they say that Eve was seduced by its deception. *Epiph.* Hær. 37, 6. *Baur*, s. 178 ff.

§ 63.

The Effects of the Fall.

Death was the punishment which Jehovah had threatened to inflict upon the transgressors of His law. Nevertheless the act of transgression was not immediately succeeded by death, but by a train of evils which came upon both the man and the woman, introductory to death, and testifying that man had become mortal. Accordingly, both death and physical evils were considered as the effects of Adam's sin; thus, *e.g.*, by *Irenæus* and others (1). But opinions were not as yet fully developed concerning the moral depravity of each individual, and the sin of the race in general, considered as the effect of the first sin. They were so much disposed to look upon sin as the free act of man's will, that they could hardly conceive of it as simply a hereditary tendency, transmitted from one to another. The sin of every individual, as found in experience, had its type in the sin of Adam, and consequently appeared to be a repetition, rather than a necessary consequence, of the first sin (2). In order to explain the mysterious power which drives man to evil, they had recourse to the influence of the demons, strong, but not absolutely compulsory, rather than to a total bondage of the will (as the result of original sin) (3). Nevertheless we meet in the writings of *Irenæus* with indications of more deep-reaching effects of the fall (4). *Tertullian* and *Origen* aided more definitely the theory of original sin, though from different points of view. Origen thought that souls were stained with sin in a former state, and thus enter into the world in a sinful condition. To this idea he added another, allied to the notions of Gnostics and Manichees, viz. that there is a stain in physical generation itself (5). According to *Tertullian*, the soul itself is propagated with all its defects as matter is propagated. The phrase " vitium originis," first used by him, is in perfect accordance with this view (6). But both were far from considering inherent depravity as involving accountability, and still farther from believing in the entire absence of human liberty (7).

(1) *Iren.* iii. 23 (*Gr.* 35), p. 221 (*Gr.* 263): Condemnationem autem transgressionis accepit homo tædia et terrenum laborem et manducare panem in sudore vultus sui et converti in terram, ex qua assumtus est; similiter autem mulier tædia et labores et gemitus et tristitias partus et servitium, *i.e.* ut serviret viro suo: ut neque maledicti a Deo in totum perirent, neque sine increpatione perseverantes Deum contemnerent (comp. c. 37, p. 264, *Grabe*). Ibid. v. 15, p. 311 (*Gr.* 423)... propter inobedientiæ peccatum subsecuti sunt languores hominibus. V. 17, p. 313 (p. 426). V. 23, p. 320 (p. 435): Sed quoniam Deus verax est, mendax autem serpens, de effectu ostensum est morte subsecuta eos, qui manducaverunt. Simul enim cum esca et mortem adsciverunt, quoniam inobedientes manducabant: inobedientia autem Dei mortem infert, et sqq. (Hence the devil is called a murderer from the beginning.) But *Irenæus* also sees a blessing in the penalty inflicted by God, iii. 20, 1: Magnanimus (*i.e.* μακρόθυμος) fuit Deus deficiente homine, eam quæ per verbum esset victoriam reddendam ei providens. He compares the fall of man to the fate of the prophet Jonah, who was swallowed by the whale in order to be saved. Thus man is swallowed by the great whale (the devil), that Christ may deliver him out of his jaws; comp. *Duncker*, s. 151. According to *Cyprian*, De Bono Patientiæ, p. 212, even the higher physical strength of man (along with immortality) was lost by the fall; *Origen* also connected the existence of evil in the world with sin. Comp. above, § 48. By *death*, however, the Alexandrians do not mean physical death, which, on their postulates, they must regard as a wise arrangement of nature (φυσικὴ ἀνάγκη θείας οἰκονομίας), and so as a blessing; but moral and spiritual death. *Clement*, Strom. iii. p. 540, and the passages from *Origen* in Gieseler's Dogmengesch. s. 182. [Comm. in Matt. xiii. § 7, in Joan. xvii. § 37. On the Ep. to the Romans, lib. vi. § 6, *Origen* declares the death effected by sin to be the separation of the soul from God: Separatio animæ a Deo mors appellatur, quæ per peccatum venit.]

§ 63.] THE EFFECTS OF THE FALL. 233

(2) Though *Justin M.* uses strong expressions in lamenting the universal corruption of mankind (Dial. c. Tryph. c. 95), yet original sin, and the imputation of Adam's guilt, are conceptions foreign to him. At least man has still such right moral feelings, that he judges and blames the sin of others as his.—Dial. c. Tryph. c. 93 : Τὰ γὰρ ἀεὶ καὶ δι' ὅλου δίκαια καὶ πᾶσαν δικαιοσύνην παρέχει ἐν παντὶ γένει ἀνθρώπων· καὶ ἔστι πᾶν γένος γνωρίζον ὅτι μοιχεία κακόν, καὶ πορνεία, καὶ ἀνδροφονία, καὶ ὅσα ἄλλα τοιαῦτα. Compare what follows, according to which only those filled with the evil spirit, or wholly corrupted by bad education (and hence not the posterity of Adam as such), have lost this feeling. Accordingly every man deserves death, because in his obedience he *resembles* the first man. Dial. c. Tr. c. 88 : Ὁ (scil. γένος ἀνθρώπων) ἀπὸ τοῦ Ἀδὰμ ὑπὸ θάνατον καὶ πλάνην τὴν τοῦ ὄφεως ἐπεπτώκει, παρὰ τὴν ἰδίαν αἰτίαν ἑκάστου αὐτῶν πονηρευσαμένου. C. 124 : Οὗτοι (scil. ἄνθρωποι) ὁμοίως τῷ Ἀδὰμ καὶ τῇ Εὐᾳ ἐξομοιούμενοι θάνατον ἑαυτοῖς ἐργάζονται κ.τ.λ. Compare *Semisch*, l.c. s. 397–399, who goes into the interpretation of these passages. See ibid. p. 401, in reference to the difficult passage, Dial. c. Tr. c. 100, in which many have found an argument for original sin : Παρθένος οὖσα Εὔα καὶ ἄφθορος τὸν λόγον τὸν ἀπὸ τοῦ ὄφεως συλλαβοῦσα, παρακοὴν καὶ θάνατον ἔτεκε (is τέκτειν here metaphorical ?). [On the difficult passage, Apol. i. cap. 61, see *Rudelbach*, Zeitschrift f. luth. Theol. 1841, s. 171 : especially *Landerer*, Jahrb. f. deutsche Theol. 1857, s. 518 ff.; Just. M. on Erbsünde, Theol. Quartalschrift, 1859. The passage in the First Apology, ch. 61, reads : ἐπειδὴ τὴν πρώτην γένεσιν ἡμῶν ἀγνοοῦντες κατ' ἀνάγκην γεγεννήμεθα ἐξ ὑγρᾶς σπορᾶς κατὰ μίξιν τὴν τῶν γονέων πρὸς ἀλλήλους, καὶ ἐν ἔθεσι φαύλοις καὶ πονηραῖς ἀνατροφαῖς γεγόναμεν, ὅπως μὴ ἀνάγκης τέκνα μηδὲ ἀγνοίας μένωμεν ἀλλὰ προαιρέσεως καὶ ἐπιστήμης ἀφέσεώς τε ἁμαρτιῶν ὑπὲρ ὧν προημάρτομεν τύχωμεν ἐν τῷ ὕδατι ἐπονομάζεται τῷ ἑλομένῳ ἀναγεννηθῆναι . . . τὸ τοῦ πατρὸς . . . θεοῦ ὄνομα. That Justin taught the necessity of internal grace, see *Landerer* in the same essay, s. 522.] According to *Clement* of Alexandria, man now stands in the same relation to the tempter in which Adam stood prior to the fall, Coh. p. 7 : Εἷς γὰρ ὁ ἀπατεὼν, ἄνωθεν μὲν Εὔαν, νῦν δὲ ἤδη καὶ τοὺς ἄλλους ἀνθρώ-

πούς εἰς θάνατον ὑποφέρων; comp. Pæd. i. 13, 158, 159. *Clement*, indeed, admits the universality of sin among men, Pæd. iii. 12, p. 307: Τὸ μὲν γὰρ ἐξαμαρτάνειν πᾶσιν ἔμφυτον καὶ κοινόν; but the very circumstance that some appear to him by nature better than others (Strom. i. 6, p. 336), shows that he did not consider man as absolutely depraved, nor throw all into one corrupt mass. No one commits iniquity for its own sake, Strom. i. 17, p. 368. But he rejects the idea of original sin, as already imputed to children, most strongly, in Strom. iii. 16, p. 556, 557: Λεγέτωσαν ἡμῖν· Ποῦ ἐπόρνευσεν τὸ γεννηθὲν παιδίον, ἢ πῶς ὑπὸ τὴν τοῦ Ἀδὰμ ὑποπέπτωκεν ἀρὰν τὸ μηδὲν ἐνεργῆσαν. He does not regard the passage, Ps. li. 5, as proof. (Comp. the above passages on liberty and sin in general.)

(3) *Athen.* Leg. c. 25. *Tatian*, Contra Græc. c. 7, and the passages quoted, § 58. Besides the influence of Satan, *Justin M.* also mentions bad education and evil examples, Apol. i. 61: Ἐν ἔθεσι φαύλοις καὶ πονηραῖς ἀνατροφαῖς γεγόναμεν.

(4) *Irenæus*, Adv. Hær. iv. 41, 2, and other passages quoted by *Duncker*, s. 132 ff. According to *Duncker*, the doctrine of original sin and hereditary evil is so fully developed in the writings of *Irenæus*, "*that the characteristic features of the western type of doctrine may be distinctly recognised.*" *Irenæus* indeed asserts that man, freely yielding to the voice of the tempter, has become a child, disciple, and servant of the devil, etc. He also thinks that, in consequence of the sin of Adam, men are already in a state of guilt. On the question whether *Irenæus* understands by that death which we have inherited, merely physical death (v. 1, 3, and other passages), see *Duncker*, l.c. [The doctrine of *Irenæus*, in its approximation to Augustinianism, is given in the following passages (*Landerer* in Jahrb. für deutsche Theologie, 1857, s. 528):— Adv. Hær. v. 16: ἐν τῷ πρώτῳ Ἀδὰμ προσεκόψαμεν, μὴ ποιήσαντες αὐτοῦ τὴν ἐντολήν, ἐν δὲ τῷ δευτέρῳ Ἀδὰμ ἀποκατηλλάγημεν ὑπήκοοι μέχρι θανάτου γενόμενοι. Οὐδὲ γὰρ ἄλλῳ τινὶ ἦμεν ὀφειλέται ἀλλ' ἢ ἐκείνῳ, οὗ καὶ τὴν ἐντολὴν παρέβημεν: so in iii. 18: Perdideramus in Adam—secundum imaginem et similitudinem Dei esse; and in iii. 22: Quemadmodum illa (Eva) inobediens facta et sibi et universo generi humano causa est facta mortis; v. 19: et quemadmodum

adstrictum est morti genus humanum per virginem, salvatur per virginem.]

(5) On the one hand, *Origen*, by insisting upon the freedom of the human will, forms a strong contrast with Augustine; as he also maintains that concupiscence is not reckoned as sin, so long as it has not ripened into a purpose; guilt arises only when we yield to it, De Princip. iii. 2, 2 (Opp. t. i. p. 139, *Red.* p. 179), and iii. 4 (de Humanis Tentationibus). But, on the other, he formally adopts the idea of original sin, by asserting that the human soul does not come into the world in a state of innocence, because it has already sinned in a former state ($\mu\nu\sigma\tau\acute{\eta}\rho\iota o\nu\ \gamma\epsilon\nu\acute{\epsilon}\sigma\epsilon\omega\varsigma$); De Princip. iii. 5 (Opp. t. i. p. 149, 150, *Redep.* p. 309 ff.); comp. also *Redep.* ii. 322 ff.; concerning the generation of man, see Hom. xv. in Matth. § 23 (Opp. iii. p. 685); Hom. viii. in Lev. (Opp. ii. p. 229, and xii. p. 251): Omnis qui ingreditur hunc mundum in quadam contaminatione effici dicitur (Job xiv. 4, 5) ... Omnis ergo homo in patre et in matre pollutus est, solus vero Jesus Dominus meus in hanc generationem mundus ingressus est, et in matre non est pollutus. Ingressus est enim corpus incontaminatum. See, further, in *Baur*, Dg. s. 589 ff. And yet subsequent times, especially after Jerome, have seen in *Origen* the precursor of Pelagius. *Jerome* (Ep. ad Ctesiphont.) calls the opinion, that man can be without sin—Origenis ramusculus. Comp. in reply, *Wörter*, u. s., s. 201 [and *Landerer*, u. s.].

(6) *Tert.* De Anima, c. 40: Ita omnis anima eo usque in Adam censetur, donec in Christo recenseatur; tamdiu immunda, quamdiu recenseatur. Peccatrix autem, quia immunda, recipiens ignominiam ex carnis societate. Cap. 41, he makes use of the phrase *vitium originis*, and maintains that evil has become man's second nature, while his *true* nature (according to Tertullian) is the good. He therefore distinguishes *naturale quodammodo* from *proprie naturale*. Quod enim a Deo est, non tam extinguitur, quam obumbratur. Potest enim *obumbrari*, quia non est Deus, *extingui non potest, quia a Deo est*.

(7) That, *e.g.*, *Tertullian* was far from imputing original sin to children as real sin, may be seen from his remarkable expression concerning the baptism of infants; De Bapt. 18, comp. § 72, and *Neander*, Antignostikus, s. 209 ff., 455 ff.— His disciple *Cyprian* also acknowledges inherent depravity,

and defends infant baptism on *this ground;* but yet only to purify infants from a *foreign* guilt which is imputed to them, but not from any guilt which is properly *their own.* Ep. 64. Comp. *Rettberg,* s. 317 ff. *Cyprian* calls original sin, contagio mortis antiquæ, in Ep. 59; but says that it does not annul freedom; De Gratia Dei, ad Donatum, c. 2.

FOURTH DIVISION.

CHRISTOLOGY AND SOTERIOLOGY.

§ 64.

Christology in General.

Martini, Versuch einer pragmatischen Geschichte des Dogma von der Gottheit Christi, Rostock 1800. *Dorner, Entwicklungsgeschichte der Christologie, Stuttgardt 1839, 2d edit. 2 Bde. 1845, 46, 3d edit. 1853–56. [*Baur*, Dreieinigkeitslehre, 3 Bde. Tübing. 1841–43. *G. A. Meier*, Trinitat. 2 Bde. 1844. *L. Lange*, Antitrinitar. 1851.]

THE manifestation of the Logos in the flesh is the chief dogmatic idea around which this period revolves. This fact, unveiling the eternal counsels of God's love, was regarded by the first teachers of the Church, not under a partial aspect as the mere consequence of human sin, nor as exclusively conditioned and brought about by sin, but also as a free revelation of God, as the summit of all earlier revelations and developments of life, as the completion and crown of creation. Thus the *Christology* of this period forms at once the continuation of its *theology*, and the supplement and counterpart of its *anthropology*.

Irenæus decidedly keeps in view the twofold aspect under which Christ may be considered, as both *completing* and *restoring* human nature. Both are expressed by the terms ἀνακεφαλαιοῦν, ἀνακεφαλαίωσις (*i.e.* the repetition of that which formerly existed, renovation, restoration, the reunion of that which was separated, comp. *Suicer*, Thesaurus, s.v.). Christ is the sum of all that is human in its highest significance, both the sum total and the renovation of mankind, the new Adam; comp. v. 29, 2, iii. 18, 7, and other passages quoted by *Duncker*, s. 157 ff. He frequently repeats the proposition, that Christ became what *we* are, that *we* might be what *He* is, *e.g.* iii. 10, 20, and in the Præfatio: Jesus Christus, Dominus noster, propter immensam suam dilectionem factus est quod sumus nos, uti nos perficeret esse, quod est ipse. [*Irenæus*, iii. 18: Filius Dei, existens semper apud patrem, incarnatus est et homo factus, longam hominum expositionem in se ipso recapitulavit, in compendio nobis salutem præstans, et quod perdideramus in Adam, *i.e.* secundum imaginem et similitudinem esse, hoc in Christo Jesu reciperemus. Comp. v. 16.] *Irenæus* also says that Christ represents the perfect man in all the stages of human life. Similar views were entertained by the theologians of the Alexandrian school; see the passages quoted on the Logos. — On the other hand, *Tertullian*, De Carne Christi, c. 6, thinks that the incarnation of Christ had reference to the sufferings He was to endure. (At vero Christus, mori missus, nasci quoque necessario habuit, ut mori posset.) According to *Cyprian*, the incarnation was necessary, not so much on account of the sin of Adam, as because of the disobedience of the later generations, on whom the former revelations did not produce their effect (Heb. i. 1), De Idol. Van. p. 15: Quod vero Christus sit, et quomodo per ipsum nobis salus venerit, sic est ordo, sic ratio. Judæis primum erat apud Deum gratia. Sic olim justi erant, sic majores eorum religionibus obediebant. Inde illis et regni sublimitas floruit et generis magnitudo provenit. Sed illi negligentes, indisciplinati et superbi postmodum facti, et fiducia patrum inflati, dum divina præcepta contemnunt, datam sibi gratiam perdiderunt. . . . Nec non Deus ante prædixerat, fore ut vergente sæculo, et mundi fine jam proximo, ex omni gente et populo et loco cultores sibi allegeret Deus multo fideliores et melioris obsequii; qui indulgentiam de divinis muneribus haurirent, quam acceptam Judæi contemtis religionibus perdidissent. Hujus igitur indulgentiæ, gratiæ disciplinæque arbiter et magister, sermo et filius Dei mittitur, qui per prophetas omnes retro illuminator et doctor humani generis prædicabatur. Hic est virtus Dei, hic ratio, hic sapientia ejus et gloria. Hic in virginem illabitur, carnem, Spiritu Sancto coöperante, induitur. Deus cum homine miscetur. Hic Deus noster, hic Christus est, qui, mediator duorum, hominem induit, quem perducat ad patrem. *Quod homo est, esse Christus voluit, ut et homo possit esse quod Christus est.* Comp. *Rettberg,* s. 305. In this last position he coincides with *Irenæus.*

§ 65.

The God-man.

Along with more indefinite and general expressions concerning the higher nature of Jesus (1), the elevation of His doctrine and person (2), and His Messianic character (3), we find even in the primitive Church allusions to the intimate union between the divine and the human in His person. But the relation in which they stand to each other is not exactly defined, nor is the part which each takes in the formation of His personality sharply or philosophically determined (4). The earlier Fathers endeavoured, on the one hand, to avoid the low views of the Ebionites and Artemonites (Alogi), who considered Jesus as only the son of Joseph and Mary (while the more moderate Nazarenes, in accordance with the Catholic confession, admitted a supernatural conception) (5). On the other hand, they combated still more decidedly the tendency of the Docetæ, who rejected the true humanity of Christ (6). They also opposed the opinion (held by Cerinthus and Basilides) that the Logos (Christ) had descended upon the man Jesus at His baptism, according to which the divine and human are united only in an external, mechanical way; and the still more fanciful notions of Marcion, according to which Christ appeared as Deus ex machina (7); and lastly, the view of Valentinus (also docetic), who admitted that Christ was born of Mary, but maintained that He made use of her only as of a channel, by which He might be introduced into this finite life (8).

(1) Thus in the letter of Pliny to Trajan (Ep. x. 97): Carmen Christo quasi Deo dicere.—The usual doxologies, the baptismal formulas, the services of the Christian festivals and of divine worship, bear witness to the divine homage paid to Christ by the primitive Church; comp. *Dorner*, l.c. s. 273 ff. Even art and Christian customs testify the same; ibid. s. 290 ff. [Comp *Münter, Schöne, Bingham, Piper, Didron, Jameson*, in their works, referred to § 8; also, especially, *Louis Perret*, Catacombes de Rome, 5 vols. fol. Paris 1851 (by the Institute).] The calumnies which the Jew of Celsus brings against the person of Christ, that He was born from the adulterous intercourse of Mary with a Roman soldier, Pantheras, are refuted by *Origen*, and the miraculous birth of the Saviour vindicated in view of His high destination (in connection with the doctrine of the pre-existence of the soul); Contra Cels. i. 32 (p. 345-351).

(2) According to *Justin Martyr*, the excellency of His *doctrine* elevates Christ over the rest of mankind (Apol. i. 14): Βραχεῖς δὲ καὶ σύντομοι παρ' αὐτοῦ λόγοι γεγόνασιν· οὐ γὰρ σοφιστὴς ὑπῆρχεν, ἀλλὰ δύναμις θεοῦ ὁ λόγος αὐτοῦ ἦν, and this human wisdom would be sufficient by itself (according to c. 22) to secure to Jesus the predicate of the Son of God, even though He were a mere man. But He is *more* than this: ibidem. *Origen* also appeals to the extraordinary personal character of Jesus (apart from His divine dignity), which he considers as the bloom and crown of humanity; Contra Cels. i. 29 (Opp. t. i. p. 347, in reference to *Plato*, De Rep. i. p. 329, and *Plutarch* in Vita Themistoclis): "Jesus, the least and humblest of all Seriphii, yet caused a greater commotion in the world than either Themistocles, or Pythagoras, or Plato, yea more than any wise man, prince or general." He unites in Himself all human excellences, while others have distinguished themselves by particular virtues, or particular actions; He is the miracle of the world! c. 30 (altogether in the sense of the modern apologists). *Minucius Felix* does not go beyond the negative statement, that Jesus *was more than a mere man;* generally speaking, we find in his writings little or nothing positively Christological; Octav. 29, § 2, 3 (comp. with 9, 5): Nam quod religioni nostræ hominem noxium et crucem ejus adscribitis, longe de vicinia

veritatis erratis, qui putatis Deum credi aut meruisse noxium aut potuisse terrenum. Næ ille miserabilis, cujus in homine mortali spes omnis innititur; totum enim ejus auxilium cum extincto homine finitur. Comp. *Novatian,* De Trin. 14: Si homo tantummodo Christus, cur spes in illum ponitur, cum spes in homine maledicta referatur? *Arnobius,* Adv. Gentes, i. 53: Deus ille sublimis fuit, Deus radice ab intima, Deus ab incognitis regnis, et ab omnium principe Deus sospitator est missus, quem neque sol ipse, neque ulla, si sentiunt, sidera, non rectores, non principes mundi, non denique dii magni, aut qui fingentes se deos genus omne mortalium territant, unde aut qui fuerit, potuerunt noscere vel suspicari. On the Christology of the apostolical Fathers, see *Dorner,* l.c. s. 144 ff.

(3) *Justin M.* Apol. i. 5, 30 ff.; Dial. c. Tryph. in its whole bearing. *Novatian,* De Trin. c. 9. *Orig.* Contra Cels. in various places.

(4) Thus *Justin M.* defended, on the one hand, the birth of Christ of a Virgin, in opposition to the Ebionites; and, on the other, His true humanity, in opposition to the Gnostics; Dial. c. Tryph. c. 54: Οὐκ ἔστιν ὁ Χρ. ἄνθρωπος ἐξ ἀνθρώπων, κατὰ τὸ κοινὸν τῶν ἀνθρώπων γεννηθείς. Apol. i. 46: Διὰ δυνάμεως τοῦ λόγου κατὰ τὴν τοῦ πατρὸς πάντων καὶ δεσπότου θεοῦ βουλὴν διὰ παρθένου ἄνθρωπος ἀπεκυήθη. Comp. *Semisch,* ii. s. 403 ff. *Iren.* iii. 16 (*Gr.* 18), 18 (*Gr.* 20), p. 211 (*Gr.* 248): "Ἥνωσεν οὖν καθὼς προέφαμεν, τὸν ἄνθρωπον τῷ θεῷ... Εἰ μὴ συνηνώθη ὁ ἄνθρωπος τῷ θεῷ, οὐκ ἂν ἠδυνήθη μετασχεῖν τῆς ἀφθαρσίας. Ἔδει γὰρ τὸν μεσίτην θεοῦ τε καὶ ἀνθρώπων διὰ τῆς ἰδίας πρὸς ἑκατέρους οἰκειότητος εἰς φιλίαν καὶ ὁμόνοιαν τοὺς ἀμφοτέρους συναγαγεῖν καὶ θεῷ μὲν παραστῆσαι τὸν ἄνθρωπον, ἀνθρώποις δὲ γνωρίσαι θεόν, c. 19 (21), p. 212, 213 (250): "Ὥσπερ γὰρ ἦν ἄνθρωπος, ἵνα πειρασθῇ, οὕτως καὶ λόγος, ἵνα δοξασθῇ· ἡσυχάζοντος μὲν τοῦ λόγου ἐν τῷ πειράζεσθαι... καὶ σταυροῦσθαι καὶ ἀποθνήσκειν· συγγινομένου δὲ τῷ ἀνθρώπῳ ἐν τῷ νικᾶν καὶ ὑπομένειν καὶ χρηστεύεσθαι καὶ ἀνίστασθαι καὶ ἀναλαμβάνεσθαι. *Irenæus* also advocates the true manhood of the Saviour in opposition to the Docetæ, and His true Godhead in opposition to the Ebionites. As Adam had no human father, so Christ is begotten without the act of a man; as the former was

formed from the virgin soil, so the latter is born of a pure virgin. Contrasted with the sinful flesh of Adam is this sinless nature; a spiritual (πνευματικός) man is set over against the carnal (psychical, ψυχικός), iii. 21, 10. *Duncker*, s. 218 ff. Comp. *Novatian*, De Trin. c. 18: Quoniam si ad hominem veniebat, ut mediator Dei et hominum esse deberet, oportuit illum cum eo esse et verbum carnem fieri, ut in semetipso concordiam confibularet terrenorum pariter atque coelestium, dum utriusque partis in se connectens pignora, et Deum homini et hominem Deo copularet, ut merito filius Dei per assumtionem carnis filius hominis, et filius hominis per receptionem Dei verbi filius Dei effici possit. Hoc altissimum atque reconditum sacramentum ad salutem generis humani ante saecula destinatum, in Domino Jesu Christo Deo et homine invenitur impleri, quo conditio generis humani ad fructum aeternae salutis posset adduci.

(5) Comp. § 23, 24, and 42, note 1. On the mild manner in which *Justin M.* (Dial. c. Tryph. § 48) and *Origen* (in Matt. t. xvi. c. 12, Opp. iii. p. 273, comparison with the blind man, Mark x. 46) judged of the view of the Ebionites, see *Neander*, Kirchg. i. s. 616, 617. But *Origen* expresses himself in stronger terms against them in Hom. xv. in Jerem. ib. p. 226: Ἐτόλμησαν γὰρ μετὰ τῶν πολλῶν τῶν ἀνθρωπίνων κακῶν καὶ τοῦτο εἰπεῖν, ὅτι οὐκ ἔστι θεὸς ὁ μονογενὴς ὁ πρωτότοκος πάσης κτίσεως· ἐπικατάρατος γὰρ, ὃς τὴν ἐλπίδα ἔχει ἐπ' ἄνθρωπον. But even common Ebionites supposed that a higher power had united itself with Jesus at His baptism, though it was indeed only an (abstract) power. The Ebionites, whose views are represented by the Clementine Homilies, differed from the former by asserting that Jesus had from the beginning been penetrated with this higher power; hence He is in one rank with Adam, Enoch, and Moses, who all had the same prophetic character; comp. *Schliemann*, s. 200 ff., 483 ff., 523 ff. *Dorner*, s. 296 ff. Concerning the birth from the Virgin, it is remarkable how little the primitive Church hesitated about adducing analogies from pagan myths as a kind of evidence, though the reality of the fact was held fast. Thus *Orig.* Contra Cels. i. 37 (Opp. t. i. p. 355—Plato, a son of Apollo and Amphictyone); in the same connection an analogy is drawn from nature (in the case of the hawk), in

opposition to the blasphemy of Celsus, c. 32, p. 350, mentioned above; comp., however, c. 67, p. 381.[1]

(6) Against the Docetæ, comp. the Epistles of *Ignatius*, especially ad Smyrn. 2 and 3, ad Ephes. 7, 18, ad Trall. 9, also the before-cited passage of *Irenæus*, as well as *Tert*. Adv. Marc. and De Carne Christi; *Novatian*, De Trin. c. 10: Neque igitur eum hæreticorum agnoscimus Christum, qui in imagine (ut dicitur) fuit, et non in veritate; nihil verum eorum quæ gessit, fecerit, si ipse phantasma et non veritas fuit. Some have thought that there is a leaning towards Docetism in the Epistle of Barnabas, c. 5. But it is only the same idea of the κρύψις which occurs in later times, *e.g.* in the (apocryphal) oration of Thaddeus to Abgarus, apud *Euseb*. 1, 13: Ἐσμίκρυνεν αὐτοῦ τὴν θεότητα, and elsewhere.

(7) *Tertull*. De Carne Christi, c. 2: Odit moras Marcion, qui subito Christum de coelis deferebat. Adv. Marc. iii. 2: Subito filius, et subito missus, et subito Christus; iv. 11: Subito Christus, subito et Johannes. Sic sunt omnia apud Marcionem, quæ suum et plenum habent ordinem apud creatorem. [On Basilides and Marcion, see *Neander*, l.c.]

(8) Καθάπερ ὕδωρ διὰ σωλῆνος ὀδεύει, comp. *Neander*, gnost. Systeme, s. 136 ff. On the Docetism of the Gnostics in general, see *Baur*, s. 258 ff.: "*Basilides is nearest to the orthodox view; Marcion departs farthest from it; and Valentinus, with his psychical Christ, occupies an intermediate position.*" Comp. also *Baur*, Dg. s. 610.

§ 66.

Further Development of this Doctrine.

* *J. C. L. Gieseler*, Commentatio, qua Clementis Alexandrini et Origenis doctrinæ de corpore Christi exponuntur, Götting. 1837, 4to. [*Lämmer*, Clem. Alex. Doctrina de λογῷ, 1855.]

---

[1] On the different recensions of what is commonly called the Apostles' Creed, comp. *King*, p. 145. The phrase: conceptus de Spiritu Sancto, is wanting in the earlier recensions, and one reads: qui natus est de Spiritu Sancto ex Maria virg. Comp. *King*, p. 145. [Comp. also *Swainson* on the Nicene and Apostles' Creeds, Lond. 1875.]

244   FIRST PERIOD.—CHRISTOLOGY AND SOTERIOLOGY.   [§ 66.

Though the Christian and Catholic doctrine, in opposition to all these heretical theories, rested upon the simple declaration of John: ὁ λόγος σὰρξ ἐγένετο, and thus preserved the idea which is peculiar to Christianity, viz. that of a necessary union between the divine and the human (1); yet the doctrine of the God-man was modified by the influence of various modes of thought and speculation. Thus it is not quite clear from the phraseology of the Fathers *prior* to Origen (2) (with the exception of *Irenæus* (3) and *Tertullian* (4)) how far they thought the soul of Jesus to be a part of His humanity. Nor does *Clement* of Alexandria make a strict distinction between the human and divine in Christ (5). Concerning His body, the theologians of the Alexandrian school adopted views essentially allied to those of the Docetæ, although they opposed the grosser forms of Docetism. *Clement* maintained that the body of Jesus was not subject to the accidents and influences of the external world with the same physical necessity as other human bodies (6); and *Origen* went so far as to ascribe to it the property of appearing to different persons under different forms (7). On the other hand, Origen was very definite upon the doctrine of the human soul of Jesus (8), and, generally speaking, endeavoured, more exactly than his predecessors, to define in a dialectic method the relation between the divine and the human in the person of Christ (9). He also first made use of the expression θεάνθρωπος (10).

(1) *Novat.* De Trin. c. 10 : Non est ergo in unam partem inclinandum et ab alia parte fugiendum, quoniam nec tenebit perfectam veritatem, quisquis aliquam veritatis excluserit portionem. Tam enim scriptura etiam Deum adnuntiat Christum, quam etiam ipsum hominem adnuntiat Deum, etc.

(2) According to *Justin M.*, Christ had a soul, but not a νοῦς. Its place was supplied by the λόγος. In his view, Christ is composed of λόγος, ψυχή, and σῶμα, Apol. min. c. 10, comp. *Semisch*, s. 410.

(3) *Duncker* (p. 207 ff.) endeavours to make it probable,

from passages quoted by him (especially iii. 22, 1, v. 6, 1), that *Irenæus* taught the perfect humanity of Christ as regards body, soul, and spirit; he also adduces the passage, v. 1, 3, to which others have attached the opposite sense, comp. *Gieseler* on the passage, Dogmengesch. s. 187. [*Gieseler* here states that the Fathers of the Church soon came to feel the necessity, in a doctrinal point of view, of maintaining that Christ had a proper human soul, as otherwise He could not be a real man, nor our example, and His sufferings must be wholly denied, or else ascribed to the Logos. *Irenæus* first refers to it distinctly, v. c. 1; He gave His soul for our souls, His flesh for our flesh; and ψυχή here cannot mean merely the sensuous soul, for *Irenæus* does not distinguish between ψυχή and πνεῦμα. *Tertullian* expressly says that Christ assumed a human soul as well as a human body; De Carne Christi, c. 11, 13; Adv. Prax. c. 16. *Origen*, De Princip. ii. c. 6, first goes into full investigations on this point, making the rational human soul the necessary medium of the incarnation, since God could not be immediately united with a body, etc. Comp. also *Neander*, Dg.] According to a fragment in *Massuet*, p. 347, *Irenæus* taught a ἕνωσις καθ' ὑπόστασιν φυσική—a partial anticipation of that was afterwards called the communicatio idiomatum. See *Baur*, Dg. s. 627.

(4) *Tert.* Adv. Prax. c. 30, takes the exclamation of Christ on the cross: My God, my God, why hast Thou forsaken me! as a vox carnis et animæ; cf. De Carne Christi, c. 11–13: Non poterat Christus inter homines nisi homo videri. Redde igitur Christo fidem suam, ut, qui homo voluerit incedere, animam quoque humanæ conditionis ostenderit, non faciens eam carneam, sed induens eam carne. Comp. De Resurr. Carn. c. 34, and other less definite passages (only in relation to the assuming of the flesh) which are given by *Münscher* (von *Cölln*), i. s. 261–263.

(5) He indulges in sharp contrasts, *e.g.* in Coh. p. 6 and p. 84: Πίστευσον, ἄνθρωπε, ἀνθρώπῳ, καὶ θεῷ· πίστευσον, ἄνθρωπε, τῷ παθόντι καὶ προσκυνουμένῳ θεῷ ζῶντι· πιστεύσατε, οἱ δοῦλοι, τῷ νεκρῷ· πάντες ἄνθρωποι, πιστεύσατε μόνῳ τῷ πάντων ἀνθρώπων θεῷ· πιστεύσατε, καὶ μισθὸν λάβετε σωτηρίαν· ἐκζητήσατε τὸν θεόν, καὶ ζήσεται ἡ ψυχὴ ὑμῶν.

He does not make the distinction drawn by others, according to which the name Ἰησοῦς is used only of the *man*: on the contrary, Pæd. i. 7, p. 131, he says: Ὁ δὲ ἡμέτερος παιδαγωγὸς ἅγιος θεὸς Ἰησοῦς, ὁ πάσης τῆς ἀνθρωπότητος καθηγεμὼν λόγος. He also applies the subject, ὁ λόγος, to His humanity, Pæd. i. 6, p. 124 : Ὁ λόγος τὸ αὐτοῦ ὑπὲρ ἡμῶν ἐξέχεεν αἷμα; comp. iii. 1, p. 251, and *Gieseler*, l.c. On the question whether *Clement* of Alex. believed that Christ had a human soul, see *Gieseler*, Dogmengesch. s. 187. [*Clement*, Strom. vi. p. 775, says that the God-man had no πάθη; in Pædag. iii. 250, he distinguishes in the human soul the rational (λογιστικόν), the principle of resentment (θυμικόν), and the principle of desire (ἐπιθυμητικόν), and says that the two last were not in Jesus.]

(6) Pæd. ii. 2, p. 186 (*Sylb.* 158), he most decidedly maintains, in opposition to the Docetæ, that Jesus ate and drank like other men, but very moderately; comp. Strom. vii. 17, p. 900, where he calls the Docetæ heretics; hence the charge which *Photius* (Bibl. Cod. 109) brought against him, viz. that the doctrine that Christ's body was a phantasm, is propounded in his work entitled the Hypotyposes (μὴ σαρκωθῆναι τὸν λόγον, ἀλλὰ δόξαι), is justly considered as unfounded. But, after all, Clement refines the true human body of Jesus into little more than a kind of phantom, Strom. vi. 9, p. 775 (*Sylb.* p. 158, given by *Gieseler*, l.c. 12), where he speaks of the eating and drinking of our Lord as only an accommodation to human nature, and calls it even *ridiculous* (γέλως) to think otherwise; for, according to him, the body of Jesus was sustained by a divine power, but not by meats and drinks. *Clement* admits that His body was bruised and died; but still he maintains that the passion was only apparent, inasmuch as the suffering Redeemer felt no pains; comp. Pæd. i. c. 5, p. 112, and *Gieseler* on the passage, p. 13. *Clement* also teaches that His divinity was veiled during His manifestation (κρύψις) in the flesh, Strom. vii. 2, p. 833, though he does not use these very words. In accordance perhaps with these views, he asserts that Jesus was without comeliness, Pæd. iii. 1, sub finem, p. 252, in deference to the passage, Isa. liii.; yet, on the other hand, he elevates the body of Jesus far above all other human organisms; for the

§ 66.]   THE GOD-MAN.   247

Saviour did not manifest that beauty of the flesh which strikes the senses, but the beauty of the soul, and the *true* beauty of the body, viz. immortality.¹ The assumption of the perpetual virginity of Mary (Strom. vii. 16, p. 889, 890, and the (apocryphal) passage there cited: Τέτοκεν καὶ οὐ τέτοκεν) may be traced to the same docetic tendency. Different views are entertained by *Tertull.* De Carne Christi, sub finem (in *Potter's* edition, on the passage from the Clementines), who nevertheless quotes the same dictum. A real Docetism has been inferred from the Coh. ad Græcos, p. 86, where the assumption of humanity on the part of the Logos is compared to the putting on of a mask, and the taking a part in a drama: at any rate, this is no real *becoming* man. Comp. *Gieseler*, Dogmengesch. s. 191.

(7) *Gennadius*, De Dogm. Eccles. c. 2, incorrectly numbers *Origen* among those, qui Christum carnem de cœlo secum afferre contenderint (cf. *Gieseler*, Dogmengesch. s. 191); but his doctrine too is not quite free from Docetism. It is most fully given in the Comment. in Ep. ad Gal., preserved by Pamphilus; in *Gieseler*, Comm. p. 16, 17, and Contra Cels. i. 69, 70 (Opp. i. p. 383, 384); ibid. iii. 42 (p. 474); De Princip. ii. 6, 6. Hom. in Gen. i. (Opp. ii. p. 55): Non æqualiter omnes, qui vident, illuminantur a Christo, sed singuli secundum eam mensuram illuminantur, qua vim luminis recipere valent. Et sicut non æqualiter oculi corporis nostri illuminantur a sole, sed quanto quis in loca altiora conscenderit, et ortum ejus editioris speculæ intuitione fuerit contemplatus, tanto amplius et splendoris ejus vim percipiet et caloris: ita etiam mens nostra quanto altius et excelsius appropinquaverit Christo, ac se viciniorem splendori lucis ejus objecerit, tanto magnificentius et clarius ejus lumine radiabitur. With this view he connects the transfiguration on the mount, Contra Cels. ii. 64 (Opp. i. p. 435), and Comment. in Matth. (Opp. iii. p. 906); *Gieseler*, p. 19 ss. Comp. Contra Cels. iv. 16, p. 511: Εἰσὶ γὰρ διάφοροι οἱονεὶ τοῦ λόγου μορφαί, καθὼς ἑκάστῳ τῶν εἰς ἐπιστήμην ἀγομένων φαίνεται ὁ λόγος, ἀνάλογον τῇ ἕξει τοῦ εἰσαγομένου, ἢ ἐπ'

¹ This is also alleged by *Tertullian*, De Carne Christi, c. 9: Adeo nec humanæ honestatis corpus fuit, nedum cœlestis claritatis. For had it been otherwise, how could the soldiers have dared to pierce this fair body ?

ὀλίγον προκόπτοντος, ἢ ἐπὶ πλεῖον, ἢ καὶ ἐγγὺς ἤδη γινομένου τῆς ἀρετῆς, ἢ καὶ ἐν ἀρετῇ γεγενημένου.

(8) De Princip. iv. 31: Volens Filius Dei pro salute generis humani apparere hominibus et inter homines conversari, suscepit non solum corpus humanum, ut quidam putant, sed et animam, nostrarum quidem animarum similem per naturam, proposito vero et virtute similem sibi, et talem, qualis omnes voluntates et dispensationes verbi ac sapientiæ indeclinabiliter possit implere (Joh. x. 18, xii. 27; Matt. xxvi. 38). *Origen* held it to be impossible that the Logos should be directly united with the body: the soul is the intermediate link: De Princip. ii. 6. Comp. Contra Cels. ii. 9, quoted by *Münscher* (*von Cölln*), i. s. 263, where he infers the human soul of the Saviour from Matt. xxvi. 38.— *Origen's* theory of pre-existence would force him to ask why the Son of God assumed *this* very soul, and not any other? comp. Contra Cels. i. 32 (Opp. i. p. 350); De Princip. ii. 6, 3, quoted in *Münscher* (*von Cölln*), s. 265 ff.; comp. *Dorner*, ii. 677 ff.; *Baur*, Dg. 622. According to *Socrat.* iii. 7, the Synod of Bostra, A.D. 240, maintained, in opposition to Beryllus, the proposition: ἔμψυχον εἶναι τὸν ἐνανθρωπήσαντα.—On the Christological views of *Origen* in general, see *Dorner*, ii. 2, s. 942 ff.

(9) *Origen* observes that in the Christology a twofold error is to be guarded against: (1) that of excluding the Logos from Christ, as if the eternal Logos and the historical Christ were two distinct personalities; (2) that of including the Logos wholly in the man, as if He did not exist apart from him; De Princip. iv. c. 30: . . . Non ita sentiendum est, quod omnis divinitatis ejus majestas intra brevissimi corporis claustra conclusa est, ita ut omne verbum Dei et sapientia ejus ac substantialis veritas ac vita vel a patre divulsa sit, vel intra corporis ejus coërcita et conscripta brevitatem, nec usquam præterea putetur operata: sed inter utrumque cauta pietatis esse debet confessio, ut neque aliquid divinitatis in Christo defuisse credatur, et nulla penitus a paterna substantia, quæ ubique est, facta putetur esse divisio . . . Cap. 31: Ne quis tamen nos existimet per hæc illud affirmare, quod pars aliqua deitatis filii Dei fuerit in Christo, reliqua vero pars alibi vel ubique: quod illi sentire possunt, qui naturam

substantiæ incorporeæ atque invisibilis ignorant. Comp. also Contra Cels. iv. 5 : Κἂν ὁ θεὸς τῶν ὅλων τῇ ἑαυτοῦ δυνάμει συγκαταβαίνῃ τῷ Ἰησοῦ εἰς τὸν τῶν ἀνθρώπων βίον, κἂν ὁ ἐν ἀρχῇ πρὸς τὸν θεὸν λόγος, θεὸς καὶ αὐτὸς ὤν, ἔρχηται πρὸς ἡμᾶς, οὐκ ἔξεδρος γίνεται, οὐδὲ καταλείπει τὴν ἑαυτοῦ ἕδραν· ὥς τινα μὲν τόπον κενὸν αὐτοῦ εἶναι, ἕτερον δὲ πλήρη, οὐ πρότερον αὐτὸν ἔχοντα. The Logos in His incarnate state is like the sun, whose beams remain pure wherever they may shine (Contra Cels. vi. 73). Nevertheless, *Origen* asserts that He laid aside His glory, in Jerem. Hom. x. 7 (Opp. iii. p. 186). The Father is the light as such, the Son is the light which shines in darkness; comp. Comm. in Joh. ii. 18 (Opp. iv. p. 76), and De Princip. i. 2, 8. The humanity of Christ ceased to exist after His exaltation; comp. Hom. in Jerem. xv. (Opp. iii. p. 226): Εἰ καὶ ἦν ἄνθρωπος (ὁ σωτήρ), ἀλλὰ νῦν οὐδαμῶς ἐστιν ἄνθρωπος. Comp. Hom. in Luc. xxix. (Opp. iii. p. 967): Tunc homo fuit, nunc autem homo esse cessavit. See *Dorner*, l.c. s. 371 ff.; *Thomasius*, s. 202 ff.; *Redepenning*, ii. s. 313 ff.

(10) So *Dorner*, l.c. s. 679, Anm. 40. The phrase in question occurs (so far as we know) only in the Latin translation of the Homil. in Ezech. iii. 3 (Deus homo); but it is implied in other passages, *e.g.* Contra Cels. iii. 29, vii. 17. Comp. *Thomasius*, s. 203, Anm. c. The Greek term was first explained by Chrysostom, see *Suicer*, Thesaurus, sub voce.

<small>A special question arose concerning the *risen* body of Christ, in its relation to the body which He possessed prior to the resurrection. According to *Ignatius, Justin, Irenæus, Tertullian, Cyprian,* and *Novatian,* Jesus had the same body *after* the resurrection which He had *before* it. Comp. the passages in the work of *C. L. Müller,* De Resurrectione Jesu Christi vitam æt. excipiente et ascensu in cœlum sententiæ, quæ in ecclesia Christiana ad finem usque sæculi sexti viguerunt (Havniæ, 1836), p. 77 ; some merely modifying statements of *Irenæus* and *Tertullian*, p. 78. But *Origen* taught, on the other hand, in more definite terms, Contra Cels. ii. c. 62 (Opp. i. p. 434), that the body of Jesus had undergone a change, and, in support of his opinion, appealed to His miraculous appearance, when the doors were shut : Καὶ ἦν γε μετὰ τὴν ἀνάστασιν αὐτοῦ ὡσπερεὶ ἐν μεθορίῳ τινὶ τῆς παχύτητος τοῦ πρὸ τοῦ πάθους σώματος καὶ τοῦ γυμνὴν τοιούτου σώματος φαίνεσθαι ψυχήν. Comp. c. 64, 65, p. 436: Τὸν μηκέτι ἔχοντά τι χωρητὸν ὁραθῆναι τοῖς πολλοῖς, οὐχ οἷοί τε ἦσαν αὐτὸν βλέπειν οἱ πρότερον αὐτὸν ἰδόντες πάντες . . . Λαμπροτέρα γὰρ τὴν οἰκονομίαν τελέσαντος ἡ θειότης ἦν αὐτοῦ. *Müller*, p. 83. *Origen* does not seem to have believed that the ascension of Christ effected</small>

250 FIRST PERIOD.—CHRISTOLOGY AND SOTERIOLOGY. [§ 67.

a further change; for he probably means by the ethereal body, which he ascribes to Him in His state of exaltation (Contra Cels. iii. 41, 42, Opp. i. p. 474), the same which He had when He rose from the grave. Comp. *Müller*, p. 82 and p. 131.

§ 67.

The Sinlessness of Jesus.

Ullmann, über die Sündlosigkeit Jesu, 7th edit. 1863. [Ullmann on the Sinless Character of Jesus, Edinr.] *Fritzsche*, de ἀναμαρτησίᾳ Jesu Christi, Comment. IV. comp. § 17.

The intimate union between the divine and human in Christ, as held by the primitive Church, excluded every possible idea of the existence of sin in *Him* who was the pure image of Deity. Hence *Irenæus, Tertullian, Clement,* and *Origen* assert the sinlessness (ἀναμαρτησία) of Jesus in the strongest terms (1); and even those of the Fathers who do not expressly mention it, at least take it for granted. In the scheme of the Ebionites and Artemonites, this sinlessness was not necessarily affirmed, although there are not any definite declarations to the contrary. On the other hand, *Basilides* found it difficult to reconcile the sinlessness of Christ with his Gnostic system, according to which every sufferer bears the punishment of his own sins; though he used every possible means to conceal this defect in his scheme (2).

(1) *Justin M.* Dial. c. Tr. § 11, 17, 110, et al.; *Iren.* in the next section. *Tert.* De Anima, cap. 41: Solus enim Deus sine peccato, et solus homo sine peccato Christus, quia et Deus Christus. *Arnobius,* Adv. Gentes, i. 53: Nihil, ut remini, magicum, nihil humanum, præstigiosum, aut subdolum, nihil fraudis delituit in Christo. *Clem. Al.* derives (Pæd. i. 2, p. 99) the prerogative of Christ as the judge of all men from His sinlessness. In Pæd. iii. 12, p. 307, he speaks indeed of the *Logos* as alone ἀναμάρτητος; but as he makes no distinction between the Logos and the human nature of Christ (comp. the preceding section), it would follow that he regarded Jesus as sinless, which is confirmed by what he

says, Strom. vii. 12, p. 875 (*Sylb.* 742): Εἶς μὲν οὖν μόνος ὁ ἀνεπιθύμητος (which implies still more than ἀναμάρτητος) ἐξ ἀρχῆς ὁ κύριος, ὁ φιλάνθρωπος, ὁ καὶ δι' ἡμᾶς ἄνθρωπος. Concerning *Origen,* comp. § 63, note 5; Hom. xii. in Lev. (Opp. ii. p. 251): . . . Solus Jesus dominus meus in hanc generationem mundus ingressus est, etc. In De Princip. ii. c. 6, § 5, 6 (Opp. i. p. 91), he endeavours to remove the difficulty which arises when we assume the absolute sinlessness of our Lord, in contrast with the other assumption of His free spiritual development: Verum quoniam boni malique eligendi facultas omnibus præsto est, hæc anima, quæ Christi est, ita elegit diligere justitiam, ut pro immensitate dilectionis inconvertibiliter ei atque inseparabiliter inhæreret, ita ut propositi firmitas et affectus immensitas et dilectionis inextinguibilis calor omnem sensum conversionis atque immutationis abscinderet, et quod in arbitrio erat positum, longi usus affectu jam versum sit in naturam: ita et fuisse quidem in Christo humana et rationabilis anima credenda est, et nullum sensum vel possibilitatem eam putandum est habuisse peccati (comparison with iron always in the fire). Christ possesses sinlessness as something peculiar to Himself and specific: Sicut vas ipsum, quod substantiam continet unguenti, nullo genere potest aliquid recipere fœtoris, hi vero qui ex odore ejus participant, si se paulo longius a fragrantia ejus removerint, possibile est, ut incidentem recipiant fœtorem: ita Christus velut vas ipsum, in quo erat unguenti substantia, impossibile fuit, ut contrarium reciperet odorem. Participes vero ejus quam proximi fuerint vasculo, tam odoris erunt participes et capaces. Comp. Contra Cels. i. 69 (Opp. i. p. 383): Διὸ πρὸς τοῖς ἄλλοις καὶ μέγαν ἀγωνιστὴν αὐτόν φαμεν γεγονέναι, διὰ τὸ ἀνθρώπινον σῶμα, πεπειρασμένον μὲν ὁμοίως πᾶσιν ἀνθρώποις κατὰ πάντα, οὐκέτι δὲ ὡς ἄνθρωποι μετὰ ἁμαρτίας, ἀλλὰ πάντη χωρὶς ἁμαρτίας. (Hebr. iv. 15, where 1 Pet. ii. 22 and 2 Cor. v. 21 are also quoted.) The term ἀναμάρτητος first occurs in the writings of Hippolytus (*Gallandii,* Bibl. ii. p. 466).

(2) Comp. *Clem.* Strom. iv. p. 600 (*Sylb.* 506); and the comment of *Jacobi* in *Neander's* Dg. s. 219, in connection with the statement of Hippolytus. Comp. also *Neander,* Gnost. Syst. s. 49 ff. *Baur,* Versöhnungslehre, s. 24; Dg. s. 609.

§ 68.

Redemption and Atonement.

(*The Death of Jesus.*)

Dissertatio Historiam Doctrinæ de Redemtione Ecclesiæ, Sanguine Jesu Christi facta, exhibens, in *Cotta's* edition of *Gerhard's* Loci Theologici, t. iv. p. 105–132. *W. C. L. Ziegler*, Historia Dogmatis de Redemtione, etc., inde ab ecclesiæ primordiis usque ad Lutheri tempora, Gött. 1791 (in Comment. Theol. ed. *A. Velthusen*, t. v. p. 227 seq.). **K. Bähr*, die Lehre der Kirche vom Tode Jesu in den ersten 3 Jahrhunderten, Sulzb. 1832, reviewed in the Neue Kirchenzeitung, 1833, No. 36. *F. Ch. Baur*, die christliche Lehre von der Versöhnung in ihrer geschichtlichen Entwickelung von der ältesten Zeit bis auf die neueste, Tübingen 1838 (s. 1–67). [*Thomasius*, Christi Person und Werk, iii. s. 158 ff. 1859. *William Thomson* (now Archbishop of York), The Atoning Work of Christ; Bampton Lectures, Oxford 1853, Lect. VI., Theories in the Early Church. *H. N. Oxenham*, Catholic Doctrine of the Atonement, 2d ed. London 1869. Chap. ii. The Ante-Nicene Fathers.]

The manifestation of the God-man, in and of itself, had a redeeming and reconciling efficacy by breaking the power of evil and restoring the harmony of human nature, through the life-awakening and life-imparting influences which proceeded from Him (1). But from the very beginning, on the basis of apostolic Christianity, the redeeming element was placed chiefly in the sufferings and death of Christ. The first teachers of the Church regarded this death as a sacrifice and ransom (λύτρον), and therefore ascribed to the blood of Jesus the power of cleansing from sin and guilt (2), and attached a high importance, sometimes even a magical efficacy, to the sign of the cross (3). They did not, however, rest satisfied with such vague ideas, but, in connection with the prevailing views of the age, they further developed the above doctrine, and saw in the death of Christ the actual victory over the devil, the restoration of the divine image, and the source and condition of all happiness (4). But, however decidedly and victoriously this enthusiastic faith in the power of the Redeemer's death manifested itself in the writings and lives of the Christian Fathers, as well as in the death of martyrs;

yet this faith had not yet been developed into the form of a strict theory of satisfaction, in the sense that the sufferings of Christ were a punishment, necessarily inflicted by divine justice, and assumed in the place of the sinner, whereby the justice of God was strictly *satisfied*. At least several intermediate links were wanting ere the doctrine could assume this shape. The term *satisfactio* occurs, indeed, first in the writings of *Tertullian*, but in a sense essentially different from, and even opposed to, the idea of a *vicarious* satisfaction (5). Nor was the death of Christ, as a reconciling power, considered as an isolated truth, dissevered from other aspects of it. The same *Origen*, who, on the one hand, along with the notion that the devil had been outwitted in this matter, likewise developed the idea of sacrifice as applicable to it on the basis of the Old Testament typology (6), on the other hand spoke just as definitely in favour of the moral interpretation of Christ's death, which he did not hesitate to compare with the heroic death of other great men of primitive times (7). He also ascribed a purifying power to the blood of martyrs, as *Clement* had done before him (8). And, besides, he understood the death of Jesus in a mystic and idealistic sense as an event not limited to this world, nor to one single moment of time, but which occurred in heaven as well as on earth, embraces all ages, and is in its consequences of infinite importance even for the other worlds (9).

(1) "*Christianity is not only the religion of redemption, inasmuch as it realizes the idea of the union of the divine and the human in the person of the God-man, but also the religion of absolute reconciliation.*" Baur, l.c. s. 5. On the relation in which redemption stands to reconciliation, ibid. [*Baur* here says: The two ideas of redemption and atonement (reconciliation) are usually distinguished, by referring the former to the idea of sin, and the latter to the idea of guilt. . . . Even if one should be transferred from a state of sin to one of sinlessness, it would not follow that the guilt of his sin had been removed. . . . The removal of this guilt can be

conceived only as a divine act, and the ground of its possibility can be found only in the idea of God.] On negative and positive redemption, see *Neander*, Kg. i. s. 1070. According to *Justin M.*, the renovation and restoration of mankind is brought about by the *teaching of Jesus*, Apol. i. 23 : Γενόμενος ἄνθρωπος ταῦτα ἡμᾶς ἐδίδαξεν ἐπ᾽ ἀλλαγῇ καὶ ἐπαναγωγῇ τοῦ ἀνθρωπείου γένους. Comp. Apol. ii. 6 (see note 4, below); Coh. ad Græc. 38, Dial. c. Tryph. § 121 and § 83 : Ἰσχυρὸς ὁ λόγος αὐτοῦ πέπειθε πολλοὺς καταλιπεῖν δαιμόνια, οἷς ἐδούλευον, καὶ ἐπὶ τὸν παντοκράτορα θεὸν δι᾽ αὐτοῦ πιστεύειν. Also § 30 : Ἀπὸ γὰρ τῶν δαιμονίων, ἅ ἐστιν ἀλλότρια τῆς θεοσεβείας τοῦ θεοῦ, οἷς πάλαι προσεκυνοῦμεν, τὸν θεὸν ἀεὶ διὰ Ἰησοῦ Χριστοῦ συντηρηθῆναι παρακαλοῦμεν, ἵνα μετὰ τὸ ἐπιστρέψαι πρὸς θεὸν δι᾽ αὐτοῦ ἄμωμοι ὦμεν. Βοηθὸν γὰρ ἐκεῖνον καὶ λυτρωτὴν καλοῦμεν· οὗ καὶ τὴν τοῦ ὀνόματος ἰσχὺν καὶ τὰ δαιμόνια τρέμει κ.τ.λ. If *Justin* emphasizes the negative, *Irenæus* speaks rather of the positive aspect, iii. 18 (20), quando filius Dei incarnatus est et homo factus, longam hominum expositionem in semet ipso recapitulavit; 20 (22), p. 214 : . . . Filius hominis factus est, ut assuesceret hominem percipere Deum et assuesceret Deum habitare in homine, sec. placitum Patris. The work of redemption was carried on through all the ages and stages of life, which Christ represented in Himself, so that death appears as the crown of the entire redemptive work. ii. 22, 4, p. 147 : Omnes enim venit per semetipsum salvare : omnes, inquam, qui per eum renascuntur in Deum, infantes et parvulos et pueros et juvenes et seniores. Ideo per omnem venit ætatem, et infantibus infans factus, sanctificans infantes ; in parvulis parvulus, sanctificans hanc ipsam habentes ætatem, simul et exemplum illis pietatis effectus et justitiæ et subjectionis : in juvenibus juvenis, exemplum juvenibus fiens, eosque sanctificans Domino ; sic et senior in senioribus, ut sit perfectus magister in omnibus, non solum secundum expositionem veritatis, sed et secundum ætatem, sanctificans simul et seniores, exemplum ipsis quoque fiens ; deinde et usque ad mortem pervenit, ut sit primogenitus ex mortuis, ipse primatum tenens in omnibus, princeps vitæ, prior omnium et præcedens omnes [v. 23, 2 : Recapitulans autem universum hominem in se ab initio usque ad finem, recapitulavit et mortem ejus]. Comp. v. 16. [Comp. also *Irenæus,* Contra Hæres. v. 16: Ἐν τοῖς πρόσθεν χρόνοις ἐλέγετο μὲν κατ' εἰκόνα θεοῦ γεγονέναι τὸν ἄνθρωπον, οὐκ ἐδείκνυτο δέ· ἔτι γὰρ ἀόρατος ἦν ὁ λόγος, οὗ κατ' εἰκόνα ὁ ἄνθρωπος ἐγεγόνει διὰ τοῦτο δὴ καὶ τὴν ὁμοίωσιν ῥᾳδίως ἀπέβαλεν, ὁπότε δὲ σὰρξ ἐγένετο ὁ λόγος τοῦ θεοῦ, τὰ ἀμφότερα ἐπεκύρωσε· καὶ γὰρ τὴν εἰκόνα ἔδειξεν ἀληθῶς, αὐτὸς τοῦτο γενόμενος, ὅπερ ἦν ἡ εἰκὼν αὐτοῦ· καὶ τὴν ὁμοίωσιν βεβαίως κατέστησε, συνεξομοιώσας τὸν ἄνθρωπον τῷ ἀοράτῳ Πατρί.]—Comp. Tert. Adv. Marc. 12.—*Clem.* Coh. p. 6, p. 23: Ἡμεῖς δὲ οὐκ ὀργῆς θρέμματα ἔτι, οἱ τῆς πλάνης ἀπεσπασμένοι, ᾄσσοντες δὲ ἐπὶ τὴν ἀλήθειαν. Ταύτῃ τοι ἡμεῖς, οἱ τῆς ἀνομίας υἱοί ποτε, διὰ τὴν φιλανθρωπίαν τοῦ λόγου νῦν υἱοὶ γεγόναμεν τοῦ θεοῦ. Pæd. i. 2, p. 100: Ἔστιν οὖν ὁ παιδαγωγὸς ἡμῶν λόγος διὰ παραινέσεων θεραπευτικὸς τῶν παρὰ φύσιν τῆς ψυχῆς παθῶν ... Λόγος δὲ ὁ πατρικὸς μόνος ἐστὶν ἀνθρωπίνων ἰατρὸς ἀρρωστημάτων παιώνιος καὶ ἐπῳδὸς ἅγιος νοσούσης ψυχῆς. Comp. i. 9, p. 147, i. 12, p. 158; Quis Div. salv. p. 961 s. (Comparison with the merciful Samaritan.) *Origen* also, Contra Cels. iii. 28 (Opp. i. p. 465), sees in the union of the divine and the human in Christ the beginning of an intimate connection between the one and the other, which is to be progressively developed in mankind: Ὅτι ἀπ' ἐκείνου ἤρξατο θεία καὶ ἀνθρωπίνη συνυφαίνεσθαι φύσις· ἵν' ἡ ἀνθρωπίνη τῇ πρὸς τὸ θειότερον κοινωνίᾳ γένηται θεία οὐκ ἐν μόνῳ τῷ Ἰησοῦ, ἀλλὰ καὶ πᾶσι τοῖς μετὰ τοῦ πιστεύειν ἀναλαμβάνουσι βίον, ὃν Ἰησοῦς ἐδίδαξεν.[1]

(2) *Barnabas,* c. 5: Propter hoc Dominus sustinuit tradere corpus suum in exterminium, ut remissione peccatorum sanctificemur, quod est sparsione sanguinis illius, etc., comp. c. 7, 11, and 12. *Clemens Rom.* ad Cor. i. c. 7: Ἀτενίσωμεν εἰς τὸ αἷμα τοῦ Χριστοῦ καὶ ἴδωμεν, ὡς ἔστιν τίμιον τῷ θεῷ (αἷμα) αὐτοῦ, ὅτι διὰ τὴν ἡμετέραν σωτηρίαν ἐκχυθὲν παντὶ τῷ κόσμῳ μετανοίας χάριν ὑπήνεγκεν, comp. i. c. 2, where the παθήματα αὐτοῦ grammatically refer to θεός. (*Möhler,* Patro-

---

[1] "Inferences might be drawn from these ideas of Origen, not in accordance with the simple truth of Scripture; but they may also be so interpreted as to agree with the example of wholesome doctrine. *The latter is undoubtedly better and more charitable than the former.*" Mosheim, s. 297.

logie, i. s. 61.) [Comp. also *Clem. Rom.* c. 49: Διὰ τὴν ἀγάπην, ἣν ἔσχεν πρὸς ἡμᾶς, τὸ αἷμα αὐτοῦ ἔδωκεν ὑπὲρ ἡμῶν ὁ Χριστὸς ὁ κύριος ἡμῶν ἐν θελήματι θεοῦ, καὶ τὴν σάρκα ὑπὲρ τῆς σαρκὸς ἡμῶν, καὶ τὴν ψυχὴν ὑπὲρ τῶν ψυχῶν ἡμῶν.] *Dorner* in his Christol. i. 138, says: "*Every interpretation of these passages is forced, which does not find in them the idea of substitution; and this, not only subjectively, the vicarious satisfaction of Christ, but also, objectively, that His substituted experience and acts also had their corresponding objective consequences.*" *Ignatius*, ad Smyrn. 6: Μηδεὶς πλανάσθω. Καὶ τὰ ἐπουράνια καὶ ἡ δόξα τῶν ἀγγέλων, καὶ οἱ ἄρχοντες ὁρατοί τε καὶ ἀόρατοι, ἐὰν μὴ πιστεύσωσιν εἰς τὸ αἷμα Χριστοῦ, κἀκείνοις κρίσις ἐστιν. (He also defends the reality of His bodily sufferings in opposition to the Docetæ, c. 2.) Comp. *Höfling*, die Lehre der Apostolischen Väter vom Opfer im Christlichen Cultus, 1841. The following passage, from the Epistle to Diognetus (c. 9), is peculiar, from its pure apprehension of the redemption that is in Christ, as an act of love proceeding from the divine compassion, not as reconciling His wrath; Ἐπεὶ δὲ πεπλήρωτο μὲν ἡ ἡμετέρα ἀδικία καὶ τελείως πεφανέρωτο ὅτι ὁ μισθὸς αὐτῆς κόλασις καὶ θάνατος προσεδοκᾶτο, ἦλθε δὲ ὁ καιρὸς, ὃν θεὸς προέθετο λοιπὸν φανερῶσαι τὴν ἑαυτοῦ χρηστότητα καὶ δύναμιν (ὢ τῆς ὑπερβαλλούσης φιλανθρωπίας καὶ ἀγάπης τοῦ θεοῦ), οὐκ ἐμίσησεν ἡμᾶς, οὐδὲ ἀπώσατο, οὐδὲ ἐμνησικάκησεν, ἀλλὰ ἐμακροθύμησεν, ἠνέσχετο, ἐλεῶν αὐτὸς τὰς ἡμετέρας ἁμαρτίας ἀνεδέξατο· αὐτὸς τὸν ἴδιον υἱὸν ἀπεδότο λύτρον ὑπὲρ ἡμῶν, τὸν ἅγιον ὑπὲρ ἀνόμων, τὸν ἄκακον ὑπὲρ τῶν κακῶν, τὸν δίκαιον ὑπὲρ τῶν ἀδίκων, τὸν ἄφθαρτον ὑπὲρ τῶν φθαρτῶν, τὸν ἀθάνατον ὑπὲρ τῶν θνητῶν. Τί γὰρ ἄλλο τὰς ἁμαρτίας ἡμῶν ἠδυνήθη καλύψαι ἢ ἐκείνου δικαιοσύνη; ἐν τίνι δικαιωθῆναι δυνατὸν τοὺς ἀνόμους ἡμᾶς καὶ ἀσεβεῖς, ἢ ἐν μόνῳ τῷ υἱῷ τοῦ θεοῦ;[1] comp. also c. 7 and 8: ... ὡς σώζων ἔπεμψεν, ὡς πείθων, οὐ βιαζόμενος. βία γὰρ οὐ πρόσεστι τῷ θεῷ. ... God is rather called by him ἀόργητος (c. 8). According to *Justin M.*, the object of Christ's incarnation was to *suffer* for mankind, Apol. iii. 13: Δι' ἡμᾶς ἄνθρωπος γέγονεν, ὅπως καὶ τῶν παθῶν τῶν ἡμετέρων συμμέτοχος γενόμενος καὶ ἴασιν ποιήσηται. Comp. Apol. i. 32:

---

[1] [The reader is probably aware that this passage has been adduced, among other reasons for doubting the genuineness of this Epistle.]

Δι' αἵματος καθαίρων τοὺς πιστεύοντας αὐτῷ, i. 63 ; Dial. c. Tryph. § 40–43, and § 95. *Justin* also calls the death of Jesus a sacrifice (προσφορά); comp. the passages quoted by *Bähr*, s. 42, and *Semisch*, ii. s. 418 ff. On the question whether *Justin* referred the power of the death of Christ in cancelling sin to the whole life of the believer, or restricted it to the epoch preceding His deliberate entrance into the church, see *Semisch*, s. 422 ff.; comp. Ep. ad Diognetum, c. 9. The writings of *Clement* of Alexandria also abound in passages upon the efficacy of the death of Jesus; Coh. p. 86 (comp. *Bähr*, s. 76); ibid. 88; Pæd. i. 9, p. 148, ii. 2, p. 177 (διττὸν τὸ αἷμα τοῦ κυρίου), and other passages. A mystical interpretation of the crown of thorns, Pæd. ii. 8, p. 214, 215 (with reference to Heb. ix. 22), a passage which *Bähr* has overlooked. In the treatise, Quis Dives Salvus, 34, p. 954, the phrase occurs: αἷμα θεοῦ παιδός (not παιδὸς τοῦ θεοῦ); hence the assertion of *Bähr* (s. 116), that the Lutheran phrase, "*the blood of God,*" would have met with opposition on the part of all the Fathers of this period, must be restricted. On the efficacy of His death, see Strom. iv. 7, 583, and other passages. On the other hand, it is worthy of notice that *Clement*, as *Philo* had done before him, and *Origen* did after him, applies the idea of the high-priesthood of Christ in an ideal sense to the Logos, without reference to the death which He suffered in His human nature; comp. *Bähr*, s. 81.

(3) The fact that the heathen charged the Christians with rendering homage to all that were crucified (*Orig.* c. Cels. ii. 47, Opp. i. p. 422), shows, to say the least, that the latter held the cross in high esteem. On the symbolical signification of the cross, and the earlier fanciful interpretations of the allegorists concerning the blood of Jesus, comp. § 29, note 3 ; and *Gieseler*, Dogmengesch. s. 196 f. On the effects of the cross upon the demons, see § 52, note 4.

(4) "*The viewing of the death of Christ as a victory over the devil was so congruous with the entire circle of ideas in which that time moved, that they could not miss it.*" *Baur*, l.c. s. 28. *Baur* also maintains that this mode of considering the death of Christ was transplanted from the Gnostics to the Church, by simply converting the person of the demiurge into that of

the devil (?). This view is represented in this period by *Irenæus*. His train of thought is the following: Man came under the dominion of the devil by violating the divine commandment. This state of bondage lasted from Adam to Christ. The latter delivered men by rendering perfect obedience on the cross, and paying a ransom with His blood. God did not rescue their souls from the power of the devil by force, as the devil himself had done, but *secundum suadelam*. All depends upon the explanation of this word. According to *Baur*, l.c., the devil was himself convinced of the justice of the manner in which he was treated. But *Duncker*, s. 237, and *Gieseler*, Dogmengesch. s. 201, refer the *suadela* more correctly to man, who was delivered from the power of the devil by the better conviction he had gained through the teaching of Christ. Comp. the passage, on the previous page, from the Ep. ad Diognetum, ὡς πείθων, οὐ βιαζ. [Comp. *Dorner*, i. 479 (also against *Baur*). *Dorner* makes use of the passage from the Ep. ad Diog. to refute *Baur's* interpretation of *Irenæus*.] And as man now voluntarily abandoned the service of the devil, under whose sway he had voluntarily placed himself, the relation of Ruler in which God stands to man was restored; comp. *Iren.* Adv. Hær. v. 1, 1: [Et quoniam injuste dominabatur nobis apostasia, et cum natura essemus Dei omnipotentis, alienavit nos contra naturam, suos proprios nos faciens discipulos, potens in omnibus Dei verbum, et non deficiens in sua justitia, juste etiam adversus ipsum conversus est apostasiam, ea quæ sunt sua redimens ab eo non cum vi, quemadmodum ille initio dominabatur nostri, ea quæ non erant sua insatiabiliter rapiens; sed *secundum suadelam*, quemadmodum decebat Deum suadentem, et non vim inferentem, accipere quæ vellet, ut neque quod est justum confringeretur, neque antiqua plasmatio Dei deperiret.] From this *Irenæus* infers the necessity of the Saviour's twofold nature (here the views of *Irenæus* approach most nearly those of *Anselm* in a later period), iii. 18, 7: "Ἥνωσεν τὸν ἄνθρωπον τῷ θεῷ. Εἰ γὰρ μὴ ἄνθρωπος ἐνίκησε τὸν ἀντίπαλον τοῦ ἀνθρώπου, οὐκ ἂν δικαίως ἐνικήθη ὁ ἐχθρός; comp. v. 21, 3; iii. 19, 3: "Ὥσπερ γὰρ ἦν ἄνθρωπος ἵνα πειρασθῇ, οὕτως καὶ λόγος ἵνα δοξασθῇ, etc. (comp. § 65, note 4). Both elements are here, viz. the perfect obedience of Christ, and the shedding of His blood as a ransom (v. 1, 1: Τῷ ἰδίῳ οὖν αἵματι λυτρωσαμένου ἡμᾶς τοῦ κυρίου, καὶ δόντος τὴν ψυχὴν ὑπὲρ τῶν ἡμετέρων ψυχῶν, καὶ τὴν σάρκα τὴν ἑαυτοῦ ἀντὶ τῶν ἡμετέρων σαρκῶν, etc.): and thus *Irenæus* has in his system the negative aspect of the doctrine of redemption; and to this is added the positive one, the communication of a new principle of life, iii. 23, 7. Comp. *Baur*, l.c. s. 30–42. *Bähr*, s. 55–72. On the other hand, the idea of a sacrifice is in his writings kept in the background, see *Duncker*, s. 252 : " *The idea of the vicarious sufferings of the Lord, in the sense that thereby satisfaction is rendered to the divine justice, which had been offended by our sins, and that thus the punishment, which ought in justice to have been inflicted upon all men, is cancelled —this idea is not found in Irenæus, any more than the corresponding notion of an exchange or compact with the devil, by which he receives, as it were, a legal compensation for the men he gives up.*" *Neander* qualifies this statement of the views of *Irenæus*, by adding, " but doubtless there is lying at the bottom the idea of a perfect fulfilment of the law by Christ; of His perfect obedience to the holiness of God in its claims to satisfaction due to it from mankind." And *Thomasius*, iii. 176, cites from *Irenæus*, iii. 18: " We were God's enemies and debtors, and Christ in His priestly work fulfilled the law "— propitians pro nobis Deum; and also xvii. 1: Et propter hoc in novissimis temporibus in amicitiam nos restituit Dominus per suam incarnationem, mediator Dei et hominum factus; propitians quidem pro nobis Patrem, in quem peccaveramus, et nostram inobedientiam consolatus, etc.

(5) On the peculiar usage of the term " satisfactio," comp. *Münscher*, Handb. i. s. 223. *Bähr*, s. 90 ff. On the question whether *Justin M.* propounded the doctrine of satisfaction, see *Semisch*, s. 423, 424. The answer to it must mainly depend on the interpretation of ὑπέρ, which frequently occurs in his writings, Apol. i. 63; Dial. c. Tryph. § 88, and other passages quoted by *Semisch*. He distinctly says that the curse under which Christ was laid was only apparent (δοκοῦσαν κατάραν), Dial. c. Tryph. § 90; comp. § 94: ῎Ονπερ οὖν τρόπον τὸ σημεῖον διὰ τοῦ χαλκοῦ ὄφεως γενέσθαι ὁ θεὸς ἐκέλευσε, καὶ ἀναίτιός ἐστιν, οὕτω δὴ καὶ ἐν τῷ νόμῳ κατάρα κεῖται κατὰ τῶν σταυρουμένων ἀνθρώπων· οὐκ ἔτι δὲ καὶ κατὰ τοῦ

Χριστοῦ θεοῦ κατάρα κεῖται, δι' οὗ σώζει πάντας τοὺς κατάρας ἄξια πράξαντας. § 96 : Καὶ γὰρ τὸ εἰρημένον ἐν τῷ νόμῳ, ὅτι ἐπικατάρατος πᾶς ὁ κρεμάμενος ἐπὶ ξύλου οὐχ ὡς τοῦ θεοῦ καταρωμένου τούτου τοῦ ἐσταυρωμένου, ἡμῶν τονοῖ τὴν ἐλπίδα ἐκκρεμαμένην ἀπὸ τοῦ σταυρωθέντος Χριστοῦ, ἀλλ' ὡς προειπόντος τοῦ θεοῦ τὸ ὑφ' ὑμῶν πάντων καὶ τῶν ὁμοίων ὑμῖν . . . μέλλοντο γίνεσθαι. § 111: Ὁ παθητὸς ἡμῶν καὶ σταυρωθεὶς Χριστὸς οὐ κατηράθη ὑπὸ τοῦ νόμου, ἀλλὰ μόνος σώσειν τοὺς μὴ ἀφισταμένους τῆς πίστεως αὐτοῦ ἐδήλου. The agony of soul in Gethsemane, too, according to *Justin*, only made indubitable the fact of Christ's human nature, and set aside the subterfuge that, because He was the Son of God, He could not feel pain as well as other men; cf. Dial. c. Tryph. § 103. *Neander* says: "In Justin Martyr may be recognised the idea of a satisfaction rendered by Christ through suffering—at least lying at the bottom, if it is not clearly unfolded and held fast in the form of conscious thought." So, too, *Thomasius*, Christologie, iii. 169. From *Tert*. De Pœn. 5, 7, 8, 9, 10; De Pat. 13; De Pud. 9, it is evident "*that he applies the term satisfaction to such as make amends for their own sins by confession and repentance, which shows itself in works;*" but he never understands by it *satisfactio vicaria* in the sense afterwards attached to it. That *Tertullian* was far from entertaining this view may be proved from De Cultu Fem. i. 1, and the interpretation which he gives to Gal. iii. 13, Contra Judæos, 10. He there represents the crime that had been committed as a curse, but not the hanging on the tree (for Christ was not accursed by God, but by the Jews); thus also Contra Marc. v. 5, and other passages which are quoted by *Bähr*, s. 89 ff. In other points his views resemble those of *Irenæus*, ibid. s. 100–104.

(6) On the relation of these two representations of the matter, viz. that of *Irenæus*, that it was a victory over the devil (which assumes in *Origen* the still more mythical character of an intentional deception on the part of God), and that it was a voluntary sacrifice, not having respect, like the former, to the idea of justice, but resting rather on the love of God, compare *Baur*, s. 43–67; *Bähr*, s. 111 ff.; *Thomasius*, s. 214 ff.; *Redepenning*, ii. s. 405; *Gieseler*, Dogmengesch. s. 203. On the question whether *Origen* taught an intentional decep-

tion on the part of God, see (against *Baur*) *Redepenning*, s. 406, Anm. 5. The idea is original that it was a *torment* to the devil to be obliged to keep near him so pure a soul as that of Jesus; he *could not* keep it, because it did not belong to him. Comp. *Origen's* Comm. in Matt. t. xvi. 8 (Opp. i. 726) and the other passages, Comment. series, § 75 (on Matt. xxvi. 1, Opp. i. 819), and on Matt. t. xiii. 8 and 9, in which the giving up of the Son by the Father appears as an act of love, in distinction from the treachery practised on Him by Satan through his agents (different interpretations of the expression παραδίδοσθαι used in both places). *Origen's* interpretation of Isa. liii. 5 comes nearest to the view entertained in later times by *Anselm*, Comment. in Joh. t. xxviii. 14, Opp. iv. p. 392. (*Bähr*, s. 151.)[1] But still *Origen* differs from the Church doctrine of satisfaction in the manner in which he explains, *e.g.*, the sufferings in Gethsemane, and the forsaking of Christ on the cross: My God, my God, etc. (*Bähr*, s. 147–149, and *Redepenning*, s. 408 ff.) [On *Origen's* views, comp. *Thomson's* Bampton Lectures, ubi supra; and *Origen* in Joan. t. ii. 21, in Matt. xvi. 8, and in Rom. ii. 13 (p. 493): Si ergo pretio emti sumus, ut etiam Paulus adstipulatur, nec ab aliquo sine dubio emti sumus cujus eramus servi, qui et pretium poposcit quod voluit, ut de potestate dimitteret quos tenebat. Tenebat autem nos Diabolus, cui distracti fueramus peccatis nostris. Poposcit ergo pretium nostrum sanguinem Christi. That *Origen* also brought the death of Christ into relation to God, see his Comment. on Rom. iii. 24 (*Thomasius*, iii. 180): Nunc addit [Paulus] aliquid sublimius et dicit: proposuit eum Deus *propitiationem*, quo scilicet per hostiam sui corporis *propitium hominibus faceret Deum* ; and his Hom. in Lev. ix. 10: Tu, qui ad Christum venisti, qui sanguine suo *Deum tibi propitium* fecit, et reconciliavit te patri, etc. See also *Oxenham*, u. s. p. 112 ff.]

(7) Comp. t. xix. in Joh. (Opp. iv. p. 286), and the passage before quoted from t. xxviii. p. 393 ; Contra Cels. i. 1, p. 349 : Ὅτι ὁ σταυρωθεὶς ἑκὼν τοῦτον τὸν θάνατον ὑπὲρ τοῦ τῶν ἀνθρώπων γένους ἀνεδέξατο, ἀνάλογον τοῖς ἀποθανοῦσι ὑπὲρ

---

[1] But it should not be overlooked that Origen immediately afterwards connects this passage with 1 Cor. iv. 13, and applies to Christ in a *higher degree* what is there said in reference to the apostles, and also adduces still other examples from ancient times.

πατρίδων ἐπὶ τῷ σβέσαι λοιμικὰ κρατήσαντα καταστήματα ἢ ἀφορίας ἢ δυσπλοίας. These human sacrifices were thought to be connected with the influence exerted by the demons, which was to be removed by them; see *Baur*, s. 45, and *Mosheim*, in a note to the translation of that passage, s. 70. The death of Christ also gave an additional weight to His *doctrine*, and was the cause of its propagation; Hom. in Jerem. 10, 2, comp. *Bähr*, s. 142, who observes that no ecclesiastical writer of this period besides Origen distinctly mentions this point. This idea bears, indeed, the greatest resemblance to the modern rationalistico-moral notions concerning the death of Christ. He also compares the death of Jesus with that of Socrates, Contra Cels. ii. 17, Opp. i. p. 403, 404, and represents it as a moral lever to elevate the courage of His followers (ibid. 40–42, p. 418, 419).

(8) *Clement*, too, saw in the death of the martyrs a reconciling power, Strom. iv. 9, p. 596, comp. p. 602, 603; likewise *Orig.* Comm. in Joh. (Opp. iv. p. 153, 154), Exhort. ad Martyr. 50, Opp. i. p. 309: Τάχα δὲ καὶ ὥσπερ τιμίῳ αἵματι τοῦ Ἰησοῦ ἠγοράσθημεν . . . οὕτως τῷ τιμίῳ αἵματι τῶν μαρτύρων ἀγορασθήσονταί τινες.

(9) On the basis of Col. i. 20 (Comment. in Joh. i. 40, Opp. iv. p. 41, 42): *Οὐ μόνον ὑπὲρ ἀνθρώπων ἀπέθανεν, ἀλλὰ καὶ ὑπὲρ τῶν λοιπῶν λογικῶν.* De Princip. iv. 25 (Opp. i. p. 188; *Redep.* p. 79 and 364). There are two altars on which sacrifice is made, an earthly and a heavenly; Hom. in Lev. i. 3 (Opp. ii. p. 186), ii. 3 (ibid. p. 190); comp. *Bähr*, s. 119 ff. *Baur*, s. 64. *Thomasius*, s. 214–217. *Redepenning*, Orig. ii. s. 403.

From all that has been said in reference to the subject in question, it would follow that the primitive Church held the doctrine of vicarious *sufferings*, but not that of vicarious *satisfaction*. But we should not lay too much stress upon the negative aspect of this inference, so as to justify or to identify it with that later interpretation of the death of Jesus which excludes everything that is mysterious. Comp. *Bähr*, s. 5–8, and 176–180.

§ 69.

Descensus ad Inferos.

J. A. *Dietelmaier*, Historia Dogmatis de Descensu Christi ad Inferos, Altorf. 1762. J. S. *Semler*, Observatio historico-dogmatica de vario et impari veterum Studio in recolenda Historia Descensus Christi ad Inferos, Hal.

§ 69.]   DESCENSUS AD INFEROS.   263

1775. *J. Clausen*, Dogmatis de Descensu Jesu Christi ad Inferos historiam biblicam atque ecclesiasticam composuit, Havn. 1801. *Pott* in the Epp. cath. Exc. iii. [Comp. also *Pearson* on the Creed, V. art., and *Heylyn* on the Creed, VI. art.] *J. L. König*, die Lehre von Christi Höllenfahrt, nach der h. Schrift, der ältesten Kirche, den christlichen Symbolen und nach ihrer viel umfassenden Bedeutung, Frankf. 1842. *E. Güder*, Die Lehre von d. Erscheinung Christi unter den Todten, Berl. 1853. *F. Huidekoper*, The Belief of the first Three Centuries concerning Christ's Mission to the Under-World, Boston 1854. [*Archd. Blackburn*, Hist. Account of Views about the Intermed. State, 1770. The Revealed Economy of Heaven and Earth, Lond. 1853. *V. U. Maywahlen*, Tod, Todtenreich, etc., Berl. 1854; transl. by J. F. Schön, The Intermed. State, Lond. 1856. The Intermed. State, by the late *Duke of Manchester*, Lond. 1856. *T. Körber*, Die kath. Lehre d. Höllenfahrt Jes. Christi, Landshut 1860.]

We have seen that the Fathers of this period, with the exception of *Origen*, limited the direct efficacy of Christ's death to this world. But several writers of the second and third centuries thought that it was also retrospective in its effects, and inferred from some allusions in Scripture (1) that Christ descended into the abode of the dead (under-world, Hades), to announce to the souls of the patriarchs, etc., there abiding, the accomplishment of the work of redemption, and to conduct them with Him into the kingdom of His glory (2).

(1) Acts ii. 27, 31 (Rom. x. 6, 7, 8); Eph. iv. 9; 1 Pet. iii. 19, 20 (in connection with Ps. xvi. 10).—On the clause " descendit ad inferos " in the Apostles' Creed, which is of later origin, see *Rufin.* Expos. p. 22 (ed. *Fell*). *King*, p. 169 ff. *Pott*, l.c. p. 380. *G. H. Waage*, De Ætate Articuli, quo in Symb. Apost. traditur Jesu Christi ad Inferos Descensus, Havn. 1836. This clause is first found in the creed of the Church of Aquileia, and was brought into wider use through Rufinus. [Comp. Harvey on the Three Creeds; *Pearson*, l.c. p. 237; *Swainson*, u. s.]

(2) Apocryphal narrative, in the Ev. Nic. c. 17–27. (*Thilo*, Cod. Ap. i. p. 667 ff.) *Ullmann*, Historisch oder mythisch? s. 220. An allusion is found in the Testament of the XII. Patriarchs (*Grabe*, Spic. PP. Sæc. i. p. 250). On the passage in the oration of Thaddeus, quoted by *Eus.* i. 13: Κατέβη εἰς τὸν ᾅδην καὶ διέσχισε φραγμὸν τὸν ἐξ αἰῶνος μὴ σχισθέντα, καὶ ἀνέστη καὶ συνήγειρε νεκροὺς τοὺς ἀπ' αἰώνων κεκοιμημένους, καὶ πῶς κατέβη μόνος, ἀνέβη δὲ μετὰ πολλοῦ

264   FIRST PERIOD.—CHRISTOLOGY AND SOTERIOLOGY.   [§ 70.

ὄχλου πρὸς τὸν πατέρα αὐτοῦ, comp. Vales.—The passage from the fuller recension of *Ign*. Ep. ad Trall. c. 9 (ii. p. 64), is doubtful; and that from the Shepherd of *Hermas*, Sim. ix. c. 16, refers properly to the apostles. *Justin M*. also supposes that Christ preached in the nether world (Dial. c. Tryph. § 72); though He was not compelled to this, on account of His views respecting the λόγος σπερματικός, in relation to the heathen; comp. *Semisch*, ii. s. 414. More definite language is first used by *Iren*. iv. 27 (45), p. 264 (347), v. 31, p. 331 (451). *Tert*. De Anim. 7 and 55. *Clem*. Strom. vi. 6, p. 762–767, and ii. 9, p. 452 (where he quotes the passage from Hermas); the latter is inclined to extend the preaching of the gospel to the Gentiles in Hades. *Orig*. Contra Cels. ii. 43 (Opp. i. p. 419), in libr. Reg. Hom. ii. (Opp. ii. p. 492–498), especially towards the close. Comp. *König*, s. 97. Among the heretics we may mention the opinion of Marcion, that Christ did not deliver the patriarchs, but Cain, the people of Sodom, and all those who had been condemned by the demiurge. *Iren*. i. 27 (29), p. 106 (*Gr*. 104); *Neander*, Dg. s. 222. [On the opinions of the Fathers, comp. also *Pearson*, l.c. p. 238, 245 ff., and *Heylyn*, l.c. p. 264 ff.] Other Gnostics wholly rejected the doctrine of the Descensus, and explained the passage in Peter of Christ's appearance on the earth.

§ 70.

The Economy of Redemption.

H. L. Heubner, Historia antiquior Dogmatis de modo salutis tenendæ et justificationis, etc., Wittenb. 1805, 4to. † *Wörter*, Die christl. Lehre über das Verhältniss von Gnade u. Freiheit, etc., Freib. 1856. *Landerer*, das Verhältniss der Gnade und Freiheit in der Aneignung des Heils (Jahrb. deutsch. Theol. 1857, 2, s. 500 ff.). † *P. J. Haber*, Theologiæ Græcorum Patrum vindicatæ circa universam materiam gratiæ, libri iii., Würzburg 1863.

From what precedes, it is evident that the primitive Church universally believed that Jesus Christ was the only ground of salvation, and the Mediator between God and man. But all were required to appropriate to themselves, by a free act, the blessings which Christ obtained for them (1); and the forgiveness of sins was made dependent both on true repentance (2), and the performance of good works (3). Sometimes expressions are used which seem to favour the doctrine of the meritoriousness of good works (4). Nevertheless all agreed in making *faith* (in accordance with the apostolic doctrine) the conditio sine qua non of salvation (5), and in celebrating its blessed power in bringing about an intimate union (unio mystica) between man and God (6). Though the will of man was admitted to be free, yet it was also felt that it must be assisted by divine grace (7), and this, when carried out, led to the idea of an eternal decree of God (*predestination*), which, however, was not yet viewed as unconditional (8). *Origen*, in particular, endeavoured to explain the relation of predestination to the freedom of the human will so as not to endanger the latter (9).

(1) This follows from the passages above cited on human liberty. *Justin M.* Dial. c. Tryph. § 95 : Εἰ μετανοοῦντες ἐπὶ τοῖς ἡμαρτημένοις καὶ ἐπιγνόντες τοῦτον εἶναι τὸν Χριστὸν καὶ φυλάσσοντες αὐτοῦ τὰς ἐντολὰς ταῦτα φήσετε, ἄφεσις ὑμῖν τῶν ἁμαρτιῶν ὅτι ἔσται, προεῖπον. Comp. *Orig.* Contra Cels. iii. 28, Opp. i. p. 465 (in connection with what is cited § 68, note 1), according to whom, every one who *lives* in compliance with the precepts of Christ obtains through Him friendship with God, and has living communion with Him.

(2) The very circumstance that, in the belief of the primitive Church, sins committed *after* baptism are less easily pardoned (*Clem.* Strom. iv. 24, p. 634, *Sylb.* 536 C), and the entire ecclesiastical discipline of the first ages, prove this. —As regards μετάνοια, *Clement* knows the distinction afterwards made between contritio and attritio, Strom. iv. 6, p. 580 : Τοῦ μετανοοῦντος δὲ τρόποι δύο· ὁ μὲν κοινότερος, φόβος ἐπὶ τοῖς πραχθεῖσιν, ὁ δὲ ἰδιαίτερος, ἡ δυσωπία ἡ πρὸς ἑαυτὴν τῆς ψυχῆς ἐκ συνειδήσεως.—On μετάνοια, comp. also Pæd. i. 9, p. 146, and Quis Div. Salv. 40, p. 957.

(3) *Hermas*, Pastor, iii. 7 : Oportet eum, qui agit pœnitentiam, affligere animam suam, et humilem animo se præstare in omni negotio, et vexationes multas variasque perferre. *Justin M.* also lays great stress upon the external manifestation of

repentance by tears, etc., Dial. c. Tryph. § 141. *Tertullian* has left us a book (De pœnitentia) which contains the elements of the later ecclesiastical theory of penance. Already he attributes great value to *confessio* and *satisfactio*. Cap. 8 : Confessio satisfactionis consilium est, dissimulatio contumaciæ. Cap. 9 : Quatenus satisfactio confessione disponitur, confessione pœnitentia nascitur, pœnitentia Deus mitigatur. Itaque exomologesis prosternendi et humilificandi hominis disciplina est, conversationem injungens misericordiæ illicem, de ipso quoque habitu atque victu mandat, sæco et cineri incubare, corpus sordibus obscurare, animum mœroribus dejicere . . . pastum et potum pura nosse, jejuniis preces alere, ingemiscere, lacrymari et mugire dies noctesque ad Dominum Deum suum . . . Cap. 10 : In quantum non peperceris tibi, in tantum tibi Deus, crede, parcet. Similarly *Cyprian*, De Opere et Eleem. p. 167 (*Bal.* 237); Loquitur in scripturis divinis Spir. S. et dicit (Prov. xv. 29): Eleemosynis et fide delicta purgantur ; non utique illa delicta, quæ fuerunt ante contracta, nam illa Christi sanguine et sanctificatione purgantur. Item denuo dicit (Eccles. iii. 33): Sicut aqua extinguit ignem, sic eleemosyna extinguit peccatum. Hic quoque ostenditur et probatur, quia sicut lavacro aquæ salutaris gehennæ ignis extinguitur, ita eleemosynis atque operationibus justis delictorum flamma sopitur. Et quia semel in baptismo remissio peccatorum datur, assidua et jugis operatio baptismi instar imitata Dei rursus indulgentiam largitur (with a further appeal to Luke xi. 41). Tears are of much avail, Ep. 31, p. 64, *Rettb.* s. 323, 389. *Origen*, Hom. in Lev. ii. 4, Opp. ii. p. 190, 191, enumerates seven remissiones peccatorum : (1) that which is granted in baptism ; (2) that which is obtained by martyrdom ; (3) by alms (Luke xi. 41); (4) by the forgiveness which we grant to those who have trespassed against us (Matt. vi. 14) ; (5) by the conversion of others (Jas. v. 20) ; (6) by exceeding great love (Luke vii. 47 ; 1 Pet. iv. 8); (7) by penance and repentance : Est adhuc et septima, licet dura et laboriosa, per pœnitentiam remissio peccatorum, cum lavat peccator in lacrymis stratum suum, et fiunt ei lacrymæ suæ panes die ac nocte, et cum non erubescit sacerdoti Domini indicare peccatum suum et quærere medicinam. On the merit of the martyrs, comp. § 68. The intercession of con-

§ 70.]   THE ECONOMY OF REDEMPTION.   267

fessors yet living is opposed by *Tertull.* De Pud. 22. *Cyprian* also limits their influence to the day of judgment, De Lapsis, p. 129 (187).—Concerning *a first* and *second penance,* see *Hermæ* Pastor, Mand. iv. 3 ; *Clem.* Strom. ii. 13, p. 459: Καὶ οὐκ οἶδ' ὁπότερον αὐτοῖν χεῖρον ἢ τὸ εἰδότα ἁμαρτάνειν ἢ μετανοήσαντα ἐφ' οἷς ἥμαρτεν πλημμελεῖν αὖθις. The different views of *Tertullian before* and *after* his conversion to Montanism may be seen by comparing De Pœnit. 7 with De Pud. 18. On the controversy between Cyprian and the Novatians, see the works on ecclesiastical history.

(4) Even in the Epistle of *Polycarp* the giving of alms is praised as a work that saves from death (appealing to Tob. xii. 9); and a tendency towards the doctrine of works of supererogation (opera supererogatoria) is found in the Shepherd of *Hermas,* Simil. Lib. iii. 5, 3 : Si præter ea quæ non mandavit Dominus aliquod boni adjeceris, majorem dignitatem tibi conquires et honoratior apud Dominum eris, quam eras futurus. *Origen* speaks in a similar manner, Ep. ad Rom. Lib. iii. Opp. t. iv. p. 507 (he makes a subtle distinction between the *unprofitable* servant, Luke xvii. 10, and the *good* and *faithful* servant, Matt. xxv. 21, and appeals to 1 Cor. vii. 25 concerning the command to the virgins).

(5) During this period, in which theoretical knowledge was made prominent, *faith* was for the most part considered as historico-dogmatic faith in its relation to γνῶσις (comp. § 34). Hence the opinion that *knowledge* in divine things may contribute to justification,[1] while ignorance condemns. *Minucius Fel.* 35 : Imperitia Dei sufficit ad pœnam, notitia prodest ad veniam. *Theophilus* of Antioch also distinctly recognizes only a fides historica, upon which he makes salvation to depend, i. 14 : Ἀπόδειξιν οὖν λαβὼν τῶν γινομένων καὶ προαναπεφωνημένων, οὐκ ἀπιστῶ, ἀλλὰ πιστεύω πειθαρχῶν θεῷ, ᾧ εἰ βούλει, καὶ σὺ ὑποτάγηθι, πιστεύων αὐτῷ, μὴ νῦν ἀπιστήσας, πεισθῇς ἀνιώμενος τότε ἐν αἰωνίοις τιμωρίαις. But though it was reserved for later times to investigate more profoundly the idea of justifying faith in the

[1] As the Gnostics carried out the theory of salvation by knowledge to its full extent, and looked down with contempt alike on the faith and works of the Catholic Christians; so the Clementines depreciated faith for the benefit of works. See *Baur,* Dg. s. 657.

Pauline sense, yet correct views on this subject were not entirely wanting during this period, comp. *Clem. Rom.* Ep. i. ad Cor. 32 and 33: Ἡμεῖς οὖν διὰ θελήματος αὐτοῦ [sc. θεοῦ] ἐν Χριστῷ Ἰησοῦ κληθέντες οὐ δι' ἑαυτῶν δικαιούμεθα, οὐδὲ διὰ τῆς ἡμετέρας σοφίας ἢ συνέσεως ἢ εὐσεβείας ἢ ἔργων, ὧν κατειργασάμεθα ἐν ὁσιότητι καρδίας· ἀλλὰ διὰ τῆς πίστεως, δι' ἧς πάντας τοῦ ἀπ' αἰῶνος ὁ παντοκράτωρ θεὸς ἐδικαίωσεν. Comp. 37–39. *Irenæus*, too (iv. 13, 2 sq.), distinguishes clearly between the righteousness of the law, and the new obedience which comes from faith; *Neander*, Dg. s. 228. *Baur*, Dg. s. 659. Grace, he says, is the dew of heaven which falls upon the withered field to fertilize it (Adv. Hær. iii. 17). *Tertull.* Adv. Marc. v. 3: Ex fidei libertate justificatur homo, non ex legis servitute, quia justus ex fide vivit.[1] According to *Clement* of Alexandria, *faith* is not only the key of knowledge (Coh. p. 9), but by it we are also made the children of God, ib. p. 23 (comp. § 68, note 1), and p. 69. Clement accurately distinguishes between theoretical and practical unbelief, and understands by the latter the want of susceptibility to divine impressions, a carnal mind which would have everything in a tangible shape, Strom. ii. 4, p. 436. *Origen* in Num. Hom. xxvi. (Opp. iii. p. 369): Impossibile est salvari sine fide. Comm. in Ep. ad Rom. Opp. iv. p. 517: Etiamsi opera quis habeat ex lege, tamen, quia non sunt ædificata supra fundamentum fidei, quamvis videantur esse bona, tamen operatorem suum justificare non possunt, quod eis deest fides, quæ est signaculum eorum, qui justificantur a Deo.

(6) *Clement*, Coh. p. 90: Ὦ τῆς ἁγίας καὶ μακαρίας ταύτης δυνάμεως, δι' ἧς ἀνθρώποις συμπολιτεύεται θεός κ.τ.λ. Quis Div. salv. p. 951: Ὅσον γὰρ ἀγαπᾷ τις τὸν θεόν, τοσούτῳ καὶ πλέον ἐνδοτέρω τοῦ θεοῦ παραδύεται. Ideal quietism, Pæd. i. 13, p. 160: Τέλος δέ ἐστι θεοσεβείας ἡ ἀΐδιος ἀνάπαυσις ἐν τῷ θεῷ. Comp. iii. 7, p. 277, 278 (in reference to riches in God), Strom. ii. 16, p. 467, 468, iv. 22, p. 627, 630.

(7) *Tert.* Ad Uxor. i. 8: Quædam sunt divinæ liberalitatis, quædam nostræ operationis. Quæ a Domino indulgentur, sua gratia gubernantur; quæ ab homine captantur, studio perpetrantur. Cf. De Virg. Vel. 10; De Patient. 1, Adv.

[1] It was natural, too, that *Marcion* should insist upon the Pauline view, in opposition to the Jewish dependence on works; see *Neander*, Dg. s. 229.

§ 70.] THE ECONOMY OF REDEMPTION. 269

Hermog. 5. *Justin M.* and *Clement* of Alexandria are favourable to synergism. Comp. *Just.* Apol. i. 10, Dial. c. Tryph. § 32. *Clem. Alex.* Coh. i. 99. Strom. v. 13, p. 696, vii. 7, p. 860: Ὡς δὲ ὁ ἰατρὸς ὑγείαν παρέχεται τοῖς συνεργοῦσι πρὸς ὑγείαν, οὕτως καὶ ὁ θεὸς τὴν ἀΐδιον σωτηρίαν τοῖς συνεργοῦσι πρὸς γνῶσίν τε καὶ εὐπραγίαν. Quis Div. salv. p. 947: Βουλομέναις μὲν γὰρ ὁ θεὸς ταῖς ψυχαῖς συνεπιπνεῖ. So, too, *Orig.* Hom. in Ps. (Opp. t. ii. p. 571): Τὸ τοῦ λογικοῦ ἀγαθὸν μικτόν ἐστιν ἔκ τε τῆς προαιρέσεως αὐτοῦ καὶ τῆς συμπνεούσης θείας δυνάμεως τῷ τὰ κάλλιστα προελομένῳ; comp. De Princip. iii. 1, p. 18 (Opp. i. p. 129), and 22, p. 137 (on Rom. ix. 16, and the apparent contradiction between 2 Tim. ii. 20, 21, and Rom. ix. 21). *Cyprian*, De Gratia Dei ad Donat. p. 3, 4: Ceterum si tu innocentiæ, si justitiæ viam teneas, si illapsa firmitate vestigii tui incedas, si in Deum viribus totis ac toto corde suspensus, hoc sis tantum quod esse cœpisti, tantum tibi ad licentiam datur, quantum gratiæ spiritalis augetur. Non enim, qui beneficiorum terrestrium mos est, in capessendo munere cœlesti mensura ulla vel modus est: profluens largiter spiritus nullis finibus premitur, nec coërcentibus claustris intra certa metarum spatia frænatur, manat jugiter, exuberat affluenter. Nostrum tantum sitiat pectus et pateat; quantum illuc fidei capacis afferimus, tantum gratiæ inundantis haurimus. De Orat. dom. p. 144 (208); Adv. Jud. iii. 25 ss., p. 72, 42 ss., p. 77 ss.

(8) *Hermas* represents the predestination of God as dependent on His *foreknowledge*, Lib. iii. Simil. 8, 6, likewise *Justin M.* Dial. c. Tryph. § 141. *Iren.* iv. 29, 2, p. 267. *Minuc. Fel.* c. 36. *Tert.* Adv. Marc. ii. 23. *Clem. Al.* Pæd. i. 6, p. 114: Οἶδεν οὖν (ὁ θεὸς) οὓς κέκληκεν, οὓς σέσωκεν. According to Strom. vi. 6, p. 763, it is men's own fault if they are not elected. They resemble those who voluntarily jump out of the vessel into the sea. *"Thus the practical sense of Cyprian rebelled against the doctrine of rigid predestination, of irresistible grace; he could not so boldly face all the consequences which are found in the stupendous fabric of Augustine's system."—" That the Bishop of Hippo still thought that he discovered his own orthodoxy in the writings of Cyprian, may perhaps be ascribed to his joy at finding in him the premises for his own conclusions,"* Rettberg, s. 321.

(9) *Origen* is far from believing in the doctrine of reprobation. De Princip. iii. 1 (Opp. i. p. 115; *Redep.* p. 20), he calls those heterodox who adduce the passage relative to the hardening of Pharaoh's heart, and other passages of the Old Testament of similar import in opposition to the αὐτεξούσιον of the human soul. He explains God's dealings with Pharaoh from physical analogies: the rain falls upon different kinds of soil, and causes different plants to grow; the sun both melts wax and hardens clay. Even in common life it sometimes happens that a good master says to his lazy servant, spoiled by indulgence: I have spoiled you, not meaning that such was his intention. *Origen* (as *Schleiermacher* in later times) sees in what is called *reprobatio*, only a longer delay of the grace of God. As a physician often employs those remedies which at first apparently produce bad effects, but heal the disease (homœopathically?) radically, instead of using such as effect a speedy cure, so God acts in His long-suffering; He prepares souls not only for the span of this short life, but for eternity, ibid. p. 121. (*Redep.* p. 26.) He adduces a similar illustration from the husbandman (after Matt. xiii. 8), and then goes on, p. 123: Ἄπειροι γὰρ ἡμῖν, ὡς ἂν εἴποι τις, αἱ ψυχαὶ, καὶ ἄπειρα τὰ τούτων ἤθη καὶ πλεῖστα ὅσα τὰ κινήματα καὶ αἱ προθέσεις καὶ αἱ ἐπιβολαὶ καὶ αἱ ὁρμαὶ, ὧν εἷς μόνος οἰκονόμος ἄριστος, καὶ τοὺς καιροὺς ἐπιστάμενος, καὶ τὰ ἁρμόζοντα βοηθήματα καὶ τὰς ἀγωγὰς καὶ τὰς ὁδοὺς, ὁ τῶν ὅλων θεὸς καὶ πατήρ. See ibid. the interpretation of Ezek. xi. 19, and other passages. On the connection between *Origen's* doctrine of predestination and his doctrine of the preexistence of the soul, comp. De Princip. ii. 9, 7 (Opp. i. p. 99; *Redep.* p. 220), in reference to Jacob and Esau. *Origen* also held, like the other Fathers prior to the time of Augustine, that predestination was dependent on foreknowledge, Philoc. c. 25, on Rom. viii. 28, 29 (quoted by *Münscher, Von Cölln,* i. s. 369). "*All the Fathers of this period agree that God so far predestines men to blessedness or condemnation as He foresees their free acts, by which they are made worthy of reward or punishment; but the foreseeing of these acts is not the cause of them, but the acts are the cause of the foreknowledge.*" *Gieseler,* Dg. s. 212. Cf. also *Baur,* Dg. s. 663.

FIFTH DIVISION.

THE CHURCH AND ITS MEANS OF GRACE.

§ 71.

The Church.

H. Th. C. Henke, Historia antiquior Dogmatis de Unitate Ecclesiæ, Helmst. 1781. †Möhler, die Einheit der Kirche, Tüb. 1825. *Rich. Rothe, die Entwicklung des Begriffs der Kirche in ihrem ersten Stadium. (The third book of his work: die Anfänge der christlichen Kirche und ihrer Verfassung, Wittenb. 1837, 1 vol.) Gess, die Einheit der Kirche im Sinne Cyprians (in Studien der evangelischen Geistlichkeit Würtembergs, Stuttgart 1831, ii. 1, p. 147). Huther, Cyprian, comp. § 26, note 9. Schenkel, see § 30. In reference to Rothe's work: A. Petersen, die Idee der christlichen Kirche, Leipz. 1839-44, 3 vols. Jul. Müller, Die unsichtbare Kirche (in the Deutsche Zeitschrift f. chr. Wiss. 1850, No. 2). J. Köstlin, Die katholische Auffassung von d. Kirche (ibid. 1855, Nos. 33 ff., 46 ff., 1856, No. 12). Münchmeier, von der sichtbaren und unsichtbaren Kirche, Götting. 1854. [F. C. Baur, Ueber den Episcopat. W. Palmer, Treatise on the Church. Th. Kliefoth, Acht Bücher von d. Kirche, 1854 sq. Hauber in Herzog's Realencyclop. Bd. vii. Ritschl, Die Begriffe sichtbare und unsichtbare Kirche, in Stud. u. Krit. 1859, reviewing Münchmeier. J. H. Friedlieb, Schrift, Tradition, etc., Breslau 1854. Thos. Greenwood, Cathedra Petri, 4 vols. Lond. 1856-60. Bishop Kaye, Government and Discipline of the Church in the First Three Centuries, Lond. 1855. F. C. Baur, Das Christenthum d. drei ersten Jahrh. 1853, s. 239 ff.]

A holy Catholic Christian Church, which is the communion of saints, was the expression used in the Christian confession of faith to denote the feeling of Christian fellowship which prevailed in the primitive Church, though no exact definitions concerning the nature of the Church are found before the time of *Cyprian* (1). Among the many images under which the Church was represented, none was so frequently employed as that of a mother, or of Noah's ark. The Fathers uniformly asserted, both in opposition to heretics and to all who were not Christians, that there is no salvation out of the Church,[1] but that all the fulness of divine grace is to be found in it (2). *Clement* of Alexandria, too, and *Cyprian*, yet more emphatically and in a realistic sense, gave prominence to the unity of the Church (3). The definitions of the latter make an epoch in the history of this doctrine. But he did not sufficiently distinguish between the historico-empirical, visible existence of the Church (its corporeal embodiment), and the idea of a Church which is above the change of mere forms, and which is ever struggling for a complete expression of its essence. This is shown in the Novatian controversy. Thus it happened that the apostolic Christian doctrine of a universal priesthood was more and more superseded by the hierarchial aspirations of the bishops, and the internal was converted into the external (4). The false idealism of the Gnostics, and the subjective, heretical, and schismatical tendencies of separate sects, especially of the Montanists and the Novatianist Puritans, form a striking contrast with this false external unity of the Catholic Church (5).

(1) "*The general character of the earlier period (previous to the time of Cyprian) is that of abstract indefiniteness. What the theologians of this period say concerning the nature of the Church is so frequently void of clearness and precision, that it is almost impossible fully to ascertain their real sentiments on this point; it is not uncommon to see the same Fathers evading, or even rejecting, consequences which necessarily follow from their general reasonings. They thus evince a fickleness* (?) *which prevents us from forming any decided and certain opinion as to their ideas of the nature of the Church*," *Rothe*, l.c. s. 575.

(2) On the term ἐκκλησία in general (corresponding to the Hebrew קְהַל יְהֹוָה, עֲדַת, מִקְרָא), Matt. xvi. 18, xviii. 17; 1 Cor. x. 32; Eph. i. 22; Col. i. 18, 24; comp. *Suicer*, Thes. sub voce; *Rothe*, s. 74 ff.; and the anonymous work, Zukunft d. evang. Kirche (Leipz. 1849), s. 42: "*The solemn and em-*

[1] This strongly defined Church feeling is very marked in the writings of *Irenæus*.

§ 71.] THE CHURCH. 273

phatic meaning of the words, call, calling, called (καλεῖν, κλῆσις, κλητοί), *which sound out to us from all parts of the writings of the New Testament, may have essentially contributed in lending to the word* ecclesia, *formed from the same root, its significance, as designating the whole company of the elect, the called.*" The phrase ἐκκλησία καθολική first occurs in the inscription of the Ep. Smyrn. de mart. Polycarpi about the year 169 (Eus. iv. 15). Comp. *Ign.* ad Smyrn. 8: "Ὥσπερ ὅπου ἂν ᾖ Χριστὸς Ἰησοῦς, ἐκεῖ ἡ καθολικὴ ἐκκλησία. How great an importance the Fathers were accustomed to attribute to the Church may be seen from *Irenæus,* Adv. Hær. iii. 4, 1, and iii. 24 (40). In the *Church* alone all the treasures of truth are deposited; out of her are thieves and robbers, pools with foul water: Ubi enim ecclesia, ibi et spiritus Dei, ubi spiritus Dei, illic ecclesia et omnis gratia (comp. *Huther,* l.c. s. 4, 5), iv. 31, 3, where the pillar of salt into which the wife of Lot was transformed, represents the imperishableness of the Church; and other passages (comp. § 34, notes 1 and 2). *Clement* of Alexandria derives the term and the idea of ἐκκλησία from the elect forming a society, Coh. p. 69, and Pæd. i. 6, p. 114: Ὡς γὰρ τὸ θέλημα αὐτοῦ ἔργον ἐστὶ καὶ τοῦτο Κόσμος ὀνομάζεται· οὕτως καὶ τὸ βούλημα αὐτοῦ ἀνθρώπων ἐστὶ σωτηρία, καὶ τοῦτο Ἐκκλησία κέκληται· οἶδεν οὖν οὓς κέκληκεν, οὓς σέσωκεν. Comp. Strom. vii. 5, p. 846: Οὐ γὰρ νῦν τὸν τόπον, ἀλλὰ τὸ ἄθροισμα τῶν ἐκλεκτῶν Ἐκκλησίαν καλῶ κ.τ.λ. *Clement* describes the Church as a mother, Pæd. i. 5, p. 110; and as both a mother and a virgin, c. 6, p. 123; in speaking of this subject in other places he indulges in allegories, p. 111 ss. The Church is the *body* of the Lord, Strom. vii. 14, p. 885; comp. p. 899, 900 (*Sylb.* 765). Though *Clement* asserts that only the *true* Gnostics (οἱ ἐν τῇ ἐπιστήμῃ) form the Church, yet he does not so much contrast with them those who have only *faith,* as the heretics who have only *opinions* (οἴησις), and the heathen who live in total ignorance (ἄγνοια), Strom. vii. 16, p. 894 (*Sylb.* 760). *Origen* also, though, generally speaking, he judges mildly of heretical or sectarian opinions (Contra Cels. iii. § 10–13), knows of no salvation out of the Church, Hom. iii. in Josuam (Opp. ii. p. 404): Nemo semetipsum decipiat, extra hanc domum, *i.e.* extra ecclesiam, nemo salvatur, and Selecta in Iob. ibid. iii. p. 501, 502. Yet with him everything turns upon a living union with Christ: *Christus est lux vera* . . . ex cujus lumine illuminata ecclesia etiam ipsa lux mundi efficitur, illuminans eos qui in tenebris sunt: sicut et ipse Christus contestatur discipulis suis, dicens: Vos estis lux mundi; ex quo ostenditur, quia Christus quidem lux est Apostolorum, Apostoli vero lux mundi. *Ipsi enim sunt non habentes maculam vel rugam aut aliquid hujuscemodi vera ecclesia* (Hom. i. in Gen. Opp. i. p. 54). Consequently, a distinction between the true and the false Church! As to the views of *Tertullian*, we must make a distinction between those which he held previously, and those which he entertained subsequently to his conversion to Montanism. Comp. *Neander*, Antign. s. 264 ff. The principal passages relative to his early opinions are: De Præscript. c. 21 ss., 32, 35; De Bapt. c. 8; De Orat. c. 2, where the above figures of the ark of Noah, and the mother, are carried out at length (see *Münscher, von Cölln*, i. s. 70). So, too, *Cyprian*, Ep. 4, p. 9: Neque enim vivere foris possunt, cum domus Dei una sit, et nemini salus esse, nisi in ecclesia possit. He, too, adduces a profusion of similar images. Comp. note 3.

" *The common opinion, that the proposition :* quod extra ecclesiam nulla salus, *or :* de ecclesia, extra quam nemo potest esse salvus, *was for the first time laid down by Augustine, in the fourth century, in the Donatist controversy, is incorrect. It was only the necessary consequence and application of earlier principles, and was distinctly implied in the form which the doctrine of the Church had assumed since the time of Irenæus. Hence we find in the writings of the latter many allusions to it, though he does not make use of this formula of terror.*" *Marheineke* (in Daub und Creuzers Studien, iii. s. 187).

(3) On the *unity* of the Church, see *Clem. Al.* Pæd. i. 4, p. 103, c. 6, p. 123 : 'Ω θαύματος μυστικοῦ· εἷς μὲν ὁ τῶν ὅλων πατήρ· εἷς δὲ καὶ ὁ τῶν ὅλων λόγος· καὶ τὸ πνεῦμα τὸ ἅγιον ἓν καὶ τὸ αὐτὸ πανταχοῦ· μία δὲ μόνη γίνεται μήτηρ παρθένος κ.τ.λ. Strom. i. 18, p. 375, vii. 6, p. 848, and other passages. Concerning the opinion of *Tertull.*, comp. the passages before cited. *Cyprian* wrote a separate work on the doctrine of the *unity* of the Church about the year 251 : De Unitate Ecclesiæ, with which, however, several of his extant letters (see note 4) should be compared. He adds some new images to those used by Tertullian, as illustrative of this unity : the sun which

breaks into many rays; the tree with its many branches, and the *one* power in the tough root; the *one* source which gives rise to many brooks: Avelle radium solis a corpore, divisionem lucis unitas non capit: ab arbore frange ramum, fractus germinare non poterit; a fonte præcide rivum, præcisus arescet. Sic ecclesia Domini luce perfusa per orbem totum radios suos porrigit, etc. He also carries out at great length the image of the *one* mother: Illius fœtu nascimur, illius lacte nutrimur, spiritu ejus animamur. He who has not the Church for his mother, has no longer God for his father (De Unit. Eccles. 5, 6). After the analogy of the Old Test., faithlessness toward the Church is compared to adultery. The Trinity itself is an image of the unity of the Church (comp. Clement, l.c.); also the coat of Christ which could not be rent; the passover which must be eaten in *one* house; the *one* dove in Solomon's Song; the house of Rahab which was *alone* preserved, etc. With peculiar harshness, but quite in consistency with such notions, he maintains that martyrdom out of the Church, so far from being meritorious, is rather an aggravation of sin: Esse martyr non potest, qui in ecclesia non est.... Occidi talis potest, coronari non potest, etc. Comp. *Rettb.* s. 241 ff., 355 ff., 367 ff.; *Huther,* s. 52–59. [Comp. the passages quoted by *Münscher,* l.c. s. 70 ff.]

(4) If the genuineness of the epistles of *Ignatius* (even of the shorter recension) were fully established, they would prove beyond all dispute that submission to the bishops was considered as a *doctrine* of the Church at a very early period. Comp. Ep. ad Smyrn. c. 8 : Πάντες τῷ ἐπισκόπῳ ἀκολουθεῖτε, ὡς Ἰησοῦς Χριστὸς τῷ πατρί, etc., ad Polyc. c. 6 : Τῷ ἐπισκόπῳ προσέχετε, ἵνα καὶ ὁ θεὸς ὑμῖν; ad Eph. c. 4 : Πρέπει ὑμῖν συντρέχειν τῇ τοῦ ἐπισκόπου γνώμῃ, ὅπερ καὶ ποιεῖτε. Τὸ γὰρ ἀξιονόμαστον ὑμῶν πρεσβυτέριον, τοῦ θεοῦ ἄξιον, οὕτως συνήρμοσται τῷ ἐπισκόπῳ, ὡς χορδαὶ κιθάρᾳ; ad Magn. c. 6 ; ad Philad. c. 7; ad Trall. c. 2 : Ἀναγκαῖον οὖν ἔστιν . . . ἄνευ τοῦ ἐπισκόπου μηδὲν πράσσειν ὑμᾶς, ἀλλ' ὑποτάσσασθε καὶ τῷ πρεσβυτερίῳ. Comp. *Rothe,* s. 445 ff., and Bunsen, s. 93. *Iren.* iii. 14, iv. 26 (43), v. 20. On the succession of the bishops: iii. 3 (primacy (?) of the Roman Church); comp. with it, *Neander,* Kg. i. 3, s. 318, Anm. [*Gieseler,* i. 150, note 10; †*Kuhn* in Theol. Quartalschrift,

276 FIRST PERIOD.—THE CHURCH, ITS MEANS OF GRACE. [§ 71.

1858, s. 205.] Though *Tertullian* at first appeared willing (De Præscr. c. 32) to concede to the Church of Rome the precedence over other Churches, yet, after his conversion to Montanism, he combated the pretensions of the Roman bishops, De Pud. 21; he there alludes particularly to the words of Christ addressed to Peter: dabo tibi claves ecclesiæ —and maintains that the word *tibi* refers to Peter alone, and not to the bishops. He supposed that the spiritually-minded (πνευματικοί) were the successors of Peter, and distinguished between the ecclesia spiritus per spiritales homines (in which the Trinity dwells), and *that* ecclesia which is composed of the sum total of the bishops (numerus episcoporum). On this ground (but not in the purely apostolic sense) he defended the idea of a spiritual priesthood. *Neander,* Antignostikus, s. 258, 259, and s. 272. On the contrary, *Cyprian* conceives that the true priestly dignity is expressed in the *episcopal* power itself (not indeed in that of the Roman bishops exclusively, but in that of all the bishops collectively, which he views in its solidarity, as if it were one man), and thinks that the unity of the Church is represented by the successors of the apostles; so that he who is not with the bishops, is not with the Church. Comp. especially the following epistles: 45, 52, 55, 64, 66, 67, 69, 74, 76 (c. 2), see *Huther,* s. 59 ff. *Rettberg,* s. 367 ff. *Gess,* s. 150 ff. *Neander,* Kg. i. 1, s. 404– 407. Here, however, the Alexandrian school takes a different and contrasted view. According to *Origen* (Comment. in Matt. xii. 10), all true believers are also πέτροι, of whom holds good the word spoken to Peter. Comp. De Orat. c. 28, and *Neander,* Dg. s. 227.

(5) Wherever the term ἐκκλησία occurs in the Clementine Homilies (Hom. iii. 60, 65, 67, p. 653 ss., vii. 8, p. 680; *Credner,* iii. s. 308; *Baur,* s. 373), it is to be understood in a limited sense. They do not rise to the idea of a *Catholic* Church, although they indicate the tendency to a strict, hierarchical Church constitution; comp. *Schliemann,* u. s., s. 4, 247 ff. Concerning the Ebionites, *Epiphanius* observes, Hær. 30, 18, p. 142: Συναγωγὴν δὲ οὗτοι καλοῦσι τὴν ἑαυτῶν ἐκκλησίαν καὶ οὐχὶ ἐκκλησίαν. Comp. *Credner,* ii. s. 236. If in the Ebionitic tendency the idea of a Church shrivelled up into that of a Jewish synagogue sect, among the Gnostics

it was dissipated into an idealistic world of æons (*Baur*, s. 172); there a body without a soul, here a phantom without a body. For the views of the Montanists concerning the Church (vera, pudica, sancta, virgo: *Tertull. De Pudic.* 1), which, as a spiritual Church, is composed of homines pneumatici, see *Schwegler*, Montanismus, s. 47 ff., 229 ff. The Montanists made no more distinction between the *visible* and *invisible* Church than did the Catholic Church; but they prepared the way for it. See *Schwegler*, s. 232.

§ 72.

Baptism.

G. J. Voss, De Baptismo, disputt. xx. Opp., Amstel. 1701, fol. t. vi. *C. St. Matthies*, Baptismatis Expositio biblica, historica, dogmatica, Berol. 1831. *J. G. Walch*, Historia Pædo-baptismi 4 priorum sæcul., Jen. 1739, 4to. (Misc. Sacr., Amstel. 1744, 4to.) [*Robinson*, The History of Baptism, Lond. 1790. *R. Halley*, The Sacraments. P. I. Baptism, Lond. 1844.] *J. W. F. Höfling*, Das Sacrament der Taufe, nebst andern damit zusammenhangenden Acten der Initiation, 2 Bde. Erl. 1846. [*Edward Beecher*, Baptism with reference to its Import and Modes, New York 1849. *Bunsen's* Hippolytus, vol. iii. *W. Wall*, Hist. of Infant Baptism, 2 vols. 1705, 4 vols. 1845. *E. B. Pusey* in Tracts for the Times, No. 67. Chronological Catena on Baptism, Lond. 1852. *W. Goode*, Effects of Infant Baptism, 1851. *R. J. Wilberforce*, Doctrine of Holy Baptism, 1851. *J. B. Mozley*, Primitive Doctrine of Baptismal Regeneration, Lond. 1856. *J. Gibson*, Testimony of Script. and Fathers of First Five Centuries to Nature and Effects of Baptism, Lond. 1854; cf. also *Hooker*, Eccl. Polity, Bk. v.]

The doctrine of baptism stands in intimate connection with the doctrine of the Church. From the founding of Christianity great efficacy was attached to baptism in relation to the forgiveness of sins and to regeneration (1). Some of the Fathers, especially *Irenæus, Tertullian*, and *Cyprian*, in treating of this subject, as well as of the doctrine of the Church, often indulged in exaggerated, fanciful, and absurd allegories and symbolisms (2), while *Origen* draws a more distinct line between the external sign and the thing signified (3). Infant baptism was not universal until the time of *Tertullian;* and this Father, though a strenuous advocate of the doctrine of original sin, nevertheless opposed pædo-baptism, on the ground that an innocent age needs no cleansing from sins (4). *Origen*, on the contrary, is in favour of infant baptism (5). In the time of *Cyprian* it became more general in the African Church, so that the African bishop *Fidus* appealed to the analogy of circumcision under the Old Testament dispensation, and proposed to delay the performance of the ceremony of baptism to the eighth day, which, however, Cyprian did not allow (6). The baptism of newly converted persons was still frequently deferred till the approach of death (Baptismus Clinicorum) (7). During this period a question arose, intimately connected with the doctrine of the nature of the Church, viz. whether the baptism of heretics was to be accounted valid, or whether a heretic who returned to the Catholic Church was to be rebaptized? In opposition to the usage of the Eastern and African Churches, which was defended by *Cyprian*, the principle was established in the Roman Church under *Stephen*, that the rite of baptism, if duly performed, was always valid, and its repetition contrary to the ecclesiastical (that is, the Roman) tradition (8). Baptism was entirely rejected by some Gnostic sects, while it was held in high esteem by the Marcionites and Valentinians. But the mode of baptism which they adopted was altogether different from that of the Catholic Church, and founded upon quite another principle (9). The idea of a *baptism of blood* originated with martyrdom, and found a response in the sympathies of the age (10).

(1) Concerning the baptism of Christ and of the apostles, comp. the works on Biblical Theology; and in reference to the mode of baptism (immersion, formula, etc.), see the works on Archæology (*Augusti*, vol. vii.), [*Martigny*, Antiquités Chrétiennes, Paris 1865. *Smith's* Dictionary of Christian Antiq.]. As to the words used at baptism, baptism in the name of Christ alone seems to be more ancient than in the name of the three persons of the Trinity; comp. *Höfling*, s. 35 ff. [*Hefele*, Hist. of Councils, i. p. 98 ff., Eng. transl.] On the terms: βάπτισμα, βαπτισμός, λοῦτρον, φωτισμός, σφραγίς,

§ 72.]   BAPTISM.   279

and others, comp. the Lexicons. Respecting baptism as it was practised before the coming of Christ, see *Schneckenburger*, über das Alter der jüdischen Proselytentaufe und deren Zusammenhang mit dem johanneischen und christlichen Ritus, Berlin 1828, where the literature is given. Like the apostles, the first teachers of the Church regard baptism not as a mere ritual act, but as having its objective results. *" Baptism was to them not merely a significant symbol, representing to the senses the internal consecration and renewal of the soul, but an efficacious medium for conveying objectively to believers the blessings of the gospel, and especially the benefits of the sacrificial death of Christ."* Semisch, Justin d. Mart. ii. s. 426.

(2) On the magical influence which the Clementine Homilies ascribe to water, in connection with the notions widely spread in the East, comp. *e.g.* Hom. ix. and x.; see *Baur*, Gnos. s. 372. *Credner*, l.c. ii. s. 236, and iii. s. 303. Concerning the Ebionites, it is said by *Epiph.* Indicul. ii. p. 53: Τὸ ὕδωρ ἀντὶ θεοῦ ἔχουσι, comp. Hær. 30. Together with the symbolism of the cross, we find in the writings of the apostolical Fathers a symbolical interpretation of water: *Barn.* 11. *Hermas*, Pastor, Vis. iii. 3; Mand. iv. 3; Simil. ix. 6. *Justin M.* (Apol. i. 61) contrasts regeneration by the baptismal water with natural birth ἐξ ὑγρᾶς σπορᾶς. By the latter we are τέκνα ἀνάγκης, ἀγνοίας; by the former τέκνα προαιρέσεως καὶ ἐπιστήμης, ἀφέσεώς τε ἁμαρτιῶν; hence the λοῦτρον is also called φωτισμός. Comp. Dial. c. Tryph. c. 13 and 14, where the contrast between baptism and Jewish lustrations is urged. *Theoph.* Ad Aut. ii. 16, applies the blessings God pronounced on the fifth day of the work of creation upon the creatures which the waters brought forth, to the water used in baptism. *Clem.* of Alex. (Pæd. i. 6, p. 113) connects the baptism of Christians with the baptism of Jesus. He became τέλειος only by it. And so it is with us: Βαπτιζόμενοι φωτιζόμεθα, φωτιζόμενοι υἱοποιούμεθα, υἱοποιούμενοι τελειούμεθα, τελειούμενοι ἀπαθανατιζόμεθα. Baptism is a χάρισμα. Comp. also p. 116, 117, where the baptized, in allusion to the cleansing power of water, are called διυλιζόμενοι (filtered). On account of the union between the element and the Logos, or His power and spirit, he also calls baptism ὕδωρ λογικόν; Coh. p. 79. All former

lustrations are abolished by baptism, being all included in it, Strom. iii. 12, p. 548, 549. *Iren.* iii. 17 (19), p. 208 (224). As dough cannot be made of dry flour without the addition of some fluid, so we, the many, cannot be united in one body in Christ without the cement of water which comes down from heaven; and as the earth is quickened and rendered fruitful by dew and rain, so Christianity by the heavenly water, etc. *Tertullian* wrote a separate treatise on this subject, entitled De Baptismo. Though he rejects the notion of a merely magical and mechanical blotting out of sins by baptism, and makes the efficacy of baptism dependent on repentance (De Pœnitentia, c. 6), yet he takes occasion, from the cosmical and physical significance of water, to adduce numerous analogies. Water (felix sacramentum aquæ nostræ, qua abluti delictis pristinæ cæcitatis in vitam æternam liberamur!) is in his view the element in which Christians alone feel at home, as the small fishes which follow the great fish (ΙΧΘΤΣ). Heretics, on the contrary, are the amphibious generation of vipers and snakes that cannot live in wholesome water. Water is of great importance for the whole universe. The Spirit of God moved upon the face of the waters—so upon the waters of baptism. As the Church is compared with the ark (see the previous section), so the water of baptism is contrasted with the deluge, and the dove of Noah is a type of the dove—the Spirit.[1] As power is inherent in all water, it is indifferent what kind of water is used. The water of the Tiber possesses the same power as the water of Jordan; still water produces the same effects as running water, De Bapt. 4: Omnes aquæ de pristina originis prærogativa sacramentum sanctificationis consequuntur, invocato Deo. Supervenit enim statim Spiritus de cœlis et aquis superest, sanctificans eas de semetipso, et ita sanctificatæ vim sanctificandi combibunt. He also compares (c. 5) the baptismal

---

[1] Concerning these manifold allegorical interpretations of fish, dove, etc., comp. *Münter*, Sinnbilder der Christen, and *Augusti* in his essay: Die Kirchenthiere, in vol. xii. of his work on the Antiquities of the Christian Church. But *Tertullian* rightly says in reference to himself: Vereor, ne laudes aquæ potius quam baptismi rationes videar congregasse! [See also the works of *Didron, Piper, Twining*, etc., as referred to in § 8, supra. On the representation of baptism in the Catacombs, see *Perret's* work, ubi supra, and Dublin Review, Dec. 1858.]

water with the pool of Bethesda; as the latter was troubled by an angel, so there is a special angel of baptism (angelus baptismi), who prepares the way for the Holy Spirit. (Non quod in aquis Spiritum Sanctum consequamur, sed in aqua emundati sub angelo Spiritui Sancto præparamur.) — [On *Tertullian*, comp. *Leopold* in Zeitschrift f. Hist. Theol. 854.] Cyprian spoke of the high importance of baptismal water from his own experience, de Grat. ad Donat. p. 3. He does not indeed maintain that water purifies *as such* (peccata enim purgare et hominem sanctificare aqua sola non potest, nisi habeat et Spiritum S., Ep. 71, p. 213), but his comparisons give the impression of a magical efficacy of water. The devil was cast out of Pharaoh, when he and all his hosts were drowned in the Red Sea (the sea is a symbol of baptism, according to 1 Cor. x.); for the power of the devil only reaches to the margin of the water. As scorpions and snakes are strong on dry land, but lose their strength, and must vomit their poison, when thrown into water, so the unclean spirits. In short, whenever water is mentioned in the sacred Scriptures, the Punic symbolism is at once applied to it; "*it is therefore not at all surprising that the rock in the wilderness, as well as the Samaritan woman at Jacob's well, and many others, are regarded as types of baptism,*" Rettberg, s. 332.

(3) The term σύμβολον itself, which *Origen* uses, Adv. Cels. iii. (Opp. i. p. 481), and Comment. in Joh. (Opp. iv. p. 132), indicates a more or less distinct consciousness of the difference between the image and the thing which it represents. Nevertheless (οὐδὲν ἧττον), from the last-mentioned passage it is evident that he also considers baptism as something κατ᾽ αὐτό, viz. ἀρχὴ καὶ πηγὴ χαρισμάτων θείων, because it is administered in the name of the divine Trias. Comp. Hom. in Luc. xxi. (Opp. i. p. 957).

(4) The passages from Scripture cited in favour of infant baptism as a usage of the primitive Church are doubtful, and prove nothing: viz. Mark x. 14; Matt. xviii. 4, 6; Acts ii. 38, 39, 41, x. 48; 1 Cor. i. 16; Col. ii. 11, 12. [*R. Wardlaw*, Scriptural Authority of Infant Baptism. *R. Halley* on the Sacraments. I. Baptism (Cong. Lect.). *Waterland's* Works, ii. 171 ff.] *Justin M.* Apol. i. 15, speaks of μαθητεύεσθαι ἐκ παίδων, but this does not necessarily involve

baptism; comp. *Semisch,* ii. s. 431 ff. Nor does the earliest definite passage in the writings of the Fathers, *Iren.* Adv. Hær. ii. 22, 4, p. 147 (see § 68, note 1), afford any absolute proof. It only expresses the beautiful idea that Jesus was Redeemer *in* every stage of life, and *for* every stage of life; but it does not say that He redeemed children by the *water of baptism*, unless baptism is interpreted into the term *renasci* (comp., however, *Thiersch* in the Zeitschrift f. d. Luth. Theol. 1841, 2, s. 177, and *Höfling,* Die Taufe, s. 112).[1] Just as little can this passage prove anything *against* the usage. A reference to infant baptism is found in a passage of *Clem. Alex.* (Pæd. iii. 11), according to which the fish on the signet-ring of Christians should remind us of the children drawn out of the water (τῶν ἐξ ὕδατος ἀνασπωμένων παιδίων). The expression παιδία may, however, apply to Christians generally, with reference to the Pædagogue. That, on the other hand, infant baptism was customary in *Tertullian's* times, is proved by his opposition to it. De Bapt. 18. He alleges the following reasons against it:—(1) The importance of baptism—not even earthly goods are entrusted to those under age; (2) The consequent responsibility of the sponsors; (3) The innocence of children (quid festinat innocens ætas ad remissionem peccatorum?); (4) The necessity of being previously instructed in religion (Ait quidem Dominus: nolite eos prohibere ad me *venire*. Veniant ergo dum adolescunt, veniant dum discunt, dum quo veniant docentur; fiant Christiani cum Christum nosse potuerint); (5) The great responsibility which the subject of baptism takes upon him (Si qui pondus intelligant baptismi, magis timebunt consecutionem, quam dilationem). For the last-mentioned reason he recommends even to grown-up persons (single persons, widows, etc.) to delay baptism till they are either married, or have formed the firm resolution to live a single life. Comp. *Neander,* Antignostikus, s. 209, 210.

(5) The views of *Origen,* Comm. in Ep. ad Rom. v. (Opp. iv. p. 565), in Lev. Hom. viii. (Opp. i. p. 230), in Lucam (Opp. iii. p. 948), were connected with his notions respecting the stain in natural generation (comp. § 63, note 4). But it

---

[1] *Gieseler* in his Dogmengesch. maintains that *renasci* can here be understood only of baptism; *Neander* is more reserved.

is worthy of notice, that in the first of the above passages he calls infant baptism *a usage derived from the apostles:* Ecclesia ab apostolis traditionem accepit etiam parvulis baptismum dare. Sciebant enim illi quibus mysteriorum secreta commissa sunt divinorum, quod essent in omnibus genuinæ sordes peccati, quæ per aquam et spiritum ablui deberent. And so it was held to be, in the third century, in the North African, Alexandrian, and Syro-Persian Church; Mani among the Persians appealed to infant baptism as customary (*August. c. Julian*, iii. 187); comp. *Neander*, Dg. s. 247. [On *Origen's* views, compare *Bunsen's* Hippolytus, vol. iii.]

(6) See *Cypr.* Ep. 59 (written in the name of 66 occidental bishops; Ep. 64, edit. *Fell*, Oxon.). *Cyprian* maintains that infants should be baptized as soon as is possible: it is, however, remarkable that his argument in favour of infant baptism is not founded upon the *guilt* of original sin, but upon the *innocence* of infants. *Tertullian*, on the other hand, urges this very reason in opposition to infant baptism. But *Cyprian* looks more at the beneficial effects it is designed to produce, than at the responsibility which is attached to it. As we do not hesitate to salute the new-born yet innocent babe with the kiss of peace, "*since we still see in him the fresh handiwork of God*," so we should not raise any objection to his being baptized. Comp. *Rettb.* s. 331. *Neander*, Kg. i. 2, s. 554. The reproach of Stephen against *Cyprian* for re-baptizing, was regarded by the latter as quite inapplicable, since, in his view, heretical baptism was no baptism. Cf. Ep. 71 (Eus. vii. 5).

(7) On this custom, comp. the works on ecclesiastical history and antiquities; *Cyprian*, Ep. 76 (*Fell*, 69, p. 185), where some very thorny questions are raised respecting sprinkling. *Münscher*, l.c. i. s. 464. Against the delay: Const. Apost. vi. 15, so far as it proceeds from depreciation or levity. *Tertullian* allows even laymen, but not women, to administer the rite of baptism in cases of emergency; de Bapt. c. 17. Comp. Const. Apost. iii. c. 9–11.

(8) *Clement* of Alexandria recognises only *that* baptism as valid which is administered in the Catholic Church: Τὸ βάπτισμα τὸ αἱρετικὸν οὐκ οἰκεῖον καὶ γνήσιον ὕδωρ, Strom. i. 19, p. 375; so, too, *Tert.* De Bapt. c. 15: Unus omnino baptismus est nobis tam ex Domini evangelio, quam ex

Apostoli literis, quoniam unus Deus et unum baptisma et una ecclesia in cœlis.... Hæretici autem nullum habent consortium nostræ disciplinæ, quos extraneos utique testatur ipsa ademptio communicationis. Non debeo in illis cognoscere, quod mihi est præceptum, quia non idem Deus est nobis et illis, nec unus Christus, *i.e.* idem: ideoque nec baptismus unus, quia non idem. Quem quum rite non habeant, sine dubio non habent. Comp. De Pud. 19; De Præscr. 12.— The Phrygian synods of Iconium and Synnada (about the year 235) pronounced the baptism of heretics invalid, see the letter of *Firmilian*, Bishop of Cæsarea, to *Cyprian* (Ep. 75), *Eus.* vii. 7. [*Münscher, von Cölln*, i. s. 473.] A synod held at Carthage (about the year 200), under Agrippinus, had used similar language; see *Cypr.* Ep. 73 (ad Jubianum, p. 129, 130, *Bal.*). Cyprian adopted the custom of the Asiatic and African Churches, and insisted that heretics should be re-baptized; though according to him this was not a repetition of the act of baptism, but the *true* baptism; comp. Ep. 71, where he requires *non re-baptizari, sed baptizari* of heretics. Concerning the subsequent controversy with Stephen, comp. *Neander*, Church Hist. i. 563, 577. *Rettberg*, s. 156 ff. The Epistles 69–75 of *Cyprian* refer to this subject. *Stephen* recognised baptism administered by heretics as valid, and merely demanded the laying on of hands as significant of *pœnitentia* (with indirect reference to Acts viii. 17). The African bishops, on the other hand, restricted this latter rite to those who had once been baptized in the Catholic Church, but had afterwards fallen away and returned again; and they appealed to the custom observed by the heretics themselves in confirmation of their view. Such *lapsi* could not, of course, be re-baptized. The old African usage was confirmed by the synods of Carthage (held in the years 255 and 256). Comp. Sententiæ Episcoporum lxxxii. de baptizandis hæreticis, in *Cypr.* Opp. p. 229 (*Fell*). [On the whole controversy, comp. *Münscher (von Cölln)*, i. s. 472–475. *Hefele*, Hist. of Councils, u. s. *Lawrence*, Lay Baptism invalid, 1712 ff. Anonymi Scriptoris de Rebaptismate liber, in *Routh's* Reliquiæ Sacræ, v. 283–328. *Waterland's* Letters on Lay Baptism, Works, vi. 73–235.]

(9) *Theod.* Fab. Hær. i. c. 10. On the question whether

the sect of the Cainians (vipera venenatissima, *Tert.*), to which Quintilla of Carthage, an opponent of baptism, belonged, was identical with the Gnostic Cainites, see *Neander*, Antignostikus, s. 193, Dg. 241. Some of the objections to baptism were the following: It is below the dignity of the divine to be represented by anything earthly: Abraham was justified by faith alone; the apostles themselves were not baptized,[1] and Paul attaches little importance to the rite (1 Cor. i. 17). —That the majority of the Gnostics held baptism in high esteem, is evident from the circumstance that they laid great stress on the baptism of Jesus, see *Baur*, Gnosis, s. 224; but they advocated it on very different grounds from those of the orthodox Church. On the threefold baptism of the Marcionites, and further particulars, comp. the works treating on this subject: respecting the Clementine Homilies, see *Credner*, iii. s. 308.

(10) *Orig.* Exh. ad Mart. i. p. 292, with reference to Mark x. 38; Luke xii. 50. *Tertull.* De Bapt. 16 : Est quidem nobis etiam secundum lavacrum, unum et ipsum, *sanguinis* scilicet. . . . Hos duos baptismos de vulnere perfossi lateris emisit: quatenus qui in sanguinem ejus crederent, aqua lavarentur; qui aqua lavissent, etiam sanguinem potarent. Hic est baptismus, qui lavacrum et non acceptum repræsentat, et perditum reddit. Comp. Scorp. c. 6. *Cyprian*, Ep. 73, and especially De Exh. Martyr. p. 168, 169. According to him, the baptism of blood is in comparison with the baptism of water, in gratia majus, in potestate sublimius, in honore pretiosius; it is baptisma, in quo angeli baptizant, baptisma in quo Deus et Christus ejus exultant, bap. post quod nemo jam peccat, b. quod fidei nostræ incrementa consummat, b. quod nos de mundo recedentes statim Deo copulat. In aquæ baptismo accipitur peccatorum remissio, in sanguinis corona virtutum. Heretics are profited neither by the baptism of blood nor by that of water, but the former is of some service to the catechumens who are not yet baptized. *Rettberg*, s. 382. Comp. also Acta Martyr. Perpet. et Fel., ed. Oxon. p. 29, 30,

---

[1] To the remark of some : Tunc apostolos baptismi vicem implesse, quum in navicula fluctibus adspersi operti sunt, ipsum quoque Petrum per mare ingredientem satis mersum, *Tertullian* replies (De Bapt. 12) : aliud est adspergi vel intercipi violentia maris, aliud tingui disciplina religionis.

286 FIRST PERIOD.—THE CHURCH, ITS MEANS OF GRACE. [§ 73.

and *Dodwell,* De secundo Martyrii Baptismo, in his Diss.
Cypr. XIII.[1]

§ 73.

The Lord's Supper.

D. Schulz, die christl. Lehre vom Abendmahl, nach dem Grundtexte des
N. Test., Leipz. 1824, 1831 (exegetical and dogmatic). *Works on the History
of this Doctrine:* **Phil. Marheineke,* Ss. Patrum de Præsentia Christi in
Cœna Domini sententia triplex, s. sacræ Eucharistiæ Historia tripartita,
Heidelb. 1811, 4to. *Karl Meyer,* Versuch einer Geschichte der Transsub-
stantiationslehre, mit Vorrede von *Dr. Paulus,* Heidelb. 1832. †*J. J. v.
Döllinger,* die Lehre von der Eucharistie in den 3 ersten Jahrhunderten,
Mainz 1826. *F. C. Baur,* Abhandlung in der Tüb. Ztschr. 1839, ii. 2, s.
56 ff. **A. Ebrard,* das Dogma vom h. Abendmahl und seine Geschichte,
Frankf. 1845. *J. G. W. Engelhardt,* Bemerkungen über die Gesch. d.
Lehre vom Abendmahl in den drei ersten Jahrh. in Illgen's Zeitschrift f. d.
hist. Theol. 1842. **J. W. F. Höfling,* Die Lehre der ältesten Kirche vom
Opfer im Leben und Cultus der Christen, Erlang. 1851. *Kahnis,* Lehre
vom Abendmahl, Leipz. 1851. *L. J. Rückert,* Das Abendmahl, sein
Wesen und seine Gesch. in der alten Kirche, Leipz. 1856. *H. J. Holtzmann,* De corpore et sanguine Christi quæ statuta fuerint ·in ecclesia
examinantur, Heidelb. 1858. **Steitz,* die Abendmahlzlehre in der griech.
Kirche (theol. Jahrb. ix. 3 and x. 1-3). [*W. F. Rinck,* Lehrbegriff vom
heilig. Abendmahl in den ersten Jahrh., in Zeitschrift f. d. hist. Theol.
1853, p. 331-334. *Julius Müller,* article *Abendmahl* in Herzog's Realencyclop., cf. *Ströbel* in the Zeitschrift f. luth. Theol. 1854. *Jeremy
Taylor* on the Real Presence. *Waterland* on the Eucharist, Works, iv.
476-798, v. 125-292. *Hampden's* Bampton Lectures (3d ed. 1848),
Lect. viii. *Robert Halley,* The Sacraments, Part II. (Cong. Lect. 1851).
Robt. J. Wilberforce, Doctrine of Eucharist, 1853 (cf. Christian Rembr.
1853). *W. Goode,* Nature of Christ's Presence in Euch. 2, 1856. *E. B.
Pusey,* The Real Presence, 1853-1857. *Philip Freeman,* Principles of Divine
Service, Lond. 1855-1857 (cf. Christ. Rembr. Jan. 1858). *Turton* (Bp.) on
the Eucharist, and *Wiseman's* reply (rep. in his Essays), 1854. *Vogan,*
True Doctrine of the Eucharist, Lond. 1871. *Dimock,* Eucharistic
Worship, Lond. 1876.]

---

[1] Though the parallel drawn between the baptism of blood and that of water
has a basis in the whole symbolical tendency of the age, yet in its connection
with the doctrine of the Fathers it appears to be more than a mere rhetorical
figure. Like the comparison instituted between the death of the martyrs and
that of Jesus, as well as the notions concerning penance, it rests upon the
equilibrium which the writers of that period were desirous to maintain between
the free-will of man and the influence of divine grace. In the baptism of water
man appears as a passive recipient, in the baptism of blood he acts with
spontaneity.

§ 73.] THE LORD'S SUPPER.

The Christian Church attached from the beginning a high and mysterious import (1) to the bread and wine used in the Lord's Supper, as the symbols of the body and blood of Christ, to be received by the Church with thanksgiving (Eucharist) (2). It was not the tendency of the age to analyse the symbolical in a critical and philosophical manner, and to draw metaphysical distinctions between its constituent parts, viz. the outward sign on the one hand, and the thing represented by it on the other. On the contrary, the real and the symbolical were so blended that the symbol did not supplant the fact, nor did the fact dislodge the symbol (3). Thus it happens that in the writings of the Fathers of this period we meet with passages which speak distinctly of *signs*, and at the same time with others which speak openly of a *real participation* in the body and blood of Christ. Yet we may already discern some leading tendencies. *Ignatius*, as well as *Justin* and *Irenæus* (4), laid great stress on the mysterious connection subsisting between the Logos and the elements; though this union was sometimes misunderstood in a superstitious sense, or perverted in the hope of producing magical effects (5). *Tertullian* and *Cyprian*, though somewhat favourable to the supernatural, are nevertheless representatives of the symbolical interpretation (6). The Alexandrian school, too, espoused the latter view, though the language of *Clement* on this subject (intermingling an ideal mysticism) is less definite than that of *Origen* (7). In the apostolical Fathers, and, with more definite reference to the Lord's Supper, in the writings of *Justin* and *Irenæus*, the idea of a *sacrifice* already occurs; by which, however, they did not understand a daily repeated propitiatory sacrifice of Christ (in the sense of the later Roman Church), but a thankoffering to be presented by Christians themselves (8). This idea, which may have had its origin in the custom of offering oblations, was brought into connection with the service for the commemoration of the dead, and thus imperceptibly prepared the way for the later doctrine of masses for the deceased (9). It further led to the notion of a sacrifice which is repeated by the priest (but only symbolically), an idea first found in *Cyprian* (10). It is not quite certain, but probable, that the Ebionites celebrated the Lord's Supper as a commemorative feast; the mystical meals of some Gnostics, on the contrary, bear only a very distant resemblance to the Lord's Supper (11).

(1) " *That the body and blood of Christ were given and received in the Lord's Supper was from the beginning the general faith, and this, too, at a time when written documents were not yet extant or not widely diffused. And this faith remained in subsequent times; the Christian Church has never had any other; no one opposed this in the ancient Church, not even the arch-heretics,*" Rückert, Abendmahl, s. 297.

(2) Respecting the terms εὐχαριστία, σύναξις, εὐλογία, see *Suicer* and the Lexicons. With the exception of the *Hydroparastates* (Aquarii, *Epiph.* Hær. 46, 2), all Christians, in accordance with the original institution, used wine and bread; the wine was mixed with water (κρᾶμα), and dogmatical significancy was attributed to the mingling of these two elements (*Justin M.* Apol. i. 65; *Iren.* v. 2, 3; *Cypr.* Epist. 63). The *Artotyrites* are said to have used cheese along with bread (*Epiph.* Hær. 49, 2). Comp. the Acts of Perpetua and Felicitas in *Schwegler*, Montanismus, s. 122. *Olshausen*, Monumenta, p. 101: Et clamavit me (Christus) et de caseo, quod mulgebat, dedit mihi quasi buccellam, et ego accepi junctis manibus et manducavi, et universi circumstantes dixerunt Amen. Et ad sonum vocis experrecta sum, commanducans adhuc dulcis nescio quid. Concerning the celebration of the Lord's Supper in the age of the Antonines, and the custom of administering it to the sick, etc., see *Justin M.* Apol. i. 65: Προσφέρεται τῷ προεστῶτι τῶν ἀδελφῶν ἄρτος, καὶ ποτήριον ὕδατος καὶ κράματος· καὶ οὗτος λαβὼν, αἶνον καὶ δόξαν τῷ Πατρὶ τῶν ὅλων διὰ τοῦ ὀνόματος τοῦ Υἱοῦ καὶ τοῦ Πνεύματος τοῦ Ἁγίου ἀναπέμπει, καὶ εὐχαριστίαν ὑπὲρ τοῦ κατηξιῶσθαι τούτων παρ' αὐτοῦ ἐπὶ πολὺ ποιεῖται . . . εὐχαριστήσαντος δὲ τοῦ προεστῶτος, καὶ ἐπευφημήσαντος παντὸς τοῦ λαοῦ, οἱ καλούμενοι παρ' ἡμῖν διάκονοι διδόασιν ἑκάστῳ τῶν παρόντων μεταλαβεῖν

§ 73.] THE LORD'S SUPPER. 289

ἀπὸ τοῦ εὐχαριστηθέντος ἄρτου καὶ οἴνου καὶ ὕδατος, καὶ τοῖς οὐ παροῦσιν ἀποφέρουσι, 66. Καὶ ἡ τροφὴ αὕτη καλεῖται παρ' ἡμῖν Εὐχαριστία. . . . On the liturgical part of this ordinance in general, see *Augusti*, viii. On the communion of children, *Neander*, Dg. s. 254.

(3) "*It is only in consequence of the more abstract tendency of the West and of modern times that so many different significations are assigned to what the early Eastern Church understood by the phrase* τοῦτο ἐστί. *If we would fully enter into its original meaning, we must not separate these possible significations. To say that the words in question denote transubstantiation is too definite and too much said; to interpret them by the phrase* cum et sub specie *is too artificial; the rendering:* this signifies, *says too little, and is too poor. In the view of the writers of the Gospels (and after them of the earliest Fathers),* THE BREAD IN THE LORD'S SUPPER WAS THE BODY OF CHRIST. *But if they had been asked whether the bread was changed? they would have replied in the negative; if they had been told that the communicants partook of the body with and under the form of the bread, they would not have understood it; if it had been asserted that then the bread only signifies the body, they would not have been satisfied,*" Strauss, Leben Jesu, 1st ed. ii. s. 437. Comp. *Baumgarten-Crusius*, ii. s. 1211 ff. and 1185 ff. It is also noteworthy that in this period there is not as yet any proper *dogma* on the Lord's Supper. "*There had been no controversy; no council had spoken,*" Rückert, s. 8. Only the germs of later opinions were certainly there.

(4) *Ignat.* ad Rom. 7: Ἄρτον θεοῦ θέλω κ.τ.λ.; this is incorrectly referred to the Lord's Supper; it can only be understood of that internal and vital union with Christ, after which the martyr longed; comp. *Rückert*, p. 302. But here is pertinent, ad Smyrn. 7, where *Ignatius* objects to the Docetæ: Εὐχαριστίας καὶ προσευχῆς ἀπέχονται διὰ τὸ μὴ ὁμολογεῖν τὴν εὐχαριστίαν σάρκα εἶναι τοῦ σωτῆρος ἡμῶν Ἰησοῦ Χριστοῦ, τὴν ὑπὲρ ἁμαρτιῶν ἡμῶν παθοῦσαν, ἣν τῇ χρηστότητι ὁ πατὴρ ἤγειρεν. Some understand the word εἶναι itself as symbolical. Comp. *Münscher (von Cölln)*, i. s. 495; and, on the other side, *Ebrard*, l.c. 254, and *Engelhardt*, in Illgens Hist. Theol. Zeitschrift. "*Ignatius teaches that flesh and blood are present in the Lord's Supper; but he does*

not teach how they came to be there, nor in what relation they stand to the bread and the wine," *Rückert*, s. 303. *Justin*, Apol. i. 66, is the first to make a strict distinction between the bread and wine used in the Lord's Supper and common bread and wine: Οὐ γὰρ ὡς κοινὸν ἄρτον, οὐδὲ κοινὸν πόμα ταῦτα λαμβάνομεν, ἀλλ' ὃν τρόπον διὰ λόγου θεοῦ σαρκοποιηθεὶς Ἰησοῦς Χριστὸς ὁ σωτὴρ ἡμῶν καὶ σάρκα καὶ αἷμα ὑπὲρ σωτηρίας ἡμῶν ἔσχεν, οὕτως καὶ τὴν δι' εὐχῆς λόγου τοῦ παρ' αὐτοῦ εὐχαριστηθεῖσαν τροφήν, ἐξ ἧς αἷμα καὶ σάρκες κατὰ μεταβολὴν τρέφονται ἡμῶν, ἐκείνου τοῦ σαρκοποιηθέντος Ἰησοῦ καὶ σάρκα καὶ αἷμα ἐδιδάχθημεν εἶναι. He does not speak of a change of the bread and wine into the flesh and blood of Christ, see *Ebrard*, s. 257 (against *Engelhardt*). In *Ebrard's* view, the phrase κατὰ μεταβολήν is the opposite of κατὰ κτίσιν, and denotes that natural food is accompanied by that provided by our Saviour for our new life, comp. also *Semisch*, ii. s. 439 ff., and *Rückert*, s. 401. The passage is obscure, and it is remarkable that all the three (later) confessions—the Roman Catholic, the Lutheran, and the Reformed —find their doctrine expressed in *Justin*, while his doctrine is fully expressed by none of them. *" That he teaches a change is not to be denied, but yet only a change into flesh that belongs to Christ, not into the flesh born of Mary ; there is not to be found in him a word about what the Church afterwards added to the doctrine,"* *Rückert*, s. 401. *Irenæus*, iv. 18 (33), p. 250 (*Gr.* 324), also thinks that the change consists in this, that common bread becomes bread of a higher order—the earthly, heavenly; but it does not, therefore, cease to be bread. He draws a parallel between this change and the transformation of the mortal body into the immortal, p. 251 : Ὡς γὰρ ἀπὸ γῆς ἄρτος προσλαμβανόμενος τὴν ἔκκλησιν [ἐπίκλησιν] τοῦ θεοῦ οὐκέτι καινὸς ἄρτος ἐστίν, ἀλλ' εὐχαριστία, ἐκ δύο πραγμάτων συνεστηκυῖα, ἐπιγείου τε καὶ οὐρανίου, οὕτως καὶ τὰ σώματα ἡμῶν μεταλαμβάνοντα τῆς εὐχαριστίας μηκέτι εἶναι φθαρτά, τὴν ἐλπίδα τῆς εἰς αἰῶνας ἀναστάσεως ἔχοντα. Comp. v. 2, p. 293, 294 (396, 397), and *Massueti*, Diss. iii. art. 7, p. 114. *Irenæus* also defends the real presence of the body of Christ in the Lord's Supper in opposition to the Docetæ and Gnostics, iv. 18, § 4 : Quomodo constabit eis, eum panem, in quo gratiæ actæ sint, corpus esse Domini sui et calicem [esse calicem] sanguinis ejus, si non ipsum fabricatoris mundi filium dicunt? Comp. the Greek passage from Joh. Dam. Parall.: Πῶς τὴν σάρκα λέγουσιν εἰς φθορὰν χωρεῖν καὶ μὴ μετέχειν τῆς ζωῆς, τὴν ἀπὸ τοῦ σώματος τοῦ Κυρίου καὶ τοῦ αἵματος αὐτοῦ τρεφομένην; ἢ τὴν γνώμην ἀλλαξάτωσαν, ἢ τὸ προσφέρειν τὰ εἰρημένα παραιτείσθωσαν· ἡμῶν δὲ σύμφωνος ἡ γνώμη τῇ εὐχαριστίᾳ, καὶ ἡ εὐχαριστία βεβαιοῖ τὴν γνώμην. Comp. 33, § 2 (*Münscher, von Cölln,* i. s. 496). But the reason which he urges in favour of his views, viz. that *the Gnostics cannot partake of the bread and wine with thanksgiving because they despise matter,* shows that he regarded the elements as more than merely accidental things, though they are not merely bread and wine. Comp. *Thiersch,* die Lehre des Irenæus von der Eucharistie, in Rudelbach and Guericke's Zeitschrift, 1841, 4to, s. 40 ff.; in reply, *Ebrard,* l.c. s. 261.

(5) The pain produced by spilling any part of the wine (*Tert.* De Corona Mil. 3: Calicis aut panis nostri aliquid decuti in terram anxie patimur, and *Orig.* in Exod. Hom. xiii. 3) may have originated in a deeper feeling of propriety, but it degenerated into superstitious dread. Thus, too, the fair faith in an inherent vital power in the elements (φάρμακον ἀθανασίας, ἀντίδοτον τοῦ μὴ ἀποθανεῖν) was gradually converted into the belief of miraculous cures being effected by them, which easily made the transition to gross superstition. The practice of administering the Lord's Supper to children may also be ascribed to the expectation of magical effects. Comp. the anecdotes of *Cyprian,* De Lapsis, p. 132. *Rettberg,* p. 337. — The separation of the Lord's Supper from the Agapæ, which had become necessary, the custom of preserving the bread, the communion of the sick, etc., tended to further such views.

(6) It is remarkable that *Tertullian,* whose views, generally speaking, are so realistic, shows in this instance a leaning towards the mere symbolical interpretation according to which the Lord's Supper is *figura corporis Christi,* Adv. Marc. i. 14, iv. 40. In the latter place (see the connection) he urges the *symbolical* sense to refute Marcion: if Christ had not possessed a real body, it could not have been represented (vacua res, quod est phantasma, figuram capere non potest;—how near to

saying, it is *impossible to partake* of a phantom as such!)[1] This sentiment accords with what is said as to its significance as a memorial in De 'Anima, c. 17: Vinum in sanguinis sui memoriam consecravit. Nevertheless *Tertullian* speaks in other places (De Resurr, c. 8, De Pud. c. 9) of the participation of the Lord's Supper as an opimitate dominici corporis vesci, as a de Deo saginari; with these expressions, comp. De Orat. 6: Christus enim panis noster est (spoken in reference to the daily bread in the Lord's Prayer), quia vita Christus et vita panis. Ego sum, inquit, panis vitæ. Et paulo supra: Panis est sermo Dei vivi, qui descendit de cœlis. Tum quod et corpus ejus in pane *censetur* (not *est*):[2] Hoc est corpus meum. Itaque petendo panem quotidianum perpetuitatem postulamus in Christo et individuitatem a corpore ejus. He also is not wanting in mystical allusions (*e.g.* Gen. xlix. 11: Lavabit in vino stolam suam, is, in his opinion, a type, etc.), and adopts the notions of his age concerning the magical effects of the Lord's Supper. But these do not prove that the doctrine of transubstantiation, or any of similar import, was known at that time, since the same expressions are used of the baptismal water. Comp. *Neander*, Antignostikus, s. 547, and *F. Baur*, Tertullian's Lehre vom Abendmahl (Tübing. Zeitschr. 1839, 2, s. 36 ff.), in opposition to *Rudelbach*, who finds (as Luther had done before him) in Tertullian the Lutheran view of the point in question. On the other hand, Œcolampadius and Zwingli appealed to the same Father in support of their opinions; comp. also *Ebrard*, s. 289 ff., and *Rückert*, s. 305 ff., against Rudelbach, Scheibel, and Kahnis. *Cyprian's* doctrine of the Lord's Supper is set forth in the sixty-third of his epistles, where he combats the irregularity of those who used water instead of wine (see note 1), and proves the necessity of employing the latter. The phrase

---

[1] Respecting the manner in which *Tertullian* viewed the relation between the *sign* and the *thing signified*, comp. as a parallel passage, De Resurr. Carnis, p. 30. *Rückert* (s. 307) correctly remarks that Tertullian here follows the usus loquendi of the New Testament, and that any one might just as well in all simplicity speak of the body of the Lord, as of the Good Shepherd and the true vine, without being obliged always to say, in the way of caution, that it is meant figuratively.

[2] Comp., however, De Anima, 40 (above, § 63, Note 6), and *Rückert*, s. 210–212 (with reference to *Döllinger*, s. 52).

ostenditur, used in reference to the wine as the blood of Christ, is somewhat doubtful. But the comparison which Cyprian makes of the water with the people is rather *for* than *against* the symbolical interpretation, though in other places (like Tertullian) he calls the Lord's Supper outright the body and blood of Christ, Ep. 57, p. 117. The rhetoric, bordering on the dithyrambic, with which he speaks of the effects of the Lord's Supper (the blessed inebriation of the communicants contrasted with the drunkenness of Noah), and the miraculous stories he relates, should protect him from the charge of an excessively prosaic view. But in connection with the doctrine of the unity of the Church, he attaches great practical importance to the idea of a *communio*, which was afterwards abandoned by the Roman Church, but on which much stress was again laid by the Reformed Church, Ep. 63, p. 154: Quo et ipso sacramento populus noster ostenditur adunatus, ut quemadmodum grana multa in unum collecta et commolita et commixta panem unum faciunt, sic in Christo, qui est panis cœlestis, unum sciamus esse corpus, cui conjunctus sit noster numerus et adunatus. Comp. *Rettberg*, s. 332 ff.

(7) In *Clement* the mystical view of the Lord's Supper preponderates, according to which it is heavenly meat and heavenly drink; but he looks for the mystical not so much in the elements (bread and wine), as in the spiritual union of the soul with the Logos; and thinks that effects are produced only upon the mind, not upon the body. *Clement* also considers the Lord's Supper as a σύμβολον, but a σύμβολον μυστικόν, Pæd. ii. 2, p. 184 (*Sylb.* 156); comp. Pæd. i. 6, p. 123: Ταύτας ἡμῖν οἰκείας τροφὰς ὁ Κύριος χορηγεῖ καὶ σάρκα ὀρέγει καὶ αἷμα ἐκχεῖ, καὶ οὐδὲν εἰς αὔξησιν τοῖς παιδίοις ἐνδεῖ· ὦ τοῦ παραδόξου μυστηρίου κ.τ.λ. The use of the terms ἀλληγορεῖν, δημιουργεῖν, αἰνίττεσθαι, clearly shows that he sought the mystery, not in the material elements, but in the spiritual and symbolical interpretation of the idea hidden in the elements. His interpretation of the symbols is peculiar: the Holy Spirit is represented by the σάρξ, the Logos by the αἷμα, and the Lord, who unites in Himself the Logos and Spirit, by the mixture of the wine and the water. A distinction between the blood *once* shed on the cross and that represented in the Lord's Supper is found in Pæd. ii. 2, p. 177 (*Sylb.* 151):

Διττόν τε τὸ αἷμα τοῦ Κυρίου· τὸ μὲν γάρ ἐστιν αὐτοῦ σαρκικὸν, ᾧ τῆς φθορᾶς λελυτρώμεθα· τὸ δὲ πνευματικὸν, τουτέστιν ᾧ κεχρίσμεθα. Καὶ τοῦτ' ἐστὶ πιεῖν τὸ αἷμα τοῦ Ἰησοῦ, τῆς κυριακῆς μεταλαβεῖν ἀφθαρσίας· ἰσχὺς δὲ τοῦ λόγου τὸ πνεῦμα, ὡς αἷμα σαρκός. Comp. *Bähr*, vom Tode Jesu, s. 80: "The meaning of Clement is, that what the blood is for the flesh and the body, its life and power, that is the πνεῦμα for the Logos. It is, as it were, the blood of the Logos. By the blood of Christ poured out upon the cross we are ransomed; by the blood of the Logos, through the πνεῦμα, we are anointed and sanctified." In what follows, the mixture of the wine and water is again said to be a symbol of the union of the πνεῦμα with the spirit of man. Lastly, *Clement* also finds in the Old Test. types of the Lord's Supper, *e.g.* in Melchisedec, Strom. iv. 25, p. 637 (*Sylb.* 539 B).—Among the Ante-Nicene Fathers, *Origen* is the only one who decidedly opposes those who take the external sign for the thing itself, as ἀκεραιοτέροις in Hom. xi. on Matt. (Opp. iii. p. 498–500): "As common food does not defile, but rather unbelief and the impurity of the heart, so the food which is consecrated by the word of God and by prayer does not by itself (τῷ ἰδίῳ λόγῳ) sanctify those who partake of it. The bread of the Lord profits only those who receive it with an undefiled heart and a pure conscience." In connection with such views, *Origen* (as afterwards Zwingli, and still more decidedly the Socinians) did not attach so much importance to the actual participation of the Lord's Supper as the other Fathers: Οὕτω δὲ οὔτε ἐκ τοῦ μὴ φαγεῖν παρ' αὐτὸ τὸ μὴ φαγεῖν ἀπὸ τοῦ ἁγιασθέντος λόγῳ θεοῦ καὶ ἐντεύξει ἄρτου ὑστερούμεθα ἀγαθοῦ τινος, οὔτε ἐκ τοῦ φαγεῖν περισσεύομεν ἀγαθῷ τινι· τὸ γὰρ αἴτιον τῆς ὑστερήσεως ἡ κακία ἐστὶ καὶ τὰ ἁμαρτήματα, καὶ τὸ αἴτιον τῆς περισσεύσεως ἡ δικαιοσύνη ἐστὶ καὶ τὰ κατορθώματα, ib. p. 898: Non enim panem illum visibilem, quem tenebat in manibus, corpus suum dicebat Deus Verbum, sed verbum, in cujus mysterio fuerat panis ille frangendus, etc. Comp. Hom. vii. 5, in Lev. (Opp. ii. p. 225): Agnoscite, quia figuræ sunt, quæ in divinis voluminibus scripta sunt, et ideo tamquam spiritales et non tamquam carnales examinate et intelligite, quæ dicuntur. Si enim quasi carnales ista suscipitis, lædunt vos et non alunt. Est enim et in evangeliis littera ... quæ

§ 73.] THE LORD'S SUPPER. 295

occidit eum, qui non spiritaliter, quæ dicuntur, adverterit. Si enim secundum literam sequaris hoc ipsum, quod dictum est: Nisi manducaveritis carnem meam et biberitis sanguinem meum, occidit hæc littera. Comp. *Redepenning's* Origenes, ii. s. 438 ff. On other passages, in which *Origen* seems to incline to the conception of a *real* body (especially Cont. Celsum, viii. 33), see *Rückert*, s. 343.

(8) Concerning the oblations, see the works on ecclesiastical history, and on antiquities.—The apostolical Fathers speak of sacrifices, by which, however, we are to understand either the sacrifices of the heart and life (*Barn.* c. 2), or of alms (*Clem.* of Rome, c. 40–44), which may also include the gifts (δῶρα) offered at the Lord's Supper, and certainly the offerings of prayer; comp. also *Ignat.* ad Ephes. 5; ad Trall. 7; ad Magn. 7. Only in the passage ad Philad. 4, the εὐχαριστία is mentioned in connection with the θυσιαστήριον, but in such a manner that no argument for the later theory of sacrifice can be inferred from it; see *Höfling*, die Lehre der apostolischen Väter vom Opfer im christlichen Cultus, 1841. More definite is the language of *Justin M.* Dial. c. Tryph. c. 117, who calls the Lord's Supper θυσία and προσφορά, and compares it with the sacrifices under the Old Testament dispensation.[1] He connects with this the offering of prayers (εὐχαριστία), which are also sacrifices. But Christians themselves are the sacrifices; there is not the slightest allusion to a repeated sacrifice of Himself on the part of Christ. Comp. *Ebrard*, l.c. s. 236 ff. *Irenæus*, Adv. Hær. iv. 17, 5, p. 249 (*Gr.* 324), teaches, with equal clearness, that Christ had commanded, not for the sake of *God*, but of the *disciples*, to offer the first-fruits; and thus, breaking the bread and blessing the cup with thanksgiving, He instituted oblationem, quam ecclesia ab Apostolis accipiens in universo mundo offert Deo, ei qui alimenta nobis præstat, primitias suorum munerum, etc. The principal thing, too, is the disposition of the person who makes the offering. On the difficult passage, iv. 18, p. 251 (*Gr.* 326): Judæi autem jam non offerunt, manus enim eorum sanguine plenæ sunt: non enim

[1] Namely, "*as a thankoffering for the gifts of nature, to which was then added thanksgiving for all other divine blessings. . . . The primitive Church had a distinct conception of this connection between the Lord's Supper and what might be called the natural aspect of the Passover.*"—*Baur*, l.c. s. 137.

receperunt verbum, quod (per quod ?) offertur Deo.[1] Comp. *Massuet*, Diss. iii. in Iren. *Deylingii* Obss. sacr. P. iv. p. 92 ss., and *Neander*, Kg. i. 2, s. 588, Dg. s. 251.[2] *Origen* knows only the *one* sacrifice offered by Christ. It is fitting, however, for Christians to offer spiritual sacrifices (sacrificia spiritualia). Hom. xxiv. in Num. et Hom. v. in Lev. (Opp. ii. p. 209): Notandum est quod quæ offeruntur in holocaustum, interiora sunt; quod vero exterius est, Domino non offertur. Ibid. p. 210: Ille obtulit sacrificium laudis, pro cujus actibus, pro cujus doctrina, præceptis, verbo, et moribus, et disciplina laudatur et benedicitur Deus (as in Matt. v. 16). Comp. *Höfling*, Origenis Doctrina de Sacrificiis Christianorum in examen vocatur, parts 1 and 2 (Erl. 1840, 1841), especially part 2, p. 24 ss. *Redepenning*, Origen. ii. 437, and *Rückert*, s. 383.

(9) *Tert.* De Cor. Mil. 3: Oblationes pro defunctis, pro natalitiis annua die facimus. De Exh. Cast. 11: Pro uxore defuncta oblationes annuas reddis, etc., where he also uses the term sacrificium. De Monog. 10, he even speaks of a *refrigerium*, which hence accrues to the dead, comp. de Orat. 14 (19). Here also we might be reminded that Tertullian, as Christians in general, called prayers "sacrifices" (even the whole Christian worship is called by Tertullian sacrificium, see *Ebrard*, s. 224); on the other hand, it should not be overlooked that in the above passage, De Monogamia, prayers and sacrifices are distinctly separated. *Neander*, Antignostikus, s. 155. *Höfling*, s. 207–215. *Rückert*, s. 376 ff.

(10) *Cyprian* is the first of all the Fathers who, in accordance with his hierarchical tendency, gave to the idea of sacrifice such a turn, that it is no longer the congregation that brings the thankoffering, but the *priest* taking the place of Christ who offered Himself a sacrifice: vice Christi fungitur, id quod Christus fecit, imitatur, et sacrificium verum et plenum tunc offert in ecclesia Deo Patri. But even *Cyprian* does not go beyond the idea of the sacrifice being *imitated*, which is very different from that of its actual *repetition*.

---
[1] Just before, it is said: Offertur Deo ex creatura ejus; and § 6: per Christum offert ecclesia.
[2] Neander considers the reading *per quod* offertur as unquestionably the correct one.

Comp. *Rettberg*, s. 334, and *Neander*, l.c. i. 2, s. 588. *Ebrard*, l.c. s. 249, directs attention to the obliquities in *Cyprian's* modes of statement. [Comp. *Marheineke*, Symbolik, iii. 420.]

(11) Concerning the Ebionites, see *Credner*, l.c. iii. s. 308; on the Ophites, *Epiph.* Hær. 37, 5. *Baur*, Gnosis, s. 196. As the result of more recent examinations, it may be stated that generally " *the idea of a real presence, and of a real participation of the actual body and blood of Christ, is entirely foreign to the Greek Fathers of this period*" (*Steitz*, l.c. x. 3, s. 401). Even when they speak of eating the body and drinking the blood of Christ, they are thinking not of a corporeal, but of a spiritual food. " *Beside the glory of the Logos, the corporeal and human in Christ stepped into the background, in order that His Godhead might be made more manifest*," ibid.

If we compare the preceding statements with the doctrines afterwards set forth in the confessions of faith, we arrive at the following conclusions :—1. The Roman Catholic notion of transubstantiation is as yet altogether unknown ; yet there are tendencies that way, as well as to the theory of sacrifice. 2. The views of *Ignatius, Justin,* and *Irenæus* (which last *Rückert* calls *metabolism*) can be compared with the Lutheran, only so far as they stand in the middle between strict transubstantiation and the merely symbolical view, and hold fast to an objective union of the sensible with the supersensible. 3. The theologians of North Africa and Alexandria represent the type of doctrine in the Reformed Church, in such a way that the positive side of the Calvinistic doctrine may be best seen in *Clement*, the negative view of Zwingli in *Origen;* and both the positive and the negative aspects of the Reformed doctrine are united in *Tertullian* and *Cyprian*. The Ebionites might then be considered as the forerunners of the Socinians, the Gnostics of the Quakers. Yet caution is needed in instituting such comparisons, for no phase of history is entirely identical with any other, and partisan prejudices have always disturbed the historical point of view.

§ 74.

Idea of the Sacrament.

Steitz, Article " Sacramente," in Herzog's Realencyklopädie, xiii. s. 226 ff. *G. L. Hahn*, Die Lehre v. den Sacramenten in ihrer geschichtlichen Entwicklung innerhalb der abendl. Kirche. See below, § 136.

The two ordinances of Baptism and the Lord's Supper

existed before a systematic definition of the term Sacrament had been formed, so as to include both (1). The terms μυστήριον and *sacramentum* are, indeed, already used to designate both (2); but they are quite as frequently applied to other religious symbols and usages, which implied a high religious idea, and also to the more profound doctrines of the Church (3).

(1) The New Testament does not contain the idea of *sacrament*, as such. Baptism and the Lord's Supper were not instituted by Christ as two connected rites; but each in its own place and time, without a hint of a relation of the one to the other. In the apostolical epistles, it has been thought that a connection of the two is indicated in 1 John v. 6: that it does not refer to the two sacraments, see *Lücke's* commentary on the passage [in the same sense, *Estius, Düsterdieck*, etc.]. More pertinent is 1 Cor. x. 4 (comp. 1 Cor. xii. 13). These two rites, however, having been instituted by Christ, assumed special prominence, as did also their relation to each other.

(2) As *Tertullian*, generally speaking, is the author of the later dogmatic terminology (comp. the phrases: novum Testamentum, Trinitas, peccatum originale, satisfactio), so he is the first writer who uses the phrase sacramentum baptismatis et eucharistiæ, Adv. Marc. iv. 30. Comp, *Baumgarten-Crusius*, ii. s. 1188, and the works quoted by him. The corresponding Greek term μυστήριον occurs in *Justin*, Apol. i. 66, and *Clem.* Pæd. i. p. 123. Comp. *Suicer*, sub voce; and, on the Latin expressions, *Hahn*, l.c. 5 ff., and in his treatise, "Sacrament im sinne der alten Kirchl." (in the Theol. kirch. Annal., Breslau 1849, 1).

(3) *Tertullian* also uses the word "sacramentum" in a more general sense, Adv. Marc. v. 18, and Adv. Prax. 30, where he uses the word for religion in general. Comp. the Indices Latinitatis Tertullianeæ by *Semler* and *Oehler*. Equally varied is the use of the term μυστήριον. *Cyprian* knows nothing of an exclusive terminology on this point. He speaks, indeed (Ep. 63), of a sacrament of the Lord's Supper, but also of a sacrament of the Trinity (De Orat. Dom.,

§ 74.]   IDEA OF THE SACRAMENT.   299

where the Lord's Prayer itself is called a sacrament). On the twofold sense of the Latin word, sometimes denoting an oath, sometimes used as the translation of the Greek term μυστήριον, see *Rettberg*, s. 324, 325, and compare *Rückert*, s. 315.

SIXTH DIVISION.

THE LAST THINGS.
(ESCHATOLOGY.)

§ 75.

The Second Advent of Christ—Millenarianism. (Chiliasm.)

(*Corrodi*) Kritische Geschichte des Chiliasmus, Zür. 1781–1785, iii. 1794. W. *Münscher*, Entwicklung der Lehre vom tausendjährigen Reiche in den 3 ersten Jahrhunderten, in Henke's Magazin. Bd. iv. s. 233 ff. [Cf. *Smith, Herzog*, etc., s.v. W. *Floerke*, Die Lehre vom tausendjährigen Reiche, Marb. 1859.] *M. Kirchner*, die Eschatologie des Irenæus (Stud. u. Kritik. 1863, 2, s. 315 ff.).

THE disciples of Christ having received from their Master the promise of His second coming (παρουσία), the first Christians looked upon this event as near at hand, and, in connection with it, the resurrection of the dead and the judgment (1). The Book of Revelation (which many ascribed to the Apostle John, while others denied this, and even contested its canonicity) (2), in its 20th chapter, gave currency to the idea of a millennial kingdom, together with that of a double resurrection, also found in the same book (3); and the imagination of those who dwelt fondly upon sensuous impressions, delineated these millennial hopes in the most glowing terms. This was the case not only with the Judaizing Ebionites (4) and *Cerinthus* (5) (according to the testimony of some writers), but also with several orthodox Fathers, such as *Papias* of Hierapolis, *Justin, Irenæus* (6), and *Tertullian.* The millennial notions of the latter were supported by his Montanistic views (7). In *Cyprian* we find only an echo in a more subdued tone of the ideas of *Tertullian* (8). The Gnostics were from the first unfavourable to millenarian tendencies (9), which were also opposed by some orthodox writers, *e.g.* the Presbyter *Caius* in Rome, and by the theologians of the Alexandrian school, especially *Origen* (10).

(1) Comp. the works on Biblical Theology. On the importance of eschatology in the first period, and its necessary connection with Christology, see *Dorner's* Person Christi, i. 232 ff. [" The Christian hope in the Christ that was to come grew out of faith in the Christ who had already come." " The Christian principle celebrated its apotheosis in the eschatology. For the whole universe is ordered in reference to Christ. What is not a part of the eternal kingdom, must at the end of all things be entirely rejected, become powerless and worthless."] The distinction between the second coming of Christ and the first was founded on the New Testament. *Justin M.* Apol. i. 52: Δύο γὰρ αὐτοῦ παρουσίας προεκήρυξαν οἱ προφῆται· μίαν μὲν τὴν ἤδη γενομένην, ὡς ἀτίμου καὶ παθητοῦ ἀνθρώπου, τὴν δὲ δευτέραν, ὅταν μετὰ δόξης ἐξ οὐρανῶν μετὰ τῆς ἀγγελικῆς αὐτοῦ στρατιᾶς παραγενήσεσθαι κεκήρυκται, ὅτε καὶ τὰ σώματα ἀνεγερεῖ πάντων τῶν γενομένων ἀνθρώπων κ.τ.λ. Cf. Dial. c. Tryph. 32, 45, 49, 51. *Iren.* i. 10 (he makes a distinction between ἔλευσις and παρουσία), iv. 22, 2.

(2) See above, § 31, note 7, especially *Euseb.* vii. 25, and the introductions to the commentaries on the Book of Revelation (*Lücke*). According to the latest criticism, the author of the Apocalypse was, indeed, the real John; but because entangled in the Ebionitish and Jewish modes of thought, he cannot be the same with John the Evangelist; compare *Baur* (in *Zellers* Theol. Jahrb. 1844) and *Schwegler's* Nachapost. Zeitalter, s. 66 ff. In opposition to them, *Ebrard* endeavours to harmonize the standpoint of the Apocalypse with that of the Gospel; see his Evangel. Johannes und die neueste Hypothese über seine Entstehung (Zürich 1845), s. 137 ff.—We cannot regard the acts in this controversy as definitely closed. [The latest criticism is decidedly in favour of the opinion, that the Apostle John wrote the Apocalypse. Cf. *Hilgenfeld*, Einleitung in d. N. T. 1875. Passages in Register ad fin.]

(3) Comp. the commentaries on this chapter. From *Justin's*

larger Apology, c. 52, it has been inferred that, though a millenarian, he held to only *one* resurrection (τὰ σώματα ἀνεργεῖ πάντων τῶν γενομένων ἀνθρώπων); so *Münter* (älteste Dogmengesch. ii. 2, s. 269), and also *Gieseler*, Dogmengesch. s. 241 and 247. But in the Dial. c. Tryph. c. 81, *Justin* teaches a double resurrection; comp. *Semisch*, ii. s. 471 ff. He calls the *first* resurrection *holy* (Dial. c. Tryph. c. 113), but the *second*, the *general*. *Irenæus*, too (v. c. 32), and *Tertullian* (De Resur. Carn. c. 42, and De Anima, c. 58) teach a double resurrection, or (in the case of *Tertull.*) a progressive resurrection (?); comp. *Gieseler*, u. s., s. 241. [" The wholly pure will rise at once; those, however, who have contracted great guilt, must make amends by staying a longer time in the under-world, and rising later;" and thus he interprets Matt. v. 26. Comp. also *Maitland's* Apostle's School of Prophetic Interpretation, 1849. *Auberlen*, Der Prophet Daniel und die Offenbarung Johannis, 3 Ausg. Basel 1874. *Alford's* Greek Test. in loc. *Reuss*, Théologie Chrétienne, vol. i. p. 429 ss., 3d ed. Stras. et Paris 1864.]

(4) *Jerome*, in his Comment. on Isa. lxvi. 20, observes that the Ebionites understand the passage, " And they shall bring all your brethren for an offering unto the Lord out of all nations upon horses, and in chariots, and in litters, and upon mules, and upon swift beasts," in its literal sense, and apply it to chariots drawn by four horses, and conveyances of every description. They believe that at the last day, when Christ shall reign at Jerusalem, and the temple be rebuilt, the Israelites will be gathered together from all the ends of the earth. They will have no wings to fly, but they will come in carriages of Gaul; in covered chariots of war, on horses of Spain and Cappadocia; their wives will be carried in litters, and ride upon mules of Numidia instead of horses. Those who hold offices, dignitaries and princes, will come in chariots from Britain, Spain, Gaul, and the regions where the river Rhine is divided into arms; the subdued nations will hasten to meet them. But the Clementine Homilies and the Gnostic Ebionities, far from adopting this gross chiliasm (*Credner*, l.c. iii. s. 289, 290), even oppose it; see *Schliemann*, s. 251 and 519.

(5) *Euseb.* iii. 28, from the accounts given by *Caius* of Rome and *Dionysius* of Alexandria. According to *Caius*,

§ 75.] THE SECOND ADVENT OF CHRIST. 303

Cerinthus taught: Μετὰ τὴν ἀνάστασιν ἐπίγειον εἶναι τὸ βασίλειον τοῦ Χριστοῦ καὶ πάλιν ἐπιθυμίαις καὶ ἡδοναῖς ἐν Ἱερουσαλὴμ τὴν σάρκα πολιτευομένην δουλεύειν, this sta!e would last a thousand years; according to *Dionysius:* ἐπίγειον ἔσεσθαι τὴν τοῦ Χριστοῦ βασιλείαν· Καὶ ὧν αὐτὸς ὠρέγετο φιλοσώματος ὢν καὶ πάνυ σαρκικὸς, ἐν τούτοις ὀνειροπολεῖν ἔσεσθαι, γαστρὸς καὶ τῶν ὑπὸ γαστέρα πλησμονῶν, τουτέστι σιτίοις καὶ πότοις καὶ γάμοις καὶ δι' ὧν εὐφημότερον ταῦτα ᾠήθη ποριεῖσθαι, ἑορταῖς καὶ θυσίαις καὶ ἱερείων σφαγαῖς. Comp. iii. 25, and *Theodoret*, Fab. Hær. ii. 3, and the works referred to in § 23. [*Burton*, Bampton Lecture, Lect. VI. p. 177-179, and note 76.] But that chiliasm did not come into the orthodox Church through *Cerinthus* is shown by *Gieseler*, Dogmengesch. s. 234. [This is declared by *Eusebius*, Hist. Eccl. iii. c. 28, and *Theodoret* and others. But *Eusebius* (iii. 39) accuses *Papias* of having spread millenarianism, from a misunderstanding of the apostles, and calls him on this very account σφόδρα σμικρὸς τὸν νοῦν. But *Justin* (Dial. p. 306), writing at the time of *Papias,* says that it was the general faith of all orthodox Christians, and that only the Gnostics did not share it. Comp. *Irenæus*, v. 25, 26. *Tertull.* c. Marc. iii. 24, and the apocryphal books of the period.]

(6) " *In all the works of this period (the first two centuries) millenarianism is so prominent, that we cannot hesitate to consider it as universal in an age, when such sensuous motives were certainly not unnecessary to animate men to suffer for Christianity,*" *Gieseler*, Kg. Bd. i. s. 166 ; Dogmengesch. s. 231 ff. Comp., however, the writings of *Clement* of Rome, *Ignatius, Polycarp, Tatian, Athenagoras*, and *Theophilus* of Antioch, in none of which millenarian notions are propounded. May anything be inferred from this silence ? On the millennial views of *Papias*, see *Euseb*. iii. 39 : Χιλιάδα τινά φησιν ἐστῶν ἔσεσθαι μετὰ τὴν ἐκ νεκρῶν ἀνάστασιν, σωματικῶς τῆς τοῦ Χριστοῦ βασιλείας ἐπὶ ταυτησὶ τῆς γῆς ὑποστησομένης. Comp. *Barn*. c. 15 (Ps. xc. 4); *Hermas*, lib. i. Vis. i. 3, and the observations of *Jachmann,* s. 86.—*Justin*, Dial. c. Tr. 80, 81, asserts that, according to his own opinion and that of the other orthodox theologians (εἴ τινές εἰσιν ὀρθογνώμονες κατὰ πάντα χριστιανοί), the elect will rise from the

dead, and spend a thousand years in the city of Jerusalem, which will be restored, changed, and beautified (in support of his views he appeals to Jeremiah and Ezekiel) ; at the same time, he admits that even orthodox Christians (τῆς καθαρᾶς καὶ εὐσεβοῦς γνώμης[1]) entertain different views. Comp. Apol. i. 11, where he opposes the hope of a human political kingdom, but not that of a millennial reign of Christ. *Justin* holds an intermediate position between a gross, sensuous view (συμπιεῖν πάλιν καὶ συμφαγεῖν, Dial. c. Tr. § 51) on the one hand, and a spiritualizing idealism on the other. Comp. *C. Semisch*, Justin Martyr, l.c. *Irenæus*, Adv. Hær. v. 33, p. 332 (*Gr.* 453), defends chiliasm, especially in opposition to the Gnostics. He appeals, *e.g.*, to Matt. xxvi. 29 and Isa. xi. 6.—On the highly sensuous and fantastical description (carried out with genuine Rabbinic taste) of the fertility of the vine and of corn, which is said to have originated with *Papias* and the disciples of John, see *Münscher, von Cölln*, i. s. 44. *Grabe*, Spic. Sæc. 2, p. 31 and 230. *Corrodi*, ii. s. 406. *Iren.* Adv. Hær. v. 33 : " The days will come in which vines will grow, each having ten thousand branches ; and on each branch there will be ten thousand twigs, and on each twig ten thousand clusters of grapes, and in each cluster ten thousand grapes ; and each grape, when expressed, will yield twenty-five μετρῆται of wine. And when any one of the saints shall take hold of a cluster of grapes, another (cluster) will cry out : I am a better cluster, take me, and on my account give thanks to the Lord. In like manner, a grain of wheat will produce ten thousand heads, and each head will have ten thousand grains ; and each grain will yield ten pounds of the finest wheaten flour ; and other fruits will yield seeds and herbage in the same proportion." This fruitfulness of the corn he regards as necessary on account of the lion eating straw ; and

---

[1] Various writers have endeavoured to remove the contradiction between these two views. *Rössler*, i. s. 164, interpolates thus : many *otherwise* orthodox Christians ; *Dallæus, Münscher* (Handbuch, ii. s. 420), *Münter, Schwegler* (Montan. s. 137), interpolate the word μή [comp. *Gieseler*, l.c. i. § 52, note 19]. *Semisch*, in opposition to this, ii. s. 469, note : "*Justin does not assert that all, but that only the all-sided, the complete believers, are chiliasts.*" According to *Baur* (Dg. s. 701), the passage can only be understood to say that chiliasm (millenarianism) is the faith of all true Christians, and that only the Gnostics are excluded from it. (Comp. theol. Jahrb. 1857, s. 218 ff.)

§ 75.]   THE SECOND ADVENT OF CHRIST.   305

the wheat must also be such " cujus palea congrua ad escam erit leonum." See also *Corrodi*, ii. s. 496 ; *Gieseler*, Dogmengesch. s. 235 ; *Kirchner*, l.c. *Dorner* tries to give a more spiritual turn to this chiliasm ; he does not view it as necessarily connected with Judaizing tendencies ; see his Lehre von d. Person Christi, i. 240 f. note. [He views it as the counterpoise to the Gnostic abstractions, and as containing a genuine historical element ; and particularly opposes the views of *Corrodi*, which have been too implicitly followed by many German Church historians.] On the Sibylline Oracles, the Book of Enoch (probably a purely Jewish product), the Testaments of the XII. Patriarchs, and the New Testament Apocrypha, see *Gieseler*, Dogmengesch. s. 243 ff. [also *Hilgenfeld*, Die Jüdische Apocalypse, 1859].

(7) *Tertullian's* views are intimately connected with his Montanistic notions. His treatise, De Spe Fidelium (Hieron. de Vir. illus. c. 18, and in Ezech. c. 36), is indeed lost ; but comp. Adv. Marc. iii. 24. *Tertullian*, however, speaks not so much of sensual enjoyments, as of a copia omnium bonorum spiritualium, and even opposes the too sensuous interpretations of Messianic passages, De Resurr. Carn. c. 26, though many sensuous images pervade his own expositions ; comp. *Neander*, Antignostikus, s. 499 ; Kg. i. 3, s. 1092. On the question, how far we may implicitly rely on the assertion of *Euseb.* v. 16, that Montanus had fixed upon the city of Pepuza, in Phrygia, as the seat of the millennial kingdom, and on the millenarian notions of the Montanists in general, see *Gieseler*, Kg. i. s. 152.

(8) Respecting his doctrine of Antichrist, and his belief that the end of the world was near, comp. Ep. 58 (p. 120, 124), Ep. 61 (p. 144) ; Exh. Mart. ab. init. p. 167. Tert. Adv. Jud. iii. § 118 (p. 91), see *Rettberg*, s. 340 ff.

(9) This is evident both from the nature of Gnosticism itself, and the opposition which *Irenæus* made to it. Some have even ascribed the origin of *Marcion's* system to his opposition to millenarianism ; comp. however, *Baur*, Gnosis, s. 295.

(10) Concerning *Caius* and his controversy with the Montanist *Proclus*, see *Neander*, Kg. i. s. 1093.—*Origen* speaks in very strong terms against the millenarians, whose opinions

he designates as ineptæ fabulæ, figmenta inania, δόγματα ἀτοπώτατα, μοχθηρά, etc., De Princip. ii. c. 11, § 2 (Opp. i. p. 164); Contra Cels. iv. 22 (Opp. i. p. 517); Select. in Ps. (Opp. t. ii. p. 570); in Cant. Cant. (Opp. t. iii. p. 28). *Münscher, von Cölln,* i. p. 44–46. Respecting *Hippolytus,* who wrote a treatise on Antichrist without being a real millenarian, comp. *Photius,* Cod. 202. *Haenell,* de Hippolyto (Gött. 1838), p. 37, 60. *Corrodi,* ii. s. 401, 406, 413, 416.

§ 76.

The Resurrection.

G. A. Teller, Fides Dogmatis de Resurrectione Carnis per 4 priora secula, Hal. et Helmst. 1766. *Ch. W. Flügge,* Geschichte der Lehre vom Zustände des Menschen nach dem Tode, Leipz. 1799, 1800. †*Hubert Beckers,* Mittheilungen aus den merkwürdigsten Schriften der verflossenen Jahrhunderte über den Zustand der Seele nach dem Tode, Augsb. 1835, 1836. † *C. Ramers,* des Origenes Lehre von der Auferstehung des Fleisches, Trier. 1851. [*Bush,* Anastasis, New York, 3d ed. 1845. *Robt. Landis,* Doctrine of the Resurr., Phila. 1848. *Delitzsch,* Bibl. Psychol., Leipz. *Rinck,* Zustand nach dem Tode, Ludgwigsb. 1861.]

Though traces of the doctrine of the resurrection of the body, which is set forth by the Apostle Paul in such a majestic manner, may be found in some conceptions of greater antiquity (1), yet it received a personal centre, and was made popular even among the uneducated, only after the resurrection of Christ (2). During the period of Apologetics this doctrine of the resurrection (of the flesh) was further developed on the basis of the Pauline teaching (3). The objections of its opponents, proceeding from a tendency limited to sense and the understanding, were more or less fully answered in the Epistle of *Clement* of Rome to the Corinthians, as well as in the writings of *Justin, Athenagoras, Theophilus, Irenæus, Tertullian, Minucius Felix, Cyprian,* and others (4). Most of the Fathers believed in the resuscitation of the body, and of the very same body which man possessed while on earth (5). The theologians of the Alexandrian school, however, formed an exception; *Origen*, in particular (6), endeavoured to clear the doctrine in question from its false additions, by reducing it to the genuine idea of Paul; but, at the same time, he sought to refine and to spiritualize it after the manner of the Alexandrian school. The Gnostics, on the other hand, rejected the doctrine of the resurrection of the body entirely (7); while the false teachers of Arabia, whom *Origen* combated, asserted that both soul and body fall into a sleep of death, from which they will not awake till the last day (8).

(1) Comp. *Herder*, Von der Auferstehung (Werke, Zur Religion und Theologie, vol. xi.).—*G. Müller*, über die Auferstehungslehre der Person, in the Studien und Kritiken, 1835, 2d part, s. 477 ff. *Corrodi*, l.c. s. 345. On the doctrine of Christ and of the Apostle Paul (1 Cor. xv., 2 Cor. v.), and on the opponents of the doctrine in the apostolic age (Hymenæus and Philetus), see the works on Biblical Theology. [*Fries*, Ueber Auferstehung, in the Jahrb. f. deutsche Theol. 1856. *Delitzsch*, Bibl. Psychol. 1855, p. 400 ff. *John Brown*, Resurrection to Life, Edin. 1852.]

(2) It naturally excites surprise that, while Paul represents *the resurrection of Christ* as the central point of the whole doctrine, the Fathers of the present period keep this fact so much in the background; at least it is not, with all of them, the foundation of their opinions concerning the resurrection of the body. Some, *e.g. Athenagoras*, who yet devoted a whole book to the subject, and *Minucius Felix*, are entirely silent on the resurrection of Christ (see below); the others also rest their arguments chiefly upon reason and analogies from nature (the change of day and night, seed and fruit, the phœnix, etc., *Clement* of Rome, c. 24, and Ep. 11, 9).

(3) It belongs to exegetical theology to inquire how far the New Testament teaches an ἀνάστασις τῆς σαρκός, and what is the relation of the σάρξ to the σῶμα, and to the ἀνάστασις τῶν νεκρῶν. Comp. *Zyro*, Ob Fleisch oder Leib das Auferstehende, in Illgens Zeitschrift, 1849, s. 639 ff. At any rate, the expression resurrectio carnis soon became current, and thus it passed over into the so-called Apostles' Creed.

(4) *Clement*, Ep. i. ad Cor. c. 24 (comp. note 2). *Justin*

M. adopts the literal interpretation of the doctrine of the resurrection of the body, and, in the form that it will rise again with all its members, Fragm. de Resurr. c. 3 (edited as a separate programme by *Teller,* 1766; extracts in *Rössler,* Bibl. i. 174). Comp. *Semisch,* ii. s. 146 ff. Even cripples will rise as such, but at the moment of the resurrection be restored by Christ, and put into a more perfect condition; De Resurr. c. 4, and Dial. c. Tryph. § 69. *Justin* founds his belief in the resurrection of the body chiefly upon the omnipotence, justice, and benevolence of God, upon the miracles of Jesus in raising the dead while He was upon the earth, and also, in fine, upon the resurrection of Christ Himself;[1] and shows, in connection with it, that the body must necessarily participate in future rewards or punishments, for body and soul necessarily constitute one whole; like two bullocks, they make one team. Alone, they can accomplish as little as one ox in ploughing. According to *Justin,* Christianity differs from the systems of both *Pythagoras* and *Plato,* in that it teaches not only the immortality of the soul, but also the resurrection of the body. But as *Justin* investigated this subject more thoroughly, he was necessarily led to the discussion of certain questions which have generally been reserved for scholastic acumen, *e.g.* relating to the sexual relations of the resurrection-bodies, which he compares to mules! [Quæst. et Resp. p. 423: Tametsi membra genitalia post resurrectionem, ad prolificationem utilia non erunt: ad reminiscentiam tamen ejus facient, quod per ea membra mortales acceperint generationem, auctum, et diurnitatem. Inducimur namque per ea ad cogitationem tam prolixæ sapientiæ *Christi,* quæ illa hominibus per mortem intercedentibus attribuit, ad eorum per generationem augendorum conservationem, ut, sobolis creatæ successione, genus nostrum in immortalitatem (perduceret).]— The arguments which *Athenagoras* adduces in his treatise De Resurr. (especially c. 11) are partly the same which were in after ages urged by natural theology in support of the doctrine of immortality; the moral nature of man, his liberty, and the retributive justice of God. Concerning the resurrection of the body, he has regard to the objections which have been made

---

[1] On the other hand, he fails to take notice of the analogies from nature, which others adduce; as *Semisch* (s. 148) has remarked.

to it at all times, on the ground of the natural course of things (the fact that the elements of one organism may enter into the composition of another, etc.). He is, however, comforted by the idea that at the resurrection all things will be restored, πρὸς τὴν τοῦ αὐτοῦ σώματος ἁρμονίαν καὶ σύστασιν.—*Theophilus*, Ad Aut. i. 8, uses similar language.—*Irenæus*, Adv. Hær. v. 12 and 13, also asserts the identity of the future with the present body, and appeals to the analogous revivification (not new creation) of separate organs of the body in some of the miraculous cures performed by Christ (*e.g.* of the blind man, the man with the withered hand). He alludes particularly to those whom Christ raised from the dead, the son of the widow at Nain, and Lazarus (but makes no mention of the body of Christ Himself!).[1] That *Tertullian*, who wrote a separate work on this subject (De Resurrectione Carnis), believed in the resurrection of the body, is what we might expect, especially as he made no strict distinction between the body and the soul. In illustration, he acutely points out the intimate connection existing between the one and the other during the present life: Nemo tam proximus tibi (animæ), quem post Dominum diligas, nemo magis frater tuus, quæ (sc. caro) tecum etiam in Deo nascitur (c. 63). In his opinion, the flesh participates in spiritual blessings, in the means of grace presented to us in unction, baptism, and the Lord's Supper; it even participates in martyrdom (the baptism of blood)! The body, too, is created after the image of God! (comp. above, § 56, note 3). He uses the same illustrations of day and night, the phœnix, etc., which we find in the writings of others, and maintains the identity of the future with the present body, c. 52: Certe non aliud resurgit quam quod seminatur, nec aliud seminatur quam quod dissolvitur humi, nec aliud dissolvitur humi quam caro, cf. 6, cap. 63. He endeavours to meet the objection, that certain members will be of no use in the future life, by saying that the members of the human body are not only designed for the mean service of the visible world, but also for something higher. Even on earth the mouth serves, not only for the purpose of eating, but also to speak and praise God, etc., c. 60 and 61.

[1] *Irenæus* takes the word "flesh" in 1 Cor. xv. 50, which was often quoted against the doctrine of the resurrection of the flesh, to mean *fleshly mind*.

Highly suggestive is the thought of *Tertullian* (De Res. c. 12), that inasmuch as a resurrection takes place in nature *for* man (omnia homini resurgunt), he himself, as the end of all nature and its metamorphoses, must also rise. The ordo revolubilis rerum is to him a testatio resurrectionis mortuorum. *Minucius Felix* makes Cæcilius bring forward the objections of the heathen to the possibility both of an incorporeal immortality and of a resurrection of the body, c. 11: Vellem tamen sciscitari, utrumne sine corpore, an cum corporibus, et corporibus quibus, ipsisne an innovatis resurgatur? Sine corpore? hoc, quod sciam, neque mens, neque anima, nec vita est. Ipso corpore? sed jam ante dilapsum est. Alio corpore? ergo homo novus nascitur, non prior ille reparatur. Et tamen tanta ætas abiit, sæcula innumera fluxerunt; quis unus ab inferis vel Protesilari sorte remeavit, horarum saltem permisso commeatu, vel ut exemplo crederemus?—Every one expects that Octavius will name *Christ* as this Protesilaus! But in vain. The arguments which he adduces, c. 34, in reply to these objections are restricted to the omnipotence of God, which created man out of nothing, and this is certainly more difficult than the mere restoration of his body; to the above analogies from nature (expectandum nobis etiam corporis ver est), and to the necessity of retribution, which those who deny the resurrection are anxious to escape.—The notions of *Cyprian* on this subject are formed after those of *Tertullian*, comp. De Habitu Virg. p. 100, and *Rettberg*, s. 345.

(5) See the passages quoted in the preceding note.

(6) *Clement* of Alexandria had intended to write a separate work περὶ ἀναστάσεως, comp. Pæd. i. 6, p. 125 (*Sylb.* 104); according to *Euseb.* vi. 24, and *Hieron.* apud Rufinum, *Origen* composed not only two books, but also (according to the latter) two dialogues (?) on this subject, comp. Contra Cels. v. 20 (Opp. i. p. 592), De Princip. ii. 10, 1, p. 100, and the Fragments, Opp. t. i. p. 33-37. *Clement* of Alexandria, in such of his writings as are yet extant, only touches upon the doctrine of the resurrection without discussing it. The passage, Strom. iv. 5, p. 569 (*Sylb.* 479), where he represents the future deliverance of the soul from the fetters of the body as the object of the most ardent desire of the wise man, does

§ 76.] THE RESURRECTION. 311

not give a very favourable idea of his orthodoxy on this point. But his disciple *Origen* maintains, Comm. in Matt. (Opp. iii. p. 811, 812), that we may put our trust in Christ without believing the resurrection of the body, provided we hold fast the immortality of the soul. Nevertheless he defended the doctrine of the Church against Celsus, but endeavoured to divest it of everything which might give a handle to scoffers: on this account he rejected the doctrine of the identity of the bodies (which is not that of Paul). Contra Cels. iv. 57 (Opp. i. p. 548, v. 18 (ibid. p. 590): Οὔτε μὲν οὖν ἡμεῖς, οὔτε τὰ θεῖα γράμματα αὐταῖς φησὶ σαρξὶ μηδεμίαν μεταβολὴν ἀνειληφυίαις τὴν ἐπὶ τὸ βέλτιον, ζήσεσθαι τοὺς πάλαι ἀποθανόντας, ἀπὸ τῆς γῆς ἀναδύντας. Ὁ δὲ Κέλσος συκοφαντεῖ ἡμᾶς ταῦτα λέγων. Cap. 23, p. 594: Ἡμεῖς μὲν οὖν οὔ φαμεν τὸ διαφθαρὲν σῶμα ἐπανέρχεσθαι εἰς τὴν ἐξ ἀρχῆς φύσιν, ὡς οὐδὲ τὸν διαφθαρέντα κόκκον τοῦ σίτου ἐπανέρχεσθαι εἰς τὸν κόκκον τοῦ σίτου. Λέγομεν γὰρ ὥσπερ ἐπὶ τοῦ κόκκου τοῦ σίτου ἐγείρεται στάχυς, οὕτω λόγος τις ἔγκειται τῷ σώματι, ἀφ' οὗ μὴ φθειρομένου ἐγείρεται τὸ σῶμα ἐν ἀφθαρσίᾳ. The appeal to the omnipotence of God appeared to him an ἀτοπωτάτη ἀναχώρησις, p. 595, according to the principle εἰ γὰρ αἰσχρόν τι δρᾷ ὁ θεὸς, οὔκ ἐστι θεός; but the biblical doctrine of the resurrection, if rightly interpreted, includes nothing that is unworthy of God, comp. viii. 49, 50 (Opp. i. p. 777 s.); Selecta in Psalm (Opp. ii. p. 532–536), where he designates the literal interpretation as φλυαρία and πτωχῶν νοημάτων, and proves that every body must be adapted to the surrounding world. If we would live in water, we ought to be made like fish, etc. The heavenly state also demands glorified bodies, like those of Moses and Elias. In the same place *Origen* gives a more correct interpretation of Ezek. xxxvii.; Matt. viii. 12; Ps. iii. 5, and other passages, which were commonly applied to the resurrection of the body. Comp. De Princip. ii. 10 (Opp. i. p. 100, *Redep.* p. 223); *Schnitzer*, s. 147 ff.; *Baur*, Dg. 711. On the other side, *Hieron.* ad Pammach. ep. 38 (61); *Photius* (according to Method.), Cod. 234. The opinion held by *Origen's* later followers, and of which he himself was accused, that the resurrection bodies have the shape of a sphere, is supported, as far as he is concerned, by only a single passage, De Oratione (Opp. i. 268), in which, moreover, he refers to other (Platonic?) authorities; comp. *Redep.* ii. s. 463; *Ramers,* ubi supra, s. 69.

(7) Thus the Gnostic *Apelles* maintained that the work of Christ had reference only to the soul, and rejected the resurrection of the body. (*Baur,* Gnosis, s. 410.) A natural opinion of the Docetæ, as connected with their contempt for matter. [That the Gnostics believed in the immortality of the soul, appears certain; but their notions concerning matter made them shrink from the idea of a reunion of the body with the soul, and led them to reject the doctrine of the resurrection of the former. But they have unjustly been charged by the Fathers with a denial of the resurrection in general. Comp. *Burton,* Bampton Lecture, notes 58 and 59, and *Münscher, von Cölln,* i. s. 51, 52. *Mansel,* Gnostics, p. 50, 58 ff.]

(8) Respecting the error of the *Thnetopsychites* (as John Damascene first calls them) about the year 248, comp. *Euseb.* vi. 37: Τὴν ἀνθρωπείαν ψυχὴν τέως μὲν κατὰ τὸν ἐνεστῶτα καιρὸν ἅμα τῇ τελευτῇ συναποθνήσκειν τοῖς σώμασι καὶ συνδιαφθείρεσθαι, αὖθις δέ ποτε κατὰ τὸν τῆς ἀναστάσεως καιρὸν σὺν αὐτοῖς ἀναβιώσεσθαι.

§ 77.

The last Judgment—Hades—Purgatory—Conflagration of the World.

J. F. *Baumgarten,* Historia Doctrinæ de Statu Animarum separatarum, Hal. 1754. J. A. *Ernesti,* de veterum Patr. Opinione de Statu Medio Animarum a corpore sejunct. Excurs. in lectt. academ. in Ep. ad Hebr., Lips. 1795. [*Jac. Windet,* Στρωματεὺς ἰστπολικός, de Vita Functorum Statu ex Hebræorum et Græcorum comparatis Sententiis concinnatus, Lond. 1663, 1664. *Thom. Burnet,* De Statu Mortuorum et Resurgentium, Lond. 1757. Comp. *Knapp,* l.c. p. 463, 464, and 478, and the references § 69.]

The process of the general judgment, which was thought to be connected with the general resurrection, was depicted in various ways. Some ascribe the office of judge to the Son, others to the Father, both in opposition to the Hellenistic myth of the judges in the under-world (1). The idea of a *Hades* (שאול), known to both the Hebrews and the Greeks, was transferred to Christianity, and the assumption that the real happiness or the final misery of the departed did not commence till after the general judgment and the resurrection of the body, appeared to necessitate the belief in an intermediate state, in which the soul was supposed to remain from the moment of its separation from the body to this last catastrophe (2). *Tertullian*, however, held that the martyrs went at once to Paradise, the abode of the blessed, and thought that in this they enjoyed an advantage over other Christians (3); while *Cyprian* does not seem to know of any intermediate state whatever (4). The Gnostics rejected the belief in Hades, together with that of the resurrection of the body, and imagined that the spiritually-minded (the pneumatic) would, immediately after death, be delivered from the kingdom of the demiurge, and elevated to the πλήρωμα (5). The ancient Oriental and Parsic idea of a purifying fire already occurs during this period in the writings of *Clement* of Alexandria and *Origen*. This purifying fire, however, is not yet transferred to this intermediate state, but is either taken in a very general sense, or supposed to be connected with the general conflagration of the world (6).

(1) *Justin M.* Apol. i. 8 : Πλάτων δὲ ὁμοίως ἔφη 'Ραδάμανθον καὶ Μίνω κολάσειν τοὺς ἀδίκους παρ' αὐτοὺς ἐλθόντας, ἡμεῖς δὲ τὸ αὐτὸ πρᾶγμά φαμεν γενήσεσθαι, ἀλλ' ὑπὸ τοῦ Χριστοῦ. For the further views of *Justin* respecting the judgment, see Apol. ii. 9 ; *Semisch*, ii. s. 474, 475. Tatian, Contra Gr. 6 : Δικάζουσι δὲ ἡμῖν οὐ Μίνως, οὐδὲ 'Ραδάμανθος ... δοκιμαστὴς δὲ αὐτὸς ὁ ποιητὴς θεὸς γίνεται. Comp. c. 25.

(2) *Justin M.* Dial. c. Tryph. § 5, makes the souls of the pious take up a temporary abode in a better, those of the wicked in a worse place. He even stigmatizes as heretical (§ 80) the doctrine that souls are received into heaven immediately after death; but he admits that they possess a presentiment of their future destiny, Coh. ad Græc. c. 35 ; comp. *Semisch*, s. 464, note 3. The good, even before the final division, dwell in a happier, the evil in a more wretched abode; Dial. cum Tryph. § 5. On his opinion that, at the departure of the

soul from the body, the former fall into the hands of evil angels (Dial. c. Tryph. § 105), see *Semisch*, ii. s. 465. *Iren.* v. 31, p. 331 (*Gr.* 451): Αἱ ψυχαὶ ἀπέρχονται εἰς τὸν τόπον τὸν ὡρισμένον αὐταῖς ἀπὸ τοῦ θεοῦ, κἀκεῖ μέχρι τῆς ἀναστάσεως φοιτῶσι, περιμένουσαι τὴν ἀνάστασιν· ἔπειτα ἀπολαβοῦσαι τὰ σώματα καὶ ὁλοκλήρως ἀναστᾶσαι, τουτέστι σωματικῶς, καθὼς καὶ ὁ Κύριος ἀνέστη, οὕτως ἐλεύσονται εἰς τὴν ὄψιν τοῦ θεοῦ (in connection with this, the decensus Christi ad inferos, and Luke xvi. 22 ff.). *Irenæus* regards it as an evidence of pride, that the Gnostics held, with reference to the *pneumatic*, that they go, immediately after death, to the Father. According to *Irenæus*, however, the martyrs go direct to Paradise, which, however, he seems to distinguish from heaven. *Tertullian* mentions (De Anima, 55) a treatise in which he says he has proved, omnem animam apud inferos sequestrari in diem Domini. The treatise itself is no longer extant; but comp. De Anima, c. 7 (aliquid tormenti sive solatii anima præcerpit in carcere seu diversorio inferum, in igni, vel in sinu Abrahæ) and c. 58. *Tertullian* rejects the notion of *the sleep of the soul*, which is not to be confounded with the error of the Arabian false teachers; he also opposes the opinion, founded upon 1 Sam. xxviii., that spirits might be conjured up from the abode of the dead, by appealing to Luke xvi. 26 (comp. *Orig.* Hom. ii. in 1 Reg. Opp. ii. p. 490–498).

(3) *Tert.* De Anim. 55, De Resurr. 43: Nemo peregrinatus a corpore statim immoratur penes Dominum, nisi ex martyrii prærogativa, paradiso scilicet, non inferis deversurus. — On the meaning of the different terms: inferi, sinus Abrahæ, Paradisus, see Adv. Marc. iv. 34; Apol. c. 47; *Orig.* Hom. ii. in 1 Reg. l.c. and Hom. in Num. xxvi. 4; *Münscher, von Cölln,* i. s. 57, 58; *Gieseler*, Dogmengesch. s. 225 ff. [*Tertullian* says most on the subject of the under-world. He describes it (De Anim. 55) as an immense space in the depths of the earth, divided by an impassable gulf into two parts. The part assigned to the righteous he calls sinus Abrahæ, that of the wicked ignis, and sometimes inferi. So, too, *Hippolytus*, in a fragment, Opp. ed. *Fabricius*, i. 220. Paradise was a different place from this under-world; it is far above this earth, separated from it by a glowing girdle: thither Christ

went; and there, too, martyrs go at once; Enoch and Elijah were also transported thither. *Origen* held that before Christ no souls, not even those of the prophets and patriarchs, went to Paradise; but when Jesus descended to Hades He transferred them into the lower Paradise (in contrast with the upper), or the third heaven. The souls of pious Christians also go to this Paradise—which Origen identifies with the bosom of Abraham. Comp. *Delitzsch*, Bib. Ps. ut s.]

(4) *Cypr.* Adv. Demetr. p. 196, and Tract. de Mortalitate in various places; he expresses, *e.g.*, his hope that those who die of pestilence will come at once to Christ, p. 158, 164 (where he appeals to the example of Enoch), 166. *Rettberg*, s. 345.

(5) *Neander*, Gnost. Systeme, s. 141 ff. [" *The Gnostics taught that the soul of the perfect Gnostic, having risen again at baptism, and being enabled by perfection of knowledge to conquer the demiurge, or principle of evil, would ascend, as soon as it was freed from the body, to the heavenly pleroma, and dwell there for ever in the presence of the Father; while the soul of him who had not been allowed while on earth to arrive at such a plenitude of knowledge would pass through several transmigrations, till it was sufficiently purified to wing its flight to the pleroma.*" *Burton*, Bampton Lecture, Lect. V. p. 131.]

(6) The views of *Clement* on this subject are expressed in still more general terms, Pæd. iii. 9, towards the end, p. 282 (*Sylb.* p. 241), and Strom. vii. 6, p. 851 (*Sylb.* 709): Φαμὲν δ᾽ ἡμεῖς ἁγιάζειν τὸ πῦρ, οὐ τὰ κρέα, ἀλλὰ τὰς ἁμαρτωλοὺς ψυχάς· πῦρ οὐ τὸ πάμφαγον καὶ βάναυσον, ἀλλὰ τὸ φρόνιμον λέγοντες, τὸ διϊκνούμενον διὰ ψυχῆς τῆς διερχομένης τὸ πῦρ. From the whole context it appears that he speaks of the purifying efficacy of a mystical fire, even *during the present life*, perhaps in allusion to Matt. iii. 11; Luke iii. 16.— *Origen*, on the other hand, referring to 1 Cor. iii. 12, considers the fire which will consume the world at the last day as at the same time a πῦρ καθάρσιον, Contra Cels. v. 15. No one (not even Paul or Peter himself) can escape this fire, but it does not cause any pain to the pure (according to Isa. xliii. 2). It is a second sacramentum regenerationis; and as the baptism of blood was compared with the baptism of water (see above, § 72, note 10), so *Origen* thought that this *baptism of fire* at

the end of the world would be necessary in the case of those who have forfeited the baptism of the Spirit; in the case of all others it will be a testing fire. Comp. in Exod. Hom. vi. 4; in Psalm. Hom. iii. 1; in Luc. Hom. xiv. (Opp. iii. p. 948), xxiv. p. 961; in Jerem. Hom. ii. 3; in Ezech. Hom. i. 13; comp. *Redepenning*, s. 235. *Guericke*, De Schola Alexand. ii. p. 294. *Thomasius*, s. 250.

In respect to the *end of the world*, opinions wavered between *annihilation* and *transformation*. Most of the Fathers seem to have held to the latter view, but *Justin* (in opposition to the Stoic tenet) believed in a real annihilation; Apol. i. 20 and ii. 7. Comp. *Semisch*, ii. 475.

§ 78.

State of the Blessed and the Condemned.—Restitution of all Things.

J. F. *Cotta*, Historia succincta Dogmatis de Pœnarum Infernalium Duratione, Tüb. 1744. J. A. *Dietelmaier*, Commenti fanatici ἀποκαταστάσεως πάντων Historia antiquior, Altorf. 1769. [*Jukes*, Restitution of all Things, London, var. ed.]

Various expressions were used in religious language to denote the state of the blessed. The idea that different degrees of blessedness are proportionate to the different degrees of virtue exhibited in this life, was in harmony with the views of most of the Fathers of this period concerning the doctrine of moral freedom (1); and was also congruous with the idea of further progress after the present life. *Origen*, in particular, developed this latter notion (2), and also endeavoured to avoid as much as possible all sensuous representations of the pleasures of the future world, and to place them in purely spiritual enjoyments (3). Notions more or less gross prevailed concerning the punishment of the wicked, which most of the Fathers regarded as *eternal* (4). From the very nature of the case, it is evident that purely spiritual views on this subject could not reasonably be expected. Even *Origen* imagined the bodies of the damned to be black (5). But as he looked upon evil rather as a

§ 78.]   STATE OF THE BLESSED AND THE CONDEMNED.   317

negation and privation of good, he was induced, by his idealistic tendency, to set limits even to hell, and to hope for a final remission of the punishment of the wicked at the restitution of all things,, although in popular discourse he retained the common idea of eternal punishment (6).

(1) According to *Justin M.*, the blessedness of heaven consists mainly in the continuation of the blessedness of the millennial reign, the only difference being the enjoyment of immediate intercourse with God, Apol. i. 8. *Semisch*, ii. s. 477. According to *Irenæus* also (v. 7), communion with God and the enjoyment of His blessings (ἀπόλαυσις τῶν παρ' αὐτοῦ ἀγαθῶν) is the substance of all blessedness. Different names were given even to the intermediate states before the resurrection (comp. the preceding section, note 6). This was also the case with the abode of the blessed. Thus *Irenæus*, v. 36, p. 337 (*Gr.* 460), makes a distinction between οὐρανός, παράδεισος, and πόλις, and endeavours to prove the existence of different habitations from Matt. xiii. 8 and John xiv. 2. *Clement* of Alexandria also adopted the idea of different degrees of blessedness, Strom. iv. 6, p. 579, 580 (*Sylb.* 488, 489), which he compared with the degrees of the ecclesiastical hierarchy, Strom. vi. 13, p. 793 (*Sylb.* 668); and *Orig.* De Princip. ii. 11 (Opp. i. p. 104).

(2) According to *Origen*, l.c., the blessed dwell in the aerial regions (1 Thess. iv. 17), and take notice of what happens in the air. Immediately after their departure from this earth, they go first to Paradise (eruditionis locus, auditorium vel schola animarum), which (like Plato) he imagined to be a happy island; as they grow in knowledge and piety, they proceed on their journey from Paradise to higher regions; and having passed through various mansions which the Scriptures call heavens, they arrive at last at the kingdom of heaven, properly so called. He, too, appeals to John xiv. 2, and maintains that progress is possible even in the kingdom of heaven (effort and perfection). The perfection of blessedness ensues only after the final judgment. Even the glory of Christ will be completed only when He celebrates His victory as the Head of the Church, dwelling entirely in those who are His. Comp. in Lev. Hom. vii.

(Opp. ii. 222). Comp. *Redepenning*, Origenes, ii. s. 340 ff. *Gieseler*, Dogmengesch. s. 230.

(3) In the same place, De Princip. ii. 11, 2, *Origen* describes in strong terms the sensuous expectations of those, qui magis delectationi suæ quodammodo ac libidini indulgentes, solius litteræ discipuli arbitrantur repromissiones futuras in voluptate et luxuria corporis expectandas. He himself, attaching too much importance to the intellectual, supposes the principal enjoyment of the future life to consist in the gratification of the desire after knowledge, which God would not have given us if He had not designed to satisfy it. While on earth, we trace the outlines of the picture which will be finished in heaven. The objects of future knowledge are, as we might naturally expect, for the most part of a theological character; as an allegorical interpreter, he would think it of great importance that we should then fully understand all the types of the Old Testament, p. 105: Tunc intelliget etiam de sacerdotibus et Levitis et de diversis sacerdotalibus ordinibus rationem, et cujus forma erat in Moyse, et nihilominus quæ sit veritas apud Deum jubilæorum, et septimanas annorum; sed et festorum dierum et feriarum rationes videbit et omnium sacrificiorum et purificationum intuebitur causas; quæ sit quoque ratio lepræ purgationis et quæ lepræ diversæ, et quæ purgatio sit eorum, qui seminis profluvium patiuntur, advertet; et agnoscet quoque, quæ et quantæ qualesque virtutes sint bonæ, quæque nihilominus contrariæ, et qui vel illis affectus sit hominibus, vel istis contentiosa æmulatio. The knowledge, however, of metaphysics, and even of natural philosophy, is not excluded: Intuebitur quoque, quæ sit ratio animarum, quæve diversitas animalium vel eorum, quæ in aquis vivunt, vel avium, vel ferarum, quidve sit, quod in tam multas species singula genera deducuntur, qui creatoris prospectus, vel quis per hæc singula sapientiæ ejus tegitur sensus. Sed et agnoscet, qua ratione radicibus quibusdam vel herbis associantur quædam virtutes, et aliis e contrario herbis vel radicibus depelluntur. We shall also have a clear insight into the destinies of man and the dealings of Providence. Among the teachings of God in that higher state will also be instruction about the stars, "why a star is in such and such a position, why it stands at such and such a

§ 78.] STATE OF THE BLESSED AND THE CONDEMNED. 319

distance from another," etc. But the highest and last degree is the intuitive vision of God Himself, the elevation of the Spirit above all the limitations of sense. The blessed need no other nourishment. Comp. De Princip. iii. 318, 321, and Hom. xx. in Joh. (Opp. iv. p. 315): "Ὅτε μὲν ὁ ἑωρακὼς τὸν υἱὸν, ἑώρακε τὸν πατέρα· ὅτε δὲ ὡς ὁ υἱὸς ὁρᾷ τὸν πατέρα, καὶ τὰ παρὰ τῷ πατρὶ ὄψεταί τις, οἱονεὶ ὁμοίως τῷ υἱῷ αὐτόπτης ἔσται τοῦ πατρὸς καὶ τῶν τοῦ πατρὸς, οὐκέτι ἀπὸ τῆς εἰκόνος ἐννοῶν τὰ περὶ τούτου, οὗ ἡ εἰκών ἐστι. Καὶ νομίζω γε τοῦτο εἶναι τὸ τέλος, ὅταν παραδίδωσι τὴν βασιλείαν ὁ υἱὸς τῷ θεῷ καὶ πατρί, καὶ ὅτε γίνεται ὁ θεὸς τὰ πάντα ἐν πᾶσιν (1 Cor. xv. 28). *Redep.* Orig. ii. 283 ff. The views of *Origen* form a remarkable contrast to the sensuous and rhetorical description of *Cyprian,* which are indeed connected with his hierarchical and ascetic tendency, but also have a more churchly character, and enjoy greater popularity, because they are adapted to the wants of the heart (personal reunions, etc.); De Mortalitate, p. 166: Quis non ad suos navigare festinans ventum prosperum cupidius optaret, ut velociter caros liceret amplecti? Patriam nostram Paradisum computamus; parentes Patriarchas habere jam coepimus: quid non properamus et currimus, ut patriam nostram videre, ut parentes salutare possimus? Magnus illic nos carorum numerus expectat, parentum, fratrum, filiorum frequens nos et copiosa turba desiderat, jam de sua immortalitate secura, et adhuc de nostra salute sollicita. Ad horum conspectum et complexum venire quanta et illis et nobis in commune lætitia est! Qualis illic coelestium regnorum voluptas sine timore moriendi et cum æternitate vivendi! quam summa et perpetua felicitas! Illic apostolorum gloriosus chorus, illic prophetarum exultantium numerus, illic martyrum innumerabilis populus ob certaminis et passionis victoriam coronatus; triumphantes illic virgines, quæ concupiscentiam carnis et corporis continentiæ robore subegerunt; remunerati misericordes, qui alimentis et largitionibus pauperum justitiæ opera fecerunt, qui dominica præcepta servantes ad coelestes thesauros terrena patrimonia transtulerunt. Ad hos, fratres dilectissimi, avida cupiditate properemus, ut cum his cito esse, ut cito ad Christum venire contingat, optemus.

(4) *Clement* of Rome, Ep. 2, c. 8 (comp. c. 9): Μετὰ γὰρ

τὸ ἐξελθεῖν ἡμᾶς ἐκ τοῦ κόσμου οὐκ ἔτι δυνάμεθα ἐκεῖ ἐξομολογήσασθαι ἢ μετανοεῖν ἔτι. *Justin M.* also asserts the eternity of future punishments in opposition to Plato's doctrine, that they would last a thousand years, Apol. i. 8, Coh. ad Gr. c. 35. So *Minuc. Fel.* c. 35: Nec tormentis aut modus ullus aut terminus. Also *Cyprian,* ad Demetr. p. 195: Cremabit addictos ardens semper gehenna, et vivacibus flammis vorax pœna, nec erit, unde habere tormenta vel requiem possint aliquando vel finem. Servabuntur cum corporibus suis animæ infinitis cruciatibus ad dolorem. P. 196: Quando istinc excessum fuerit, nullus jam pœnitentiæ locus est, nullus satisfactionis effectus: hic vita aut amittitur, aut tenetur, hic saluti æternæ cultu Dei et fructu fidei providetur.—The idea of eternal punishments is different from that of a total annihilation, which was propounded by *Arnobius* at the commencement of the following period. Some are disposed to find the first traces of this doctrine in *Justin M.* (Dial. cum Tryph. § 5), where it is said that the souls of the wicked should be punished as long as ἔστ' ἂν αὐτὰς καὶ εἶναι καὶ κολάζεσθαι ὁ θεὸς θέλῃ. (Comp. on this passage, *Semisch,* ii. s. 480, 481.) Comp. also *Iren.* ii. 34: Quoadusque ea Deus et esse et perseverare voluerit; and *Clement,* Hom. iii. 3.

(5) In accordance with the analogy of Scripture, fire was commonly represented as the instrument by which God executes His punishments. *Justin M.* speaks in various places of a πῦρ αἰώνιον, ἄσβεστον (Apol. ii. 1, 2, 7, Dial. c. Tryph. § 130). *Clement* of Alexandria, Coh. 47 (35), calls it πῦρ σωφρονοῦν; *Tert.* Scorp. 4, and *Minuc. Fel.* 35 (afterwards also *Jerome* and others), call it an ignis sapiens. It will be sufficient here to quote the passage of *Minucius*: Illic sapiens ignis membra urit et reficit, carpit et nutrit, sicut ignes fulminum corpora tangunt, nec absumunt. Sicut ignes Ætnæ et Vesuvii montis et ardentium ubique terrarum flagrant nec erogantur, ita pœnale illud incendium non damnis ardentium pascitur, sed inexesa corporum laceratione nutritur. Comp. also *Tert.* Apol. c. 48, and *Cypr.* ad Demetr. l.c., who thinks that the sight of these punishments is a kind of satisfaction to the blessed for the persecution which they had to suffer while on earth. [*Cyprian,* Ep. 55 (*Baluz.* 52, c. 17): Aliud

est ad veniam stare, aliud ad gloriam pervenire, aliud missum in carcerem non exire inde, donec solvat novissimam quadrantem, aliud statim fidei et virtutis accipere mercedem, aliud pro peccatis longo dolore cruciatum emundari et *purgari diu igne* (another reading is, *purgari diutine*), aliud peccata omnia passione purgasse, aliud denique pendere in diem judicii ad sententiam Domini, aliud statim a Domino coronari.] Hell was represented as a place; thus by *Justin M.* Apol. i. 19 : Ἡ δὲ γεέννά ἐστι τόπος, ἔνθα κολάζεσθαι μέλλουσι οἱ ἀδίκως βιώσαντες καὶ μὴ πιστεύοντες ταῦτα γενήσεσθαι, ὅσα ὁ θεὸς διὰ τοῦ Χριστοῦ ἐδίδαξε.—As *Origen* imagined that future blessedness consists in spiritual enjoyments, so he believed the condemnation of the wicked to consist in separation from God, remorse of conscience, etc., De Princip. ii. 10 (Opp. i. p. 102). The eternal fire is not a material substance, kindled by another, but the combustible materials are our sins themselves, coming up before the conscience: the fire of hell resembles the fire of passion in this world. The separation of the soul from God may be compared with the pain which we suffer when all the members of the body are torn out of their joints (an endless dissolution of our very essence!). By "outer darkness" *Origen* does not so much understand a place devoid of light as a state of ignorance; so that his notion about *black bodies* seems to be an accommodation to popular ideas. It should also be borne in mind that *Origen* supposed that the design of all these punishments was remedial or disciplinary, in expectation of future reformation.

(6) De Princip. i. 6 (Opp. i. p. 70, 71, quoted by *Münscher, von Cölln,* i. s. 64, 65). The ideas here expressed are connected with *Origen's* general views of the character of God, the design of the divine punishments, liberty and the nature of evil, as well as with his demonology, and especially with his triumphant faith in the power of redemption to overcome all things (according to Ps. cx. 1 and 1 Cor. xv. 25). At the same time, he frankly confessed that his doctrine might easily become dangerous to the unconverted; contra Celsum, vi. 26 (Opp. i. p. 650). He therefore speaks at the very commencement of the xix. Hom. in Jerem. (Opp. t. iii. p. 241) of an eternal condemnation, and even of the impossibility of being converted in the world to come. Nevertheless, in the

same Hom. (p. 267) he calls the fear of eternal punishment (according to Jer. xx. 7) ἀπάτη, beneficial indeed in its effects, and appointed by God Himself (a pedagogical artifice, as it were). For, he says, many wise men, or such as thought themselves wise, after having apprehended the (theoretical) truth respecting the divine punishments, and rejected the delusion (beneficial in a practical point of view), have given themselves up to a vicious life; so that it would have been much better for them to believe in the eternity of the punishments of hell. Comp. *Redep.* ii. 447.

SECOND PERIOD.

FROM THE DEATH OF ORIGEN TO JOHN DAMASCENE, FROM THE YEAR 254–730.

THE AGE OF POLEMICS.

A. GENERAL HISTORY OF DOCTRINES IN THE SECOND PERIOD.

§ 79.

Introduction.

De Wette, Christliche Sittenlehre, Bd. ii. s. 294 ff. *Münscher,* Handbuch, Bd. iii. Abschn. 1. [*F. C. Baur,* Die Christliche Kirche vom Anfang des vierten bis zum Ende des sechsten Jahrh., Tübingen 1859. *E. von Lasaulx,* Der Untergang des Hellenismus, München 1854. *Isaac Taylor,* Ancient Christianity, 4th ed. 2 vols. 1844.] *Gieseler,* Dg. s. 252 ff. *Neander,* Dg. s. 269 ff. [*Klee,* u. s. *Shedd,* u. s.]

DURING the considerable space of time embraced in this period, the *Polemics* of the Church were developed much more prominently than either the apologetical tendency as in the preceding, or the systematic tendency as in the next period. In the time which elapsed between the Sabellian and the Monothelite controversies, which nearly coincides with the limits here assigned, an unbroken series of contests is carried on *within* the Church respecting the most important doctrinal points. While, in the preceding period, heretical tendencies separated from the Church, as a matter of course; here, on the contrary, victory for a long time wavers, and inclines now to the one side, and again to the other. Orthodoxy, however, prevailed at last, partly from an internal necessity, yet not without the aid of the secular power and of external circumstances.

It is just as one-sided to ascribe the victory of orthodoxy to the combination of political power and monkish intrigues, as it is to deny these factors altogether. Much as there was of human passion and dogmatism intermingled with this strife, it is not to be wholly derived from such impure sources; but there must also be recognized a law of internal progress, determining the gradual and systematic unfolding of the dogmas.

§ 80.

Doctrinal Definitions and Controversies.

The three main pillars of the Christian system, *Theology*, *Christology*, and *Anthropology*, were the principal points debated in the councils, and defined in symbols [creeds]. The controversies here to be considered are the following: (*a*) *In reference to the Doctrine of the Trinity* (Theology): the Sabellian and the Arian controversies, with their branches, the Semi-Arian and the Macedonian; (*b*) *Relative to the Two Natures of Christ* (Christology): the Apollinarian, Nestorian, Eutychian-Monophysite, and Monothelite controversies; (*c*) *Concerning Anthropology and the Economy of Redemption*: the Pelagian, Semi-Pelagian, and (in reference to the Church) the Donatist controversies. The first eight took their rise in the East; the last three originated in the West, but both east and west reciprocally felt their effects; so that there were frequent divisions between the oriental and occidental Church, till at last the controversy respecting the procession of the Holy Ghost brought about a lasting schism.

The controversy about the *Worship of Images*, carried on

in the East, and partly, too, in the West (only the beginning of which falls into this period), belongs, in the first instance, to the history of worship; but it also had an influence, especially in the West, upon the doctrinal definitions of the nature of God, the person of Christ, and the significance of the sacraments. But the further development of the doctrine of the sacraments, and of eschatology, was reserved for the next period. Concerning the external history of those controversies, see the works on ecclesiastical history.

§ 81.

The Dogmatic Character of this Period—The Fate of Origenism.

In proportion to the development of ecclesiastical orthodoxy into fixed and systematic shape, was the loss of individual freedom in respect to the formation of doctrines and the increased peril of becoming heretical. The more liberal tendency of former theologians, such as *Origen*, could no longer be tolerated, and was at length condemned. But, notwithstanding this external condemnation, the spirit of *Origen* continued to animate the chief theologians of the East, though it was kept within narrower limits. The works of this great teacher were also made known in the West by *Jerome* and *Rufinus*, and exerted an influence even upon his opponents.

The principal *followers* of *Origen* were *Dionysius*, Bishop of Alexandria, *Pamphilus* of Cæsarea, *Gregory Thaumaturgus*, Bishop of Neocæsarea, and others. Among his opponents *Methodius* (Bishop of Lycia, and afterwards of Tyrus, died in the Diocletian persecution, A.D. 311) occupied the most conspicuous position, although he too adopted many of *Origen's* views, *e.g.* in his *Symposion;* see *Neander*, Kg. i. 3, s. 1232 ff.; *S. Methodii*, opera et S. Methodius Platonizans edid. *Alb. Jahnius*, Halle 1865. On the further controversies relative to the doctrinal tenets of *Origen* under the Emperor Justinian I., and their condemnation brought about (A.D. 544) by *Mennas*, Bishop of Constantinople, see the works on ecclesiastical

326 SECOND PERIOD.—THE AGE OF POLEMICS. [§ 82.

history; *Ramers*, u. s. (§ 76), in his first part, or historical introduction.

§ 82.

Church Teachers of this Period.

Among the theologians of the East who either exerted the greatest influence upon the development of the system of doctrines, or composed works on the subject, are the following: *Eusebius* of Cæsarea (1), *Eusebius* of Nicomedia (2), but principally *Athanasius* (3) and the three Cappadocians, *Basil* the Great (4), *Gregory* of Nyssa (5), and *Gregory* of Nazianzus (6); next to them: *Chrysostom* (7), *Cyril* of Jerusalem (8), *Epiphanius* (9), *Ephræm Syrus* (10), *Nemesius* (11), *Cyril* of Alexandria (12), *Theodore* of Mopsuestia (13), *Theodoret*, Bishop of Cyrus (14); in the West: *Arnobius* (15), *Lactantius* (16), *Hilary* of Poitiers (17), *Jerome* (18), *Ambrose* (19), and above all, *Augustine* (20). These were followed by others of greater or less importance: *John Cassian* (21), *Vincentius* of Lérins (22), *Salvian* (23), *Leo I.*, surnamed *the Great* (24), *Prosper* of Aquitaine (25), *Gennadius* (26), *Fulgentius* of Ruspe (27), *Boëthius* (28), *Gregory* the Great (29), and *Isidore* of Seville (30). The last is of importance, as he brought together the dogmatic material already in existence, and was thus the forerunner of *John Damascene* (in the East).

(1) *Eusebius* (Pamphili), Bishop of Cæsarea (author of the Ecclesiastical History), was born about the year 261, and died 340. Of his dogmatical works the following may be mentioned (in addition to the prologue to his Ecclesiastical History): Εὐαγγελικῆς ἀποδείξεως παρασκευή (Præparatio Evangelica), Ed. i. of Steph. 1544 s. Cum not. *F. Vigeri*, 1628, Col. 1688, fol.—Εὐαγγελικὴ ἀπόδειξις (Demonstratio Evangelica), Ed. of Steph. 1545. Cum not. *Rich. Montacutii*, 1628, Lips. 1688, fol.—Κατὰ Μαρκέλλου, ii.—Περὶ τῆς ἐκκλησιαστικῆς θεολογίας, τῶν πρὸς Μάρκελλον.—Epistola de Fide Nicæna

§ 82.] CHURCH TEACHERS OF THIS PERIOD. 327

ad Cæsarienses. Some exegetical treatises also belong here. [Eccles. Hist. edited by *E. Burton*, 4 vols. with notes, Oxford 1841 and 1845 ; Annotationes ad Eus. Hist. ed. Burton, 2 vols. Oxon. 1841. Præp. Evang. ed. *E. Burton*, 4 vols. Oxon. 1841 ; this and the Demonstr. Evangelica, and Contra Hieroclem et Marcellum, ed. *T. Gaisford*, Oxon.; on the Theophania, Syriac version, by *S. Lee*, Lond. 1842, and translation by the same, Cambr. 1843. Treatises by Eusebius in *Mai's* Patrum Nov. Bibliotheca, tom. 3, 1853.—The first fasciculus of a new, critical edition of the Eccles. Hist. of Eusebius, by *Hugo Læmmer*, Berl. 1859. Transl. into Eng., Bagster and Bohn's Eccl. Lib.]

(2) *Eusebius* of Nicomedia, at first Bishop of Berytus, and afterwards of Constantinople, died A.D. 340. He was the leader of the Eusebian party in the Arian controversy. His opinions are given in the works of *Athanasius*, *Sozomen*, *Theodoret* (comp. especially his Epistola ad Paulianum Tyri Episcopum, in *Theod.* i. 6), and *Philostorgius*. Comp. *Fabric.* Bibl. Gr. vol. vi. p. 109 ss.[1] [Comp. *Semisch* in Herzog's Realencyklop.]

(3) *Athanasius*, called the father of orthodoxy, was born at Alexandria about the year 296, was bishop of that city from the year 326, and died A.D. 373. He exerted an important influence in the formation of the Nicene Creed, and took a prominent part in the Arian controversy. " *The devotion with which he contended for the cause of orthodoxy, and the importance of the dogma which occasioned the controversy, have made his name one of the most venerated in the Church,*" Baur, Dg. i. 2, s. 41. Of his numerous dogmatical works the most important are : Λόγος κατὰ Ἑλλήνων (an apologetical treatise) ; Λόγος περὶ τῆς ἐνανθρωπήσεως τοῦ θεοῦ λόγου καὶ τῆς διὰ σώματος πρὸς ἡμᾶς ἐπιφανείας αὐτοῦ.—Ἔκθεσις πίστεως (Expositio Fidei Nicænæ).—Πρὸς τοὺς ἐπισκόπους Αἰγύπτου καὶ Λιβύης, ἐπιστολὴ ἐγκυκλικὸς κατὰ Ἀριανῶν.—Oratt. V. contra Arianos.—Homilies, Letters, etc. The principal *editions* are: the Benedictine (by *Montfaucon*),1689-1698, 2 vols.fol. ed.

---

[1] The homilies of *Eusebius* of Emisa (who died A.D. 360) are only of secondary importance in relation to the doctrine of the descensus ad inferos. Opusc. ed. *Augusti*, Elberf. 1829. *Thilo*, über die Schriften des Euseb. von Alex. und des Euseb. von Emisa, Halle 1832.

N. A. Giustiniani, Patav. et Lips. 1777, 4 vols. fol. [reprinted by *Migne*, 4 vols.]. Festal Letters, by *Cureton*, from the Syriac; in German, by *Larsow*, Götting. 1852. Comp. *Tillemont*, t. viii. *Rössler*, Bibliothek der Kirchenväter, vol. v.—MONOGRAPHS: †*Möhler*, Athanasius der Grosse und die Kirche seiner Zeit, Mainz 1827, new ed. 1844, 2 vols. *Böhringer*, die Kirche Christi, i. 2, s. 1 ff. *Hesler*, Athanasius als Vertheidiger der Homoousie im Kampfe mit den Arianern (in *Niedner's* Ztschr. für hist. Theol. 1856, iii. s. 331 ff.). *H. Voigt*, die Lehre des Athanasius von Alexandrien, Bremen 1861. [On Athanasius, comp. *Bishop Kaye* in his Council of Nice, 1853; his treatises against the Arians, translated by *John Henry Newman*, with notes, in the Oxford Library of the Fathers, vols. viii. and xix., and his Historical Tracts in the same Library, vol. xiii.; his Four Orations against the Arians, previously translated by *S. Parker*, 2 vols. Oxford 1713; his Opera Dogmatica Selecta, ed. by *Thilo*, in his Bibl. Patr. Græc. Dogmatica, vol. i. Leipz. 1853.]

(4) *Basil* of Neocæsarea, surnamed the Great, was born A.D. 316, and died A.D. 379. He is of importance in the Arian and Macedonian controversies. His *principal writings* are: Ἀνατρεπτικὸς τοῦ ἀπολογητικοῦ τοῦ δυσσεβοῦς Εὐνομίου (libri v. contra Eunomium), Περὶ τοῦ ἁγίου πνεύματος, numerous Letters and Homilies (in Hexaëmeron 11; in Ps. xvii.; Diversi Argumenti 31; Sermones 25). *Editions* of his works were published by *Fronto Ducæus* and *Morellius*, Par. 1618, 38, 2 (3) vols. fol.; by the Benedictine monks in the year 1688, 3 vols. fol., and by *Garnier, Paris 1721–1730, 3 vols. fol.; by *De Sinner*, Paris 1839, 3 vols.—MONOGRAPHS: *Feisser*, De Vita Basilii, Gron. 1828. **C. R. W. Klose*, Basilius der Gr. nach seinem Leben und seiner Lehre, Stralsund 1835. *A. Jahn*, Basilius M. platonizans, Bern. 1838, 4to. Animadvers. in S. Bas. Opera, 1843. *Böhringer*, i. 2, s. 152 ff. [*Basilii* Opera Dogmat., ed. *Thilo* in Bibl. Patr. Græc. Dogm. vol. ii. 1854. Select Passages from Basil, Lond. 1810. Complete works, ed. *Gaume*, Paris.]

(5) *Gregory* of Nyssa, a brother of Basil, a native of Cappadocia, died about the year 394. His principal work is: Λόγος κατηχητικὸς ὁ μέγας.—He also composed dogmatical and exegetical treatises on the creation of the world and of man, wrote

§ 82.] CHURCH TEACHERS OF THIS PERIOD. 329

against Eunomius and Apollinaris, and was the author of several homilies, ascetic tracts, etc. Though he strictly adhered to the Nicene doctrine, he was yet distinguished for the mildness of his disposition; *"the profoundness of his scientific knowledge, as well as his peculiarities, assign to him the place nearest to Origen"* (*Hase*). His works were edited by *Morellius*, Par. 1615, ii. f. Append. by *Gretser*, Par. 1618. Of the Benedictine edition (Paris 1780), only the first volume appeared. Some newly discovered treatises against the Arians and Macedonians were published in *A. Maii* Scriptt. Vet. Coll. Rom. 1834, t. viii.; new ed. by *F. Oehler*, Halle 1865.— MONOGRAPHS: *Jul. Rupp*, Gregors, des Bischofs von Nyssa, Leben und Meinungen, Leipz. 1834. *Böhringer*, i. 2, s. 275 ff. *Heyns*, De Greg. Nyss. Lugd. Bat. 1835. [*E. G. Möller*, Greg. Nyss. Doctrina de hominis natura, cum Origen. comparat., Halle 1854. *J. N. Stigler*, Die Psychol. des Greg. v. N., Regensb. 1857. *Gregory* on Celibacy, and eight discourses Gr. and Ger. in *Oehler's* Bibl. d. Kirchenväter, 1859.]

(6) *Gregory* of Nazianzus, surnamed the theologian [an intimate friend of Basil], was born about the year 300 at Arianzus, near Nazianzus, was afterwards Bishop of Constantinople, and died A.D. 390. His *principal works* are: In Julianum Apostatam Invectiva duo (published separately by *Montague*, 1610, 4to).—Λόγοι θεολογικοί.—He also composed numerous orations, letters, poems, and shorter treatises. His works were published by *Morellius*, Paris 1630, 2 vols. fol. (Lips. 1690). Of the Benedictine edition only the first volume appeared [vol. ii. 1840].—MONOGRAPHS: *Ullmann*, Gregor von Nazianz. der Theologe, Darmst. 1825. *Böhringer*, i. 2, s. 357 ff. [*Ullmann's* Life of Greg. Naz. transl. in part by *G. V. Cox*, Lond. 1851. His dogmatic works in *Thilo's* Bibl. (u. s.). *Hergenröther*, Greg. Lehre von d. Dreieinigkeit, Regensb. 1850.]

(7) *Chrysostom* was born at Antioch in Syria about the year 344, occupied the episcopal see of Constantinople, and died A.D. 407. His practico-exegetical and homiletical writings are more valuable than his strictly dogmatical works; at the same time, he is of importance in the History of Doctrines on account of this very practical tendency, *e.g.* his views on the freedom of the will are in strong contrast with

those of Augustine. In addition to his numerous homilies and sermons, he wrote: Περὶ ἱεροσύνης, lib. vi. (edited by *Bengel*, Stuttg. 1825 ; by *Leo*, Lips. 1834), De Providentia, lib. iii.— *Editions of his complete works* were published by *Savile*, Eton. 1612. *Fronto Ducæus*, Par. 1609–1636. **Bern. de Montfaucon*, Paris 1718–1731, 13 vols. fol.; Venet. 1755, 13 vols. fol.; ib. 1780, 14 vols. fol. [repub. in 8vo by *Gaume* and *Migne*, Greek and French ed. by *Vivès*, Paris, 20 vols.].—MONOGRAPHS : *Neander, der heil. Chrysostomus und die Kirche des Orients in dessen Zeitalter, Berlin 1821, 1822, 2 vols. 2d edit. 1833. *Böhringer*, i. 4, s. 1 ff. [*Neander's* monograph, vol. i. transl. by *J. C. Stapleton*, Lond. 1845. *Perthes*, Leben Chrysost. 1854. Homiliæ in St. Matt., Gr. cum variis Lection., ed. *F. Field*, 4 vols. Cantab. 1829 ff.; Homiliæ in Ep. ad Corinth. cura. *F. Field*, Oxon. 1845–1849, 4 vols.; in Ep. ad Gal., ad Ephes. Phil. Col. etc., ed. *F. Field*, 1850–1855. His Homilies, transl. in Oxford Lib. of Fathers, vols. 4, 5, 6, 7, 9, 11, 12, 14, 15, 27, 28, 33, 34. *Abbé J. B. Bergier*, Histoire de St. Jean Chrys., sa vie, ses œuvres, son siècle, Paris 1856. Life of C. by *J. D. Butler*, Bibl. Sacra, vol. i. Life by *Stephens*, Lond. 1872. His work on the Priesthood, transl. by *H. Hollier*, Lond. 1728; by *J. Bunce*, Lond. 1759; by *H. M. Mason*, Philad. 1826.]

(8) *Cyril* of Jerusalem, at first a Eusebian, went over to the Nicene party; he had already combated the strict Arian Acacius; he died A.D. 386. He was distinguished for his catechetical lectures (347), in which he propounded the doctrines of the Church in a popular style. His five Mystagogical Discourses are of most importance from the dogmatic point of view. His works were edited by *Mills*, Oxon. 1703 f., and by **Ant. Aug. Touttée* (after his death by *Prud. Maran*), Par. 1720 f., Ven. 1763 f. Comp. *von Cölln* in Ersch u. Grubers Encyklopädie, Bd. xxii. s. 148 ff. *Van Vellenhoven*, Specim. theol. de Cyril. Hieros. Catechesibus, Amst. 1837. [The Lectures of Cyril, transl. in Oxford Lib. of Fathers, 1838, vol. iii. Extracts from thirteen works in *Mai's* Nova Bibliotheca, vol. ii. 1853. De Cyril. Hierosol. Orationibus, *J. T. Plitt*, Heid. 1855.]

(9) *Epiphanius* of Besanduc, near Eleutheropolis in Palestine, Bishop of Constantia in the isle of Cyprus, died at the age of nearly one hundred years, A.D. 404. His work against heretics,

§ 82.] CHURCH TEACHERS OF THIS PERIOD. 331

Αἱρεσέων LXXX. ἐπικληθὲν πανάριος εἴτ᾽ οὖν κιβώτιος (Adv. Hær.), is among the secondary sources of the History of Doctrines. The theology of Epiphanius consisted in rigid adherence to the orthodox system rather than in the development of original thought. It is represented in the treatise: Περιοχὴ λόγου τοῦ Ἐπιφ. τοῦ ἀγκυρωτοῦ καλουμένου, with which may be compared his Λόγος εἰς τὴν Κυρίου ἀνάστασιν, εἰς τὴν ἀνάληψιν τοῦ Κυρίου λόγος, etc. There is an *edition* of his works by *Petavius*, Par. 1622, fol., ib. 1630, fol. Edit. auct. Colon. (Lips.) 1682, 2 vols. fol. By *G. Dindorf*, 5 vols. Lips. 1859–1863. [*Eberhard*, Betheiligung Epiph. am Streit über Origenes, Trier. 1859.] Cf. *R. A. Lipsius*, zur Quellen-Kritik des Epiphanios, Wien 1865.

(10) *Ephraem*, Propheta Syrorum, of Nisibis in Mesopotamia, abbot and deacon in a monastery at Edessa, died about the year 378. He gained a high reputation by his exegetical works, and rendered signal service to Syria by the introduction of Grecian science and dogmatic terminology. Opp. ed. *J. S. Assemani*, Rom. 1732, 1746, 6 vols. fol. Comp. *C. A. Lengerke*, de Ephraemo Sc. S. interprete, Hal. 1828, 4to. [*H. Burgess*, Transl. of Ephraem's Hymns and Homilies, 2 vols. Lond. 1853, and of his Repentance of Nineveh, 1854. *J. Alsleben*, Das Leben des Eph. Syr. Berl. 1853. Comp. *Cardinal Wiseman*, Essays, vol. iii. (from Dublin Review); *Rödiger* in Herzog's Realencyclop., and in the Hall. Encyclop.; *Aschbach's* Allg. Kirchen-Lexicon; Zeitschrift d. deutschen morgenländ. Gesellschaft, Bd. ix. *S. Ephraemi*, S. Carmina nisibena, etc. *G. Bickell*, Lips. 1866.]

(11) *Nemesius*, Bishop of Emisa in Phœnicia (?), lived about the year 400. His treatise, Περὶ φύσεως ἀνθρώπου, was formerly attributed to *Gregory* of Nyssa, Oxon. 1671. Ed. *Matthæi*, Hal. 1802. Comp. *Schröckh*, Kirchengeschichte, vii. s. 157.

(12) *Cyril* of Alexandria (died A.D. 444) is well known by his violent proceedings against Nestorius, and by his Monophysite tendency. Besides homilies and exegetical works, he wrote Anathematismata against Nestorius, treatises on the Trinity and the Incarnation of Christ, Περὶ τῆς ἐν πνευματι καὶ ἀληθείᾳ προσκυνήσεως καὶ λατρείας, xvii. books—Κατὰ ἀνθρωπομορφιτῶν—and a work in defence of Christianity

against the Emperor Julian in 10 books.—Extracts of it are given by *Rössler*, vol. viii. p. 43–152. *Editions* of his works were published by **J. Aubertus*, Lut. 1638, 7 vols. fol., and *A. Maii*, Collectio t. viii. s. 43–152. [By *Migne*, 10 vols. Par. His Comm. on S. Luke, ed. by R. Payne Smyth: Syriac, 1858, in Eng. 1859.] In *Baur's* judgment (Dg. i. 2, s. 47), " *C. deserves a higher position, in reference to doctrine, than is generally assigned to him.*"

(13) *Theodore* of Mopsuestia was born about the year 350, and died A.D. 429. Of his writings we have scarcely more than fragments. Theodori quæ supersunt omnia, ed. *A. F. Wegnern*, Berol. 1834 ss. Comp. *Assemani*, Bibl. Orient. t. iii. pars i. p. 30. Theod. Ep. in Nov. Test. Comment. collegit, *O. F. Fritzsche*, Turin 1847; De Incarn. lib. xv. frag., ibid. Comp. *R. E. Klener*, Symbolæ, liter. ad Theod. etc., Gött. 1836, and *O. F. Fritzsche*, de Theodori Mopsvhesteni Vita et Scriptis. Comment. Hist., Hal. 1836. A sketch of his (liberal) theology is given by *Neander*, Kg. ii. 3, s. 928–944. [In the Spicileg. Solesmense of *Pitra*, i. 1853, fragments of a commentary on Paul are ascribed to Hilary, which *Jacobi* vindicates for Theod. Mops. in the Deutsche Zeitschrift, 1854. *Theod. Mops.* Doctrina de Imagine Dei, by *Dorner*, 1844.—Comp. *Dorner's Person Christi*.]

(14) *Theodoret* was born at Antioch, and died about the year 457. His dogmatico-polemical writings are of importance in the Nestorian and Monophysite controversies. *Theodoret* and *Theodore* are the representatives of the liberal tendency of the school of Antioch. The following work is one of the sources of the History of Doctrines: Αἱρετικῆς κακομυθίας ἐπιτομή, Lib. v. (Fabulæ Hæreticæ). He also composed several exegetical writings. There are *editions* of his works by *J. Sirmond*, Lutet. 1642, 4 vols. fol. Auctuarium cura. *J. Garnerii*, ib. 1684, fol., and *J. L. Schulze* and *Nösselt*, Hal. 1768–74, 5 vols. [*Migne*, 5 vols. *Theod.* Comm. in omnes beati Pauli Epistolas, in Bibl. Patrum, Oxf. 1852. *Theod.* Græcarum Affectionum Curatio, ed. *J. Gaisford*, Oxf. 1839. *Theod.* Eccl. Hist. libri v. ed. *J. Gaisford*, Oxf. 1854; translated in the edition of Eusebius, etc., 6 vols. Lond. 1847.]

(15) *Arnobius* (in part considered in the previous period), born at Sicca Veneria in Numidia, the teacher of Lactantius,

lived towards the close of the third, and at the commencement of the fourth century. He wrote a work under the title: Adv. Gentes, libr. vii., which was edited by *J. C. Orelli, Lips. 1816, Add. 1817. Hildebrand, Hal. 1844. Oehler, Lips. 1846.— His writings contain many heterodox assertions, like those of his disciples.

(16) *Lucius Cœlius Firmianus Lactantius* (Cicero Christianus) was born in Italy, became a rhetorician in Nicomedia, was tutor of *Crispus* (the eldest son of the Emperor Constantine the Great), and died about the year 330. He wrote: Divinarum Institutt. libri vii.; De Ira Dei; De Opificio Dei vel de formatione hominis.—*Editions* of his works were published by *Bünemann*, Lips. 1739, by *Le Brun* and *Dufresnoi*, Par. 1748, 2 vols. 4to, and *O. F. Fritzsche, Lips. 1842-1844. Comp. F. G. Ph. Ammon, Lactantii Opiniones de Religione in Systema redactæ, Diss. ii. Erl. 1820. *Spyker*, de pretio institutionibus Lactantii tribuendo, Lugd. 1826. On the position of *Arnobius* and *Lactantius* in the Church development, see *Meier*, Trinitätslehre, i. 91, note: " *Coming out of time, blossoms appearing in the autumn, disfigured imitations of a period long since past.*"

(17) *Hilary* (*Hilarius*), Bishop of Pictavium (Poitiers) in Gaul, died A.D. 368. Besides commentaries on the Psalms and on Matthew, and several minor treatises, he wrote: De Trinitate, libr. xii. *Editions* of his works were published by the Benedictines, Par. 1693, fol.; by *Maffei*, Ver. 1730, 2 vols. fol.; and by *Oberthür*, Würzb. 1785-1788, 4 vols. *A. Maii*, Scriptt. Vet. Coll. t. vi. [*Hilar*. Pictav. Opera, *Migne*, 2 vols. Paris 1844. Fragments ascribed to him in Spicileg. Solesm. i. 1853; see above, note 13.]

(18) *Sophronius Eusebius Hieronymus* (*Jerome*) was born about the year 331 [according to *Thierry*, 346; according to *Prosper*, 331: there are difficulties about both dates], at Stridon in Dalmatia, and died as a monk in a monastery at Bethlehem, A.D. 420. In his earlier years he was a disciple of *Origen*, but became his opponent, and a blind zealot for orthodoxy; he possessed great talents, and was a man of profound learning. (" *He made the West acquainted with Greek ecclesiastical erudition, and with the Hebrew,*" *Hase.*) He rendered greater service to biblical criticism and exegesis (by the Vulgate version), as well as to literary history (by his work, De Viris

Illustribus), than to dogmatic theology. As to the latter, he rather preserved it like an antiquarian relic, rescued from the Origenistic deluge, than exerted any living and original influence upon the healthy development of doctrines. His controversial writings are partly directed against those who opposed Monachism, the worship of relics, celibacy, Mariolatry (of which he was a great friend), etc., and in part have respect to the Pelagian and Origenist controversies. The following are the principal *editions* of his works: Opp. cura. *Erasmi*, Bas. 1516, 9 vols. fol.; the Benedictine (by *Martianay* and *Pouget*), Par. 1693–1706, 5 vols. fol.; and that of *Vallarsius*, Veron. 1734–1742, 11 vols. fol.; ed. 2, Venet. 1766–1772, 4 vols. [*Migne*, 9 vols.] (*Luther* judged unfavourably of him.) Comp. *Fricke*, Kirchengesch. i. s. 104. [*Collembet*, Gesch. des Hieron. nach d. Franz. 1847. *Osgood* in Bib. Sacra, v.] *O. *Zöckler*, Hieronymus, sein Leben u. Wirken aus seinen Schriften dargestellt, Gotha 1865. [*Thierry*, St. Jerome, Paris 1867.]

(19) *Ambrose* was born A.D. 340, was Archbishop of Milan from the year 374, and died A.D. 398. He was the chief pillar of Nicene orthodoxy in the West, and was important through his practical influence upon *Augustine*. His doctrinal writings are: Hexaëmeron, libb. vi.; De Officiis, iii.; De Incarnationis dominicæ Sacramento; De Fide, libri v.; de Spiritu, lib. iii., and several others. He also composed some exegetical works, though some, under his name, are spurious (Ambrosiaster). The principal *editions* of his works are that of *Amerbach*, Bas. 1492; and the Benedictine edition, cura. *N. Nurriti* et *Jac. Frischii*, Par. 1686–1690, 2 vols. fol. [ed. of *Migne*, 4 vols.]. Comp. *Böhringer*, i. 3, s. 1 ff. [Herzog's Realencycl. by *Böhringer*. His De Officiis Ministr. ed. by *Krabinger*, from new MSS. Tüb. 1857.]

(20) *Aurelius Augustine* was born at Thagaste in Numidia, A.D. 354, died as Bishop of Hippo Regius, A.D. 430; on his eventful and deeply interesting life, compare his autobiography, entitled Confessiones, libri xiii. (a manual edition of which was published at Berlin 1823, with a preface by *Neander*, also at Paris and Leipzig), and his life by *Possidius* (*Possidonius*); on his writings compare his own Retractationes. A great part of his works consists of his many-sided polemical writings against the *Manichæans*, the *Donatists*, and the *Pelagians*. All

his works, and their different editions, are enumerated in the work of *Schönemann*, t. ii. p. 8 ff.—A. PHILOSOPHICAL WORKS: Contra Academicos—De Vita Beata—De Ordine, ii.—Soliloquia, ii.—De Immortalitate Animæ, etc.—B. POLEMICAL WRITINGS: (*a*) *Against the Manichæans:* De Moribus Ecclesiæ Cathol. et Manichæorum, ii.—De Libero Arbitrio, iii.—De Genesi contra Manich.—De Genesi ad Litteram, xii.—De Vera Religione—De Utilitate credendi—De Fide et Symbolo, et al. (*b*) *Against the Donatists:* (in vol. ix.) contra Parmenianum, iii. —De Baptismo, vii.—Contra Litteras Petiliani, iii.—Ep. ad Catholicos (de unitate ecclesiæ), et al. (*c*) *Against the Pelagians and Semi-Pelagians* (they are contained for the most part in vol. x. of the Benedictine edition): De Gestis Pelagii —De Peccatorum Meritis et Remissione—De Natura et Gratia—De Perfectione Justitiæ Hominis—De Gratia Christi et de Peccato Originali—Contra duas Epistolas Pelagianorum —Contra Julian. lib. vi.—De Gratia et Libero Arbitrio—De Correptione et Gratia—De Prædestinatione Sanctorum—De Dono Perseverantiæ—Contra secundam Juliani Responsionem, opus imperfectum.—C. DOGMATICAL WORKS: De Civitate Dei ad Marcellin. libr. xxii. (*A manual edition was published by *Tauchnitz*, Lips. 1825, 2 vols.)—De Doctrina Christiana, lib. iv.—Enchiridion ad Laurentium, s. de fide, spe et caritate —De Fide—De Trin. xv.—D. PRACTICAL WORKS (De Catechizandis rudibus).—E. EXEGETICAL WRITINGS, LETTERS, SERMONS, etc. *Editions* of his works were published by *Erasmus*, Bas. 1529,10 vols.; 1543,1556,1569, in 11vols.; by the *Benedictines, Paris 1679–1701, 11 vols. (in 8) [reprinted by *Gaume*, Paris, and by *Migne*, 16 vols.]; Antwerp 1700–1703, 11 vols. fol., Append. by *Clericus*, ib. 1703, fol.—*J. B. Albrizzi*, Ven. 1729–1735, 12 vols. fol.; 1756–1769, 18 vols. 4to. Opp. Omnia, supplem. ed. *Hier Vignier*. Par. 1654, 1655, 2 vols. fol. —*Wiggers*, pragmatische Darstellung des Augustinismus und Pelagianismus, Berl. 1821, Hamb. 1833, 2 vols. *Bindemann*, der h. Augustin, 2 Bde. Berl. 1844–1854. *Poujoulat*, Histoire de St. Augustin, 2 vols. 6 ed. Tours 1875. *Böhringer*, i. 3, s. 99 ff. [new ed. i. 11]. *Kling* in Herzog's Realenc. i. s. 616 ff.

[In the Oxford Library of Fathers, vol. i., Augustine's Conf. edited by *E. B. Pusey*, who also edited the original, 1842; his Sermons, vols. xvi. and xx.; his Treatises, xxii.; Psalms, in

4 vols.; and John, 3 vols. The principal works: Confessions —De Trin.—Civ. Dei—Doctr. Christ.—Tract. in Joann.— Letters—Works on the three great controversies, pub. in Eng. by Clark, Edinb. *Kloth*, der Kirchenlehrer, Augustinus, Aachen 1854. Life and Times of A. by *Philip Schaff*, 1854. Life, etc., London 1853 (Bagster). *Trench*, Essay on August. as Interpreter, etc.—*J. B. Mozley*, The August. Doctrine of Predestination, Lond. 1855. *Th. Gangauf*, Die metaph. Theol. des heil. August. 1851-1853. *J. Nirschl*, Wesen des Bösens nach Aug. Regensb. 1854. *Roulet*, De l'Idée du Péché dans St. August., Montauban 1856. Aug. Confessions, with Introd. by *Prof. Shedd*, Andover 1860. A new ed. of Aug. published in Paris 1836-1840, 11 vols.; 1849 in 16 vols., and at Venice, in 8 vols. 1854. Two hundred new sermons, in *Mai*, Patrum Nov. Biblioth. vol. i. Aug. De Civit. Dei, ed. *Strange*, Col. 1850, 1; transl. by *Saisset*, Paris 1855. "*There is no Church teacher of early times, who, in respect of intellect and of breadth and consistency of view, could with more propriety be placed by the side of Origen, than Augustine; no one who, with all his difference of individuality and of mental tendency, had so great similarity to him,*" Baur, Dg. i. 2, s. 30.]

(21) *John Cassian*, a pupil of *Chrysostom*, probably a native of the West, founded Semi-Pelagianism, and died about the year 440. De Institut. Coenob. lib. xii.—Collationes Patrum, xxiv.—De Incarnatione Christi, adv. Nestorium, libr. vii. The principal *editions* of his works are: Ed. princ., Bas. 1485, Lugd. 1516, Lips. 1733. Comp. *Wiggers*, vol. ii. and his Diss. de Joanne Cassiano, Rost. 1824, 5. *L. F. Meier*, Jean Cassien, Strasb. 1840.

(22) *Vincent* of Lérins (*Lirinensis*), a monk and presbyter of the monastery in the isle of Lerinum, near the coast of Gallia Narbonica, died about the year 450. Commonitoria duo pro Catholicæ Fidei Antiquitate et Universitate adv. profanas omnium Hæreticorum Novitates. There is an *edition* of this work by *Jo. Costerius*, et *Edm. Campianus*, Col. 1600, denuo edid. *Herzog*, Vratislav. 1839. Commonitor. adv. Hæres. juxta editt. optim. recognitum, Notisque brev. illustr. a clerico diocesis Augustanæ, Aug. Vind. 1844; comp. *Wiggers*, ii. s. 208 ff., and *Gengler*, Ueber die Regel des Vincenz, in the Tüb. Quartalschrift, 1853, 1. Der Katholik, 1837, 2. [*Hefele*

in Theol. Quartalschrift, 1854. His Commonitory, transl. by *Reeves*, 1716, and at Oxford 1841.]

(23) *Salvian*, a native of Gaul, wrote: Adv. Avaritiam, libb. iv.; and a work on the doctrine of Providence, which is of importance in dogmatic theology: De Gubernatione Dei (de providentia). *Editions:* Bas. 1550. *Venet. (*Baluz.*) 1728 (together with Vinc. Lerin., Par. 1684).

(24) *Leo the Great*, Bishop of Rome, died A.D. 461. He is of importance in the Monophysite controversy, by the influence which he exerted upon the decrees of the Council of Chalcedon. He wrote Sermons and Letters, Ed. 1, Rom. 1479; Rom. 1753–1755, cura. *P. Th. Cacciari*. Comp. *Griesbach*, Loci Theologici collecti ex Leone Magno. (Opusc. t. i. ab init.) *Arendt*, Leo d. Grosse u. seine Zeit, Mainz 1835. *Perthel*, Pabst Leo's I. Leben und Lehren. Jena 1843. *Böhringer*, i. 4, s. 170 ff. [*Migne's* edition, 3 vols. 1845. *St. Cheron*, Vie de Leo. Comp. *Greenwood's* Cathedra Petri, i. 1856.]

(25) *Prosper* of Aquitaine opposed the Pelagians in several writings; Carmen de ingratis, and others. Opp. by *Jean Le Brun de Maret* and *Mangeant*, Par. 1711, fol. Cf. *Wiggers*, ii. s. 136 ff.

(26) *Gennadius*, a presbyter of Massilia, died about the year 493. He wrote: De ecclesiasticis Dogmatibus, edited by *Elmenhorst*, Hamb. 1616, 4to; it is also found among the works of *Augustine* (t. viii.).

(27) *Fulgentius*, born A.D. 468, at Telepte in Africa, and died A.D. 533, as Bishop of Ruspe. Works: Contra Objectiones Arianorum—De Remissione Peccatorum—Ad Donatum, de Fide orthod. et de diversis Erroribus Hæreticorum. An edition of his works by *J. Sirmond*, Par. 1623, fol. (Bibl. Max. Patr. Lugd. t. ix. p. 1), Ven. 1742, fol.

(28) *Anicius Manlius Torquatus Severianus Boëthius*, born at Rome A.D. 470, and beheaded A.D. 524, under Theodoric. He wrote: De Trin. etc.; De Persona et Natura (contra Eutychem et Nestorium):—Fidei Confessio, s. brevis Fidei Christianæ Complexio. He also composed several philosophical writings, among which that entitled De Consolatione Philosophica, lib. v., is remarkable, inasmuch as it shows how the ancient philosophy of the Stoics was associated with the speculative dogmatic theology of the Church without being

much influenced by the spirit of true Christianity. *Schleiermacher* even questions "*whether Boëthius ever was in earnest about Christianity;*" Geschichte der Philosophie, s. 175. *F. Nitzsch* (Das System des Boëthius, 1860) shows that *Boëthius* must be for ever struck out of the number of Christian and ecclesiastical writers. The doctrinal writings ascribed to him, which are certainly not without significance for the history of doctrine (1. De Trinitate; 2. Utrum pater et filius ac Spiritus de divinitate substantialiter prædicentur; 3. De persona et natura, contra Eutychem et Nestorium; 4. Fidei Confessio s. brevis fidei Christianæ complexio), are by other authors, who are distinct from each other in time, but may possibly all belong to this period.

(29) *Gregory the Great* (Bishop of Rome, A.D. 590) died A.D. 604. Protestants commonly, but arbitrarily, regard him as closing the patristic period. Opp. Par. 1675, Venet. 1768-1776.—*Wiggers*, de Gregorio Magno ejusque placitis anthropologicis, Comment. 1, 1838, 4to. *G. J. Th. Lau*, Gregor I. der Grosse, nach seinem Leben und seiner Lehre, Leipz. 1845. *Böhringer*, i. 4, s. 310 ff. [*G. Pfahler*, Gregor d. Grosse und seine Zeit, Bd. i. Frankf. 1852. *Neander* in his History, and in his Memorials of Christ. Life (Bohn), p. 386 ff. *Markgraf,* De Greg. Mag. Vita, Berol. 1845. Gregory's Augustinianism, *Wiggers* in Zeitschrift, f. d. hist. Theol. 1854. *V. Luzarche,* Vie de Grég. le Grand, Paris 1857. G.'s Morals on Job, in Oxf. Libr. of Fathers, 18, 21, 23, 31. King *Alfred* transl. Gregory's Pastoral (in Alf. Regis Res Gestæ), Lond. 1574.—Opera Omnia, ed. *Migne,* 5 vols. imp. 8vo, Paris 1849.]

(30) *Isidore* of Seville (*Hispalensis*) died A.D. 663; he attempted previously to the time of *John Damascene* to arrange the doctrines of the Church in the form of a system, but his work is only a compilation: Sententiarum sive de Summo Bono, libri iii. Opp. ed. *Faust Arevalo,* Rom. 1797, 7 vols. 4to. He wrote, moreover, some independent works on doctrinal subjects: Liber Quæstionum sive Expositionis Sacramentorum—De Natura Rerum—Exhort. ad Pœnitentiam—De ecclesiasticis officiis—and also several historical, canonical, and practical treatises, particularly Originum sive Etymologiarum libri xx. (ed. *Otto,* Lips. 1833). *Oudin,*

Comment. vol. i. p. 1582-1596. [*Isid. Hisp.* De Natura Rerum, recens. *G. Becker,* Berol. 1857 ; comp. *Gersdorf's* Rep. Oct. 1857.]

§ 83.

The Eastern Church from the Fourth to the Sixth Century.

The Schools of Alexandria and Antioch.

F. *Münter,* über die antiochenische Schule, in Staüdlins and Tzschirners Archiv, i. 1, s. 1 ff. [*Niedner,* Kirchengeschichte, p. 317 ff.] *Baur,* Dg. i. 2, s. 10 ff.

During this period an important change took place in the theological position of the school of Alexandria. Formerly it had been the representative of a spiritual and living Christianity, and of that idealistic theology which did not rest satisfied with the popular and sensuous apprehension of truth : during the present period the dogmatic tendency of the school of Egypt reacted into a compact realism. As it had once been the task of the Alexandrian school, so it became now the office of the *School of Antioch,* to defend a more liberal theology against rude and narrow polemics. The consequence was, that the teachers of that school shared the same fate with *Origen* in being treated as heretics. The school of Antioch, however, so far from resembling the earlier Alexandrian school in giving countenance to the arbitrary system of allegorical interpretation, adopted the grammatical interpretation, to which, as well as to biblical criticism in general, they thus rendered signal service. But on this account they have also sometimes been charged with a want of spirituality.

The change of opinions respecting classical literature, which many thought irreconcilable with the spirit of the gospel (the dream of *Jerome* in his Epist. ad Eustachium, comp. *Ullmann,* Gregor von Nazianz. s. 543), could not but exert a prejudicial influence upon the critical judgment of commentators. But where this last was wanting, only a limited gain could accrue to Christian theology from speculation, even when strengthened by Christian principles.

§ 84.

The Western Church—Augustinianism.

About the same time a new epoch in the History of Doctrines begins with the appearance of Augustine. From the dogmatic point of view, the West now assumes a higher degree of importance than the East, which exhausted itself in the controversies respecting the nature of Christ and the worship of images. The Carthaginian and Roman realistic tendency (a tendency earlier represented in the western Churches) gradually gained the ascendency over the Hellenistic idealism of past ages; the philosophy of Aristotle supplanted that of Plato. Augustine embraced in his theology the germs of two systems, which more than a thousand years afterwards were to wage open war against each other. The Roman Catholic system was based on his doctrine of the Church (in opposition to the Donatists); the system of evangelical Protestantism rests upon his doctrine of sin, of grace, and predestination (in opposition to the Pelagians). But both these systems appear organically conjoined in his own person, and have a basis not only in his personal career and experience, but also in the position which he occupied in relation to the Church and to his opponents.

Comp. *Neander*, Church History, and Dg. s. 272 ff.

§ 85.

The Heresies.

[*Baur*, Epochen d. kirchlichen Geschichtschreibung, 1852; Die Christl. Kirche, vom 4n. bis 6n. Jahrh. 1859.]

Among the natural heresies which prevailed during the first period, the Ebionitic (Judaizing) may be considered as entirely suppressed (1). The Gnostic (anti-Judaizing) tendency, on the contrary, was more firmly established in the *system of Manes* (Manichæism), which, as a complete dualism, planted itself by the side of Christianity, from its very nature belonging to that form of oriental and pagan philosophy which had not yet disappeared (2). The system of the followers of *Priscillian* must be regarded as a continuation of Gnosticism, though modified by Manichæism; it spread in the West in the course of the fourth century, but was suppressed by violent persecutions (3). The *Paulicians,* too, manifested a leaning towards Gnostic and Manichæan notions, though they at first appear to have been impelled by a practical necessity to attempt a return to the simplicity of apostolical Christianity (4). These heresies, that are, as it were, the younger branches, which the old stock of Gnosticism continued to shoot forth, and which attained a higher importance in the next period, are to be carefully distinguished from the heresies which arose in consequence of dogmatic controversies; the latter, by the antagonisms which were called forth, had an essential influence upon the doctrinal definitions of the Church, and, in fact, evoked these definitions to mediate between opposite extremes. To this period belong the heresies which arose in the struggle respecting a dialectic treatment of the separate doctrines, and which essentially contributed to the doctrinal statements made in this period, viz.:—1. The heresies of *Sabellius* and *Paul* of Samosata, with their opposites, the *Arian, Semi-Arian,* and *Eusebian* heresies (which continued to prevail among the Goths, Burgundians, and Vandals long after they had been condemned). 2. The heresy of the *Pelagians,* who never were able to form a distinct sect, but by means of a modified system (*Semi-Pelagianism*) kept a backdoor open to creep now and then into the Church, from which they had been excluded by the more strict doctrinal decisions. 3. The *Nestorian* heresy, with its opposites, the *Monophysite* and *Monothelite* heresies. The Nestorians, after having been defeated in Europe, succeeded in winning over to their party the Chaldees and the Thomas-Christians in Asia. Monophysites prevailed among the *Jacobites* and *Copts*, and the Monothelites have dragged out a wretched existence even to the present day among the *Maronites in Syria* (5).

(1) A Judaizing view lies at the basis of *Sabellianism*, just as a heathen tendency is manifested in *Arianism;* but the Jewish element is no longer bound to what is national, as it was in Ebionitism. Yet the whole conflict strikes rather into the sphere of dialectic thought, than into that of primitive religious opinions. The notions of the Pelagians concerning the meritoriousness of works bore some resemblance to Judaism, but they did not in the popular mind originate with it.

(2) *Manichæism* is distinguished from *Gnosticism* by a more complete development of the dualistic principle; this also accounts for its rigid and uniform appearance, while Gnosticism is divided into many branches, and admits of more variety. There is far less of historical Christianity in Manichæism than in Gnosticism: it rests on its own historical foundation, which is here and there an imitation of Christianity, and hence it forms (like Mohammedanism at a later period) a separate system of religion rather than a sect. Comp. *Beausobre*, Histoire de Manichée et du Manichéisme, Amst. 1734, 2 vols. 4to. **Baur*, das manichäische Religionssystem, Tüb. 1831, and Dg. i. 2, s. 33 ff. *F. Trechsel*, über den Kanon, die Kritik, und Exegese der Manichäer, Bern. 1832. *F. E. Colditz*, die Entstehung des manichäischen Religionssystems, Leipz. 1837 (where Manichæism is compared with the Indian, Zoroastrian, and other systems of religion). [On the Manichæans, see Note F to *Pusey's* edition of Augustine's Confessions.]

(3) On the history of the Priscillianists, which is of more importance for the history of the Church than for the History of Doctrines, because they were the first heretics persecuted with the sword, comp. *Sulp. Sever.* Hist. Sacr. ii. 46–51. *Neander,* Kg. ii. 3, s. 1486 ff. *Baumgarten-Crusius,* i. s. 292 ff. *J. H. B. Lübkert,* De Hæresi Priscillianistarum, Havn. 1840. †*Mandernach,* Geschichte des Priscillianismus, Trier. 1851. *Vogel* in Herzog's Realencyclop. xii. s. 194.

(4) Further particulars may be found in *Fr. Schmid,* Historia Paulicianorum Orientalium, Havn. 1826; in an

essay in Winer and Engelhardt's Journal, 1827, Bd. vii. 1, 2; *Gieseler* in the Studien und Kritiken, 1829, ii. 1, and *Neander*, Kg. iii. s. 494 ff. SOURCES: Petri Siculi (who lived about the year 876) Historia Manichæorum, Gr. et Lat. ed. *M. Raderus*, Ingolst. 1604, 4to, newly edited, with a Latin translation, by *J. C. L. Gieseler*, Gött. 1846, 4to. Photius adv. Paulianistas, s. rec. Manichæorum, libb. iv., in *Gallandii* Bibl. PP. t. xiii. p. 603 ss. The clear distinctions between the Paulicians and Manichæans are pointed out by *C. Schmidt* in *Herzog*, Realencycl. xi. s. 230.

(5) On all these heresies, which have a peculiar bearing upon the development of doctrines during this period, comp. the special History of Doctrines. Concerning the external history of the controversies themselves, see the works on Ecclesiastical History.

§ 86.

Division of the Material.

Respecting the dogmatic material of this period, we have to distinguish between—1. Those doctrines which were shaped by the controversy with the last-named heresies; and 2. Those which were developed in a more quiet and gradual manner.

To the former class belong *Theology* proper (the doctrine of the Trinity), *Christology*, and *Anthropology*; to the latter, those parts of theology which treat of the nature of God, creation, providence, etc., as well as the doctrine of the sacraments and eschatology, though it must be admitted that they exerted an influence upon each other. We think it best to begin with the history of the first class of doctrines, as there was here a strictly polemic movement, and then to treat of the more esoteric (acroämatic) doctrines. The first class may be subdivided into two divisions, viz.: the Theologico-Christological on the one hand, and the Anthropological on the other. The controversies respecting the doctrines belonging to the former of these two divisions were carried on principally in the East, those concerning the latter in the West.

B. SPECIAL HISTORY OF DOCTRINES DURING THE SECOND PERIOD.

FIRST CLASS.
DOCTRINAL DEFINITIONS OF THE CHURCH IN CONFLICT WITH HERESIES.
(POLEMICAL PART.)

FIRST DIVISION.
DOCTRINES RESPECTING THEOLOGY AND CHRISTOLOGY.

A. THEOLOGY PROPER.

§ 87.

The Hypostatical Relation and Subordination of the Son.

Lactantius. Dionysius of Alexandria and the Origenists.

THE indefinite term *Logos* was one on which the earlier Fathers were so little agreed, that some understood by it the *Word*, others the *Wisdom* (reason, spirit), and even *Lactantius*, who lived on the borders of the present period, regards λόγος and πνεῦμα as identical (1). From the time of *Origen* it fell increasingly into disuse, and in its place the expression *Son*, which is used in the New Testament in direct reference to the human personality of Christ, was transferred to the second person of the Godhead (previous to His incarnation). The disciples of *Origen* (2), in accordance with the opinions of their master, understood by this second person a distinct hypostasis subordinate to the Father. Such is the view of *Dionysius* of Alexandria, though he endeavoured to clear himself from the charges brought against him by *Dionysius* of Rome, by putting forth the doctrine in a milder form (3). The doctrine of *Origen* now met with a peculiar fate. It consisted, as we have seen, of two elements, viz. the hypostasis of the Son, and His subordination to the Father. The former was maintained in opposition to Sabellianism, and received as orthodox; the latter, on the contrary, was condemned in the Arian controversy. Thus Origenism gained the victory on the one hand, but was defeated on the other; but it was thus proved to be a necessary link in the chain, and became an element by which the transition was made.

(1) The theology of *Lactantius* was an isolated phenomenon in the present period, and has always been regarded as heterodox. (Concerning his prevailing ethical tendency, see *Dorner*, s. 777.) *Lactantius*, after having opposed the gross and sensuous interpretation of the birth of Christ: ex connubio ac permistione feminæ alicujus, Instit. Div. iv. c. 8, returns to the meaning which the term *Word* (sermo) has in common life; Sermo est spiritus cum voce aliquid significante prolatus. The Son is distinguished from the angels, in that He is not only *spiritus* (breath, wind), but also the (spiritual) *Word*. The angels proceed from God only as taciti spiritus, as the breath comes out of the nose of man, while the Son is the breath which comes out of God's mouth, and forms articulate sounds; hence he identifies Sermo with the Verbum Dei, quia Deus procedentem de ore suo *vocalem* spiritum, quem non utero, sed mente conceperat, inexcogitabili quadam majestatis suæ virtute ac potentia in effigiem, quæ proprio sensu ac sapientia vigeat, comprehendit. There is, however, a distinction between the Word (Son) of God and our words. Our words being mingled with the air, soon perish; yet even

we may perpetuate them by committing them to writing— quanto magis Dei vocem credendum est et manere in æternum et sensu ac virtute comitari, quam de Deo Patre tanquam rivus de fonte traduxerit. *Lactantius* is so far from the doctrine of the *Trinity*, that he finds it necessary to defend himself against the charge of believing not so much in *three*, as in *two* Gods. To justify this dual unity (or belief in two divine persons), he makes use of the same expressions which orthodox writers employed in earlier and later times for the defence of the doctrine of the Trinity: Cum dicimus Deum Patrem et Deum Filium, non diversum dicimus, nec utrumque secernimus: quod nec Pater a Filio potest, nec Filius a Patre secerni, siquidem nec Pater sine Filio potest nuncupari, nec Filius potest sine Patre generari. Cum igitur et Pater Filium faciat et Filius Patrem, una utrique mens, unus spiritus, una substantia est. He then comes back to the illustrations previously used, *e.g.* those drawn from the fountain and the stream, the sun and its beams; and more boldly (wholly in the Arian sense) he compares the Son of God with an earthly son, who, dwelling in the house of his father, has all things in common with him, so that the house is named after the son, as well as after the father.

(2) Thus *Pierius*, the master of Pamphilus of Cæsarea, was charged by *Photius* (Cod. 119) with having maintained that the Father and the Son are two οὐσίαι καὶ φύσεις. Nevertheless, he is said to have taught εὐσεβῶς, by employing those terms in the sense of ὑποστάσεις; but, δυσσεβῶς, he made the πνεῦμα inferior to both Father and Son. In like manner *Theognostus* (about 280) was accused of making the Son a κτίσμα; but this is not in accordance with the other (more orthodox) teachings of that theologian (*Phot.* Cod. 106); comp. *Dorner*, s. 723 ff. Some disciples of *Origen, e.g. Gregory Thaumaturgus*, even manifested a leaning towards Sabellianism; according to *Basil* (Ep. 210, 5), *Gregory* taught πατέρα καὶ υἱὸν ἐπινοίᾳ μὲν εἶναι δύο, ὑποστάσει δὲ ἕν; comp., however, *Gieseler*, Dogmengesch. s. 147 f. *Methodius* of Patara avoided the use of the term ὁμοούσιος in reference to the pre-existence of the Son, yet he seems to have admitted His eternal pre-existence, though not in the sense of *Origen;*

§ 87.] THE HYPOSTASIS AND SUBORDINATION OF THE SON. 347

comp. Opp. edit. *Combefis* (Par. 1644), p. 283-474, and *Dorner*, l.c.

(3) This is obvious, particularly in the opposition of *Dionysius* to Sabellianism (see the next section). Of his work addressed to the Bishop of Rome, and entitled, Ἔλεγχος καὶ Ἀπολογία, libb. iv., fragments are preserved in the writings of *Athanasius* (περὶ Διονυσίου τοῦ ἐπ. Ἀλ. liber; Opp. i. p. 243) and *Basil;* they were collected by *Coustant* in his Epistt. Rom. Pontt. in *Gallandi*, t. iv. p. 495. See *Gieseler*, i. s. 244; *Neander*, i. 3, s. 1037; *Münscher (von Cölln)*, s. 197-200. *Schleiermacher* (see the next section), s. 402 ff. According to *Athanasius* (p. 246), *Dionysius* was charged with having compared (in a letter to Euphranor and Ammonius) the relation between the Father and the Son to that in which the husbandman stands to the vine, the shipbuilder to the ship, etc. The Arians even asserted (see *Athanasius*, p. 253) that he taught like themselves : Οὐκ ἀεὶ ἦν ὁ θεὸς πατήρ, οὐκ ἀεὶ ἦν ὁ υἱός· ἀλλ᾽ ὁ μὲν θεὸς ἦν χωρὶς τοῦ λόγου· αὐτὸς δὲ ὁ υἱὸς οὐκ ἦν πρὶν γεννηθῇ· ἀλλ᾽ ἦν ποτε ὅτε οὐκ ἦν, οὐ γὰρ ἀΐδιός ἐστιν, ἀλλ᾽ ὕστερον ἐπιγέγονεν. He also called the Son ξένος κατ᾽ οὐσίαν τοῦ πατρός. Comp., however, the expressions quoted by *Athanasius*, p. 254, which go to prove the contrary. But the Bishop of Rome (not without a Sabellian leaning, see *Dorner*, s. 754) insisted that *Dionysius* should adopt the phrase ὁμοουσία (Homoousia), to which the latter at last consented, though he did not think that it was founded either upon the language of Scripture, or upon the terminology till then current in the Church.[1] Orthodox theologians of later times (*e.g. Athanasius*), endeavouring to do more justice to *Dionysius* of Alexandria, maintained that he had used the aforesaid offensive illustrations only κατ᾽ οἰκονομίαν, and that they might be easily explained from the stand he took against Sabellianism (*Athanasius*, p. 246 ss.); see, on the other side, *Löffler*, Kleine Schriften, Bd. i. s. 114 ff. (quoted by *Heinichen* on *Euseb.* i. s. 306). It can also be justly alleged that *Dionysius* had a practical rather than a

[1] An intermediate position was taken by *Zeno* of Verona (a contemporary of Origen and Cyprian), who, in Hom. i. ad Genes. in Bibl. Max. PP. iii. p. 356 ss., compared the Father and the Son to two seas which are joined by straits; comp. *Dorner*, s. 754 ff.

speculative mind, and that his main bias and intention was different from that of *Arius*. The thesis of subordination, which was the centre of the Arian system, was to him only a "*suspicious and hasty inference from the distinction between the Father and the Son.*" See *Dorner*, s. 743 ff., and *Baur*, Dg. s. 487.

§ 88.

The Consubstantiality of the Son with the Father, with the Denial of the Hypostatic Distinction.

Sabellianism and Paul of Samosata.

Ch. Wormii, Historia Sabelliana, Francof. et Lips. 1696. * *Schleiermacher*, über den Gegensatz zwischen der sabellianischen und athanasianischen Vorstellung von der Trinität (Berlin. Theol. Zeitschr. 1822, 3). *Lange*, der Sabellianismus in seiner ursprünglichen Bedeutung (Illgens Zeitschr. für historische Theol. iii. 2, 3).—*J. G. Feuerlin*, de Hæresi Pauli Samos. 1741, 4to. *J. G. Ehrlich*, de Erroribus Pauli Samos. Lips. 1745, 4to. *Schwab*, de Pauli Sam. vita atque doctrina Diss. inaug. 1839. *Trechsel* in Herzog's Realencyc. xi. s. 249. [Comp. *Dorner*, i. 127 ff., on Sabellius; and on Paul of Samosata, i. 510 ff. *L. Lange*, Antitrin. vor d. Nic. Syn. 1851. *Waterland's* Works, i. 517 ff., ii. 703 ff.]

Sabellius, a presbyter of Ptolemais, who lived about the middle of the third century, adopted the notions of the earlier Monarchians, such as *Praxeas, Noëtus*, and *Beryllus;* and maintained, in opposition to the doctrine propounded by *Origen* and his followers, that the appellations Father, Son, and Holy Spirit were only so many different manifestations and designations of one and the same divine being. He thus converted the objective and real distinction of persons (a Trinity of essence) into a merely subjective and modalistic view (a Trinity of manifestation). In illustration of his views, he made use not only of various images which his opponents sometimes misinterpreted, but also of such expressions as were afterwards transferred to the terminology of the orthodox Church (1). Thus, while he avoided, on the one hand, the subordination of the Son to the Father, and re-

§ 88.] CONSUBSTANTIALITY OF THE SON WITH THE FATHER. 349

cognized the divinity manifested in Christ as the absolute Deity; yet, on the other hand, by annulling the personality of the Son, he gave the appearance of Pantheism to this immediate revelation of God in Christ; since, with the cessation of the manifestation of Christ in time, the Son also ceased to be Son. The doctrine of *Paul* of Samosata is not, as formerly happened, to be identified with the notions of *Sabellius*; it rather approached the earlier (Alogistic) opinions of *Artemon* and *Theodotus*, which, as regards the nature of Christ, were not so much pantheistic as deistic (2).

(1) *Eus.* vii. 6. *Epiph.* Hær. 62. *Athan.* Contra Arian. iv. 2, and other passages. *Basil*, Ep. 210, 214, 235. *Theodoret*, Fab. Hær. ii. 9. According to *Epiphanius*, *Sabellius* taught that there were ἐν μιᾷ ὑποστάσει τρεῖς ἐνέργειαι (ὀνομασίαι, ὀνόματα), and illustrated his views by adducing the human trinity of body, soul, and spirit, and the three properties of the sun, viz. the enlightening (φωτιστικόν), the warming (τὸ θαλπόν), and the periphery (τὸ περιφερείας σχῆμα). But it is difficult to determine how far he applied the one or the other of these characteristics to the persons of the Trinity, and carried out the analogy in all its particulars. According to *Athanasius*, iv. 25, he also referred to the manifold gifts coming from the *one* Spirit, as illustrative of the Trinity. What is objective in the matter consisted, in his view, in the divine economy, in the modes in which God is revealed to the human race. God is called Father in relation to the giving of the law; He is called Son in relation to the work of redemption; and Holy Spirit in relation to the inspiration of the apostles and the quickening of believers; hence the charge of the orthodox (*Athan.* iv. 25; *Basil.* Ep. 210, 214, 235; *Aug.* Tract. in Joh. § 3), that *Sabellius* had limited the doctrine of the Trinity merely to the wants of the present world (πρὸς τὰς ἑκάστοτε χρείας). These three different modes of the divine manifestation (according to *Athanasius*, iv. 13) he regarded as a πλατύνεσθαι or ἐκτείνεσθαι (the figure of an arm stretched out and brought back). But it is difficult to ascertain the precise distinction which he made between these different modes of manifestation and the " monas " (unity), the

αὐτόθεος, whom he called υἱοπάτωρ (*Athan.* De Syn. 16); and the relation in which this monas stands to these modes of manifestation, and to the Father in particular. To judge from some passages (quoted by *Athan.* iv. 25), he seems to have considered the terms πατήρ and μόνας identical; while elsewhere (iv. 13) the Father, who is designated as the μόνας, forms a part of the Trinity, comp. *Dorner*, s. 706 ff. *Voigt, Athan.* s. 268, seeks (in opposition to Schleiermacher, Baur, and others) again to establish the opinion that, according to Sabellius, the monas and the Father are identical. The Logos also occupies a peculiar position in the system of Sabellius. While, in his opinion, the Trinity only exists in relation to the world, the creation of the world is brought about by the Logos, to whom Sabellius, like the earlier writers, applies the predicates ἐνδιάθετος and προφορικός, see *Dorner*, s. 711 ff. Thus, according to Sabellius, God is inactive as silent, and active as speaking (*Athan.* iv. 11). On the entire system of Sabellius, as well as on the sense in which he used the terms πρόσωπον (whether borrowed from the theatre?) and ὁμοούσιος, see *Schleiermacher*, l.c. *Baumgarten-Crusius*, i. 1. 200 ff. *Neander*, Kg. i. 3, s. 1015 ff., and Dg. s. 175. *Möhler*, Athanasius der Grosse, i. s. 184 ff.; and *Voigt*, l.c. As regards the historical manifestation of Christ, it must be admitted that its theological significance is not impugned by Sabellius, inasmuch as he regards the Saviour as the immediate manifestation of God. But Christ possesses personality only during this historical appearance in the flesh. That personality neither existed previous to His incarnation, nor does it continue to exist in heaven, since that divine ray which had been let down into Christ returns again to God. Nevertheless, Sabellius seems to have expected the second coming of Christ (*Schleiermacher*, s. 174). It is even doubtful whether he makes the return of the Logos to God to occur at the ascension of Christ, or only when the kingdom of God is completed. On the connection between Sabellianism and Ebionitism, see *Dorner*, s. 726. [This is seen in that Sabellius makes the revelation of Christ a mere means, and not an end; in his calling the Son a ray (ἀκτῖνα) of the monas, on account of which he was accused of dividing the divine essence; and then the difficult question (since he allowed no distinctions in God), whether the whole

God was in the person (*Prosopon*) of the Son in such a way that He was not elsewhere active during the incarnation—a question which led him to speak of the Son in terms approximating to Ebionitism.] According to *Epiphanius* (l.c.), the opinions of Sabellius were principally spread in Mesopotamia, and in the vicinity of Rome. A sect of Sabellians, properly so called, has never existed.

(2) *Paul*, a native of Syria, Bishop of Antioch from the year 260, was, after 264, charged with heresy at several synods,[1] and at last removed from his office (269–272). Of his dispute with the presbyter Malchion, a fragment is preserved in *Mansi*, vol. i. p. 1001 ss. Comp. the different accounts given by *Epiph.* 65, 1, and *Euseb.* vii. 27. The writers on the History of Doctrines vary in their opinions respecting the relation in which he stands, whether to Sabellianism or to the Unitarianism of the Artemonites (see *Euseb.* v. 28, ab init.); comp. *Schleiermacher*, s. 389 ff. *Baumgarten-Crusius*, i. s. 204. *Augusti*, s. 59. *Meier*, Dogmengesch. s. 74, 75. *Dorner*, s. 510. *Baur*, Dg. 477 ff. The difference between *Sabellius* and *Paul* of Samosata may be said to have consisted in this, that the former thought that the whole substance of the divine being, the latter that only one single divine power, had manifested itself in Christ. *Trechsel* (Geschichte des Antitrinitarismus, i. s. 61) agrees with this, calling Samosatianism "*the correlate of Sabellianism, according to the measures of the mere understanding.*" The divine here comes only into an external contact with man, touches human nature only on the surface; while, on the other hand, the human element comes to its rights more than in the system of Sabellius. In other words: "*In the man Jesus, as He lived here below, there dwelt the divine Logos from above; and, in a higher degree than in the prophets and in Moses, the divine wisdom was in Christ as a Temple of God,*" Baur, s. 478.

---

[1] On the two Antiochene Synods, 265 and 270, see *Dorner*, p. 769. [Their decrees, though not in a strict dogmatic form, were received as orthodox— though containing expressions which were avoided after the Council of Nicæa. The Son is confessed to be God in essence and hypostasis (οὐσίᾳ καὶ ὑποστάσει); His pre-existence is definitely stated—He was always with the Father; through Him, not as instrument merely, nor as an impersonal Wisdom, the Father created all things, etc. Sabellianism and Samosatianism are excluded by these and like positions.]

At all events, we can hardly expect any serious and persevering attempts at a doctrinal system from a man whose vanity is so prominent. Though the charge that he countenanced Jewish errors to obtain favour with Queen Zenobia is unfounded (*Neander*, i. 3, s. 1009), yet it is quite probable that the vain show he made of free-thinking principles, and his idle pretension of taking a stand *above* the parties, were in as full accordance with his ostentatious nature, as in other times and under other circumstances this has been found to be connected with an arrogant and pretentious orthodoxy. Even to make a heresy, a definite theological character is needed; frivolity is but an external appendage of any party. At any rate, it is false to use the terms Sabellianism and Samosatianism promiscuously. It would be more accurate to say that they form a contrast, as *Baur*, l.c. s. 483, rightly shows. Generally, those who denied the distinction of persons in the Trinity were called Πατριπασσιανοί in the West, and Σαβελλιανοί in the East. Comp. *Athanasius*, de Synod. 25, 7.

§ 89.

The Subordination of the Son to the Father, and the Distinction of Persons in Arianism.

[*Newman's* Arians of the Fourth Century. *Maimbourg*, Hist. of Arianism, by *W. Webster*, 2 vols. 1768. *J. A. Stark*, Versuch einer Gesch. des Arian. *T. G. Hassencamp*, Historia Arianæ Controversiæ, 1845. *Bp. Kaye* in his Council of Nice, 1853. *Albert de Broglie*, L'Eglise et l'Empire Romain au iv. Siècle, Paris 1856, i. 329–397. *W. Klose* in Herzog's Realencycl. The preparatory history of the Council of Nicæa, in *Hefele*, Hist. of Councils, Freib. and Edinb.]

The system of *Arius*, a presbyter of Alexandria, forms the most striking contrast with that of *Sabellius*. *Arius*, in endeavouring to define objectively the distinction between the persons of the Trinity, carried the idea of a subordination of the one to the other, and, in the first place, of the Son to the Father, so far as to represent the former as a creation of the latter (1). This opinion, which he promulgated at Alexandria, met with the most decided opposition on the part of *Alexander*, bishop of that city (2). This contest, which was at first merely a private dispute, gave rise to a controversy which exerted greater influence upon the History of Doctrines than all former controversies, and was the signal for an almost endless succession of subsequent conflicts.

(1) SOURCES: *Arii* Epist. ad Euseb. Nicomed. in *Epiph.* Hær. 69, § 6. *Theodoret,* Hist. Eccles. i. 4. Epist. ad Alex. in *Athan.* De Synodis Arim. et Seleuc. c. 16, and Ep. Hær. 69, § 7. Of the work of *Arius,* entitled Θαλεία, only some fragments are preserved by *Athanasius.* — According to the Epist. ad Euseb., his opinion was: "Ότι ὁ υἱὸς οὐκ ἐστιν ἀγέννητος, οὐδὲ μέρος ἀγεννήτου κατ' οὐδένα τρόπον, ἀλλ' οὔτε ἐξ ὑποκειμένου τινός, ἀλλ' ὅτι θελήματι καὶ βουλῇ ὑπέστη πρὸ χρόνων καὶ πρὸ αἰώνων, πλήρης θεός, μονογενής· ἀναλλοίωτος, καὶ πρὶν γεννηθῇ ἤτοι κτισθῇ ἤτοι ὁρισθῇ ἢ θεμελιωθῇ, οὐκ ἦν· ἀγέννητος γὰρ οὐκ ἦν. His views are fully settled on the last (negative) point; though he is labouring, in what precedes, to discover a satisfactory mode of statement. "We are persecuted," he continues, "because we say that the Son hath a beginning, while we teach that God is ἄναρχος. We say ὅτι ἐξ οὐκ ὄντων ἐστίν, because He is no part of God, nor is He created of anything already in existence" (he rejects accordingly the theory of emanation, or the notion that Christ is created from matter). Comp. the letter to *Alexander,* l.c., where he defends his own doctrine against the notion of *Valentinus* concerning a προβολή; against that of the Manichæans about a μέρος; and lastly, against the opinions of *Sabellius;* he there uses almost the same phraseology which occurs in the letter to *Eusebius.* The same views are expressed in still stronger language in the fragments of the aforesaid work Thalia (in *Athan.* Contra Arian. Orat. i. § 9): Οὐκ ἀεὶ ὁ θεὸς πατὴρ ἦν, ἀλλ' ὕστερον γέγονεν· οὐκ ἀεὶ ἦν ὁ υἱός, οὐ γὰρ ἦν πρὶν γεννηθῇ· οὐκ ἔστιν ἐκ τοῦ πατρός, ἀλλ' ἐξ οὐκ ὄντων ὑπέστη καὶ αὐτός· οὐκ ἔστιν ἴδιος τῆς οὐσίας τοῦ πατρός. Κτίσμα γάρ ἐστι καὶ ποίημα, καὶ οὐκ ἔστιν ἀληθινὸς θεὸς ὁ Χριστός, ἀλλὰ μετοχῇ καὶ αὐτὸς ἐθεοποιήθη. Οὐκ οἶδε τὸν πατέρα ἀκριβῶς ὁ υἱός, οὔτε ὁρᾷ ὁ λόγος τὸν πατέρα τελείως· καὶ οὔτε συνιεῖ, οὔτε γινώσκει ἀκριβῶς ὁ λόγος τὸν πατέρα· οὐκ ἔστιν ὁ ἀληθινὸς καὶ μόνος αὐτὸς τοῦ πατρὸς λόγος, ἀλλ'

ὀνόματι μόνον λέγεται λόγος καὶ σοφία, καὶ χάριτι λέγεται υἱὸς καὶ δύναμις· οὐκ ἐστιν ἄτρεπτος ὡς ὁ πατήρ, ἀλλὰ τρεπτός ἐστι φύσει, ὡς τὰ κτίσματα, καὶ λείπει αὐτῷ εἰς κατάληψιν τοῦ γνῶναι τελείως τὸν πατέρα. Contra Arian. i. § 5 : Εἶτα θελήσας ἡμᾶς (ὁ θεὸς) δημιουργῆσαι, τότε δὲ πεποίηκεν ἕνα τινὰ καὶ ὠνόμασεν αὐτὸν λόγον καὶ σοφίαν καὶ υἱὸν, ἵνα ἡμᾶς δι᾽ αὐτοῦ δημιουργήσῃ. — He proves this from the figurative expression, Joel ii. 25 (the Septuagint reads, " the great power of God," instead of " locusts "). Comp. *Neander*, Kg. ii. 2, s. 767 ff.; Dg. s. 299 ff. *Dorner*, s. 849 ff. *Baur*, Trinitätl. s. 319 ff., 342 ff. *Meier*, Trinität. s. 134; the latter says (s. 137):[1] "*Arius represents the reaction of common sense against the tendency to recur to the forms of Platonic speculation.*" But compare *Baur*, ubi supra, who finds also a speculative element in *Arius*. [The previous statements had resulted only in bringing out the extreme positions, without reconciling them. Arius laid hold of one of these, that the Father alone is unbegotten, and the Son begotten, and carried it to its logical results. If begotten, then not eternal; if not eternal, then originated in time, etc. Arianism is an abstract separation between the infinite and the finite. Comp. *Baur's* Dogmengesch. s. 164.]

(2) Concerning the opinion of *Alexander*, see his letter to Alexander, Bishop of Constantinople, in *Theodoret*, Hist. Eccles. i. 4, and the circular letter Ad Catholicos, in *Socrat.* i. 6. *Münscher, von Cölln,* p. 203–206. He founds his arguments chiefly on the prologue to the Gospel of John, and shows, μεταξὺ πατρὸς καὶ υἱοῦ οὐδὲν εἶναι διάστημα. All time and all spaces of time are rather created by the Father through the Son. If the Son had had a beginning, the Father would have been ἄλογος. The generation of the Son had nothing in common with the sonship of believers. Christ is the Son of God κατὰ φύσιν. Comp. *Schleiermacher*, Kirchengesch. p. 212.

---

[1] Thus *Arius*, on the doctrine of *Origen*, contended against its speculative side, in the *eternal generation*, while he adopted his view of the subordination of the Son to the Father. Comp. *Gieseler*, Dogmengesch. s. 308; and *Neander*, Dg. s. 300: "*The profound idea first expressed by Origen, of the eternal generation of the Son, without any beginning, could not be comprehended by the commonplace understanding of Arius.*"

§ 90.

The Hypostatical Relation and Homoousia of the Son.

The Nicene Doctrine.

Münscher, Untersuchung, über den Sinn der nicäischen Glaubensformel, in *Henke's* Neues Magazin, vi. s. 334 ff. *Walch*, Bibl. Symb. Vet. Lemg. 1770, p. 75 ss. [*Fuchs*, Bibliothek d. Kirchenversammlungen der 4n. und 5n. Jahr. i. 350. *Athanasii* Epistolæ de Decret. Synod. Nic. in Oxford Lib. of Fathers, vols. 8, 19. *Kaye's* Some Account of the Council of Nice, 1853. *Petavius*, Theol. Dogm. tom. ii. *Bp. Bull*, Defensio Fid. Nic. *De Broglie*, L'Eglise et l'Empire Romain, ii. 1-71. *Möhler*, Athanasius, 2 Thle. Mainz, 2 Ausg. 1844. *K. W. T. Hessler*, Athanasius, der Vertheidiger d. Homoousia, in Zeitschrift f. d. hist. Theol. 1856, transl. in Presb. Qu. Review, 1857. *W. W. Harvey*, Hist. and Theol. of the Three Creeds, 2 vols. Lond. 1854. *Voigt*, Die Immanente Trinität, und Athanasius, in Jahrb. f. deutsche Theologie, 1858. Analecta Nicæna, fragments on the Council, from the Syriac, by *B. H. Cowper*, Lond. 1857; cf. Journal of Sacr. Lit., Lond. Jan. 1860, p. 380. *Hefele*, Hist. of Councils, vol. i.]

The Emperor Constantine the Great, and the two bishops named Eusebius (of Cæsarea and of Nicomedia), having in vain endeavoured to bring about a reconciliation between the contending parties (1), the *First Œcumenical Council of Nicæa* was held (A.D. 325), principally through the intervention of Bishop Hosius of Corduba. After several other formulas, apparently favourable to Arianism (2), had been rejected, a confession of faith was adopted, in which it was established as the inviolable doctrine of the Catholic Church, that the Son is of the *same essence* (ὁμοούσιος) with the Father, but sustaining to Him the relation of that which is begotten to that which begets (3).

(1) Comp. Epist. *Constantini* ad Alexandrum et Arium, in *Eus.* Vita Const. ii. 64–72; and on the attempts of the two bishops to bring about a reconciliation, see *Neander*, l.c. s. 783 ff.

(2) One of these is the confession of faith which Eusebius of Cæsarea proposed, *Theodor.* Hist. Eccles. i. 11, comp. *Neander*, l.c. s. 797 ff. It contained the expression: ʽΟ τοῦ θεοῦ

λόγος, θεὸς ἐκ θεοῦ, φῶς ἐκ φωτός, ζωὴ ἐκ ζωῆς, πρωτότοκος πάσης κτίσεως, πρὸ πάντων τῶν αἰώνων, ἐκ τοῦ πατρὸς γεγεννημένος. According to *Athan.* De Decret. Syn. Nic. 20, they at first only wished to decide that the Son of God is εἰκὼν τοῦ πατρός, ὅμοιός τε καὶ ἀπαράλλακτος κατὰ πάντα τῷ πατρὶ καὶ ἄτρεπτος καὶ ἀεί, καὶ ἐν αὐτῷ εἶναι ἀδιαιρέτως.

(3) Πιστεύομεν εἰς ἕνα θεόν, πατέρα παντοκράτορα, πάντων ὁρατῶν τε καὶ ἀοράτων ποιητήν· καὶ εἰς ἕνα κύριον Ἰησοῦν Χριστὸν τὸν υἱὸν τοῦ θεοῦ, γεννηθέντα ἐκ τοῦ πατρὸς μονογενῆ, τουτέστιν ἐκ τῆς οὐσίας τοῦ πατρός, θεὸν ἐκ θεοῦ, φῶς ἐκ φωτός, θεὸν ἀληθινὸν ἐκ θεοῦ ἀληθινοῦ, γεννηθέντα οὐ ποιηθέντα, ὁμοούσιον τῷ πατρί, δι' οὗ τὰ πάντα ἐγένετο, τά τε ἐν τῷ οὐρανῷ καὶ τὰ ἐν τῇ γῇ, τὸν δι' ἡμᾶς τοὺς ἀνθρώπους καὶ διὰ τὴν ἡμετέραν σωτηρίαν κατελθόντα καὶ σαρκωθέντα καὶ ἐνανθρωπήσαντα, παθόντα καὶ ἀναστάντα τῇ τρίτῃ ἡμέρᾳ· ἀνελθόντα εἰς τοὺς οὐρανούς, καὶ ἐρχόμενον κρῖναι ζῶντας καὶ νεκρούς. Καὶ εἰς τὸ ἅγιον πνεῦμα. Τοὺς δὲ λέγοντας, ὅτι ἦν ποτε ὅτε οὐκ ἦν, καὶ πρὶν γεννηθῆναι οὐκ ἦν, καὶ ὅτι ἐξ οὐκ ὄντων ἐγένετο, ἢ ἐξ ἑτέρας ὑποστάσεως ἢ οὐσίας φάσκοντας εἶναι, ἢ κτιστὸν ἢ τρεπτὸν ἢ ἀλλοιωτὸν τὸν υἱὸν τοῦ θεοῦ, ἀναθεματίζει ἡ ἁγία καθολικὴ καὶ ἀποστολικὴ ἐκκλησία. *Athan.* Epist. De Decret. Syn. Nic.—*Eus. Cæs.* Ep. ad Cæsariens.—*Socrat.* i. 8. *Theodoret*, Hist. Eccl. i. 11. *Münscher (von Cölln)*, s. 207–209. *Baur*, Trinitätl. s. 334 ff. *Meier*, s. 146 ff. *Dorner*, 849. [The Nicene Creed, says *Dorner*, showed to Christian theology the end at which it was to aim, even if it did not perfectly realize that end. Arianism had pressed back towards Ebionitism; it had lost the idea of the incarnation, putting between God and the creature a fantastic, subordinate God, which separated rather than united the infinite and finite. It made a perfect revelation or manifestation of God impossible. The Nicene Fathers met this by proclaiming the real and proper Godhead of the Son, etc.]

Respecting the definitions of the phrases ἐξ οὐσίας and ὁμοούσιος, comp. *Athanasius*, l.c. We find that even at that time a distinction was made between *sameness* and *similarity*. The Son is like the Father in a different sense from that in which we become like God by rendering obedience to His laws. This resemblance, moreover, is not external, accidental, like that between another metal and gold, tin and silver, etc.

§ 91.] HYPOSTATICAL RELATION AND HOMOOUSIA OF THE SON. 357

[*Baur*, Dg. s. 164, gives the following as the substance of the Nicene and Athanasian belief. To the Arian hypothesis it opposes the eternal generation and consubstantiality (Homoousia) of the Son, on the basis of the following arguments: 1. The Father would not be absolute God if He were not in His essence begetting, and so the Father of a Son of the same essence. 2. The idea of the Godhead of the Son is abolished, if He is not Son by nature, but only through God's grace. If created, He were neither Son nor God; to be both creature and Creator is a complete contradiction. 3. The unity of the finite with the infinite, of man with God, falls to the ground, if the mediator of this unity is only a creature, and not the absolute God.]

§ 91.

Further Fluctuations until the Synod of Constantinople.

But the phrase ὁμοούσιος did not meet with universal approval (1). In this unsettled state of affairs the party of the Eusebians (2), who had for some time previously enjoyed the favour of the court, succeeded in gaining its assent to a doctrine in which the use of the term ὁμοούσιος was studiously avoided, though it did not strictly inculcate the principles of Arianism. Thus Athanasius, who firmly adhered to this watchword of the Nicene party, found himself compelled to seek refuge in the West. Several synods were held for the purpose of settling this long protracted question; a number of formulæ were drawn up and rejected (3), till at last the Nicene and Athanasian doctrine was more firmly established by the decisions of the second Œcumenical Synod of Constantinople (A.D. 381) (4).

(1) Several Asiatic bishops took offence at the term in question; *Socrat.* i. 8, 6. *Münscher* (*von Cölln*), s. 210. They considered it unscriptural (λέξις ἄγραφος), and were afraid that it might give rise to a revival of the theory of emanation. But the expression ἐκ τῆς οὐσίας was more favourable to that

theory than the term ὁμοούσιος, comp. *Meier*, l.c. s. 147.— Respecting the further course of the external events, see the works on ecclesiastical history. LEADING HISTORICAL FACTS: I. The banishment of Arius and of the bishops Theonas and Secundus. The fate of Eusebius of Nicomedia and Theognis of Nicæa. II. Arius recalled, A.D. 330, after having signed the following confession of faith: εἰς Κύριον Ἰησοῦν Χριστὸν, τὸν υἱὸν τοῦ θεοῦ, τὸν ἐξ αὐτοῦ πρὸ πάντων τῶν αἰώνων γεγεννημένον, θεὸν λόγον, δι' οὗ τὰ πάντα ἐγένετο κ.τ.λ. (*Socr.* i. 26). Synods of Tyre and Jerusalem (A.D. 335). III. Banishment of Athanasius to Gaul. The sudden death of Arius at Constantinople (A.D. 336), prior to his solemn readmission into the Church. Different opinions concerning this event. IV. Death of the Emperor Constantine the Great at Nicomedia, A.D. 337. (*Socr.* i. 27–40.) A remarkable change had taken place in the views of Constantine towards the close of his life. The Arians were firmly supported by his son Constantius, who ruled in the East from A.D. 337.

(2) Concerning this name, see *Gieseler*, Kg. i. 2, s. 54. Athanasius himself frequently calls them οἱ περὶ Εὐσέβιον; by other writers they are classed with the Arians, whom they joined in their opposition to Athanasius.

(3) I. The four confessions of faith drawn up by the Eusebians, and presented at councils in Antioch from the year 341 (in *Athan.* De Syn. c. 22–25. *Walch*, p. 109 ss. *Münscher (von Cölln)*, s. 211 ff. *Gieseler*, Kg. i. 2, s. 51); in all of these the word ὁμοούσιος is wanting, but in other points they were not favourable to Arianism. II. The formula μακρόστιχος, by the Council of Antioch, A.D. 343, in which Arianism was condemned, Tritheism rejected, the doctrine of Athanasius found fault with, and in opposition to it, the subordination of the Son to the Father was maintained, *Athanas.* De Synod. § 26; *Walch*, Bib. Symb. p. 115; *Gieseler*, l.c. s. 55. III. The Synod of Sardica (A.D. 347, or, according to others, A.D. 344[1]), *Socrat.* ii. 20; but the western bishops alone remained at Sardica, the eastern held their assemblies in the neighbouring town of Philippopolis. The formula Philippopolitana, pre-

---

[1] Respecting the chronology, see *H. J. Wetzer*, Restitutio veræ Chronologiæ Rerum ex Controversiis Arianis inde ab anno 325 usque ad annum 350 exortarum contra chronologiam hodie receptam exhibita. Francof. 1827.

§ 91.] HYPOSTATICAL RELATION AND HOMOOUSIA OF THE SON. 359

served by *Hilary* (de Synodis contra Arianos, § 34), is partly a repetition of the formula μακρόστιχος. IV. The confession of faith adopted at the first Council of Sirmium (A.D. 351, in *Athanas.* § 27 ; in *Hilary*, § 37 ; and in *Socrat.* ii. 29, 30) was directed against Photinus; see below, § 92. V. The formula of the second Council of Sirmium (A.D. 357, in *Hilary*, § 11 ; *Athanas.* § 28 ; *Socrat.* ii. 30) was directed both against the use of the term ὁμοούσιος, and against speculative tendencies in general : Scire autem manifestum est solum Patrem quomodo genuerit filium suum, et filium quomodo genitus sit a patre (comp. above, *Irenæus*, § 42, note 10); but it also asserts the subordination of the Son to the Father in the strict Arian manner: Nulla ambiguitas est, majorem esse Patrem. Nulli potest dubium esse, Patrem honore, dignitate, claritate, majestate et ipso nomine Patris majorem esse filio, ipso testante: qui me misit major me est (John xiv. 28). Et hoc catholicum esse, nemo ignorat, duas Personas esse Patris et Filii, majorem Patrem, Filium subjectum cum omnibus his, quæ ipsi Pater subjecit. VI. The strict Arian views were rejected by the Semi-Arians at the Synod of Ancyra in Galatia (A.D. 358), under Basil, Bishop of Ancyra; the decrees of this synod are given in *Epiph.* Hær. 73, § 2–11. (*Münscher, von Cölln*, s. 213, and *Gieseler*, l.c. s. 58.) VII. The confession of faith adopted at the third Synod of Sirmium (A.D. 358), in which that agreed upon at the second synod (the Arian) is condemned, and the Semi-Arian confession of the Synod of Ancyra is confirmed (comp. *Athan.* § 8. *Socrat.* ii. 37). VIII. Assembly of westerns at Ariminum (Rimini), and of easterns at Seleucia (A.D. 359).

(4) SYMBOLUM NICÆNO-CONSTANTINOPOLITANUM : Πιστεύομεν εἰς ἕνα θεὸν, πατέρα παντοκράτορα, ποιητὴν οὐρανοῦ καὶ γῆς, ὁρατῶν τε πάντων καὶ ἀοράτων. Καὶ εἰς ἕνα κύριον Ἰησοῦν Χριστὸν, τὸν υἱὸν τοῦ θεοῦ τὸν μονογενῆ, τὸν ἐκ τοῦ πατρὸς γεννηθέντα πρὸ πάντων τῶν αἰώνων, φῶς ἐκ φωτός, θεὸν ἀληθινὸν ἐκ θεοῦ ἀληθινοῦ, γεννηθέντα οὐ ποιηθέντα, ὁμοούσιον τῷ πατρὶ, δι' οὗ τὰ πάντα ἐγένετο· τὸν δι' ἡμᾶς τοὺς ἀνθρώπους καὶ διὰ τὴν ἡμετέραν σωτηρίαν κατελθόντα ἐκ τῶν οὐρανῶν, καὶ σαρκωθέντα ἐκ πνεύματος ἁγίου καὶ Μαρίας τῆς παρθένου, καὶ ἐνανθρωπήσαντα· σταυρωθέντα δὲ ὑπὲρ ἡμῶν ἐπὶ Ποντίου Πιλάτου, καὶ παθόντα

καὶ ταφέντα καὶ ἀναστάντα ἐν τῇ τρίτῃ ἡμέρᾳ κατὰ τὰς γραφάς· καὶ ἀνελθόντα εἰς τοὺς οὐρανούς, καὶ καθεζόμενον ἐκ δεξιῶν τοῦ πατρὸς, καὶ πάλιν ἐρχόμενον μετὰ δόξης κρῖναι ζῶντας καὶ νεκρούς· οὗ τῆς βασιλείας οὐκ ἔσται τέλος. Καὶ εἰς τὸ ἅγιον πνεῦμα κ.τ.λ. (Concerning the further statements as to the nature of the Holy Spirit, see below, § 93, note 7.)

Münscher (von Cölln) compares this symbol with the Nicene Creed, s. 240. Comp. *J. C. Suicer*, Symbolum Nicæno-Constantinopolitan. expositum et ex antiquitate ecclesiastica illustratum, Traj. ad Rhen. 1718, 4to. [Comp. *Cardinal Wiseman*, Account of Council of Constantinople in the Arian Controv., in his Essays, vol. iii.; *Hefele*, History of Councils, Eng. transl., vols. i. and ii.; and *Swainson*, l.c.]

§ 92.

The Causes of these Fluctuations.

Arianism and Semi-Arianism on the one hand, and return to Sabellianism on the other (Marcellus and Photinus).

C. R. W. *Klose*, Geschichte und Lehre des Eunomius, Kiel 1833. *By the same:* Geschichte und Lehre des Marcellus und Photinus, Hamburg 1837.

From the very nature of the controversy in question, it followed that the difficult task of steering clear both of Sabellianism and Arianism devolved on those who were anxious to preserve orthodoxy in its purity. In maintaining the sameness of essence (consubstantiality), they had to hold fast to the distinction of persons (hypostases); in asserting the latter, they had to avoid the doctrine of subordination (1). The Semi-Arians (2), and with them *Cyril* of Jerusalem (3) and *Eusebius* of Cæsarea (4), endeavoured to avoid the use of the term ὁμοούσιος, lest they should fall into the Sabellian error; though the former asserted, in opposition to the strict Arians (the followers of Aëtius and the Eunomians) (5), that the Son was of *similar* essence with the Father (ὁμοιούσιος) (6). But *Marcellus*, Bishop of Ancyra, and his disciple *Photinus*, Bishop of Sirmium, carried their opposition to Arianism so far as to

§ 92.] HYPOSTATICAL RELATION AND HOMOOUSIA OF THE SON. 361

adopt in substance the principles of Sabellianism. They modified it, however, to some extent, by drawing a distinction between the terms Logos and the Son of God, and thus guarded it against all semblance of patripassianism (7).

(1) *Chrysostom* shows clearly the necessity, as well as the difficulty, of avoiding both of these dangers, De Sacerdotio, iv. 4, sub finem: Ἄν τε γὰρ μίαν τις εἴπῃ θεότητα, πρὸς τὴν ἑαυτοῦ παράνοιαν εὐθέως εἵλκυσε τὴν φωνὴν ὁ Σαβέλλιος· ἄν τε διέλῃ πάλιν ἕτερον μὲν τὸν Πατέρα, ἕτερον δὲ τὸν Υἱὸν καὶ τὸ Πνεῦμα δὲ τὸ ἅγιον ἕτερον εἶναι λέγων, ἐφέστηκεν Ἄρειος, εἰς παραλλαγὴν οὐσίας ἕλκων τὴν ἐν τοῖς προσώποις διαφοράν. Δεῖ δὲ καὶ τὴν ἀσεβῆ σύγχυσιν ἐκείνου, καὶ τὴν μανιώδη τούτου διαίρεσιν ἀποστρέφεσθαι καὶ φεύγειν, τὴν μὲν θεότητα Πατρὸς καὶ Υἱοῦ καὶ ἁγίου Πνεύματος μίαν ὁμολογοῦντας, προστιθέντας δὲ τὰς τρεῖς ὑποστάσεις. Οὕτω γὰρ ἀποτειχίσαι δυνησόμεθα τὰς ἀμφοτέρων ἐφόδους.

(2) The leaders of the Semi-Arians (ὁμοιουσιασταί, ἡμιάρειοι) were *Basil*, Bishop of Ancyra, and *Georgius*, Bishop of Laodicea. Comp. the confession of faith adopted by the Synod of Ancyra (A.D. 358), in *Athanas*. de Syn. § 41. *Münscher (von Cölln)*, s. 222.

(3) *Cyril*, Cat. xvi. 24. He rejects, generally speaking, the too fine-spun speculations, and thinks it sufficient to believe: Εἷς θεὸς ὁ Πατήρ· εἷς κύριος, ὁ μονογενὴς αὐτοῦ υἱός· ἓν τὸ πνεῦμα τὸ ἅγιον, ὁ παράκλητος. Christ says, he that believeth on Him hath eternal life—not he who knows how He was generated. We ought not to go beyond Scripture, nor turn either to the right or to the left, but keep in the via regia, μήτε διὰ τὸ νομίζειν τιμᾶν τὸν υἱόν,. πατέρα αὐτὸν ἀναγορεύσωμεν, μήτε διὰ τὸ τιμᾶν τὸν πατέρα νομίζειν, ἕν τι δημιουργημάτων τὸν υἱὸν ὑποπτεύσωμεν, xi. 17. Instead of ὁμοούσιος, he would prefer ὅμοιος κατὰ πάντα, iv. 7, but comp. the various readings in the work of *Toutée*, p. 54, and *Münscher, von Cölln*, s. 226. Socrat. iv. 25. *He* also maintains that it is necessary to hold the medium between Sabellianism and Arianism, iv. 8 : Καὶ μήτε ἀπαλλοτριώσῃς τοῦ πατρὸς τὸν υἱόν, μήτε συναλοιφὴν ἐργασάμενος υἱοπατορίαν πιστεύσῃς κ.τ.λ. Comp. xvi. 4, and *Meier*, die Lehre

von der Trinität. i. s. 170. [*Cyril's* chief aim is to hold fast the individual existence of the Son and the Father, without so annulling all internal relations, that the Trias is destroyed, and the Son degraded to the level of creatures by the ἦν ποτε οὐκ ἦν.]

(4) *Eus.* Hist. Eccl. i. 2, calls the Son τὸν τῆς μεγάλης βουλῆς ἄγγελον, τὸν τῆς ἀρρήτου γνώμης τοῦ πατρὸς ὑπουργὸν, τὸν δεύτερον μετὰ τὸν πατέρα αἴτιον, etc. In Panegyricus, x. 1, he also calls Him τῶν ἀγαθῶν δεύτερον αἴτιον, an expression which greatly offended the orthodox writers;[1] but at another place he gives Him the name αὐτόθεος, x. 4. On the formation of compound words by means of the pronoun αὐτό, of which *Eusebius* makes frequent use, comp. the Demonstr. Evang. iv. 2, 13, and *Heinichen*, l.c. p. 223. In the same work, v. 1, p. 215, the subordination of the Son to the Father is stated; he calls Him (iv. 3, p. 149) υἱὸν γεννητόν, but yet says that He is πρὸ χρόνων αἰωνίων ὄντα καὶ προόντα καὶ τῷ πατρὶ ὡς υἱὸν διαπαντὸς συνόντα; yet again he speaks of Him as ἐκ τῆς τοῦ πατρὸς ἀνεκφράστου καὶ ἀπερινοήτου βουλῆς τε καὶ δυνάμεως οὐσιούμενον. For further particulars, see *Münscher, von Cölln*, s. 227–229, and Handbuch, iii. s. 427 ff. *Martini*, Eus. Cæs. de Divinitate Christi Sententia, Rost. 1795, 4to. † *Ritter*, Eus. Cæs. de Divinitate Christi placita, Bonn 1823, 4to. *Baur*, Trin. i. s. 472 ff. *Haenell*, de Eusebio Cæs. relig. Christ. defensore. *Meier*, l.c. i. s. 167. *Dorner*, s. 792 ff.: "*His system is a play of colours, a reflex of the unsolved problems of the Church at that time.*"

(5) Respecting the strict Arians: *Aëtius* of Antioch, *Eunomius*, Bishop of Cycicum, and *Acacius*, Bishop of Cæsarea, in Palestine, comp. *Philostorg.* iii. iv., *Epiph.* Hær. 76, 10. Respecting the life, writings, and opinions of *Eunomius*, see *Klose*, l.c. *Neander*, Kg. ii. 2, s. 852 ff. Comp. *Dorner*, i. 3, s. 853 ff. *Meier*, i. s. 176 ff. *Baur*, Trin. i. 360 ff.

(6) *Athanasius* showed how little the idea of similarity of

---

[1] Comp. the note of the scholiast in the Cod. Med. (in the editions of *Valesius* and *Heinichen*, iii. p. 219): Κακῶς κἀνταῦθα θεολογιῖς, Εὐσέβιι, περὶ τοῦ συνανάρχου καὶ συναϊδίου καὶ συμποιητοῦ τῶν ὅλων υἱοῦ τοῦ θεοῦ, δεύτερον αὐτὸν ἀποκαλῶν αἴτιον τῶν ἀγαθῶν, συναίτιον ὄντα καὶ συνδημιουργὸν τῷ πατρὶ τῶν ὅλων, καὶ ὁμοούσιον, and the more recent note in the Cod. Mazarin., ibidem.

essence (homoiousianism) was adapted to satisfy the mind, when, among other things, he calls to mind that many things may be of similar nature without having sprung from each other (as silver and tin, a wolf and a dog); De Synod. § 41. The Semi-Arians, with the Arians, maintained that the Son was created from the will of the Father; the opposite of this appeared to them to be mere compulsion or force. In reply, *Athanasius* held up the idea of an internal necessity, founded in the very nature of God, to which the category of force does not apply. He compared the relation to that of the shining of the light. Orat. contr. Ar. ii. 2. Comp. *Gieseler*, Dogmengesch. s. 311. *Neander*, Dg. 311. [*Voigt* on Athanasius and the Immanent Trinity, in Jahrb. f. deutsche Theologie, 1858. *Baur*, Dogmengesch. s. 165, says of the Semi-Arians, that they had a half-way position, reducing the absolute ideas of the two parties to indeterminate terms, and running back into the old subordination and emanation views.]

(7) The opinions of *Marcellus* (who died about the year 374) are derived partly from the fragments of his treatise against Asterius (de Subjectione Domini, edited by *Rettberg*, under the title "Marcelliana," Gött. 1791), partly from the writings of his opponents, *Eusebius* (κατὰ Μαρκέλλου, lib. ii., and περὶ τῆς ἐκκλησιαστικῆς θεολογίας) and *Cyril* of Jerusalem (Cat. xv. 27, 33), and partly from his own letter to Julius, Bishop of Rome (*Epiph.* Hær. 72, 2). The earlier writers are divided in their opinions concerning the orthodoxy of *Marcellus*: the language of *Athanasius* is very mild and cautious (διὰ τοῦ προσώπου μειδιάσας, *Epiph.* Hær. 72, 4), though he does not directly approve of his sentiments. *Basil the Great*, on the other hand (according to *Epiphanius*, 69, 2, and 263, 5), and most of the other Eastern bishops, insisted upon his condemnation; most of the later writers considered him a heretic, comp. *Montfaucon*, Diatribe de Causa Marcelli Ancyrani (in Collect. Nova Patr. 1707, t. ii. p. li.); *Klose*, s. 21-25; *Gieseler*, Kg. ii. 1, s. 51, Anm. *Marcellus* had formerly defended the term ὁμοούσιος at the Council of Nicæa. When, in the course of the controversy, and of his opposition to the Arian sophist *Asterius*, he seemed to lean more towards Sabellianism, this may have occurred without his being directly conscious of it; comp. *Baumgarten-Crusius*, i. s. 277,

278. [Ueber die Orthodoxie des Marc., *von F. A. Willenberg,* Münster 1859.] Concerning the doctrine itself, *Marcellus* returned to the old distinction made between λόγος ἐνδιάθετος and προφορικός; he imagined, on the one hand, that the λόγος was ἡσυχάζων in God, and, on the other, that it was an ἐνέργεια δραστική proceeding from Him. Inasmuch as he maintains the reality of the Logos (whom he does not consider to be a mere name), in opposition to the Sabellian view of a τριὰς ἐκτεινομένη καὶ συστελλομένη, and rejects the idea of *generation* adopted by the Council of Nicæa (because it seemed to him to infringe upon the Godhead of the Logos), he occupies an intermediate position between the one and the other. He also endeavoured to reintroduce the older historical signification of the phrase υἱὸς θεοῦ, as applying to the personal manifestation of the historical Christ, and not to the pre-existence of the Logos, to whom the idea of generation cannot be applied. He consequently referred the biblical phrases, Col. i. 15, and the like, in which Christ is spoken of as the image of God, to the incarnate Logos; so, too, the πρωτότοκος πάσης κτίσεως; comp. *Neander*, Dg. s. 315. His disciple *Photinus*, Bishop of Sirmium (to whom his opponents, with poor wit, gave the nickname Σκοτεινός), adopted similar views, but carried them to a much greater extent; he died about the year 376. His doctrine was condemned in the aforesaid formula μακρόστιχος, and again at the Council of Milan (A.D. 346). He himself was dismissed from his office by the Council of Sirmium (A.D. 351). The sect of the Photinians, however, continued to exist till the reign of Theodosius the Great. From what has been said concerning him by *Athan.* de Syn. § 26, *Socrat.* ii. 19, *Epiph.* Hær. 70, *Hilary* (Fragm. and De Synodis), *Marius Mercator* (Nestorii Sermo IV.), and *Vigil. Tapsens.* (Dialogus), it cannot be fully ascertained how far *Photinus* either adhered to the principles of his master or deviated from them. Comp. on this point, *Münscher*, Handbuch, iii. s. 447. *Neander*, Kg. ii. 2, s. 908, 425. *Baumgarten-Crusius*, s. 279. *Gieseler*, l.c. *Hase*, Kg. (6 Auf.), s. 116. *Klose*, s. 66 ff. *He* too asserted the co-eternity of the Logos (but not of the Son) with the Father, and employed the term λογοπάτωρ to denote their unity, as *Sabellius* had used the word υἱοπάτωρ. He applied the name

"Son of God" only to the incarnate Christ. The only difference between *Marcellus* and *Photinus* probably was that the latter developed the negative aspect of Christology more than his master, and consequently considered the connection of the Logos with the historical Christ to be less intimate. Hence his followers were called Homuncionitæ (according to *Mar. Mercator*, quoted by *Klose*, s. 76). Thus *Photinus* corresponds more with *Paul* of Samosata, and *Marcellus* with *Sabellius*. So, too, *Photinus* viewed the pre-existence of Christ in a merely ideal way, referring it (as the Socinians afterwards did) to predestination. In these controversies it is very striking, as *Münscher* has said, "*that theologians then but little understood the distinction made by Marcellus and Photinus between the terms* LOGOS *and* SON OF GOD. *In refuting their opponents, they invariably confounded these expressions, and thus might easily draw dangerous and absurd inferences from their propositions. But, at the same time, it is evident that their own arguments would take a wrong direction, and thus lose the greatest part of their force,*" Münscher, Handbuch, l.c. Comp., however, *Dorner*, i. 3, s. 864 ff. *Baur*, Trinit. i. s. 525 ff. *Meier*, i. s. 160 ff., especially on the transverse relations in which *Photinus* stood to his teacher in respect to Christology. [*Baur*, Dogmengesch. s. 168: "*Marcellus* distinguishes the Son from the Logos, and makes the Logos itself to be both quiescent and active; the Sonship of the Logos has both a beginning and an end. The doctrine of *Marcellus* is partly Arian and partly Sabellian. With Arianism he sundered God and the world as far as possible. The doctrine of *Paulinus* is the same, excepting that, like *Paul* of Samosata and *Arius*, he adopted the view that the human Christ was deified by means of His moral excellences."]

§ 93.

Godhead of the Holy Spirit.

[*Kahnis*, Gesch. d. Lehre vom Heiligen Geiste. *Burton*, Test. of Ante-Nicene Fathers to the Divinity of the Holy Ghost, 1831 (Works, vol. ii.). *Hare's* (*Archd.*) Mission of the Comforter, 2d ed. 1851. *Gaume*, Traité du Saint Esprit, 2 vols. var. ed. *Swete*, Early History of the Doctrine of the Holy Spirit, Camb. 1873.]

The Nicene Creed decided nothing concerning the Holy Spirit (1). While *Lactantius* still identified the Word with the Spirit (2), other theologians regarded the Spirit as a mere divine power or gift, or at least did not venture to determine His nature in any more definite way, though accustomed to teach the Godhead of the Son in unequivocal terms (3). But *Athanasius* correctly inferred from his premises the Godhead of the Holy Spirit (4), and was followed by *Basil*, surnamed *the Great*, as well as by *Gregory* of Nazianzus and *Gregory* of Nyssa (5). At last the Synod of Constantinople (A.D. 381), influenced by *Gregory* of Nazianzus, adopted more precise doctrinal definitions concerning the Holy Spirit, especially in opposition to the Macedonians ($\pi\nu\epsilon\nu\mu\alpha\tau o\mu\acute{a}\chi o\nu s$) (6). Though the term $\acute{o}\mu oo\acute{v}\sigma\iota os$ itself was not applied to the Spirit in the canons of this council, yet, by determining that He proceeds from the Father, they prepared the way for further definitions, in which honour and power, equal in every respect to those of the Father and the Son, were ascribed to Him (7).

(1) The opposition to Arius would necessarily lead to more precise definitions; for *Arius* (according to *Athan.* Orat. 1, § 6) maintained that the Spirit stood as far below the Son as the Son was below the Father, and that He was the first of the creatures made by the Son. But it did not appear wise to complicate the matter in question still more by contending about the Godhead of the Spirit, since many of the Nicene Fathers, who consented that the term $\acute{o}\mu oo\acute{v}\sigma\iota os$ should be applied to the Son, would not have so easily admitted it in reference to the Spirit. See *Neander*, Kg. ii. 2, s. 892.

(2) See above, § 87, note 1.

(3) There were here again two ways—the one falling back into Sabellianism, the other a continuation of Arianism. *Lactantius*, on the one hand, separated the Son from the Father (after the manner of the Arians); and, on the other, confounded the Spirit with the Son (as the Sabellians did). Some writers followed the same course, while others ascribed a distinct personality to the Spirit, but asserted that He was subordinate to both the Father and the Son (the Arian view).

Gregory of Nazianzus gives a summary of the different views entertained in his time in the fifth of his theological orations, which was composed about the year 380 (De Spir. S. Orat. xxxi. p. 539): "Some of the wise men amongst us regard the Holy Spirit as an energy (ἐνέργεια), others think that He is a creature, some again that He is God Himself, and, lastly, there are some who do not know what opinion to adopt, from reverence, as they say, for the sacred Scriptures, because *they* do not teach anything definite on this point." *Eustathius* of Sebaste belonged to this latter class. He said in reference to the Macedonian controversy (*Socr.* ii. 45): Ἐγὼ οὔτε θεὸν ὀνομάζειν τὸ πνεῦμα τὸ ἅγιον αἱροῦμαι, οὔτε κτίσμα καλεῖν τολμήσαιμι. Comp. *Ullmann*, Gregor von Nazianz. s. 380. *Neander*, Kg. ii. 2, s. 892. *Eusebius* of Cæsarea was the more willing to subordinate the Spirit to both the Father and the Son, as he was disposed to admit the subordination of the Son to the Father. He thinks that the Spirit is the first of all rational beings, but belongs nevertheless to the Trinity, De Theol. Eccles. iii. 3, 5, 6. *Hilary* was satisfied that that which searcheth the deep things of God must be itself divine, though he could not find any passage in Scripture in which the name *God* was given to the Holy Spirit, De Trin. lib. xii. c. 55; Tuum est, quicquid te init; neque alienum a te est, quicquid virtute scrutantis inest. Comp. de Trin. ii. 29 : De spiritu autem sancto nec tacere oportet, nec loqui necesse est, sed sileri a nobis eorum causa, qui nesciunt, non potest. Loqui autem de eo non necesse est, quia de patre et filio auctoribus confitendum est, et quidem puto an sit, non esse tractandum. Est enim, quandoquidem donatur, accipitur, obtinetur, et qui confessioni patris et filii connexus est, non potest a confessione patris et filii separari. Imperfectum enim est nobis totum, si aliquid desit a toto. De quo si quis intelligentiæ nostræ sensum requirit, in Apostolo legimus ambo: Quoniam estis, inquit, filii Dei, misit Deus spiritum filii sui in corda vestra clamantem: Abba pater. Et rursum : Nolite contristare Spir. S. Dei, in quo signati estis. . . . Unde quia est et donatur et habetur et Dei est, cesset hinc sermo calumniantium, cum dicunt, per quem sit et ob quid sit, vel qualis sit. Si responsio nostra displicebit, dicentium : Per quem omnia et in quo omnia sunt, et quia spiritus est Dei, donum fidelium ; displiceant et apostoli et evangelistæ et prophetæ, hoc tantum de eo quod esset loquentes, et post hæc pater et filius displicebit. He also advises us not to be perplexed by the language of Scripture, in which both the Father and the Son are sometimes called "Spirit." "*He grossly confounds the terms: Deus Spiritus, Dei Spiritus, and Spiritus S.; and, though he believes in the separate subsistence of the Spirit, he does not go beyond the idea that he is a donum, a munus,*" Meier, Trinitätsl. i. s. 192.—*Cyril* of Jerusalem, too, endeavours to avoid all further definitions as to the nature of the Holy Spirit not contained in the Scriptures, though he distinctly separates him from all created beings, and regards him as an essential part of the Trinity; but he urges especially the practical aspect of this doctrine in opposition to the false enthusiasm of heretical fanatics, Cat. 15 and 17.[1]

(4) *Athanasius* (Epp. 4, ad Serap.) endeavoured to refute those who declared the Holy Ghost to be a κτίσμα, or the first of the πνευμάτων λειτουργικῶν, and who were called τροπικοί, πνευματομαχοῦντες. He shows that we completely renounce Arianism only when we perceive in the Trinity nothing that is foreign to the nature of God (ἀλλότριον ἢ ἐξώθεν ἐπιμιγνύμενον), but one and the same being, which is in perfect accordance and identical with itself. Τριὰς δέ ἐστιν οὐχ ἕως ὀνόματος μόνον καὶ φαντασίας λέξεως, ἀλλὰ ἀληθείᾳ καὶ ὑπάρξει τριάς (Ep. i. 28, p. 677). He appealed both to the declarations of Holy Writ, and to the testimony of our own Christian consciousness. How can that which is not sanctified by anything else, which is itself the source of sanctification to all creatures, possess the *same* nature as those who are sanctified by it? We have fellowship with God, and participate in the divine life by means of the Holy Spirit; but this could not be if the Spirit were a creature. As certain as it is that we through Him become partakers of the divine nature, so certain is it that He must Himself be one with the divine essence (εἰ δὲ θεοποιεῖ, οὐκ ἀμφίβολον, ὅτι ἡ τούτου φύσις

---

[1] As *one* shower waters flowers of the most different species (roses and lilies), so *one* Spirit is the author of many different graces, etc. Cat. xvi. 12. He is τίμιον, τὸ ἀγαθόν, μέγας παρὰ θεοῦ σύμμαχος καὶ προστάτης, μέγας διδάσκαλος ἐκκλησίας, μέγας ὑπερασπιστὴς ὑπὲρ ἡμῶν, etc., ibid. c. 19. Hence His glory far surpasses that of all angels, c. 23.

θεοῦ ἐστί). Ep. i. ad Serap. § 24, p. 672. The Holy Ghost is the image of the Son, as the Son is the image of the Father, ib. § 26. *Neander*, l.c. s. 895. *Meier*, i. s. 187 ff. *Voigt* on Athanasius in the Jahrb. f. deutsche Theol. 1858, s. 81 ff.

(5) *Basil the Great* on a particular occasion composed his treatise, De Spiritu Sancto, addressed to the Bishop Amphilochius of Iconium (comp. with it Ep. 189; Homilia de Fide, t. ii. p. 132; Hom. contra Sab. t. ii. p. 195). He too maintained that the name *God* should be given to the Spirit, and appealed both to Scripture in general, and to the baptismal formula in particular, in which the Spirit is mentioned together with the Father and the Son. He did not, however, lay much stress upon this express designation, but simply required that the Spirit should not be regarded as a creature, but be considered as inseparable from both the Father and the Son. He spoke in eloquent language of the practical importance of the doctrine of the Holy Spirit (as the sanctifier of men), De Spir. S. c. 16 : Τὸ δὲ μέγιστον τεκμήριον τῆς πρὸς τὸν πατέρα καὶ υἱὸν τοῦ πνεύματος συναφείας, ὅτι οὕτως ἔχειν λέγεται πρὸς τὸν θεὸν, ὡς πρὸς ἕκαστον ἔχει τὸ πνεῦμα τὸ ἐν ἡμῖν (1 Cor. ii. 10, 11). In answer to the objection that the Spirit is called a *gift*, he remarks that the Son is likewise *a gift of God*, ibid. c. 24; comp. *Klose*, Basilius der Grosse, s. 34 ff. His brother, *Gregory* of Nyssa, in the second chapter of his Larger Catechism, starts from ideas similar to those of Lactantius, that the *Spirit* (breath) must be connected with the *Word*, since it is so even in the case of man. He does not, however, like Lactantius, identify the Spirit with the Word, but keeps them distinct. The Spirit is not to be considered as anything foreign which enters from without into the Deity (comp. Athanasius); to think of the Spirit of God as similar to our own, would be to detract from the glory of the divine omnipotence. "On the contrary, we conceive that this *essential power, which manifests itself as a distinct hypostasis*, can neither be separated from the Godhead in which it rests, nor from the Divine Word which it follows. Nor does it cease to exist, but, being self-existing (αὐτοκίνητον), like the Divine Word, it is ever capable of choosing the good, and of carrying out all its purposes." Comp. *Rupp*, Gregor von Nyssa, s. 169, 170.—The views of *Gregory* of Nazianzus

agreed with those of these two writers, though he clearly perceived the difficulties with which the doctrine in question was beset in his time. He anticipated the objection that it would introduce a θεὸν ξένον καὶ ἄγραφον (Orat. xxx. 1, p. 566. *Ullmann*, s. 381). He also acknowledged that the doctrine in this particular form was not expressly contained in Scripture, and therefore thought that we must go beyond the letter.[1] He therefore had recourse to the idea of a gradual revelation, which, as he conceived, stood in connection with a natural development of the Trinity. "The Old Testament set forth the Father in a clear, but the Son in a somewhat dimmer light: the New Testament reveals the Son, but only indicates the Godhead of the Spirit; but now the Spirit dwells in the midst of us, and manifests Himself more distinctly. It was not desirable that the Godhead of the Son should be proclaimed as long as that of the Father was not fully recognized; nor to add that of the Spirit as long as that of the Son was not believed." Gregory numbered the doctrine of the Holy Spirit among those things of which Christ speaks, John xvi. 12, and recommended, therefore, prudence in bringing forward this dogma. He himself developed it principally in his controversy with Macedonius, and showed, in opposition to him, that the Holy Spirit is neither a mere power nor a creature, and, accordingly, that there is no other alternative except that He is God Himself. For further particulars, see *Ullmann*, s. 378 ff.

(6) The word Πνευματομάχοι has a general meaning, in which it comprehends, of course, the strict Arians. But the Godhead of the Spirit was equally denied by the *Semi-Arians*, while their views concerning the nature of the Son approximated to those of the orthodox party; the most prominent theologian among them was *Macedonius*, Bishop of Constantinople (A.D. 341–360). *Sozom.* iv. 27, says of him: Εἰσηγεῖτο δὲ τὸν υἱὸν θεὸν εἶναι, κατὰ πάντα τε καὶ κατ' οὐσίαν ὅμοιον τῷ πατρί· τό τε ἅγιον πνεῦμα ἄμοιρον τῶν αὐτῶν πρεσβείων

---

[1] Comp. *Meier*, Trinit. Lehre, i. s. 190: "*The want of a sufficiently definite interpretation of Scripture was one of the chief hindrances to the recognition of the consubstantiality (Homoousia) of the Son. To conduct the proof from the depths of the Christian consciousness appeared to many too adventurous, especially in view of the tendencies of the East at that epoch; they had doubts about ascribing to the Holy Spirit identity of essence, and paying worship to Him without express declaration of Christ and the apostles.*"

ἀπεφαίνετο, διάκονον καὶ ὑπηρέτην καλῶν. *Theodoret*, ii. 6, adds that he did not hesitate to call the Spirit a creature. His opinion was afterwards called the *Marathonian*, from *Marathonius*, Bishop of Nicomedia. His followers appear to have been very numerous, especially in the vicinity of Lampsacus, see *Meier*, i. s. 192. The Macedonians, though condemned at the second Œcumenical Council, continued to exist as a separate sect in Phrygia down to the fifth century, when they were combated by *Nestorius*. The objections which the Macedonians either themselves made to the Godhead of the Spirit, or with which they were charged by their opponents, are the following: "The Holy Spirit is either begotten or not begotten; if the latter, we have two unoriginated beings (δύο τὰ ἄναρχα), viz. the Father and the Spirit; if begotten, he must be begotten either of the Father or of the Son: if of the Father, it follows that there are two Sons in the Trinity, and hence brothers (the question then arises, Which is the elder of the two, or are they twins?); but if of the Son, we have a grandson of God (θεὸς υἰωνός)," etc. *Greg.* Orat. xxxi. 7, p. 560, comp. *Athanas.* Ep. i. ad Serapion. c. 15. In opposition to this, *Gregory* simply remarks, that not the idea of generation, but that of ἐκπόρευσις, is to be applied to the Spirit, according to John xv. 26; and that the procession of the Spirit is quite as incomprehensible as the generation of the Son. To these objections was allied another, viz. that the Spirit is wanting in something, if He is not Son. But the Macedonians chiefly appealed to the absence of decisive scriptural testimony. Comp. *Ullmann*, s. 390, 391.

(7) Τὸ κύριον, τὸ ζωοποιόν, τὸ ἐκ τοῦ πατρὸς ἐκπορευόμενον, τὸ σὺν πατρὶ καὶ υἱῷ συμπροσκυνούμενον, καὶ συνδοξαζόμενον, τὸ λαλῆσαν διὰ τῶν προφῆτων. Comp. § 91, note 4.

§ 94.

Procession of the Holy Spirit.

J. G. *Walch*, Historia Controversiæ Græcorum Latinorumque de Processione Spir. S., Jenæ 1751. *Chr. Matth. Pfaff*, Historia succincta Controversiæ de Processione Spir. S., Tüb. 1749, 4to. [*Swete*, u. s. *Pusey* on the clause: "And the Son," Oxf. 1876.]

The formula of the Council of Constantinople, however, did not fully settle the point in question. For though the relation of the Spirit to the Trinity in general was determined, yet the particular relation in which He stands to the Son and the Father respectively, still remained to be decided. Inasmuch as the formula declared that the Spirit proceeds from the Father, it did not indeed expressly deny the procession from the Son; but yet it could be taken in a negative (exclusive) sense. On the one hand, the assertion that the Spirit proceeds *only* from the Father, and not from the Son, seemed to favour the notion that the Son is subordinate to the Father; on the other, to maintain that He proceeds from both the Father and the Son, appeared to place the Spirit in a still greater dependence (viz. on two instead of one). Thus the attempt to establish the full Godhead of the Son would easily detract from the Godhead of the Spirit; the effort, on the contrary, to give greater independence to the Spirit, would tend to throw the importance of the Son into the shade. The Greek Fathers, *Athanasius*, *Basil the Great*, *Gregory* of Nyssa, and others, asserted the procession of the Spirit from the Father, without distinctly denying that He also proceeds from the Son (1). *Epiphanius*, on the other hand, derived the Spirit from both the Father and the Son, with whom *Marcellus* of Ancyra agreed (2). But *Theodore* of Mopsuestia and *Theodoret* would not in any way admit that the Spirit owes His being in any sense to the Son (3), and defended their opinion in opposition to *Cyril* of Alexandria (4). The Latin Fathers, on the contrary, and *Augustine* in particular (5), taught the procession of the Spirit from both the Father and the Son. This doctrine became so firmly established in the West, that, at the third Synod of Toledo (A.D. 589), the clause *filioque* was added to the confession of faith of the Council of Constantinople, and so the dogmatic basis was laid for a schism between the eastern and western Churches (6).

(1) In accordance with the prevailing notions of the age,

the Father was considered as the only efficient principle (μία ἀρχή) to whom all other things owe their existence, of whom the Son is begotten, and from whom the Holy Spirit proceeds, who works all things *through* the Son, and *in* the Holy Spirit. The phrase, that the Holy Spirit proceeds from the Father, was maintained especially against the *Pneumatomachi.* It was asserted, in opposition to them, " *that the Holy Spirit does not derive His essence from the Son in a dependent manner, but that He stands in an equally direct relation to the Father, as the common first cause; that, as the Son is begotten of the Father, so the Holy Spirit proceeds from the Father,*" Neander, Kg. ii. s. 897.

(2) *Epiphan.* Ancor. § 9, after having proved the Godhead of the Spirit (among other passages) from Acts v. 3, says: ἄρα θεὸς ἐκ πατρὸς καὶ υἱοῦ τὸ πνεῦμα, without expressly stating that He ἐκπορεύεται ἐκ τοῦ υἱοῦ. Comp. Ancor. 8: Πνεῦμα γὰρ θεοῦ καὶ πνεῦμα τοῦ πατρὸς καὶ πνεῦμα υἱοῦ, οὐ κατά τινα σύνθεσιν, καθάπερ ἐν ἡμῖν ψυχὴ καὶ σῶμα, ἀλλ' ἐν μέσῳ πατρὸς καὶ υἱοῦ, ἐκ τοῦ πατρὸς καὶ τοῦ υἱοῦ, τρίτον τῇ ὀνομασίᾳ. Marcellus inferred, from the position that the Spirit proceeds from the Father and the Son, the sameness of the last two in the Sabellian sense. *Eusebius,* De Eccles. Theol. iii. 4, p. 168 (quoted by *Klose,* über Marcell. s. 47). Concerning the views of *Photinus,* see *Klose,* l.c. s. 83.

(3) *Theodore* of Mopsuestia, in his confession of faith (quoted by *Walch,* Bibl. Symb. p. 204), combated the opinion which represents the Spirit as διὰ τοῦ υἱοῦ τὴν ὕπαρξιν εἰληφός. On the opinion of *Theodoret,* comp. the IX. Anathematisma of *Cyril,* Opp. v. p. 47.

(4) *Cyril* condemned all who denied that the Holy Spirit was a *proprium* of Christ. *Theodoret,* in reply, observed that this expression was not objectionable, if nothing more were understood by it than that the Holy Spirit is of the same essence (ὁμοούσιος) with the Son, and proceeds from the Father; but that it ought to be rejected if it were meant to imply that He derives His existence from the Son, or through the Son, either of which would be contrary to what is said, John xv. 26; 1 Cor. ii. 12. Comp. *Neander,* l.c. s. 900.

(5) *Augustine,* Tract. 99, in Evang. Joh.: A quo autem

habet filius, ut sit Deus (est enim de Deo Deus), ab illo habet utique, ut etiam de illo procedat Spir. S. Et per hoc Spir. S. ut etiam de filio procedat, sicut procedit de patre, ab ipso habet patre. Ibid.: Spir. S. non de patre procedit in filium, et de filio procedit ad sanctificandam creaturam, sed simul de utroque procedit, quamvis hoc filio Pater dederit, ut quemadmodum de se, ita de illo quoque procedat. De Trin. 4, 20: Nec possumus dicere, quod Spir. S. et a filio non procedat, neque frustra idem Spir. et Patris et Filii Spir. dicitur. 5, 14: ... Sicut Pater et Filius unus Deus et ad creaturam relative unus Creator et unus Deus, sic relative ad Spiritum S. unum principium. (Comp. the whole section, c. 11 and 15.)

(6) This additional clause made its appearance at the time when Recared, king of the Visigoths, passed over from the Arian to the Catholic doctrine. This synod of Toledo pronounced an anathema against all who did not believe that the Spirit proceeded from both the Father and the Son. Comp. *Mansi*, ix. p. 981.

§ 95.

Final Statement of the Doctrine of the Trinity.

The more accurately the Godhead both of the Holy Spirit and of the Son was defined, the more important it became to determine exactly the relation in which the different persons stood to each other, and to the divine essence itself, and then to settle the ecclesiastical terminology. *Athanasius, Basil the Great, Gregory* of Nazianzus, and *Gregory* of Nyssa, in the Greek, *Hilary, Ambrose, Augustine,* and *Leo the Great* in the Latin Church, exerted the greatest influence upon the formation of the said terminology. According to this usage, the word οὐσία (essentia, substantia) denotes what is common to the Father, the Son, and the Holy Spirit; the word ὑπόστασις (persona) what is individual, distinguishing the one from the other (1). Each person possesses some peculiarity (ἰδιότης), by which it is distinguished from the other persons,

§ 95.] FINAL STATEMENT OF THE DOCTRINE OF THE TRINITY. 375

notwithstanding the sameness of essence. Thus, underived existence (ἀγεννησία) belongs to the Father, generation (γέννησις) to the Son, and procession (ἐκπόρευσις, ἔκπεμψις) to the Holy Spirit (2). When *Augustine* rejected all the distinctions which had been formally made between the different persons, and referred to the triune Godhead what had been before predicated of the separate persons (particularly creation), he completely purified the dogma from the older vestiges of subordinationism (3); but, as he reduced the persons to the general idea of divine relations, he could not entirely avoid the appearance of Sabellianism (4). (*Pseudo-*)*Boëthius* and others adopted his views on this point (5).

(1) The writers of this period avoided the use of the term πρόσωπον, which would have corresponded more exactly with the Latin word *persona*, while ὑπόστασις means literally *substantia*, lest it might lead to Sabellian inferences; but they sometimes confounded ὑπόστασις with οὐσία, and occasionally used φύσις instead of the latter. This was done, *e.g.*, by *Gregory* of Nazianzus, Orat. xxiii. 11, p. 431, xxxiii. 16, p. 614, xiii. 11, p. 431; Ep. 1, ad Cledonium, p. 739, ed. Lips. (quoted by *Ullmann*, s. 355, Anm. 1, and s. 356, Anm. 1). *Gregory* also sometimes attaches the same meaning to ὑπόστασις and to πρόσωπον, though he prefers the use of the former; Orat. xx. 6, p. 379. *Ullmann*, s. 356, Anm. 3. This distinction is more accurately defined by *Basil*, Ep. 236, 6 (quoted by *Münscher, von Cölln*, s. 242, 243): Οὐσία δὲ καὶ ὑπόστασις ταύτην ἔχει τὴν διαφοράν, ἣν ἔχει τὸ κοινὸν πρὸς τὸ καθ' ἕκαστον· οἷον ὡς ἔχει τὸ ζῶον πρὸς τὸν δεῖνα ἄνθρωπον. Διὰ τοῦτο οὐσίαν μὲν μίαν ἐπὶ τῆς θεότητος ὁμολογοῦμεν, ὥστε τὸν τοῦ εἶναι λόγον μὴ διαφόρως ἀποδιδόναι· ὑπόστασιν δὲ ἰδιάζουσαν, ἵν' ἀσύγχυτος ἡμῖν καὶ τετρανωμένη ἡ περὶ Πατρὸς καὶ Υἱοῦ καὶ ἁγίου Πνεύματος ἔννοια ἐνυπάρχῃ κ.τ.λ. Comp. *Greg. Naz.* Orat. xxix. 11, p. 530 (in *Ullmann*, s. 355, Anm. 3), and Orat. xlii. 16, p. 759 (quoted by *Ullmann*, s. 356, Anm. 3), where the distinction between οὐσία and ὑπόστασις is prominently brought forward. *Jerome*, moreover, had objections to the statement that there were three hypostases, because it seemed to lead to Arianism; but he submitted on

this point to the judgment of the Roman See; comp. Ep. xv. and xvi. ad Damasum.

(2) *Greg. Naz.* Orat. xli. 9 : Πάντα ὅσα ὁ πατὴρ, τοῦ υἱοῦ, πλὴν τῆς ἀγεννησίας· πάντα ὅσα ὁ υἱὸς, τοῦ πνεύματος, πλὴν τῆς γεννήσεως κ.τ.λ. Orat. xxv. 16 : Ἴδιον δὲ πατρὸς μὲν ἡ ἀγεννησία, υἱοῦ δὲ ἡ γέννησις, πνεύματος δὲ ἡ ἔκπεμψις; but the terms ἰδιότης and ὑπόστασις were sometimes used synonymously, *e.g. Greg. Naz.* Orat. xxxiii. 16, p. 614. *Ullmann*, s. 357.

(3) Such vestiges are unquestionably to be found even in the most orthodox Fathers, not only in the East, but also in the West. Thus, for instance, in *Hilary*, De Trin. iii. 12, and iv. 16. He designates the Father as the jubentem Deum, the Son as facientem. And when even *Athanasius* says that the Son is at once greater than the Holy Spirit and equal to Him (μείζων καὶ ἴσος), and that the Holy Spirit, too, is related to the Son as is the Son to the Father (Cont. Arian. Orat. ii.), "*the idea of a subordination lies at the basis of such statements*," *Gieseler*, Dogmengesch. s. 315.

(4) *Augustine*, Contra Serm. Arian. c. 2, n. 4 (Opp. t. viii.) : Unus quippe Deus est ipsa trinitas, et sic unus Deus, quomodo unus creator.— He also referred the theophanies, which were formerly ascribed to the Logos alone, to the whole Trinity. In support of this view, he appeals to the three men who appeared to Abraham, De Trin. ii. 18. He also thinks that the sending of the Son is not only a work of the Father, but of the whole Trinity. The Father alone is not sent, because He is unbegotten (comp. the passages quoted by *Meier*, i. s. 206 ff.). [Nec pater sine filio, nec filius sine patre misit Spirit. S., sed eum pariter ambo miserunt. Inseparabilis quippe sunt opera trinitatis. Solus pater non legitur missus, quia solus non habet auctorem, a quo genitus sit, vel a quo procedat. Contra Serm. Arian. c. 2, n. 4. Opp. tom. viii.] The distinctions between the persons are, in his opinion, not distinctions of *nature*, but of *relation*. But he is aware that we have no appropriate language to denote those distinctions, De Trinit. v. 10 : Quum quæritur, quid tres, magna prorsus inopia humanum laborat eloquium. Dictum est tamen : tres personæ, non ut illud diceretur, sed ne taceretur. The persons are not to be regarded as species, for we

do not say, tres equi are unum animal, but tria animalia. Better would be the comparison with three statues from one mass of gold; but this too halts, since we do not necessarily connect the conception of gold with that of statues, and the converse; l.c. vii. 11. He brings his views concerning the Trinity into connection with anthropology; but by comparing the three persons with the *memoria, intellectus,* and *voluntas* (caritas) of man (l.c. ix. 11, x. 10, 18, xv. 7), he evidently borders upon Sabellianism; it has the appearance of mere relations, without personal shape. [Conf. 13, cap. 11: Vellem ut hæc tria cogitarent homines in seipsis. Longe alia sunt ista tria quam illa Trinitas: sed dico ubi se exerceant et ibi probent, et sentiunt quam longe sunt. Dico autem hæc tria; esse, nosse, velle. Sum enim, et novi, et volo; sum sciens et volens; et scio esse me, et velle; et volo esse, et scire. In his igitur tribus quam sit inseparabilis vita, et una vita, et una mens, et una essentia, quam denique inseparabilis distinctio, et tamen distinctio, videat qui potest.] On the other hand, the practical and religious importance of the doctrine of the Trinity appears most worthily where he reminds us that it is of the very nature of disinterested (unenvious) love to impart itself, De Trin. ix. 2 : Cum aliquid amo, tria sunt; ego, et quod amo, et ipse amor. Non enim amo amorem, nisi amantem amem : nam non est amor, ubi nihil amatur. Tria ergo sunt: amans, et quod amatur, et (mutuus) amor. Quid si non amem nisi meipsum, nonne duo erunt, quod amo et amor? Amans enim et quod amatur, hoc idem est, quando se ipse amat. Sicut amare et amari eodem modo id ipsum est, cum se quisque amat. Eadem quippe res bis dicitur, cum dicitur: amat se et amatur a se. Tunc enim non est aliud atque aliud amare et amari, sicut non est alius atque alius amans et amatus. At vero amor et quod amatur etiam sic duo sunt. Non enim cum quisque se amat, amor est, nisi cum amatur ipse amor. Aliud est autem amare se, aliud est amare amorem suum. Non enim amatur amor, nisi jam aliquid amans, quia ubi nihil amatur, nullus est amor. Duo ergo sunt, cum se quisque amat, amor et quod amatur. Tunc enim amans et quod amatur unum est. . . . . Amans quippe ad amorem refertur et amor ad amantem. Amans enim aliquo amore amat, et amor alicujus amantis est.... Retracto amante nullus est amor, et retracto amore nullus et amans. Ideoque quantum ad invicem referuntur, duo sunt. Quod autem ad se ipsa dicuntur, et singula spiritus, et simul utrumque unus spiritus, et singula mens et simul utrumque una mens. Cf. lib. xv.[1] See, further, † *Gangauf,* Des h. Augustinus speculative Lehre von Gott, dem Dreieinigen, Mainz 1865.

(5) (*Pseudo-*)*Boëthius,* De Trin. (Ad Symmach.)[2] c. 2 : Nulla igitur in eo (Deo) diversitas, nulla ex diversitate pluralitas, nulla ex accidentibus multitudo, atque idcirco nec numerus. Cap. 3 : Deus vero a Deo nullo differt, nec vel accidentibus vel substantialibus differentiis in subjecto positis distat; ubi vero nulla est differentia, nulla est omnino pluralitas, quare nec numerus; igitur unitas tantum. Nam quod tertio repetitur, Deus; quum Pater et Filius et Spir. S. nuncupatur, tres unitates non faciunt pluralitatem numeri in eo quod ipsæ sunt.... Non igitur si de Patre et Filio et Spir. S. tertio prædicatur Deus, idcirco trina prædicatio numerum facit.... Cap. 6 : Facta quidem est trinitatis numerositas in eo quod est *prædicatio relationis;* servata vero unitas in eo quod est indifferentia vel substantiæ vel operationis vel omnino ejus, quæ secundum se dicitur, prædicationis. Ita igitur substantia continet unitatem, relatio multiplicat trinitatem, atque ideo sola sigillatim proferuntur atque separatim quæ relationis sunt; nam idem Pater qui Filius non est, nec idem uterque qui Spir. S. Idem tamen Deus est, Pater et Filius et Spir. S., idem justus, idem bonus, idem magnus, idem omnia, quæ secundum se poterunt prædicari.—*Boëthius* falls into the most trivial Sabellianism, by drawing an illustration of the Trinity from the cases in which we have three names for the same thing, *e.g.* gladius, mucro, ensis ; see *Baur,* Trin.-Lehre, ii. s. 34. —The orthodox doctrine of the western Church is already expressed in striking formulas by *Leo the Great, e.g.* Sermo LXXV. 3 : Non alia sunt Patris, alia Filii, alia Spiritus Sancti, sed omnia quæcunque habet Pater, habet et Filius, habet et

---

[1] As to the mode in which *Augustine* made his doctrine of the Trinity intelligible to the congregation, in his sermons, see *Bindemann,* ii. 205 ff. On *Jerome's* doctrine of the Trinity, see *Zöckler,* l.c. s. 434.

[2] It is doubtful whether the work De Trin. was really by *Boëthius;* we cite it under the customary name.

Spiritus S.; nec unquam in illa trinitate non fuit ista communio, quia hoc est ibi omnia habere, quod semper existere. LXXV. 1, 2: Sempiternum est Patri, coæterni sibi Filii sui esse genitorem. Sempiternum est Filio, intemporaliter a Patre esse progenitum. Sempiternum quoque est Spiritui Sancto Spiritum esse Patris et Filii. Ut nunquam Pater sine Filio, nunquam Filius sine Patre, nunquam Pater *et Filius* fuerint sine Spiritu Sancto, et, omnibus existentiæ gradibus exclusis, nulla ibi persona sit anterior, nulla posterior. Hujus enim beatæ trinitatis incommutabilis deitas una est in substantia, indivisa in opere, concors in voluntate, par in potentia, æqualis in gloria. Other passages are quoted by *Perthel*, Leo der Grosse, s. 138 ff.

§ 96.

Tritheism, Tetratheism.

In keeping the three persons of the Godhead distinct from each other, much care was needed, lest the idea of οὐσία (essence), by which the unity was expressed, should be understood as the mere concept of a species, and the ὑπόστασις viewed as an individual falling under this species; for this would necessarily call up the idea of three Gods. Another misunderstanding was also to be obviated; for, in assigning to God Himself (the αὐτόθεος) a logical superiority above Father, Son, and Spirit, it might appear as though there were *four* persons, or even four Gods. Both of these results followed. *John Ascusnages* of Constantinople (1) and *John Philoponus* (2) of Alexandria were the leaders of the Tritheites; while the monophysite patriarch of Alexandria, *Damianus* (3), was accused of being the head of the Tetratheites (Tetradites), but probably by unfair inference.

(1) *John Ascusnages* of Constantinople, when examined by the Emperor Justinian concerning his faith, is said to have acknowledged one nature of the incarnate Christ, but asserted three natures, essences, and deities in the Trinity. The

Tritheites, *Conon* and *Eugenius*, are said to have made the same statements before the Emperor Justin.

(2) The opinion of *Philoponus* can be seen from a fragment (Διαιτητής) preserved by *John Damascene* (De Hæresib. c. 83, p. 101 ss. *Phot.* Bibl. Cod. 75. *Niceph.* xviii. 45–48, extracts from which are quoted by *Münscher, von Cölln,* i. 251). In his view, the φύσις is the species which comprehends individuals of the same nature. The terms essence and nature are identical; the term ὑπόστασις, or person, denotes the separate real existence of the nature, that which philosophers of the peripatetic school call ἄτομον, because there the separation of genus and species ceases. Comp. *J. G. Scharfenberg*, de Jo. Philopono, Tritheismi defensore, Lips. 1768 (Comm. Theol., ed. *Velthusen*, etc., t. i.), and *Trechsel* in the Studien und Kritiken, 1835, i. s. 95 ff. *Meier*, Trin.-Lehre, i. s. 195 ff. [*Philoponus* applied the ideas of *Aristotle* to the Trinity; he connected the two notions φύσις and εἶδος—confounding the common divine essence with the notion of species. Cf. *Baur*, Dogmengesch. s. 170 : *Philoponus* maintained that nature in the Church usage signified the special as well as the general, and that we might as well speak of three natures as of three hypostases; but yet he did not say there were three Gods.]

(3) In his controversy with *Peter* of Callinico, patriarch of Antioch, *Damianus* maintained that the Father is one, the Son another, and the Holy Ghost another, but that no one of them is God as such; they only possess the subsisting divine nature in common, and each is God, in so far as he inseparably participates in it. The Damianites were also called Angelites (from the city of Angelium). Comp. *Niceph.* xiii. 49. *Schröckh*, xviii. s. 624. *Münscher, von Cölln,* s. 253. *Baumgarten-Crusius*, i. s. 364. *Meier*, Trin.-Lehre, s. 198 : "*Such systems of dissolution are the signs of the life of these times; they exercised themselves upon dead forms, seeking help in them instead of first trying to fill out the stiff definitions of the dogma with the living contents of the Christian ideas, which sustain the dogma.*"—Tritheism may be viewed as the extreme of Arianism, and Tetratheism as the extreme of Sabellianism; comp. *Hasse*, Anselm, 2 Thl. s. 289.

§ 97.

Symbolum Quicumque.

J. G. *Vossius,* De tribus Symbolis, Amst. 1642, Diss. ii. *Dan. Waterland,* Critical History of the Athanasian Creed, Cambridge 1724, 1728. [Works, 1843, vol. iii. p. 97-273.] *John Dennis,* The Athanasian Creed, 1815. Comp. *Münscher, von Cölln,* i. s. 249, 250. *Baumgarten-Crusius,* i. 124, 231, ii. 124. [*Wm. Whiston,* Three Essays, 1713. *J. Redcliff,* The Creed of Athanasius illustrated, etc., Lond. 1844. *W. W. Harvey,* Hist. and Theol. of the Three Creeds, 2 vols. *E. S. Ffoulkes,* The Athan. Creed, Lond. (n. d. 187?). *C. A. Swainson,* Nicene and Apostles' Creeds, Lond. 1875.]

The doctrine of the Church concerning the Trinity appears most fully developed and defined in a perfect symbolical form in what is called the *Symbolum quicumque* (commonly, but erroneously, called the Creed of St. Athanasius). It originated in the school of Augustine, and is ascribed by some to *Vigilius Tapsensis,* by others to *Vincentius Lerinensis,* and by some again to others (1). By its repetition of positive and negative propositions, its perpetual assertion, and then again, denial of its positions, the mystery of the doctrine is presented, as it were, in hieroglyphs, as if to confound the understanding. The consequence was, that all further endeavours of human ingenuity to solve its apparent contradictions in a dialectic way, must break against this bulwark of the faith, on which salvation was made to depend, as the waves break upon an inflexible rock (2).[1]

(1) According to the old legend, *Athanasius* drew up the creed in question at the synod held in Rome in the year 341. This, however, cannot be—*first,* because it exists only in the Latin language; *secondly,* from the absence of the term *consubstantialis* (ὁμοούσιος); and, *thirdly,* from the more fully developed doctrine concerning the Holy Spirit (the procession from the Son). It was generally adopted in the seventh century under the name of *Athanasius,* when it was classed as

[1] [*Hagenbach's* statements are, of course, strongly contested. The last books on the list above will give the present state of the controversy.]

an *œcumenical* symbol with the Apostles' and the Nicene Creed. *Paschasius Quesnel* (Dissert. xiv. in Leonis M. Opp. p. 386 ss.) first pronounced it as his opinion that it was composed by *Vigilius*, Bishop of Tapsus in Africa, who lived towards the close of the fifth century. Others attribute it to *Vincent* of Lérins, in the middle of the fifth century, *Muratori* (Anecd. Lat. t. ii. p. 212–217) conjectured that its author was *Venantius Fortunatus* (a Gallican bishop of the sixth century); and *Waterland* ascribes it to *Hilary* of Arles (who lived about the middle of the fifth century). [*Gieseler* supposes that it originated in Spain in the seventh century.]

(2) Symbolum Athanasianum:—

1. Quicumque vult salvus esse, ante omnia opus habet, ut teneat catholicam fidem. 2. Quam nisi quisque integram inviolatamque servaverit, absque dubio in æternum peribit. 3. Fides autem catholica hæc est, ut unum Deum in Trinitate et Trinitatem in unitate veneremur. 4. Neque confundentes personas, neque substantiam separantes. 5. Alia enim est persona Patris, alia Filii, alia Spiritus Sancti. 6. Sed Patris et Filii et Spiritus Sancti una est divinitas, æqualis gloria, æqualis majestas. 7. Qualis Pater, talis Filius, talis et Spir. S. 8. Increatus Pater, increatus Filius, increatus Spir. S. 9. Immensus Pater, immensus Filius, immensus Spiritus S. 10. Æternus Pater, æternus Filius, æternus et Spir. S. 11. Et tamen non tres æterni, sed unus æternus. 12. Sicut non tres increati, nec tres immensi, sed unus increatus et unus immensus. 13. Similiter omnipotens Pater, omnipotens Filius, omnipotens et Spiritus S. 14. Et tamen non tres omnipotentes, sed unus omnipotens. 15. Ita deus Pater, deus Filius, deus et Spir. S. 16. Et tamen non tres dii sunt, sed unus est Deus. 17. Ita dominus Pater, dominus Filius, dominus et Spir. S. 18. Et tamen non tres domini, sed unus Dominus. 19. Quia sicut sigillatim unamquamque personam et Deum et dominum confiteri christiana veritate compellimur, ita tres Deos aut dominos dicere catholica religione prohibemur. 20. Pater a nullo est factus, nec creatus, nec genitus. 21. Filius a Patre solo est, non factus, non creatus, sed genitus. 22. Spir. S. a Patre et Filio non creatus, nec genitus, sed procedens. 23. Unus ergo Pater, nec tres patres; unus Filius, non tres filii; unus Spiritus S., non tres spiritus sancti.

24. Et in hac Trinitáte nihil prius aut posterius, nihil majus aut minus, sed totæ tres personæ coæternæ sibi sunt et coæquales. 25. Ita ut per omnia, sicut jam supra dictum est, et unitas in Trinitate et Trinitas in unitate veneranda sit. 26. Qui vult ergo salvus esse, ita de Trinitate sentiat. (Opp. Athanasii, t. iii. p. 719.—*Walch,* Bibl. Symb. Vet. p. 136 ss.; it is also contained in the collections of the symbolical books published by *Tittmann, Hase,* and others.[1])

B. CHRISTOLOGY.

§ 98.

The True Humanity of Christ.

Traces of Docetism. — Arianism.

It was no less difficult to determine the relation of the divine to the human nature of Christ, than to define the

---

[1] While salvation at this extreme point in the development of the doctrine appears to be made dependent on the most refined points of dialectics, it is pleasing to hear other men, such as *Gregory* of Nazianzus (see *Ullmann,* s. 159, 170; *Neander,* Chrysost. ii. 19), raising their voices during this period, who did not attach such unqualified value to the mere orthodoxy of the understanding, and who were fully convinced of the limits of human knowledge and the insufficiency of such dogmatic definitions, *Greg.* Orat. 31, 33, p. 577 (*Ullmann,* s. 336, comp., however, s. 334, 335). *Rufinus* also says, Expos. p. 18 (in the sense of an *Irenæus*): Quomodo autem Deus pater genuerit filium, nolo discutias, nec te curiosius ingeras in profundi hujus arcanum (al. profundo hujus arcani), ne forte, dum inaccessæ lucis fulgorem pertinacius perscrutaris, exiguum ipsum, qui mortalibus divino munere concessus est, perdas aspectum. Aut si putas in hoc omni indagationis genere nitendum, prius tibi propone quæ nostra sunt: quæ si consequenter valueris expedire, tunc a terrestribus ad cœlestia et a visibilibus ad invisibilia properato.—Moreover, in the midst of this dialectic elaboration of the materials of the faith, we cannot mistake the presence of a yet higher aim—that, viz., of bringing to distinct consciousness, not only the unity of the divine nature, but also the living longing of divine love to impart itself; in other words, the effort to maintain both the *transcendent* nature of God and His *immanence* in His works—the former in opposition to polytheism and pantheism, and the latter to an abstract deism. So far such formulas have also their edifying side, as giving witness to the struggle of the Christian mind after a satisfactory expression of what has its full reality only in the depths of the Christian heart.

relation between the three persons and the one nature of God. For the more decidedly the Godhead of the Son was asserted in the ecclesiastical or Catholic sense, the more the doctrine of the incarnation of the Son had to be guarded, so as not to abridge either the true Godhead or the true manhood of Christ. In opposition to Docetism, the doctrine of the human nature of Christ had indeed been so firmly established, that no one was likely to deny that He possessed a human body; and when *Hilary*, orthodox on all other points, seems to border upon Docetism, by maintaining that the body of Jesus could not undergo any real sufferings (1), he only means that the sufferings of Christ are to be understood as a free act of His love. But two other questions arose, which were beset with still greater difficulties. In the first place, it was asked whether a human soul formed a necessary part of the humanity of Christ; and if so (as the orthodox maintained, in opposition to the Arians) (2), it was still asked whether this soul meant only the animal soul, or also included the rational human spirit (in distinction from the divine).

(1) *Hilary* wishes to preserve the most intimate union between the divine and human natures of Christ, so that it may be said: totus hominis Filius est Dei Filius, and vice versa; for the same reason he says concerning the God-man, De Trin. x. 23: Habens ad patiendum quidem corpus et passus est, sed non habuit naturam ad dolendum. (He compares it to an arrow which passes through the water without wounding it.)—Comment. in Ps. cxxxviii. 3: Suscepit ergo infirmitates, quia homo nascitur; et putatur dolere, quia patitur: caret vero doloribus ipse, quia Deus est (the usage of the Latin word *pati* allowed such a distinction to be made).— De Trin. xi. 48: In forma Dei manens servi formam assumsit, non demutatus, sed se ipsum exinaniens et intra se latens et intra suam ipse vacuefactus potestatem; dum se usque ad formam temperat habitus humani, ne potentem immensamque naturam assumptæ humanitatis non ferret infirmitas, sed in tantum se virtus incircumscripta moderaretur, in quantum oporteret eam usque ad patientiam connexi sibi corporis

obedire. He opposes the purely docetic interpretation of the Impassibilitas, De Synodis 49 (*Dorner*, ii. 2, 1055): Pati potuit, et passibile esse non potuit, quia passibilitas naturæ infirmis significatio est, passio autem est eorum, quæ sunt illata perpessio. He makes a distinction between passionis materia et passibilitatis infirmitas. *Hilary*, moreover, ascribes a human soul to Christ, but says that He received neither that soul nor His body from Mary; on the contrary, the Godman has His origin in Himself; comp. *Dorner*, s. 1040 ff., and the whole section. Cf. also *Hilar.* Com. in Matt. xxvi. 37; *Zöckler*, s. 213, 436.

(2) *Athan.* Contra Apollin. ii. 3 : Ἄρειος δὲ σάρκα μόνην πρὸς ἀποκρυφὴν τῆς θεότητος ὁμολογεῖ· ἀντὶ δὲ τοῦ ἔσωθεν ἐν ἡμῖν ἀνθρώπου, τουτέστι τῆς ψυχῆς, τὸν Λόγον ἐν τῇ σαρκὶ λέγει γεγονέναι, τὴν τοῦ πάθους νόησιν καὶ τὴν ἐξ ᾅδου ἀνάστασιν τῇ θεότητι προσάγειν τολμῶν. Comp. *Epiph.* Hær. 69, 19, and other passages quoted by *Münscher, von Cölln*, s. 268. This notion was very prominently brought forward by the Arians, *Eudoxius* and *Eunomius;* respecting the former, see *Cave*, Historia Script. Eccles. i. p. 219; concerning the latter, comp. *Mansi*, Conc. t. iii. p. 648, and *Neander*, Dg. s. 330. [The doctrines of *Arius* were expressed still more definitely by *Eunomius*. The Son cannot even be said to be like God, since likeness and unlikeness can only be predicated of created things. Generation from the divine essence is inconceivable; an eternal generation is unimaginable. The will is the mediating principle between the divine essence and agency. The Son of God was created according to God's will; He was eternally with God only as predestinated. Ibid. s. 336. In the confession of faith of *Eunomius*, it is stated that the Logos assumed man, both body and soul; but doubtless an οὐκ has dropped out—" *not* a man consisting of body and soul;" this appears from a citation of *Gregory* of Nyssa, from *Eunomius*, and also from a fragment lately published by *Mansi.—Baur*, Dogmengesch. s. 161, says that *Eunomius* widely diverged from the original standpoint of *Arius*, in maintaining that the essence of God could be completely conceived—particularly in reference to the point that God must be unbegotten. Thus Arianism logically leads to putting the infinite and the finite into an abstract opposition to each other.

It presents the contrast of the Aristotelian with the Platonic mode of thought.] Another party of the Arians, however, rejected the notion that the Logos had been changed into the soul of Christ, and supposed a human soul along with the Logos. Comp. *Dorner*, ii. 2, s. 1038. But even some orthodox theologians of this period used indefinite language on this point previously to the rise of the Apollinarian controversy. Comp. *Münscher, von Cölln*, s. 269. *Dorner*, l.c. s. 1071 ff. *Baur*, Dg. i. 2, s. 212.

§ 99.

The Doctrine of Apollinaris.

Apollinaris, Bishop of Laodicea, who in other respects had a high reputation among orthodox theologians, conceived that that higher life of reason, which elevates man above the rest of creation, was not needed by Jesus, in whom there is a personal indwelling of Deity; or rather, that this human reason was absolutely set aside, the Logos, as νοῦς θεῖος, being substituted (1). His intention seems to have been to honour Christ, not to detract from His dignity. He was opposed by *Athanasius*, and still more by *Gregory* of Nazianzus and *Gregory* of Nyssa, whose efforts led to the adoption of the doctrine that Christ had a perfect human nature, consisting of a body and a rational soul, together with the divine nature (2). The Council of Constantinople (A.D. 381) condemned Apollinarianism as heretical.

(1) *Apollinaris* was led by his dialectic culture[1] to suppose that he might establish his argument with mathematical precision (γεωμετρικαῖς ἀποδείξεσι καὶ ἀνάγκαις). Of the writings in which he explained his views, only fragments are extant in the works of *Gregory* of Nyssa, *Theodoret*, and *Leontius Byzantinus* (who lived about the year 590); they were the following: περὶ σαρκώσεως λογίδιον (ἀπόδειξις περὶ τῆς θείας

[1] *Baumgarten-Crusius*, ii. 160, sees here a twofold Platonism; not only the distinction between νοῦς and ψυχή, but also that in place of the νοῦς comes a higher potence, but of the same nature.

ἐνσαρκώσεως)—τὸ κατὰ κεφάλαιον βιβλίον—περὶ ἀναστάσεως—περὶ πίστεως λογίδιον—and some letters (in *Gallandii* Bibl. PP. t. xii. p. 706 ss. *Angelo Maio*, Class. Auct. t. ix. p. 495 ss.). Comp. *Dorner*, ii. 2, s. 976, and *Neander*, Dg. 334 ff. *Apollinaris* objected to the union of the Logos with a rational human soul, that the human being thus united to the Logos must either preserve his own will, in which case there would be no true interpenetration of the divine and the human, or that the human soul must lose its liberty by becoming united to the Logos, either of which would be absurd. "*He chiefly opposed the τρεπτόν, or the liberty of choice in Christology*."— *Dorner*, l.c. s. 987. In his opinion, Christ is not merely ἄνθρωπος ἔνθεος, but God *become* man. According to the threefold division of man (the trichotomistic anthropology), *Apollinaris* was willing to ascribe a soul to the Redeemer, since he thought that was only something intermediate between body and spirit, and the ἡγεμονικόν of the body. But that which itself determines the soul (τὸ αὐτοκίνητον), and constitutes the higher dignity of man, the νοῦς (the ψυχὴ λογικὴ) of Christ, could not be of human origin, but must be purely divine; for His incarnation did not consist in the Logos becoming νοῦς, but in becoming σάρξ. (Whether and how far Christ brought the σάρξ itself from heaven, or received it from Mary, see *Baur*, 595, Anm., and *Dorner*, 1007 ff. [*Dorner* says that *Apollinaris* held that the Logos was always potentially, or had the destination to be, man, since He was the type of humanity; but yet, that the assumption of the form (flesh) of man occurred only at His birth.]) But as the divine reason supplies the place of the human, there exists a specific difference between Christ and other men. In their case everything has to undergo a process of gradual development, which cannot be without conflicts and sin (ὅπου γὰρ τέλειος ἄνθρωπος, ἐκεῖ καὶ ἁμαρτία, apud *Athan.* i. 2, p. 923. Comp. c. 21, p. 939: ἁμαρτία ἐνυπόστατος). But this could not take place in the case of Christ: οὐδεμία ἄσκησις ἐν Χριστῷ· οὐκ ἄρα νοῦς ἐστιν ἀνθρώπινος. Comp. *Gregory* of Nyssa, Antirrhet. adv. Apollin. iv. c. 221. At the same time, *Apollinaris* supposed the body and soul of Christ to be so completely filled and animated with the higher life of God, that he took no offence at such expressions as " God died, God is born," etc. He in fact believed that we do not adequately express the unity unless we say: " Our God is crucified," and: " Man is raised up to the right hand of God." He even maintained that, on account of this intimate union, divine homage is also due to the human nature of Christ, l.c. p. 241, 264. His opponents, therefore, charged him with Patripassianism. But it certainly is a mere inference drawn by *Gregory* of Nazianzus, when he attributes to *Apollinaris* the assertion that Christ must have possessed an irrational, animal soul, *e.g.* that of a horse, or an ox, because He had not a rational human soul. On the other hand, *Apollinaris*, on his side, was not wanting in deducing similar consequences from his opponents' positions, accusing them of believing in two Christs, two Sons of God, etc. Comp. *Dorner*, s. 985 ff. *Ullmann*, Greg. v. Naz. s. 401 ff. *Baur*, Gesch. der Trinitätl. i. s. 585 ff.

(2) *Athanasius* maintained, in opposition to *Apollinaris*, Contra Apollinar. libri ii. (but without mentioning by name his opponent, with whom he had personal intercourse),[1] that it behoved Christ to be our example in every respect, and that His nature, therefore, must resemble ours. Sinfulness, which is empirically connected with the development of man, is not a necessary attribute of human nature; this would lead to Manichæism. Man, on the contrary, was originally free from sin, and Christ appeared on that very account, viz. in order to show that God is not the author of sin, and to prove that it is possible to live a sinless life (the controversy thus touched upon questions of an anthropological nature then debated).— *Athanasius* distinctly separated the divine from the human (comp. especially lib. ii.), but he did not admit that he taught the existence of two Christs. Comp. *Neander*, Kg. ii. 2, 923. *Möhler*, Athanasius, ii. s. 262 ff.[2] *Gregory* of Nazianzus (Ep.

[1] On the character of this book, see *Dorner*, i. 984, Anm. [It was written after the death of *Apollinaris*, and very much in it has reference rather to what the tendency became, than to views actually avowed by *Apollinaris* himself.] To what extent *Athanasius* himself approximated to Apollinarianism, see *Voigt*, l.c. s. 125, 129.

[2] *Möhler* compares the doctrine of *Apollinaris* with that of *Luther* (s. 271). This is so far correct, as that in *Luther* we certainly find similar expressions; see *Schenkel*, Das Wesen des Protest. i. 313 ff. Yet such parallels can seldom be fully carried out. Others have tried to find other correspondences with *Apollinaris* in later times; *Dorner* has compared his views with those of *Osiander* (s. 1028), and *Baur* with those of *Servetus* (Gesch. d. Trin. iii. 101).

ad Cledon. et Orat. 51) equally asserted the necessity of a true and perfect human nature. It was not only necessary, as the medium by which God might manifest Himself, but Jesus could redeem and sanctify man only by assuming his whole nature, consisting of body and soul. (Similar views had been formerly held by *Irenæus*, and were afterwards more fully developed by *Anselm*.) *Gregory* thus strongly maintained the doctrine of the two natures of the Saviour. We must distinguish in Christ ἄλλο καὶ ἄλλο, but not ἄλλος καὶ ἄλλος. Compare the Epist. ad Nectar. sive Orat. 46, with his 10 Anathematismata against *Apollinaris*, and *Ullmann*, s. 396–413. The work of *Gregory* of Nyssa, entitled λόγος ἀντιρρητικὸς πρὸς τὰ 'Ἀπολλιναρίου (which was probably composed between the years 374 and 380), may be found in *Zaccagni*, Collect. Monum. Vett., and *Gallandii* Bibl. Patr. vi. p. 517. Comp. *Gieseler*, Kg. i. s. 356; *Rupp*, s. 139.—He opposed the followers of *Apollinaris* (Συνουσιασταί, Διμοιρῖται) in his Ep. Hær. 77.—The doctrine of *Apollinaris* was also condemned in the West by *Damasus*, Bishop of Rome (comp. *Münscher, von Cölln*, s. 277), and once more by the second Œcumenical Synod of Constantinople (A.D. 381, Can. i. vii.). The later disciples of *Apollinaris* appear to have developed the doctrine of their master in a completely Docetic manner. Comp. *Möhler*, ubi supra, s. 264 ff.

§ 100.

Nestorianism.

P. E. *Jablonski*, Exercitatio historico-theologica de Nestorianismo, Berol. 1724. —Tübinger Quartalschrift, 1835, ii. part 1. W. *Möller*, Nestorius u. die nestorianische Streit., in *Herzog*, x. s. 288 ff.

The attempt to maintain the integrity of the human nature of Christ together with the divine, necessarily led from time to time to the inquiry whether that which the Scriptures relate respecting the life and actions of the Redeemer, His birth, sufferings, and death, refers only to His humanity, or to both His divine and human nature; and, if the latter, in what way it may be said to refer to both. While the teachers of the Alexandrian school asserted in strong terms the *unity* of the divine and the human in Christ, the theologians of Antioch, *Diodorus* of Tarsus and *Theodore* of Mopsuestia, made a strict distinction between the one and the other (1). At last the phrase, "mother of God" (θεοτόκος) (2), which the increasing homage paid to Mary had brought into use, gave rise to the controversy respecting the relation of the two natures in Christ. *Nestorius*, patriarch of Constantinople, disapproved of this phrase, maintaining that Mary had given birth to Christ, but not to God (3). *Cyril*, patriarch of Alexandria, opposed him, and both pronounced anathemas against each other (4). *Nestorius* supposed, in accordance with the Antiochene mode of thought, that the divine and the human natures of Christ ought to be distinctly separated, and admitted only a συνάφεια (junction) of the one and the other, an ἐνοίκησις (indwelling) of the Godhead. *Cyril*, on the contrary, was led by the tendencies of the Egyptian (Alexandrian) school (5) to maintain the perfect union of the two natures (φυσικὴ ἕνωσις). *Nestorius* was condemned by the Synod of Ephesus (A.D. 431) (6), but the controversy was not thus brought to a close.

(1) *Diodorus* died A.D. 394. Some fragments of his treatise : πρὸς τοὺς Συνουσιαστάς, are preserved in a Latin translation by *Mar. Mercator*, ed. *Baluze*, p. 349 s. (*Garner*, p. 317), and *Leontius Byzantinus*. Comp. *Münscher, von Cölln*, s. 280: Adoramus purpuram propter indutum et templum propter inhabitatorem, etc. — The opinions of *Theodore* are expressed in his confession of faith, which may be found in Acta Conc. Ephes. Actio vi. quoted by *Mansi*, t. iv. p. 1347; in *Marius Mercator* (*Garner*, i. p. 95); *Münscher, von Cölln*, s. 280. On his controversy with *Apollinaris*, see *Fritzsche*, p. 92, 101. Comp. *Neander*, Kg. ii. 3, s. 929–944. Fragmentum, ed. *Fritzsche*, p. 8 : Ἀλλ' οὐχ ἡ θεία φύσις ἐκ παρθένου γεγέννηται, γεγέννηται δὲ ἐκ τῆς παρθένου ὁ ἐκ τῆς οὐσίας τῆς παρθένου συστάς· οὐχ ὁ θεὸς λόγος ἐκ τῆς Μαρίας γεγέννηται, γεγέννηται δὲ ἐκ Μαρίας ὁ ἐκ σπέρματος Δαβίδ· οὐχ ὁ θεὸς λόγος ἐκ γυναικὸς

§ 100.] NESTORIANISM. 391

γεγέννηται, γεγέννηται δὲ ἐκ γυναικὸς ὁ τῇ τοῦ ἁγίου πνεύματος δυνάμει διαπλασθεὶς ἐν αὐτῇ· οὐκ ἐκ μητρὸς τέτεκται ὁ ὁμοούσιος τῷ πατρί, ἀμήτωρ γὰρ οὗτος κατὰ τὴν τοῦ μακαρίου Παύλου φωνήν, ἀλλ' ὁ ἐν ὑστέροις καιροῖς, ἐν τῇ μητρῴᾳ γαστρὶ τῇ τοῦ ἁγίου πνεύματος δυνάμει διαπλασθείς, ἅτε καὶ ἀπάτωρ διὰ τοῦτο λεγόμενος.

(2) Concerning the ecclesiastical meaning of this term, which came gradually into use, see *Socrat.* vii. 32; *Münscher, von Cölln,* i. 286. The absurd discussions on the partus virgineus (comp. *e.g. Rufinus,* Expos. 20), where Mary, with allusion to what Ezekiel says, is called the porta Domini, per quam introivit in mundum, etc., belong to the same class. *Neander* (Dg. s. 344) says that the controversy took an unfortunate turn from the beginning, because it started from a word and not from a doctrinal idea: "*thus the fanaticism of the multitude was inflamed, and political passions had the greater play.*"

(3) *Anastasius,* a presbyter of Alexandria (A.D. 428), preached against the use of the term in question, and thus called forth the controversy. He was followed by *Nestorius* (a disciple of *Theodore* of Mopsuestia); *Socrat.* vii. 32. *Leporius,* a presbyter and monk at Massilia, and follower of *Pelagius,* had previously propounded a similar doctrine in the West, see *Münscher, von Cölln,* s. 282. The views of *Nestorius* himself are contained in iii. (ii.) Sermones *Nestorii,* quoted by *Mar. Mercator,* p. 53–74; *Mansi,* iv. p. 1197; *Garner,* ii. p. 3 ss. He rejected the appellation "mother of God" as heathenish, and contrary to Heb. vii. 3. Resting, as he did, on the orthodox doctrine of the eternal generation of the Son, he could say (see *Garner,* p. 5): Non peperit creatura eum, qui est increabilis; non recentem de virgine Deum Verbum genuit Pater. In principio erat enim verbum, sicut Joh. (i. 1), ait. Non peperit creatura creatorem [increabilem], sed peperit hominem, Deitatis instrumentum. Non creavit Deum Verbum Spir. S. . . . sed Deo Verbo templum fabricatus est, quod habitaret, ex virgine, etc. But *Nestorius* by no means refused to worship the human nature of Christ in its connection with the divine, and strongly protested against the charge of separating the two natures: Propter utentem illud indumentum, quo utitur, colo, propter absconditum adoro, quod

foris videtur. Inseparabilis ab eo, qui oculis paret, est Deus. Quomodo igitur ejus, qui non dividitur, honorem [ego] et dignitatem audeam separare ? Divido naturas, sed conjungo reverentiam (quoted by *Garner*, p. 5). And in the fragment given by *Mansi*, p. 1201. Διὰ τὸν φοροῦντα τὸν φορούμενον σέβω, διὰ τὸν κεκρυμμένον προσκυνῶ τὸν φαινόμενον· ἀχώριστος τοῦ φαινομένου θεός· διὰ τοῦτο τοῦ μὴ χωριζομένου τὴν τιμὴν οὐ χωρίζω· χωρίζω τὰς φύσεις, ἀλλ' ἑνῶ τὴν προσκύνησιν. He preferred calling Mary Θεοδόχυς or Χριστοτόκος, instead of Θεοτόκος. Comp. the other passages in *Münscher, von Cölln*, s. 284–286. *Baur*, Gesch. d. Trinität. i. s. 727 ff.

(4) On the external history of this controversy, see the works on ecclesiastical history. — It commenced with a correspondence between *Nestorius* and *Cyril*, in which they charged each other with respectively separating and confounding the two natures of Christ. *Cyril* was supported by Cœlestine, Bishop of Rome; *Nestorius*, by the Eastern bishops in general, and John, Bishop of Antioch, in particular.—In the progress of the controversy *Nestorius* declared himself willing even to adopt the term θεοτόκος if properly explained. Comp. the Acts, and especially the Anathematismata themselves, in *Mansi*, v. p. 1 ss., and iv. p. 1099; in *Mar. Mercator*, p. 142 (*Garner*, ii. 77 ss.), reprinted in *Baumgarten's* Theologische Streitigkeiten, ii. s. 770 ff. *Gieseler*, Kirchengesch. i. s. 408. *Münscher, von Cölln*, s. 290–295.

(5) "*As the Alexandrians exalted the* ὑπὲρ λόγον, *so did the Antiochenes the* κατὰ λόγον," *Neander*, Dg. s. 349. On their differences, and the inferences which each party drew from the views of the other to its disadvantage, see ibid. The ἀντιμετάστασις τῶν ὀνομάτων was carried to an extreme by the Alexandrians, while the Antiochenes distinguished between what is spoken δογματικῶς and what πανηγυρικῶς.

(6) The acts of the synod are given in *Mansi*, iv. p. 1123; *Fuchs*, iv. s. 1 ff. The synod was organized in a partisan way by Cyril.— A counter-synod was held under John, Bishop of Antioch, in opposition to Cyril and Memnon; these in their turn excommunicated John and his party. The Emperor Theodosius at first confirmed the sentence of deposition which the two contending parties had pronounced upon

each other, but afterwards *Nestorius* was abandoned by all; for *John* of Antioch himself was prevailed upon to give his consent to the condemnation of his friend, after *Cyril* had proposed a formula, the contradictions of which with his former Anathematismata were but poorly slurred over (comp. *Münscher, von Cölln*, s. 297). The consequence was the separation of the Nestorian party (Chaldee Christians, Thomas - Christians) from the Catholic Church. On the further history of the Nestorians, see *J. S. Asseman*, de Syris Nestorianis, in Bibl. Orient., Rom. 1728, t. iii. pt. 2. " *We may call the view of Cyril (according to which the human is changed into the divine) the* MAGICAL *aspect of the union, and that of Nestorius (according to which the two natures are only joined together) the* MECHANICAL," *Dorner* (1st ed.), s. 90.

§ 101.

Eutychian-Monophysite Controversy.

Pressel in *Herzog's* Realencyclopädie, ix. s. 743 ff.

The doctrine which *separated the two natures of Christ* had been rejected by the condemnation of *Nestorius*. But with the growing influence and power of the party of *Cyril*, led by *Dioscurus, Cyril's* successor (1), the still greater danger arose of *confounding* instead of *separating* the said natures. When the party zeal of *Eutyches*, archimandrite of Constantinople, maintained the doctrine of only one nature in Christ (2), there arose new disturbances; and, when *Dioscurus* had in vain endeavoured to force the Monophysite doctrine by violent means upon the Eastern Church (3), both he and his sentiments were condemned at the Council of Chalcedon (A.D. 451). In the course of the controversy, *Leo the Great*, Bishop of Rome, addressed a letter to *Flavian*, Bishop of Constantinople (4). On the basis of this Epistola Flaviana the synod pronounced in favour of the doctrine of two natures, neither to be separated nor confounded, and, in order to prevent further errors, drew up a formula of faith, which should be binding upon all parties (5).

(1) Respecting his character and violent conduct, especially towards Theodoret, see *Neander*, Kg. ii. 3, s. 1064 ff. The original documents of this controversy are given in *Mansi*, t. vi. vii. (*Ang. Maio*, Script. Vett. Coll. t. vii. and ix. Coll. Class. Auct. t. x. p. 408 ss.). [*Liberatus*, Breviarium Causæ Nestor. et Eutychian., in *Mansi*, ix. 659. *Walch's* Ketzerhist. vi. *Baur*, Dreieinigkeit, i. 800. *Dorner*, Person Christi, ii. 99 ff.]

(2) *Eutyches* was charged by *Eusebius* of Dorylæum with the revival of Valentinian and Apollinarian errors, and deposed by a synod held at Constantinople in the year 448. See *Mansi*, vi. p. 694–754. According to the acts of this synod, he taught: Μετὰ τὴν ἐνανθρώπησιν τοῦ θεοῦ λόγου, τουτέστι μετὰ τὴν γέννησιν τοῦ Κυρίου ἡμῶν Ἰησοῦ Χριστοῦ, μίαν φύσιν προσκυνεῖν καὶ ταύτην θεοῦ σαρκωθέντος καὶ ἐνανθρωπήσαντος. He denied that the flesh of Christ was of the same essence (ὁμοούσιος) with ours, though he would not be understood to teach that Christ brought His body with Him from heaven. But when his opponents drove him at last into a corner, he went so far as to admit that the body of Christ was of the same substance with our own. But he could not be induced to confess his belief in the existence of two natures, a divine and a human. He maintained that there had been *two* natures only πρὸ τῆς ἐνώσεως; but after that he would acknowledge only *one*. On the agreement between his doctrine and that of *Cyril*, see *Münscher, von Cölln*, s. 301.

(3) These violent proceedings were carried to an extreme length at the *Robber Synod*, A.D. 449 (Latrocinium Ephesinum, σύνοδος ληστρική), the acts of which may be found in *Mansi*, vi. p. 593 ss.; *Fuchs*, iv. s. 340 ff.

(4) The epistle in question is given in *Mansi*, v. p. 1359 (separately published by *K. Phil. Henke*, Helmst. 1780, 4to, comp. *Griesbach*, Opusc. Acad. t. i. p. 52 ss. *Münscher, von Cölln*, s. 302): Salva proprietate utriusque naturæ et substantiæ et in unam coëunte personam, suscepta est a majestate humilitas, a virtute infirmitas, ab æternitate mortalitas; et ad resolvendum conditionis nostræ debitum natura inviolabilis

naturæ est unita passibili, ut quod nostris remediis congruebat, unus atque idem mediator Dei et hominum, homo Jesus Christus, et mori posset ex uno et mori non posset ex altero. In integra ergo veri hominis perfectaque natura verus natus est Deus, totus in suis, totus in nostris. . . . Qui enim verus est Deus, idem verus est homo, et nullum est in hac unitate mendacium, dum invicem sunt et humilitas hominis et altitudo Deitatis. Sicut enim Deus non mutatur miseratione, ita homo non consumitur dignitate. Agit enim utraque forma cum alterius communione, quod proprium est: Verbo scilicet operante, quod verbi est, et carne exsequente, quod carnis est, etc. He then ascribes birth, hunger, nakedness, suffering, death, burial, etc., to the human, miracles to the divine nature; the passage in John xiv. 28 refers to the former, that in John x. 30 to the latter. Comp. on *Leo's* Christology, *Perthel,* u. s. 146; *Baur,* Trin. i. 807 ff.

(5) *Mansi,* vii. 108 s.: . . . Ἑπόμενοι τοίνυν τοῖς ἁγίοις πατράσιν, ἕνα καὶ τὸν αὐτὸν ὁμολογεῖν υἱὸν τὸν κύριον ἡμῶν Ἰησοῦν Χριστὸν συμφώνως ἅπαντες ἐκδιδάσκομεν, τέλειον τὸν αὐτὸν ἐν θεότητι καὶ τέλειον τὸν αὐτὸν ἐν ἀνθρωπότητι, θεὸν ἀληθῶς καὶ ἄνθρωπον ἀληθῶς τὸν αὐτὸν ἐκ ψυχῆς λογικῆς καὶ σώματος, ὁμοούσιον τῷ Πατρὶ κατὰ τὴν θεότητα καὶ ὁμοούσιον τὸν αὐτὸν ἡμῖν κατὰ τὴν ἀνθρωπότητα, κατὰ πάντα ὅμοιον ἡμῖν χωρὶς ἁμαρτίας· πρὸ αἰώνων μὲν ἐκ τοῦ Πατρὸς γεννηθέντα κατὰ τὴν θεότητα, ἐπ' ἐσχάτων δὲ τῶν ἡμερῶν τὸν αὐτὸν δι' ἡμᾶς καὶ διὰ τὴν ἡμετέραν σωτηρίαν ἐκ Μαρίας τῆς παρθένου τῆς θεοτόκου κατὰ τὴν ἀνθρωπότητα, ἕνα καὶ τὸν αὐτὸν Χριστὸν Υἱὸν, Κύριον, μονογενῆ ἐκ δύο φύσεων (ἐν δύο φύσεσιν)[1] ἀσυγχύτως, ἀτρέπτως, ἀδιαιρέτως, ἀχωρίστως γνωριζόμενον· οὐδαμοῦ τῆς τῶν φύσεων διαφορᾶς ἀνῃρημένης διὰ τὴν ἕνωσιν, σωζομένης δὲ μᾶλλον τῆς ἰδιότητος ἑκατέρας φύσεως καὶ εἰς ἓν πρόσωπον καὶ μίαν ὑπόστασιν συντρεχούσης· οὐκ εἰς δύο πρόσωπα μεριζόμενον, ἢ διαιρούμενον, ἀλλ' ἕνα καὶ τὸν αὐτὸν Υἱὸν καὶ μονογενῆ, θεὸν λόγον, κύριον Ἰησοῦν Χριστόν· καθάπερ ἄνωθεν οἱ προφῆται περὶ αὐτοῦ καὶ αὐτὸς ἡμᾶς Ἰησοῦς Χριστὸς ἐξεπαίδευσε· καὶ τὸ τῶν πατέρων ἡμῖν παραδέδωκε σύμβολον.

We cannot fail to see a dogmatic parallel between these

---

[1] On this different reading, comp. *Mansi,* p. 106, 775, 840. *Walch,* Bibl. Symb. p. 106.

Christological decisions and the theological definitions of the Council of Nice, with this difference only (demanded by the difference of the objects in view), that the latter understood by φύσις that which belongs to each nature separately, but by ὑπόστασις, πρόσωπον, that which both have in common; the reverse is the case in the decisions of the Synod of Chalcedon.

§ 102.

Progress of the Controversy.—Theopaschites.

But the authority of the decision of the Council of Chalcedon was not at once generally acknowledged. Many conflicts ensued (1) before the doctrine of *two natures in one person* was received as the orthodox doctrine of the Church, and finally inserted into what is commonly called the Athanasian Creed (2). The exact medium, however, between the two extreme views was not strictly preserved. For by the admission of a new clause, viz. that one of the divine persons had been crucified (*Theopaschitism*), into the definitions of the fifth Œcumenical Synod (A.D. 553) (3), the Monophysite notion gained the ascendency within the pale of orthodoxy.

(1) The *Henoticon* of the Emperor Zeno, A.D. 482 (in *Evagr.* iii. c. 14; separately published by *Berger*, Wittenb. 1723, 4to), was intended to bring about a reconciliation between the contending parties, but was not followed by any permanent success. Comp. *Jablonski*, Diss. de Henotico Zenonis, Francof. ad Viadr. 1737, 4to. *Münscher, v. Cölln,* s. 306, 307. It was taught that Christ was ὁμοούσιος τῷ πατρὶ κατὰ τὴν θεότητα, καὶ ὁμοούσιος ἡμῖν κατὰ τὴν ἀνθρωπότητα. The predicate θεοτόκος was vindicated for Mary; and the Anathematismata of Cyril were justified.

(2) Symb. Athan. pars ii.—(Comp. § 97.)

27. Sed necessarium est ad æternam salutem, ut incarnationem quoque Domini nostri Jesu Christi fideliter credat. 28. Est ergo fides recta, ut credamus et confiteamur, quia Dominus noster Jesus Christus, Dei filius, Deus pariter et homo

§ 102.] PROGRESS OF THE MONOPHYSITE CONTROVERSY. 397

est. 29. Deus est ex substantia Patris ante sæcula genitus: homo ex substantia matris in sæculo natus. 30. Perfectus deus, perfectus homo, ex anima rationali et humana carne subsistens. 31. Æqualis Patri secundum divinitatem, minor Patre secundum humanitatem. 32. Qui, licet deus sit et homo, non duo tamen, sed unus est Christus. 33. Unus autem non conversione divinitatis in carnem, sed assumtione humanitatis in Deum. 34. Unus omnino non confusione substantiarum, sed unitate personæ. 35. Nam sicut anima rationalis et caro unus est homo, ita et Deus et homo unus est Christus. 36. Qui passus est pro salute nostra, descendit ad inferos, tertia die resurrexit a mortuis, 37, ascendit in cœlos, sedet ad dexteram Patris, inde venturus judicare vivos et mortuos. 38. Ad cujus adventum omnes homines resurgere debent cum corporibus suis et reddituri sunt de factis propriis rationem. 39. Et qui bona egerunt, ibunt in vitam æternam: qui vero mala, in ignem æternum. 40. Hæc est fides catholica, quam nisi quisquam fideliter firmiterque crediderit, salvus esse non poterit.

(3) *Peter Fullo* (ὁ γναφεύς) was the first who introduced the clause θεὸς ἐσταυρώθη into the Trisagion, at Antioch (463–471). The African bishops, Fulgentius, Ferrandus, and Fulgentius of Ruspe, declared in favour of the formula, that one of the Trinity was crucified. See *Gieseler*, Kg. i. 2, 365. — In the year 533 Justinian pronounced the phrase, *unum crucifixum esse ex sancta et consubstantiali Trinitate*, to be orthodox (Cod. lib. i. Tit. i. 6): he did so in agreement with John II., Bishop of Rome, but in opposition to his predecessor Hormisdas. — The decree of the council is given in *Mansi*, ix. p. 304: Εἴ τις οὐχ ὁμολογεῖ τὸν ἐσταυρωμένον σαρκὶ Κύριον ἡμῶν Ἰησοῦν Χριστὸν εἶναι θεὸν ἀληθινὸν καὶ κύριον τῆς δόξης, καὶ ἕνα τῆς ἁγίας τριάδος· ὁ τοιοῦτος ἀνάθεμα ἔστω. — This victory of the advocates of Theopaschitism was only the counterpart of the one which the friends of the phrase θεοτόκος had gained in former years. Thus such expressions as "God is born, God died," came gradually into use in dogmatic theology. It was in this sense that, *e.g.*, the author of the Soliloquia Animæ (which may be found in the works of Augustine), c. 1, offered the following prayer: Manus tuæ, Domine, fecerunt me et plasmaverunt me, manus inquam illæ,

quæ affixæ clavis sunt pro me. Cf. *Herzog,* Realenc. xvi. s. 15.

§ 103.

Various Modifications of the Monophysite Doctrine.
Aphthartodocetæ, Phthartolatri, Agnoëtæ.

J. C. L. *Gieseler,* Commentatio, qua Monophysitarum veterum Variæ de Christi Persona Opiniones inprimis ex ipsorum effatis recens editis illustrantur. Part. i. ii. Gött. 1838, 4to.

The Monophysites themselves were not agreed on the question whether Christ possessed a corruptible or an incorruptible body. The *Phthartolatri* (Severians) maintained the former; the *Aphthartodocetæ* (Julianists) asserted the latter, in accordance with their Monophysite premisses respecting the nature of Christ. Different views obtained among the Aphthartodocetæ themselves on the question whether Christ's body was created or not, and led to the formation of two distinct parties, the *Ktistolatri* and the *Aktistetæ* (1). The omniscience of Christ necessarily followed from the Monophysite doctrine. The assertion, therefore, of *Themistius,* deacon of Alexandria, that Christ as man was ignorant of many things (*Agnoëtism,* Mark xiii. 32; Luke ii. 25), was rejected by the strict Monophysites (2).

(1) SOURCES: *Leont. Byzant.* (in *Gallandii* Bibl. Patr. xii.). *Niceph. Callisti,* lib. xvii. *Gieseler* (in the 2d Part of the dissertation cited before) endeavours to prove that the view of the Julianists was by no means purely Docetic, but allied to that taken by *Clement* of Alexandria, *Hilary, Gregory* of Nyssa, etc., and that it also bore resemblance to the opinions entertained by *Apollinaris. Xenaias* (Philoxenus), Bishop of Hierapolis, and the contemporary of *Julian,* Bishop of Halicarnassus, appears as the representative of this view (*Gieseler,* s. 7). — Different meanings were attached to the word $\phi\theta o\rho\acute{a}$, which was made at one time to denote the frailty of the living body, and its susceptibility to suffering; at another, to signify the dissolubility of the corpse (ibidem, s. 4).

(2) On the orthodox side, *Gregory the Great* (Epist. x. 35, 39) declared against Agnoëtism. On the controversy in the West, with *Leporius*, a monk of Gaul (about 426), who also taught Agnoëtism in connection with the doctrines of *Theodore* of Mopsuestia, see *Neander*, Dg. s. 354. [He contended for the unconditional transference of the predicates of the human nature to the divine, and consequently for such expressions as " God was born," " God died ; " he also taught a progressive revelation of the divine Logos in the human nature to which he was united, and Agnoëtism.]

Though the orthodox Church was far from giving the least countenance to Docetism, yet the ideas entertained by *Origen* in the preceding period (see § 66, note 6), viz., *that Christ rose from the tomb with a glorified body*, found many more friends in the present period. Not only *Hilary*, whose views, generally speaking, come nearest to those of the Docetæ, but also *Chrysostom, Theodoret*, and most of the eastern theologians, with the exception of *Ephraem Syrus, Gregory* of Nyssa, and *Cyril* of Alexandria, adopted more or less the notion of Origen. Thus Chrysostom says in reference to John xxi. 10 : ἐφαίνετο γὰρ ἄλλῃ μορφῇ, ἄλλῃ φωνῇ, ἄλλῳ σχήματι ; in support of his opinion he appealed especially to the appearance of Christ when the doors were shut. On the other hand, the last-named Fathers of the Eastern Church, as well as the western theologians, *Jerome* in particular, asserted that Christ possessed the very same body both prior and anterior to His resurrection. *Cyril* firmly maintains that Christ was ἐν σώματι παχεῖ. *Augustine* and *Leo the Great*, on the contrary, endeavoured to reconcile the notion of the identity of Christ's body with the idea of its glorification. Thus *Leo* says in Sermo 69, de Resurrect. Dom. cap. 4 (t. i. p. 73): Resurrectio Domini non finis carnis, sed commutatio fuit, nec virtutis augmento consumta substantia est. Qualitas transiit, non natura deficit : et factum est corpus impassibile, immortale, incorruptibile... nihil remansit in carne Christi infirmum, ut et ipsa sit per essentiam et non sit ipsa per gloriam. *Gregory the Great* and others used similar language. — Most of the theologians of this period also adhered to the opinion that *Christ had quickened Himself by His own power*, in opposition to the notion entertained by the Arians, viz. that the Father had raised Him from the dead. For the doctrine of the two natures in Christ led them to imagine that the union subsisting between the divine and the human was so intimate and permanent, that both His body and soul, after their natural separation by death, continued to be connected with His divine nature, the body in the grave, the soul in Hades. Nor did Christ stand in need of the angel to roll away the stone ; this took place only in consequence of His resurrection.—His ascension was likewise the self-exaltation of the Godhead in Him, not a miracle wrought by the Father upon Him (generally speaking, theologians were accustomed at this time to consider the miracles of Christ as works achieved by His divine nature). The cloud which formerly enveloped all the events of Christ's life was now changed into a triumphal car (ὄχημα) accompanied by angels. Comp. *Athan.* De Assumt. Dom.; and for further particulars, see *Müller*, l.c. p. 40 ss., p. 83 ss.

§ 104.

The Doctrine of Two Wills in Christ.—Monothelites.

†. *Comlefisii*, Historia Monothelitarum, in the second volume of his Nov. Auctuarium Bibl. PP. Græco-Latin. Par. 1648, fol. *Walch*, Historie der Ketzereien, vol. ix. s. 1–606. *Pressel* in *Herzog*, Realenc. ix. s. 752 ff.

The attempt made by the Emperor Heraclius, in the seventh century, to re-unite the Monophysites with the Catholic Church, led to the controversy respecting the two wills in Christ, akin to that concerning His natures (1). In agreement with *Cyrus*, patriarch of Alexandria, the emperor, hoping to reconcile the two parties, adopted the doctrine of only one divine-human energy (ἐνέργεια), and of one will in Christ (2). But *Sophronius*, an acute monk of Palestine, afterwards patriarch of Jerusalem (A.D. 635), endeavoured to show that this doctrine was inadmissible, since the doctrine of two natures, set forth by the Synod of Chalcedon, necessarily implied that of two wills (3). After several fruitless attempts had been made to establish the Monothelite doctrine (4), the sixth Œcumenical Council of Constantinople (A.D. 680), with the co-operation of the Bishop of Rome (5), adopted the doctrine of *two* wills and *two* energies as the orthodox doctrine, but decided that the human will must always be conceived as subordinate to the divine (6).

(1) In this way the controversy was removed from the province of pure metaphysics into the moral and practical sphere, and thus brought into connection with the anthropological disputes, as there had also been occasion for this in the Apollinarist strife (see above). But this did not help the matter itself.

(2) When the Emperor Heraclius, in the course of his campaign against Persia, passed through Armenia and Syria, he came to an understanding with the Monophysite leaders of the Severians and Jacobites, and induced *Sergius*, the orthodox patriarch of Constantinople, to give his assent to the

doctrine of ἓν θέλημα καὶ μία ἐνέργεια, or of an ἐνέργεια θεανδρική. *Cyrus* (a Monophysite), whom the emperor had appointed patriarch of Alexandria, effected, at a synod held in that place (A.D. 633), a union between the different parties. The acts of this synod are given by *Mansi*, Conc. xi. p. 564 ss., as well as the letters of *Cyrus*, ibid. p. 561.

(3) See *Sophronii* Epist. Synodica, which is given in *Mansi*, xi. 461. Those Monophysites who maintained the doctrine of two natures, and of only *one* will, were quite as inconsistent as most of the orthodox theologians in the Arian controversy, who held that the Son was of the same essence with the Father, but asserted a subordination of the Spirit.

(4) The Greek emperor at first endeavoured to settle the matter amicably by the Ἔκθεσις [an edict issued by the Emperor Heraclius, A.D. 638, in which he confirmed the agreement made by the patriarchs for the preservation of ecclesiastical union] and the Τύπος [an edict issued by the Emperor Constans II., A.D. 648, in which the contending parties were prohibited from resuming their discussions on the doctrine in question]. See *Mansi*, x. p. 992, p. 1029 ss. Afterwards Martin I. and Maximus were treated with the most shameful cruelty; for further particulars, see *Neander*, Kg. iii. s. 377 ff.

(5) Pope *Honorius* was in favour of the union, but his successors, *Severinus* and *John* IV., opposed it. The latter condemned the doctrine of the Monothelites, and *Theodore* excommunicated *Paul*, patriarch of Constantinople, till the doctrine of *two* wills and *two* energies was at last adopted at the first synod of the Lateran, held under *Martin* I., Bishop of Rome, in the year 649; see *Mansi*, x. p. 863 s.: Si quis secundum scelerosos hæreticos cum una voluntate et una operatione, quæ ab hæreticis impie confitetur, et duas voluntates, pariterque et operationes, hoc est, divinam et humanam, quæ in ipso Christo Deo in unitate salvantur, et a sanctis patribus orthodoxe in ipso prædicantur, denegat et respuit, condemnatus sit. (Comp. *Gieseler*, Kg. i. s. 666. *Münscher, von Cölln*, ii. 78, 79.)

(6) This council (also called the First Trullan) was summoned by *Constantinus Pogonatus*. The decision of the synod was based upon the epistle of *Agatho*, the Roman bishop, which

was itself founded upon the canons of the above Lateran synod (*Agathonis* Ep. ad Imperatores, in *Mansi*, xi. 233–286), confessing belief in duæ naturales voluntates et duæ naturales operationes, non contrariæ, nec adversæ, nec separatæ, etc. This was followed by the decision of the council itself (see *Mansi*, xi. 631 s. *Münscher, von Cölln*, ii. s. 80. *Gieseler*, l.c.). Δύο φυσικὰς θελήσεις ἤτοι θελήματα ἐν Χριστῷ καὶ δύο φυσικὰς ἐνεργείας ἀδιαιρέτως, ἀτρέπτως, ἀμερίστως, ἀσυγχύτως, κατὰ τὴν τῶν ἁγίων πατέρων διδασκαλίαν κηρύττομεν· καὶ δύο φυσικὰ θελήματα οὐχ ὑπεναντία, μὴ γένοιτο, καθὼς οἱ ἀσεβεῖς ἔφησαν αἱρετικοί· ἀλλ' ἑπόμενον τὸ ἀνθρώπινον αὐτοῦ θέλημα, καὶ μὴ ἀντιπαλαῖον, μᾶλλον μὲν οὖν καὶ ὑποτασσόμενον τῷ θείῳ αὐτοῦ καὶ πανσθενεῖ θελήματι. —Respecting the insufficiency of these, and the indefiniteness of the other canons of the council, see *Dorner* (1ste Ausg.), s. 99 ff.—The Reformers did not accept the decisions of this council. The Monothelites (Pope Honorius included) were condemned. They continued to exist as a distinct sect in the mountains of Lebanon and Anti-Lebanon under the name of Maronites (which was derived from their leader, the Syrian abbot *Marun*, who lived about the year 701). Comp. *Neander*, l.c. s. 398. [*Baur*, Dogmengesch. s. 211, says of this controversy: " Its elements on the side of the Monothelites were, the unity of the person or subject, from whose one will (the divine will of the incarnate Logos) all must proceed, since two wills also presuppose two personal subjects (the chief argument of Bishop Theodore of Pharan, in *Mansi*, tom. xi. p. 567); on the side of the Duothelites, the point was the fact of two natures, since two natures cannot be conceived without two natural wills and two natural modes of operation. How far, then, two wills can be without two persons willing, was the point at which they slipped away by mere assumptions."]

§ 105.

Practical and Religious Significance of Christology during this Period.

Unedifying as is the spectacle of these manifold controversies, in which the person of the Redeemer is dragged down

§ 105.] SIGNIFICANCE OF CHRISTOLOGY DURING THIS PERIOD. 403

into the sphere of passionate conflicts, it is still cheering to see how the faith of Christians in those times was supported by that idea of the God-man, which was above all such strife, and how it attributed to the doctrine of the one and undivided person of Christ its due significance in the history of the world.

"*All the Fathers agreed, as it were with one mind and one mouth, that to Christ belongs not merely the limited importance attached to every historical personage, but that His person stands in an essential relation to the* WHOLE HUMAN RACE; *on this account alone could they make a* SINGLE INDIVIDUAL *the object of an article of faith, and ascribe to him a lasting and eternal significancy in relation to our race.*" Dorner (1ste Ausg.), s. 78: compare the passages from the Fathers there cited. [They say, *e.g.*, that Christ is the primitive type after which Adam and the whole of humanity were created; the principle, the ἀρχή, of the whole new creation, in which the old is first completed; the ἀπαρχή of the whole φύραμα of humanity, penetrating all; the eternal head of the race—a member of it indeed, but yet its plastic and organizing principle, in virtue of the union between divinity and humanity in Him perfectly realized, etc.]

SECOND DIVISION.

ANTHROPOLOGICAL DEFINITIONS.

§ 106.

On Man in General.

THE Platonic doctrine of a pre-existence of the human soul, which none but *Nemesius* and *Prudentius* favoured (1), was almost unanimously rejected as Origenistic (2). Along with physical *Traducianism* (favourable as was this doctrine in certain aspects to the idea of original sin, see § 55), *Creatianism* was also able to obtain more authority. According to this view, every human soul was created as such, and at a certain moment of time united with the body, developing itself in the womb. Yet the most influential teachers of the Church, as *Augustine* and *Gregory the Great*, expressed themselves with reserve on this point (3). In the West the threefold division of man (§ 54) gave way to the simpler division into body and soul (4), on the mutual relation of which different views obtained among the Fathers of the present period (5). Nor did they agree in their opinions respecting the image of God, though most of them admitted that it consisted in reason imparted to man, in his capacity of knowing God, and in his dominion over the irrational creation (6). There were still some who imagined that the image of God was also reflected in the body of man; but while the *Audiani* perverted this notion in support of a gross anthropomorphism (7), others gave to it a more spiritual interpretation. The immortality of the soul was universally believed (8); *Lactantius*, however, did not regard it as a natural property of the soul, but as the reward of virtue (9).

§ 106.] ON MAN IN GENERAL. 405

(1) The former did so as a philosopher (De Humana Natura, ii. p. 76 ss. of the Oxford edit.), the latter as a poet (Cathemerin. Hymn. x. 161–168). [Cf. *Aur. Prudent.* Carmina, ed. *Alb. Dressel*, Lips. 1860.]

(2) Conc. Const. A.D. 540 (*Mansi*, ix. p. 396 s.) : Ἡ ἐκκλησία τοῖς θείοις ἑπομένη λόγοις φάσκει τὴν ψυχὴν συνδημιουργηθῆναι τῷ σώματι· καὶ οὐ τὸ μὲν πρότερον, τὸ δὲ ὕστερον, κατὰ τὴν Ὠριγένους φρενοβλάβειαν.

(3) *Lactantius* maintains, Inst. iii. 18, that the soul is born with the body, and distinctly opposes Traducianism, De Opif. Dei ad Demetr. c. 19 : Illud quoque venire in quæstionem potest, utrum anima ex patre, an potius ex matre, an vero ex utroque generetur. Nihil ex his tribus verum est, quia neque ex utroque, neque ex alterutro seruntur animæ. Corpus enim ex corporibus nasci potest, quoniam confertur aliquid ex utroque; de animis anima non potest, quia ex re tenui et incomprehensibili nihil potest decedere. Itaque serendarum animarum ratio uni ac soli Deo subjacet:

"Denique cœlesti sumus omnes semine oriundi,
Omnibus ille idem pater est,"

ut ait Lucretius; nam de mortalibus non potest quidquam nisi mortale generari. Nec putari pater debet, qui transfudisse aut inspirasse animam de suo nullo modo sentit; nec, si sentiat, quando tamen et quomodo id fiat, habet animo comprehensum. Ex quo apparet, non a parentibus dari animas, sed ab uno eodemque omnium Deo patre, qui legem rationemque nascendi tenet solus, siquidem solus efficit; nam terreni parentis nihil est, nisi ut humorem corporis, in quo est materia nascendi, cum sensu voluptatis emittat vel recipiat, et citra hoc opus homo resistit, nec quidquam amplius potest; ideo nasci sibi filios optant, quia non ipsi faciunt. Cetera jam Dei sunt omnia: scilicet conceptus ipse et corporis informatio et inspiratio animæ et partus incolumis et quæcunque deinceps ad hominem conservandum valent; *illius* munus est, quod spiramus, quod vivimus, quod vigemus.—In opposition to Traducianism, he appeals to the fact that intelligent parents have sometimes stupid children, and *vice versa*, which could not well be ascribed to the influence of the stars!—In accordance with this opinion, *Hilary* asserts, Tract. in Ps. xci. § 3: Quotidie animarum origines [et corporum figulationes] occulta et incognita nobis divinæ virtutis molitione procedunt. See also Tract. in Ps. cxviii. cap. i.: Igitur vel quia in terræ hujus solo commoramur, vel quia ex terra instituti conformatique sumus, anima quæ alterius originis est, terræ corporis adhæsisse creditur. *Pelagius*, and the Semi-Pelagians, *Cassian* and *Gennadius*, adopted substantially the same view, see *Wiggers*, Augustin und Pelagius, i. s. 149, ii. s. 354. *Pelagius* taught (in Symb. quoted by *Mansi*, iv. p. 355): Animas a Deo dari credimus, quas ab ipso factas dicimus, anathematizantes eos, qui animas quasi partem divinæ dicunt esse substantiæ; *Augustine* agreed with him as far as the negative aspect of this proposition was concerned: Retract. i. 1: (Deus) animum non de se ipso genuit, sed de re nulla alia condidit, sicut condidit corpus e terra; he here refers, however, directly to the creation of our first parents. But *Augustine* does not expressly state whether he thinks that the soul is newly created in every case; on the contrary, he declined to investigate this point: Nam quod attinet ad ejus (animi) originem, qua fit ut sit in corpore, utrum de illo uno sit, qui primum creatus est, quando factus est homo in animam vivam, an semper ita fiant singulis singuli, nec tunc sciebam (in his treatise Contra Academicos) nec adhuc scio. Comp. Ep. 140 (al. 120), ad Honorat. (t. ii. p. 320). When *Jerome* (Contra Error. Joann. Hierosolym. § 22) derives Creatianism from the words of Christ (John v.): "My Father worketh hitherto," *Augustine* will not allow *this* argument to be valid, since the working of God is not excluded even upon the Traducian hypothesis; comp. *Neander*, Dg. 381. [The opinion of *Augustine* upon this point has been much debated: *Bellarmine* and *Staudenmaier* contend that he was for creation; *Melanchthon, Klee*, and others reckon him among the Traducianists; *Gangauf* (u. s.), *Wiggers*, and *Ritter* say that he was undecided. *Bellarmine* cites for Creatianism, Epist. 190, ad Optat. cap. 14: Illi, qui animas ex una propagari asserunt, quam Deus primo homini dedit, atque ita eas ex parentibus trahi dicunt, si Tertulliani opinionem sequuntur, profecto eas, non spiritus, sed corpora esse contendunt, et corpulentis seminibus exoriri, quo perversius quod dici potest? But this applies strictly only to *Tertullian's* corpulenta semina. He recognizes the connection between Traducianism and original sin, De Lib.

Arb. lib. iii. cap. 56 : Deinde si una anima facta est, ex qua omnium hominum animæ trahuntur nascentium, quis potest dicere, non se pecasse, cum primus ille peccavit? In his De Anima et ejus Orig. lib. i. cap. 19, Num. 34, he says that he could accept Creatianism if four difficulties were removed; and in De Orig. Anim. cap. 28, he designates the chief of these difficulties, in connection with the doctrine of the salvation of children not baptized: Sed antequam sciam, quænam earum potius eligenda sit, hoc me non temere sentire profiteor, eam, quæ vera est, non adversari robustissimæ ac fundatissimæ fidei, qua Christi ecclesia nec parvulos homines recentissime natos a damnatione credit, nisi per gratiam nominis Christi, quam in suis sacramentis commendavit, posse liberari ; comp. De Genesi ad Lit. lib. x. cap. 23, Num. 39, and Epist. 169 ad Evodium, cap. 13. In Epist. 190, ad Optat. cap. 17, he says : Aliquid ergo certum de animæ origine nondum in scripturis canonicis comperi. And in Genes. ad Lit. x. 21, he says : Jam de ceterarum animarum adventu, utrum ex parentibus an desuper, sit, vincant, qui poterunt ; ego adhuc inter utrosque ambigo, et moveor aliquando sic, aliquando autem sic.] —The phrase mentioned before (note 2) : τὴν ψυχὴν συνδημιουργηθῆναι τῷ σώματι, which was used by the Greek Church, and is also found in the works of *Theodoret* (Fab. Hær. v. 9, p. 414), implies the doctrine commonly called Creatianism. Yet Traducianism continued to be professed not only by heterodox writers, *e.g. Eunomius* and *Apollinaris*, but also by some orthodox theologians. Thus *Athanasius*, the father of orthodoxy, favoured it, saying of Adam : ἐν αὐτῷ ἦσαν οἱ λόγοι τῆς διαδοχῆς παντὸς τοῦ γένους (C. Arian. ii. 48); and so *Gregory* of Nyssa (De Hom. Opif. c. 29) directs attention to the fact that body and soul belong essentially together, and cannot possibly be imagined to be separated from each other : Ἀλλ' ἑνὸς ὄντος τοῦ ἀνθρώπου, τοῦ διὰ ψυχῆς τε καὶ σώματος συνεστηκότος, μίαν αὐτοῦ καὶ κοινὴν τῆς συστάσεως τὴν ἀρχὴν ὑποτίθεσθαι, ὡς ἂν μὴ αὐτὸς ἑαυτοῦ προγενέστερός τε καὶ νεώτερος γένοιτο, τοῦ μὲν σωματικοῦ προτερεύοντος ἐν αὐτῷ, τοῦ δὲ ἑτέρου ἐφυστερίζοντος κ.τ.λ., which he proves by analogies drawn from nature. Cf. *Möller*, Gregorii Nysseni doctrina de hominis natura, Hal. 1854. The views of *Anastasius Sinaïta* on this point are very materialistic (Hom. in *Bandini* Monum.

Eccles. Gr. t. ii. p. 54, in *Münscher, von Cölln*, i. s. 332): Τὸ μὲν σῶμα ἐκ τῆς γυναικείας γῆς (*Thiersch* conjectures γονῆς, see the review in Zeitschrift f. d. luth. Theol. 1841, s. 184) καὶ αἵματος συνίσταται· ἡ δὲ ψυχὴ διὰ τῆς σπορᾶς, ὥσπερ διά τινος ἐμφυσήματος ἐκ τοῦ ἀνθρώπου ἀρρήτως μεταδίδοται. According to *Jerome*, Ep. 78, ad Marcellin. (Opp. t. iv. p. 642, ap. *Erasm*. ii. p. 318), even maxima pars occidentalium (probably of earlier times?) held the opinion, ut quomodo corpus ex corpore, sic anima nascatur ex anima et simili cum brutis animantibus conditione subsistat. But *Jerome* himself rejects all other systems, and designates *Creatianism* as the orthodox doctrine;[1] Epist. ad Pammach. (Opp. t. iv. p. 318, ap. *Erasm*. ii. p. 170): Quotidie Deus fabricatur animas, cujus velle fecisse est et conditor esse non cessat. . . . Noli despicere bonitatem figuli tui, qui te plasmavit et fecit ut voluit. Ipse est Dei virtus et Dei sapientia, qui in utero virginis ædificavit sibi domum. The advocates of Creatianism saw in the birth of every human being something analogous to the miracle of Christ's incarnation on its physical side, without putting the one on a level with the other (which *Jerome* would have been the last to do); those who adopted Traducianism were compelled to consider Christ's birth as an exception to the rule; and even this exception seemed to require some limitation of the position, that Christ's human nature is consubstantial with ours. Many theologians, therefore, preferred obviating these difficulties, following *Augustine's* example, by directing attention to the impossibility of comprehending the origin and processes of existence. Thus *Gregory the Great*, Ep. vii. 59, ad Secundinum (Opp. ii. p. 970), says: Sed de hac re dulcissima mihi tua caritas sciat, quia de origine animæ inter sanctos Patres requisitio non parva versata est; sed utrum ipsa ab Adam descenderit, an certe singulis detur, incertum remansit, eamque in hac vita insolubilem fassi sunt esse quæstionem. Gravis enim est quæstio, nec valet ab homine comprehendi, quia si de Adam substantia cum carne nascitur, cur non etiam cum carne moritur? Si vero cum carne non nascitur, cur in ea carne,

---

[1] *Leo the Great* likewise declares it to be the doctrine of the Church (Ep. 15, ad Turrib. Opp. *Quesnel*, p. 229), quoted in *Münscher, von Cölln*, s. 331, note 11: Catholica fides . . . omnem hominem in corporis et animæ substantiam *formari* intra materna viscera confitetur.

quæ de Adam prolata est, obligata peccatis tenetur? (he thus deduces Traducianism from the doctrine of original sin, the correctness of which he assumes; while the latter, on the contrary, was generally inferred from the former). Cf. *Leo*, s. 391 ff.

(4) *Athanasius* adopted the bipartite division. He distinguishes simply body and soul; the former is to him ὁ ἔσωθεν ἄνθρωπος, the latter ὁ ἔξωθεν (Contra Apoll. i. 13–15). The soul is to him not merely the blossom of the life of the body, but a principle distinct from the body, coming from above. See *Voigt*, s. 104.

(5) *Hilary* of Poitiers asserts (in Matth. Can. v. § 8) that the soul, whether in the body or out of the body, must always preserve its corporeal substance, because everything that is created must exist in some form or other (in aliquo sit necesse est); reminding us of the views of *Tertullian*. Yet elsewhere he views the soul as a spiritual, incorporeal being; comp. in Ps. lii. § 7, in Ps. cxxix. § 6 (nihil in se habens corporale, nihil terrenum, nihil grave, nihil caducum).—*Augustine* frankly acknowledges the difficulty of defining the relation in which the soul stands to the body, De Morib. Eccles. Cath. c. 4: Difficile est istam controversiam dijudicare, aut si ratione facile, oratione longum est. Quem laborem ac moram suscipere ac subire non opus est. Sive enim utrumque sive anima sola nomen hominis teneat, non est hominis optimum quod optimum est corporis, sed quod aut corpori simul et animæ aut soli animæ optimum est, id est optimum hominis.—On the psychological views of *Augustine*, comp. *Schleiermacher*, Geschichte der Philosophie, s. 169 ff., and *Heinichen*, De Augustini doctrinæ anthropologicæ origine (Histor.-theolog. Studien, 1 Hft. 1862); on those of *Claudius Mamertus* and *Boëthius*, *Schleierm.* s. 174.— According to *Gregory the Great*, man is composed of body and soul (Mor. xiv. c. 15). The principal properties of the soul are, mens, anima, et virtus; comp. *Lau*, s. 370.

(6) *Greg. Nyss.* in verba: "Faciamus hominem," Orat. 1 (Opp. i. p. 143): Ποιήσωμεν ἄνθρωπον κατ' εἰκόνα ἡμετέραν· τουτέστι· δώσομεν αὐτῷ λόγου περιουσίαν ... Οὐ γὰρ τὰ πάθη εἰς τὴν τοῦ θεοῦ εἰκόνα παρελήφθη, ἀλλ' ὁ λογισμὸς τῶν παθῶν δεσπότης. *Athanasius* speaks in the same manner, Orat. contra Gent. § 2, *Cyrill. Hier.* Cat. xiv. 10. The dominion over the animals was included. *Gregory*, l.c., says: ὅπου ἡ τοῦ

ἄρχειν δύναμις, ἐκεῖ ἡ τοῦ θεοῦ εἰκών. Comp. *Theodoret* in Genes. Quæst. 20. *Chrys.* Hom. viii. in Genes. (Opp. ii. p. 65 s.). *August.* De Catechizandis Rudib. xvii. 20; De Genesi contra Manich. c. 17; De Trin. xii. 2; Sermo xlviii. (De Cura Animæ): Quæ est imago Dei in nobis, nisi id quod melius reperitur nobis, nisi ratio, intellectus, memoria, voluntas. —The Semi-Pelagians, *Gennadius* and *Faustus*, made a distinction between *imago* and *similitudo*, see *Wiggers*, ii. s. 356. —*Gregory the Great* regards the image of God, in which man was created, as soliditas ingenita (Mor. ix. c. 33), which was lost by sin (Mor. xxix. c. 10), see *Lau*, s. 371. On the other traits of the first man as to body and soul, ibid. s. 372 ff. Whether there is here a hint of the doctrine of donum superadditum, afterwards fully developed, ibid. s. 376.

(7) *Audæus* (Udo), who lived at the beginning of the fourth century in Mesopotamia, a rigid and zealous ascetic, seems to have fallen into these notions through his essentially practical tendency; comp. *Epiph.* Hær. 70, who speaks very mildly of Audæus and his followers: οὔ τι ἔχων παρηλλαγμένον τῆς πίστεως, ἀλλ' ὀρθότατα μὲν πιστεύων αὐτός τε καὶ οἱ ἅμα αὐτῷ. *Theodoret* takes the opposite view, Hist. Eccles. iv. 10 (καινῶν εὑρετὴς δογμάτων), comp. Fab. Hær. iv. 10. *Schröder*, Diss. de Hæresi Audianor. Marb. 1716, 4to. *Neander*, Kirchengeschichte, ii. 3, s. 1465.

(8) *Augustine*, Sermo xlviii.: Anima enim non moritur, nec succumbit per mortem, cum omnino sit immortalis, nec corporis materia, cum sit una numero.

(9) *Lact.* Instit. Div. vii. 5 (in *Münscher, von Cölln,* s. 336, comp. s. 338). *Nemesius* likewise (cap. i. p. 15) accedes in this point to the opinion of the earlier Greek theologians: Ἑβραῖοι δὲ τὸν ἄνθρωπον ἐξ ἀρχῆς οὔτε θνητὸν ὁμολογουμένως, οὔτε ἀθάνατον γεγενῆσθαί φασιν, ἀλλ' ἐν μεθορίοις ἑκατέρας φύσεως, ἵνα ἂν μὲν τοῖς σωματικοῖς ἀκολουθήσῃ πάθεσιν, περιπέσῃ καὶ ταῖς σωματικαῖς μεταβολαῖς· ἐὰν δὲ τὰ τῆς ψυχῆς προτιμήσῃ καλά, τῆς ἀθανασίας ἀξιωθῇ κ.τ.λ. On the other hand, *Gregory the Great* teaches that, even if the soul lose the blessed life, it cannot lose the essentialiter vivere (Dial. iv. c. 45). The body of man, too, was originally immortal (potuit non mori), and became mortal through sin; comp. Moral. iv. c. 28 s. *Lau*, ubi supra, s. 371 f.

§ 107.

On the Doctrine of Sin in general.

Concerning the nature of sin, the generally received opinion was, that it has its seat in the will of man, and stands in the most intimate connection with his moral freedom. *Augustine* himself defended this doctrine (at least in his earlier writings) (1), which was opposed to the Manichæan notion, that evil is inherent in matter. *Lactantius*, on the contrary, manifested a strong leaning towards Manichæism by designating the body as the seat and organ of sin (2). The ascetic practices then so common sufficiently indicate that the Church tacitly approved of this view. *Athanasius* regarded sin as something negative, and believed it to consist in the blindness and indolence of man, which prevent him from elevating himself to God. Similar (negative) definitions were given by *Basil the Great* and *Gregory* of Nyssa (3). But sin was most frequently looked upon as opposition to the law of God, and rebellion against His holy will (4), analogous to the sin of Adam, which was now generally viewed as an historical fact (in contradiction of the allegorical interpretation of Origen) (5).

(1) *Aug.* De Duab. Animab. contra Manich. § 12 : Colligo nusquam nisi in *voluntate* esse peccatum ; De Lib. Arb. iii. 49 : Ipsa *voluntas* est prima causa peccandi.—In many other passages he regards sin from the negative point of view as a conversio a majori bono ad minus bonum, defectio ab eo, quod summe est, ad id, quod minus est, perversitas voluntatis a summa substantia detortæ in infimum. See the passages in *Julius Müller*, l.c. s. 69.

(2) *Lact.* Inst. Div. ii. 12, vi. 13 ; De Ira Dei, 15 : Nemo esse sine delicto potest, quamdiu indumento carnis oneratus est. Cujus infirmitas triplici modo subjacet dominio peccati : factis, dictis, cogitationibus.

(3) *Athan.* Contra Gent. c. 4 (Opp. i. p. 4) : Ὄντα δέ ἐστι τὰ καλά, οὐκ ὄντα δὲ τὰ φαῦλα· ὄντα δέ φημι τὰ καλά, καθότι

ἐκ τοῦ ὄντος θεοῦ τὰ παραδείγματα ἔχει· οὐκ ὄντα δὲ τὰ κακὰ λέγω, καθότι ἐπινοίαις ἀνθρώπων οὐκ ὄντα ἀναπέπλασται. Ibid. c. 7, p. 7 : Ὅτι τὸ κακὸν οὐ παρὰ θεοῦ οὐδὲ ἐν θεῷ, οὔτε ἐξ ἀρχῆς γέγονεν, οὔτε οὐσία τίς ἐστιν αὐτοῦ· ἀλλὰ ἄνθρωποι κατὰ στέρησιν τῆς τοῦ καλοῦ φαντασίας ἑαυτοῖς ἐπινοεῖν ἤρξαντο καὶ ἀναπλάττειν τὰ οὐκ ὄντα καὶ ἅπερ βούλονται. Comp. that which follows. *Athanasius* traces the sinful propensity of man to indolence, c. 3, p. 3 : Οἱ δὲ ἄνθρωποι κατολιγωρήσαντες τῶν κρειττόνων, καὶ ὀκνήσαντες περὶ τὴν τούτων κατάληψιν, τὰ ἐγγυτέρω μᾶλλον ἑαυτῶν ἐζήτησαν. Sensuality is allied with indolence, because this clings to what is nearest, viz. the bodily and the visible. Comp. the subsequent part of the chapter. In the same manner *Basil M.*, Hexaëmeron Hom. ii. p. 19 (Paris edit. 1638), says : Οὐ μὴν οὐδὲ παρὰ θεοῦ τὸ κακὸν τὴν γένεσιν ἔχειν εὐσεβές ἐστι λέγειν, διὰ τὸ μηδὲν τῶν ἐναντίων παρὰ τοῦ ἐναντίου γίνεσθαι, οὔτε γὰρ ἡ ζωὴ θάνατον γεννᾷ, οὔτε ὁ σκότος φωτός ἐστιν ἀρχὴ, οὔτε ἡ νόσος ὑγείας δημιουργός. . . . Τί οὖν φαμεν; Ὅτι κακόν ἐστιν οὐχὶ οὐσία ζῶσα καὶ ἔμψυχος, ἀλλὰ διάθεσις ἐν ψυχῇ ἐναντίως ἔχουσα πρὸς ἀρετὴν διὰ τὴν ἀπὸ τοῦ καλοῦ ἀπόπτωσιν τοῖς ῥαθύμοις ἐγγινομένη.—*Greg. Nyss.* Orat. Catechet. c. 5 (Opp. iii. p. 53) : Καθάπερ γὰρ ἡ ὅρασις φύσεών ἐστιν ἐνέργεια, ἡ δὲ πήρωσις στέρησίς ἐστι τῆς φυσικῆς ἐνέργειας, οὕτως καὶ ἡ ἀρετὴ πρὸς τὴν κακίαν ἀνθέστηκεν· οὐ γὰρ ἔστιν ἄλλην κακίας γένεσιν ἐννοῆσαι, ἢ ἀρετῆς ἀπουσίαν. Comp. c. 6, c. 22, c. 28, and the Dial. de Anima et Resurrectione. *J. Müller*, l.c. s. 132.

(4) That sin was *in contradiction* with God's purposes, was the practically weighty position held fast by the Church in all its different definitions of sin. "*Augustine, too, everywhere remains true to this denial of the divine origination of sin. Though the opposite opinion has been often imposed upon him in past and present times, on account of his doctrines of the moral incapacity of human nature and of divine predestination, yet this belongs to those groundless inferences which have been so freely drawn, especially with reference to this great teacher of the Church,*" Julius *Müller*, l.c. s. 308. A more precise definition is given by the theologians after the time of *Augustine.* Thus *Gregory* I. makes a distinction between peccatum and delictum: Peccatum est mala facere, delictum

vero est bona relinquere, quæ summopere sunt tenenda. Vel certe peccatum in opere est, delictum in cogitatione; in Ezech. lib. ii. Hom. 9, p. 1404. He also distinguishes between peccatum et crimen;[1] every crimen is a peccatum, but not *vice versa*. No one is sine peccato, but many are sine crimine (Tit. i. 6; 1 John i. 8). The peccata only stain the soul, the crimina kill it; Moral. xxi. c. 12. The iniquitas, impietas, etc., are also represented as modifications of sin; Moral. xi. 42, xxii. 10. The deepest root of all sin, according to *Gregory*, is pride; pride produces envy, wrath, etc. The seat of sin is both in the soul and in the body; the devil is one of the chief agents in inducing man to commit sin; comp. *Lau*, s. 379 ff.

(5) *Augustine* still endeavours to reconcile the mystic interpretation of Paradise with the historical; De Civit. Dei, xiii. 21. Moreover, he sees all individual sins comprised in the primitive sin; comp. Enchiridion ad Laurentium, c. 45: In illo peccato uno . . . possunt intelligi plura peccata, si unum ipsum in sua quasi membra singula dividatur. Nam et *superbia* est illic, quia homo in sua potius esse quam in Dei potestate dilexit; et *sacrilegium*, quia Deo non credidit; et *homicidium*, quia se præcipitavit in mortem; et *fornicatio* spiritalis, quia integritas mentis humanæ serpentina suasione corrupta est; et *furtum* quia cibus prohibitus usurpatus est; et *avaritia*, quia plus quam illi sufficere debuit, adpetivit; et si quid aliud in hoc uno admisso diligenti consideratione inveniri potest. *Gregory the Great* adopts the literal interpretation; Mor. xxxi., comp. *Lau*, s. 377 ff. The devil tempted our first parents in a threefold manner, gula, vana gloria, and avaritia. The attack itself was fourfold, by suggestio, delectatio, consensus, and defensionis audacia; Mor. iv. c. 27.

§ 108.

Consequences of the First Sin, and Freedom of the Will (according to the Teachers of the Greek Church).

A. Hahn, Ephräm der Syrer über die Willensfreiheit des Menschen, nebst den Theorien derjenigen Kirchenlehrer bis zu seiner Zeit, welche hier besondere

---

[1] This distinction, however, had been already made by *Augustine*; see below, § 111, 2.

Berücksichtigung verdienen (in Illgens Denkschrift der hist. theol. Gesellschaft zu Leipzig 1819, 2, s. 30 ff.). [Comp. *Landerer*, Verhältniss von Gnade und Freiheit, in Jahrb. f. deutsche Theologie, 1857, s. 556, 572, on *Chrysostom*, s. 549-561. *Kuhn*, d. angebliche Pelagianismus der voraugustinischen Kirchenväter, in Theol. Quartalschrift, 1853. *Wörter*, Christl. Lehre über d. Verhältniss von Gnade u. Freiheit, Band i. 1856, Band ii. 1, 1860.]

Even those theologians who kept themselves free from the influence of the *Augustinian* system, held that the sin of Adam was followed by disastrous consequences to the human race; but restricted these evil consequences (as the Fathers of the preceding period had done) to the mortality of the body, the hardships and miseries of life, also admitting that the moral powers of man had been enfeebled by the fall. Thus *Gregory* of Nazianzus, in particular (to whom *Augustine* appealed in preference to all others), maintained that both the νοῦς and the ψυχή have been considerably impaired by sin, and regarded the perversion of the religious consciousness seen in idolatry, which previous teachers had ascribed to the influence of demons, as an inevitable effect of the first sin. But *he* was far from asserting the total depravity of mankind, and the entire loss of free-will (1). On the contrary, the doctrine of the freedom of the will continued to be distinctly maintained by the Greek Church (2). *Athanasius* himself, the father of orthodoxy, maintained in the strongest terms that man has the ability of choosing good as well as evil, and even allowed exceptions from original sin, alleging that several individuals, even before Christ, had remained free from it (3). *Cyril* of Jerusalem also maintained that the life of man begins in a state of innocence, and that sin enters only with the use of free-will. Similar views were entertained by *Ephraem Syrus*, *Gregory* of Nyssa, *Basil the Great*, and others (4). *Chrysostom*, whose whole tendency was of a practical and moral kind, insisted most of all upon the liberty of man and his moral self-determination, and passed a severe censure upon those who endeavoured to excuse their own defects by ascribing the origin of sin to the fall of Adam (5).

(1) Orat. xxxviii. 12, p. 670, xliv. 4, p. 837, xiv. 25, p. 275, xix. 13, p. 372; Carmen iv. v. 98, and other passages quoted by *Ullmann*, s. 421 ff. Comp. especially the interesting parallel which is there drawn between *Gregory* and *Augustine*, as well as between the expressions of the former in the original, and the (corrupt) translation of the latter. " *Gregory by no means taught the doctrines afterwards propounded by Pelagius and his followers; but if all his sentiments be duly considered, it will be found that he is far more of a Pelagian than of an Augustinian,*" *Ullmann*, l.c. s. 439 f.

(2) According to *Methodius* (in *Phot.* Bibl. Cod. 234, p. 295), man does not possess the power either of *having* desires, or of not having them (ἐνθυμεῖσθαι ἢ μὴ ἐνθυμεῖσθαι), but he is at liberty either to gratify (χρῆσθαι) them or not. Comp. *Nemes.* De Nat. Hom. c. 41: Πᾶσα τοίνυν ἀνάγκη τὸν ἔχοντα τὸ βουλεύεσθαι καὶ κύριον εἶναι πράξεων. Εἰ γὰρ μὴ κύριος εἴη πράξεων, περιττῶς ἔχει τὸ βουλεύεσθαι.

(3) *Athan.* Contra Gent. c. 2, p. 2: Ἐξ ἀρχῆς μὲν οὐκ ἦν κακία, οὐδὲ γὰρ οὐδὲ νῦν ἐν τοῖς ἁγίοις ἐστὶν, οὐδ' ὅλως κατ' αὐτοὺς ὑπάρχει αὐτή, cf. Contra Arian. Or. 3 (4). Opp. t. i. p. 582, 583: Πολλοὶ γὰρ οὖν ἅγιοι γεγόνασι καθαροὶ πάσης ἁμαρτίας. (He alludes to Jeremiah and John the Baptist; but they cannot properly be called πολλοί.) " Nevertheless, death reigned . . . even over them that had not sinned after the similitude of Adam's transgression" (Rom. v. 14).

(4) *Cyr.* Cat. iv. 19: Ἐλθόντες εἰς τόνδε τὸν κόσμον ἀναμάρτητοι, νῦν ἐκ προαιρέσεως ἁμαρτάνομεν. 21: Αὐτεξούσιός ἐστιν ἡ ψυχὴ, καὶ ὁ διάβολος τὸ μὲν ὑποβάλλειν δύναται· τὸ δὲ καὶ ἀναγκάσαι παρὰ προαίρεσιν οὐκ ἔχει τὴν ἐξουσίαν. Cat. xvi. 23: Εἰ γάρ τις ἀβλεπτῶν μὴ καταξιοῦται τῆς χάριτος, μὴ μεμφέσθω τῷ πνεύματι, ἀλλὰ τῇ ἑαυτοῦ ἀπιστίᾳ. (*Oudin*, Comm. p. 461–464, attempted in vain to contest the genuineness of the catecheses favourable to Semi - Pelagianism.) — Concerning *Ephraem*, see the above dissertation. — *Basil the Great* delivered a discourse περὶ τοῦ αὐτεξουσίου, the authenticity of which was denied by *Garnier* (t. ii. p. xxvi.), but in modern times again defended by *Pelt* and *Rheinwald* (Homiliarium Patrist. i. 2, p. 192). In this, though he admitted the depravity of mankind, he asserted that human liberty and divine grace must co-operate.

Comp. also the Hom. de Spir. S., and *Klose*, l.c. s. 59 ff. [cf. *Landerer*, ubi supra, s. 556].—*Gregory Nyss.* also takes for granted a universal bias to sin (De Orat. Dom. Or. v. Opp. i. p. 751 s.), but finds no sin in infants; Orat. de infantibus qui præmature abripiuntur (Opp. iii. p. 317 s.).

(5) See Hom. in Ep. ad Rom. xvi. p. 241; in Ep. ad Hebr. Hom. xii. p. 805 D; in Evang. Joh. Hom. xvii. p. 115 C; in 1 Epist. ad Cor. Hom. ii. p. 514 D; in Ps. l. Hom. ii. (Opp. t. iii. p. 869 D); all of which are quoted by *Münscher, von Cölln,* i. s. 363; see also Ep. ad Phil. Hom. i. (especially on Phil. i. 6). "*Chrysostom was so zealous for morality, that he must have considered it a point of special importance to deprive men of every ground of excuse for the neglect of moral effort. His practical sphere of labour in the cities of Antioch and Constantinople gave a still greater impulse to this tendency. For in these great capitals he met with many who sought to attribute their want of Christian activity to the defects of human nature, and the power of Satan or of fate,*" Neander, Kg. iii. 2, s. 1369 f. Comp. his Chrysostomus, i. s. 51, 283 ff. But *Chrysostom* urged quite as strongly the existence of depravity in opposition to a false moral pride. Hom. vi. Montf. t. 12 (in *Neander*, Chrysostomus, ii. s. 36, 37), comp. *Wiggers,* i. s. 442.

§ 109.

The Opinions of the Latin Teachers before Augustine, and of Augustine before the Pelagian Controversy.

During this period, as well as the preceding, the theologians of the western Church were more favourable than those of the eastern to the Augustinian doctrine. Even *Arnobius* speaks of a connatural infirmity, making man prone to sin (1). *Hilary* and *Ambrose* of Milan taught the defilement of sin by birth; *Ambrose* appealed especially to Ps. li. 5 in support of original sin, but without determining to what extent every individual shares in the common guilt (2). Nevertheless, neither of them excluded the liberty of man from the work of moral reformation (3). Even *Augustine* himself, at an earlier period of his life, defended human freedom, in opposition to the Manichæans (4).

(1) *Arnobius*, Adv. Gentes, i. 27: Proni ad culpas et ad libidinis varios appetitus, vitio sumus infirmitatis ingenitæ.

(2) *Hilar.* Tract. in Ps. lviii. p. 129; in Ps. cxviii. litt. 22, 6, p. 366; in Matt. xviii. 6: Ovis una, homo intelligendus est, et sub homine uno, universitas sentienda est; sed in unius Adæ errore omne hominum genus aberravit; and some other passages (in *Münscher, von Cölln*, s. 354). Cf. *Neander*, Dg. s. 357. *Ambrose,* Apol. David. c. 11 (Opp. i. p. 846): Antequam nascamur, maculamur contagio, et ante usuram lucis, originis ipsius excipimus injuriam; in iniquitate concipimur: non expressit, utrum parentum, an nostra. Et in delictis generat unumquemque mater sua; nec hic declaravit, utrum in delictis suis mater pariat, an jam sint et aliqua delicta nascentis. Sed vide, ne utrumque intelligendum sit. Nec conceptus iniquitatis exsors est, quoniam et parentes non carent lapsu. Et si nec unius diei infans sine peccato est, multo magis nec illi materni conceptus dies sine peccato sunt. Concipimur ergo in peccato parentum et in delictis eorum nascimur. Sed et ipse partus habet contagia sua, nec unum tantummodo habet ipsa natura contagium. [*Ambrose*, Apol. David. § 71: Omnes in primo homine peccavimus et per naturæ successionem culpæ quoque ab uno in omnes transfusa est successio.] Comp. De Pœnit. i. 3 (Opp. iii. p. 498): Omnes homines sub peccato nascimur, quorum ipse ortus in vitio est, sicut habes lectum, dicente David: *Ecce enim in iniquitatibus conceptus sum, et in delictis peperit me mater mea.* — In Ev. Luke i. 17 (Opp. i. p. 737); Epp. Class. ii. (Opp. iii. p. 1190), and some other passages (in *Münscher, von Cölln*, s. 355; after another edition ?).

(3) *Hilar.* Tract. in Psalm. cxviii. lit. 15, p. 329: Est quidem in fide *manendi* a Deo munus, *sed incipiendi a nobis origo est.* Et voluntas nostra hoc proprium ex se habere debet, ut velit. Deus incipienti incrementum dabit, quia consummationem per se infirmitas nostra non obtinet; meritum tamen adipiscendæ consummationis est ex initio voluntatis. Comp.

also *Arnobius*, Adv. Gentes, ii. 64 : Nulli Deus infert necessitatem, imperiosa formidine nullum tenet ... 65 : Quid est enim tam injustum, quam repugnantibus, quam invitis extorquere in contrarium voluntates, inculcare quod nolint et quod refugiant animis.

(4) De Gen. contra Manich. ii. 43 (c. 29): Nos dicimus nulli naturæ nocere peccata nisi sua; nos dicimus, nullum malum esse naturale, sed omnes naturas bonas esse. — De lib. Arb. iii. 50 (c. 17): Aut enim et ipsa voluntas est et a radice ista voluntatis non receditur, aut non est voluntas, et peccatum nullum habet. Aut igitur ipsa voluntas est prima causa peccandi. Non est cui recte imputetur peccatum, nisi peccanti. Non est ergo, cui recte imputetur, nisi volenti ... Quæcunque ista causa est voluntatis : si non ei potest resisti, sine peccato ei ceditur; si autem potest, non ei cedatur, et non peccabitur. An forte *fallit* incautum ? Ergo caveat, ne fallatur. An tanta fallacia est, ut caveri omnino non possit ? Si ita est, nulla peccata sunt : quis enim peccat in eo, quod nullo modo caveri potest ? Peccatur autem; caveri igitur potest. Comp. de Duab. Animab. contra Manich. 12 ; and, on the other hand, the Retractationes on the different passages; also de nat. et grat. 80 (c. 67). On the relation between the earlier and the later views of *Augustine* on the nature of sin, comp. also *Baur*, Dg. i. 2, s. 294 ff.

§ 110.

The Pelagian Controversy.

*G. F. Wiggers, Versuch einer pragmatischen Darstellung des Augustinismus und Pelagianismus, Berlin 1821, Hamburg 1833, ii. 8. †*J. A. Lentzen*, de Pelagianorum doctrinæ principiis, Colon. ad Rhen. 1833. *J. L. Jacobi*, die Lehre des Pelagius, Lpz. 1842. [*Theod. Gangauf*, Metaph. Psychologie des heil. Augustinus, Augsb. 1852. *Jul. Müller*, Der Pelagianismus, in Deutsche Zeitschrift, 1855. *Hampden's* Bampton Lectures, Lect. iv.] *W. Möller*, Pelagius und die pelagianischen Streitigkeiten, in *Herzog's* Realencykl. xi. s. 268 ff.

Towards the commencement of the fifth century *Cœlestius* and *Pelagius* (Briton, Morgan ?) made their appearance in the

§ 110.] THE PELAGIAN CONTROVERSY. 419

West (1). The views which they held were partly in accordance with the opinions hitherto entertained by the theologians of the Greek Church, but in part carried to a much greater length in the denial of natural depravity. Some of the propositions, on the ground of which the presbyter *Paulinus* accused *Cœlestius* at the Synod of Carthage (A.D. 412), had been previously defended by orthodox theologians; others were directly opposed both to the doctrine of Scripture (and especially that of Paul) and to the general belief of the Church, and thus threatened the fundamental doctrines of the gospel (2). It is, however, difficult to decide how far *Pelagius* accorded with all these assertions, since he expressed himself very cautiously (3). But it is certain that what is commonly called *Pelagianism* does not so much represent the single notions of a single individual as a complete *moral and religious system*, which formed a decided contrast to *Augustinianism*. In this conflict the former system was vanquished so far as this, that, in consequence of the turn which the controversy took, and of the great authority of *Augustine* in the West, his doctrine gained the victory over that of *Pelagius* (4). The followers of *Pelagius* did not form a sect properly so called. But Pelagianism, though condemned, retained its advocates, especially as but few could fully enter into all the consequences of the Augustinian system, and find in them real inward satisfaction. It will be necessary, in order to examine more fully the antagonistic elements, to divide the subject-matter of controversy into three leading sections, viz.: 1. Sin; 2. Grace and Liberty; and 3. Predestination.

(1) On the personal character and history of *Cœlestius* and *Pelagius*, see *Wiggers*, s. 33 ff., and *Neander*, Dg. s. 361.

(2) The 6 or 7 Capitula (the numbers vary according as several propositions are separated or joined together) are preserved in *Augustine*, De Gestis Pelagii, cap. 11 (comp. De Peccato Originali, 2, 3, 4, 11, c. 2–10), as well as in the two commonitoria of *Marius Mercator* [comp. *Gieseler*, § 87, note 4] They are the following (comp. *Wiggers*, i. s. 60):—

1. Adam was created mortal, so that he would have died whether he had sinned or not.
2. Adam's sin injured only himself, and not the human race.
3. New-born infants are in the same condition in which Adam was previous to the fall (ante prævaricationem).
4. Neither does the whole human race die in consequence of Adam's death or transgression; nor does it rise from the dead in consequence of Christ's resurrection.
5. Infants obtain eternal life, though they be not baptized.
6. The law is as good a means of salvation (lex sic mittit ad regnum cœlorum) as the gospel.
7. There were some men, even before the appearance of Christ, who were without sin.

If we compare these propositions with the doctrines of the earlier theologians, we find that the third was held by some of the Greek Fathers (*e.g.* *Theophilus* of Antioch and *Clement* of Alexandria, see above, § 62, note 1); that the fifth, in a modified form, was substantially defended by *Gregory* of Nazianzus and others, viz. that unbaptized children are at least not condemned on that account (comp. § 72 on baptism); and even as to the seventh, bold as it may appear, something like it, though in a different connection, was maintained by the father of orthodoxy himself (§ 108, note 3). On the other hand, the isolated way in which the sin of Adam is viewed in the first two and the fourth propositions, all connection between this sin and that of his posterity, even in relation to the mortality of the body, being denied, would have been condemned as heresy before the tribunal of the earlier theologians. But none appears so heretical, so much opposed to the doctrine of Paul and the gospel, as the sixth. And, lastly, the denial of the connection subsisting between the resurrection of Christ and ours (in the fourth proposition) must have offended the common feelings and consciousness of Christians. Yet it may still be a question, how much here is to be ascribed to inferences, made for them by their opponents. See *Neander*, Kg. ii. 3, s. 1219, and Dg. s. 360 ff.

(3) *Augustine* perceives no other difference between *Pelagius* and *Cœlestius* (De Pecc. Orig. c. 12) than that the latter was more open, the former more guarded; the latter more obstinate,

the former more deceitful,—or, to say the least, that the latter was more straightforward (liberior), the former more cunning (astutior). *Prosper* of Aquitaine calls him, therefore, coluber Britannus (in his poem De Ingratis, append. 67 ; comp. *Wiggers,* s. 40). — *Neander* (Chrysostomus, Bd. ii. s. 134) judges more mildly of him : " *Pelagius is deserving of all esteem on account of his honest zeal ; his object was to combat the same perverse anti-Christian tendency which Augustine opposed. But he was wrong in the manner in which he sought to attain his object,*" etc. Comp. Kg. ii. 3, s. 1195 ff., Dg. s. 365. "*As far as we know him through his writings, he was a clear-headed, intelligent man, who possessed rather a serious and moral turn of mind, than that disposition which feels itself compelled to dive into the depths of the soul and spirit, and to bring to light hidden things,*" s. 1199.

(4) THE PRINCIPAL POINTS IN THE EXTERNAL HISTORY OF THE CONTROVERSY ARE: The condemnation of the doctrine of *Pelagius* at Carthage, A.D. 412. He repairs to Palestine, where *Jerome* becomes one of his most zealous opponents, and, conjointly with *Paulus Orosius,* a disciple of *Augustine,* accuses him at a synod held at Jerusalem (A.D. 415), under *John,* Bishop of Jerusalem. John, however, did not pronounce his condemnation, but reported the whole matter to Innocent, Bishop of Rome. — Synod at Diospolis (Lydda), under *Eulogius* of Cæsarea. The accusers were *Heros* of Arles, and *Lazarus* of Aix. Acquittal of *Pelagius.* Dissatisfaction of *Jerome* with the decisions of this synod (Synodus miserabilis ! Ep. 81). — Under *Zosimus,* the successor of Innocent, *Pelagius* and *Cœlestius* entertain new hopes. — Synod of the North African bishops at Carthage, A.D. 418, and condemnation of *Pelagius.* — The Emperor Honorius decides the controversy. — *Zosimus* is induced to change his view, and publishes his Epistola Tractoria, in which also the Pelagian doctrine is condemned. *Julian,* Bishop of Eclanum in Apulia, undertakes to defend Pelagianism (respecting him, see *Wiggers,* i. s. 43 ff.). — He was anathematized at the Synod of Ephesus (A.D. 431), in (accidental ?) connection with *Nestorius.* Still the opposite system of *Augustine* was not accepted in the East. [See the Pelagian controversy in *St. Augustine*—The Fathers for English readers. Lond. S. P. C. K.]

§ 111.

First Point of Controversy.

Sin.—Original Sin and its Consequences.

[*J. Nirschl,* Ursprung und Wesen der Sünde nach d. Lehre des heiligen Augustinus, Regensb. 1854. *Julius Müller,* Lehre· von d. Sünde, ii. 417–494. *Voigt,* De Theoria Aug. Pelag., Götting. 1829. *Lentzen,* De Pelag. Doctr. Principiis, Colon. 1833.]

Pelagius, starting from the standpoint of mere reflection, or of the understanding in distinction from the reason, with a tendency preponderating to the ethical view of man's nature, looked upon every human individual as a moral personality, complete in and bounded by himself, and sharply separated from all others. Hence sin would necessarily appear to him as the free act of the individual, so that in his view there could be no other connection between the sin of the one (Adam) and the sin of the many (his posterity), than that which exists between an example on the one hand, and a voluntary imitation of it on the other. Every man at his birth is accordingly in the same condition in which Adam was. Neither sin nor virtue is inborn, but the one as well as the other developes itself in the use of freedom, and is to be put to the account only of him who exercises this freedom (1). *Augustine,* on the contrary, with more profound conceptions, which, however, might easily prevent a clear insight into the personal and moral relations of man, considered the human race as a compact mass, a collective body, responsible in its unity and solidarity. With a predominant bias towards religion, he directed his attention more to the inner and permanent state of the soul and its absolute relation to God, than to the passing and external actions of the individual. This tendency, proceeding from the experience of his own heart and life, led him to conjecture a mysterious connection subsisting between the transgression of Adam and the sin of all men—a connection which loses itself in the dim beginnings of nature no less than of history. Mere suppositions, however, did not satisfy his mind; but, carrying out his system in all its logical consequences, and applying a false exegesis to certain passages, he laid down the following rigid proposition as his doctrine:—"*As all men have sinned in Adam, they are justly subject to the condemnation of God on account of this hereditary sin and the guilt thereof*" (2).

(1) *Pelag.* lib. 1, De Lib. Arb., in Aug. De Pecc. Orig. c. 13: Omne bonum ac malum, quo vel laudabiles, vel vituperabiles sumus, non nobiscum *oritur*, sed *agitur* a nobis: *capaces* enim utriusque rei, non *pleni* nascimur, et ut sine virtute, ita et sine vitio procreamur, atque ante actionem propriæ voluntatis id solum in homine est, quod Deus condidit; he even admits the preponderance of *good* in man, when he (according to *August.* De Nat. et Grat. c. 21) speaks of a *naturalis quædam sanctitas*, which dwells in man, and keeps watch in the castle of the soul over good and evil, and by which he means *conscience.* Comp. *Julian* (quoted by *August.* in Op. Imp. i. 105): Illud quod esse peccatum ratio demonstrat, inveniri nequit in seminibus. 122: Nemo naturaliter malus est: sed quicunque reus est, moribus, non exordiis accusatur. Other passages may be found in *Münscher, von Cölln*, i. s. 375 ff. [L. ii. 66: *In omnes* autem *homines* mors *pertransiit*, quia una forma judicii prevaricatores quosque etiam reliquæ comprehendit ætatis; quæ tamen mors nec in sanctos, nec in innocentes ullos sævire permittitur, sed in eos pervadit quos prævaricationem viderit æmulatos.] Comp. *Wiggers*, s. 91 ff. *Augustine* himself protested against the expression peccatum naturæ or peccatum naturale which the Pelagians imputed to him, and always substituted his phrase—peccatum originale. The Pelagians considered bodily death not as a punishment of the first sin, but as a physical necessity, though *Pelagius* himself conceded, at the Synod of Diospolis, that the death of Adam was a punishment inflicted upon Adam, but only upon him. *Aug.* De Nat. et Gr. 21 (c. 19); Op. Imp. i. 67, vi. 27, 30. Yet *Pelagius* did not deny the power of sin; he even asserted an increasing degradation of the human race; but he explained

this from the long habit of sinning and bad example. Epist. ad Demetriadem, c. 8 : Longa consuetudo vitiorum, quæ nos infecit a parvo paulatimque per multos corrupit annos, et ita postea obligatos sibi et addictos tenet, ut *vim quodammodo videatur habere naturæ.* Cf. *Schröckh,* Kg. xiv. s. 344.

(2) A list of the works in which *Augustine* combated the Pelagians will be found in *Münscher, von Cölln,* s. 373. The passages bearing on this question, which can be understood, however, only in their connection, are also given there, s. 377 ff. (Comp. De Pecc. Mer. i. 2, 4, 21 ; Opus Imp. vi. 30 ; De Pecc. Mer. i. 10 ; De Nupt. et Concup. i. 27, ii. 57–59 ; Op. Imp. i. 47 ; De Nupt. et Concup. i. 26 ; De Pecc. Orig. 36 ; De Con. et Grat. 28. In support of his views he appealed to infant baptism: De Pecc. Mer. i. 39, iii. 7 ; Contra Jul. vi. 6 ; De Pecc. Mer. i. 21 ; Enchirid. 93 ; to the formulas of exorcism: De Pecc. Orig. 45 ; and principally to Rom. v. 12.) *Wiggers,* s. 99 ff. [De Civit. Dei, xiv. 1 : A primis hominibus admissum est tam grande peccatum, ut in deterius eo natura mutaretur humana, etiam in posteros *obligatione peccati et mortis necessitate transmissa.*—De Corrept. et Grat. x. (28) : Adam, quia per liberum arbitrium Deum deseruit, justum judicium Dei expertus est ; ut *cum tota sua stirpe,* quæ in illo adhuc posita tota cum illo peccaverat, damnaretur. —De Pecc. Orig. c. 38 : Deus nihil fecit nisi quod hominem voluntate peccantem justo judicio cum stirpe damnavit, et ideo ibi quidquid etiam nondum erat natum, merito est in prævaricatrice radice damnatum ; in qua stirpe damnata, tenet hominem generatio carnalis. De Nupt. et Concup. 11, c. 5 : Per unius illius voluntatem malam omnes in eo peccaverunt, quando omnes ille unus fuerunt, de quo propterea singuli peccatum originale traxerunt. De Civit. Dei, viii. 14 : Deus enim creavit hominem rectum, naturarum auctor non utique vitiorum ; sed sponte depravatus justeque damnatus, depravatos damnatosque generabit. *Omnes enim fuimus in illo, quando fuimus ille unus.* Nondum erat nobis singillatim creata et distributa forma, in qua singuli viveremus ; sed jam natura erat seminalis, ex qua propagaremur ; qua scilicet propter peccata vitiata, et vinculo mortis obstricta, justeque damnata, non alterius conditionis homo ex homine nascetur. Ibid. xiv. 15 : Adam faciendo voluntatem suam non ejus, a quo

factus est, universum genus humanum, propagine vitiata, *culpæ et pœnæ fecit obnoxium.* Ibid. xxii. 24: In originali malo duo sunt, *peccatum atque supplicium.*]—On *Augustine's* interpretation of Rom. v. 12 (*in quo* omnes peccaverunt, Vulg.), see Op. Imp. ii. 47 ss., 66, contra duas Epp. Pel. iv. 7 (c. 4); *Julian*, on the other hand, gives the following explanation: *in quo* omnes peccaverunt nihil aliud indicat, quam: quia omnes peccaverunt. *Augustine's* exposition was confirmed by the Synod of Carthage (A.D. 418). Comp. *Münscher, von Cölln*, s. 381, 382. But it would be a great mistake, a merely atomistic procedure, to ascribe the whole theory of *Augustine* to this exegetical error. Deeper causes gave rise to that theory, viz.: (1) His own experience, moulded by the remarkable events in the history of his external and internal life; (2) Perhaps some vestiges of his former Manichæan notions, of which he might himself be unconscious, *e.g.* that of defilement in the act of generation (comp. De Nupt. et Concup. i. 27: Concupiscence, he says, is not attributed to the regenerate as sin; but in its own nature it is not without sin, it is the daughter and the mother of sin: hence every one conceived and born in the way of nature, is under sin until he is born again through *Him*—quem sine ista concupiscentia virgo concepit[1]); (3) His realistic mode of thinking, which led him to confound the abstract with the concrete, and to consider the individual as a transient and vanishing part of the whole (massa perditionis). In connection with this mode of thinking, other causes might be: (4) His notions of the Church as a living organism, and of the effects of infant baptism; (5) The opposition which he was compelled to make to Pelagianism and its possible consequences, threatening to destroy all deeper views of the Christian system. — Thus, according to *Augustine*, not only was physical death a punishment inflicted upon Adam and all his posterity, but he looked upon *original sin itself as being in some sense a punishment of the first transgression,* though it was also a real sin (God punishes sin by sin), and can therefore be imputed to every

---

[1] "However little *Augustine* was satisfied by Manichæism, it is probable that the attraction, which at one period of his life he felt towards this system, proceeded from his consciousness of the power of evil in man's nature, a consciousness by which he was throughout his life deeply penetrated," *Baur*, Dg. i. 2, s. 29.

individual. But it is on this very point, first, strongly emphasized by him, viz. the *imputation* of original sin, that his views differed from all former opinions, however strict they were, on the fall of man.—He endeavoured to clear himself from the charge of Manichæism (in opposition to *Julian*) by designating sin not as a *substance*, but as a *vitium*, a languor; he even charged his opponent with Manichæism. So, too, *Augustine* could very well distinguish between the *sin*, which is common to all men, and personal crime, from which the pious are preserved. Enchir. 64: Neque enim quia peccatum est omne crimen, ideo crimen est etiam omne peccatum. Itaque sanctorum hominum vitam, quam diu in hac mortali (*al.* morte) vivitur, inveniri posse dicimus sine crimine; "*peccatum autem, si dixerimus quia non habemus, nosmet ipsos seducimus, et veritas in nobis non est*" (1 John i. 8).—Respecting his views of the insignificant remnant (lineamenta extrema) of the divine image left in man, and of the virtues of the heathen, see *Wiggers*, s. 119, Anm.

§ 112.

Second Point of Controversy.

Liberty and Grace.

Pelagius admitted that man, in his moral activity, stands in need of divine aid, and could therefore speak of the *grace of God* assisting the weakness of man by a variety of provisions (1). He supposed, however, this grace of God to be something external, and added to the efforts put forth by the free will of man; it can even be merited by man's good will (2). *Augustine*, on the other hand, looked upon grace as the creative principle of life, which generates as an abiding good that freedom of the will which is entirely lost in the natural man. In the power of the natural man to choose between good and evil, to which great importance was attached by *Pelagius*, as well as by the earlier Church, he saw only a liberty to do evil, since the regenerate man alone can actually will the good (3).

(1) On this point *Pelagius* expresses himself clearly, as follows (in *August. De Grat.* c. 5): Primo loco posse statuimus, secundo velle, tertio esse. Posse in natura, velle in arbitrio, esse in effectu locamus. Primum illud, *i.e.* posse ad Deum proprie pertinet, qui illud creaturæ suæ contulit; duo vero reliqua, h. e. velle et esse, ad hominem referenda sunt, quia de arbitrii fonte descendunt. Ergo in voluntate et opere laus hominis est, immo et hominis *et* Dei, qui *ipsius* voluntatis et operis possibilitatem dedit, quique ipsam possibilitatem gratiæ suæ adjuvat semper auxilio. Quod vero *potest* homo velle bonum atque perficere, solius Dei est. Hence man also owes to God, that he *can* will, as is said in what follows: quod possumus omne bonum facere, dicere, cogitare, illius est, *qui hoc posse donavit*, qui hoc posse adjuvat. Comp. c. 18: Habemus autem possibilitatem a Deo insitam, velut quandam, ut ita dicam, radicem fructiferam atque fecundam, etc. The freedom of the will is common to Jews, Gentiles, and Christians; *grace*, according to *Pelagius* himself, is something exclusively Christian. *Pelagius* also rejected the proposition of *Cœlestius:* " gratiam Dei non ad singulos actus dari." [*Münscher, von Cölln*, i. s. 386.]

(2) *Pelagius* considered as means of grace, especially *doctrine*, as the manifestation of the divine will, promises, and trials (to which belong the wiles of Satan); but *Julian* strongly denied that the will of man is first created by grace (fabricetur, condatur); he sees in them nothing but an *adjutorium* of the undisturbed free will. Comp. *Aug. De Grat. Chr.* c. 8, Op. Imp. i. 94, 95. [*Münscher*, l.c. s. 387, 388.] *Julius Müller* justly remarks (in his work on Sin, 1st ed., s. 475) that *Pelagius* has not the idea of development: " *he has not the conception of a life unfolding itself; he only recognizes the mechanical concatenation of single acts.*" Distinction of real and formal freedom. Comp., too, *Neander*, Dg. 385, on the different stages of the divine revelation of grace [corresponding in the view of *Pelagius* to its progressive deterioration].

(3) *Augustine*, on the contrary, maintains: Non lege atque doctrina insonante forinsecus, sed interna et occulta, mirabili ac ineffabili potestate operari Deum in cordibus hominum non solum veras revelationes, sed bonas etiam voluntates (De Grat. Chr. 24). He recognizes in the grace of God an inspiratio

dilectionis, and considers this as the source of everything. Nolentem prævenit, ut velit; volentem subsequitur, ne frustra velit (Enchir. c. 32).—He understands by freedom the being free from sin, that state of mind in which it is no longer necessary to choose between good and evil. The same view is expressed in his treatise De Civit. Dei, xiv. 11, which was not written against the Pelagians : Arbitrium igitur voluntatis tunc est vere liberum, cum vitiis peccatisque non servit. Tale datum est a Deo: quod amissum proprio vitio, nisi a quo dari potuit, reddi non potest. Unde Veritas dicit: *Si vos Filius liberavit, tunc vere liberi eritis.* Idque ipsum est autem, ac si diceret: si vos Filius salvos fecerit, tunc vere salvi eritis. Inde quippe liberator, unde salvator. Comp. contra duas Epp. Pel. i. 2. The freedom of the will is greater in proportion as the will itself is in a state of health; its state of health depends on its subjection to the divine mercy and grace.— Contra Jul. ii. c. 8, he calls the human will servum propriæ voluntatis arbitrium.—Such expressions were so much misused by the monks of Adrumetum (about the year 426), that *Augustine* himself was compelled to oppose them (especially in his treatise De Correptione et Gratia); in general, he himself frequently appealed from a practical point of view to the will of man (see the next section). [For a more detailed statement of *Augustine's* views respecting grace and the freedom of the will, see *Münscher, von Cölln,* i. § 93, and s. 388–398, where further passages are quoted.] At any rate, it was not the view of *Augustine* that man is like a stone or stick, upon whom grace works externally; he could conceive of grace as working only in the sphere of freedom. Comp. Contra Julianum, iv. 15: Neque enim gratia Dei lapidibus aut lignis pecoribusve præstatur, sed quia imago Dei est (homo), meretur hanc gratiam. De Peccat. Merit. et Remiss. ii. § 6 : Non sicut in lapidibus insensatis aut sicut in iis, in quorum natura rationem voluntatemque non condidit salutem nostram Deus operatur in nobis. [*Julius Müller* in his work on Sin, i. 458 ff., shows that *Augustine* spoke of freedom under three aspects : (1) As spontaneity, in contrast with external force. This always exists in all men. (2) Power of choice, liberum arbitrium,—as in Adam before the fall,—an equal power of deciding between the alternatives of good and evil. But this is a low, weak state of the will. (3) The freedom with which the Son makes us free—the determination of the soul to what is good and holy—the non posse peccare—the felix necessitas boni—the union of freedom and necessity.]

[*Baur*, Dogmengesch. s. 179 ff.: In the system of Pelagius everything depends upon the principle of the freedom of the will; this is the determining and fundamental conception in his doctrine of sin and of grace. Freedom, as the absolute capacity of choice (liberum arbitrium), to determine equally for good or evil, appeared to him in such a degree to be the substantial good of human nature, that he even reckoned the capacity for evil as a *bonum naturæ*, since we cannot choose good without in like manner being able to choose evil (Epist. ad Demetr. c. 2, 3).]

§ 113.

Third Point of Controversy.

Predestination.

[*J. B. Mozley*, Augustinian Doctrine of Predestination, Lond. 1855.]

Augustine held the doctrine of hereditary depravity, the guilt of which man has himself incurred, and from which no human power or human determination can deliver; from which only the grace of God can save those to whom it is imparted. From these premises it would necessarily follow that God, in consequence of an eternal decree, and without any reference to the future conduct of man, has elected (1) some out of the corrupt mass to become vessels of His mercy (vasa misericordiæ), and left the rest as vessels of His wrath (vasa iræ) to a just condemnation. Augustine called the former *predestinatio*, the latter *reprobatio*, and thus evaded the necessity of directly asserting the doctrine of a predestination to evil (predestinatio duplex) (2). On the whole, he endeavoured to soften the harshness of his theory by practical cautions (3). But the doctrine in question became to many a stone of stumbling, which orthodox theologians themselves (especially those of the Greek Church) endeavoured by every possible means to remove (4). This prepared the way for those practically well-meant but theoretically vague and unfounded schemes, which *Semi-Pelagianism* (see the following section) brought to light.

(1) De Præd. Sanctorum, 37 (c. 18): Elegit nos Deus in Christo ante mundi constitutionem, prædestinans nos in adoptionem filiorum : non quia per nos sancti et immaculati futuri eramus, sed elegit prædestinavitque, ut essemus. Fecit autem hoc secundum placitum voluntatis suæ, ut nemo de sua, sed de illius erga se voluntate glorietur, etc. In support of his views he appealed to Eph. i. 4, 11, and Rom. ix.: he spoke, too, of a *certus numerus electorum, neque augendus, neque minuendus*, De Corrept. et Gr. 39 (c. 13). [De Dono Perseverantiæ, c. 14 : Hæc est prædestinatio sanctorum, nihil aliud; præscientia scilicet et præparatio beneficiorum Dei, quibus certissime liberantur, quicunque liberantur. Cæteri autem ubi nisi in massa perditionis justo divino judicio relinquuntur ? De Corrept. et Gratia, c. 13 : Hi ergo, qui non pertinent ad istum certissimum et felicissimum numerum (prædestinatorum) pro meritis justissime judicantur. De Præd. Sanc. c. 19: Dicet (apostolus) ideo nos electos in Christo et prædestinatos ante mundi constitutionem, ut essemus sancti et immaculati ... non quia futuros tales nos esse præscivit, sed ut essemus tales per electionem gratiæ suæ ... c. 10 : Si quæratur, unde quisque sit dignus, non desunt, qui dicunt, voluntate humana ; nos autem dicimus, gratia vel prædestinatione divina. *Schmid*, Dogmengesch. s. 59. *Baur*, in his Dogmengesch. s. 184, cites the following passage from De Corrept. et Gratia, c. 9, as bringing together the series of divine acts in respect to the elect : Quicunque in Dei providentissima dispositione præsciti, prædestinati, vocati, justificati, glorificati sunt, non dico etiam nondum renati, sed etiam nondum nati, jam filii Dei sunt et omnino perire non possunt. This, says *Baur*, exhibits what is hardest and most incomprehensible in the doctrine of Augustine.]—He refutes the objections of the understanding by quoting Rom. ix. 20, and adducing examples from sacred history. Even in *this* life, worldly goods, health, beauty, physical and intellectual powers, are distributed unequally,

§ 113.]   PREDESTINATION.   431

and not always in accordance with human views of merit, ibid. 19, c. 8. Christ Himself was predestinated to be the Son of God, De Pred. 31 (c. 15). De Corr. et Grat. § 30. He even calls Christ the præclarissimum lumen prædestinationis et gratiæ. *Neander,* Dg. s. 394.

(2) *Augustine* teaches a predestination to punishment and condemnation, but not a direct predestination to sin; comp. Enchiridion, c. 100. The passage 1 Tim. ii. 4, brought to prove the universality of grace, he explains as meaning that no age, condition, sex, etc., is excluded from grace, and adduces in illustration Luke xi. 42, where "omne olus" means every kind of herbs; comp. Enchiridion, c. 103, and Epist. 107 (Ad Vitalem): comp. *A. Schweizer,* Centraldogmen. i. s. 45. [De Dono Perseverantiæ, c. 8: Cur gratia non secundum merita hominum datur? Respondeo, quoniam Deus misericors est. Cur ergo, inquit, non omnibus? Et hic respondeo, quoniam Deus judex est.]

(3) De Dono Persev. 57 (c. 22): Prædestinatio non ita populis prædicanda est, ut apud imperitam vel tardioris intelligentiæ multitudinem redargui quodammodo ipsa sua prædicatione videatur; sicut redargui videtur et præscientia Dei (quam certe negare non possunt) si dicatur hominibus: "Sive curratis, sive dormiatis, quod vos præscivit qui falli non potest, hoc eritis." Dolosi autem vel imperiti medici est, etiam utile medicamentum sic alligare, ut aut non prosit, aut obsit. Sed dicendum est: "Sic currite, ut comprehendatis, atque ut ipso cursu vestro ita vos esse præcognitos noveritis, ut legitime curreretis," et si quo alio modo Dei præscientia prædicari potest, ut hominis segnitia repellatur, 59 . . . *de ipso autem cursu vestro bono rectoque condiscite vos ad prædestinationem divinæ gratiæ pertinere.*

(4) Notwithstanding the condemnation of Pelagius at the Synod of Ephesus, the system of Augustine did not exert any influence upon the theology of the Eastern Church. *Theodore* of Mopsuestia wrote (against the advocates of Augustinianism): πρὸς τοὺς λέγοντας φύσει καὶ οὐ γνώμῃ πταίειν τοὺς ἀνθρώπους, 5 books (*Photii* Bibl. Cod. 177, some Latin fragments of which are preserved by Mar. Mercator, ed. *Baluze; Fritzsche,* p. 107 ss.). On the question whether it was directed against Jerome or against Augustine, see

Fritzsche, l.c. p. 109 ss., and *Neander,* Kg. ii. s. 1360 ff., Dg. s. 405. *Theodoret, Chrysostom, Isidore* of Pelusium, and others continued to follow the earlier line of the dogmatic development. See the passages in *Münscher, von Cölln,* i. s. 408–410, and comp. § 108.

§ 114.

Semi-Pelagianism and the later Teachers of the Church.

J. *Geffcken,* Historia Semi-Pelagianismi Antiquissima, Gött. 1826, 4to. *Wiggers,* de Joh. Cassiano Massiliensi, qui Semi-Pelagianismi auctor vulgo perhibetur. Rost. 1824, 1825, 4to. *By the same:* Versuch einer pragmat. Darstellung des Augustinismus und Pelagianismus, Th. ii. *Neander,* Denkwürdigkeiten, Bd. iii. s. 92 ff.

In opposition both to the extreme Augustinians (Predestinarians) (1), and to Augustinianism itself, a new system was formed upon which Monachism undoubtedly exerted a considerable influence (as its deepest roots are essentially Pelagian), but which also proceeded in part from a more healthy, practical, and moral tone. Its advocates endeavoured to pursue a middle course between the two extremes of Pelagianism and Augustinianism, and to satisfy the moral as well as the religious wants of the age, by the partial adoption of the premises of both systems, without carrying them out to all their logical consequences (2). The leader of the Gallican theologians (Massilienses) who propounded this new system, afterwards called *Semi-Pelagianism,* was *John Cassian,* a disciple of Chrysostom (3), whom *Prosper Aquitanus* and others combated (4). He was followed by *Faustus,* Bishop of Rhegium (5), who gained a victory over *Lucidus,* a hyper-Augustinian presbyter, at the Synod of Arles (A.D. 472). For several decades Semi-Pelagianism continued to be the prevailing form of doctrine in Gaul (6), till it met with new opposition on the part of *Avitus* of Vienne (7), *Cæsarius* of Arles (8), *Fulgentius* of Ruspe (9), and others. After a variety of fortunes, Augustinianism obtained the preponderance even in Gaul, by means of the Synods of *Arausio* (Orange) and *Valence* (A.D.

§ 114.] SEMI-PELAGIANISM. 433

529), but with the important restriction that the doctrine of predestination to evil should not be taught (10). Boniface II., Bishop of Rome, in accordance with the measures adopted by his predecessors, confirmed these decisions (A.D. 530) (11). *"Gregory the Great transmitted to subsequent ages the milder aspect of the Augustinian doctrine, in its relations to practical Christianity rather than to speculation"* (12).

(1) Under (doctrinal) Predestinarians are usually included the monks of Adrumetum, in the province of Byzacene in North Africa, and Lucidus, mentioned below, who taught the doctrine of a prædestinatio duplex; still it is satisfactorily proved that (historically) *"a sect, or even a separate party of Predestinarians who dissented from Augustine never existed"* (as was formerly erroneously supposed). Comp. *Wiggers*, ii. s. 329 ff., 347. This error was spread by *J. Sirmond*, Historia Prædestinatiana (Opp. t. iv. p. 267 ss.), and the work edited by him under the title Prædestinatus, 1643, in which the Prædest. Hæresis is mentioned as the ninetieth in the order of heresies (reprinted in *Gallandii* Bibl. x.). Comp. also *Walch*, Historie der Ketzereien, v. s. 218·ff. '*Neander*, Kg. ii. 3, s. 1339 ff. *Gieseler*, i. § 113, notes 4, 9–11. [On this work, Prædestinatus, see *Neander*. The Jesuits were charged with having forged it. *Baur*, Dg. s. 155, note, says that Neander maintains, without sufficient reason, that the second part of the book (it is in three parts) was not by the author himself, but was a current Augustinian treatise. *Baur* says that the whole work was really by a Semi-Pelagian, and intended to make Predestinarianism odious by carrying it out to the most revolting consequences: *e.g.*, "the predestined may sin ever so much, since without his own will he will attain salvation; and, on the other hand, he who is destined to death strives in vain;" illustrated in the instances of Judas and Paul.]

(2) According to the reports made by *Prosper* and *Hilary*, scil. Prosperi (428, 429), to *Augustine* (in *Wiggers*, s. 153, *Münscher, von Cölln*, i. s. 411), the treatise of *Augustine*, titled De Correptione et Gratia, had excited some commotion among the Gallican theologians and monks, in consequence of which he wrote the further treatises, De Præd. Sanctorum,

and De Dono Perseverantiæ. Though these Gallican theologians differed in some particulars from Cassian (see *Wiggers*, s. 181), yet there was a considerable agreement between their doctrine and his. Comp. also *Neander*, s. 1315 ff.

(3) Comp. above, § 82, note 21. Of his Collationes, the thirteenth is the most important. *Prosper* complains of his syncretism, Contra Collatorem, c. 5: Illi (Pelagiani) in omnibus justis hominum operibus liberæ voluntatis tuentur exordia, nos bonarum cogitationum ex Deo semper credimus prodire principia, tu *informe* nescio quid *tertium* reperisti.— This *tertium* consisted in the following particulars:— (*a*) *Cassian*, who detested the profana opinio and impietas Pelagii (see *Wiggers*, ii. s. 19, 20), regarded the natural man neither as morally healthy (as Pelagius did) nor as morally dead (like Augustine), but as diseased and morally weakened (dubitari non potest, inesse quidem omnia animæ naturaliter virtutum semina beneficio creatoris inserta, sed nisi hæc opitulatione Dei fuerint excitata, ad incrementum perfectionis non poterunt pervenire, Col. xiii. 12). (*b*) He insisted so much more than Pelagius on the necessity and spiritual nature of divine grace (Col. xiii. 3), that he even ventured to assert that men are sometimes drawn to salvation against their will (nonnunquam etiam inviti trahimur ad salutem, comp. Inst. Cœn. xii. 13; *Wiggers*, s. 85). But, in opposition to Augustine, he restricted only to a few (*e.g.* Matthew and Paul) what the latter would extend to all, and appealed to the example of Zacchæus, Cornelius the centurion, the thief on the cross, and others, in proof of his opinion. In general, he ascribed the *ascensus* to God, as well as the *descensus* to earthly things, to the free will of man, and looked upon grace as rather *co-operans*, though he does not express himself very distinctly. Only we must take care not to refer all the merits of the saints to God, so as to leave to human nature nothing but what is bad. (*c*) He understood the redemption through Christ as universal, and thus rejected the doctrine of predestination (in the sense of Augustine and the hyper-Augustinians). The assertion that God would save only a few, appeared to him an ingens sacrilegium (Col. xiii. 7). An outline of his complete system is given by *Wiggers*, s. 47–136, and *Baur*, Dg. i. 2, s. 360 ff. [1. Man is not

dead in sin, but diseased; freedom is not lost, but lamed. 2. Freedom and grace concur, sometimes the one leading, and again the other; the initiation is usually in the will, but God draws some against their will; grace is internal. 3. Predestination on the basis of prescience. Comp. *Baur* (Dg. s. 187), who says that the result was merely that the two antagonistic positions of predestination and free will stood over against each other unreconciled. But still the result was to show that as the divine always stands above the human, so it is essential to the Church system that the absolute importance of grace should not be yielded, at least in the formal statements of doctrine.]

(4) *Augustine* himself combated Semi-Pelagianism in the above works. *Wiggers* gives a sketch of the controversy between Prosper on the one hand, and Cassian and the Semi-Pelagians on the other (s. 136 ff.).

(5) *Faustus* first presided over the monastery of Lerinum, which was for some time the chief seat of Semi-Pelagianism. On *Vincentius Lerinensis*, comp. *Wiggers*, s. 208 ff.; on *Faustus* and his doctrine, ibid. s. 224 ff., 235 ff. Respecting the doctrine of original sin, the views of Faustus come nearer to Augustine's opinions than do those of Cassian; on the other hand, his ideas of the nature of grace are more external (Pelagian) than those of the latter; comp. *Wiggers*, s. 287.— But he bestows more attention upon the third point of the controversy, the doctrine of predestination. He decidedly rejects the doctrine of unconditional election by making a distinction between predetermination and foreknowledge, the former of which is independent of the latter; De Grat. et Lib. Arbitrio, i. *Wiggers*, s. 279 ff. Faustus uses, *e.g.*, the following arguments, which savour strongly of anthropomorphism: When I accidentally cast my eyes upon a vicious action, it does not follow that I am guilty of it because I have seen it. Thus God foresees adultery, without exciting man to impurity; He foresees murder, without exciting in man the desire for its commission, etc., *Wiggers*, s. 282, 283. In speaking of the doctrine of unconditional predestination, as propounded by his opponent Lucidus, he used the strongest terms: lex fatalis, decretum fatale, fatalis constitutio, originalis definitio vel fatalis, and looked upon it as some-

thing heathenish, *Wiggers*, s. 315. He believed in universal atonement. [Among the modifying Augustinians, says *Baur* (Dg. s. 187), was the author of the work De Vocatione omnium Gentium, who, in a peculiar manner, while holding Augustine's view of grace, conceived of original sin in a merely negative way, as the want of good, or as the mere following of natural instinct. The will remains the same, its object is different; to the good it can be directed only by God; but every one can obtain this direction, since there is a universal as well as a special efficacy of grace.]

(6) Comp. Gennadius Massiliensis and Ennodius Ticinensis, in *Wiggers*, s. 350 ff. On Gennadius, see *Neander*, Dg. s. 401. A summary view of the Semi-Pelagian doctrine in general, and its relation to both Augustinianism and Pelagianism, is given in the form of a table by *Wiggers*, s. 359–364.

(7) *Wiggers*, s. 368.

(8) *Wiggers*, s. 369, concerning his book De Gratia et Lib. Arbitrio.

(9) *Wiggers*, s. 369 ff. *Fulgentius*, carrying the doctrine of imputation still farther than *Augustine*, consigned to everlasting fire not only those infants that died without being baptized, but also the immature fœtus; De Fide ad Petrum, c. 30, quoted by *Wiggers*, s. 376. But in reference to predestination, he endeavoured carefully to avoid all exaggerations which might give offence to Christian feelings (*Neander*, Kg. l.c. 1354). After the interference of the Scythian monks, he expressly blamed those who asserted the doctrine of predestination to evil, though he maintained himself a prædest. duplex (but in a different sense). *Neander*, l.c. s. 1357. Grace is in his opinion præveniens, as well as comitans and subsequens. (Ep. ad Theodorum de Conversione a Seculo, quoted by *Wiggers*, s. 386.)

(10) *Mansi*, t. viii. p. 711 ss. *Aug.* Opp. t. x. part ii. Append. p. 157 ss. *Wiggers*, s. 430. *Münscher, von Cölln*, s. 417. The conclusion is the most important part: [Hoc etiam secundum catholicam fidem, credimus, quod accepta per baptismum gratia omnes baptizati, Christo auxiliante et co-operante, quæ ad salutem pertinent, possint et debeant, si fideliter laborare valuerint, adimplere]. Aliquos vero ad malum divina potestate prædestinatos esse non solum non

credimus, sed etiamsi sunt, qui tantum malum credere velint, cum omni detestatione illis anathema dicimus. On the Synod of Valence, see *Mansi,* viii. 723 ss.; App. p. 162.

(11) Among the earlier popes, *Cœlestine* and *Gelasius I.* had condemned Semi-Pelagianism; *Hormisdas,* on the contrary, pronounced a very mild judgment in opposition to the Scythian monks, without, however, denying the doctrine of *Augustine.* See *Bonifacii II.* Epist. ad Cæsarium, given by *Mansi,* t. viii. p. 735, and App. p. 161 ss.

(12) Comp. *Neander,* Kg. iii. s. 287. *Wiggers,* de Gregorio M. ejusque Placitis Anthropologicis, Rost. 1838. *Lau,* s. 379 ff. The views of *Gregory* are most fully developed in Moralia, iv. c. 24; comp. xv. c. 15, 51, ix. c. 21, 34, and many other passages. Along with strict Augustinianism, we find in his writings Semi-Pelagian modifications. See *Lau,* s. 400 f. For his views respecting the doctrine of grace, see Mor. xx. 4; Hom. in Ezech. i. 5 (*Lau,* s. 403 ff.). He also distinguishes between gratia præveniens and subsequens. The former is operans, but at the same time co-operans. The gratia subsequens is a help: ne inaniter velimus, sed possimus implere. See Mor. xxii. c. 9: Sancti viri sciunt, post primi parentis lapsum de corruptibili stirpe se editos, et non virtute propria, sed præveniente gratia superna ad meliora se vota et opera commutatos: et quidquid sibi mali inesse conspiciunt, de mortali propagine sentiunt meritum; quidquid vero in se boni inspiciunt, immortalis gratiæ cognoscunt donum, eique de accepto munere debitores fiunt, qui et præveniendo dedit iis bonum velle quod noluerunt, et subsequendo concessit bonum esse, quod volunt.—*Gregory* further maintains that grace can be lost, Mor. xxv. 8 (we know what we are, but we do not know what we shall be); while, on the other hand, he appears to assert the irresistibility of grace (Mor. ix. 9: sicut nemo obstitit largitati vocantis, ita nullus obviat justitiæ relinquentis), again, he says that the humble will accept, the proud reject, the gift of God (Mor. xxx. 1; Evang. lib. ii.; Hom. 22); comp. *Lau,* s. 410, 411. [On *Gregory,* compare *Wiggers* in the Zeitschrift f. hist. Theologie, 1854, on the History of Augustinian Anthropology after the Condemnation of Semi-Pelagianism, s. 7–43. *Gregory* agrees with *Augustine* on the primitive state. As to the fall, he asserts a primitive

weakness in Adam; he calls original sin a disease, and admits a certain necessity of sinning; free will is not annulled, but weakened; man can withstand grace; predestination is only of the elect, yet he denies the absolute decree. Bonum quod agimus, et Dei est, et nostrum; Dei, per præveníentem gratiam; nostrum, per obsequentem liberam voluntatem. Suprema pietas prius agit in nobis aliquid sine nobis, ut subsequente quoque nostro libero arbitrio bonum, quod jam appetimus, agat nobiscum: quod tamen per impensam gratiam in extremo judicio ita remunerat in nobis, ac si solis præcessisset ex nobis.]

It is worthy of notice that in this protracted controversy the objective aspect of anthropology was far more developed than the subjective. The doctrine of the economy of redemption still remains in an imperfect state, as may be seen, *e.g.*, from the indefinite manner in which the terms justificare and justificatio (= justum facere, see *Wiggers*, s. 380) were used, and from the want of proper definitions of the nature of faith. *Wiggers* therefore justly closes his account of this controversy by saying: "*A more profound examination of the nature of faith would even then have given a very different appearance to Christian anthropology.*" It should further be observed that the Augustinian doctrine of predestination rested on the premisses contained in his views of original sin. Adam was free *before* the fall, and consequently stood out of the sphere of predestination, though God *foreknew* his transgression (*Aug.* de Civ. Dei, xii. 21). Later theologians (the supralapsarians) first extended predestination even to Adam, and so completed the doctrine of predestination in a speculative way. Thus it was reserved for the Reformation to finish the work which *Augustine* left incomplete; the *Lutherans*, by developing the doctrine of faith and justification; the *Calvinists*, by developing that of absolute predestination. On the other hand, the Roman Catholic Church either placed itself in opposition to its own Father (in the Council of Trent and among the Jesuits), or simply adhered to the doctrine propounded by him (the Jansenists). *Neander* (Dg. 387) has drawn attention to the fact that with Augustine justification and sanctification run into each other, while Pelagius views justification in a more external manner. Comp. also *Baur*, Dg. i. 2, s. 395 ff.

END OF VOLUME I.

Printed in the United States
121143LV00002B/19/A